THE UNIVERSITY OF
WINCHESTER

PUBLICATIONS

OF THE

NAVY RECORDS SOCIETY

VOL. 130

ANGLO-AMERICAN NAVAL RELATIONS

1917–1919

THE NAVY RECORDS SOCIETY was established in 1893 for the purpose of printing unpublished manuscripts and rare works of naval interest. The Society is open to all who are interested in naval history, and any person wishing to become a member should apply to the Hon. Secretary, c/o Barclays Bank PLC, Murray House, 1, Royal Mint Court, London EC3 4HH. The annual subscription is £15, which entitles the member to receive one free copy of each work issued by the Society in that year, and to buy earlier issues at much reduced prices.

SUBSCRIPTIONS and orders for back volumes should be sent to Mrs Annette Gould, 5, Goodwood Close, Midhurst, West Sussex GU29 9JG.

THE COUNCIL OF THE NAVY RECORDS SOCIETY wish it to be clearly understood that they are not answerable for any opinions and observations which may appear in the Society's publications. For these the editors of the several works are entirely responsible.

ANGLO-AMERICAN NAVAL RELATIONS

1917–1919

edited by

MICHAEL SIMPSON, M.A., M.Litt, F.R.Hist.S.,
Senior Lecturer in History and American Studies,
University College of Swansea
in the University of Wales

PUBLISHED BY SCOLAR PRESS
FOR THE NAVY RECORDS SOCIETY
1991

Published by
SCOLAR PRESS
Gower Publishing Company Limited
Gower House
Croft Road
Aldershot
Hants GU11 3HR
England

Gower Publishing Company
Old Post Road
Brookfield
Vermont 05036
USA

British Library Cataloguing in Publication Data
   Anglo-American naval relations 1917–1919. –
   (Publications of the Navy Records Society; v. 130)
   1. Great Britain. Naval policies, history   2. United
   States Military
   I. Simpson, Michael   II. Navy Records Society III. Series
   359.030941

   ISBN 0–85967–863–6

Printed and bound in Great Britain by
Billing and Sons Limited, Worcester.

CONTENTS

LIST OF MAPS

PREFACE

This volume derives from a long-term study, *FDR's Navy: Franklin D. Roosevelt and the United States Navy, 1913–1945*. The Anglo-American naval relationship naturally forms a substantial part of this work, though it went through stormy waters quite as much as calm seas. The present collection traces only a small part of that developing relationship, though it is hoped ultimately to carry the story down to 1945.

The present harmonious and well integrated association between the Royal Navy and the US Navy is taken so much for granted that it is instructive to see how it all began, in such tentative and stuttering fashion, in the dark days of 1917. Several objects have governed the selection of documents. I have sought to show the nature and development of the relationship at both the policy-making and the operational levels and to illuminate both the harmonies and the disharmonies. The accent in 1917–18 was naturally on the means of defeating the U-boats and there was considerable disagreement over anti-submarine policies. An attempt has been made to illustrate co-operation in each of the major theatres – the North Sea, the Western Approaches, the Mediterranean and the Western Hemisphere. The documents reveal the often uncomplimentary thoughts of one service about the other and demonstrate something of the naval thinking on strategic and material issues of the day. Although a close and successful partnership at sea was established by the end of 1917, a spirit of suspicion and rivalry underlay the whole relationship and this surfaced quickly once the guns fell silent. Although the collection ends on a relatively happy note, there was in fact an uneasy truce from 1919 to the Washington Conference of 1921–22. The issue of parity was in large part resolved there, but the relationship was a generally hostile one throughout the 1920s and warmed up again only after the appearance of threats to world peace from the dictators.

The collection breaks new ground for the Society in that about half of the sources, inevitably, are American. Extensive use has been made of the Navy Department records at the National Archives and of the Papers of the Secretary of the Navy Josephus Daniels, Admirals W. S. Benson and W. S. Sims (Library of Congress) and Admiral W. V. Pratt (Naval Historical Center), all in Washington, DC. Further material has come from the Papers of President Franklin D. Roosevelt at Hyde Park, New York. On the British side, one is fortunate to have the handy and extensive collection of Admiralty records gathered together for the official history (*The History of the Great War, Naval Operations*, 5 volumes: 1–3 by Sir Julian S. Corbett, 4–5 by Sir Henry Newbolt, London: Longmans Green, 1920–31), ADM 137, supplemented by the official papers of two First Lords, Sir Eric Geddes and Walter Long (ADM 116). I have drawn extensively on the Society's earlier volumes on this period – those on the Royal Navy in the Mediterranean, the Royal Naval Air Service, and the Papers of Admirals Beatty, Jellicoe and Keyes. The late Professor Arthur Marder's interpretations of British naval history in this period may now lack universal acceptance but his books remain a rich quarry of information (*From the Dreadnought to Scapa Flow: the Royal Navy in the Fisher Era, 1904–1919*, 5 volumes, especially volume 4, *1917: Year of Crisis* (1969) and volume 5, *Victory and Aftermath: January 1918 to June 1919* (1970), London: Oxford University Press). I owe a particular debt to Professor David F. Trask, not only for his highly perceptive and thoroughly authoritative study *Captains and Cabinets: Anglo-American Naval Relations, 1917–1918* (Columbia, Missouri: Missouri University Press, 1972) but also for his warm encouragement and sage advice. I have provided brief introductions to each Part but I take the view that the documents should largely speak for themselves and more detailed discussion of major issues is available in Professor Trask's monograph. As readers on one side of the Atlantic may not be familiar with the naval history of the other party, I have included references to a number of works to assist them.

In general the papers fall naturally into the individual Parts but there are a number of documents which relate to two or more Parts; they have been placed in the Part which seems most appropriate. Part I charts the hesitant contacts between the two powers in the period immediately preceding American entry into the war (January–April 1917). Part II shows the two navies struggling to integrate their activities while desperately staving off defeat by the U-boats (April–June 1917). Part III follows the gradual development of a harmonious relationship, a path marked by mutual complaints, from the beginning of real American engagement in the war (July 1917) to her total commitment (November 1917); for the last year of the war, the relationship enjoyed a honeymoon period. Part IV deals with the central naval issue of these years, the German submarine campaign and Allied counter-measures. In Part V, the role played by US battleships in European waters (chiefly the 6th Battle Squadron of the Grand Fleet) is portrayed. Part VI looks at the boldest joint operation, the North Sea mine barrier between Scotland and Norway. In Part VII, we move to shared operations in the Mediterranean, principally at Gibraltar but including discussion of the Adriatic situation and the overall picture of Allied naval activity in that sea. Part VIII crosses the Atlantic to discover the nature of the relationship on America's eastern seaboard and in the Caribbean. Finally, Part IX deals with the fashioning of a naval armistice and then of a peace treaty; in this period (October 1918–May 1919), the warmth of wartime co-operation was replaced by an atmosphere of suspicion, rivalry, acrimony, jingoism and chauvinism which threatened to make enemies of the two powers.

The documents have been edited with as light a hand as possible. The punctuation has been left as in the originals with very few exceptions; in some documents, chiefly signals, punctuation is entirely absent. Insertions to cover missing or illegible words are in square brackets, sometimes accompanied by a question mark. Headings have been kept as simple as possible. Except where stated it should be assumed that British documents originate in London, as do those from Sims and his staff, while American documents are generally from Washington, as are most of the communications from the British Commanders-in-Chief North America and West Indies and the British Naval Attaché. Omissions of parts of sentences are indicated by an ellipsis (...) and of whole paragraphs by four asterisks (****). Place names have been left as they were in 1914–1918, though many have subsequently changed, notably in the Adriatic. Biographical details have been culled from a variety of sources: the *Navy List*, the US *Navy Register*, Marder's volumes, *Who Was Who*, the *Dictionary of National Biography*, the *Dictionary of American Biography*, and A. J. P. Taylor's *English History, 1914–1945*. Information on warships has been obtained from the relevant issues of *Jane's Fighting Ships*. Individuals and ships are identified on the page on which they are first mentioned. The numerals in square brackets in the introductions to the Parts refer to documents in the text dealing with particular issues.

The Royal Navy and the US Navy were largely unacquainted prior to American entry into World War I. Relations between individual members of the two services in distant waters appear to have been cordial and even warm but at the highest level there was no real contact. The Royal Navy appears to have paid little attention to the US Navy in the early part of the twentieth century since its chief concern was with the much more menacing Imperial German navy, and in any case the USA was regarded officially as a friendly power with whom war was unthinkable from at least 1900 onwards. On the American side there were both strong Anglophiles, such as Sims, and strident Anglophobes, like Rear-Admiral French Ensor Chadwick. Between 1914 and 1916 the United States Government had at least as much cause to protest at Britain's arbitrary behaviour on the high seas as at the German submarine campaign, and towards the end of 1916 it was not inconceivable that the US Navy might have fought the Royal Navy, as it had in similar circumstances during the Napoleonic era, rather than co-operating with it. It was the German announcement of the resumption of unrestricted submarine warfare from 1 February 1917 which ensured that the two would work together. As Part I demonstrates, America's entry into the war was remarkably gradual and even uncertain until late in March, largely due to the personality and policies of President Woodrow Wilson. Others, like Assistant Secretary of the Navy Franklin D. Roosevelt, Wilson's confidant Edward M. House and the strongly Anglophile US Ambassador to the Court of St James, Walter Hines Page, were impatient for the declaration of war. The first Part shows how these two attitudes were held in an uneasy balance between 1 February and 6 April 1917, when the United States at last took the plunge into belligerency.

ACKNOWLEDGMENTS

I must thank first those institutions without whose generous financial assistance the research for the present volume would have been
impossible: the British Academy; the Franklin and Eleanor Roosevelt Institute; and the Research Support Fund of the University
College of Swansea.

In common with all historians, I am deeply indebted to many
archivists and librarians in both the United Kingdom and the
United States, at: the Public Record Office, Kew; the library of the
National Maritime Museum, Greenwich; the library of the Ministry
of Defence; Dr Barry Zerby, and the genial staff of the research
room at the National Archives, Washington; the Manuscript Division, Library of Congress, Washington; Operational Archives,
Naval Historical Center, Washington Navy Yard; the Widener
Library, Harvard University; the library of the Naval War College;
and Dr William Emerson, Mr Robert Parks, Mrs Susan Elter and
their colleagues at the Franklin D. Roosevelt Library, Hyde Park,
New York – now as much good friends as professional associates.

I am equally grateful to fellow historians for sharing with me on
such a generous scale their wisdom, experience and knowledge: from
the Navy Records Society, Mr Eric Grove, Mr Allan Pearsall, Lt-
Cdr Lawrence Phillips and Dr Nicholas Rodger, among others, and
most of all the indefatigable Honorary General Editor Mr Anthony
Ryan. I wish to thank also Dr Alex Danchev of the University of
Keele and Dr Fiona Venn of the University of Essex, and from my
own University Professors Muriel Chamberlain and Richard Shan-
non, Dr Alan Dobson, Mr Michael Collins and Mr. Guy Lewis who
drew the maps. In the United States, I have benefitted greatly from
the assistance of Dr Dean C. Allard, Professor William R. Braisted,
Professor Paul Halpern, Professor Paul M. Kennedy, Professor Jon
T. Sumida and Professor David F. Trask. I am particularly pleased
to acknowledge the early encouragement to pursue naval history of
the late Captain Stephen Roskill.

The Papers of the Hon Josephus Daniels, Admiral W. S. Benson
and Admiral W. S. Sims are in the public domain but I am indebted

to the Manuscript Division of the Library of Congress for facilitating their use. I have used the Papers of Admiral W. V. Pratt, housed in the Operational Archives of the Naval Historical Center, but have been unable to trace his descendants to secure formal permission to publish extracts from them. I acknowledge the assistance of the National Archives in Washington in obtaining access to the Navy Department records. Crown Copyright material in the Public Record Office is reproduced by permission of the Controller of Her Majesty's Stationery Office.

Thanks are due to *The Times* and the *Daily Telegraph* for permitting reproduction of certain reports from those newspapers.

Once again, my family has borne patiently my absorption in yet another book and I owe them far more than a mere note of thanks can convey.

GLOSSARY OF ABBREVIATIONS

ACNS	Assistant Chief of Naval Staff
AEF	American Expeditionary Forces
ANC	Allied Naval Council
bt	baronet
BCS	Battle Cruiser Squadron
BS	Battle Squadron
BEF	British Expeditionary Force
C-tube	US anti-submarine listening device
CNO	Chief of Naval Operations
CoS	Chief of Staff
Cdr	Commander
CinC	Commander-in-Chief
CO	Commanding Officer
Commodore (F)	Commodore, Grand Fleet Destroyer Flotillas
Conn	Connecticut
CS	Cruiser Squadron
DCT	Depth Charge Thrower
DCNS	Deputy Chief of Naval Staff
D1SL	Deputy First Sea Lord
DASD	Director of Anti-Submarine Division
DNI	Director of Naval Intelligence
DOD	Director of Operations Division
DOP	Director of Plans
DSO	Distinguished Service Order
DC	District of Columbia
Div	Division
FO	Foreign Office
FDR	Franklin D. Roosevelt
GSO	General Staff Officer
GMT	Greenwich Mean Time
HC	Halifax-UK convoys (troops)
HX	Halifax/New York-UK convoys
HS	Sydney, Nova Scotia-UK convoys
HMS	His Majesty's Ship

j.g.	junior grade
K-tube	US anti-submarine listening device
Lieut	Lieutenant
Lt-Cdr	Lieutenant-Commander
LCS	Light Cruiser Squadron
Md	Maryland
MTB	Motor Torpedo Boat
NJ	New Jersey
NY	New York
NID	Naval Intelligence Division
NIP	Naval Institute Press
NC	North Carolina
ONO	Office of Naval Operations (Opnav), Navy Department
P-boat	Patrol-boat (corvette)
Q-ship	merchant vessel with hidden armament; 'mystery' ship
Rear-Admiral (M)	Rear-Admiral (Mining)
RAF	Royal Air Force
RM	Royal Marines
RMA	Royal Marine Artillery
RMLI	Royal Marine Light Infantry
RCN	Royal Canadian Navy
RN	Royal Navy
RNAS	Royal Naval Air Service
RNR	Royal Naval Reserve
RNVR	Royal Naval Volunteer Reserve
RMS	Royal Mail Steamer
SNO	Senior Naval Officer
shp	shaft horse power
SOS	distress signal
Sqdn	Squadron
SS	Steam Ship
S/M	Submarine
Tenn	Tennessee
TBD	Torpedo Boat Destroyer
tt	torpedo tubes
U-boats	German submarines (U, UB, UC varieties)
US	United States
USNAF	United States Naval Air Forces
USS	United States Ship
UP	University Press

Va	Virginia
W/T	Wireless Telegraphy
Y-gun	a form of depth charge thrower
1913	year of completion of a ship
4in	4-inch (or 6-inch, etc) gun

PART I

PRELIMINARY DISCUSSIONS
JANUARY TO APRIL 1917

INTRODUCTION

On 31 January 1917 the German Ambassador in Washington, Count Johann von Bernstorff, informed President Wilson that on 1 February Germany would resume unrestricted submarine warfare against all shipping, neutral and Allied. The German high command recognised that this presented Wilson with a *casus belli* but did so in the firm belief that Britain would have been starved into surrender within six months and that her defeat would precipitate the collapse of the other Entente powers, long before the United States could mobilise her enormous resources, a process estimated accurately at eighteen months.[1] For his part, the pacific Wilson moved slowly and reluctantly towards hostilities, hoping against hope that the Germans did not mean what they said and that it was still possible to shore up the fragile *modus vivendi* which had endured virtually since the *Lusitania* Notes of 1915.[2] Wilson, who was determined to carry a united nation with him, waited for 'overt acts' of war, that is for American ships to be sunk without warning. In the meantime, he adopted means short of war to express his disgust at the German policy and to protect American shipping. Diplomatic relations with Germany were broken off on 3 February [1] and on 26 February Congress was asked for authority to arm merchant vessels. When eleven non-interventionist senators filibustered the bill to death, Wilson exercised his executive powers and ordered the arming of merchantmen on 9 March. From then until 20 March Wilson underwent what Arthur Link has called his own Gethsemane,[3] waiting for news of sinkings and noting the public's overwhelming clamour for peace. On 18 March, three American steamers were sunk without

[1] H. H. Herwig, *The Politics of Frustration: The United States in German Naval Planning, 1889–1941* (Boston: Little Brown, 1976), pp. 117–22, 126–8; Trask, *Captains and Cabinets*, p. 31; Marder, vol. 4, pp. 49–53.

[2] Trask, *Captains and Cabinets*, p. 40. Thomas Woodrow Wilson (1856–1924): President, 1913–1921; historian, political scientist and university president; Governor of New Jersey, 1910–12; won Presidency for Democrats 1912; re-elected 1916.

[3] A. S. Link, *Woodrow Wilson and the Progressive Era, 1910–1917* (New York: Harper & Row, 1963), pp. 275–7.

warning and with heavy casualties; their twisted plates formed Wilson's cross. With as heavy a heart as history can have known, the man who had for two years pursued peace with unexampled zeal now decided that the nation could no longer avoid war and on 21 March he called Congress into special session for 2 April. Following Wilson's call for a crusade not only against German militarism but also to 'make the world safe for democracy', prominent figures in both houses rejected belligerency but the President's confidence that events had united the nation behind him was borne out. By 82 votes to six the Senate supported him on 4 April and the House of Representatives, by 373 votes to 50, followed on 6 April. Wilson signed the Congressional resolution at lunchtime on that day and the United States accepted belligerency as an Associated Power, asserting its independence of Allied war aims.[1]

Wilson's watchful waiting and desire to avoid provoking Germany militated against preparations for war and official conversations with the Allies about wartime co-operation. Secretary of the Navy Daniels, even more pacific than Wilson, adhered loyally to the President's hesitant course. He 'consistently refused to the eve of American entry into the war either to admit the possibility of American entry or to place the Navy in readiness for war'.[2] Preparedness advocates like ex-President Theodore Roosevelt complained 'We are terribly unprepared, more unprepared than our people have any idea of.'[3] Defence chiefs and some civilian members of the administration, notably Colonel House[4] and young Franklin Roose-

[1] R. H. Ferrell, *Woodrow Wilson and World War I, 1917–1921* (New York: Harper & Row, 1985), pp. 1–3.

[2] P. E. Coletta, *The American Naval Heritage in Brief* (University Press of America, 1980), p. 260. Josephus Daniels (1862–1948): newspaper editor and proprietor, N. Carolina; Democratic politician; Secretary of the Navy 1913–1921; author of several books on the era; Ambassador to Mexico, 1933–1942.

[3] Theodore Roosevelt, *Report of a Special Meeting of the Union League Club of New York*, 20 March 1917, p. 30. Theodore Roosevelt (1858–1919): historian, natural historian, explorer, outdoor pursuits fanatic, rancher, country gentleman and Republican politician; after apprenticeship in New York politics (city and state), became Asst Secretary of Navy, 1897–8; resigned to head volunteer cavalry unit in Spanish–American War 1898; compiled heroic record and exploited it to become Governor of NY, 1899–1900; elected Vice-President 1900 and succeeded assassinated President McKinley September 1901; won election in own right 1904; retired from Presidency 1909 but tried again with own Progressive party 1912; lost to Wilson but active in politics to death; an early advocate of Preparedness; elder cousin of Franklin Roosevelt.

[4] Edward Mandell ('Colonel') House (1858–1938): well-to-do Texan, prominent Democrat; intimate associate of Wilson 1911–19; enjoyed especially close relations with British representatives in US; undertook several diplomatic missions to Europe; member of US delegation to Paris Peace Conference 1918–19; Wilson dropped him from team – probably a matter of egotism on both sides.

velt,[1] as much a firebrand as his older cousin, raged inwardly and undertook such preparation as they thought they could get away with, which was precious little, and pursued clandestine discussions with the British [4, 6, 8, 10] Tentative but strategically sensible memoranda, both official [11] and unofficial [3], were prepared outlining the necessary steps to mobilisation, strategic priorities and possible modes of co-operation with the Allies. Both sets of memoranda clearly identified the defence of North Atlantic shipping as the most urgent requirement and both proved remarkably prescient; their advice formed the basis of American interaction with the Entente powers throughout the conflict. Though the United States was ignorant of the true extent of the crisis into which the resumption of unrestricted submarine warfare was plunging the Allies, the General Board's eve-of-war paper [11] reflected a widespread American fear, heightened by the recent Zimmermann telegram,[2] that the Allies might be defeated, leaving the United States alone to face its recurrent nightmare – war on three fronts against Germany, Mexico and Japan.

It was characteristic that Assistant Secretary of the Navy Roosevelt, 'without doubt the least neutral official in all Washington',[3] should take the lead in exploring co-operation with the British [3, 8, 10] but he was ably abetted from London by Walter Hines Page,[4] the fervently Anglophile American Ambassador [6]. The British, delighted but somewhat embarrassed at these eager but unofficial advances, responded coyly and with punctilious adherence to diplomatic protocol [4, 5, 8, 9]. There was, after all, no guarantee that the United States would enter the war; until then the British 'could only stand and wait'.[5] They went to some lengths to hide their despe-

---

[1] Franklin Delano Roosevelt (1882–1945): country gentleman; entered NY politics 1910 and early supporter of Wilson; Asst Secretary of Navy 1913–20; Democratic Vice-Presidential candidate 1920 (badly beaten); polio summer 1921, thereafter mostly confined to wheelchair; Governor of New York 1929–32; President 1933–45, elected to record 4 terms; promulgator of New Deal. See M. A. Simpson, *Franklin D. Roosevelt* (Oxford: Blackwell, 1989).

[2] A telegram from German Foreign Minister Alfred Zimmermann to his Minister in Mexico City, sent on 19 February, intercepted, decoded and passed to US by British. It proposed, in event of war between Germany and USA, that Mexico should intervene on Germany's behalf and secure adherence also of Japan.

[3] R. G. Tugwell, *The Democratic Roosevelt* (Baltimore, Md: Penguin Books, 1969), p. 99; C. Seymour, *Woodrow Wilson and the World War* (New Haven, Conn: Yale UP, 1921), p. 144.

[4] Walter Hines Page (1855–1918): publisher, editor of *World's Work*; N. Carolina Democratic politician; Ambassador to UK 1913–18.

[5] Trask, *Captains and Cabinets*, p. 42.

ration but their outline proposals for US naval assistance accorded closely with those of the Americans [4, 6, 9].

At this juncture, the Royal Navy was demonstrably failing what was arguably its greatest ever test, the German submarines' counter-blockade. Sinkings of British, Allied and neutral merchant vessels had increased steadily from the onset of submarine warfare in February 1915, but after the resumption of the unrestricted campaign in February 1917, losses topped the 500000 tons mark in both February and March. Most sinkings took place at the focal point of sea lanes to and from the British Isles, the Western Approaches, though the Mediterranean was almost as dangerous; there, the British maintained only a small force of largely superannuated warships and lacked effective co-operation from their French and Italian allies.[1] Germany, which possessed about 120 submarines, maintained an average of 46 at sea and was adding about five per month; losses ran at about three per month. Longer daylight would shortly assist the U-boats, the newer ones having greater endurance, better armament, higher speeds and more strength than the pre-war force. Allied countermeasures, ingenious, extensive, determined and varied as they were – mines, nets, air patrols, Q-ships, hunter-killer submarines, defensively armed merchant ships, hydrophone hunting units, zig-zagging, course alterations, camouflage, smokescreens, depth charges and swarms of surface patrol vessels – had palpably little effect on U-boat operations and depredations. The Admiralty, which apparently had no fresh ideas of its own, was prepared to listen to any boy scout, old lady or crank inventor who claimed to have a sovereign remedy. Neutral masters were refusing to sail, yards were clogged with damaged vessels and ports congested with ships held back because of reports of submarines beyond the bar. The Admiralty was in bleak despair; its heads, the First Lord, Sir Edward Carson[2] and the First Sea Lord, Admiral Sir John Jellicoe,[3] though mutually compatible, were not inspiring, imaginative or dynamic leaders. Neither was a good admi-

---

[1] Marder, vol. 4, chs. 4 and 5.

[2] Sir Edward Henry (later Baron) Carson (1854–1935): First Lord of Admiralty December 1916–June 1917; Ulster protestant and Unionist leader; barrister; Attorney-General 1915; member of War Cabinet 1917–18; Lord of Appeal and baron 1921.

[3] Admiral Sir John Rushworth Jellicoe (later Admiral of the Fleet Earl Jellicoe of Scapa) (1859–1935): First Sea Lord December 1916–December 1917; Rear-Admiral 1907; Controller and 3rd Sea Lord 1908; Vice-Admiral and CinC Atlantic Fleet 1910; 2nd Sea Lord 1912; Acting Admiral and CinC Home Fleets (later Grand Fleet) August 1914–November 1916; reported on naval defence of Empire 1919; Governor-

nistrator, Jellicoe in particular being addicted to detail. Both were somewhat self-effacing and Jellicoe was rather inclined to pessimism.[1]

Given this sense of foreboding, the note of half-suppressed anxiety and anticipation in the British responses to American overtures is understandable [4, 9]. However, even after Wilson had decided to ask Congress for a declaration of war, both parties proceeded warily [7, 8, 9]. Nevertheless, the pace quickened. The Americans, responding to the promptings of Page and Franklin Roosevelt, despatched Rear-Admiral William S. Sims[2] to London. Daniels's first choice had been Rear-Admiral Henry B. Wilson, who preferred a sea-going appointment.[3] Sims, a notorious Anglophile, a devotee of the gospel of efficiency, an advocate of a naval 'general staff', and a publicist for the Naval War College (of which he had recently assumed the presidency), was a gunnery specialist and had recently shaken up the Atlantic Fleet's destroyer force with his imaginative and vigorous leadership, raising it to a high pitch of efficiency and morale – qualities which served its flotillas well when they were flung, piecemeal, into the grind of anti-submarine warfare. Like Nelson, an inspiration to junior officers, Sims surrounded himself with a devoted 'band of brothers'. Following service in Chinese waters, he had become acquainted with Admiral Sir Percy Scott[4] and Jellicoe and he had an open admiration of most things

General of New Zealand 1920–4; viscount 1917, earl 1925. See A. T. Patterson, ed. *The Jellicoe Papers*, 2 vols. (London; Allen & Unwin for Navy Records Society, 1966, 1968) and his *Jellicoe: A Biography* (London: Macmillan/St Martin's Press, 1969).

[1] Marder, vol. 4, pp. 57–8.

[2] Rear-Admiral William Sowden Sims, US Navy (1858–1936): graduated from Annapolis, 1880; Naval Attaché, Paris 1898; gunnery expert who complained to President T. Roosevelt of poor gunnery standards in fleet; jumped over the heads of many seniors to Commander; Roosevelt's Naval Aide 1907–09; Naval War College course 1912, stayed on as instructor; Captain 1913; commanded Destroyer Force, Atlantic Fleet 1913–15; captain of new battleship *Nevada* 1915–16; Rear-Admiral and President, Naval War College February 1917; sent to London as liaison officer March 1917, shortly after becoming Vice-Admiral and Force Commander, US Naval Forces in European Waters; returned home March 1919, to Naval War College; promoted Admiral for war services; launched Senate investigation of Navy Dept.'s conduct of war spring 1920; retired 1922. See his *The Victory at Sea* (Garden City, NY: Doubleday Page, 1920; repr. Annapolis, Md: NIP, 1984, with new intro. by D. F. Trask) and his son-in-law's fine biography, E. E. Morison, *Admiral Sims and the Modern American Navy* (Boston: Houghton Mifflin 1942).

[3] Rear-Admiral Henry B. Wilson, US Navy: Captain and commander, 3rd Sqdn, Patrol Force, Atlantic Fleet, May 1917; in August 1917 a Rear-Admiral and appointed commander, US Forces, Gibraltar; in November 1917 transferred to Brest as commander, US Naval Forces, Coast of France; in 1919 commanded Atlantic Fleet. Ironically, therefore, Wilson did spend most of the war ashore.

[4] Admiral Sir Percy Scott, bt (1853–1924): entered RN 1866; gunnery specialist;

British, notably the Royal Navy. This bias, while endearing him to those with whom he was to work in London, rendered his independence of mind suspect in Washington. There is little doubt that Sims was the ablest of the small band of American flag officers, a man of charm, dignity, tact, humour, shrewd judgement, dynamism and forthrightness.

Sims's instructions were vague in the extreme. This is not surprising. When he was summoned to Washington on 28 March the situation was still clouded with uncertainty and the Navy Department wisely required him to be simply 'a transmitter of information', enabling Washington to grasp the nature of a form of warfare of which it was almost totally ignorant and to respond to Allied plans and requests for assistance, then largely unknown in detail. Sims's role could be expanded and defined in the light of subsequent events. At a post war Senate investigation of the Navy Department's conduct in the first few months of hostilities, instigated by Sims himself,[1] he made much of a statement allegedly made by the Chief of Naval Operations, Rear-Admiral Benson: 'don't let the British pull the wool over your eyes. We would as soon fight the British as the Germans.' By any standard the remark was infelicitous and Benson defended himself somewhat lamely at the hearings. It has led historians to polarize the two men; since Sims was avowedly, perhaps excessively, Anglophilic, then Benson must be as determinedly, perhaps maliciously, Anglophobic. This is too neat a judgement. Sims certainly believed in the congruity of the British and American world views and looked to a post-war Anglo-American condominium over the world. He was convinced that the correct wartime strategy was to accept the Admiralty emphasis on distant blockade and the defence of trade, to integrate American forces with British commands and to reinforce the Allies at their weakest points. Nevertheless, Sims, a man of broad strategic vision, a disciplined military mind and a relentlessly probing spirit, rarely took Admiralty statements entirely at face value and subtly pressed his own

---

Egypt 1882; Captain 1893; pioneer of modern director firing system; S. Africa 1899–1900; Boxer Rising 1900; captain of *Excellent* 1903–05; Rear-Admiral 1905 and Inspector of Target Practice 1905–07; 2nd Cruiser Sqdn 1907–09; Vice-Admiral 1908; Admiral on retired list and baronet 1913; special service, Admiralty 1914–18: dummy fleet, gunnery, anti-submarine warfare, air defence of London.

[1] For Sims's position, see Morison; for Benson, see M. Klachko with D. F. Trask, *Admiral William Shepherd Benson: First Chief of Naval Operations* (Annapolis, Md: NIP, 1987), hereafter Klachko; for Daniels, P. E. Coletta, 'Josephus Daniels', in Coletta, ed., *American Secretaries of the Navy* (Annapolis, Md: NIP, 1980), vol. 2, pp. 564–72.

views on his hosts, notably with regard to convoy.[1]

Benson,[2] on the other hand, though rather slow of wit and unversed in strategic doctrine, was a devoted nationalist and, by virtue of his office, had perforce to take into account the whole spectrum of American naval responsibilities, present and future. As CNO since 1915, he had been as galled as Wilson by the high-handed treatment of American shipping and maritime rights by both the British and the Germans, Moreover, he endorsed Wilson's general approach to the current crisis. Wilson had hoped to become the impartial chairman of the peace conference he had endeavoured to bring about, to no avail, in 1915–16. Even after America entered the war, Wilson maximised his independence, co-operating with the Allies only to the degree necessary to defeat the submarine menace and root out Wilhelmine militarism. Otherwise, the United States refused to endorse Allied war aims and pointedly identified itself only as an Associated Power. Like Wilson, if unlike Sims, Benson was prepared to shore up the Allies only if that served America's own cause. The United States should commit to the Entente powers only such resources as were necessary to a joint victory over the Central Powers. Apart from his support of Wilsonian mediation, Benson had other grounds for hesitation. The victory of either side might have dangerous implications for the United States. Freed of their European enemies, the victorious coalition might then assert itself elsewhere on the globe, since all European powers nursed extensive imperial ambitions – economic, territorial or strategic in character. More immediately, Benson shared the common American fear of a sudden Allied collapse, leaving America facing the dreaded triple threat of Germany, Mexico and Japan. In any case, the CNO's primary responsibility in war was the defence of America's coasts, possessions, ships and sea lanes. Even if he shared Sims's conviction that the cockpit of war was in the Western Approaches, Benson's political masters, not to mention the largely ignorant but jittery American public, would hold him to that priority and thus limit the US Navy's commitment to the European theatre. It is true that Benson continued to nurse dark suspicions of British competence,

---

[1] See document no 19. See also D. F. Trask, 'W. S. Benson', in R. W. Love, ed., *American Chiefs of Naval Operations* (Annapolis, Md: NIP, 1980), pp. 8–11; D. C. Allard, 'Admiral W. S. Sims and US Naval Policy in World War I', *American Neptune*, vol. 35, no. 2, April 1975, pp. 97–102.

[2] Rear-Admiral William Shepherd Benson, US Navy (1855–1932): Chief of Naval Operations, 1915–19; graduated from Annapolis 1877; Commander 1906; Commandant of Midshipmen, Naval Academy 1907; commanded *Albany* 1908–09; Captain 1909; commanded *Utah* 1911–13; Commandant, Philadelphia Navy Yard and 4th

strategy and global policy, as later Parts demonstrate, yet there is much evidence of his will to co-operate, and his commitment to the support of the Allies following his visit to Europe in November 1917 [Part III] cannot be questioned.[1]

While welcoming the despatch of Sims, the Admiralty hesitated to reciprocate, in part because they had an efficient Naval Attache, Captain Gaunt [1], well liked in the Navy Department and enjoying the confidence of Jellicoe, and partly because of the diplomatic caution imposed by the Foreign Office. However, once the French intimated that they were sending their flag officer in the Caribbean, Rear-Admiral Grasset, to negotiate naval assistance in the event of war, the Admiralty, determined to secure the lion's share of American maritime resources for Britain, alerted Vice-Admiral Browning, CinC North America and West Indies, enjoining him to reach Washington no later than Grasset and preferably in advance of the Frenchman [9].

As two months of confusion, uncertainty and almost furtive conversations drew to an end early in April, concrete arrangements for co-operation got under way. The US Navy, however, was almost hopelessly unready for the great burdens about to be thrust upon it. There was no co-ordination between the nation's policy-makers and its defence forces. The Navy Department was deficient in organisation and, in some respects, in leadership. The war plan against Germany was now patently irrelevant, if indeed it had ever been otherwise. The fleet was seriously unbalanced; the 1916 building programme designed to correct its lopsidedness in favour of heavy ships, was scarcely under way and little could be looked for before 1919. Officers were in desperately short supply and the Navy fell 35 000 below its manpower establishment of 87 000. In consequence only 10 per cent of its ships were fully manned and only one-third were ready for service.[2] Senior officers (notably Benson) had no realistic conception of the nature of submarine warfare nor of effective countermeasures. The world's third largest navy, the American fleet list read impressively: 15 dreadnoughts, 20 pre-dreadnoughts, 10 armoured cruisers, 25 light cruisers, 7 monitors, 74 destroyers, 19

Naval District 1913–15; Chairman and member, US Shipping Board 1920–8.
    [1] Trask, *Captains and Cabinets*, p. 48; Klachko, p. 60.
    [2] Trask, 'Benson', p. 8; A. S. Link et al., *The Papers of Woodrow Wilson* (Princeton, NJ: Princeton UP, relevant vols. from 1979), vol. 40, p. 238, extract from E. M. House's diary, 14 December 1916 (hereafter *Wilson Papers*) Coletta, *Naval Heritage*, p. 260; A. Westcott et al., *American Sea Power since 1775* (Philadelphia: Lippincott, 1952), pp. 312, 314; P. C. MacFarlane, 'The State of the Navy: Is this Country Ready for War?', *Collier's Magazine*, 31 March 1917, pp. 5–7, 21, 24–5.

torpedo boats, and 66 submarines, with 6 battleships, 10 light cruisers, 10 destroyers and 34 submarines under construction.[1] While the dreadnoughts ranked among the world's best and the latest classes of destroyers were probably the finest of their type, the pre-dreadnoughts and armoured cruisers were of limited utility; the light cruisers were a heterogenous assortment – ageing, slow, and militarily puny – while the monitors and torpedo boats were useful for only the most local defence and the submarines remained a constant source of anxiety, exasperation and embarrassment. Most crucially, only 51 of the 74 destroyers were modern craft suitable for the gruelling patrol and convoy duties in the Eastern Atlantic which was to be the United States Navy's principal contribution to the war at sea. Moreover, there was no naval aviation service of any consequence.

[1] N. Lloyd, *How We Went to War* (New York: Scribners, 1919), p. 109.

1. *Captain Guy Gaunt[1] to Captain W. R. Hall[2]*

New York,
3 February 1917

Have just been informed by House[3] that Bernstorff[4] has been given his passports and will leave at once.
I shall probably get drunk tonight.

2. *Senior Member Present, General Board of the Navy,[5] to the Secretary of the Navy*

4 February 1917

Steps to be taken to meet a possible condition of war with the Central Powers

****

22.   And as most important arrange, as soon as possible, plans of co-operation with the naval forces of the allies for the joint protection of trans-Atlantic commerce and for offensive naval operations against the common enemy.

---

[1] Later Admiral Sir Guy Gaunt: an Australian who began his career at sea in the merchant service; Sub-Lieut, RNR; service in Pacific 1897–9; Captain 1907; Naval Attaché, Washington 1914–18; Commodore 1917; served in NID 1918; knighted, promoted to Rear-Admiral and retired list at end of war; Conservative MP for Buckrose (Yorkshire); later retired to Tangier; published racy autobiography, *The Yield of the Years: Adventures Ashore and Afloat* (London: Hutchinson, 1940).

[2] Later Admiral Sir William Reginald Hall (1870–1943): Captain 1905; Inspecting Captain of Mechanical Training Establishments 1906–7; commanded *Natal* 1911; Naval Asst to Controller 1911–13; Director of Naval Intelligence 1914–19; Rear-Admiral April 1917; Conservative MP after war; the famous 'Blinker' Hall.

[3] Colonel House.

[4] Count Johann von Bernstorff, German Ambassador to USA.

[5] Rear-Admiral Charles Johnston Badger, US Navy (1853–1932): graduated from Annapolis 1873; Naval War College 1897; Cuba and Puerto Rico 1898; commanded *Chicago*; service in San Francisco earthquake 1906; Captain 1907; commanded *Kansas* 1909–11; Rear-Admiral and commanded Battleship Div. 2 1911–13; CinC Atlantic Fleet 1913–14; at Tampico, Mexico 1914; General Board 1914–21 (Chairman 1917–21); retired 1916. The rest of the memorandum outlined steps to be taken to prepare the US Navy for war. The General Board was the Navy's advisory council on policy.

3. *Captain T. P. Magruder, U.S. Navy,[1] to Franklin D.*
Roosevelt

5 February 1917

Naval Estimate of the Situation

****

... Cooperation with the Entente Allies in this war is the first and
great mission of the Navy and the Navy Department of the United
States. Such cooperation shall be absolute and entails, besides cooperation in the usual sense of the word, coordination, and in many
respects, subordination.

****

Own Forces, Strength

... Keeping in mind the nature of the war and its possibilities, it is
apparent that the only operations that may be undertaken immediately in order to bring about the objects of the war are those projected
against the enemy submarines that are being used to maintain restricted zones surrounding Britain, France, Italy and the eastern
Mediterranean. Whatever methods have been applied thus far in this
war by the Allies with success against submarines are the methods
which we must adopt at once. This denotes that immediate consul-
tations shall be had with British Naval authorities in order that we
may gain from their experience and not waste time and energy on
discredited methods. Whatever ways and means experience has
taught to be most successful against submarines, those ways and
means must be adopted by the United States and used with the
utmost energy.

****

Courses of Action Open

****

... it is unthinkable that Germany can win this war against the
major portion of the civilized world, if the submarine campaign

---

[1] Captain T. P. Magruder, US Navy: Director of Naval Militia Affairs 1917;
Commander, Sqdn 4, Patrol Force and District Commander, Lorient, France, February 1918.

against Great Britain – the foundation of Allied Strength – meets prompt and decisive defeat.

****

... That can be done in *one* way only, viz.: To place at the disposal of the British Admiralty such of our Naval Forces as are ready and suitable for aggressive action against German Submarines. The reasons for this action, unusual and drastic as it may appear from casual consideration, are as follows:

In the first place no campaign may be properly directed without *Unity of Command*. That is an elemental strategic conception.

Secondly: ... we have had no practice in the type of warfare in which we are about to enter. ... It is the part of wisdom for us to profit by Britain's experience. ... [we may] be expected to furnish for operations in the ensuing campaign:

1. Fast motor boat squadrons.
2. Destroyer flotillas.
3. Scout and cruiser squadrons.

****

Decisions

****

3. Seek immediately from British Admiralty information as to types, methods and operations best to combat submarines.
4. Ask for Entente Allies' needs and supply them wholeheartedly and entirely.
5. Harmonise plans, for carrying out or otherwise maintaining maritime commerce in accordance with existent plans of the Entente.

****

6. Send a Committee of naval officers (three) to advise with the Admiralty.

4. *Admiralty to Gaunt*

22 March 1917

Foreign Office are replying that question of co-operation cannot be discussed officially with United States Naval Department until our counsel has been sought formally through usual diplomatic channels. But Secretary of State for Foreign Affairs[1] has no objection to your communicating privately views of British Admiralty to Authorities of Navy Department if and when your advice is sought. If therefore you are asked you may say that the Admiralty would afford all necessary facilities for basing United States Destroyers on coast of Ireland for operating against submarines and protecting trade. A memorandum embodying Admiralty views of further assistance is being sent you for your personal guidance.

5. Foreign Office to Colville Barclay[2]

22 March 1917

In view of the hesitating attitude of the President and, as you say, of the 'jealousy and anti-British sentiment which pervades the United States Navy', there are obvious objections to discussing schemes of co-operation with American Naval Authorities unless we are officially approached in this sense through the proper channel. It is most desirable that such schemes should be formulated, but United States of America should call us into counsel.

6. Ambassador Walter Hines Page to Secretary of State Robert Lansing[3]

American Embassy,
Grosvenor Square,
London.
23 March 1917

Mr Balfour has shown me the informal suggestion conveyed by the Navy Department through Gaunt regarding closer naval relations and his reply. The British Government will heartily fall in with any plan we propose as soon as cooperation can be formally established. It was intimated to me that a[n anti-] submarine base on the

[1] Arthur James Balfour (1848–1930): Foreign Secretary 1916–19; notable scholar; Conservative MP; nephew of Lord Salisbury and Chief Secretary for Ireland in Salisbury cabinet 1887–91; succeeded Salisbury as Prime Minister 1902–05; deposed as Conservative leader 1911; First Lord of Admiralty in Asquith coalition 1915–16; Lord President of the Council, 1919–22 and 1925–29; earldom 1922.

[2] Colville Barclay: First Secretary, British Embassy, Washington.

[3] Robert Lansing (1864–1928): Secretary of State 1915–20; international lawyer and Counsellor of the State Department 1914–15; dismissed by Wilson in 1920 for displaying too much independence.

coast of Ireland would then be assented to.

The whole subject of active cooperation and the best methods to bring it about have been informally discussed by me with Mr Balfour, Mr Bonar Law,[1] the Prime Minister,[2] Admiral Jellicoe and others at their invitation; and they will most gladly assent to any proposals that we are likely to make. They with-held proposals of their own until the way has been formally opened by us, lest they should seem to push themselves upon us which they of course do not wish to do.

I know personally and informally that they hope for the establishment of full and frank naval interchange of information and cooperation. Knowing their spirit and their methods, I cannot too strongly recommend that our Government send here immediately an Admiral of our Navy who will bring our Navy's plans and inquiries. The coming of such an officer of high rank would be regarded as a compliment and he would have all doors opened to him and a sort of special staff appointed to give him the results and methods of the whole British naval work since the war began. Every important Ally has an officer of such high rank here. In a private conversation with me today at luncheon Mr Balfour expressed his enthusiastic hope that such a plan would be immediately carried out. Many things of the greatest value would be verbally made known to such an officer which would never be given out in a routine way nor reduced to writing.

Admiral Jellicoe has privately expressed the hope to me that our Navy may see its way to patrol our coast and possibly relieve the British cruisers, now on our side [of] the Atlantic. He hopes, too, that in case more German raiders go out we may help capture them in waters where they prey on shipping from Mexico or South America.

If our Navy Department will send an Admiral, it would be advantageous for me to be informed as soon as possible. The confidential information that he will come would be of immediate help. Such an officer could further definite plans for full cooperation.

---

[1] Andrew Bonar Law (1858–1923): Chancellor of the Exchequer 1916–19; Canadian-born businessman and Conservative MP; succeeded Balfour as Conservative leader 1911; Colonial Secretary in Asquith coalition 1915–16; Lord Privy Seal 1919–21; Conservative Prime Minister 1922–23.

[2] David Lloyd George (1863–1945): Prime Minister of coalition government 1916–22; Liberal MP, Caernarvon Boroughs, 1890–1945; Chancellor of the Exchequer 1908–15; Minister of Munitions 1915–16; Secretary of State for War 1916; earldom 1945.

7.   *President Wilson to Daniels*

The White House,
Washington,
24 March 1917

****

The main thing is no doubt to get into immediate communication with the Admiralty on the other side (through confidential channels until the Congress has acted) and work out the scheme of cooperation. As yet sufficient attention has not been given, it seems to me, by the authorities on the other side of the water to the routes to be followed or to plans by which the safest possible approach may be made to the British ports. As few ports as possible should be used, for one thing, and every possible precaution thought out. Can we not set this afoot at once and save all the time possible?

8.   *Barclay to Foreign Office*

25 March 1917

I have spoken privately to Counsellor of State Department[1] and Assistant Secretary of the Navy.[2] They quite understand the initiative should come from the United States Government. Difficulty is that until actual state of war is proclaimed they are unable to approach us officially.

Assistant Secretary of Navy suggests unofficially it might be advisable to send as soon as possible expert Naval officer from London also one from Commander-in-Chief's staff in American waters whose advice would be invaluable to Naval Department as regards netting and mining methods against submarines and coast patrol, etc. Danger of waiting to send these officers until after actual declaration of war would be that much valuable time would be lost. There is of course an off chance that war will not be declared on 2 April but strongest probabilities are that it will.[3]

[1] Frank Lyon Polk (1871–1943): Counsellor of the State Department 1915–18; lawyer, municipal reformer and diplomat; army service in Spanish–American War; friend of Franklin Roosevelt; Acting Secretary of State December 1918–July 1919; Under-Secretary July 1919–June 1920; peace commissioner at Paris July to December 1919; thereafter active in law, politics and business.

[2] Roosevelt was serving his own purpose here. He wanted to mobilise the yachtsmen of America in a motor boat patrol of the East Coast.

[3] The Constitutional position was that the President had to recommend to Congress the passage of a resolution declaring war upon Imperial Germany. Wilson went before Congress on 2 April but the resolution was not passed by the Senate until 5 April and by the House of Representatives until 6 April. Wilson signed it at once and

9. *Admiralty to Vice-Admiral Sir Montague Browning*[1]

29 March 1917

Foreign Office have instructed Ambassador Washington[2] that question of co-operation with United States Navy cannot be discussed officially until we are approached by them through diplomatic channel but a memorandum is being telegraphed to our Naval Attache New York stating Admiralty views as to the assistance which would be most useful so that he can use it if and when his advice is sought. Substance of Memorandum is as follows[:] United States flying squadron to be based on port in North Atlantic and kept ready to proceed immediately on receiving news of escape of raider; operations of squadron to be co-ordinated with those of allied squadrons; a further squadron to be employed on East Coast of South America particularly on shipping routes from Plate to American and European ports. Facilities would be given to United States to base destroyers on Irish coast for operating against submarines. It would be useful if United States Navy can look after West Coast of North America particularly Mexico as far South as Panama Canal; co-operation on West Coast of South America would depend on relations of United States with Chile. Desired that United States squadron in China seas should be maintained in view of withdrawal of British China squadron. Supervision is desirable by United States Navy of Gulf [of] Mexico and East Coast of Central America as far as Trinidad with view to preventing enemy bases [;] Memorandum ends. In event of break between United States and Germany it is probable you will be requested to go to United States and make arrangements as regards British co-operation. Meanwhile Commander Eldridge[3] Naval Staff Officer Halifax has been directed to be ready [to] proceed and advise United States Navy Authorities as regards Boom defence when so ordered by Admiralty. Third Light Division are at Brest. French are being asked to furnish

the United States thus entered the war formally on 6 April 1917.

[1] Later Admiral Sir Montague E. Browning (1863–1947): Egyptian war 1882; lost left hand in accident 1889, thereafter known as 'Hooky'; at relief of Peking 1900; Captain 1902; Rear-Admiral and Inspector of Target Practice 1911–13; commanded 3rd Battle Squadron 1913; at this time CinC, North America and West Indies; Acting Vice-Admiral 1916 and permanently raised April 1917; commanded 4th Battle Squadron 1918; head of Allied Naval Armistice Commission 1918–19; 2nd Sea Lord 1919.

[2] Sir Cecil Arthur Spring-Rice (1859–1918): Ambassador to USA 1913–January 1918; entered Foreign Office 1882; poet; close friend of Theodore Roosevelt; retired as Ambassador January 1918 but died 14 February 1918 before he could sail home.

[3] Commander G. B. Eldridge, RN (retd).

definite date of sailing.[1]

10.   *Gaunt to Hall*

29 March 1917

I have had long private conversation with Assistant Secretary of Navy who is very anxious for some private advice as to disposition of United States cruisers for patrol work and also area to be covered observing he would like to take over as far North as Cape Sable.

****

I would be grateful if America Section could send me by telegraph [?] a more or less detailed scheme for cruiser patrol as a suggestion.

Sims[2] who is detailed for London in strictest secrecy and sails *incognito* 31 March is I think a very good man.

11.   *General Board to Daniels*

5 April 1917

Assistance that United States can give Allies upon declaration of War

****

3. The General Board suggests that consideration be given to the following measures in anticipation of cooperation with the Allies:

  (a) Protect shipping to and from our ports from submarine or other attack;

  (b) Prevent the use of unfrequented bays or harbors on our own coasts, in the Gulf of Mexico and the Caribbean ... by submarines as bases;

  (c) Take over as far as may be desired and practicable the patrol of trade routes in the western north and south Atlantic and eastern Pacific, and prevent the exit of enemy merchant ships now finding asylum in the South American ports;

  (d) There is no doubt that, if desired by the Allies, sending immediately a number of destroyers to cooperate with the Allied

[1] Third Light Division was a French cruiser squadron detailed for anti-raider duties in the Caribbean and adjacent waters.
[2] Rear-Admiral William Sowden Sims, US Navy.

powers in the barred zones would greatly add to the moral effect, at home and abroad, of the participation of the United States in the war. The numbers of this type which may eventually be sent abroad will depend upon the development of a German offensive on this side of the Atlantic, our immediate needs, and the increase of this type in our Navy;

(e) Should United States troops be sent to Europe it will be necessary to escort the transports from shore to shore. At present we are short of transports and convoying vessels, and cooperation in this duty with the Allies would be necessary;

(f) The transportation of supplies for the Entente Allies is of the first importance. Requisition all enemy merchant ships detained in our ports, and seize enemy converted ships interned, repair them and place them in service as transports or supply ships;

(g) Mobilize the shipbuilding industries, both commercial and governmental, so that the energies of the nation [will] be extended in the directions needed to provide vessels to combat submarines, to escort merchant shipping, to replace shipping destroyed and for other necessary additions to the fleet;

(h) Keep constantly in view the possibility of the United States being in the not distant future compelled to conduct a war single handed against some of the belligerents[1] and steadily increase the ships of the fighting line, large as well as small but doing this with as little interference with the building of destroyers and other small craft for the Navy and cargo ships for the Merchant Marine as possible.

(i) Manufacture the number of medium caliber guns which will be needed for merchant shipping and patrol craft.

---

[1] Germany, Austria-Hungary and Japan. The fear of a two-ocean war had preoccupied American war planners since the Spanish–American War of 1898.

PART II

AMERICAN ENTRY INTO THE WAR
APRIL TO JUNE 1917

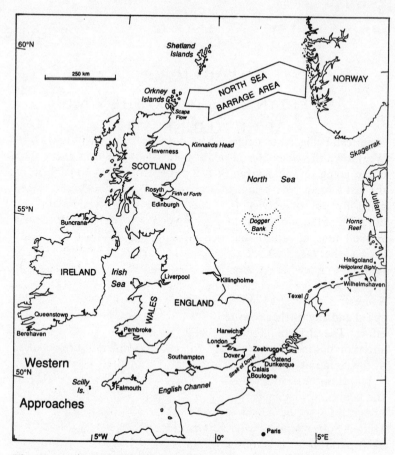

The North Sea and Western Approaches.

INTRODUCTION

American belligerency coincided with the deepest maritime crisis of World War I, when the U-boats were sinking one in every four ocean-going vessels clearing British ports. Only some 10 per cent of the lost tonnage was being replaced; moreover, damaged ships were generally out of service for several months and some for the duration of the war. In the month of America's intervention, almost 900 000 tons of Allied and neutral shipping was lost by enemy action, the vast bulk of it to the submarines. The British were reduced to a few weeks' supply of grain and only ten days' stock of sugar but the most serious shortage was that of oil, vital to all arms. Successful interdiction of the supply reduced the Grand Fleet to half speed and any further constriction would cripple the anti-submarine effort. The British public was kept in the dark about this dire situation but ministers and shipping officials were becoming restless at the Admiralty's self-confessed incapacity to discover a solution.[1]

It was in these doom-laden circumstances that a new member of the coalition, distant from it in more than one sense, had to be integrated into the Allied war effort. The disturbing fact that the United States was so woefully unprepared for war rendered her absorption into the coalition all the more difficult. For a time the Americans were likely to prove a military liability and a drain on resources until their own war effort had taken off. Moreover, the Americans, half afraid that they might soon find themselves alone against the power of Germany and her allies, remained wary of committing themselves too deeply to their new associates. They clung to as high a degree of independence as seemed consistent with ensuring the Allies' survival and an ultimate victory. As Benson's biographers explain:

American leaders possessed only the vaguest notion of the military and naval situation in Europe as the United States entered the war in April 1917. Neither the army nor the navy had made extensive efforts to analyse the conflict, a consequence of Wilson's

[1] Marder, vol. 4, chs. 4 & 5.

desire to maintain his credibility as a mediator and of European censorship, which withheld accurate information.[1]

Spring-Rice and other British observers noted that the American government and people were extraordinarily slow both to understand the seriousness of the situation and to grasp the breathtaking demands of total war on even the unmatched resources of the United States; and though the nation had gone to war united behind its President, there was little enthusiasm for the war and certainly no élan.[2]

The first months of American participation were spent in mutual explorations and inquisitions by the partners on both sides of the Atlantic. As the documents in this Part indicate, there was a series of missions to Washington and London. These sought to establish warm or at least harmonious working relationships at both policy-making and operational levels, to elucidate the truth about each partner's situation and to formulate joint plans, distribute forces to the best advantage, present shopping lists of material requirements and to concentrate their combined energies and minds on solving the current shipping crisis.

The first of the major missions was actually a joint Anglo-French exercise, the visit paid by Browning and Grasset to Hampton Roads, Virginia, and Washington on 10 and 11 April. They presented Entente proposals for American naval assistance, requesting in particular American assumption of responsibility for the protection of Western Atlantic waters against both surface and submarine raiders, the retention of the US China squadron and the drafting of American anti-submarine craft to European waters [12, 13, 14]. The atmosphere at the meetings, cool at first, warmed considerably before they concluded, and Browning's reports [17, 18] indicate steady progress towards the Allied aims. They demonstrate, too, the shortage of available American forces and the Navy Department's grudging initial response to the Allied request for anti-submarine craft to be sent to Europe. Benson suggested that two destroyers would be sufficient to show the flag; the remainder he proposed to retain for local defence and as a screen for the Atlantic Fleet.[3] Roosevelt and Admiral Mayo[4] appear to have grasped the vital strategic fact that

[1] Klachko, p. 62.
[2] E. B. Parsons, *Wilsonian Diplomacy: Allied-American Rivalries in War and Peace* (St Louis, Mo: Forum, 1978), pp. 35–6.
[3] Klachko, pp. 63, 65.
[4] Admiral Henry Thomas Mayo, US Navy (1856–1937): graduated from Annapolis 1876; hydrography specialist; Captain 1908; commanded *California* 1909–10; Commandant, Mare Island Navy Yard, San Francisco 1911–13; Aide for Personnel to

the war would be won or lost three thousand miles to the east, in the Western Approaches, and that America's true defensive frontier lay there [18]. The conferences represented a substantial success for the Allies, though rather more so for the British than for the French. Grasset seems to have been less impressed with the Americans than Browning, who struck up a deep and lasting friendship with Benson. The British also obtained substantially more assistance than the French. This was strategically sound, since the Royal Navy bore the principal responsibility for the defence of the Atlantic, but the French felt somewhat aggrieved.[1]

Meanwhile, Sims had arrived in London, meeting with a warm and no doubt heartfelt welcome from Jellicoe [15, 19]. Sims, quickly apprised of the gloomy situation, was profoundly shocked, the more so because Jellicoe confessed to knowing of no solution [19]. The British had been somewhat reluctant to unveil the true extent of the crisis but the forthright Sims properly insisted on being taken fully into the Admiralty's confidence, a demand the beleagured officials were in no position to refuse [19, 20]. Jellicoe presented a request for American assistance more comprehensive than that outlined by Browning but equally emphatic on the need to reinforce Allied measures against both surface and sub-surface raiders [16]. On Sims raising the possibility of a convoy system, Jellicoe offered the Admiralty's stock answers as to its impracticability. Here the American showed his mettle and independence, refusing to be put off by the Admiralty's uncritical fatalism and turning to the Ministry of Shipping, where convoy was already seen as the likely answer to the U-boat problem [19].

Even as Browning and Sims were arriving at their respective destinations, the British and French Governments were organising more august and more comprehensive missions to Washington. The Entente Powers' intentions were to provide the Americans with detailed information, further requests for assistance (particularly light craft and merchantmen) and, in the case of the British, to persuade the United States to abandon the construction of heavy ships in favour of anti-submarine vessels. It is likely, too, that the Allies felt that America's accession to their side should be marked by high-level missions, though Wilson seems to have regarded them as

Secretary of Navy 1913; Rear-Admiral 1913; commanded Battleship Div. 4, 1913; tough line with Mexicans provoked Tampico incident 1914; Vice-Admiral 1915; and 2nd-in-command Atlantic Fleet; CinC Atlantic Fleet 1916–19; retired 1920.

[1] Klachko, p. 65.

unnecessary and received them with some reluctance.[1] In lengthy negotiations, Arthur Balfour, the British Foreign Secretary, and his Naval Advisor, Rear-Admiral de Chair[2] pressed hard but with little concrete success. The Americans remained wedded to their 1916 dreadnought programme and were unable to release yards for Allied orders. American shipbuilding capacity was in fact extremely limited and the vast emergency yards planned for Hog Island and other places took many months to come into production. De Chair also worked manfully to arouse the Congress, the Navy Department and the American public to the critical nature of the situation and to induce a greater sense of urgency in the nation's war effort [21, 22].

Balfour's attempt to inveigle the Americans into switching their naval programme from heavy ships to destroyers ran up against the American fear of a two-ocean war. House, who had 'no authorization' to do so, boldly if covertly offered a secret deal by which Britain would transfer dreadnoughts to America after the war if the latter were threatened by hostile powers in both the Atlantic and the Pacific. In return the Americans would suspend dreadnought construction in favour of destroyers for the duration of the war. The whole scheme, which may have originated in the fertile mind of the ever-resourceful Franklin Roosevelt, was taken seriously enough to reach the War Cabinet but fell before Wilson's adamant refusal to contract the secret treaties and binding alliances which he felt were the bane of European diplomacy and a major cause of the present conflict. [The matter is discussed fully in Part IX].[3]

The Americans, too, had their demands [22], notably for a greater flow of information (particularly on plans for offensive action), for the secondment of experienced British officers, and for Admiralty consideration of a proposed North Sea Barrage [see Part VI]. However, neither they nor the British could claim any firm commitments or substantial concessions from the exhaustive talks. Nevertheless,

[1] Parsons, p. 40.

[2] Rear-Admiral (later Admiral) Sir Dudley R. S. de Chair (1864–1958): Naval Advisor to FO 'on matters concerning enemy trade' 1916–17; born in Canada; entered RN 1878; Captain 1902; Naval Attaché, Washington 1902–04; Asst Controller 1908–11; Rear-Admiral 1912; Naval Secretary to First Lord 1913; 6th Cruiser Sqdn 1913; Rear-Admiral, Training Service 1914; 10th Cruiser Sqdn and Northern Patrol 1914–March 1916; 3rd Battle Sqdn, Channel Fleet September 1917; in protest at Jellicoe's dismissal, refused Wemyss's invitation to serve on Board, relieved and placed on half pay; Vice-Admiral 1917; Admiral Commanding Coastguard and Reserves July 1918; Admiral 1920; President, Inter-Allied Commission on Enemy Warships 1921–23; retired list 1923; Governor of New South Wales 1923–30. See his *The Sea is Strong* (London: Harrap, 1961).

[3] Trask, *Captains and Cabinets*, pp. 102–25; W. R. Braisted, *The United States Navy in the Pacific, 1909–1922* (Austin, Texas: University of Texas Press, 1971), *passim*.

Balfour, a statesman of rare charm, sharp intellect, vast experience, infinite patience and considerable tact, was entitled to feel satisfied with his delegation's efforts. Both sides had opened their minds with great frankness and each knew the other's priorities, strengths and weaknesses with absolute clarity. With the departure for home of the Balfour mission the first phase of wartime co-operation was over. The problems and possibilities having been laid out uncompromisingly by both partners, the task now was to settle down to a harmonious and successful partnership.

12. *Admiralty to Browning and Gaunt*

2 April 1917

French Admiral Grasset[1] is directed by Minister of Marine to await orders Martinique to proceed to U.S. Port to be arranged by French Ambassador[2].

Desired that Commander-in-Chief North America should arrive Washington at same time as French Admiral or before him.

Inform British Ambassador and ask him to arrange for arrival of C-in-C at U.S. Port in *Leviathan*[3] when situation requires it.

Ask him to inform Admiralty and C-in-C direct of Port proposed.

After disembarking C-in-C *Leviathan* can proceed if desired to Halifax to await his return.

13. *Admiralty to Browning and Gaunt*

3 April 1917

We attach greatest importance to having as many U.S. Destroyers as possible in our waters to assist in protection of trade and will give them all facilities.

You should endeavour to get U.S. to send them at earliest possible date.

The second important point is the immediate organisation of sweeping squadrons to pick up raiders.

14. *Admiralty to Gaunt*

7 April 1917

Besides the points already communicated to you, you should ascertain how the U.S.A. intend to employ their submarines, informing them that we are using some of our submarines in operations against similar hostile craft. We have obtained some successes.[4] The moral effect on the enemy submarines is very consider-

---

[1] Contre-Amiral Maurice-Ferdinand-Albert Grasset, commanding French naval forces in North American waters. In 1916 he served in the Ministry of Marine.

[2] Jules Jusserand, who served in Washington for over 25 years.

[3] HMS *Leviathan*: cruiser, 1901; 14000 tons; 2 × 9.2 in., up to 14 × 6 in.; Browning's flagship.

[4] The use of submarines against U-boats was frequently advocated but it was not easy to avoid accidental clashes with one's own surface forces or aircraft. Allied submarines were credited with 18 successes; more U-boats were destroyed by mines, depth charges and gunfire. See Marder, vol. 5, pp. 119–20.

28

able and it cramps their activities.

Any such operations by the U.S. submarines would be welcomed by us in the vicinity of West Indies or Canadian coast if any [hostile] submarines should appear there.

To avoid mistakes, it is of course imperative that surface patrol vessels and submarines should work in entirely distinct areas.

15. *Jellicoe to Sims*

7 April 1917

Welcome to England! I am exceedingly glad that you have been selected by the Government to come here and I feel sure that we shall be able to establish close co-operation between the two countries so far as naval matters are concerned.

I have sent Captain Hope[1] to meet you so that you can discuss matters on your way to London, and I shall hope to have the pleasure of seeing you very shortly.

The situation is far from easy, solely on account of the submarine question, but the difficulties are only there to be overcome, and that they will be overcome I am convinced, although I fully expect our losses to be very heavy before all is over.

My one regret is that I shall not be actively co-operating with the United States Naval Forces although it is possible that the Grand Fleet may not see much of them.

I am of course very anxious of hearing your views.[2]

16. *Memorandum by Jellicoe*

9 April 1917

The question of the assistance which might be given by the United States Navy and by the United States generally from the Naval point of view

****

1. There is no doubt that the whole efforts of the U.S. Navy as well as of other navies of the Allies, should be devoted at the present time

[1] Later Admiral Sir George Price Webley Hope (1869–1959): at this time on Admiralty operations staff and appointed Director of Operations May 1917; Captain 1905; Assistant Director of Naval Mobilisation 1911; Assistant Director, Operations 1912–13; commanded *Queen Elizabeth* 1916; Rear-Admiral April 1917; Deputy First Sea Lord January 1918.

[2] Sims and Jellicoe had first met in China in 1901, when the former was a Lieut.-Cdr. and Jellicoe a Captain. Both were gunnery specialists and therefore had much in common. See Sims, *The Victory at Sea*, p. 5.

to attacking submarines and protecting merchant ships from their attack, as it appears most probable that the war will be decided by the ability of the Allies to preserve sufficient shipping for the import of food and other essentials, as well as for the maintenance of the overseas armies. The direction therefore in which the U.S. can help us best is by the provision of the vast numbers of small craft for these two purposes. For the efficient protection of our trade on this side, and for a really vigorous offensive against the enemy submarines, we require at least twice as many patrol craft such as trawlers, sloops, etc., as we have at present, and we require at least another 100 destroyers. Anything therefore that the U.S. can do in the way of providing us with these craft, either by sending them now, or by building them very rapidly, will be of inestimable value to the Allied cause. I realise, of course, that 'charity begins at home', and that the first care of the U.S. must be for the protection of shipping off their own shores, but it is obvious that submarines will have very great difficulty in maintaining themselves off the American coast unless they are provided with supply ships or supply bases, and with the whole of the North American continent opposed to Germany there ought to be great difficulty to the Germans in maintaining such bases. Therefore the number of submarines that are likely to work in U.S. waters is very small indeed compared to the numbers which will work on this side, and consequently the number of anti-submarine craft required is correspondingly less. This is a point which should be pressed strongly. No doubt the Germans will endeavour to establish bases on the Mexican coast, but it is a very long way from Germany to Mexico, and the submarine which makes this journey will certainly require considerable repairs before she is fit for use again, and it should not be difficult to ensure that, at any rate, repair facilities in Mexico would be a matter of great difficulty for the Germans to obtain.

2. The resources of the U.S. in the direction of rapid shipbuilding must be very considerable. The proof of this is forthcoming in the rapidity with which Mr Schwab of the Bethlehem Steel Works[1]

---

[1] Charles Michael Schwab (1862–1939): Chairman of Bethlehem Steel 1904–39; Director-General, Emergency Fleet Corporation 1917–18; industrialist; executive with Carnegie Steel Co.; President, US Steel Corp. 1901–03; Schwab was certainly efficient but Jellicoe was over-optimistic in expecting all American yards to match Bethlehem's record. Moreover, the USA had a relatively small shipbuilding capacity in pre-war days. Finally, Jellicoe seems to have taken little account of possible American wartime programmes for both mercantile and naval vessels; as events proved, such programmes were likely to be enormous.

built 10 'H' class submarines for us in the early part of the war.[1] His promise was five months and he fulfilled it. If he can produce submarines quickly, it is probable that he can produce other small craft equally quickly, and if it is found that he, or any other firm in the United States can build for us with great rapidity destroyers, trawlers, sloops or 'H' class submarines, it is desirable that you [Gaunt] should telegraph at once direct to me, giving particulars.

3. It is of course most desirable that the U.S. should immediately repair and get running all the interned German merchant ships, and should build merchant ships for us. This no doubt is a matter which the representative of the Shipping Controller[2] will take up.

4. The U.S. Navy might help us very much by hunting down in a systematic manner the raiders now at large. It is believed that there is one in the Indian Ocean, and one either in the Pacific or the Atlantic.[3] No doubt the U.S. will have facilities for obtaining information as to the whereabouts of the raider, and the bases which she or they have been using, which will be greater than the facilities possessed by us. If they can give any valuable information of this sort, it will be of inestimable value.

Action against Raiders

I am very anxious to strengthen our blockading squadron in order to establish a second line to minimize the chances of further raiders breaking out. Undoubtedly the best type of vessel for the work is the armed merchant ship, and it would be of great assistance to us if I could withdraw from service abroad the armed merchant ships which we now have there for service in Home waters. I cannot however do this unless they are relieved by vessels of a similar type, because the qualities which render them useful in the blockading squadron, namely great fuel endurance and sea-keeping capacity, render them equally valuable on foreign stations. It will probably be more acceptable to the U.S., if they intend commissioning any armed merchant steamers, to use them in the Atlantic and Pacific, and not to join our blockading squadron, as they may not see eye to

[1] 'H' class submarines: 440/500 tons; 4 tt; 13/10.5 knots. Ten built by Fore River S.B. Co.; on US entry into war, 6 transferred to Chile, 2 to Canada; others built in Canada, 1915–19. Gaddis Smith, *Britain's Clandestine Submarines* (New Haven, Conn: Yale UP, 1964).

[2] Sir Joseph Paton Maclay (1857–1951): appointed Shipping Controller December 1916; Glasgow shipowner; baronetcy 1914 for public and political services in Scotland; a Liberal; baron 1922.

[3] Two raiders, the *Wolf* and the sailing ship *Seeadler*, were out at this time. See Marder, vol. 4, pp. 99–101.

eye with us in blockade matters,[1] but in either capacity they could render us very great service, and similarly their cruiser squadrons could be of great help in taking over from us some of the foreign work. This would relieve our own cruisers for blockade work nearer Home and for preventing the escape of raiders.

****

The Employment of American Submarines

No doubt at first the US authorities will desire to keep their submarines in Home waters. If they do so, and if German submarines do make their appearance in American waters, their best role would be to act offensively against the German submarines. This is not a method which produces any great material effect unless the enemy submarines attack on the surface, but it does exercise a considerable moral effect and it cramps the activities of the German submarines. If however it is found, as I anticipate, that German submarines do not appear on the American coast, the US submarines would be of very great assistance to the Allied cause in Home waters. I should recommend that some of them should be employed in Mexican waters in case of an attempt on the part of Germany to establish a base in those waters. The best place for American submarines to start work would be in the vicinity of the Canary Islands and Madeira, and for this purpose they could be based on Gibraltar.[2]

Mine Laying

I presume that the US authorities have made a provision for a force of mine sweepers in the vicinity of their principal ports. I imagine that this form of attack is one which the Germans will

[1] It was a considerable understatement on Jellicoe's part to observe that the US might not accept British blockade policy, for this had been the source of major diplomatic friction between the two nations since the French Revolutionary wars and tension ran as high as ever in the period from August 1914 to April 1917. The US believed in freedom of the seas in both peace and war, ultimately enshrining the principle in the second of Wilson's Fourteen Points of January 1918. At the Paris peace conference, the two countries clashed head-on, as detailed in Part IX. For the duration of the war, however, the Americans acquiesced in British policy.

[2] America's early submarines were extremely unreliable vessels in the main and the submarine service remained the despair of the naval authorities until well after the war. See Rear-Admiral Yates Stirling, US Navy, *Sea Duty. Memoirs of a Fighting Admiral* (New York: Putnam's, 1939), pp. 154–60. Stirling had commanded the Submarine Force shortly before America joined the war. For the employment of American submarines in the eastern Atlantic, see documents nos. 158, 160, 183, 187, 237, 243.

endeavour to put into force in American waters. A submarine mine-layer could get to US and back without the assistance of a depot ship.[1]

Mines

It is desirable to ascertain to what extent the US Navy is provided with mines, and the type in use. Possibly they may feel inclined to assist us in this direction. The loan of some mine layers would be of great help to us, as we are rather short of this type of vessel.

****

17. *Browning to Admiralty*

13 April 1917

Following points of agreement have been arrived at with United States Navy Dept. French Admiral sending similar telegram to Paris. Questions raised by British Admiralty:

First: One squadron immediately ready to proceed from North Atlantic port on receipt of information of escape of raider. Operations of ships of this squadron will be co-ordinated with those of Allied squadrons. Area of operations from parallel of Cape Sable to longitude 5° West thence South to parallel of 20° North.

Second: Second squadron on the East Coast of South America will be provided as soon as possible in the near future. Area of operations from Brazillian Coast along parallel 5° South to meridian 30° West thence South to 15° South then parallel with coast to latitude of 35° South then along that parallel to the coast.

Third: Six destroyers will be sent over in the immediate future; these will be based on a British or French port as may be considered most necessary.[2]

Fourth: United States will look after West Coast of North America from Canadian to Colombian boundaries.

Fifth: Relations with Chile excellent. United States armed govt. nitrate vessels will maintain continuous service for the present which will be utilised.

Sixth: United States China Squadron will be maintained for the

---

[1] Mines were laid off the US east coast by cruiser submarines. On 19 July 1918, the USS *San Diego* (cruiser, 1904; 13 680 tons; 4 x 8in, 14 x 6in) was mined and sunk off Fire Island, NY, but this was the Germans' only major success. The mines were laid by U-156.

[2] See document no. 128.

present.

Seventh: United States will supervise Gulf of Mexico and Central America as far as Colombian boundary thence to West Point of Jamaica along North coast of Jamaica to East point of Virgin Islands thence North to South Eastern limit of area referred to in first.

Eighth: If and when enemy's submarines appear they will attempt to send several submarines to the Canadian coast but this only possible if a parent ship or accommodation of men on shore provided.

****

18.   *Browning to Secretary of the Admiralty*[1]

British Embassy,
Washington, D.C.,
13 April 1917

Report of Proceedings since arrival in the United States[2]

****

3. ...

It was evident that they were really desirous to co-operate, but the provision of Destroyers seemed to be unacceptable, and also the institution of a South Atlantic Squadron was viewed with some doubt. All the U.S. officers however expressed a general wish to receive as much information as could be afforded them, and some points prepared by Admiral Grasset and by me were stated to be exactly those upon which they especially desired guidance.

During the meeting their attitude became more and more cordial, especially in the cases of Admirals Benson and Mayo.

It was generally evident that the U.S. Navy had a deep respect for our experience gained during the War, and an anxious desire to be afforded advice. There was no trace of any feeling to the contrary.

****

[1] Sir William Graham Greene (1857–1950): entered Admiralty 1881; Private Secretary to First Lord 1887–1902; Principal Clerk 1902–07; Asst. Secretary 1907–11; knighted 1911; Permanent Secretary 1911–17; ousted in re-organisation of Admiralty by Geddes in 1917; Permanent Secretary, Ministry of Munitions 1917–20.

[2] On 10 April Browning had conferred at Hampton Roads, Va., with Admiral Henry T. Mayo, Commander of the Atlantic Fleet, and other senior US officers. He was accompanied by Captain Gaunt, Rear-Admiral Grasset and the French Naval Attache, Cdr Blanpre.

5. This meeting[1] was markedly an advance upon that of the previous day. Mr. Daniels made a short speech expressing the entire readiness of the U.S. Navy to co-operate to the utmost of its power.
...

6. *Two* Destroyers were stated to be in readiness to leave forthwith; Admiral Mayo expressed his desire to send six. As this proposal was not to any degree backed up, I expressed grateful thanks for the two (Mr Franklin Roosevelt having whispered to me that more would most certainly be forthcoming).

7. The provision of the South Atlantic Squadron had been reconsidered and it was now stated that it would be sent as soon as possible, but that it was not immediately ready like the North Atlantic Squadron.

I enquired whether it was desired that my own opinion as to the desired strength of these squadrons should be stated, and their reply being that that was what they wished I mentioned the number as four ships for each. Admiral Mayo immediately said that six ships should be detailed for each squadron in order that four should be constantly maintained. and this was implicitly accepted by the Conference as a necessary condition.

It was stated that the four North Atlantic ships will be distributed along the coast ports with their respective patrol squadrons, but that they would act in conjunction on a contingency arising. I suggested, and so did Admiral Grasset, that it would be best to concentrate them, but as soon as it appeared that this was not acceptable, it was not pressed. They will find out the disadvantages later. An attitude of acquiesence to their wishes was evidently the best to adopt.

8. I expressed the opinion that Armed Merchant Cruisers are especially suitable for anti-raider operations, and why; but they said they must consider the debit balance of the advantage in withdrawing them from freight duties, etc., and this point was set aside for consideration.

9. They enquired whether Trinidad, etc., could be used by such a squadron if found desirable. This I said could certainly be done, but that I would suggest their providing their own colliers. This they agreed to do.

10. At present there are political difficulties which stand in the way of U.S. ships of war visiting the ports of Colombia.[2]

[1] Report of a formal meeting at Washington on 11 April attended by Daniels, Roosevelt, Benson, Badger and other senior US officers, together with Browning, Gaunt, Grasset and Blanpre.
[2] Colombia was still aggrieved at the high-handed actions of President Theodore

11. The present intention is not to send any United States men-of-war south to the west coast of South America, but meantime there are armed nitrate transports, working under both War and Navy Departments, which will be utilised, and ships of war could be sent south if the situation required it.

We were informed that the feeling in Chile was excellent.[1]

12. The U.S. China squadron will be maintained. This was at the first meeting stated to be permanently, but at the final conference on 12 April Admiral Benson stated that in consequence of certain information received that morning from Japan,[2] the maintenance of the squadron might have to be modified, but that due notice would be given of withdrawal.

13. There seemed to be a readiness to send submarines to Halifax if and when required, but they did not care about sending them to the West Indies.

They acknowledged that their submarine service is inefficient, but it was pointed out to them that the moral effect of the presence of such craft at Canadian ports would be useful, and they quite realise it.

14. Admiral Grasset was very anxious to fix the exact limits of action of the allied squadrons, and pressed the point so much that Admiral Benson and I agreed, although at this stage it seemed undesirable, and as Admiral Benson remarked, the U.S. ships would not cease to chase a raider if she left their areas. Areas were accordingly drafted for consideration at the final meeting.

15. On 12 April a final smaller naval meeting took place in Admiral Benson's room to decide upon the exact terms in which the Admiralty and the Ministry of Marine should be informed of the result of the conference.

****

16. I was agreeably surprised and impressed with the warm recep-

---

Roosevelt in 1903, when he boasted 'I took Panama and let Congress debate'. The Colombians had held out for a more favourable deal on the proposed Panama Canal, angering Roosevelt. When the Colombian province of Panama revolted and proclaimed its independence, Roosevelt promptly accorded recognition, signed a canal treaty on the terms rejected by Colombia and effectively prevented the Colombians from crushing the rebellion. It took almost 20 years to assuage the Colombian grievances..

[1] Chile was a vital source of nitrates for explosives.

[2] The fact that the British wanted the Americans to maintain a squadron in Chinese waters suggests that they were suspicious of the ambitions of their ally, Japan. The Americans were equally suspicious of the Japanese but Benson's statement referred to

tion given to us by the Civil and Naval sides of the U.S. Navy Department, and especially by Mr Daniels himself, with whom I became on completely friendly terms. I had been led to believe, even from hints dropped by their own officers, that he might prove difficult, but, from first to last, he has not only made friendly speeches, but repeatedly impressed upon me the anxious desire of the Department for full co-operation, and their keenness to do all that is possible to injure the enemy.[1]

I expected to find that advice might not be acceptable, but both he and the officers repeatedly asked me for advice on many points which I gave to the best of my ability.

Admiral Benson also became completely friendly as soon as the first meeting at Hampton Roads was over, and he has talked to me confidentially upon many matters.[2]

The attitude of Admiral Mayo, Commander-in-Chief of the Atlantic Fleet, from first to last has been that of a brother officer. He is reserved, and a man of few words, but he has always intervened in the discussions with the most timely suggestions, and to him and to Mr Franklin Roosevelt is chiefly due the change in attitude in the provision of destroyers on our side; the latter official is my authority for the statement that eighteen would actually come over, and that soon. He also told me that Admiral Mayo had wished to do this at the meeting on 11 April, as he understood the urgency of the matter. Mr Roosevelt told me particularly that he was completely aware of the necessity for more of these craft in our home waters, but understood the advisability of my not pressing the matter at the meetings.

****

17. ... Commodore Gaunt has been most invaluable, and it is to his able, careful and thorough work as Naval Attaché, and to the friendly relations he has established with the United States Navy and the Department, that our reception was of so satisfactory a character, and the result so much above my own, and even his, expectations.

an overture from Japan which resulted in the Lansing–Ishii Agreement of November 1917, by which relations between the two powers were improved, at least for a few years.
    [1] Daniels, like Wilson himself, a near-pacifist, was loath to enter the war but ultimately manifested a spirit as warlike as any blue-water sailor. See Josephus Daniels, *Our Navy at War* (New York: Doran, 1922).
    [2] Browning and Benson became firm friends. See Klachko, pp. 63–5, 192.

19. *Sims to Daniels*

American Embassy,
London
19 April 1917

*Confirmation and elaboration of recent cablegrams concerning War
situation and recommendations for U.S. Naval cooperation*

1. *Reception*

My reception in this country has been exceptionally cordial and
significant of the seriousness of present situation and importance to
be attached to United States entry into the war.

I was met at Liverpool by Rear-Admiral Hope, R.N., a member
of Admiral Jellicoe's staff, and the Admiral of the Port,[1] the former
having been sent by the Admiralty to escort me to London. A special
train was provided which made a record run, and within a few hours
after arrival in London I was received by the First Sea Lord and his
principal assistants in a special conference.

2. *Conferences*

More or less hesitancy was noted at first in presenting a full
statement of the true situation, particuarly (as it developed later) on
account of its seriousness combined with a natural reluctancy
against appearing to seek assistance, and a hesitancy on taking
chances of allowing information indirectly to reach the enemy, and
thereby improve enemy morale.

I therefore positively took the position that I must be considered a
part of the Admiralty organisation, and that it was essential to safe
and efficient cooperation that I be trusted with full knowledge of the
exact situation.

They finally consented, only after reference to the Imperial War
Council, to my exposing the true state of affairs both as regards the
military situation and rate of destruction of merchant shipping.

I have had daily conferences with the First Sea Lord, both at his
office and residence, and also have been given entire freedom of the
Admiralty and access to all Government Officials. I have freely
consulted with such officials as the following:

Prime Minister
First Lord of Admiralty[2]
Ministers of Munitions, Shipping, Trade and other Cabinet
officials

---

[1] Rear-Admiral Harry Hampson Stileman, a retired officer.
[2] Sir Edward Henry, later Baron, Carson.

First Sea Lord and his assistants
Chief of Naval Staff[1]
Directors (corresponding our Chiefs of Bureaus) of Intelligence,
Antisubmarine operations, Torpedoes, Mines, Mining, etc.

3. *General Statement of the Situation*
Since the last declaration of the enemy Government, which from
intelligence information was anticipated, the submarine campaign
against merchant shipping of all Nations has resolved itself into the
real issue of the war and, stated briefly, the Allied Governments have
not been able to, and are not now,effectively meeting the situation
presented.

****

8. With improved weather and the shorter nights now coming on we
may expect even more enemy submarine success.
9. The Commander-in-Chief of the Grand Fleet[2] was yesterday in
conference in the Admiralty as to what greater extent destroyers and
auxiliaries of the Fleet may be utilised without endangering its
power in the remote possibility of another Fleet engagement.
The consensus of opinion seems to be that the latter will not
occur, but there is not complete unanimity in this belief, and of
course, in any case, the possibility must be adequately and continuously provided against.
10. *General discussion of situation*

****

11. The evidence is conclusive that, regardless of any enemy diver-

[1] It is difficult to know to whom Sims refers, unless it is the Chief of the Admiralty
War Staff, November 1914–May 1917, Acting Vice-Admiral Sir Henry F. Oliver
(1865–1965): Captain 1903; commanded Navigation School, Portsmouth 1905–07;
Naval Assistant to First Sea Lord 1908–11; Director of Intelligence 1913; Rear-
Admiral 1913; Naval Secretary to First Lord 1914; DCNS June 1917; commanded 1st
Battle Cruiser Squadron 1918; ultimately an Admiral of the Fleet.
[2] Later Admiral of the Fleet Sir David, later Earl, Beatty (1871–1936): Acting
Admiral and CinC Grand Fleet November 1916–April 1919; entered RN 1884; won
DSO in Nile operations 1898; gallantry in Boxer campaign, China 1900; rapid
promotions, viz. Commander 1898, Captain 1900, Rear-Admiral 1 January 1910;
Naval Secretary to First Lord (Churchill) 1912–13; commanded battle cruiser forces
of Grand Fleet 1913–16; Acting Vice-Admiral 2 August 1914, confirmed 9 August
1915; Admiral 1 January 1919; Admiral of the Fleet 3 April 1919; First Sea Lord
1919–27; earldom 1919. See S. W. Roskill, *Admiral of the Fleet Earl Beatty, the Last
Naval Hero* (London: Collins, 1980); B. McL. Ranft, *The Beatty Papers: Selections
from the Private and Official Correspondence of Admiral of the Fleet Earl Beatty*
(Aldershot: Scolar Press for Navy Records Society, vol. 1 (1902–1918) 1989; vol. 2
(1919–1936) forthcoming).

sions such as raids on our coasts or elsewhere, the critical area in which the war's decision will be made is in the eastern Atlantic at the focus of all lines of communications.

****

12. Even in this critical area, it is manifest that the field is relatively large for the maximum number of submarines which the enemy can maintain in it. For example, with the present Admiralty policy (explained below), they are forced to cover all the possible trade routes of approach between the north of Scotland and Ushant.

13.   From consideration of the above and all other essential information available, it is apparent that the enemy could not disperse his main submarine campaign into other quarters of the Globe without diminishing results in this and all areas to a degree which would mean failure to accomplish the Mission of the submarine campaign, which can be nothing else than a final decision of the War.

14. Considerable criticism has been, and still is, concentrated upon the Admiralty for not taking more effective steps and for failing to produce more substantial and visible results. One of the principal demands is for convoys of merchant shipping, and more definite and real protection within the war zone.

The answer, which manifestly is not publicly known, is simply that the necessary vessels are not available and further those which are available are suffering from the effects of three years of arduous service.

15. It is insistently asked (was asked by myself) why shipping is not directed to and concentrated at various rendezvous and from these convoyed through the dangerous areas. The answer is the same – the area is too large; the necessary vessels are not available.

16. However, I am now consulting with the Director of Shipping[1] as to the practicability and advisability of attempting some new approach to such a plan in case the United States is able to put in operation sufficient tonnage to warrant it.

17. After trying various methods of controlling shipping, the Admiralty now believes the best policy to be one of dispersion. They use about six relatively large avenues or arcs of approach to the United Kingdom and Channel, changing their limits or areas periodically if necessity demands.

****

20. The Admiralty has had frequent conferences with Merchant

[1] Presumably Sir Joseph Maclay, the Controller of Shipping.

masters and sought their advice. Their most unanimous demand is 'Give us a gun and let us look out for ourselves'. They are also insistent that it is impracticable for merchant vessels to proceed in formation, at least in any considerable numbers, due principally to difficulty in controlling their speed [and] to the inexperience of their subordinate officers. With this view I do not personally agree but believe that with a little experience merchant vessels could safely and sufficiently well steam in open formations.

21. The best protection against the submarine menace for all classes of ships, merchant as well as Naval, is SPEED and ZIGZAGGING, not more than fifteen minutes on a course. Upon this point no one disagrees, but on the contrary there is absolute unanimity of opinion.

22. In the absence of adequate patrol craft, particularly destroyers, and until the enemy submarine morale is broken, there is but one sure method of meeting the submarine issue upon which there is also complete unanimity – increased number of merchant bottoms, preferably small.

'More Ships! More Ships! More Ships!' is heard on every hand.

****

24. The Prime Minister only two days ago expressed to me the opinion that it ought to be possible to find physical means of absolutely sealing up all escape for submarines from their own ports. The fact that all such methods (nets, mines, obstructions, etc.) inherently involve the added necessity of continuous protection and maintenance by our own Naval forces is seldom understood and appreciated. I finally convinced the Prime Minister of the fallacy of such propositions by describing the situation into which we would be led, namely that in order to maintain our obstructions we would have to match the forces the enemy brought against them until finally the majority if not all of our forces would be forced into dangerous areas where they would be subject to continual torpedo and other attack, in fact in a position more favorable to the enemy.

25. Entirely outside of the fact that the enemy does, and always can force exits, and thereby nullify the close blockade, the weather is a serious added difficulty. The heaviest anchors obtainable have been used for nets, mines and obstructions, only to have the arduous work of weeks swept away in a few hours of heavy weather. Moorings will not hold. They chafe through. In this respect we could be of great assistance, i.e., in supplying moorings and buoys.

26. The Channel is not now, and never has been completely secure

against submarine egress, let alone the vaster areas of escape to the north. Submarines have gone under mine fields, and have succeeded in unknown ways in evading and cutting through nets and obstructions.

27. In addition to submarines, heavy forces are free to raid and in fact escape through the Channel at any time when the enemy decides that the necessity or return will justify the risk. Hence the suggestion that two divisions of our fast Dreadnoughts might be based upon Brest primarily for the resulting moral effect against such possible raids.

****

28. *Submarine Losses*

It has been found necessary to accept *no* reports of submarine losses as authentic and certain unless survivors are captured or the submarine itself definitely located by dragging. No dependence is placed upon evidence of oil on the surface after a submarine has been attacked and forced down as there is reason to believe that when an enemy submarine dives to escape gunfire she is fitted to expel oil for the particular purpose of conveying the impression that she has been sunk and thereby avoids further pursuit.

It has been shown that the amount of damage a submarine can stand is surprising and much more than was anticipated before the experience of the war. ...

29. *Best anti-submarine weapons*

One of the most efficient weapons now used by all destroyers and patrol craft against submarines is the so-called 'Depth Charge', sample and drawings of which have been forwarded by our Naval Attaché.[1] These are merely explosive charges designed to explode at a certain depth, formerly eighty feet, now about one hundred feet. They are dropped overboard where a submarine that has submerged is assumed to be and are counted upon to badly shake up and demoralise [the crew] if they do not actually cause serious damage.

Howitzers and Bomb-throwers of large calibre are under construction designed to throw similar depth charges to distances of about 2000 yards. Details will be forwarded.

****

34. *Submarine versus Submarine*

There has always been opposition to using submarines against submarines principally on the grounds that the possibilities of their

[1] Captain William D. MacDougall, US Navy: later commanded USS *North Carolina*.

accomplishment would not be sufficiently great to justify the risk involved of mistaken identity and damage to friends.

The Director of Anti-Submarine Warfare[1] believes, however, that such operations promise well and the experiment is now being tried with as many submarines as can be spared from the Grand Fleet. Some enemy submarines have been destroyed by this method, usually torpedoed. One valuable feature of this method lies in the fact that as long as our submarines are not so used, the enemy submarine is always perfectly safe in assuming that all submarines sighted are friends. If this certainty is removed the enemy will be forced to keep down more and to take much greater precautions against detection. This is an advantage of no small amount.

****

20.   *Office Memorandum by Graham Greene*

20 April 1917

Admiral Sims, of the United States Navy, having been appointed to represent the American Navy Department in London, it has been decided that he should be placed in a confidential position in regard to the Admiralty Departments dealing with war operations, and arrangements are to be made to provide him with a room at the Admiralty (Room 63, Old Building).

In view of the importance of obtaining every possible assistance from the United States in connection with submarine warfare and other important war operations, all information that may be of use to the United States Navy should be communicated to the Admiralty Secretary, it being understood that the First Sea Lord is to be consulted should there be any doubt as to the expediency of communicating any particular item of secret information.

****

21.   *Rear-Admiral Sir Dudley De Chair to Graham Greene*

Washington, D.C.,
15 May 1917

General Report on the Progress of Negotiations with the United States Navy Department, etc., in connection with Mr Balfour's Mission

****

[1] Later Admiral Sir Alexander Ludovic Duff (1862–1933): Director of Anti-Sub-

3. At first the Navy Department did not seem to be alive to the gravity of the submarine menace and the inclination was to keeping their forces, particularly the Destroyers, within the limits of American Waters, but after repeated representations this view altered. On 25 April the first Flotilla of Six boats was despatched to Queenstown[1] followed on 8 May by Six more and on 13 May by a third division of Six. Meanwhile 18 boats were ordered to their Dockyards in order to be in readiness to proceed to European Waters with their tenders *Melville* and *Dixie*,[2] one of the latter being designated as the flagship of the Squadron.

4. Some difficulty was experienced in securing that these boats should all go to British Waters as there was a large section of the Navy Department in favour of Destroyers being sent to assist French Patrols, but after it had been pointed out how fatal this policy would be, it was decided to send the Flotillas to the South West Coast of Ireland where they would be placed under the Orders of an United States Flag Officer (probably Rear-Admiral Sims) and would work from there.

5. As I telegraphed on 4 May the Navy Department expressed their willingness to forward at once 2000 ELIA Mines of an improved type, together with 2000 Mines of an earlier type, and they stated they were prepared to start manufacturing 10,000 Mines of this type if required, promising that delivery should commence in July.[3]

6. I have frequently touched on the question of the arming of Merchant Ships, pointing out the obvious desirability so often proved by our experience, of providing all shipping with some means of defence against submarines, and I am now informed that it has been decided to remove the light guns from several of the older ships of the Fleet and to reduce the light armament of the newer vessels in order to provide for the requirements of Merchant Vessels in this direction.

7. On 4 May, accompanied by Admiral Benson, I attended a meet-

marine Division January to June 1917; entered RN 1875; Captain 1902; Naval Assistant to 3rd Sea Lord 1905–08; Commodore, RN Barracks, Portsmouth 1910–11; Director of Naval Mobilisation 1911–14; Rear-Admiral 1913; 2nd-in-command, 4th Battle Squadron 1914–17; Assistant Chief of Naval Staff June 1917–1919; Vice-Admiral 1918; CinC, China Station 1919–22; Admiral 1921; retired list 1925.

[1] See documents nos. 134, 137, 142, 143.

[2] USS *Melville*: 1915; 7150 tons; 8 x 5 in.; 15 knots. USS *Dixie*: 1893; 6114 tons; 10 x 3 in.; 14.5 knots.

[3] The standard British mine at that time was of the ELIA type but was not very efficient. The British ultimately adopted the successful German pattern. They politely declined the American offer. See Marder, vol. 4, pp. 86–88.

ing of the Naval Committee of Congress[1] behind closed doors and explained the situation and answered questions, and I understand that it was practically decided after I left to proceed with the 'Ship Appropriation Bill', and to requisition all necessary small craft in United States harbours, which would probably mean approximately 150 vessels of varying types.

8. I have been informed by the Navy Department that they are most anxious to co-operate with us in the efficient direction and control of Merchant Shipping, and it appears to me that the United States Government is prepared to adopt many of our measures to secure the stoppage of supplies to Germany.

9. In the matter of Mercantile Ship Construction and the building of small craft I have experienced some difficulty for the following reasons:-

(a) the policy of the United States Government as to building is not yet decided on, and it remains uncertain whether heavy Warship construction, wooden or steel merchant ship building, or the building of Destroyers and small craft is to be given preference.

(b) the relations between the Shipping Board and Mr Schwab are far from good, and the latter is practically debarred from accepting any contracts except for Patrol Craft and Submarines to which he does not seem anxious to confine himself though I am urging him to do so.

I am however hopeful of gaining some concession from the Shipping Board through General Goethals,[2] the most practical man on that body, which may enable us to obtain the type of vessel we need.

****

11. At Mr Balfour's request I visited the Minister of Commerce[3] and discussed with him a projected plan for blocking the passage of the North Sea by means of nets stretched from the North of Shetland to a point on the Norwegian Coast south of Bergen – roughly 150 miles. This project, concerning which I am telegraphing, is much favoured by the Navy Department, and if it is considered feasible

[1] Presumably the Naval Affairs Committee of the House of Representatives.

[2] General George Washington Goethals, US Army (1858–1928): at this time head of Emergency Fleet Corporation but resigned in July 1917, unable to co-operate with US Shipping Board; renowned as builder of Panama Canal; retired as Major-General 1916; recalled in 1917 to help organise Army's supplies.

[3] William C. Redfield (1858–1932): Secretary of Commerce 1913–19; former Democratic member of House of Representatives from Brooklyn, NY. His Department's Bureau of Coast and Geodetic Survey had devised the scheme. See Part VI for a full discussion of the project.

they propose to put it into execution and maintain it with their own resources in the way of personnel, small craft and other necessary materiel. The question of the violation of Territorial Waters is involved in this scheme but the United States Authorities appear to have no scruples and they are prepared to take the consequences as regards Norway provided we favour the scheme.

****

13. At the request of Rear-Admiral Badger I delivered a short lecture at the Navy Board Office[1] to some seventy Officers in which I outlined generally our Naval Policy and emphasised the need of immediate co-operation on the part of the United States Navy.

14. In common with other Heads of the Mission I have given interviews to members of the American Press in which I have endeavoured to impress on the American Public through their readers the necessity of prompt and decisive action against Germany. It is of course understood that the information given to the Press has been of a more general and optimistic nature than the details which I have placed at the disposal of the Navy Department.

15. Many inventions and so-called sovereign remedies applicable to the present critical situation have been sent to the Mission for consideration and some of them may be worthy of notice though most seem wildly impracticable. I am forwarding them to the Assistant Naval Attache who has dealt with such matters in the past.

16. With reference to your telegram of 20 April, I have repeatedly asked the Navy Department whether two of the ex-German Passenger Liners[2] could be turned over to us for use as Mine-Layers. The Department is favourable to the request, but the matter, together with several others, is being held up in Congress where there is still a certain anti-British Party which endeavours to block measures intended in any way to facilitate our operations in the War.

17. During a short visit to New York I took an opportunity of going over the Brooklyn Navy Yard and saw several Destroyers completing for service in European Waters. I also noticed a dozen 100-foot

[1] Probably the General Board of the Navy, of which Badger was the Chairman.
[2] Almost 700000 tons of German merchant shipping was trapped in American ports in 1914. When the United States entered the war, the German crews wrecked the machinery but Yankee ingenuity overcame the sabotage and the ships were a priceless bonus for the rapidly dwindling Allied shipping pool. Sixteen were passenger liners, later used for transporting the American Expeditionary Forces to France. See R. H. Ferrell, *Wilson and World War I*, p. 39.

wooden motor boats (chasers)[1] being built in this Yard. They are to have a speed of 18 knots and appear to be too small for their work. Work was proceeding on the battleship *New Mexico*[2] which was lately launched.

22.   De Chair to Admiralty

Washington, D.C.,
7 June 1917

Continuation of General Report

1. With a view to eliciting definite information as to the Shipbuilding situation, I obtained an interview with General Goethals and ascertained that all the plant in the United States was fully occupied both by Naval and Merchant Ship construction. This state of affairs seems likely to continue, even if the work on capital ships is dropped. As reported in my telegram of 24 May, there is no plant at present which exists for building 35,000-ton ships except at Newport News which is at present congested. At the same time General Goethals informed me that the Shipping Board had given an estimate that subject to possible difficulties in the transportation of steel to the seaboard it was hoped to build 3,000,000 tons of steel shipping in the next eighteen months, exclusive of vessels now actually under construction.

A further appeal to Mr Schwab with reference to the construction of sloops and minesweepers only elicited the reply that until the needs of the United States Government had been clearly defined it would be impossible for his firm to take up the question of any new ship construction. Details of the vessels required have however been left with Commodore Gaunt, who will again take up the matter as soon as there is a possibility of the Bethlehem Steel Works being free to accept orders.

2. In connection with the Destroyer Force already despatched to British waters, the Navy Department informed me that they intended to send the necessary oilers and repair ships together with six small craft to act as sweepers.

The construction of Destroyers is proceeding and it is understood that orders for an additional twenty have been placed with various

[1] Submarine chasers: 1917–18; 110 ft; 60–65 tons; 16.85 knots; 1 x 3 in; depth charges.
[2] USS *New Mexico*: 1918; 32000 tons; 12 × 14in; 21.3 knots; 2 turbine-driven generating units and 4 propelling motors.

firms. Eight boats should be ready in October, the remaining 36 in twelve months....

3. The provision of small armed craft for patrol work is being energetically pushed by the Assistant Secretary of the Navy, and as soon as Congress gives permission he hopes to send over fifty of these vessels. ...

****

5. I communicated to Admiral Benson your request that fast light cruisers of the *Birmingham* type[1] should be sent to assist the Allies in the Adriatic, and he stated that he had put the matter before the Secretary of the Navy, who would bring it to the notice of the President. I consider that a favourable decision will be given and with this hope I have reminded the Secretary of the Navy of the matter in a letter which will be referred to later.[2]

6. The question of the continuation or stoppage of work on capital ships for the United States Navy had not been settled when I left Washington. In view of the susceptibilities of the authorities, and a certain anti-British element in Congress, coupled with the fear of a Japanese Naval expansion, I did not think it wise to press for definite information on this point. Not only Naval but also important political considerations are obviously involved and I discussed the matter with Mr Balfour, who decided that it was of such importance that it must be referred to the War Cabinet.[3]

****

9. I was requested by the Navy Department to lay before the Admiralty a scheme for using Aeroplanes carrying large charges of T.N.T. to blow up Zeebrugge, the Kiel Canal or German Naval Bases. I was informed that experiments which had been made had proved most successful, and a surprising degree of accuracy of flight had been achieved. This device is considered superior to the Sperry-Cooper invention. As the accuracy of flight is a matter of dead reckoning which would be considerably at fault in cross winds I do not altogether credit the perfection of the device at present. Mr Hays

[1] *Birmingham* class: light cruisers; other ships *Chester* and *Salem*; 1907; 3750 tons; 4 x 5 in; 2 t.t.; 24 knots. They were no faster than the British cruisers already employed in the Adriatic, themselves slower than their Austrian opponents. See Paul G. Halpern, ed., *The Royal Navy in the Mediterranean, 1915–1918* (London: Temple Smith for Navy Records Society, 1987), p. 8.

[2] One problem was that the United States was not at war with Austria–Hungary (war was declared in December 1917). More to the point, Benson was exceedingly cautious and referred most matters to Daniels, who was a procrastinator.

[3] See documents nos. 377–83.

Hammond,[1] who is also experimenting in this matter, told me that he had under trial a scheme for directing one aeroplane by wireless telegraphy from another, and if this is successful it could be applied with great effect to the present device.

10. Experiments with microphones for the detection of submarines are being conducted by Admiral Grant, U.S. Navy,[2] and Professor Fessenden[3] at Newport [Rhode Island], and it is understood that they have been successful up to a distance of from five to ten miles, but the noises of the ship in which the microphone is fixed remain a difficulty which must be eliminated. Mr Fessenden has an idea that he will be able to overcome this in some way of which he at present prefers to retain the secret. It would be very useful if an expert officer could be sent out to the United States to get in touch with Mr Fessenden and investigate the matter.

****

12. Before finally leaving the United States I addressed a letter to the Secretary of the Navy in which I detailed the requirements of the Admiralty. I attach a copy hereto, together with a copy of a memorandum which I left with Commodore Gaunt informing him of outstanding matters which the departure of the Mission prevented me from carrying to a satisfactory conclusion.

****

18. In concluding this Report I desire to lay stress on the fact that the United States Navy Department has shown an unmistakeable desire to welcome advice and information from expert British Officers who have first-hand knowledge of present war conditions.

[1] John Hays Hammond (1855–1936): mining engineer and inventor; South Africa in 1890s; implicated in Jameson Raid 1895, sentenced to death by Boers but later released; consulting engineer, London and New York; associated with Guggenheim interests to 1907; strong interest in peace movement after war.

[2] Vice-Admiral Albert Weston Grant, US Navy (1856–1930): Vice-Admiral 1917 and commanded Battleship Division 1, Atlantic Fleet 1917–19; graduated from Annapolis 1877; Cuba 1898; Naval War College 1907; commanded *Arethusa*; chief of staff of 'Great White Fleet' on world voyage 1908–09; Captain and commanded *Connecticut* 1909–10; Commandant, Philadelphia Navy Yard 1910–12; commanded *Texas* 1914–15; Rear-Admiral and Commander of Submarine Flotilla 1915–17; Commandant, Washington Navy Yard 1919–20; retired 1920.

[3] Professor Reginald Aubrey Fessenden (1866–1932): inventor, pioneer of radio communications; associate of Edison; employed by Westinghouse 1890–93; successively Professor of Electrical Engineering, Purdue and Pittsburgh Universities; formed National Electric Signalling Co. in 1902; inventor sonic depth finder, submarine communication devices, turbo-electric drive for ships. See Willem Hackmann, *Seek and Strike: Sonar, Anti-Submarine Warfare and the Royal Navy, 1914–1954* (London: HMSO, 1984), pp. 6, 7, 74, 79, 115, 224.

They have in fact written officially to me asking for the services of specialists in Gunnery, Torpedo, Submarine work and Naval Construction, the Ordnance specialist to be an expert in the matter of fuses. Should a Naval Mission be asked for by the United States at any time it should certainly include such officers, who would confer great benefit on the United States Navy if their services could be spared.

Admiral Benson, the Chief of Naval Operations, also evinced a keen desire to be informed of our Naval policy and in a personal letter to me made the following remarks:–

> I wish to emphasize the fact that we have been obliged
> to come to our conclusions from very meagre information
> on the subject, and for this reason desire to be put
> in touch as closely as possible with the operations
> of the Allied Naval forces, in order to more intelligently
> study the situation and render all possible assistance.
>
> It would be a material assistance if this
> Department could be fully informed as to the prospective
> plans of the Allied Admiralties, in regard to the possible action
> of the vessels of the main fleets, in order that we might
> more efficiently utilize all of our various naval forces.
> It is needless to add that the United States Navy
> is not only ready but anxious to cooperate to the very fullest in
> every possible way with the Allies' Naval forces in clearing
> the seas of the present enemy and establishing the freedom
> of the seas for all time.

****

[Attached]

Vessels Urgently required by the British Admiralty – To obtain which they hope for the assistance of the Navy Department

20 sloops
20 convoy sloops
50 Destroyers (new)

200 Trawlers
Tugs – as many as can be procured.
Note. Orders would be placed as soon as permission is obtained
from Navy Department.
2 German vessels as Mine Layers.
2 Light Cruisers of *Denver*[1] or *Birmingham* Class to assist the
Allies in the Adriatic

[1] *Denver* class: light cruisers, 1903–05; 3 200 tons; 8 x 5in; 16.5 knots.

PART III

GENERAL CO-OPERATION
MAY 1917 TO MAY 1919

INTRODUCTION

This part revolves around Rear-Admiral Sims, as indeed did Anglo–American naval relations in general throughout 1917–18. Despatched originally simply to channel information on Allied naval plans and requirements back to the Navy Department, Sims became by stages a fully-fledged and essentially independent theatre commander. The first six American destroyers for service in European waters left for Queenstown on 24 April 1917 and Sims was given over all responsibility for them. By increments the force under his command grew until by Armistice Day his writ ran to 45 bases and he commanded 375 naval vessels, 5000 officers and 75000 men. Naval air forces in Europe alone comprised 570 aircraft, 50 kite balloons and three airships manned and maintained by 1300 officers and 15000 men on 27 stations.[1] Sims never received a set of orders outlining his authority and responsibilities but ultimately he was designated Force Commander, US Naval Forces in European Waters. He never felt secure – Franklin Roosevelt and Admiral Mayo both aspired to supplant him or at least to become his overlord; fortunately for Sims, Daniels and Benson, though both thought him far too subservient to the British, retained enough faith in his ability and utility to veto such designs.[2] After the war, Sims told the story of his London-based command, though as Frederic Paxson remarked: 'His powers and mission were somewhat less impressive than he described them in *The Victory at Sea* but they were real.'[3] Sims gradually established his autonomy but the Navy Department retained control over the key strategic decisions (such as devoting the greater part of its limited destroyer force to the protection of US troopships rather than, as Sims wished, to cargo vessels supplying Britain). The high command in Washington did not consult him over other flag appointments within his bailiwick and Sims experienced friction with some of them (notably Rear-Admiral Wilson at Brest). He was often unable to exercise effective

[1] Trask, *Captains and Cabinets*, p. 363; Klachko, pp. 111–2; *Annual Report of the Secretary of the Navy, 1919* (Washington: Govt. Printing Office, 1919), p. 41.

[2] Trask, *Captains and Cabinets*, pp. 138, 148, 166, 198.

[3] Sims, *The Victory at Sea*; F. L. Paxson, *American Democracy and the World War*,

authority over them, partly because they related more properly to local Allied commands and partly because they were determined to enjoy their prerogatives as flag officers. Only at Queenstown did Sims have his way, persuading the Navy Department that appointing a flag officer there would disturb the smooth but delicately poised integrated command structure headed by the British Admiral Bayly, whose Chief of Staff was Captain Joel Pringle, US Navy.[1] Sims also had to endure four major missions from home which, though all of them endorsed his policies, disrupted his activities, caused him anxiety and undoubtedly irritated him, however, courteous he appeared to be – and he never let slip his mask of dignity, good humour and charm during his two years in London.

Justly noted for his ability to cut to the heart of a matter, Sims began his tour of duty with a grand ambition, happily one nobly fulfilled, to make history by ensuring absolute harmony and complete unity of purpose in Anglo–American naval co-operation [23,25]. Within a few weeks of his arrival it was widely acknowledged that he was unquestionably the right man for the job [30, 31, 67, 68]. The British were unreserved in their appreciation of him. Jellicoe told Browning that Sims was 'perfectly invaluable to me. His ideas are as sound as a bell. He and I see eye to eye in everything.'[2] Therein lay Sims's greatest problem, one which, despite his protestations, he never overcame. The very qualities which endeared him to the British rendered him suspect in Washington and militated against the United States committing its resources unreservedly to the Allied side. Doubts about his independence of mind were present before he set off for London and surfaced shortly after his arrival [26]. From time to time Sims attempted to reassure Washington on this point [35, 40]. His doubtful allegiance was only one of a number of handicaps he had to overcome. Much of his time and energy (and that of Ambassador Page) in the early months were spent in desperate pleas to the Navy Department to understand how close to defeat

vol. 1, *The Pre-War Years, 1913–1917* (Boston: Houghton Mifflin, 1936). p. 407.

[1] Allard, p. 106; M. A. Simpson, 'Admiral W. S. Sims, Admiral Sir L. Bayly, an Unlikely Friendship and Anglo–American Cooperation, 1917–1919', *Naval War College Review*, spring 1988, pp. 66–80. Captain (later Vice-Admiral) Joel Roberts Poinsett Pringle, US Navy (1873–1932): graduated from Annapolis 1892; Acting Captain 1917, SNO US Forces, Queenstown, CoS to Sims and Bayly; captain, USS *Melville*; Captain 1918; Naval War College staff 1919; captain of *Idaho*; CoS Naval War College 1923–5; CoS Battleship Divs 1925; CoS Battlefleet 1926; Rear-Admiral 1926; President, Naval War College 1927–30; Advisor, London Naval Conference 1930; commanded Battleship Div 3 1930–2; Vice-Admiral and commanded battleships of US Fleet 1932.

[2] Jellicoe to Browning,7 July 1917, *Jellicoe Papers*, vol. 2, p. 181.

the Allies were and to despatch anything that could float, make 12 knots, mount a gun and stow depth charges [26, 27, 29]. Page gave Sims's tireless efforts his full support, though noting that the Navy Department felt that Sims had been 'completely led astray by British guile' – a charge of which the Ambassador himself stood accused.[1] By the end of June, Page and Sims, exasperated by the Navy Department's apparent indifference to Britain's fate. resorted in desperation to a direct message from Balfour to Wilson; thereafter the President ensured that the US Navy committed itself wholeheartedly to co-operation in the British convoy system.[2] For much of 1917, through to November, Sims's relations with Washington were strained, not simply because of his Anglophilism and the refusal of his superiors to believe his alarmist signals but also because there is 'an inherent tendency to disagreement between a theatre commander and general headquarters at home'.[3]

Sims naturally viewed the situation from an Allied, especially British, perspective. Though he recognised that the United States had a distinct purpose to fulfil in the war, he seemed at times more concerned that America should altruistically save the Allies from defeat. The United States Government, equally naturally, took a broader and more self-interested stance. It had not only to consider the immediate security of the United States and its possessions and interests but also to safeguard the nation's position in an uncertain postwar world. America would help the Allies to survive if their survival was essential to the attainment of its own war aims; otherwise, the United States had no direct concern with the well-being of its associates. Benson, a patriot of Patrick Henry stature, embraced that strategic vision with total fidelity [36, 39]. Even when he gave up his initial opposition to convoy, he found a new obligation which precluded complete acquiescence in Sims's and the Admiralty's policies – the defence of the troopships carrying the American Expeditionary Forces to France. This became the US Navy's greatest single commitment in 1918 and as such is beyond this story, for the organisation was in Washington and the route direct to Brest (though many of the troopers and supply vessels were British, as were the majority of the escorts).[4] Apart from Washington's

[1] B. J. Hendrick, *The Life and Letters of Walter Hines Page* (London: Heinemann, 1924), pp. 277, 284.

[2] Jellicoe to Browning, 7 July 1917, *Jellicoe Papers*, vol. 2, p. 181; Trask, *Captains and Cabinets*, pp. 91, 95; Hendrick, pp. 285–6.

[3] Trask, *Captains and Cabinets*, pp. 100. 193–5.

[4] Admiral W. V. Pratt, US Navy, *Autobiography* (typescript, 1939), *Pratt Papers*, ch. 14; Allard, pp. 75–6.

doubts about Sims and the British, America in the spring and early summer of 1917 was 'still unwarlike' and made only 'a half-way covenant' with the war until July.[1] A greater resolve and readier co-operation materialised thereafter, notably following Captain Pratt's elevation to Assistant Chief of Naval Operations [36, 39, 40]. Pratt 'had a clearer conception of what was going on both in Washington and London than any other man in the Department' and has been described as 'one of the unsung naval statesmen of the war and postwar years'; he made possible a tolerable working relationship between Sims and Benson, as he was trusted by both men.[2] In particular Pratt hastened reinforcements to Europe and persuaded Daniels to stop work on battleships and order 200 emergency destroyers.[3]

In July 1917, then, America at last began to apply the spurs to her war effort.[4] Nevertheless, her reaction had been unwontedly tardy and after the war Sims excoriated the Navy Department for its lethargy. He estimated that shortcomings in Washington had caused the loss of 500 000 lives, 2 500 000 tons of shipping and the waste of $15 billion.[5] At the Senate investigation, the Navy Department focused on what it regarded as Sims's shortcomings, charging that he represented only the Admiralty view. It insisted that it sent all available men and ships once it understood Allied requirements but the Allies themselves were slow to formulate and explain their requirements adequately. Though the Navy was acutely short of officers, Sims was sent many of the ablest junior officers [62, 67, 72, 88, 89]. As with so many ex post facto enquiries, this one generated as much heat as light, pointed up personal and partisan differences and produced little but a mass of paper. There was slack administration in Washington and the urgency of the situation only sank in slowly, but the Department was generally anxious and genuine in its desire to assist the Allies and it had to create a war machine practically from scratch, besides retaining a broad and long-term perspective.[6] Given the nation's profound desire to remain at peace until the very last moment, thus inhibiting adequate preparedness, it is

[1] S. Morison, 'Personality and Diplomacy in Anglo-American Relations 1917', in R. Pares and A. J. P Taylor, eds., *Essays Presented to Sir Lewis Namier* (London: Macmillan, 1956), p. 449; Trask, *Captains and Cabinets*, p. 95.
[2] Braisted, p. 296; E. Morison, p. 396.
[3] Trask, *Captains and Cabinets*, p. 96.
[4] Jellicoe to Browning, 7 July 1917, *Jellicoe Papers*, vol. 2, p. 181.
[5] Klachko, pp. 169–80; E. Morison, pp. 439–61.
[6] T. G. Frothingham, *The Naval History of the World War*, vol. 3, *The United States in the War, 1917–1918* (Cambridge, Mass: Harvard UP, 1926), p. 85; Coletta, 'Daniels', pp. 554, 566–72.

not surprising that the American naval effort was 'barely hitting its stride' by the time of the Armistice.[1]

If the Navy Department responded sluggishly to Sims, to the Allies and to the maritime crisis, it was in large measure the fault of the men at the top. Daniels, most unwarlike at the outset (yet a rumbustious publicist for the Navy's glorious deeds by the war's end) was suspicious of gold braid, determined to avoid scandal and a notoriously 'slow decider' [26]. Benson, wrote his friend Browning to Jellicoe, 'is most anxious to co-operate and as nice as he can be to me personally, but he is simply buried in details and has nothing like the freedom of action or general position which you have. I think he tries to do too much himself; they all say so.'[2] This was unconscious irony – Jellicoe was just as prone to immerse himself in detail, as Sims, in turn, told Benson! [86]. The Admiralty itself was a creaking giant, as Marder's work testifies.[3] Matters improved in both high commands from the summer of 1917 [36] but it was not until the close of the year that a highly efficient new team was formed in Whitehall. Sims lamented Jellicoe's summary dismissal but welcomed Admiral Wemyss's promotion to First Sea Lord [81, 82, 86].[4] Wemyss, 'a naval statesman', was a man after Sims's own heart – a manager with the capacity to take the large view and to delegate detailed administration to subordinates. The new First Lord, Sir Eric Geddes, a first-rate executive, now had a naval colleague of comparable efficiency. 'The New Order,' wrote Marder, 'was overall a smashing success.'[5]

The Admiralty may have shaken off the Victorian dust under

[1] D. W. Knox, *A History of the United States Navy* (New York: Putnams, 1948), p. 418.

[2] Browning to Jellicoe, 31 July 1917, *Jellicoe Papers*, vol. 2, pp. 191–2.

[3] Marder, vol. 4, chs. 3, 5, 7.

[4] Marder, vol. 4, ch. 12 (esp. pp. 390–4); vol. 5, ch. 1 (esp. pp. 3–9).

[5] Marder, vol. 5, p. 9. Sir Eric Campbell Geddes (1875–1937): First Lord of the Admiralty, 20 July 1917–11 December 1918; born in India; varied occupational experience – labouring, lumbering, railways including a spell in USA; managed a timber estate in India; joined North Eastern Railway 1906, Deputy General Manager by 1914; Deputy Director General of Munitions Supply 1915; Director General of Transportation, later Inspector-General with rank of Major-General, BEF, France 1915–17; persuaded by Lloyd George to become Controller of Navy May 1917; demanded and received rank of Vice-Admiral; first Minister of Transport 1919–22; Conservative MP, Cambridge 1917–22; chairman, Cabinet economies committee, February 1922 ('Geddes axe'); Chairman, Imperial Airways and Dunlop Rubber Co. thereafter. Vice-Admiral Sir Rosslyn Erskine Wemyss (later Admiral of the Fleet 1st Baron Wester Wemyss) (1864–1933): Captain 1901; Rear Admiral 1911; E. Mediterranean 1914–15; CinC E. Indies 1916–17; appointed CinC Mediterranean June 1917 but moved immediately to 2nd Sea Lord; Deputy 1st Sea Lord September 1917; 1st Sea Lord December 1917–November 1919. See Lady Wester Wemyss, *The Life and*

imminent threat of defeat but that did not save it from a constant barrage of American doubts, suspicions and criticisms by civilian and naval observers (except for Sims, who delicately avoided all but the most oblique adverse comments); over thirty documents contain substantial American complaints about the Admiralty and another dozen or so contain its responses and those of its American friends, Page and Sims. The burden of the American charges, other than initial doubts abut the Royal Navy's competence in the face of the submarine crisis [26, 30], was centered on three principal themes: the Admiralty's lack of a coherent strategy, its refusal to consider offensive operations and its unwillingness to consult the Americans or even to keep them fully informed.

To American naval staff, many of them graduates of the rather rigid and Mahanite Naval War College, the Admiralty seemed to conduct operations on an *ad hoc* basis, making little use of staff planning and indeed having almost nothing in the way of a planning staff. There seemed to be no governing strategy other than the bleakly defensive and basic concept of denying the enemy use of the oceans while retaining full use of the high seas for the Allies. The distant blockade of Germany and the various measures for the defence of trade, such as convoy, were the means to this end. The Admiralty seemed to assume that this was sufficient in the way of a grand strategic design, that the Navy Department automatically recognised and approved it, and that the US Navy was simply a source of materiel to be drawn upon as required. The US Navy's leaders, however, continued to press for a comprehensive plan [31, 36, 47, 58, 68] and to this end sponsored the Allied Naval Council [79] and set up a Planning Section in Sims's headquarters to work in conjunction with the Admiralty's Plans Division [62, 72, 76, 77]. It was designed in part to enhance the Plans Division's own marginal position in the Admiralty [94, 110, 118].

The establishment of the Planning Section represented the culmination of several months of disquiet that the United States was not consulted on plans and operations and a strong suspicion that the British were more than economical with information for their associates. Frequent grumbles from both official and press sources in Washington were reported by British diplomats and naval officers, or recorded by the Americans themselves [30, 31, 36, 37, 52, 53, 55, 59, 61, 64, 65, 78]. American ire rose steadily until it reached a climax at 'a very stormy meeting' between the British Naval

Letters of Lord Wester Wemyss (London: Eyre & Spottiswoode, 1935).

Attaché, Captain Gaunt, and Navy Department heads on 12 September 1917 [55]. Thereafter, the situation improved, albeit with painful gradualness, thanks to a visit to the Admiralty by Gaunt [56] and missions to Britain by Mayo and Benson. The British journalist Arthur Pollen,[1] no friend of the Admiralty, who wrote frequently for American papers, visited the USA regularly and was well connected all the way up to the White House, prompted much of the criticism, official and otherwise [28, 59, 70]. When the British expressed surprise and hurt that the Americans should feel left in the dark, the Navy Department, somewhat disingenuously, moved to correct malicious rumours in the press and express full confidence in the Admiralty's integrity [61, 62, 65]. The American novelist and journalist Winston Churchill,[2] who had already exposed the deficiencies of the Navy Department[3] and who had Wilson's ear, investigated the Admiralty and made a number of adverse observations [68], though Sims was rather scathing about Churchill's bumptiousness [45]. Following Benson's visit in November 1917, the Navy Department seemed rather more assured about Admiralty attitudes and the rumblings from Washington petered out.[4]

The most persistent American complaint was that the Admiralty was obsessively defensive and disinclined to consider offensive measures. This was an area in which two very different traditions of warmaking clashed. The British, long practised in the art of blockade as their principal weapon, recognised that this weapon was slow to act and had become accustomed to a policy of watchful waiting. They did not neglect offensive strategies but, instead of assaulting the

[1] Arthur Joseph Hungerford Pollen (1866–1937): at this time Pollen was naval correspondent of *Land and Water* and made several visits to USA; businessman and inventor; head of Argo Co., formed to promote his system of facilitating long-range gunfire; after trials Admiralty rejected his system but used elements of it (leading to a successful claim for compensation by Pollen) and the system in a modified form was adopted by the Navy after the war; Pollen had by then returned to ordinary business life. See Jon T. Sumida, *The Pollen Papers: the Privately Circulated Printed Works of Arthur Hungerford Pollen, 1901–1916* (London: Allen & Unwin for Navy Records Society, 1984) and his *In Defence of Naval Supremacy: Financial Limitation, Technical Innovation and British Naval Policy, 1899–1914* (London: Unwin Hyman, 1989).
[2] Winston Churchill (1871–1947): American journalist, novelist and Progressive Republican politician; graduated from Annapolis 1894 but resigned commission immediately to pursue writing career; conservationist and thereby friend of Theodore Roosevelt; endeared himself to Wilson with a critical but constructive report on Navy Dept. in summer of 1917; then went to Europe to report on Admiralty; returned ill and career and life thereafter went downhill. See his 'Naval Organization: American and British', *Atlantic Monthly*, vol. 120, August 1917, pp. 277–84.
[3] Churchill to Wilson, July 1917, *Wilson Papers*, vol. 43, pp. 344–5, 354, 358.
[4] C. Seymour, ed., *The Intimate Papers of Colonel House*, vol. 3, *Into the War* (Boston: Houghton Mifflin, 1928), p. 300; Trask, 'Benson', p. 13.

enemy in his heartland, they preferred to wear him down by peripheral attacks at his weakest points. These policies, handed down from the age of sail, were in fact reinforced by the impact of modern technology and the evident military puissance and prowess of Imperial Germany. The American tradition in warfare was to go at once for the enemy's jugular, and submarines, mines, long-range coastal artillery and aircraft appeared to have little infuence on their strategic thinking; the sentiment was still that of Admiral Farragut[1] in the Civil War: 'Damn the torpedoes!' Naïveté, youthful vim and vigour, the boldness born of the breathtaking subjugation of a vast sub-continent and the characteristic American fascination with technological wizardry, all prompted thoughts of an immediate, swift and decisive offensive both on land and at sea. From Wilson, Benson and General Pershing[2] downwards, Americans asked their European partners why offensives had not been launched, or why certain techniques had not been adopted, and they devised and carried out offensive operations themselves. Wilson set the tone from an early date, demanding from Sims on 4 July 1917 a comprehensive report on British plans and activities and demonstrating an impatience and exasperation reflected in so many of these documents [28, 33, 34]. Addressing officers of the Atlantic Fleet on 11 August 1917, Wilson called for fresh offensive ideas to end U-boat warfare. 'We are hunting hornets all over the farm,' he declared, 'and letting the nest alone.' He was prepared to sacrifice half of the coalition's naval strength in a frontal assault on German submarine bases.[3] Though Admiral Mayo was reportedly shocked by his Commander-in-Chief's irresponsibility, Wilson's views were widely shared among senior officers.[4] It is not surprising that Jellicoe told Browning that there were 'some extraordinarily wild theories going about over there'.[5]

Benson was particularly insistent on an offensive strategy [39] but when Jellicoe produced a proposal evidently along Wilsonian lines, the Navy Department quickly drew back from sacrificing its old cruisers and pre-dreadnoughts in a vain attempt to block the hornets' nests [49, 50, 51]. Commander Ernest J. King, US Navy, of

[1] Admiral David G. Farragut, US Navy (1802–70): the immortal phrase is said to have been uttered when his Union ironclads ran past Confederate defences to take New Orleans in April 1862.
[2] General John J. Pershing (1860–1948): Commander of AEF, France 1917–18.
[3] Joseph P. Tumulty, *Woodrow Wilson as I Know Him* (Garden City, NY: Doubleday Page, 1921), pp. 296–8.
[4] Parsons, pp. 75–6.
[5] Jellicoe to Browning, 7 July 1917, *Jellicoe Papers*, vol. 2, p. 181.

Mayo's staff, dismissed the plan contemptuously as 'a straw man', designed to be impracticable.[1] Winston Churchill, the American journalist and other press sources maintained the pressure for offensive action [68, 69, 70] and Benson began his visit to the Admiralty in November 1917 with a further call for an attacking policy [72] but afterwards left the initiative in the hands of the new Planning Section, though its concentration was on anti-submarine hunting groups, the North Sea Barrage and a joint Allied–US offensive in the Mediterranean [90, and Parts IV, VI, and VII].

In their replies to Washington's demand for an offensive strategy, Jellicoe, Sims and Page pointed out the vital necessity of maintaining the Grand Fleet's blockade of the High Seas Fleet, the linchpin of the coalition's whole strategy, and of ensuring the safe arrival of troops and supplies from overseas; there were simply no forces to spare in 1917 for any substantial offensive operations and in any case most of those suggested were impracticable [35, 38, 42, 47]. Nevertheless, the British, anxious for American naval assistance, attempted to meet them half way, in particular embracing the suggestion of the North Sea Barrage and endorsing American efforts to raise the tempo of the war in the Mediterranean and even offering to plan an assault on German bases [35, 51, 60]. In general, however, the Admiralty's accent was on Britain's widespread naval commitments, the vital necessity to hold the ring in the North Sea and the equally crucial need to defend the United Kingdom's lifelines, as well as the need for more light craft from the United States. No fundamental change in strategy seemed either possible or desirable [60, 74, 75]. Indeed, the results of Mayo's and Benson's visits were to grant this essentially defensive posture American endorsement.[2] The British also took pains to answer American complaints about lack of information from, and consultation by, the Admiralty [38, 42, 57, 61, 64] and took the opportunity of Mayo's visit to establish personal correspondence between Geddes and Daniels and between Jellicoe and Benson [66, 67]. When Geddes attempted to make Sims an honorary member of the Board of Admiralty, however, Wilson demurred, fearing that Sims would become totally subservient to the British point of view; his refusal was a grievous disappointment to

[1] Cdr. Ernest J. King, US Navy (1878–1956): graduated from Annapolis 1901; Commander 1917; Captain 1918; inter-wars service in submarine and aviation commands; Rear-Admiral and Chief, Bureau of Aeronautics 1933; Admiral and CinC Atlantic Fleet 1940; CinC US Fleet 30 December 1941; CNO 18 March 1942–15 December 1945. See T. B. Buell, *Master of Sea Power: A Biography of Fleet Admiral Ernest J. King* (Boston: Little Brown, 1980).
[2] Trask, *Captains and Cabinets*, pp. 153, 164; Parsons, pp. 75–6.

the King, Geddes, Page and to Sims himself [73,75, 78, 91] and illustrates Wilson's fervent desire to maintain America's semi-autonomous position within the coalition.

The fact that the Mayo and Benson missions were despatched in the summer and autumn of 1917 respectively indicates a lack of full confidence in Sims's independence of thought and information and a criticism of his failure to swing Admiralty policy towards the offensive. Mayo, though critical of the Admiralty [48], also failed to shift British thinking,[1] though he could have no complaint about British courtesy or willingness to consult and inform [43, 44, 46, 47, 60, 64]. Benson came as part of a high-powered team headed by Wilson's confidant and roving ambassador Colonel House. The Allies, under the pressure of adverse events, were beginning to co-ordinate their economic and military efforts and requested American participation. Wilson was reluctant to become tied to Allied strategy and aims and the essentially technical nature of the delegation was an indication of his willingness to co-operate militarily without sacrificing his political independence. As Daniels put it, 'All possible cooperation but we must be free.'[2] The high point of Mayo's visit was the first Allied naval conference [51]; though it achieved nothing substantial, Benson capitalized on it, contributing to the formation of a formal Allied Naval Council [79]. Like Mayo, Benson visited American and Allied bases and units and came away with a substantially better opinion of the Royal Navy. More importantly, his visit broke the log-jam (mostly of his own making) on several matters. Sims obtained a planning staff, he was made American Naval Attaché *vice* Captain McDougall,[3] who was rather less enthusiastic about the British, and he became a regular attender at Admiralty councils. The North Sea Barrage was agreed to [Part VI] and American battleships were sent to join the Grand Fleet [Part V]. Benson appreciated his cordial reception in Britain [80] and Jellicoe found him 'very willing to help, but very ignorant of sea warfare. He has never had his flag up afloat and has odd ideas.'[4] For Sims, the visits by Mayo and Benson resulted in vindication of his tireless work for harmonious Anglo–American naval relations and in fact from the time of Benson's visit until the Armistice there was an almost honeymoon atmosphere in the transatlantic partnership [73, 79, 80].

[1] Trask, *Captains and Cabinets*, pp. 146–7, 153; Parsons, pp. 75–6.
[2] Klachko, pp. 86–90; Trask, *Captains and Cabinets*, pp. 172, 174–5, 193–5.
[3] Trask, 'Benson', p. 13; *Captains and Cabinets*, pp. 177, 180; Klachko, pp. 95–6; *House Papers*, vol. 3, p. 300.
[4] Jellicoe to Beatty, 9 November 1917, *Jellicoe Papers*, vol. 2, pp. 225–6; Braisted, p. 304.

The two later visits, by Assistant Secretary of the Navy Roosevelt and the Naval Affairs Committee of the House of Representatives, both of them in the summer of 1918, were of much less consequence. In fact there was a strong air of junketing about both of them.[1] Nevertheless, both Sims and the Royal Navy took them seriously, consulted them and showed them as many aspects of the maritime effort as possible [99, 101, 102, 104–9, 113]. Roosevelt and the Congressmen seem to have been particularly impressed with the very successful Anglo–American escort force at Queenstown.[2] Both were left in no doubt, however, about the disparity of naval effort as between the two navies [105] and Geddes began negotiations with the Assistant Secretary with a view to 'dovetailing' the two nations' naval and mercantile building programmes [Part IX].

By the summer of 1918 the American naval air force was at last beginning to arrive in Europe. Captain H. I. Cone, US Navy,[3] was appointed to command US Naval Aviation forces in Europe in September 1917. His proposals for an essentially offensive strategy against U-boats and their bases [92, 95], though endorsed by the Admiralty [100] was never put into operation because of delays in establishing bases and equipping them with trained personnel and aircraft. The Americans were just beginning to take full responsibility for all naval air operations in Ireland and had two substantial bases in England, though neither was fully operational, when the war ended.[4]

After the Armistice, Sims wound up his extensive command, leaving for home in March 1919, two years after his arrival in London. As good an indication as any of his remarkable ability to get on with his hosts was the fact that he managed to make friends with both Admiral of the Fleet Lord Fisher and Admiral Lord Beresford! [83, 117]. He also retained his friendship with both Jellicoe and Wemyss [115, 120] but most of all his extraordinary bond

[1] G. C. Ward, *A First-Class Temperament: The Emergence of Franklin Roosevelt* (New York: Harper & Row, 1989), p. 398.

[2] See documents nos. 102, 107, 108; J. Daniels, *Our Navy at War* (New York: Doran, 1922), p. 365; F. D. Roosevelt, 'Foreword' to Admiral Sir Lewis Bayly, *Pull Together!*, pp. 5–6.

[3] Captain (later Rear-Admiral) Hutchinson Ingram Cone, US Navy (1871–1941): graduated from Annapolis 1894; at Battle of Manila Bay 1898; Commander and Chief of Bureau of Steam Engineering 1909–13; Marine Superintendent, Panama Canal 1915–17; Captain and CO, US Naval Aviation Forces, Foreign Service 1917–19; Asiatic Fleet 1919–21; Rear-Admiral and retired list 1922; Vice-President and General Manager, US Shipping Board–Emergency Fleet Corporation, Merchant Fleet Corporation, and US Shipping Board 1924–33; Chairman, Moore–McCormack Lines 1937.

[4] Klachko, pp. 111–2; *Annual Report of Secretary of the Navy, 1919*, p. 41.

with Admiral Bayly at Queenstown [121, 122]. The tributes to Sims and Bayly were no mere formalities [123–5]; they ring true. At the operational level there was little friction between the two navies, and that there was in the end a fruitful working relationship between the senior officers is due as much to their professionalism and goodwill as to the fierce enemy pressure under which the bonds of Anglo–American naval co-operation in World War I were forged. Having outlined the general problems and the overall nature of that co-operation, it is time to study specific aspects and areas of maritime operations in which the two navies served together.

23. *Sims to Daniels*

8 May 1917

****

...changes of a radical nature are impending as regards the British Admiralty, and perhaps the Government.[1] The press has been more and more outspoken in its criticisms, and information which was known only in official circles is now becoming general.

****

You will, I am sure, be pleased to know that my visit to Paris was very successful, as it resulted in a complete agreement between the French and British Navy Departments as to the manner in which our destroyers and other forces should be employed in the campaign against the enemy submarines. It was agreed that the destroyer force and its supply train should act as a unit in the area of the greatest activity of the submarines.

I am also glad to be able to report that the British have within the past week been very successful in destroying submarines. No less than five were surely sunk and probably three others.[2]

24. *Admiralty to De Chair*

25 May 1917

Please ask Mr Balfour to represent to United States Government the grave situation with which His Majesty's Government are faced as regards shortage of Tankers. The shortage is in danger of imperilling the activity of the Fleet. The only immediate relief possible is to purchase or charter immediately in the United States the greatest possible number of such vessels. Royden[3] we understand arrives

---

[1] The reorganisation of the Admiralty which, among other changes, brought in Geddes as Controller and paved the way for his promotion to First Lord two months later. See Marder, vol. 4, pp. 167–81.

[2] It has always been notoriously difficult to confirm the destruction of submarines. Sims's figures are almost certainly wild exaggerations. See Marder, vol. 4, pp. 105–6, where it is suggested that sinkings averaged no more than three per month in the first half of 1917.

[3] Sir Thomas Royden (1871–1950): Chairman of UK Chamber of Shipping and advisor to HM Government during the war; visited USA to arrange for the transportation of American troops and supplies; Liverpool shipowner, particularly associated with Cunard (Chairman 1922–30); Conservative MP for Bootle (Liverpool) 1918–22; baron 1944.

about 2 June with full particulars and with instructions to press for assistance. Admiralty think it of importance that Mr Balfour before he leaves America should urge our requirements to the utmost on United States Government.

25.   *Sims to Captain William V. Pratt, U.S. Navy*[1]

7 June 1917

****

...I believe there is no case on record where Allies have operated together for any considerable length of time without more or less serious friction. I am out to make an exception in this mater....

26.   *Lieut. R. R. M. Emmet, U.S. Navy*[2] *to Sims*

Washington,
22 June 1917

****

...I touched on frank exchange information between the Department and Admiralty. Assured him [Benson] I was certain in long run we would find British had more to give than ourselves due three years' war experience. He seemed to think Admiral Sims and our officers abroad in danger of becoming obsessed with all things British to detriment of clear judgement. Mentioned Admiral Sims very anxious to obtain services of Captain Pratt. Replied, with a smile, he needed him in Operations. Wanted to know if British contemplated offensive warfare and what they were doing against

---

[1] Later Admiral William Veazie Pratt, US Navy (1869–1957): Assistant Chief of Naval Operations 1917–19; graduated from Annapolis 1889; service in Asian waters and at Naval Academy; attended Naval War College 1912–13; on Sims's staff in Atlantic Fleet Destroyer Force 1913; Captain 1917; commanded *New York* 1919; commanded Destroyer Force, Pacific Fleet; General Board; advisor on naval limitation 1920s; Rear-Admiral and commanded a battleship division; President, Naval War College; commanded Pacific Fleet Battleship Divisions; Admiral and CinC, US Fleet 1929; Chief of Naval Operations 1930–33; retired 1933; recalled to active service 1941. See W. V. Pratt, *Autobiography* (unpublished typescript, 1939, in Naval Historical Center, Washington); Gerald E. Wheeler, *Admiral William Veazie Pratt, US Navy: A Sailor's Life* (Washington: US Govt. Printing Office, 1974); Craig L. Symonds, 'William Veazie Pratt as CNO', *Naval War College Review*, vol. 33, no. 2, March 1980, pp. 17–33; a fuller version is in Robert W. Love, ed., *The Chiefs of Naval Operations*.

[2] Lieut. Robert R. M. Emmet, US Navy: *Arizona* 1917; later Lieut. -Cdr., *Canonicus*; Experimental Station, New London, Conn., February 1918. Emmet had evidently spent some time at Sims's headquarters in London.

submarines. Referred him to Admiral Sims's dispatches for complete answer to this question. Touched briefly on substance dispatches. Stressed vital need destroyers and patrol craft. Touched on possible ease up heavy ship construction in favor destroyers. [Benson] Said we were building all destroyers we could....

****

[Reporting a conversation with Rear-Admiral McGowan[1]]:
The last thing that seemed to interest the Secretary was to fight a war.... That Secretary considers Mr Roosevelt, Assistant Secretary and McGowan dangerous war mad lunatics... That he was perfectly certain Mr Wilson had no adequate idea just how bad the Navy Department was. That people running government didn't seem to have faintest idea we were in midst of a great war. That Navy Department is certainly not being run as if anything momentous was going on. Operations supposed to coordinate all bureaus and don't coordinate their own office. Was opinion this was entirely due to Chief. The invariable formula is 'Let's wait a while and think it over'. There needs to be a lot less talk and oceans more action. ... most serious condition ... to be overcome, is the lack of realization of the wicked serious fix we are in and the need for real efficient decisive action. I undoubtedly drew the impression from Admiral Benson, and the Secretary doubtless has it too, that Admiral Sims is all mugged up with British ideas and perspective and that therefore to a degree his judgement is warped and the weight of what he advocates lessened.
... [Benson] Told me British Navy had impressed him so badly during the war that he was doubtful whether we could gain anything of value.
... I am quite confident: (1) That Admiral Benson has not an adequate idea of the magnitude of your task. (2) That he is gravely worried about the ability of the British Navy ... (4) That the Navy Department end of the game is so big to him he can't see much farther.
The Department is accomplishing things but with groans and sweat. All the reins are still tight in the Secretary's hands and he is a slow decider. ...

---

[1] Rear-Admiral Samuel McGowan, US Navy: Paymaster-General of the Navy since 1913; a close friend of F. D. Roosevelt and a marvellously efficient head of the Navy Department's Bureau of Supplies and Accounts.

****

27. *Page to Lansing*

American Embassy.
London,
26 June 1917

I have just received from the Admiralty the following startling information:

Tank steamers of sixty thousand tons capacity have been torpedoed since the first of this month. This heavy loss comes upon the top of arrangements which at best would have brought an insufficient supply. The result is stock now England for the use of British Navy will last only six weeks at the lowest conventional rate of consumption. If any special demand should be made by navy the entire supply might be used up at once. No such dangerous situation has [arisen?] during the war. All the oil that can be carried to this country by the tankers available for naval use is only two thirds of required amount even when fleet activities are curtailed as at the present time. This perilous situation seems to me to warrant the following recommendations:

First: That ships at the present time carrying oil in bulk to neutral countries be diverted to the United Kingdom.

Second: That tank ships doing any service other than directly aiding European military situation be taken for this purpose.

Third: That construction and conversion of oilers be hastened to the extreme limit and if necessary regardless of cost for bonuses. A failure quickly to replenish stock here may at any time cause disaster.

Two hundred thousand tons must be delivered by August thirtieth and an additional [similar quantity?] by September thirtieth and the vessels which bring these quantities must be continued in the service. These quantities must be in addition to shipments already arranged for. Of course I need not [stress?] the necessity for absolute secrecy regarding this matter.

The Admiralty will highly appreciate an answer saying what can be done. This message is sent after consulting the First Lord of the Admiralty and Admiral Jellicoe who expressed gratitude for sending it.[1]

---

[1] This was almost certainly a message from Sims to Daniels and Wilson via the State Dept.

28. *Joseph Tumulty[1] to Wilson*

29 June 1917

****

Mr Pollen[2] suggested that our Admiral Sims be requested to let the President know, through the Secretary of the Navy, what plans the British Admiralty has in mind, and what Admiral Sims thinks of them. He says that the British Admiralty has done nothing of a constructive character since the war began and that if we act on the assumption that they have, we will face disaster.

29. *Sims to Daniels*

29 June 1917

General report concerning military situation

****

2. ... I consider that the military situation is very grave indeed on account of the success of the enemy submarine campaign.

If the shipping losses continue as they have during the past four months, it is submitted that the Allies will be forced to dire straits indeed, if they will not actually be forced into an unsatisfactory peace.

The present rate of destruction is very much greater than the rate of building, and the shortage of tonnage is already so great that the efficiency of the naval forces is already reduced by lack of oil. Orders have just been given to use three-fifths speed, except in cases of emergency. This simply means that the enemy is winning the war.

3. My reasons for being so insistent in my cable despatches have been because of my conviction that measures of cooperation which we may take will be inefficient if they are not put into operation immediately, that is within a month.

There is every reason to believe that the maximum enemy submarine effort will occur between now and the first of November, reaching its height probably during the latter part of July, if not earlier.

****

---

[1] Joseph Patrick Tumulty (1879–1954): President Wilson's Secretary; New Jersey Democratic politician; lawyer; early association with Wilson; a 'conservative progressive'; his influence decreased in the second term and he finally broke with the ex-President in 1922, though he remained an admirer; thereafter practised law in Washington.

[2] Arthur Pollen, the British journalist, a regular visitor to the USA.

6. We are dispersing our forces while the enemy is concentrating his. The enemy's submarine mission is and must continue to be the destruction of merchant shipping. The limitations of submarines and the distances over which they must operate prevent them from attacking our naval forces that is, anti-submarine craft. They cannot afford to engage anti-submarine craft with guns; they must use torpedoes. If they should do so to any considerable extent their limited supply would greatly reduce their period of operation away from base, and the number of merchantmen they could destroy. Their object is to avoid contact with anti-submarine craft. This they can almost always do, as the submarine can see the surface craft at many times the distance the surface craft can see a periscope, particularly one less than two inches in diameter.

Moreover the submarine greatly fears the anti-submarine craft because of the great danger of the depth charges. Our tactics should therefore be such as to force the submarine to incur this danger in order to get within range of merchantmen.

7. It therefore seems to go without question that the only course for us to pursue is to revert to the ancient practice of convoy. This will be purely an offensive measure because if we concentrate our shipping into convoys and protect it with our naval forces we will thereby force the enemy in order to carry out his mission to encounter naval forces, which are not embarrassed with valuable cargoes, and which are a great danger to the submarine. At present our naval forces are wearing down their personnel and material in an attempted combination of escorting single ships, when they can be picked up, and also of attempting to seek and offensively engage an enemy whose object is to avoid such encounters. With the convoy system, the conditions will be reversed. Although the enemy may easily know when our convoys sail, he can never know the course they will pursue or the route of approach to their destinations. Our escorting forces will thus be able to work on a deliberate prearranged plan, preserving their oil supplies and energy, while the enemy will be forced to disperse his forces and seek us. In a word, the handicap we now labor under will be shifted to the enemy; we will have adopted the essential principle of concentration while the enemy will lose it.

8. The most careful and thorough study of the convoy system by the British Admiralty shows clearly that while we may have some losses under this system, owing to lack of adequate number of anti-submarine craft, they nevertheless will not be critical as they are at present.

9. I again submit that if the Allied campaign is to be viewed as a whole, there is no necessity for any high sea protection on our own coast. The submarine as a type of war vessel possesses no unusual characteristics different than those of other naval craft, with the single exception of its ability to submerge for a limited time. The difficulty of maintaining distant bases is the same for the submarine as it is for other craft. As long as we maintain control of the sea as far as surface craft are concerned there can be no fear of the enemy establishing submarine bases in the Western Hemisphere.

10. To take an extreme illustration, if the enemy could be led or forced into diverting part of his submarine effort to the United States coast, or to any other area distant from the critical area surrounding the coast of France and the United Kingdom, the anti-submarine campaign would at once be won. The enemy labors under severe difficulties in carrying out his campaign even in this restricted area, owing to the material limitations and the distances they must operate from their bases, through extremely dangerous localities. The extent of the United States coastline and the distance between its principal commerical ports, preclude the possibility of any sub-marine effort in that part of the world except limited operations of diversion designed to affect public opinion, and thereby hold our forces from the vital field of action.

11. The difficulties confronting the convoy system are, of course, considerable. They are primarily involved in the widely dispersed ports of origin of merchant shipping; the difficulty of communication by cable; the time involved by communication by mail; and the difficulties of obtaining a cooperation and coordination between allied governments.

As reported by cable despatch, the British Government has definitely reached the decision to put the convoy system into operation as far as its ability goes. Convoys from Hampton Roads, Canada, Mediterranean and Scandinavian countries are already in operation. Convoys from New York will be put into operation as soon as ships are available. The British Navy is already strained beyond its capacity, and I therefore urgently recommend that we cooperate at least to the extent of handling convoys from New York.

12. The danger to convoys from high sea raiders is remote, but, of course, must be provided against, and hence the necessity for escorting cruisers or reserve battleships. The necessity is even greater, however, for anti-submarine craft in the submarine war zone.

13. As stated in my despatches, the arming of merchant-men is not a solution of the submarine menace, it serves the single purpose of

forcing the submarine to use torpedoes instead of guns and bombs. The facts that men-of-war cannot proceed safely at sea without escort, and that in the Queenstown avenue of approach alone in the past six weeks there have been thirty armed merchantmen sunk, without having seen the submarine at all before the attack, seems to be conclusive evidence. A great mass of other evidence and war experience could be collected in support of the above.

14. The week ending 19 June has been one of great submarine activity. Evidence indicates that fifteen to nineteen of the largest and latest submarines have been operating in the critical area to the west and south west of the British Isles. The above numbers are exclusive of the smaller and earlier type of submarines and submarines carrying mines alone. Two submarines are working to the westward of the straits of Gibraltar. A feature of the week was the sinking of ships as far west as 19 degrees. Three merchant ship convoys are en route from Hampton Roads, the last one, consisting of eighteen ships, having sailed on 19 June. One hundred and sixteen moored mines have been swept up during the week.

****

30. *Winston Churchill (US)*[1] *to Wilson*

July 1917

****

The extreme danger of the present submarine situation is known to you, and nowhere it is more sharply realised than amongst the experts in our Service. The tonnage destroyed fluctuates; but it may be said that the Germans are at present sinking some 500,000 tons a month, while we have it on good authority that the submarine building programme now being pushed forward in Germany will probably in the near future act to increase this destruction. If the current rate of destruction continues, the Allies will not be able to replace more than one third of the amount destroyed. The present necessities of England and France are about 32,000,000 tons a year; and when the available shipping is reduced below the amount adequate to transport this tonnage, the war will be lost. It will be impossible to maintain the population and the armies at the front, or to export the ore required for munitions, or the coal demanded by Italy and France. According to the calculations made by the British Government, if the present rate of destruction continues, the crisis

---

[1] Winston Churchill, the US author and journalist.

will come in December. And that Government, I understand, has so
informed our Ambassador. The information has also been conveyed
to our Navy Department.

For two years the British Admiralty has failed to realise the
significance of the submarine, has placed dependence on a naval
policy that in past wars would have been adequate, but which in this
war has not been adequate. Britain has retained command of the
surface of the seas, has adhered to a naval policy known among
naval men as the *material* policy – that a preponderance of ships
would bring victory without a battle. The best expert naval opinion,
both here and abroad, is agreed that Admiral Jellicoe, if he had not
been imbued with this policy, might in the battle of Jutland have
destroyed the German fleet. And the German fleet destroyed, the
submarines could have been stopped up in their bases at Zeebrugge
and elsewhere. I have touched on this question in an article to
appear in the *Atlantic Monthly* for August.[1] On this account there
has been a campaign of publicity in England in all respects deplor-
able in a country at war, and one if possible to be avoided here since
we are in a position to profit by the British experience. That experience, briefly, has been this; the incumbency of a First Lord with
strong ideas of his own, who chose his subordinates with a view of
dominating them.[2] This led to disaster. He was followed by other
Sea Lords who, for one reason or another, were unequal to the
position. The Admiralty, while more efficiently organised than our
own Navy Department, continued to ignore the main principle of
naval strategy as laid down by Admiral Mahan[3] and others, that it
is the main business of a navy to fight, to be aggressive, to meet new
problems as they arise precisely as, in our Civil War, the *Merrimac*
was met by the *Monitor*;[4] that naval strategy is the province of
seamen. The talent, the creative imagination of the British Service
was not taken advantage of but ignored; and although the expert of

[1] 'Naval Organisation: American and British', *Atlantic Monthly*, August 1917, pp.
277–84.
[2] Presumably referring to his namesake, the British Winston Churchill who was
First Lord from 1911 to 1915.
[3] Captain Alfred Thayer Mahan, US Navy (1840–1914): naval historian and
defence strategist; pioneer geopolitical thinker; author of numerous works on sea
power; an early supporter of Rear-Admiral Stephen B. Luce's fight to establish and
maintain the Naval War College, Newport, RI, and served on the staff there; though
retired, called back to serve on naval strategy board during Spanish–American War
1898; retired rank of Rear-Admiral.
[4] A reference to the famous if inconclusive battle between these two ships in
Hampton Roads, 9 March 1862, during the American Civil War, and the first
encounter between ironclads.

the greatest genius in the British Navy, Admiral Sir Percy Scott,[1]
(whose career has been coincident with that of Vice-Admiral Sims,
and who has been his intimate friend and collaborator) warned the
Admiralty that it would have to deal with the submarine, nothing
important was done towards following his advice. As a result there
grew up among the British public a general feeling of dissatisfaction
and unrest, of discouragement among the progressive, imaginative
officers of the British Service; and at length there came the inevitable
upheaval in the British Admiralty, which has now been reorganized.

****

The problem, as I have said, is one of making our American
genius count, of having as the authority behind any plans or suggestions sent to Admiral Sims for submission to the British Admiralty,
the voice and opinion of the American Navy. In order to win this
war a new strategy is needful, and coordination in this strategy
between America and Great Britain. In Vice-Admiral Sims it is
generally agreed that we have the right man in the right place.

31.   *Pratt to Sims*

2 July 1917

****

Our Policy in Building
   ... England's Fleet must never go elsewhere except to join our
own, ...
Cooperating Officers
   ... I feel that we do not get enough of the POINT OF VIEW
OVER THERE. ... the facts, the cold facts are what we need. ... We
are more than willing to cooperate in every sense of the word. This
office does not have to be scared into sending ships because we do
not realise the seriousness of the situation. We do. ... The Admiral is
willing to recommend anything, any forces, so long as he knows, and
he wants to know not in any critical spirit, but in the spirit of utmost
cooperation, what the Admiralty's strategical and tactical conceptions are. Just what is the major plan? ... What are the tactical
details in general by which this plan is to be solved [?] Those are the
things we have a right to know, ... especially as we are directing
every effort, building, conserving of shipping, to arrive at a successful conclusion of this war, even to the possible sacrifice of our own
individual good later. We could work so much more intelligently

[1] Admiral Sir Percy Scott, the father of modern naval gunnery.

toward the same united ends, if we knew a little more. And this is where a big Admiralty Staff man comes in. The liaison on little things is all right, but this war won't be won so much by the collection of details properly arranged as it will by the correct conceptions of the proper strategy and policy to pursue. It will be won all right, England can do it herself, but we can shorten the process. There are many problems, present and future, which can't go down in black and white on paper, but which might be more satisfactorily approached had we a MAN on the spot in the full confidence of the Admiralty, and representing them.

****

Escort and Convoy

In your cables you have insisted upon the necessity of adopting what you call convoy. Your assumption that merchant shipping should be escorted through the danger zone is absolutely correct. There has been no dissent there. ...

****

Finally

I met Arthur Pollen for a moment the other day. He said 'That man Sims has simply taken the country by storm; besides he is so preposterously good looking, over 6 feet 3 inches'. There speaks the Englishman, and we realize the pith of your statements when you say that whoever we send over must have a good presence. He said, as an example, and it takes one who knows the English character to appreciate the foothold you have gained, 'I say, do you realize that Sims is the only foreigner that has commanded a Fleet practically entirely made up of British units for over 400 years?'[1] That tells the story as nothing else could do it. It shows, and I think everybody here realises that you are the essential man for the job. ...

32. *Sims to Navy Department*

3 July 1917

... The order of importance of British needs for assistance in naval aeronautics is as follows:

(1) Sea Plane carrier ships, to the number of four, with capacity for carrying six two-seater seaplanes, and six single-seater seaplanes or land machines. Speed should be eighteen knots or more.

(2) Four or more vessels for use as depot ships in conjunction

[1] This refers to Sims's temporary command of British and American forces at Queenstown in June 1917; see documents nos. 147–8.

with large seaplanes on anti-submarine boat work;

(3) One hundred large kite balloon units, complete with trained men and officers, kite balloons being much more desirable than 'blimps'. It is recommended that construction of kite balloons be started immediately as they are very valuable for submarine work and can be provided quickly;

(4) Complete squadrons of large seaplanes from personnel [to] equipment;

(5) Satisfactory engines which should not be of less than 300 horse power. British Admiralty has no knowledge of any satisfactory American aeroplane engine of this size. Rolls Royce best engine in England;

(6) Units of trained pilots and mechanics for anti-submarine work, to operate under their own officers. Admiralty will provide every possible assistance should the United States decide upon proceeding with any part of the above program, and to that end will send experts in each branch concerned to America, ... [I recommend] that no aeronautic developments be undertaken which would interfere in any way with completion of available anti-submarine craft and equipment, in view of necessity of quick action in anti-submarine boat campaign, and in view of time required for aeronautic construction.[1]

33.   *Wilson to Daniels*

2 July 1917

****

As you and I agreed the other day, the British Admiralty had done nothing constructive in the use of their navy and I think it is time we were making and insisting upon plans of our own, even if we render some of the more conservative of our own naval advisors uncomfortable. What do you think?

34.   *Wilson to Sims*

4 July 1917

From the beginning of the war I have been greatly surprised at the failure of the British Admiralty to use Great Britain's naval superiority in an effective way. In the presence of the present submarine

---

[1] The USA had an ambitious programme of aircraft construction, bases and personnel training but virtually none of the many units intended were operational by the time the war ended.

emergency they are helpless to the point of panic. Every plan we suggest they reject for reason of prudence. In my view this is not a time for prudence but for boldness even at the cost of great losses. In most of your despatches you have quite properly advised us of the sort of aid and cooperation desired from us by the Admiralty. The trouble is that their plans and methods do not seem to us very effective. I would be very much obliged to you if you would report to me, confidentially, of course, exactly what the Admiralty has been doing and what they have accomplished and add to the report your own comments and suggestions based upon independent study of the whole situation without regard to the judgements already arrived at on that side of the water. The Admiralty was very slow to adopt the practice of convoy and is not now, I judge, supplying convoys on an adequate scale within the danger zone, seeming to prefer to keep its small craft with the fleet. The absence of craft for convoy is even more apparent on the French coast and in the Channel. I do not see how the necessary military supplies and supplies of food and fuel oil are to be delivered at British ports in any other way within the next few months than under adequate convoy. There will presently not be ships or tankers enough and our shipbuilding plans may not begin to yield important results in less than eighteen months. I beg that you will keep these instructions absolutely to yourself and that you will give me such advice as you would give if you were handling an independent navy of your own.

35. *Sims to Wilson*

[after 4] July 1917

I have sent by the last mail to the Secretary of the Navy an official paper dated July and giving the present British Naval policy, the disposition of the vessels of the fleet, and the manner and method of their employment.

This will show to what extent the various units of the fleet, particularly destroyers, are being used to oppose the submarines, protect shipping and escort convoys.

It is hoped and believed that the convoy system will be successful. It is being applied as extensively as the number of available escorting cruisers and destroyers will permit. The paper shows also that there remains with the main fleet barely sufficient destroyers and auxiliary forces to meet on equal terms a possible sortie of the German Fleet. The opposition to submarines and the application of the convoy system are rendered possible solely by the British Main Fleet and its continuous readiness for action in case the German Fleet comes out or attempts any operations outside the shelter of its fortifications and their mine fields.

I am also forwarding by next mail copy of a letter dated 27 June from the Minister of Shipping[1] to the Prime Minister, showing the present shipping situation and forecasting the result of a continuation of the present rate of destruction. Briefly this shows that this rate is more than three times as great as the rate of building. A certain minimum amount of tonnage is required to supply the allied countries and their armies. This letter shows that at the present rate of destruction this minimum will be reached about next January. This is not an opinion, it is a matter of arithmetic. It simply means that if this continues the Allies will be forced to an unsatisfactory peace.

The North Sea is mined by British and German mines for more than one hundred miles north and west of Heligoland up to the three mile limits of Denmark and Holland; over thirty thousand mines and additional mines are being laid.

It is through these neutral waters that almost all submarines have been passing.

A sea attack alone upon German ports or any heavily fortified ports could not succeed against the concealed guns of modern defenses.

I have just been informed that preparations are now being made for a combined sea and land attack to force back the German right flank and deny them the use of Zeebrugge as a destroyer base,[2] though not yet definitely decided by the war council; this would have been done long ago but for disagreements between the Allies.

The German Fleet has not left the neighborhood of Heligoland for about a year.

I am aware of but two plans suggested by our Government for preventing the egress of German submarines. These were contained in the Department's despatches of 17 April and 11 May and were answered in my despatches of 18 April and 14 May respectively.[3] These same suggestions and many similar ones have been and continue to be made by people of all classes since the beginning of the war. I have been shown the studies of the proposed plans and consider them impracticable.

It is my opinion that the war will be decided by the success or

[1] Sir Joseph Maclay.
[2] The attack was not carried out until 23 April 1918. See Marder, vol. 5, pp. 45–66.
[3] Not reproduced.

failure of the submarine campaign.

Unless the Allies' lines of communication can be adequately protected all operations on shore must eventually fail. For this reason, and as further described in my various despatches, the sea war must remain here in the waters surrounding the United Kingdom. The latest information is available here and can be met only by prompt action here.

It is wholly impossible to attempt to direct or to properly coordinate operations through the medium of communications by letter or cable.

Therefore as requested by you, if I had complete control of our Sea Forces, with the success of the Allied cause solely in view, I would immediately take the following steps:-

1st. Make immediately preparations to throw into the war area our maximum force. Prepare the Fleet immediately for distant service. As the Fleet, in case it does move, would require a large force of protective light craft, and as such craft would delay the Fleet's movements we should advance to European waters all possible craft of such description, either in service or which can be immediately commandeered and put into service. That is, destroyers, armed tugs, yachts, Light Cruisers, Revenue Cutters, Mine Layers, Mine Sweepers, Trawlers, Gun Boats and similar craft.

2nd. Such a force while waiting for the Fleet to move should be employed to the maximum degree in putting down the enemy submarine campaign and in escorting convoys of merchant ships and troops, and would be in position at all times to fall back on our Main Fleet if it approached these waters.

3rd. Prepare the maximum number of supply and fuel ships and be prepared to support our heavy forces in case they are needed.

4th. Concentrate all naval construction on destroyers and light craft. Postpone construction of heavy craft and depend upon the fact which I believe to be true that regardless of any future developments we can always count upon the support of the British Navy. I have been assured of this by important Government officials.

5th. As far as consistent with the above building program of light craft, particularly destroyers, concentrate all other shipbuilding on merchant tonnage. Divert all possible shipping to supplying the Allies.

6th. As the convoy system for merchant shipping at present affords better promise than any other means for ensuring the safety of lines of communications to all military and naval forces on all Fronts, we should lend every support possible to ensure success. To this end we should co-operate with British authorities in the United States, and here, who are attempting to carry out the convoy system.

I believe the above advice to be in accordance with the fundamental principles of Military Warfare. The first step is to establish here in London a branch of our War Council upon whose advice you can thoroughly depend. Until this is done, it will be impossible to ensure that the part which the United States takes in this war, whether it is won or lost, will be that which the future will prove to have been the maximum possible. It is quite impracticable for me, nearly single handed, to accumulate all the necessary information and it is not only impracticable but unsafe to depend upon decisions which must necessarily be based upon incomplete information since such information cannot be efficiently communicated by letter or cable.

****

I wish to make it perfectly clear that my reports and despatches have been in all cases an independent opinion based upon specific and official facts and data which I have collected in the various Admiralty and other Government Departments. They constitute my own conviction and hence comply with your request for an independent opinion.

36.   Gaunt to Admiralty

5 July 1917

Remarks on the General Naval Situation

****

The appointment of Captain Pratt as Chief of Staff in place of Captain Chase,[1] who died suddenly last week, has made a very great difference to everything. The difficulty before has always been that Admiral Benson dealt with the matters directly himself; he has a very great deal to do, practically no staff, and although he means to help in every possible way, requests get put on one side, after an answer has been promised for the following day. When the next day arrives he has probably temporarily forgotten all about the matter, and it was very difficult to strike the border between reminding him of his promise of an answer and appearing to be continually asking for or urging things. Again, he is very loyal to his Chief, the Secre-

---

[1] Captain Volney O. Chase, US Navy: Assistant Chief of Naval Operations, died June 1917.

tary of the Navy and felt that he ought to put even the smallest matter before him, which led to delay and things getting sidetracked. As an example of the difficulties of the situation, I had some secret documents to turn over to him, but he asked me not to do so, implying he would have to show them to his Chief and that meant a leak straight away, therefore, in reply to my query he felt that he could not be responsible for them being kept secret, and I still have them in my safe. He always consulted Captain Chase, but I think that was about all. Under the new regime Captain Pratt is a strong man; I can discuss things with him and he is very glad to do so, and he will go into details with me, and once having decided that such a thing can be done, I have a strong advocate who takes the matter up, puts in on paper, and will get it done at once. As an instance, – before he took over, I went into details as much as I could with Admiral Benson, who insisted that the United States had no cruisers to spare, so long as a fixed patrol remained, and in fact, many other reasons why more vessels of all sorts could not be supplied. I could not argue with him, but directly Captain Pratt took office we went over the lists together and the result was at once cruisers for convoy work, release of destroyers, and, I hope, several other items; but the great point is that it is done immediately.

I know that Vice-Admiral Sims is very anxious to get Captain Pratt on his staff. I sincerely trust he will be left here. I am sure he is a much greater asset to us over here than he would be on the other side.

I urge that some settled policy, as far as possible, be telegraphed to me. Admiral Benson does not exactly complain, but points out that all we do is to ask for things as they come along, but there is no settled policy that he can put forward and say we are working along those lines. For instance, what is the Admiralty idea as to the future of the American capital ships in the event of the Norwegian situation developing? Are they likey to require them? I think that he has a sort of feeling that he should be taken closer into the general scheme of the Allies' sea policy, instead of, as at present, just being asked from time to time to supply units which have no connection with one another.

The Americans were very anxious to leave the question of routing ships as at present, but to move all the officers into the various custom houses, and to appoint an American staff to assist the British. I think there is a sort of feeling that it is wrong that the Masters of other nations should have to go to the British Consulate (where our officers now are) in an American port. They promise that if this was done they would appoint a staff with instructions from our people for the examination of ships, and so relieve Halifax; with this reservation that they would not deal with neutral ships bound for a neutral port.

The foregoing is not official, but I know it is their wishes in the matter.

37. *Lord Northcliffe*[1] *to War Cabinet*

Washington,
5 July 1917

Though beyond my instructions, I cannot refrain from reporting current American opinion on naval matters.

Our alleged inactivity in dealing with submarines hampers our work as much as question of Ireland. Both in New York and here [by] members of Government, general public and relations of officers of new army I am constantly interrogated about progress of submarine destruction. Optimistic statements as given to Associated Press Correspondents in London on 4 July merely confuse and do harm.

All observers of war foresee that if American army, supplies, aeroplanes, food, railway material, are to be available on Western Front, they will create fresh demands for shipping, and note that losses exceed replacements so greatly that it is possible that necessary tonnage may not exist when all is ready here to intervene militarily with effect.

Secondly, naval observers point out three possible policies to end or lessen losses, all or one of which must be pursued with utmost vigour. First policy, build special unsinkable monitors and other necessary craft to enter zone outside enemy harbours and attack fleet and forts, with assistance of aircraft, while effort is made to blockade exits of enemy battle fleet. Then, under cover of capital ships, establishment of mine barriers which cannot be swept. Suggested this policy would, if feasible and carried out at Zeebrugge and all German ports combined with barrier to exclude submarines from Baltic, be completely effective. It is asked, has Admiralty considered any such scheme? If so, can they submit it to Navy Department?

Second Policy; by continuous nets, each mesh of which at all depths carry a mine, to block northern exit North Sea, or alternati-

---

[1] Alfred C. W. Harmsworth, 1st Baron Northcliffe (1865–1922): head of British mission to USA 1917; founder of *Daily Mail* 1896 and thus of popular journalism in Britain; baron 1905; viscount 1917; Director of Propaganda 1918.

vely by continuous wall of mines at either end North Sea.

Third policy; to devote shipbuilding capacity of both countries in much greater proportion to producing convoying or patrolling craft suitably armed with howitzer type of guns, depth charges, etc., with which to control lane down which all trade is directed. Most important these or any other plans should be discussed promptly and fully by Admiralty with American Navy.

Thirdly, Chief of Navy Dept. is reluctant to devote labour and material to inshore monitor or patrolling or convoying craft which will delay any part of capital ship programme, on ground that if war ends in compromise that leaves German Fleet intact or in defeat of Allies, danger to U.S. so great that utmost battleship and battle cruiser strength would be necessary in view of possible S. Atlantic and Pacific developments. Suggested this labour and material could be released by British offering latest type of battleships or battle cruisers in exchange ton for ton against anti-submarine product of labour, etc., so displaced from capital ship programme here.

Very big depth charge and mine policy adopted last week, first open sign of naval initiative and very important to acknowledge this suitably. While verbally favouring enterprise, Navy Dept. is really waiting for Admiralty to lead the way to formulate any forward strategy. *Scientific American* is dealing with subject; will cable date of article.[1]

On 30 June order was given for mines and depth charges 50,000 each, as no doubt you are aware. These supposed to be made and given free to British Government.

Submarine question mentioned at every interview I have had with President and members of his Cabinet.

38.   *Jellicoe to Northcilffe*

c. 10 July 1917

As the transport of troops is mentioned it is necessary to give a reminder of the fact that between the commencement of the War and 31 March 1917, the British Navy has safeguarded the transport overseas of ten and a half million troops from the attacks of both surface vessels and submarines, together with their equipment, munitions, stores and a large proportion of their food.

The loss incurred amounted to less than 1,000 lives.

This not inconsiderable achievement is very apt to be forgotten as

---

[1] Not traced.

is the fact that the work itself is the principal factor which has handicapped the Navy in every direction when an offensive is planned.

The ever increasing demands on the resources of the Navy are shown by the fact that the number of vessels working from Portsmouth alone to supply the needs of the Army had more than doubled between June 1916 and June 1917, and the number of fast craft required to safeguard these vessels on passages had similarly more than doubled. The same figures apply to other cross channel passages to at least an equal extent.

The 'alleged inactivity' of the Navy in dealing with the Submarine exists only in the imagination of those not acquainted with the facts.

There are certainly more submarines now, but the means of dealing with them have increased very considerably and are increasing, otherwise the losses would have been far greater. The resources of the U.S.N. are being added to those of the British and Allied Navies. *Firstly*:-

The construction of unsinkable monitors in the numbers required would take the steel and labour which is essential for the construction of merchant vessels, tankers, destroyers and anti-submarine craft. Monitors capable of withstanding the gunfire of modern forts and capital ships would require heavier armour than has yet been used in warship construction, and the manufacture of the armour plates, ordnance and ships themselves would occupy from 18 months to 2 years.

The number of large merchant vessels or old Men of War required to block the German Fleet into North Sea harbours is approximately 220.

Experience of blocking passages in a strong tideway shows that the operation is most difficult and that gaps are certain.

Submarines would not be kept in by these means and a passage would be cleared for heavy ships after a short time.

No mine barrier that cannot be swept has yet been devised. Many ideas of this nature have been put forward but no practical scheme has been evolved.

The establishment of mine barriers and their protection by capital ships necessitates a number of modern destroyers which is far in excess of the numbers in the U.S. and British Navies and supposing the increased numbers required could be built the trained personnel to man them could not be provided.

Schemes of the class mentioned put forward by Naval Officers have been constantly considered and Admiral Sims has seen them and professional seamen have in addition wasted much valuable time in considering further impracticable schemes put forward by landsmen.

Secondly:–

It is impracticable to block the northern exit from the North Sea by mine nets owing to the weather conditions and wave motion. This opinion is based on the experience gained since the War commenced. The wave motion in Dover Straits was sufficient to chafe through heavy links of chain cable in a few weeks during winter gales. On account of the greater depth and higher waves conditions in the North Sea are worse.

It must not be forgotten also that no net or mine barrier is efficient against submarines unless there are sufficient surface craft patrolling the barrier to force the submarines to dive into it. The distance from Scotland to Norway is 240 miles and the number of small craft necessary to maintain an efficient patrol on this line would be at least 150 in addition to those required for its maintenance supposing the scheme to be practicable.

Howitzers and also devices for projecting depth charges are being manufactured in large quantities for patrol vessels and merchant vessels. Shipbuilding capacity is carefully allotted according to the various types of vessels required, an undue proportion cannot be devoted to one type of vessel at the expense of equally important vessels without disaster.

Thirdly:–

The obvious course is for Great Britain to guarantee naval assistance to the U.S.A. after the War. Great Britain cannot exchange modern battleships or battle cruisers for anti-submarine craft while the German Fleet remains intact.

With regard to the construction of large number of mines in the U.S.A. it is most desirable that they should be of the H. type and not the Elia type. Plans of the H. type have been sent to the U.S.A.

Finally, Admiral Sims and his staff are in daily personal contact with the First Sea Lord and Naval Staff and meetings at which all kinds of plans are discussed take place frequently.

39.   *Daniels to Lansing*

9 July 1917

After careful consideration of the present naval situation, taken in connection with possible future situations which might arise, the Navy Department is prepared to announce its policy in so far as it relates to the Allies:–

1. The heartiest cooperation with the Allies to meet the present submarine situation, in European or other waters, compatible with an adequate defense of our own home waters.

2. The heartiest cooperation with the Allies to meet any future situation arising during the present war.

3. A realization that while a successful termination of the present war must always be the first allied aim and will probably result in diminished tension throughout the world, the future position of the United States must in no way be jeopardised by any disintegration of our main fighting fleets.

4. The conception that the present main military role of the United States Naval Forces lies in its safeguarding the lines of communication of the Allies. In pursuing this aim there will, generally speaking, be two classes of vessels engaged – minor craft and major craft – and two roles of action: first offensive, second defensive.

5. In pursuing the role set forth in paragraph 4, the Navy Department cannot too strongly insist that in its opinion, the offensive must always be the dominant note in any general plans of strategy prepared. But, as the primary role in all offensive operations must perforce belong to the Allied powers, the Navy Department announces as its policy that, in general, it is willing to accept any joint plan of action of the Allies, deemed to meet immediate needs.

6. Pursuant to the above general policy, the Navy Department announces as its general plan of action the following:

    (a) Its willingness to send its minor fighting forces, comprised of [sic] destroyers, cruisers, submarine chasers, auxiliaries, in any numbers not incompatible with home needs, and to any field of action deemed expedient by the joint Allied Admiralties, which would not involve a violation of our present States policy.

    (b) Its unwillingness, as a matter of policy, to separate any division from the main fleet for service abroad, although it is willing to send the entire battleship fleet abroad to act as a united but cooperating unit when, after joint consultation of all Admiralties concerned, the emergency is deemed to warrant it, and the entire tension imposed upon the line of communications due to the increase in the number of fighting ships in European waters will stand the strain upon it.

    (c) Its willingness to discuss more fully plans for joint operations.

40. *Sims to Daniels*

16 July 1917

****

14. The Department's policy refers to willingness to extend hearty cooperation to the Allies, and to discuss plans for joint operations, and also to its readiness to consider any plans which may be submitted by the joint allied Admiralties.

15. I submit that it is impossible to carry out this cooperation, to discuss plans with the various Admiralties, except in one way – and that is, to establish what might be termed an advance headquarters in the war area, composed of the Department's representatives upon whose recommendations the Department can depend.

****

17. One of the greatest military difficulties of this war and perhaps of all Allied wars, has been the difficulty of coordination and cooperation in military effort. I am aware of a great mass of information in this connection which it is practically impossible to impart except by personal discussion.

18. ****

I fully realize the pressure, and the influence, which must have been brought to bear upon the Department from all of the Allies and from various, and perhaps conflicting sources.

I also realise that my position here in England renders me open to suspicion that I may be unduly influenced by the British viewpoint of the war. It should not be necessary to state, however, that I have done everything within my ability to maintain a broad viewpoint, with the above stated mission constantly in mind.

19. From the *naval* point of view, it would seem evident that London is the best and most central location in the war area for what I have termed above the Advance Branch of our Naval War Council.

The British Navy, on account of its size alone, is bearing the brunt of the naval war, and hence all naval information concerning the war reaches and centres in London.

It will be quite possible for all of our advanced headquarters staff, or parts or divisions thereof, to visit Paris and other allied Admiralties at any time.

****

41.   *Browning to Jellicoe*

Halifax, Nova Scotia,
20 July 1917

There is evidently some feeling in United States Navy Dept. that they are not being taken into complete confidence of Admiralty in regard to Naval operations and following is an extract from private letter from Admiral Benson dated 9 July to me received 17 July, it appears important you should know his opinions, they are given verbatim to show the friendly spirit in which he writes, quote 'It was very good of you to write to me and I am sorry not to have shown my appreciation in writing in reply sooner. I was particularly anxious to run down to see you at Hampton Roads but it was simply impossible; under any circumstances it would have been difficult but just after losing poor Chase[1] it was not to be considered. I very much wanted to have a heart to heart talk with you on the entire subject of naval side present war. I sometimes wonder if your service realises how much in earnest we are and fully and heartily we want to cooperate with you; we get very little, in fact nothing about what your policy is except to have us send over as many tugs, anti-submarine craft as we can. Personally I am in favour of a strong offensive of some kind. I know that sounds rather indefinite but could we not get together and devise scheme or work out plan that could be carried out in the North Sea. We will never starve Germans out; it will take us long time to put a large enough land force to so strengthen allied armies to enable them to drive German armies before them; in other words I think it better to lose some of our older battleships and other fighting craft than to remain on the defensive and let them continue sink our ships. I hope you will not take this as criticism but as expression of my views on some of points I wanted to discuss with you. We are arranging to aid in the Convoy and will every possible way cooperate with you to the fullest. I trust you will not have the slightest hesitancy in calling upon us for anything you think we can be of assistance in. Our Squadron [off] Brazil seems to have accomplished its object and I hope ere this reaches you Argentina has thrown down the bars. You know we have 10 of her commissioned officers in our fighting ships so she cannot draw too fine a line on the question of neutrality.[2] We are fitting out most of the gunboats, small cruisers that were on the Patrol to send over the

[1] See note 1 on p. 82.
[2] Argentina remained neutral but Brazil declared war on Germany (26 October 1917).

other side. Admiral Jellicoe has asked for them to operate in vicinity of Gibraltar; the larger and faster cruisers will form a convoy for our troop ships and seven intermediate class will be assigned to merchant convoy – one of them took convoy yesterday from New York or was supposed to.[1] We will keep at least three fast cruisers distributed along the coast to go out if a raider is reported, we are sending coal Halifax, St. John's [Newfoundland], St. Lucia, Kingston.'

42. *Browning to Benson*

Halifax
26 July 1917

I ... think it is very kind of you to write to me at all with the load of work upon you.

I need scarcely say that it gave me much concern to hear that you felt in any way in the dark in regard to the general Admiralty policy. ... I have taken the liberty of putting the matter before Admiral Jellicoe personally, and he informs me that a copy of a recent paper written by him has been sent through Admiral Sims to the Navy Department; also that he has suggested to your Ambassador in London that perhaps the best way of attaining close co-operation would be for a certain number of Officers of the United States Navy, in the confidence of the Department, to come over and work at the Admiralty in London; any scheme of operations could then be discussed, and (he says), the sooner the better. I understand we are sending a mission over to you. Admiral Jellicoe recognises the difficulty.of stating general questions of naval policy by telegraph, and I gather from his cable that he is writing personally to you.

The problem of acting directly against the enemy is most difficult. I am no believer in obstructions against submarines, mined or otherwise, as a counter-stroke against the form of war these craft pursue. (you will remember what our submarines did in the Sea of Marmora through a mined and netted channel only 1400 yards wide)[2]; nor that any number of fast patrols, ships with concealed armaments, etc., will be any more than a palliative. The ONLY root and branch action against them is an attack on their bases; but, and it is a big but, history teaches us that without an army in conjunction, the

---

[1] USS *Albany*: cruiser, 1900; 3430 tons; 8 x 5in; 20 knots.
[2] See Paul G. Halpern, *The Naval War in the Mediterranean, 1914–1918* (Annapolis, Md: Naval Institute Press, 1987), pp. 68, 113, 116, 161–2.

navy will fail. The enemy has the most powerful fortresses in Europe in Wilhelmshaven and Kiel, backed by their massed fleet. Both are unfortunately remote from our army positions, and, even if an army could be spared, there would be no reasonable chance of landing them, either on the Frisian coast or in the Baltic. I believe that we are quite ready, as at Gallipoli, to risk and lose our older battleships, and I feel that you would come in with us tomorrow, but the operation must afford some reasonable chance of success. There may be some other decisive action possible against the submarines, but if there is we don't know it.

As I write, I have had a letter from Admiral Jellicoe. He says that the convoy system is successful up to the present, and that you are helping us very much in undertaking the convoys from New York in addition to everything else. We are now sending convoys of about 20 ships each from:–

Hampton Roads every 4 days
New York every 8 days
Sydney C[ape] B[reton] every 8 days.

My squadron has been increased considerably to provide the escort ships. So far convoys have been successful; one oiler however was torpedoed in the convoy reaching the United Kingdom on 7 July but she reached Falmouth under her own steam.

Our political people are however inclined to be too optimistic about the system; it is only a defensive solution at the best.

The Armed Merchant Cruisers acting as escorts are all taking in as much cargo as possible on this side.

Admiral Jellicoe tells me convoys are working on the United Kingdom–Scandinavian route, and he hopes to begin others weekly from Gibraltar and South America.

I should like to tell you that Captain Hines[1] is a real help at Halifax. I send all my messages to Navy Department through him; he is always most prompt and business-like; and he keeps his mouth very firmly closed in this land of indiscreet talk!

Please let me thank you for being so very good in rendering help at New York in repairing *Devonshire*.[2] Why she went into the convoy

---

[1] Captain J. F. Hines, US Navy: previously, as a Commander, captain of *Cleveland*; later chief of staff, Division 4 of Cruiser Force; at this point US liaison officer at Halifax, NS; in February 1918 commanding *Charleston*.

[2] HMS *Devonshire* cruiser, 1902; 9 800 tons; 2 x 11in, 4 x 6in; 23 knots. Damaged in a collision off eastern seaboard, she was repaired at the US Navy's Brooklyn yard.

track I do not yet know, ...

43. *Sims to Daniels*

31 July 1917

Referring recent cable from Secretary of State to Ambassador recommending naval conference London, Department to be represented by Admiral Mayo, am sure conference would result in great benefit all concerned. Admiralty cordially welcomes suggestion. Admiral Jellicoe suggests Mayo's staff be sent week or so ahead 'to get spade work done by time Admiral arrives'.

44. *Browning to Jellicoe*

10 August 1917

Admiral Benson came to Hampton Roads to see me. I found it had been arranged that Admiral Mayo was to take over a mission and leaves New York in *Philadelphia*[1] 18 August. Benson told me it had been intimated to Navy Department that Admiralty proposed to send Naval Mission short time ago but matter had not developed. He considers question might now stand over for discussion with Mayo but he (Benson) considers it would be advisable particularly if an Officer can be spared who has recently served in Grand Fleet. Sending of Mayo is intended to be greatest compliment they can pay. They wish to be made acquainted with our Grand Fleet procedure as much as can be permitted [so as to be?] ready to co-operate at any time. Benson then took me to Fleet Base to see Mayo. I found Mayo very pleased at idea of going and seeing you. He hopes to be allowed to visit Grand Fleet, see Home Port Defence organisation, U.S. Destroyer Base and perhaps Dover or Harwich. He expects to be away from United States 5 or 6 weeks. Mission mainly consists of his staff and is not intended to be permanent. President personally approved of his going. Matter is kept most secret. Suggest advisability of communicating through Gaunt as early as possible special arrangements meeting and escorting *Philadelphia* at submarine zone. Mission will at my suggestion bring special radio operators and A.F.R. Signal Book. Mayo would I gather appreciate being told his [place of?] residence in London. Benson likes Gaunt and considers him most businesslike clear and prompt.

[1] SS *Philadelphia*, US Atlantic liner.

45.   *Sims to Pratt*

18 August 1917

****

Churchill is, as you know, living up in the clouds. He denounces everybody and everything. He can and does tell you and everybody else not only that everything is all wrong, but he can explain to you just exactly what should be done both in the military and naval way, to win the war right away.[1]

46.   *Sir Eric Geddes[2] to Lloyd George*

29 August 1917

****

Admiral Mayo has had a thorough talk with the First Sea Lord and with Sir David Beatty[3] who has met him in London. He has described on the attached memorandum the purpose of his visit, and we hope very much that it will bear fruit.

****

Admiral Mayo tells me that he has come over with the instructions of President Wilson that he is to ascertain in what possible way the Americans can more fully come into Naval warfare, and that President Wilson has told him that in discussing the co-operation of the American Naval Forces with the Allies he is not to be too much influenced by the fear of running risks. He told me that President Wilson's words were – that you can't make omelettes without breaking eggs, and that war is made up of taking risks; so that we hope to be able to get more co-operation from them both now and in the future.

[Enclosure]

Admiral Mayo's Notes on the Purpose of His Visit

The purpose of the present visit of the Commander-in-Chief of the United States Atlantic Fleet is, in general terms, as follows:-

---

[1] Judging by the familiarity of tone, it is almost certainly the all-American, not the half-American Churchill who is under fire here. The American journalist was then in London, scrutinising the Admiralty (see document no. 33). Some might consider the statement applied equally well to the British Churchill.

[2] Sir Eric Geddes, First Lord from 20 July 1917 to 11 December 1918.

[3] CinC Grand Fleet.

1. To learn more fully what has happened, and what has been done.
2. To get more closely in touch with what is being done, and then
3. To discuss what it is proposed to do.

The above outline is indicated in order that the United States, first having full information as to past and present plans, may then more clearly appreciate proposals looking to future operations; all to the end that the United States may more intelligently and effectively employ its strength and its resources in cooperation with the Allies to win the war.

47.   Sims to Pratt

30 August 1917

In our weekly letter of this week, you will find a brief account of the arrival of Admiral Mayo on this side. Almost since the time I arrived here I have been suggesting and recommending that a number of officers be sent over to go into the situation, to work with the Admiralty, and dig out the information that is now wide open. It never occurred to me that Admiral Mayo might think of coming over but that of course is the best thing that could have happened. It is difficult for me to explain how much this means to the people over here. He is more than welcome, both he and his staff, and he is now in conference with the Admiralty.

****

The conference at the Admiralty was between the British Admiralty authorities, the Commander-in-Chief of the Grand Fleet, Admiral Mayo and myself. They took up a number of things for consideration and as a result the Admiral is sending a cable today. This discussion was of course only preliminary to those that will take place when the Conference meets on 4 September. France, Italy and Russia will be represented.

The Conference above referred to occupied all of the forenoon. At 1.30 we all went to lunch at the First Lord's house where Admiral Jellicoe was present and a number of Admiralty officials. In the afternoon there was an exposition of the status of the schemes of digging out tactics and so forth. I think I may safely say that it is a revelation to Admiral Mayo and his people to see what sort of a problem this would be. All of the confidential charts were shown that specified the position of all of the land and sea defences of the German Coast, including the mines that had been planted by both sides for a hundred miles out. It is really astonishing the number of shore batteries that are scattered along the coast surrounding Heligoland.

****

I have not heard Admiral Mayo express any definite opinion about the advisability of these projects, but I feel sure that he will conclude that they are not practicable. ...

Such a procedure [a landing on Heligoland and a close blockade] would be playing the game that, you may be sure, the Germans have been praying that the Allies would attempt – in order to give the former the opportunity to put into operation the attrition project formulated by Von Tirpitz.[1]

The question of sending over the four dreadnoughts that have been asked for by the British Government has been discussed to a certain extent, but without arriving at any definite conclusion. ...

... Let us suppose that the Allies lose the war. In that case what would be the position of the United States when it became known that the Allies had asked for reinforcements of their battle fleet and that America had declined for a reason believed to be unsound? The superiority of the British Fleet over the German is much less than is generally supposed. The figures were laid on the table yesterday and showed a proportion of twenty-four to nineteen dreadnoughts, with a great superiority in the matter of destroyers that the Germans could bring to bear at any particular time of their own selection.

As stated in my recent cables, it will be necessary before the end of the year to put five British pre-dreadnoughts out of commission, and replace them, in the South-east part of England by a force of a less number of dreadnoughts taken from the Grand Fleet.

Let us suppose that an action takes place and that the Germans should succeed in drawing the British Fleet over a submarine trap and damaging it to such an extent that the reinforcements would be essential to success. Where would we be in the light of history when it became known that we had declined reinforcements that might readily have turned the scale of battle? This is a matter for very earnest consideration. In my opinion not to comply with the expressed requirements of the Allies in the present situation is to take a very grave and very unnecessary risk of our fair reputation among nations.

[1] Admiral Alfred von Tirpitz, father of the German Navy; appointed State Secretary of the Navy 1897; forced out of office 1917 because he disagreed with unrestricted submarine warfare. See P. M. Kennedy, *The Rise of the Anglo–German Antagonism 1860–1914* (London: Ashfield Press, 1987).

48.   *Admiral Mayo's general impressions regarding conditions in*
the Admiralty

[?] September 1917

****

5. (a) There is little doubt that the British Admiralty is at a loss
    when asked for the history of the war to date. Reports of
    operations are so isolated and scattered and without system
    that there is not available any comprehensive record of origi-
    nal plans, the governing reasons therefore, and the degree of
    success or failure in each case. The inevitable inference is that
    the war has been carried on from day to day and not accord-
    ing to any comprehensive policy to serve as a guide to plans
    looking to the effective coordination and cooperation of
    effort against the enemy.

   (b) It is apparent that, despite the so-called war-staff arrange-
    ments put into effect in the Admiralty during the past three
    years, until very recently there has been no planning section,
    nor was there any definite body of men charged with the
    function of looking ahead, or even looking back to see where
    in lay the causes of success or failure, nor any means of
    furnishing the heads of the Admiralty with analyses and
    summaries of past operations in order that decisions as to
    continuing old operations or undertaking new ones, might be
    reached with a due sense of 'perspective' both as to past
    operations, and as to the coordination of new operations in a
    general plan.

   (c) The statement of present Admiralty policy, originally dated
    July 1917, now revised to 17 September 1917[1] is not really a
    statement of policy but rather a summary of current activi-
    ties. That these activities are based on an underlying idea of
    the defensive may readily be inferred from the leading words
    of paragraph one of the paper referred to ...

   (d) The statement of proposed future Admiralty policy dated 17
    September 1917 indicates growing appreciation of the neces-
    sity for more energetic offensive measures against the sub-
    marine in the way of preventing his egress from the North Sea.

   (e) While the development of the submarine menace has been
    gradual and the measures undertaken to meet it have had to
    be evolved and applied to new developments as they

---

[1] Not reproduced.

appeared, the present *dispersion* of allied naval effort against the submarine menace has reached large dimensions and the actual offensive against the submarine has suffered through the accumulation of large numbers of vessels to carry out protective measures. The number of vessels engaged in protective (defensive) effort includes practically the entire British Navy in northern waters except the Grand Fleet, many of whose destroyers and other small craft are also engaged in protective work.

(f) Referring again to the proposed plan of future anti-submarine operations in the North Sea, it appears that it may be necessary to withdraw some vessels engaged in protective work in order to make the offensive effective. However the effectiveness of the offensive should be cumulative thus enabling perhaps nearly all the available vessels gradually to be diverted from the protective (defensive) to the offensive.

49.   *Mayo to Benson*

London,
5 September 1917

International Naval Conference met today ... Request information whether United States willing in case there appears reasonable prospect supply twelve oldest battleships and eight oldest cruisers out of total forty battleships and forty-five cruisers to be sunk together with large number hulks and barges in blocking German Channels. Personally believe nothing will come of this proposition as consider full examination of difficulties will show impossibility of success. ...

50.   *Extract from Admiralty Operations Committee Minutes*

20 November 1917

The Employment of old Warships in German Waters

24.   It was reported to the Committee that the suggested close offensive in German Waters dealt with as Item No. 1 of the Naval Conference 4 and 5 September 1917, which would involve the sinking of old warships, was considered by the United States Navy Department to be impracticable, in which view the Committee concurred.

****

51. *Mayo to Daniels*

Carlton Hotel,
London,
8 September 1917.

Report of International Naval Conference held in London 4–5
September 1917; and kindred matters

****

6. Sir Eric Geddes, First Lord of the Admiralty, on behalf of the British Government, having offered a welcome to the representatives of the navies of the powers united against Germany, reminded them that the Conference was called at the suggestion of the United States Government and called upon the Commander in Chief of the United States Atlantic Fleet, who then stated that he had come with no definite instructions but with the desire to learn how the United States Navy could best assist and co-operate with the Allied navies, particularly in dealing with the submarine menace, which the United States regarded as particularly serious at the present time; he also emphasised his conviction of the value of personal intercourse between officers of the United States and the Allied navies.

Item 1. The Question of a Close Offensive in German Waters

8. (a)   The First Sea Lord stated in general terms that an offensive operation against German bases in the Heligoland Bight had been for some time under consideration by the British Admiralty, and said that it was essential to know, before going further, whether the powers represented would wish to have proposed in detail a scheme which would involve the sinking of approximately the following allotment of old warships, as merchant vessels could not be spared for the purpose:-

	Battleships	Cruisers
British	18	13
French	5	12
Italian	3	3
Japanese	2	7
Russian	0	0
United States	12	8
	40	43

(b) It was further stated that the operation in mind was a very difficult one and he would not go into details at this time. The primary object was to block submarines in by blocking up the German exits into the North Sea, no other object being worth the risk involved. It was repeated that further development of such a scheme was wholly dependent upon the willingness of the governments concerned to furnish the vessels indicated, which were to be loaded with concrete before sinking and were to be supplemented in the shallower parts by hulks and barges either made of concrete or partly filled with concrete.

(c) The United States representative was unable to state the views of his Government. ...

(d) The Conference, after discussion, agreed that the question should be carefully considered by the governments concerned and that they should indicate in due course to the British Admiralty the contribution of old vessels which they would be prepared to furnish, should the contemplated operation appear practicable after due consideration of all the difficulties involved.

Item 2. The Alternative of a Mine or Net Barrage Either in German Waters or Further Afield

9. (a) The British Admiralty put forward as an alternative to a close offensive in German waters, the suggestion that the activity of enemy submarines might be restricted by the laying of an effective mine field or mine-net barrage. If such an operation were undertaken it appeared that it should take the form of:

1. An efficient mine-field barrage so as to completely shut in the North Sea, which was estimated to require about 100,000 mines, a number which would not be available for some considerable time, or

2. A barrage of mine-nets for the same purpose which proposal was, in view of experience to date, deemed impracticable.

****

(c) As to the proposal to put down a mine barrage in the northern part of the North Sea, while it could be guarded against enemy sweepers, certain difficulties exist such as lack of freedom of movement of the Grand Fleet, so that a very promising degree of success should be indicated before such an undertaking was begun.

(d) The Conference, after discussion, agreed that the distant mine barrage could not well be undertaken until an adequate supply of mines of satisfactory type was assured and that, until or unless such conditions ensue, the improvement and extension of the present system of mine fields was desirable, and further, that a barrage of mine-nets was impracticable.

****

Item 3. Offensive Measures Against Enemy Submarines in the North Sea

10. (a) The British Navy was stated to be strained to such an extent in guarding and assisting to guard overseas communications that actual offensive against submarines in the North Sea was largely done by such units of the Grand Fleet as could be spared for the purpose. There was related the development of 'hunting groups' which relied chiefly upon the hydrophone or kite-balloon, or both to locate enemy submarines, and that seaplanes were very useful for this purpose and were being allotted to this duty as rapidly as the many urgent calls on the air service would permit. It was also stated that there was under construction a special type of submarine for work against enemy submarines, armed specially with a large number of smaller torpedoes with a view to discharging a 'salvo' of them at an enemy submarine which is a very difficult target for a single torpedo.[1] So far the data indicates that submarine vs. submarine is most successful, then 'mystery ships' though the latter are not now so effective as formerly due to increasing wariness of the enemy, then the destroyer and patrol boats of various kinds, the chief value of the latter appearing to be that they cause enemy submarines to dive at once in order to avoid them.

(b) After discussion, the Conference agreed that the most desirable anti-submarine measures were:-

1. to attack or block enemy submarine bases,
2. to mine the submarines in effectively,
3. to attack the submarine at sea –

and it was felt that these measures should be amplified, expanded, and improved as rapidly as the availability of vessels and material enabled the one or the other or any of them to be followed up.

---

[1] 'R' class submarines: 1917–18; 420/500 tons; 10/15 knots; 4-6tt.

*Item. 4. Measures to Deal with Enemy Submarine Cruisers of Large
Radius of Action on the High Seas*

11. (a) As six enemy submarine cruisers (so-called *Deutschland*
type)[1] are expected to be ready for sea before the end of October,
consideration must be given now to measures necessary to be
initiated very soon in readiness to deal with this matter. A striking
need is for additional long-distance radio service in arc area not now
covered by existing allied radio stations but the said area can largely
be covered by the establishment of long-distance radio service in the
Azores.

(b) The British Admiralty put forward for consideration the
following measures:–

1. Use of decoy ships, working in concert with submarines,
   which will accompany them,
2. Concerted measures for preventing the establishment of
   enemy submarine bases overseas,
3. Convoy of all craft, including friendly neutrals as far as
   possible,
4. Development of a radio warning system and of an intelligence centre in the Azores.

(c) After discussion of the several measures proposed in sub-
paragraph 10 (b) above, it was agreed that (1) thereof ought to be a
useful measure; and that (3) in view of reported armament of 6 inch
guns for cruising submarines of the *Deutschland* type, would require
larger and more powerful escort vessels than some now employed,
and that it might even become necessary to use battleships on escort
duty therefore that the governments represented should consider
whether they could provide the class of vessels deemed desirable for
escort duty. It was further agreed to refer measures (2) and (4) to a
committee composed of two British, two French, one United States,
officers, that the Portuguese Naval Attaché (Captain Lieutenant
Carvalho) should be invited to join the committee, and that the
report of the committee should be adopted as embodying the views
of the Conference in the premises.

(d) The committee report stated that they agreed:-

****

---

[1] *Deutschland* class submarines: built 1915 to carry cargo to and from USA, thus
defeating British surface blockade; converted to military use 1917; numbered U-151
to U-157; additional vessels built; clumsy craft and ineffective as commerce destroyers; 1700/2300 tons; 1 or 2 x 5.9in; 4 tt, 20 torpedoes; surface range 4500 miles
plus; larger types ready by end of war.

3. That the following steps be taken as regards the Azores, the Portuguese Government first being asked permission:-

(i) United States naval force to be based in the Azores.
(ii) A British intelligence center to be established.
(iii) British directional radio station to be established.
(iv) British long-distance radio station to be established for the war.

British units to work under the general directions of the United States senior naval officer.

****

12. An additional point touched upon (during discussion of Item 4) was the possibility of the Germans sending a battle-cruiser, accompanied by a high-speed supply vessel, to operate in the Atlantic, not only for the purpose of raiding convoys but also with a view to drawing the British battle-cruisers in pursuit. No formal opinion was recorded as varying views were expressed as to the likelihood of such an operation being attempted, but it was deemed apparent that such a move would be very difficult to deal with and that the use of battleships as escorting vessels for the convoys was indicated.[1]

Item 5. Establishment of Convoys Universally for Outward and Homeward Trade and Organization Necessary

3. (a) The First Sea Lord made a statement at length of the general arrangements for convoys in the Atlantic, inviting attention to the improvements that had been made and were making as well as to relative loss of tonnage due to delays incurred by waiting for convoys to assemble, and that all of the experience to date indicates the necessity for more frequent convoys, which will require more escorting ships and, in view of expected increase in size and effectiveness of enemy submarines, heavier ships while the need for more destroyers and small escorting vessels of that general type is not yet adequate for the convoys in operation. Difficulties are expected with the outward bound convoys which will usually be in ballast and therefore more or less unmanageable at close quarters, this being particularly true of the 'tramp' type.

(b) It was pointed out that convoy system in Atlantic had so far given good results but that lack of sufficient and suitable escort

[1] See documents nos. 259, 262–7, 269.

vessels had been the cause of considerable losses of shipping in the Scandinavian trade which has to cross the North Sea, and also that the shipping losses in the Mediterranean showed a greater percentage of loss than in any other area, although an Allied naval council now sitting at Malta was making arrangements for the establishment of a more satisfactory convoy system in the Mediterranean.[1]

(c)   Among other things the British Admiralty held the view that the following numbers of small escorting vessels were considered the minimum desirable:-

1.   Convoy of 20 ships and over – 10 to 12 escorting vessels
2.   Convoy of 12 ships and over – 6 to 8 escorting vessels
3.   Convoy of about 8 ships – 4 escorting vessels.

(d)   It was agreed that the above views of the British Admiralty were concurred in and that the governments represented had additional cause to give careful and early consideration to the furnishing of additional cruisers and other escort vessels.

****

22.   The Conference completed its sittings at about 6.30 p.m., 5 September. The fact is that, while the Conference was very useful to all concerned, it is extremely difficult to reach any conclusions other than those of a very general nature, as representatives usually lack authority to make definite arrangements and usually have been furnished with instructions to press matters which affect their own countries particularly, which tends to restrict their appreciation of the broad scope of the matters usually dealt with in conferences.

52.   *Gaunt to Jellicoe*

10 September 1917

Admiral Benson complained to me privately about being kept in the dark on important matters. Sims apparently put forward that the Americans should only be told what Admiralty think necessary.[2] Benson is very strongly against this and says they should be taken into full partnership and the information mutual. He gave two instances in 48 hours. (A) A reference by Sims to three raiders being out, of which the Americans know nothing. (B) Rumour from

[1] See Halpern, *Naval War in the Mediterranean*, pp. 369–400.
[2] This is surely a total misunderstanding on Benson's part of Sims's views on the exchange of information. See document no. 19.

apparently the same source that British are sending vessels to Azores. The conversation was a private one, but he spoke so bitterly I thought I should let you know. I respectfully submit that if information of this sort is sent through me, instead of or in conjunction with Admiral Sims it would be preferable. I will explain fully in writing.

53. *Spring-Rice to Foreign Office*

12 September 1917

United States Navy Department is anxious that Gaunt should go over at once to explain situation here.

They are willing to do everything we ask but hope that Admiralty will be more frank with them as impression prevails that we are reserved as to reasons why we make our requests. There is a suspicion that we are unwilling to take them into full partnership and they believe that Sims is too much under British influence. As Gaunt possesses their full confidence (as Sims doubtless has yours) I think his visit would have excellent effect and have given my full approval.

54. *Jellicoe to Gaunt*

14 September 1917

You should inform Admiral Benson that no information has been kept from Navy Board.

We know nothing of three raiders being sent out. Two have been out since December and it is presumed U.S.A. know this.[1]

The story about Azores is quite untrue. Suggest you should hint to Benson that many wild stories get about but that no reliable information is kept from him.

55. *Gaunt to Hall*

12 September 1917

There was a very stormy meeting at Navy Dept. today Wednesday when a number of grievances among various Departments against us were aired.[2] Afterwards Admiral Benson asked me whether it would be possible for me to go to England on a visit to explain their

---

[1] See note 3, p. 31.
[2] Gaunt presumably meant Bureaus, the principal divisions of the Navy Dept.

view of things. He told me he was wiring Mayo to the same effect. I urge that this be done as even if I cannot do much good it would at least help the situation here which is really bad as the officials of the Navy Department think that we are not playing the game. Will you place that before Admiralty and [?] wire decision as soon as possible as if concurred in I ought to be [leaving] immediately. My offices are well organised now and can carry on in my absence.

56.   *Deputy First Sea Lord[1] to Gaunt*

13 September 1917

You are to come to England as soon as possible reporting to Admiralty on arrival.

57.   *Gaunt to Benson*

17 September 1917

I have had a personal telegram from the First Sea Lord directing me to inform you that no information has been kept from the Navy Department.

58.   *Benson to Sims*

24 September 1917

****

I have also been surprised that no plan of operations has been suggested as coming either from you or the Admiralty. So far, the principal requests and suggestions have been along the line of the increase in Anti-submarine craft in European waters and increasing the personnel assistance. ...

****

We are not willing to send a portion of the battleship force and do not intend to unless very much stronger arguments are produced than have been so far set forth. It has been a surprise and disappointment that no definite plan of operation of the combined forces of the Allied naval powers has been taken up and decided upon long ere this. I consider this most urgent and certainly should be done at the earliest possible date, and if nothing can be done this fall or

---

[1] Vice-Admiral Sir Rosslyn Wemyss.

winter, preparations should be actively underway to carry out some
definite plan of operation as soon as spring 1918 opens.

59. *Arthur Pollen to Roosevelt*

Vanderbilt Hotel, 34th St.,
New York, N.Y.,
26 September 1917

I am giving a letter of introduction to you to Mr Knappen of the
New York Tribune. He will be in Washington shortly and will
present it in person.

He came to me from the paper, telling me that they had information that very serious friction had arisen between Whitehall and
the Navy Department, and asked me if I could either confirm these
reports or add anything to them. It was obviously an affair in which
I could have no information that would be useful to the paper. But,
it occurred to me that if these reports were true, it only emphasises
the high desirability of an early concentration of naval authority.
My views on the vital importance of a joint British–American conduct of the war at sea have been put forward with all the force I can
command in the *Tribune* and *Public Ledger*, and, as you will remember, in conversations with yourself, Mr Daniels, and Admiral Benson, and in memoranda which I have done my best to bring into the
most august circles. If in addition to all the other disadvantages of
the present situation, actual friction has arisen between the naval
administrations of the two countries, the case I have argued is not
only stronger than I thought, but one that should be met without
delay.

My recollection is that you and I were in practical agreement on
this point. The *Tribune* people tell me that Commodore Gaunt is
already in England to modify the position in accordance with American requirements. If I am any judge of the situation at Whitehall, he
will not have a very easy time. I very much doubt if either Spring-
Rice or Northcliffe on this side, or Sims and Mayo on the other, will
be brutal enough to bring home to Jellicoe the extraordinary folly of
their present proceedings. If I am right, a certain amount of judicious newspaper criticism might affect the situation very favourably
indeed. It would certainly impress the Prime Minister, who is extremely sensitive to indications of this sort.

From what I know of the *Tribune's* people, I should imagine that
they would be very reluctant to print anything on this subject except
with a view to strengthening the hands of those who are trying to

bring about desirable changes. If, therefore, the situation is as I am informed, and you agree that some good could be done by newspaper work of the right character, I am sure you could not allow the matter to go into better hands than those of Mr Knappen and his chiefs. My own effort has been to prevent anything being published which is simply vague and general and, therefore, mischievous. And of the specific causes of friction repeated to me, I was, of course, quite unable to distinguish which were true and which mistaken. If you decide on seeing whatever is published is true, it might be a good thing if Mr Knappen could see Admiral Benson and the Secretary.

60. *Captain Dudley Pound[1] to Wemyss*

c. 29 September 1917

Memorandum on Co-operation
Memorandum by Admiral H. T. Mayo, U.S. Navy, for First Sea Lord

The United States Navy Department intends to cooperate with the Allied Navies to the maximum of its ability, but it is convinced that effective cooperation is dependent upon:–
(a)   A mutually acceptable plan of operations.
(b)   A thorough investigation of the material and personnel requirements for the conduct of such operations.
These items divide logically into parts as follows:-
1. What is present policy and plan? What further assistance is it desired that the United States shall provide from available forces or resources?
2. What changes in that policy or plan are contemplated in the immediate future? What further assistance is it desired that the United States shall provide from present available forces or resources or from forces or resources that can be prepared in time?
3. What policy and plan is contemplated in the more distant future? What measures is it desired that the United States shall take to prepare forces and material for efficient assistance by that time?
Memorandum by Pound
    Admiral Mayo is desirous of taking back with him a statement drawn up in reply to the attached paper.

---

[1] Later Admiral of the Fleet Sir A. Dudley P. R. Pound (1877–1943): commanded *Superb* 1911; Captain 1914; Additional Naval Asst to 1st Sea Lord 1915; commanded *Colossus* 1915; Operations Division July 1917, heading Planning Section; Director of Operations (Home) September 1917; commanded Mediterranean Fleet March 1935–June 1939; First Sea Lord June 1939–September 1943.

The War Staff should prepare a paper in reply to his questions.

Question 1. – should be answered in considerable detail ...

Further assistance desired from the United States from available forces or resources are as follows:-

(1) Four coal-burning Battleships of the *Dreadnought* type to replace three or four Grand Fleet *Dreadnought* Battleships which it is desired to send to foreign waters to relieve older Battleships which are being paid off for want of personnel.[1]

(2) An increase in the number of Destroyers, in order to enlarge the Convoy system and to provide better protection for each Convoy.

(3) An increase in the number of Convoy Cruisers for the same reason.

(4) An increase in the number of Patrol craft, Tugs, etc., for anti-submarine work.

(5) The rapid building of merchant ships.

In reply to Question 2:-

The possible change in Blockade policy, due to the adoption by the United States of a system of licensing should be touched upon;

The possible changes in mining policy due to the introduction of a new type of mine, should be mentioned;

The increase in the offensive policy against submarines made possible later on by an increase in the number of anti-submarine vessels and of anti-submarine appliances, should be stated;

The co-operation with the Army in the Mediterranean consequent on certain offensive operations in prospect, should be touched upon, as well as the closer anti-submarine policy hoped for in the Adriatic.

The possibility of a close offensive action in German waters and in the Baltic should also be mentioned.

The further assistance desired from the United States in carrying out possible changes in policy might come under the heading of large supply of mines – if a successful type of mine is evolved;

An increase in the Destroyer force in British waters to enable a more offensive policy against submarines in the North Sea to be adopted;

An increase in Patrol craft to watch a possible minefield laid in northern waters;

The assistance in the shape of minelayers from the United States, etc.

Under heading 3 the following subjects might be touched upon:-

[1] J M. Winter, *The Great War and the British People* (London: Macmillan, 1985), pp. 39–48.

The policy of a possible close offensive in German waters instead of including this under Question 2, mentioning that this policy is dependent upon very extensive Air reconnaissance which cannot be carried out in the immediate future;

A close mining policy instead of under 2, because this awaits the supply of suitable mines.

Similarly the mining policy in northern waters might be transferred to Question 3.

The action contemplated if Germany sends out cruisers or other vessels as raiders.

****

Appendix II: Surface Craft Desired from United States by 15 March 1918

Destroyers or Sloops	48 in number. Coal burning if possible. Speed not less than 18 knots. Endurance – 5 or 6 days at 15 knots. Armament – not less than 2×4 inch guns. 4 Depth Charge Throwers. High-Speed Submarine sweep. Very good seakeeping qualities.
Trawlers	or similar vessels. 128 in number. Not less than 250 tons displacement. Coal burning. Speed not less than 11 knots. Armament – one four inch gun if possible. 2 Depth Charge Throwers. 1 Deep Sweep. Acoustic Apparatus – the best available. Able to keep the sea for 10 days in any weather.
Motor Launches	80 in number. 110-foot Submarine Chasers. 3 pounder or equivalent gun. Speed not less than 16 knots unless very enhanced sea-keeping qualities can be ensured with lower speed. Fitted to carry Depth Charges from chutes. Fitted for minesweeping in case they may be required for this. 40 for Mediterranean. 20 for West Indies. 20 for Canadian coast.
Tugs	20 required in addition to the 12 already being supplied.

Air Policy

****

Co-operation of the United States

In the event of the United States being in a position to co-operate in the work, it is recommended that the three main Seaplane Stations in Ireland should be taken over by them completely and equipped, manned and controlled entirely by their personnel.

It is understood that arrangements are already in progress for the establishment of an American Seaplane Station at Brest, and on this account it is not proposed to proceed with the proposed British Station at that port.

61. *Gaunt to Admiralty*

6 October 1917

Press articles with large headlines as follows:-

'Not even engendered by Britain's Navy tactics. British withhold their secrets of naval warfare. Given knowledge of American inventions, His Majesty's sea dogs reluctant to reveal their own.'

These articles appeared in the *Washington Times* of last night Thursday and *New York Evening* [?] and *Washington Post* this morning Friday. I have personally seen the Secretary, Admiral Benson, Admiral Earle,[1] and Captain Pratt and others at a [?] meeting this morning Friday. Admiral Benson made a long statement in which he asked me to assure you that they were most distressed at the articles which were totally untrue and that they were perfectly assured and confident that nothing had ever been withheld from them, he even went so far as to say that if anything at all had been withheld between the two Admiralties it had been by the United States Navy Department, and they had only done this until a definite decision had been arrived at in order that suggested inventions or alterations should not leak out at this end or in transmission. Secretary Daniels has made a statement to the Press to the above effect and I hope that it will appear in all papers tomorrow Saturday. I will cable further then.

---

[1] Rear-Admiral Ralph Earle, US Navy (1874–1939): graduated from Annapolis 1896; saw action in Spanish–American War 1898; advanced from Commander to Rear-Admiral as Chief of Bureau of Ordnance 1916; Captain in command of *Connecticut* 1919–23; commanded Torpedo Station, Newport, RI, 1923–25; retired 1925; Rear-Admiral on retired list 1930; President, Worcester Polytechnic Institute, Mass., 1925–39.

62. *Navy Department Memorandum for the Admiral [Benson] for
issue to the Press*

7 October 1917

With reference to the articles which appeared in the Washington evening papers of 4 October and in morning papers of 5 October, making certain statements about the lack of accord between the British naval authorities and our own, the Navy Department makes the following statement:

There is no foundation for such rumors and in proof of it quotes extracts from a cable prepared about a week ago by the Department for the State Department to forward to our Ambassador in London:

'Regarding the statement that the British Authorities are greatly disturbed by the information received from Washington that the United States Navy feels that the Admiralty and the Government of Great Britain have not been absolutely frank in their dealings with [us] and Admiral Sims; and do not cooperate with us in every way, there is absolutely no foundation for any such impression, and the Department of the Navy is at a loss to know where such ideas could possibly have arisen. … There has not been a time when the thought was even entertained that the British Admiralty was in any way failing to cooperate, or to give us the fullest information; not only Admiral Sims, but every representative of the Navy Department that we have sent to London has assured us of the perfect freedom in regard to all such matters; and of the fullest and heartiest cooperation from the First Lord of the British Admiralty down.'

63. *Sims to Benson*

9 October 1917

You will note, from the reports to be made by Admiral Mayo, the amount of information his large staff was able to dig out in a comparatively short space of time. That sort of work can be accomplished only by men who can devote their exclusive attention each to one specialty.

It was with the object of being able to do this, that I was so insistent in requesting more assistance when I first came over here. I am glad to say that the officers and men who have been sent over eased up things very considerably, but I think you shoud know that conditions in this respect cannot be satisfactory to the degree indicated above, unless I have a sufficient personnel to be able to keep some of the officers continually at work in departments of the Admiralty. It is only by this daily contact and association that we can keep thoroughly in touch with what is going on. The people of the Admiralty are working to the limit, and we cannot expect them to think of, and supply us, with the things which would be desirable for us.

****

64. *Page to Daniels*

[21 September 1917]

Many thanks for your cordial letter asking me to write you direct personal notes when it seems worthwhile. This is such a one. I am telegraphing the State Department – for the President and you – about a long conference that I have had with Mr Balfour, Sir Eric Geddes, the new head of the Admiralty, and Admiral Jellicoe, the First Sea Lord. They have for some time been hearing from their people in Washington of a feeling of dissatisfaction in naval circles there with the British Admiralty – that they are not frank with us, that they withhold information, and that they do not cooperate properly with us. They are much upset by these reports. These three men assure me that they have opened everything to our Admirals, and both Admiral Mayo and Admiral Sims (who this week happen to be in France) have volunteered the information to me that the British Admiralty have done what their officials say – told them and showed them everything. As for 'cooperation' I do not know what specific plans have been discussed between them but I do know that a naval problem (or any other problem) may well seem to be a very different thing here where it exists and 3000 miles away where it must be studied theoretically.

These men – Balfour, Geddes, and Jellicoe – are honorable and truthful men. They can't be concealing things which they deny concealing. They are frank and grateful and ready to receive any suggestions from us. It is impossible to believe otherwise.

Yet it seems – at least such is their information from Washington – that some sort of a grave misunderstanding has arisen. My feeling is that it has come from the lack of acquaintance and personal touch between naval authorities in Washington and in London.

They are eager for you to come here yourself. They will tell you and show you everything and discuss everything with you. If for any reason you cannot come, they hope that Admiral Benson can. They were deeply disappointed when we declined Jellicoe's invitation to have our naval officers sent to work in the Admiralty – in all its branches – and see and hear and discuss and report on everything; and they renew the invitation. They ask for specific items – *wherein* have they failed to be entirely frank? They will take up every complaint and answer it in detail.

Now when they welcome Sims and Mayo and ask for officers to work with them and ask you to come and Admiral Benson, and when they ask for specific criticisms and complaints and when both Mayo and Sims say that they have opened all doors – then something surely remains to be explained if such dissatisfaction exists at Washington as is reported to them.

My advice is

(1) Come with Benson

(2) Send the officers they asked for in July to live and work in the Admiralty.

(3) Send and bring every complaint that everybody or anybody in authority has made and take every one up with these men.

It is simply a crime to have any misunderstanding; and I believe that such as exists can in this way be cleared up completely. Our only job now – and everybody's job – is to win the war. Misunderstandings are crimes.

This is private – not for your Department's files, but only for your own eyes, confidentially. I cannot form any judgment about technical naval problems; but I have had some experience in forming judgments about men; and these men give evidence that they wish to play a square game and to play it fairly. There's a disturbing influence somewhere – apparently – that is not legitimate. I don't know what it is, unless it be the difficulty of men dealing with one another 3000 miles off, without personal touch or acquaintance.

65. *Navy Department to State Department*

10 October 1917

Cooperation with Britain

With regard to Mr Page's cable of 21 September concerning a conference with Mr Balfour, Sir John Jellicoe, and Sir Eric Geddes, the department is at a loss to understand what has given rise to such ideas as those suggested in the statement that they are disturbed by information received from Washington to the effect that the American Navy feels that in their dealings with Admiral Mayo and Vice-Admiral Sims the British Government have not been entirely frank, that they do not cooperate with us, etc., for there is absolutely no foundation for any such impression. Neither item of the two referred to was intended to be in the nature of a complaint. In regard to the first item, raiders: We had been informed by the Admiralty that no raiders were out. In one of his letters Admiral Sims stated that raiders had been operating and that in such an event the strength of the convoy escort would have to be increased. On the chance that our understanding of the situation was wrong, we referred the matter to Sims to clear up. He confirmed the Admiralty statement in his reply. The second idea – the Azores Base, was evidently a mistake and had no reference to a base in the Azores. A report we received at one time that England intended despatching some submarines to the Azores to operate in that vicinity was probably responsible for the error. It was most important for us to know whether this report was true since we were sending destroyers and other small craft en route to Europe through the Azores and we desired no unforeseen contact between our craft and the British submarines. This is the whole extent of the second item.

No thought was entertained at any time that we were not receiving the fullest information from the Admiralty or that they were failing in any way to cooperate. We have been assured of the freest and heartiest cooperation in all such matters on the part of the First Lord of the Admiralty and all his Staff not only by Admiral Sims but by every representative we have sent to London.

66.   *Geddes to Daniels*

13 October 1917

Expect that Admiral Mayo and staff have now returned from their visit here. We appreciated their visit very much and endeavoured to give them fullest information and apprise them in fullest possible way of Naval situation. After you have had an opportunity of discussing with Admiral Mayo the results of his visit hope you will cable me fully your views and also say whether in your opinion further steps can be taken to provide for full co-operation of the two Navies. My personal view is that while from time to time we can send over experts on particular subjects for short visits we must endeavour to bridge over three thousand miles of ocean by close communication between yourself and myself, Admiral Jellicoe and Admiral Benson. Would it be possible for you to send as supplementary to visit of Admiral Mayo small party composed of Navy Department Officials and naval experts to study war in the North Sea on the spot [?] If so British Admiralty would welcome this. If Admiral Benson could come he would be most warmly welcomed.

67. *Benson to Jellicoe*

22 October 1917

I do not hesitate to state that, in addition to the time worn adage that 'a fellow feeling makes us wondrous kind', there is also on my part a lively appreciation of the herculean task which you have undertaken for the past three years, and are still carrying on, together with a personal satisfaction which it gives me to be joined in the same great cause as our British cousins.

For many years I have hoped for the day when our countries would be more closely united in the common cause for the good of mankind, for I have believed that the world would be better for it. Now the time has come, – and I can assure you that it is in harmony with such sentiments as these that I shall try to reply to your most welcome letter and to carry on what I [hope] shall prove to be a most agreeable and profitable correspondence.

Admiral Mayo returned to us on the 13th instant and to me it is a source of the greatest satisfaction to feel that such cordial relations existed between the Admiral and [his] staff, and yourself, the officers in the Admiralty, and the British Service generally with whom they came in contact. His written, as well as his verbal and informal reports to me indicate the most open frankness on the part of yourself and the officers of your Service and the thought of this gives me great hopes for the future work which our two Services are, I hope and believe, destined to jointly perform.

Thus far, although I have been in conference with Admiral Mayo for three days, it has not been possible for me to thoroughly digest all of the information which he brought back, and consequently, I am not yet prepared to write you in detail regarding these matters. I assure you that we are giving the subjects which the last naval conference brought out the most earnest and serious consideration, and I hope, at an early date, that we shall be able to discuss definite propositions looking to the solution of the problems immediately confronting us.

It is my earnest desire to expedite our destroyer building program in every possible way in the hope that in a minimum time we may be able to throw a large number of such vessels into the field of operations. As you have doubtlessly been informed, the labour question here is a serious one, particularly when it comes to obtaining skilled labor for rapid ship building. We are, however, going ahead with an enormous amount of this work, although handicapped, and while we cannot get our units to sea as early as we should like, we feel that they will be there before many months, and in condition to render valuable service.

The reports which we have received from time to time from Vice-Admiral Sims's forces indicate that the spirit of cooperation for which the Admiralty and the Navy Department are striving seems to have permeated the actual fighting forces to such an extent that a very cordial feeling exists between all officers and men of the two Services. This is, to me, a source of great satisfaction and I am sure that the splendid cooperation between Admiral Sims and Admiral Bayly with the forces operating on the Irish coast is as gratifying to you as it is to me.

Our earnest desire is to do everything possible to cooperate with you and I assure you that for yourself, for the Admiralty, for the British Naval Service, and for your great country, we have nothing but the most cordial and friendly feeling and a sincere desire to see you and our other Allies triumph in the War and at the earliest possible moment.

There are many matters which it would give me a great deal of satisfaction to discuss personally and informally with you which I shall not take up in this letter. As questions arise from time to time I shall feel free to write you fully and express my opinion, and I hope that you will consider that I am only too anxious to have you do the same by me.

Please accept for yourself the assurance of my highest regard.

68. *Winston Churchill (U.S.) to President Wilson*

London,
22 October 1917

During the month or so I have been in Great Britain, as an independent observer, I have had unusual and unsought opportunities to acquire a point of view on several matters, and among these on the situation as it exists between our naval Service and the British Admiralty. I have been thrown with men engaged in many different activities, I have seen the Prime Minister and other members of the Cabinet and their assistants, I have talked with naval officers of all ranks and of both services, of progressive and conservative tendencies, including Vice-Admiral Sims and Admiral Jellicoe. The opinion I have gathered I believe to be an independent one, and I send it to you for what it is worth, trusting you will not think me presumptuous in so doing.

(1) I have become convinced that the criticism of the British Admiralty to the effect that it has been living from hand to mouth, from day to day, that it has been making no plans ahead, is justified. The several Sea Lords are of the conservative school, and they have been so encumbered with administrative and bureaucratic duties that they have found insufficient time to decide upon a future strategy. The younger and more imaginative element of that service has not been given a chance to show its powers, nor has it been consulted in matters of strategy.[1] On the other hand the British Army, under pressure of necessity, has been compelled to adopt a policy of forsightedness, and is now apparently reaping the benefits due to long preparations and the infusion of new blood.

(2) It goes without saying that any scheme of importance of an aggressive nature requires a due period of consideration by naval strategists with the aid of civilian experts, and usually involves the co-operation of sea and land forces. Such lack of cooperation has undoubtedly been a great source of weakness during the present war. And if any such scheme is adopted many months may be necessary for the collection of the material and personnel required to carry it to a successful conclusion. Sir Eric Geddes is unquestionably an able man, and apparently willing to discard precedent when necessary. There are signs that he is feeling his way, and that he is encountering a certain opposition from the Sea Lords. Not very long ago he appointed a staff of young officers who had made reputations as strategists, but both in numbers and authority it has been inadequate, and the Sea Lords have refused to support it and give its suggestions serious consideration. Its deliberations have been held in a bedroom at the top of the Admiralty building. I am informed today, however, that this staff has been increased by the First Lord, and that henceforth it will be composed of two sections, one for strategy and one for material.[2]

(3) Because all aggressive plans hitherto proposed have been found impracticable, it by no means follows that some plan may not be hit upon, especially now that we have the combined forces of the two nations to draw upon, that will accomplish the object desired of crippling or destroying the German Fleet, or of suppressing aggres-

[1] See Marder, vol. 4, *passim*.
[2] See Marder, vol. 4, chapters VII and VIII.

sively the actions of the submarines. But the accomplishment of these objects depends, first, upon due deliberation by a body of men trained for such a purpose, and who have made strategy their specialty, and second, upon the preparation of the material means called for.

I would hasten to say that I am convinced that the lack of adoption of any such aggressive plan is in no way due to a want of initiative on the part of Admiral Sims. He has urged upon the Admiralty the value of such a staff as I have described, and he was given to understand by Sir Edward Carson, before the latter's retirement as First Lord, that a staff would be established. But the Admiralty is still suffering from the inertia of a tradition that clings to the belief that the British Navy still controls the seas, and can be made to move but slowly in a new direction. In addition to this Admiral Sims has had to feel his way, he has had to build up a staff for himself, and he has been overwhelmed with work. I have visited Queenstown. I have talked with the officers of our flotilla there, with those of Admiral Sims's staff both here and in France, and the opinion is unanimous that he is the ablest officer in our Service. Their admiration for his energy and talent is unbounded, their loyalty absolute. He is extremely popular both in England and France, and his relations with the Admiralty and the French Ministry of Marine are all that could be desired. The efficiency of our flotilla, the high seamanlike qualities of our officers and their ability to make their own repairs and to keep the destroyers constantly at sea has been the subject of universal praise among British officers, and is a source of pride to Americans here.

(4) Unquestionably the most important, indeed the essential thing still to be achieved is that of a partnership between our Service and the British. It must be a full partnership. There are many good reasons why this complete cooperation has not as yet been accomplished, in addition to the situation in the Admiralty which I have described. At 30 Grosvenor Gardens I have constantly seen Admiral Sims and his staff busy from early morning until late at night, on account of the quantity of administrative work to be done. The machine has to be kept moving. This hampers them to such an extent that they find themselves, in regard to strategic matters, precisely in the condition of the Admiralty, – with this exception. There is scarcely an officer on that staff, including the Admiral himself, who is not keenly alive to the necessity of cooperation with the British Navy, of making plans a long way ahead. And we have on that staff some of the ablest strategists in our service, including

Admiral Sims and Captain Twining.[1] Officers like Captain Twining are wasted upon office work, which could equally well be done by men who have a peculiar gift for it.

It is generally agreed that what is needed is a combined staff of American and British strategists and materiel officers to sit constantly together and expend their entire energies upon making plans for the future conduct of the war. The Admiralty, in spite of their backwardness in creating such a staff for themselves, would welcome such cooperation, and indeed several times have requested it. Admiral Sims could not spare the officers. He has several times requested our Department to send him more officers. But unless the proper men are sent to such a staff, experts in their various specialties, the situation would be made worse instead of better. If more officers were sent to Admiral Sims by our Department, some of the experts on his staff could then be released for duty on the cooperative planning staff, as he has some of the best men in the Service with him today. He would need about eight more officers, in order to establish such a staff in addition to the necessary administrative staff.[2]

****

(5) I have become convinced that whatever strategic plans are made for the future prosecution of the war should be made on this side of the water, subject always, of course, to the approval of our Government. The war will be won or lost in these waters, and any aggressive policy must be staged here. New conditions will constantly arise that have to be dealt with in conjunction with the British and other forces. Besides the great difficulty of communicating in all its aspects a certain situation by cable or letter to Washington has been proved. And I may also add what seems to me the most cogent argument for the establishment of our planning staff over here that we should not merely follow the suggestions of the British Admiralty, but act with them on an equal footing. The presence on the planning staff of an energetic group of American officers and perhaps of civilian experts would strengthen the hand of Sir Eric Geddes; while any scheme they might propose, backed by our own Department and by Admiral Sims, would impel the Sea Lords to adopt it. This tendency, I think, was illustrated by their

---

[1] Captain Nathan C. Twining, US Navy: formerly on the staff of the Naval War College and by this time Chief of Staff to Sims; retired shortly after the war on grounds of ill health.

[2] See documents nos. 75–76.

agreement to our plan of a North Sea barrage of mines, a scheme to which they were formerly opposed. We are in a position to impel them to accept new ideas of value, or at least ideas worth the trying. It will do good to infuse into their councils American blood and a fresh American viewpoint; but we cannot act with the ocean between us, and under the circumstances the British cannot send a staff over there.

(6) The present very slight preponderance of the British Fleet over the German gives cause for a certain anxiety. The proportion of British super-dreadnoughts to German is now about 24 to 19 only, and three of the British dreadnoughts have to be withdrawn to replace as many vessels of the *King Edward* Class[1] now protecting the south east and the Channel from a possible raid with heavy vessels. The latter vessels must be put out of commission in order to obtain the personnel for the manning of new destroyers. It is therefore hoped that the request of the British for four of our coal burning dreadnoughts will be complied with.

The British are badly pressed for destroyers. In the past week only forty destroyers have been with the Grand Fleet in the North Sea, and at times none at all, whereas they should have one hundred and fifty in case of being called into action. Germany has one hundred and seventy which she can bring out with her fleet at her own time. While every cruiser the British Fleet is capable of sparing is at work on convoy or other duty in various localities.

(7) At present there are not enough convoying ships to take care of the merchant vessels supplying western Europe with materials and food. Except by destroyers in the zone, no ships are convoyed from Europe westward; nor, save within the zone, are those convoyed that run from the United States to Gibraltar, and from South America and the Cape of Good Hope to Dakar, on the African coast. I am also informed that none are convoyed, except by destroyers in the zone, from Gibraltar to the British Isles.

For the merchantmen now unprotected some forty odd additional cruisers are needed, including those required to make all the present convoys safe from German raiders of high gun power. The lighter armed cruisers are of no use against such raiders as evaded the North Sea patrols during the past week and sank two destroyers and many merchant ships off the coast of Norway.[2] The success of the war depends largely, of course, upon our giving Europe supplies,

[1] *King Edward VII* class: pre-dreadnought battleships; 1905–06; 16350 tons, 4 x 12in, 4 x 9.2in, 10 x 6in; 18 knots.
[2] On 17 October the German light cruisers *Brummer* and *Bremse* sank the des-

and if all ships could be convoyed and properly defended the defeat of Germany would be much more certain.

For this purpose of convoy it has been recommended to our Navy Department that our older battleships should be used, since the matter is of such grave importance that even the interference in the training of crews on these ships would in Admiral Sims's opinion be justified. The old battleships could be made into convoying vessels by the simple operation of removing the smaller batteries and of sealing up the lower ports, leaving the larger batteries, which would be ample for driving off any possible raider; while temporary bulkheads of wood could be installed to render the ships safer against torpedoes. The argument against using such vessels for convoy purposes is that a large number of trained men might be lost if a ship were to be sunk, but it would only be necessary to man them with less than one half of the ordinary crews; less than one half of the usual engineer force, since they would be steaming at convoy speed, and gun crews sufficient to man the guns remaining in use. A few of the smaller guns could be mounted on the upper deck.

(8) I think it may be said with confidence that the various plans already submitted to the British Admiralty and which have originated on this side for aggressive action against the German Navy or for making landings in the rear of the German lines are now impracticable, if indeed they were not always so. Some new plan must be devised. So also is the project of blocking in the German Fleet. I have discussed these plans with many officers, American and British, with a member of the British Cabinet and with Admiral Jellicoe, who showed me all the operations on a chart of the North Sea and the Baltic.

Along the Belgian coast the work of the British monitors has been all that could be hoped for, considerable damage has been done to the enemy, and a most ingenious plan of shelling the land batteries with the aid of a smokescreen and devices for locating these shore batteries have been adopted. Such devices were necessary because of the much greater range of the shore guns as compared with the guns ships can carry. Yet the monitors have done extremely close shooting at longer ranges than would have been thought possible – over 20,000 yards. Under the most trying circumstances barrages of mines have been laid by the British, in the darkness, close to the coast, both in the Baltic and in the North Sea. According to evidence

troyers *Mary Rose* and *Strongbow* and nine of the twelve merchantmen they were escorting from Scandinavia to Scotland. The Germans escaped unharmed and unchallenged by British light forces searching for them. See Marder, vol. 4, pp. 294–7.

from German sources, the submarines are having considerable difficulty in finding their way through these barrages.

The plan of blockading in the German Fleet by sinking ships in the channel is regarded by military men as impracticable on account of the greater range and accuracy of the shore batteries. The question of blocking these ports has several times been seriously considered by the Admiralty, and two years' preparation was made on such a plan. But it was finally abandoned because the rise of tide was found to be too great, and there was nothing to prevent the Germans blowing away the superstructures. In addition to this, eighty ships would have to be sunk in correct position at the very close range of five miles from shore under the guns of the batteries.

The plan of landing a great force behind the German lines in Belgium for the purpose of seizing the naval bases there might once have been possible before it was so strongly fortified by the Germans. Now experts of the British Army are united in discouraging it. Something like 150 ships would be needed, and they cannot at the present time be spared, while a large army would have to be put ashore. While the project of capturing Heligoland may, I think, be dismissed. If the principle that ships are powerless against strong land batteries needed to be illustrated, the unfortunate Dardanelles campaign was a case in point. And even if Heligoland could be taken it could not be held against repeated airplane attacks, since it is only 25 or 30 miles from the mainland.

****

69.   *Pratt to Daniels*

c. 12 November 1917

In the *main* and where he [Winston Churchill, the U.S. author] deals in general situations I find the letter correct.

The Admiralty situation is fairly well summed up, and coincides with my own information. This has been furnished me privately by Commodore Gaunt just back from England. He tells me that *Geddes* is the strong man – that *Jellicoe* is going – that Wemyss is to succeed.[1] The latter is not brilliant, but determined, has experience, is sound and will surround himself with an able staff. This he tells me is going into effect.

... What he says about Sims is correct. As a leader of men he is

---

[1] This msut have been the first indication of the changes that were to take place on Christmas Eve, 1917. See Marder, vol. 4, ch. XII.

without an equal in the service. He is not the keenest strategist, nor perhaps has he as much imagination as some, he is very impulsive, but as a man who can detect the right qualities in another man and use them for the good of a cause he is without equal, and his personality ensures an absolute loyalty.

****

... The barrage plan (our own) is distinctly offensive in character. It is headed by one of the most aggressive as well as one of the deepest thinkers (a War College man, Capt. Belknap) in the service.[1] ... This plan will be *dominated* by Belknap no matter whom the British select and that was one of the reasons I advocated his selection.

... The 4 dreadnoughts sail about 24 November, on them we are sending a selected group of naval men and scientists headed by Captain Leigh (a splendid officer)[2] to personally demonstrate the practical working of our C and K tubes (listening devices) in connection with the hunting groups, composed of chasers and destroyers.

The destroyers will be pushed to the fighting front as fast as practicable. The only reserve we use is that necessary to safeguard the lives of our soldiers on the transports.

****

... The Asian and South Atlantic stations are to be reduced to a shadow. All available Cruisers are being gathered in the North Atlantic. The submarines (ours) are being gathered in, both for defense and offense (when trained and ready).

He is a little off on the convoy situation. Ships westward should not be convoyed except through the danger zones, unless a raider is out. It wastes time and tonnage.

Attempted pressure is being put on all merchant ships to accept convoy Eastward.

The Gibraltar convoy will go into effect the instant the Admiralty is ready.

He is wrong on the character of cruisers we send in convoys. Their

---

[1] Captain Reginald R. Belknap, US Navy: commanding the Mine Force of the Atlantic Fleet (flagship the old cruiser *San Francisco*).

[2] Later Rear-Admiral Richard H. Leigh, US Navy: began the war as a Commander and assistant to the Chief of the Bureau of Steam Engineering; conducted trials of submarine listening devices; joined Sims's staff in December 1917; commanded a unit of destroyers and submarine chasers at Plymouth from February 1918; these were engaged in submarine hunting operations and operational trials of the new sound gear.

quality is sufficient for the German cruisers that made the North Sea raid, but they could not stand up against the German battle cruiser. Our *dreadnoughts* are ready for just that contingency. Our *old battleships* are ready to assist in convoy.

It is not the Cruiser question that hampers. It is the shortage of destroyers. The cruiser is of small use in the zone. The destroyer is absolutely necessary. It was to relieve somewhat this situation [that?] every yacht available for distant service is being sent.

****

70   *Mr Butler[1] to Colonel John Buchan[2]*

British Embassy,
Washington,
23 October 1917

Several papers including the *Tribune*[3] maintain their unappreciative attitude towards the Navy and ask specially our reasons for not adopting offensive, and for not attacking Heligoland direct and submarines at their bases.

In this connection Mr Pollen's articles are most mischievous.

As a remedy for this, Embassy suggests desirability of obtaining for publication a vigorous interview with Beatty or Jellicoe explaining attitude of Admiralty.

[Note from Buchan to Geddes]

… Mr Butler has called attention to the harm being done in America by attacks on our Naval policy. I should be very grateful if you felt able to give an interview on the subject to a representative of the American Press in order to counteract the mischief that is being done.

---

[1] Butler was evidently a British official concerned with Allied propaganda and the monitoring of the American press.

[2] Later first Baron Tweedsmuir (1875–1940): qualified as a barrister; served with Lord Milner in South Africa 1901–03; later journalist, editor, war correspondent, publisher and, most notably, novelist; commissioned as an intelligence officer in the Great War, rising to rank of Colonel; at this time Director of the Department (later Ministry) of Information; Conservative MP 1927–35; barony 1935 and appointed Governor General of Canada.

[3] It is not clear whether this was the New York *Herald Tribune* or the *Chicago Tribune*.

71.   *Sims to Secretary of Admiralty*[1]

23 October 1917

With reference to the recent Allied Naval Conference held in London 4 and 5 September I wish to furnish for the Admiralty's information, communications just received from the United States Navy Department.

****

(1) Opnav 772. 'In this cable the Department outlines a reply to specific requests made by Great Britain in a memorandum handed to Admiral Mayo by the First Sea Lord and dated 22 September.

First. The services of a division of four United States coal burning dreadnoughts to replace dreadnoughts to be withdrawn from the Grand Fleet is under serious consideration.

Second. The increase of destroyers abroad is not practicable at present but number abroad will be increased as rapidly as practicable when new destroyers become available.

Third. Re-arrangements of cruiser squadron will provide for additional cruisers for merchant convoy service. Further effort will be made to provide additional vessels.

Fourth. Arrangements made to commandeer additional yachts and tugs, fit them out and send them abroad as rapidly as possible. Fifty submarine chasers have already been assigned to France of which eleven have been delivered or are en route. Four squadrons submarine chasers of eighteen boats each will be available in the near future for service in foreign waters should they be found useful for such duty.

Fifth. The construction of merchant vessels is proceeding as fast as conditions permit.

Sixth. The contract has been let for one hundred thousand mines of American type. The United States has offered to commandeer for the British Admiralty three vessels suitable for minelaying and in addition can probably commandeer two or three more vessels suitable for mine laying to be manned by United States for employment in co-operation with British mine laying force in joint plan which may be finally agreed upon.

Seventh. The question of the proposed mine barrage Scotland to Norway as presented to Navy Department is not definitely con-

---

[1] Sir Oswyn A. R. Murray (1873–1936): entered Admiralty 1897; Director of Victualling 1905–11; Assistant Secretary 1911–17; succeeded Graham Greene on 7 August 1917, remaining Secretary until his death.

curred in but careful consideration is being given in this particular subject with a view to arrive at a definite conclusion in regard to employment of mine barrage which measure is considered in principle to promise good results. The following matters were not included in the memorandum referred to but were specifically mentioned in connection therewith.

Eighth. It is considered that American type mine is perfectly safe and inoperative upon breaking away [from] its moorings.

Ninth. Standard British Admiralty type of sinker can be used with American type mine.[1]

Tenth. Referring preceding cable regarding fuel oil situation Navy Department repeats that in [so] far as it has jurisdiction it is Department's policy to place military necessity of situation first and to settle commercial complications later. To this end Navy Department guarantee that in so far as its own efforts are concerned it will take every measure it can to assist in safeguarding military needs of the British Fleet as regards oil situation and it will requisition in addition to the six already taken over as much tanker tonnage as may be necessary to accomplish this purpose provided that by so doing the oil situation for British fleet will be improved and safeguarded.' Admiral Benson.

****

(4) Opnav 775. 'Department in this cable outlines its reply to several points brought up for consideration during international naval conference held in London, England, 5 September. Additional specific requests of Great Britain, France, Italy, will be treated in separate cable.

First. Department considers close offensive involving sinking of older battleships and cruisers to block German channel impracticable.

Second. Department will endeavor to fill any shortage in British skilled personnel for assembling mines as soon as our personnel can be collected here and arrangements made for quartering them in England.

Third. That every endeavor will be made to provide additional escorting vessels for convoy service. Rearrangement of cruiser squadron will provide four extra cruisers for merchant convoy.

Fourth. Measures are being taken to gain intelligence of and prevent establishment of enemy submarine bases. It is agreed that steps be taken to insure adequate action to prevent submarines or

---

[1] A new design with long antennae to increase the likelihood of contact.

suspicious vessels being succored or allowed to make use of neutral territory waters. Measures are being taken whereby wireless service in merchant vessels is being improved, investigation of practicability of fitting certain ships in convoy with power radio for relay work will be made but it is thought that power radio with which escort vessels are fitted should suffice.

Fifth. United States Naval Forces will be based in Azores Islands, this force will consist of division of submarines and a monitor and possibly additional ships later. United States concurs in establishment of intelligence centre, directional and long distance wireless station in Azores Islands and wishes to cooperate in these matters to fullest possible extent. Pursuant to Admiralty suggestion an American naval officer of suitable rank and attainment will be assigned as base commander in Azores Islands.[1] Question of commandeering ships building in United States for Great Britain will be referred for consideration to shipping board which has jurisdiction.' Admiral Benson.

72.   *Statement of Admiral Benson*

London,
November 1917

Naval policy of the United States

****

The Navy Department is convinced that strong offensive measures must be taken to overcome the present enemy submarine activities, and, while recognising the necessity, under the present conditions, of the defensive–offensive measures employed, does not believe that they can result in complete success. ...

To this end a definite *Naval Policy* based upon a concrete plan of operations for the forces of these countries is essential; and, it logically follows that the naval policy of each of the several powers must be based upon the grand plan with a view to its success.

In order to make any plan of offensive operations effective it should be remembered that a number of vessels will have to be taken from the present shipping for the transportation of additional supplies and for conversion as minelayers. The fuel supply will necessarily have to be tremendously increased, and at the same time an ever

---

[1] Rear-Admiral H. O. Dunn, US Navy, was appointed commander of Base 13, the Azores station, in February 1918; he had previously commanded Battleship Division 5 of the Atlantic Fleet.

increasing Army from overseas must be efficiently maintained in Europe. These and many other questions must be seriously considered and our calculations must allow a sufficient margin of safety to insure a continuation of present operations, so long as they are necessary, in addition to making the new plan effective.

The Navy Department believes that in pursuing an unrelenting and ever increasing pressure in the North Sea against the submarine, the enemy will eventually be forced to confine all his vessels to harbor, or to support the efforts of his offensive weapon (the submarine) with his main fleet. If he chooses the latter a fleet action may be brought on. If he does not, and the allied anti-submarine methods prove effective, his force will be contained within a relatively small area and the allied mission resolves itself into one of maintaining a sufficient and effective blockade and to guarding the exposed coasts from enemy raids.

This plan presupposes the effective closing of the Straits of Dover to enemy submarines. In my opinion this must be an established fact before an attempt to block the North Sea by any one or a combination of the proposals contained in Naval Staff (Operations Division) memorandum dated 17 September 1917,[1] relating to general future policy, can be in order. This does not necessarily mean that the nets, mines, or other form of barrage adopted must be located in the Straits themselves. It may be necessary to locate these at some place to the north and east, where the currents are not so strong and where the condition of the bottom is more favorable for such work.

****

The Navy of the United States is today ready to consider such plans, and it is my conviction that the matter is one of extreme urgency upon which positive action cannot be delayed. We stand ready to undertake our portion of any jointly approved plan with every resource at our command.

No doubt the first thought that occurs to everyone who attempts to solve this question is to attack the source from which the enemy vessels operate, destroy their bases, and such vessels as may be in port. I have studied the efforts that the British have made to establish mine barrages as close to the enemy defensive batteries as sea conditions and other considerations would permit, and I wish to express my admiration of the energy, skill and patience which they have displayed in these operations. These operations have been

---

[1] The Admiralty memorandum, probably prepared by Captain Pound, handed to Admiral Mayo; see document no. 60.

attended with a certain degree of success, but it is a self-evident fact that these and other measures so far made effective have failed to reduce enemy submarine activities to a point where they are not a grave menace.

****

Anti-submarine craft, such as yachts, tugs, mine-sweepers, etc., have been purchased and placed in readiness for distant service as rapidly as our facilities would permit. Sixteen yachts, ten coal burning destroyers, eleven mine-sweepers, ten gunboats, and two cruisers have been sent to operate on the French coast and from Gibraltar, and this number will be considerably augmented during the month of November. Eighteen sea-going tugs have been requisitioned and are being prepared for service in European waters and will be sent across as rapidly as completed. Eleven submarine chasers (110 footers) have been sent across to the French Government and thirty-nine more of these vessels will be turned over to the French Government as rapidly as they can be completed, which should not be later than 1 January 1918. It is hoped that during the coming winter at least two hundred and sixty of these submarine chasers will be commissioned, organised, and exercised preparatory to being taken across as early in the spring of 1918 as the weather conditions will permit. These submarine chasers have proven themselves to be particularly well suited for the use of the various submarine detectors that have been experimented with. They have not, however, proved to be as staunch and comfortable in bad weather as it was hoped they would be, although when well handled they are considered to be very good sea craft. If the drawbacks to the boats can be sufficiently overcome to make them serviceable for the purpose intended, it is the intention to use them in groups of three or possibly more, as experience will determine, for hunting submarines along the lines and in the zones which an approved plan of operations may require.

In order for these hunting groups to be effective, destroyers or some craft with heavy battery and carrying depth charges will have to be used. Preparatory to this patrol work large quantities of T.N.T. have been procured and large numbers of depth charges of 300 pounds each have been prepared, or will be prepared, also a large number of depth charges of 50 pounds each have been prepared, or will be prepared for use by the submarine chasers. Contracts have been let for the construction of 100,000 of the modified American mines; these mines to be utilized either in construction of a mine barrier in the North Sea, across the Dover Straits, or along the coast of Germany, in accordance with the approved plan of operations. Steps are being taken to prepare additional mine-planters for the purpose of assisting in laying these mines.

A division of submarines has been sent to the Azores to be prepared to operate in this region with one monitor as tender and parent ship. In addition, at least two old coal burning destroyers will be kept on this station and later on a cruiser or auxiliary will also be stationed at this place when some means of extensive radio communication will be established.

The building program of the United States contemplates at least two hundred and sixty or more additional destroyers completed within the next eighteen months. These destroyers, of course, as rapidly as completed, will be utilized wherever their services are most needed. The present indications are that at least thirty-six of these destroyers will be available by the first of June, 1918. It is possible that a larger number than this will be ready.[1]

In the very near future a division of submarines of the 'L' and 'N' types[2] will be sent to operate in the waters along the British Islands and this number will be constantly added to as the new building program is carried forward. It is impossible at this time to state how rapidly the submarine force in European waters can be augmented.

All cruisers attached to the Pacific Station, except three of the older ones, namely the *Marblehead, Yorktown,* and the *Vicksburg* have been transferred to the Atlantic for convoy duty, and all of the cruisers on the Asiatic Station, except the Flagship *Brooklyn,* have been transferred to the Atlantic for this same service. The four armored cruisers under Admiral Caperton,[3] operating in the South Atlantic, will, it is hoped, in the near future be transferred to the North Atlantic for assistance to the convoy forces. It is possible however, that one of these armored cruisers, and possibly two or three of the smaller vessels of the *Denver* class,[4] will be kept in South Atlantic waters. It will thus be seen that practically all of our cruiser force has been assigned to convoy duty.

---

[1] American destroyer production continued to be a major disappointment to Sims and the British and an embarrassment to the Navy Department. The number actually completed during hostilities was 35–45, though the total of 260 mentioned here was achieved within the 18 months. See documents nos. 388, 390–408.

[2] 'L' class submarines: 1913–16; 450/720 tons; 14/10.5 knots; 4tt. 'N' class submarines: 1915–17; 340/400 tons; 13/10 knots; 4tt.

[3] Rear-Admiral W. B. Caperton, US Navy: CinC Pacific Fleet.

[4] See note 1 on p. 47.

Reference has been made to the question of utilising some of our older battleships for various purposes, such as sinking across the entrance of channels leading from the mouths of German rivers emptying into the North Sea. Another proposal is to use them for convoy duty. In view of the urgent necessity of training a sufficient number of engine and fire-room men, with which to man new vessels, both fighting craft and transports, it has been absolutely necessary to use these older battleships almost exclusively for this purpose, at the same time attempting to keep their main batteries prepared for actual battle. It was also considered that while these vessels do not add greatly to the strength of the main fleet, yet there are certain purposes in connection with the main fleet for which they might be utilized to great advantage. It is believed that under certain conditions these vessels could be used to advantage along the German and Belgian coasts in bombarding. So far, the necessity of vessels of this type for convoy duty has not arisen, nor is it believed probable that it will arise. The conditions that probably might require the use of battleships for convoy duty would be due to the breaking out of German battle cruisers which would attack the convoys in the North Atlantic.[1] In order to meet this contingency it would be necessary to use battle cruisers against them and while they were being located it might be considered desirable to use battleships for convoy duty.

The United States is strongly, very strongly, opposed to dividing its battleship force unless for very urgent and very apparent reasons. Due, however, to the long continued holding of the battleships in readiness for battle without actual operations in or near the enemy's waters, it is believed that it would add to the morale of the battleship force, and at the same time indicate more conclusively and strongly the intentions of the United States, to unite with the battleships of our allies in naval operations, if, without waiting longer, we placed at least one division of our dreadnoughts now with the Atlantic Fleet with the Grand Fleet, while so attached to be an integral part of the Grand Fleet, subject in all respects to its routine and general service. It would be hoped, however, that this division could be relieved from time to time by other divisions until all of the battleship force would have had experience with the Grand Fleet.[2]

This arrangement would continue until such time as the shipping situation could accommodate the logistic requirements and permit

<hr>

[1] See documents nos. 259, 262–7, 269.
[2] See Part V.

the entire battleship force to be placed in close proximity to the enemy coast line, ready to cooperate with the allied naval forces.

The United States has agreed and work is being pushed as rapidly as possible toward the establishment of fifteen aviation stations along the coast of France and Southern England and Ireland; ten on the French coast and five in the British Isles. Hydroplanes are being manufactured, material for maintenance of stations and craft is being prepared, and personnel is being trained.

Every effort is being made by the United States to cooperate by its land forces, and certainly its naval forces of every character, and we only await the joint approval of a definite plan of operations in order to direct our efforts. As I have stated above, I believe that the time has come when a definite plan involving the exhaustive efforts of the United States and all her naval allies should be agreed upon; and it should be energetically pursued until enemy naval operations, actual or possible, become no longer a factor in the present conflict.

73.   Benson to Daniels

Paris,
November 1917

Upon my suggestion British Admiralty invited Vice-Admiral Sims to attend daily meetings of their naval council to keep in close touch with all matters going on in British naval service. At subsequent conferences with Sir Eric Geddes he suggested that in order that most complete cooperation could be assured the commanding officer of [American] naval forces in European waters be made an honorary member of British Admiralty Board. He stated further that they would be glad to extend same privilege to Chief of Naval Operations. He requested specially however so far this was personal suggestion and as it would be necessary eventually to refer it to the King it be most confidential. Both Sir Eric Geddes and Admiral Jellicoe are in favor of this being done and all are most anxious for closest cooperation. While my whole effort over here has been to secure this condition I feel that all questions of this kind should receive careful consideration and approval by the President before [being] completely acted upon. Due Sir Eric Geddes anxiety that this matter be kept confidential until he could refer it personally to the King it is requested that any reply be sent direct to me and that care be taken that no British Government [department ?] obtains information in regard to it either through our own or diplomatic sources.

74. *Memorandum by Admiralty Plans Division*

17 November 1917

Priority of American War Shipbuilding

It is felt that every available effort should be put into the building of merchant steamers. Without a large addition to the world's merchant tonnage the operation of American military forces in Europe will be crippled.

Next in order of priority should be ocean-going destroyers in order to escort the said merchant tonnage. Otherwise the war shipbuilding will depend largely on the success and needs of the approved strategy for 1918. This strategy, briefly, is to establish barrages across the Northern and Southern exits of the North Sea in order to prevent German submarines and other cruisers from breaking out into the Atlantic.

These barriers will consist of mines closely patrolled by surface craft and aircraft, with outposts of submarines and rearguards of hydrophone hunting flotillas.

Should these barriers be successful, we may then be able to consider direct attack on the enemy in his own territory.

In the present state of development of (a) aircraft, (b) submarines, (c) mines, (d) long-range land guns, the most promising, if not the only practicable, method of attack would appear to be by means of aircraft. As these will have to be conveyed to within reach of their objectives, it is felt that the next warship need, in order of priority, should be aeroplane carriers. It will take about eighteen months to build these specially, but large merchant ships or old cruisers could have their decks flattened and all unnecessary fittings removed, leaving only the funnels, steering wheels, telegraphs and binnacles, in four to five months.

Such ships would be quite suitable for carrying aircraft on their decks on the short sea voyage in chosen weather.

In connection with this subject special towing lighters for conveying large seaplanes to within reach of their objectives should be given priority.[1]

Minelaying Craft

The Northern Barrage will need frequent renewal and reinforcement. This will probably be resisted by the enemy – the form of resistance being submarines. Considerable losses may therefore be

[1] See Marder, vol. 4, ch. I, for a discussion of British naval air policy to the end of the war.

expected and it is felt that the conversion or building of medium-sized minelayers should be given priority after cargo steamers, destroyers and aircraft carriers.

Submarines
Submarines are not to be pushed on with at the present to the detriment of other building on account of the comparatively recent experience of the American Navy with these weapons and the perhaps peculiar difficulties of carrying out combined operations with submarines belonging to different Allies.

Light Cruisers
The combined strength of the Allied Navies in surface ships is so great that it is felt that light cruisers should not be given priority, especially in view of the probable development of aircraft in the near future.

Capital Ships
Our margin in heavy ships of the line is so fully assured, or could be assured, by efficient co-operation between the American and British navies, that it is felt that any labour or materiel put into new construction might be better employed in producing cargo steamers, destroyers and aeroplane carriers.

75.   *Memorandum on the Naval Policy of the Allies for Admiral Benson, U.S. Navy, by the Admiralty Plans Division*

17 November 1917

1. *Naval Policy of the Allies*
The ultimate objects of the Naval Policy of the Allies are, firstly, to bring pressure to bear on the enemy people so as to compel their Government to come to terms, and, secondly, to resist the pressure applied by them so that we may carry on the war undisturbed. In order to attain these objects, naval power must be directed into the following channels:-
   (a) Protection of the sea communications of the Allied armies, more particularly in France, where the main offensive lies;
   (b) Prevention of enemy trade as a means of handicapping his military operations and exerting pressure on the mass of his people;
   (c) Protection of Allied Trade, on which depends the supply of munitions and food to the Allied armies and people.
   (d) Resistance to invasion and raids.
2. *Method of Carrying Out this Policy*
The question at issue in each of these cases is the control of communications in certain areas; and in order to attain that control

136 ANGLO-AMERICAN NAVAL RELATIONS 1917-1919

permanently and completely, the enemy's naval forces both above and below water must be destroyed or effectually masked. As long as the enemy fleets refuse decisive action, the fleets of the Allies must provide against evasive attack by surface craft by guarding the exits of the North Sea and Adriatic, and by controlling the areas through which trade and transports pass.

3. *Methods of Exercising Control*

A close blockade of the German North Sea and Baltic ports is not possible in the face of the submarine menace; and the alternative of controlling the Dover and Norway–Scotland areas has been adopted. The former protects the communications of the armies in France, whilst the two combined cover the maritime communications of the world, outside the North Sea and the Baltic; and if they could be effectively guarded, three out of the four objects enumerated above would be attained.

The entry of the United States into the war on the side of the Allies has to a large extent rendered the commercial blockade of Germany in the North Sea unnecessary, but the question of preventing the escape of raiders remains a serious problem. The conflicting requirements in the use of light cruisers and destroyers precludes a systematic watch being kept on the Scotland–Norway line; and the escape of a certain number of raiders is to be expected should the enemy make the attempt. That the enemy will make such attempts is almost certain, in view of the results achieved by the *Moewe* and other raiders.[1]

It is therefore of the utmost importance that the Allies should make every effort to guard against this serious danger by utilising their surplus of cruisers on ocean escort work outside the submarine zone. The experience of the war has proved that once a raider reaches the ocean spaces, a few ships scattered about over a large area cannot hope to bring her to action. Great Britain intends to extend ocean escorts to the outward bound North Atlantic trade and the South Atlantic and Indian Oceans so far as her resources allow and it is urged that the U.S.A. and France should assist in this as far as possible by providing their surplus cruisers. In the future Great Britain intends to employ practically all her cruisers and armed merchantmen on foreign stations on convoy work.

So far as the Dover area is concerned, the narrowness of the Waters, with the consequent risk of our mines and torpedoes, have so far acted as a deterrent to the enemy's capital ships. But this may

[1] See Marder, vol. 4, pp. 99–101.

not always be so; and should the failure of the submarine campaign at a later date lead the enemy to resort to the use of his fast ships to hold up our oversea trade, capital ships (with destroyers to cover them) must be based on one of the Channel ports to frustrate any such attempt by intercepting the raiders before they can get clear of the Channel.

****

5. *Submarine Campaign against Shipping*
   In the early stages of the war the foregoing general dispositions sufficed to protect Allied communications and to throttle those of the enemy outside of the Baltic.
   With the advent of the submarine campaign however the situation has been modified and the control exercised by the Grand Fleet has been outflanked, thus enabling the enemy to threaten our vital communications without running the risk of a Fleet action. The increase in numbers and size of the enemy's submarines renders it increasingly difficult to deal with them on their hunting grounds and it has become imperative to intercept these vessels before they can reach the open seas.

6. *Future policy for dealing with the enemy submarines*
   To prevent the enemy submarines reaching their hunting grounds they must be prevented from passing out of the North Sea and the Adriatic.
   In the case of the North Sea this entails closing the Northern exit and the Strait of Dover.

The Northern Exit
   The production of mines in large quantities by the U.S.A., and Great Britain, in conjunction with the developments in hydrophones, has rendered the control of this exit a feasible proposition and preparations are being made to control this area next spring.
   The main features of the Barrage will be:-
   (a) Mining of a central area with mines of the American type in order to render this area dangerous to submarines whether on the surface or submerged.
       At such times as the output of mines warrants it, this area will be notified as dangerous and should have the effect of diverting the enemy submarines into the areas on either side of it.
   (b) The mining of the Areas on either side of the Notified Area with deep mines which will be patrolled by surface craft, and in the case of the Western Area by aircraft in addition, to

drive the submarines down onto the deep mines.

(c) The patrol of a belt of approximately 100 miles in width with a combination of slow vessels fitted with hydrophones and fast vessels to put the submarine down and fight it should it endeavour to escape on the surface.

The waters in which this patrol will be instituted are of such a depth that the submarines will not be able to take refuge on the bottom.

A hunting flotilla of four sloops and 32 trawlers on the lines of the above is now being formed and will be ready by the end of the present month.

This flotilla will form the nucleus of the patrol vessels mentioned above and valuable experience should be gained before the larger operations commence in the spring.

It is not expected that this mine barrage with its attendant patrol will ever entirely prevent any submarines reaching the Atlantic but in addition to the moral effect which it is likely to produce, it should account for sufficient submarines to render this route too dangerous to be attempted.

To pass his submarines out it will be necessary for the enemy to clear a passage through our patrol craft with his surface vessels, in which case there should be a good chance of bringing the latter to action.

The support of the patrols on the Norwegian side of the Barrier could be much more efficiently carried out should the use of a base in Norway be possible.[1]

****

Straits of Dover

The present net and mine barrage having proved ineffective principally owing to the strength of the tidal stream (note: and that mines have not been available since February), with the consequent difficulty of maintenance, plans are now being worked out for improving the present barrage and reinforcing it with a mine barrage in which new types of mines will be used.

The possibility of blocking the entrances to the enemy submarine bases on the Flanders Coast is also being considered, whilst the bombardment of the bases on the Flanders Coast is carried out whenever practicable.

The Entrance to the Adriatic

Endeavours are being made to construct a net and mine barrage

[1] See Part VI.

across the Straits of Otranto but owing to the very great depth of water it is doubtful whether this will be feasible.

This great depth of water however makes the area a very suitable one in which to operate with hydrophone hunting flotillas when these become available.

7. *Mining Policy*

In addition to the Mine Barrage across the North Sea which has already been described, ordinary moored mines will be used as opportunity offers for blocking any routes through the present mine-fields in the Heligoland Bight which the enemy are believed to use.

Mines of a special type will be laid off the entrances to German harbours.

****

10. *Possible future operations involving the co-operation of the British and American Battlefleets*

   (a) Next year there may be considerable development in the naval situation, and various contingencies may arise rendering the presence of the U.S.A. battlefleet urgently necessary in the North Sea.

   (b) Some of the situations in which the U.S.A. battlefleet might be required will now be considered.

      Opinion is tending more and more to the conclusion that future policy against the enemy attack on trade, both by surface and submarine raiders, must be directed towards securing a more effective and intensive control over the North Sea exits, and that outside those areas all forces should be employed in escorting convoys. This idea has already taken shape in the proposed mine barrage, but the chances of definitely defeating the enemy submarine by this means before next winter would be greatly increased by the use of a Norwegian harbour, and the patrol vessels on the Norwegian Coast could be effectively supported, and the danger of attacks on trade by surface vessels would be greatly reduced, as a more efficient control of the North Sea exits could be maintained. ...

   (c) The possibility of Germany or Sweden declaring war on Norway must also be taken into account as in this case it would be necessary for us to occupy a base in Norway in which either the Main Fleet or a strong detached force of capital ships should be stationed.

      Purely strategical considerations would recommend the

Main Fleet being at Stavanger for this place is nearer to both the Skager Rack and Heligoland than either Rosyth or Scapa Flow, and a fleet based there would be excellently situated for exercising an intensive control over the Norway–Scotland area and a general control over the North Sea and Kattegat. If this plan were followed, it would be desirable to base a battle squadron of about eight ships on the Humber to protect the East Coast and support the light craft in the Southern area. (note: Eight ships would not be sufficient as the H.S. Fleet always supports the raiding force).

 The alternative to the foregoing plan would be to retain the main fleet at Rosyth and to base a squadron of about eight powerful battleships in Skudaesness Fiord with a proportion of light craft for screening the battlefleet and patrolling the Norwegian side of the barrage.

(d) Whichever plan were followed, the co-operation of the U.S.A. battlefleet would just make the difference between having sufficient or insufficient forces to carry them out with confidence and success.

(e) Again no one can foresee the future of events in Russia, but the psychological moment may come next year when a diversionary effort towards the Baltic might exercise a very favourable influence on the Allied cause.

 Any move towards the Baltic, and there is no denying the possibility that at one time or another, it may become a matter of great urgency, requires a strong reserve of battleship strength.

 Investigation has shown that any operation in the Baltic in which surface vessels are employed necessitates the use of two Fleets – one to hold the Great Belt to prevent this exit being blocked – whilst the other Fleet enters the Baltic (note: and an expeditionary force to garrison the Islands).

(f) At the present time everything points to the fact that Holland will remain neutral but should they join the enemy or should the enemy seize the Scheldt it would be necessary for us to base a powerful battleship force (note: very little use under present conditions in the narrow seas) in the Southern part of the North Sea.

(g) The war on the sea cannot be separated from the war on the land; for the enemy hopes that his military power will hold out sufficiently long to enable his U-boats to bring one or more of the Allies to their knees. The Revolution in Russia and the Italian retreat[1] will probably lengthen the war and it is therefore necessary to review the situation afresh. It is now considered that 10 or 12 U.S.A. Dreadnoughts should join the Grand Fleet as soon as possible, instead of the 4 as originally suggested, in order that they may learn to co-operate with each other in a tactical and strategical sense. Thus if an emergency should arise or a redistribution of the fleet requiring an access of battleship force becomes necessary, no time will be lost in co-ordinating their action.

76. *Daniels to Benson*

17 November 1917

After thinking carefully subject feel that it would be to advantage if we have a permanent War Staff in England, as a part of the plans department of the Admiralty. If this meets your approval, additional officers will be sent to augment those already in England who are fitted for this work.

77. *Benson to Daniels*

London,
19 November 1917

I have gone over the situation fully with British Admiralty and outlined what I believe to be best plans for future Naval Operations, but am convinced now that British are not prepared now to offer definite plans of their own for our consideration. From my observations and after careful consideration I believe that such plans satisfactory to both countries cannot be developed until we virtually establish the strictly planning section for joint operations here, in order that the personnel thereof may be in position to obtain latest British and other allied information and to urge, as joint plan such plans as our estimate and policies may indicate. This action appears to be all the more necessary considering the fact that any offensive operation which we may undertake must be in conjunction with British forces, and must be from bases established or occupied within British territorial waters.

The officers detailed for this duty should come here fully imbued with our national and naval policies and ideas. Then with the intimate knowledge they can obtain here from data available actual

---

[1] Following the defeat of the Italian army by the German and Austrian forces at the battle of Caporetto, 24 October–12 November 1917.

disposition of allies' forces, reasons therefor, they will be in a position to urge upon British any plan that promises satisfactory results.

In order to initiate this policy, I recommend that Captain Schofield[1] and Commander Knox be ordered to report to Vice-Admiral Sims and Admiral Jellicoe, First Sea Lord, for this duty. A third Officer to be selected after my return.

This matter is an urgent one, and action should be taken at once. ...

78. *Daniels to Benson*

26 November 1917

President desires that heartiest cooperation should be established and maintained between our representative naval officers and British Admiralty. To effect that purpose and to keep in close touch he is glad for our officers to attend daily meetings of British Navy Council but he does not approve of their being made honorary members of British Admiralty Board.

79. *Memorandum by Geddes for War Cabinet*

11 December 1917

****

It has been decided to create a Naval Allied Council in order to ensure the closest touch and complete co-operation between the Allied Fleets. The task of the Council will be to watch over the general conduct of the Naval war and to ensure the co-ordination of effort at sea as well as the development of all scientific operations connected with the conduct of the war. The Council will make all necessary recommendations to enable the Governments to make decisions. It will keep itself in touch with their execution and the members of the Council will send to the respective Governments all the reports which may be necessary. The individual responsibility of the Chiefs of Staff, and of the Commanders in Chief at sea, towards their Governments as regards operations in hand, as well as the strategical and tactical disposition of the forces placed under their command remains unchanged. It has been decided that the Council

[1] Captain Frank H. Schofield, US Navy: began the war as a Commander in the Office of Naval Operations; served on Sims's staff for the remainder of the war.

should consist of the Ministers of Marine of the nations represented and of the Chiefs of Naval Staff.

As the meetings of the Council will of necessity be held in Europe the Chiefs of the General Naval Staffs of the United States and Japan will be represented by Flag Officers nominated by their respective Governments.

The Allied Naval Council will be provided with a permanent Secretariat whose business it will be to collect together documents, etc. The Council will meet as often as may be thought necessary under the presidency of the Minister of Marine of the Country in which the meeting is held.

The various Admiralties will furnish the Council with the information which is necessary for the work to be carried out.[1]

80.   *Benson to Daniels*

Scotland,
28 December 1917

You will be interested to know that our reception by the British, and our relations with them have been most cordial in every sense of the word; that everything has moved nicely and smoothly, and that we have been shown every kindness and consideration. Officers and men of the services from the highest to the lowest, fraternize on all occasions, and the best of feeling prevails. Our men have won the heart of the public by their exemplary behavior, and charity.

81.   *Sims to Jellicoe*

Admiralty House,
Queenstown,
29 December 1917

Here I am at Admiralty House in bed since Christmas eve with a rather painful attack of lumbago, and only just now able to sit up a bit without considerable pain, otherwise I would have written before to say how much I was distressed to learn of your leaving the Admiralty, particularly when the effects of your anti-submarine measures are showing such promise of complete success.

I assume, of course, that the Government's action is based upon the supposed political necessity of responding to the pressure of the ignorant criticisms of the 'man on the street' – a danger to which all

---

[1] This was actually a press statement submitted to the War Cabinet for information.

we military men must always be exposed in time of war.

It would appear that when the public becomes too impatient because the guns are not always firing, some of us have to be sacrificed.

However, I am confident that subsequent events will entirely justify the measures you have taken, as rapidly as practicable, to combat the common enemy.

When I return to London, within a few days, I hope to see you and thank you in person for your unfailing kindess and consideration in helping me carry out my, sometimes, difficult duties.

I hope also that I may be able to see you from time to time, and that you will permit me to benefit by your extended experience.

82. *Sims to Wemyss*

Admiralty House,
Queenstown,
29 December 1917

On Christmas eve I arrived at Queenstown and was at once put to bed with a rather severe attack of lumbago, and am only just now able to sit up a bit without considerable pain, otherwise I should have written to congratulate you upon your new honors, and to assure you of my loyal cooperation with you and the Admiralty in all measures in which the U.S. Navy Department can be of assistance to the cause of the Allies.

When I return to London within a few days, I will tell you of the very efficient cooperation of our forces with yours in this area – a cooperation carried out continuously in such harmony and with such good feeling and understanding as to leave absolutely nothing to be desired.

This is due, of course, primarily to the ability and tact of Admiral Bayly, which is such as to have won not only the sincere admiration and confidence of all of the American officers, but also their personal affection.

This has produced both a personal and an official devotion than which nothing could tend more strongly toward military efficiency.

83.   *Admiral of the Fleet Lord Fisher[1] to Sims*

undated, 1918

I am so delighted that you are coming to lunch at the above address tomorrow Wednesday at 1.30 to meet General Smuts![2] *He is a War Man! He has imagination and audacity! He understands that by Sea and Land this war is a War of Apparatus.* I presume of course that you don't put Apparatus when provided in the hands of d-d fools! (*Which alas! We have done!*) We have not shot a single General or Admiral this war! *We've promoted them!* Voltaire was right about shooting Admiral Byng.[3] ... America ought to supply *Apparatus* for the Russians. ...

84.   *Memorandum by the Planning Section, U.S. Naval Forces in European Waters*

2 January 1918

Memorandum No. 2: Duties of Planning Section

****

In conversation with the First Sea Lord on New Year's Day, he expressed the opinion that one of the Planning Section might be attached to the Staff of Rear-Admiral Keyes[4] at Dover, that

[1] Admiral of the Fleet Sir John Fisher (1st Baron Fisher of Kilverstone) (1841–1920): entered RN 1854; Rear-Admiral 1890; 3rd Sea Lord and Controller 1892; Vice-Admiral 1896; CinC North America and West Indies 1897; CinC Mediterranean 1899; Admiral 1901; 2nd Sea Lord 1902; CinC Portsmouth 1903; First Sea Lord 1904–10; Admiral of the Fleet 1905; Chairman, Royal Commission on Oil Fuel 1912; First Sea Lord 1914–15, resigning over Dardanelles fiasco; Chairman, Admiralty Board of Invention and Research 1915–18.

[2] Field-Marshal Jan Christiaan Smuts (1870–1950): Cambridge-educated barrister, Boer commando leader and South African statesman; Lieut.-Gen. commanding Imperial forces in E. Africa 1916–17; member of War Cabinet 1917; Prime Minister of South Africa 1919–24 and 1939–48; Field-Marshal 1941.

[3] Admiral George Byng, commander of the Mediterranean Fleet in the Seven Years' War, adjudged by a Court Martial to have been responsible for the loss of Minorca to the French. Byng, though certainly strategically at fault, was even more a scapegoat for an incompetent Ministry. He was executed on the quarterdeck of HMS *Monarque* by a RM firing squad in 1756.

[4] Later Admiral of the Fleet Sir Roger John Brownlow Keyes (1st Baron Keyes) (1872–1945): entered RN 1885; gallantry in Boxer campaign, China 1900; Naval Attaché, Vienna and Rome; Inspecting Captain of Submarines 1910–12 and Commo-

another might be detailed in the Material Section of the Admiralty, and that the third officer might possibly be in the Operations Section of the Admiralty. The First Sea Lord offered these suggestions as tentative only but seemed to dwell with some insistence on the Dover detail.

The proposed arrangement is not at all in accord with the expressed ideas of Admiral Benson and would but serve to nullify our usefulness as a Planning Section.

It is therefore proposed that it be pointed out to the First Sea Lord that the duties of the Planning Section must necessarily be more general. The United States is now involved in this War to an enormous degree. The Naval Vessels, and the troops on this side the water, are no correct measure of our participation in the war. Loans to the Allies aggregating Seven Billion Dollars are being made with prospect of further loans. Our entire Military effort is by way of the sea. We are intensely concerned in the measures taken to drive the Germans from the sea and in the measures taken to handle shipping at Sea.

It is therefore appropriate that the Planning Section of Admiral Sims's Staff shall be free to consider those questions that seem to him and to the members of the section, most urgent.

It appears to us that the principle that should govern our relations with the Admiralty, is –

The privileges of the Admiralty with complete freedom of action so far as the Admiralty is concerned.

These privileges and this freedom of action are essential if the Planning Section is to attain its maximum usefulness to our Joint Cause.

In presenting to the First Sea Lord such of these ideas as may be approved, we recommend that emphasis be placed upon our keen desire to be of the maximum possible usefulness to our Joint Cause.

It appears to us that we can be of most use, if we work as a unit – all of us, considering, as a rule, the same subject simultaneously.

We think it desirable that we keep a continuous General Estimate of the Naval Situation.

We think that the following special subjects should be studied by

dore (S) 1912–15; Chief of Staff to Vice-Admiral de Robeck in E. Mediterranean 1915; commanded *Centurion* 1916–17; Rear-Admiral, 4th Battle Squadron June 1917; Director of Plans October 1917; Vice-Admiral Dover January 1918; DCNS 1921; CinC Mediterranean 1925–8; Admiral 1926; CinC Portsmouth 1929–31; Admiral of the Fleet 1930; retired list 1935; Conservative MP for Portsmouth 1934–43; Director of Combined Operations 1940–41; baron 1943. See Paul G. Halpern, ed., *The Keyes Papers* (London: Allen & Unwin for Navy Records Society, 1972, 1975, 1981), 3 vols.

us very carefully at as early a date as possible:-

(1) The Northern Barrage.
(2) The English Channel.
(3) The Straits of Otranto.
(4) The tactics of contact with Submarines.
(5) The Convoy System.
(6) Co-operation of U.S. Naval Forces and Naval Forces of the Allies.
(7) A Joint Naval Doctrine.

Other subjects will undoubtedly present themselves faster than we can consider them but the above illustrates the lines along which we believe our greatest usefulness lies.

85.   *Sims to Benson*

4 January 1918

The First Sea Lord informs me King enquired as to decision concerning my appointment honorary member Admiralty Board. This honorary membership would in no sense change my present position but would permit my attending all meetings at which important matters are discussed. I would of course have no voice and the decisions would not interfere with our freedom of action. This personal message sent upon the suggestion [of] Sir Eric Geddes who believes appointment will not only result in increased efficiency of co-operation but would have good effect.

86.   *Sims to Benson*

14 January 1918

****

I have talked over the business with Admiral Wemyss quite considerably, and I am much impressed with two or three things. First, that Admiral Wemyss is a very clear headed and able man. Second, that his methods are very different from those of Admiral Jellicoe. As you know Admiral Jellicoe followed more or less minutely all of the important correspondence that came into the Admiralty and I think a good deal that was not important. He was at all times working a bit beyond the capacity of even a pretty strong man. He made many decisions himself, and sometimes the wires got crossed between him and his assistants, and sometimes the Allies.

Admiral Wemyss takes the opposite view, that is, that no question should be brought to his attention until after the people in the Admiralty whose specialty is concerned have done all the spade work, accumulated all of the information, and made a tentative decision for his approval or disapproval.

****

... Admiral Wemyss says that he does not want the subject presented to him and the Admiralty Board for decision until all this material has been accumulated and tentative decisions have been reached. ...

87.   *Sims to Benson*

15 January 1918

****

You will have seen by the papers the nature of the reorganization at the Admiralty. This is practically the same as that originally recommended and partially carried out by Sir Edward Carson, and subsequently brought up to its present condition by Admiral Jellicoe and Sir Eric Geddes.

Admiral Wemyss has been something of an unknown quantity in the Service, ...

****

The other day I took lunch with Admiral and Lady Grant.[1] The Admiral is leaving within a few days to take command of the British Squadron on our coast. He said he had been in to see Wemyss and the latter had said 'I am a little bit busy just now getting this new organisation into working order, but it won't be very long before I will have very little to do personally'.

****

---

[1] Later Admiral Sir William Lowther Grant: served in Egyptian campaign 1882; Captain 1902; commanded RN gun battery ashore in Boer War; Naval Advisor to Army Council; Rear-Admiral 1909; Home Fleet 1910–11; commanded 6th LCS 1914; Vice-Admiral 1915 and CinC China Station; CinC N. America & W. Indies 1918–19; Admiral 1918.

88. *Bayly to Sims*

16 January 1918

... I think that Jellicoe showed too much friendship and too little judgement in the appointments that followed his arrival at the Admiralty and that caused him to do most of the work himself. Hence his fall. But the silence that followed his departure was discreditable to those in high places, to the papers, and to the nation, for he has done more for the Navy since he was a captain than most people know. ...

89. *Daniels to Page*

24 January 1918

I was very glad to get your letter of the 8th and to learn of your very high opinion of Sir Eric Geddes, and of your desire that we should be in close touch. Admiral Benson and Admiral Sims both expressed to me, after talking to him, the same high opinion you have expressed of his earnestness and ability and fine spirit. I am writing him today. I wish very much that the pressure here were not so great that I could run over [for] a few days and see Sir Eric Geddes and the Minister of Marine in France[1] and have the personal touch which, after all, is the only way to get the best results through cooperation. It is impossible for me now to do so, but as I feel so much confidence in Vice-Admiral Sims, who writes me that he has been given every access and shown every courtesy by the Admiralty, my coming is not necessary.

****

The severest winter on record has made impossible the speeding up of the [shipbuilding] program as we had hoped, but work is going on more rapidly than appears on the surface and with the spring we shall be able to do much more for ourselves and the Allies and our own forces abroad than seemed possible a few months ago. No money is being spared to enlarge existing industries and creating new ones, things are moving on better every week. In spite of the setback because of the weather the destroyer program goes on apace, and in a short time the results of the intense work will be seen

[1] Georges Leygues (1857–1933): Deputy, French Parliament 1885–1933; various ministries; Minister of Marine November 1917–January 1920; Prime Minister September 1920–January 1921; Minister of Marine November 1925–January 1930, June 1932–September 1933; two French warships named after him.

in the waters across the sea.

****

90.   *Allied Naval Council*

12–14 March 1918

Memorandum by the United States of America:
The General Naval Situation at present, and Decisions that should be
taken to further successful War

Conclusions reached in the following Paper

General

(1) To provide for united action of Allied naval efforts, in conformity with the naval missions and irrespective of local situations and special interests.

(2) To unify commands where desirable in certain areas, such as the English Channel and the Adriatic.

(3) To reinforce the Grand Fleet with Japanese battle cruisers.

(4) To reinforce the Grand Fleet with United States battleships if the barrage operations require it, or if thereby troops in Great Britain can be released for service in France.

(5) To develop plans for concentrated air attacks on enemy submarine bases in the North Sea and the Adriatic.

(6) To develop plans for attacks with surface vessels against enemy Adriatic bases.

(7) To prepare to destroy Russian Baltic ships should their capture by the enemy become imminent.

(8) To give special study to the matter of mine barrages in the English Channel and the Adriatic and Aegean Seas.

(9) To acquire from Norway a base south of the proposed barrage. NOTE. – This decision to be abandoned should it appear probable that the devastation of Norway would result therefrom.

(10) To base in Norway a force of battle cruisers, light cruisers, and destroyers, superior to any similar force which the enemy is likely to employ in raiding.

Anti-Submarine

(1) To devote the maximum possible anti-submarine force to offensive operations.

(2) To divert destroyers and other anti-submarine types from Japan, and from other sources, in as great number as practicable, to anti-submarine work.

(3) To develop with the greatest possible rapidity hunting groups equipped with listening devices, and manned by the best trained personnel available from all sources.

(4) To equip vessels engaged in anti-submarine warfare with adequate means for taking the maximum tactical advantage of every contact with an enemy submarine.

(5) To arm heavily (with full gun's crews) about one merchant ship in ten, of each general class, in the North and South Atlantic; and as far as practicable to escort convoys with such heavily armed merchant ships.

****

Enemy Forces, their Strength, Disposition and Probable Intentions

Allied Naval Forces	*Enemy Naval Forces*
BRITISH ISLES	NORTH SEA
(British and United States)	
(a) *Grand Fleet (6 Jan)*	(a) *High Sea Fleet*
41 Dreadnoughts	19 Dreadnoughts
11 Battle Cruisers	5 Battle Cruisers
31 Light Cruisers	10 Light Cruisers
7 Cruisers	2 Minelaying Cruisers
13 Flotilla Leaders	88 Destroyers
111 Destroyers	50 Torpedo Boats
12 T.S. Mine Sweepers	30 Motor Boats
36 Trawlers	45 Trawlers
18 Sloops	
38 Submarines	(b) *Harbour Flotillas*
5 Hydrophone Ships	13 Destroyers
3 Seaplane Carriers	24 Trawlers
(b) *Harwich Force*	(c) *Naval Forces in Flanders*
11 Light Cruisers	15 Destroyers
4 Flotilla Leaders	16 Torpedo Boats
21 Destroyers	
(c) *Dover Force*	(d) *Naval Forces in Baltic*
15 Monitors	3 Light Cruisers
1 Light Cruiser	42 Destroyers
5 Flotilla Leaders	8 Torpedo Boats

24 Destroyers
4 Patrol Boats
2 Torpedo Boats

(d) *Portsmouth Force*
7 Destroyers
31 Patrol Boats
4 Torpedo Boats

(e) *Devonport Force*
40 Destroyers

(f) *East Coast Convoys*
28 Destroyers
4 Patrol Boats

(g) *Queenstown Force*
1 Light Cruiser
37 Destroyers (United States)
4 Torpedo Boats
11 Sloops
9 Sweepers

(h) *North Coast of Ireland*
12 Sloops
27 Destroyers

(i) *Firth of Forth*
10 Torpedo Boats

(j) *Local Defence*
10 Destroyers, Scapa Flow
12 Destroyers, The Nore
13 Torpedo Boats, The Nore
4 Destroyers, Portsmouth
18 Torpedo Boats, Portsmouth
6 Torpedo Boats, Portland
3 Destroyers, Devonport
7 Torpedo Boats, Devonport
4 Torpedo Boats, Pembroke

6 Motor Boats
116 Trawlers

(e) *Submarine Force*
(including Flanders Force)
5 Light Cruisers (old)
9 Destroyers
16 Torpedo Boats
6 U Cruisers
54 U Type
50 UB Type
20 UC Type

(f) *Training Centre*
8 Old Battleships
3 Light Cruisers
12 Destroyers
5 Torpedo Boats
20 Submarines

(g) *Vessels not Embodied in Regular Formation*
10 Old Battleships
6 Coast Defence Ships
3 Cruisers
13 Light Cruisers
2 Minelaying Cruisers
33 Mining Vessels
21 Destroyers
51 Torpedo Boats
50 Armed Merchant Vessels
6 Auxiliary Minelayers

(k) *Submarines*
68 Submarines at various ports.

****

Probable Additions by 1 July 1918
   4 Dreadnoughts (United
States)

Probable Additions by 1 July
   2 Dreadnoughts
   2 Battle Cruisers
   2 Light Cruisers
   2 Minelaying Cruisers
   12 Destroyers
     Torpedo Boats
   70 Submarines

*Possible Addition of Russian
Baltic Fleet*
It is possible that the following
units may be captured or
turned over to Germany.
   4 Dreadnoughts
   3 Pre-Dreadnoughts
   9 Cruisers
   60 Destroyers (approximately)

****

Summary of Mediterranean Forces

[Allies]	[Central Powers]
12 Dreadnoughts	4 Dreadnoughts
20 Pre-Dreadnoughts	11 Pre-Dreadnoughts
23 Cruisers	1 Battle Cruiser
22 Light Cruisers	2 Cruisers
7 Flotilla Leaders	12 Light Cruisers
181 Destroyers	24 Destroyers
92 Torpedo Boats	50 Torpedo Boats
100 Submarines	60 Submarines
	Russian Black Sea Fleet
	(probably)

****

Our Own Forces – Strength, Disposition, Courses Open to Us

****

The attainment of the *sub-surface command* of the sea is today of *paramount importance* to the Allied Forces. Victory or defeat depends upon an immediate solution of this problem. Submarines have sunk 12,000,000 tons of merchant shipping since the beginning of the war, and the sinkings continue at an average rate of about 400,000 tons per month. The effect of the shortage of shipping is apparent on the whole Allied front from the North Sea to Mesopotamia.

****

The Allies and the United States are handicapped by the lack of central direction to political, military, and naval effort, and by the difficulties of co-ordination, due to differences of language, views, and political aims, as well as to lack of common doctrines of war.

Individually we are handicapped by a less perfect system than that employed by the enemy to harmonise military effort, naval effort and State policy,and to organise and use the entire resources of the State for war. The success or failure of the present military and naval councils will depend on the extent to which they can harmonise and co-ordinate the Allied efforts and bring about unity of action for the purpose of winning the war.

****

Convoy of Shipping

This has greatly reduced the loss from enemy action, and must be adhered to until losses have been considerably reduced from the present rate. Convoy has serious disadvantages, however, among which are:-

Reduction of efficiency of shipping (estimated to be about 50 per cent).
Losses by collision.

The loss of efficiency can be decreased by:-

Better utilization of speed.
Convoys to make the best possible speed from port to port.
Thorough instruction of merchant officers in Rules for Convoy.
Placing all merchant vessels and personnel of the Allied Countries under Government control.

****

Sub-Surface Command of the Sea

****

(1) The offensive should be followed in every possible case.

(2) Greater results are promised by action close to enemy bases.

(3) A pure defensive leading to the dispersal of units over great areas has practically no hope of success. The effort involved is prohibitive as compared with that of the enemy.

(4) Every contact with a submarine should be followed by the maximum tactical offensive effort for its destruction.

The present surface command of the sea is largely a passive effort governed by the idea of an offensive whenever the opportunity presents itself. Sub-surface command can be obtained only through offensive effort. All other effort is palliative. ... When we limit our anti-submarine measures to escort duties, we do the thing most calculated to favour the morale of the submarine personnel. ...

****

To summarise our anti-submarine effort:-

(1) Emphasize the offensive as much as possible.

(2) Put the best brains and skill available into the anti-submarine service.

(3) Develop group tactics and organisation by conference and otherwise. Disseminate results.

(4) Make maximum possible use of each contact with a submarine.

(5) Always drop at least two depth charges in first salvo and as many more as possible. Expend all but two depth charges on first contact with a submarine.

(6) Fit vessels to carry the maximum possible number of depth charges in readiness for laying expeditiously. Remove after gun and torpedo tubes on destroyers if necessary.

****

91. *President Wilson to Daniels*

31 January 1918

I appreciate fully the spirit in which this honor is offered Sims, and I wish he could accept it, but I am afraid it would be a mistake for him to do so. The English persist in thinking of the United States as an English people, but of course they are not and I am afraid that our people would resent and misunderstand what they would interpret as a digestion of Sims into the British official organization. What do you think?

I would be very much obliged if you would show this note to Lansing and confer with him about this matter.

92.   *Memorandum by U.S. Navy Planning Section (London)*

15 February 1918

U.S. Naval Air Effort in European Waters

Operations

1. To make our primary air effort a continuous bombing offensive against enemy bases, avoiding sporadic offensives.

2. To make our secondary air effort a patrol in readiness for tactical offensive.

3. To depend principally upon Kite Balloons for patrol and escort work.

Areas

4. To concentrate our principal air effort in the Felixstowe–Dunkirk area in sufficient force to get local control of the air.

5. To direct all the air effort we may make in the Adriatic against enemy bases in succession, choosing areas to fit conditions.

6. To make our patrol areas, whether patrol be by flying boat or by kite balloons, coincident with the operating areas of our surface vessels, with the greatest effort where shipping is most numerous.

7. To plan and build for our air effort against the Heligoland area.

Types

8. To abandon the dirigible for use in European Waters.

9. To concentrate our efforts on bombing machines capable of:-

    (a) Great radius of action.

    (b) All around defensive fire.

    (c) Carrying the heaviest bombs.

    (d) Efficient radio work.

    (e) Efficient navigation.

10. To build fighters as necessary to get air control in the Felixstowe–Ostend area.

Note: In fighters and bombers we should endeavor to outclass the enemy.

11. To build Kite Balloons for patrol and escort work.

Auxiliary Decisions

12. To build air stations that are difficult of access to enemy aircraft, and where a great effort in a congested area is planned to scatter aerodromes in small units.

13. To build kite balloon stations at the bases of the vessels that are to use the kite balloons.

14. In the distribution of preliminary resources, and preliminary effort to give our principal attention to the Felixstowe–Dunkirk area.

15. To build as few types of aircraft as possible.

16. To consider the abandonment of the flying boat type of aircraft for bombing attack on the enemy bases, and as fighters over narrow waters.

17. To continue the seaplane stations already authorized, but to use them as auxiliaries of bombing effort against shore objectives.

18. To equip present seaplane stations with machines suitable for use in bombing enemy bases.

93. *Benson to Sims*

4 March 1918

Take up immediately with Admiralty question of preventing Russian vessels of war and particularly battle cruisers falling into hands of Germans.[1] Question most urgent. If necessary steps should be taken to insure their destruction. This refers to both Baltic and Black Sea Fleets. Keep Department fully informed regarding this question. Acknowledge.

94. *U.S. Planning Section to Sims*

7 March 1918

1. The Planning Section, in its cooperation with the Plans Division of the British Admiralty, would be of greater use if the position of the Plans Division were more firmly established. To this end we suggest:-

(a)   That the Head of the Plans Division attend all Meetings of

---

[1] The Russian Navy did not possess any battle cruisers, though it did have 4 dreadnoughts in the Baltic and 2 in the Black Sea.

the Allied Naval Council.

(b)   That all the British Agenda for the Allied Naval Council be prepared by the Plans Division.

(c)   That no plans be considered by the First Sea Lord until they have first been considered fully by the Plans Division.

(d)   That the Plans Division be encouraged to take up any and all subjects of organization, operation, or preparation, it may think need attention; and that it be directed to handle them regardless of vested interests or of precedent, being guided solely by the mission of arranging for success in the present war.

2. The above are matters wholly in the cognisance of the British Admiralty, but we think that the First Sea Lord might be susceptible to discreet suggestion on these subjects from time to time.

95.   *Memorandum by Admiralty Plans Division*

15 March 1918

Comments on U.S. Planning Section Memorandum No. 12

The comments made by the Commander, U.S. Naval Aviation Forces, Foreign Section[1] on Problem No. 6, Memo. No. 12, agree so closely with the views of the British Plans Division that they may be adopted practically in their entirety, and it is proposed to draw attention only to the few small points of divergence.

Decision

3. It is considered that kite balloons, while effective for escort work, are not so suitable for patrol, and that anti-submarine patrol work should be carried out mainly by aircraft, both heavier- and lighter than-air.

4. The Canterbury region, while most suitable for the German bases in Belgium, is not so well placed for long distance bombing raids to German bases in the [Heligoland] Bight, and it is considered that for these purposes the Felixstowe area is superior.

6. It is considered that the most economical and effective use of patrols is to maintain sea lanes rather than to patrol wide areas. It is recognised, however, that this is a matter of operational arrangement, and that the distinction is largely a verbal one.

7. The U.S. Planning Section's remarks are concurred in.

[1] Captain H. I. Cone, US Navy.

As regards the other decisions, the remarks by the Commander, U.S.N.A.F. and his final comments are concurred in.

96. *Sims to Benson*

2 April 1918

****

... Convoys when formed at sea are very seldom attacked. An incoming convoy usually reaches port without very much molestation. The trouble comes generally in forming convoys by isolated ships coming along the coast to the point of rendezvous. There are not enough destroyers to convoy these.

... the hope of the future resides in the efficiency of the listening devices, ...

****

In connection with the battle fleet, a prominent American reported to me last night a conversation he had with a British captain who was in London on a few days' leave from the Grand Fleet – the first leave that he had had since 1914. The gist of this Captain's remarks were that one of the most fortunate things that ever happened to the Grand Fleet was the arrival of the American battleships. He expressed himself as quite unable to explain the very remarkable effect that this had had on the spirits and the morale of the British officers and British men. He said they were 'fed up' to the last degree with confinement on board ship without any opportunity to go ashore sometimes for weeks at a time, and at no time more than between two and four o'clock in the afternoon. This officer spoke in the very highest terms of our vessels and their personnel.

He also expressed the general astonishment of the British Navy in pretty nearly all ranks for the accounts they now have of what they consider the taming of Admiral Bayly. There was a common saying in the British Navy that what they ought to do with Bayly was to put him in an iron cage and feed him on raw meat, until war broke out, and then turn him loose on the enemy. They can't quite understand not only the respect in which he is held by our people, but the positive affection they all have for him and he has for them.

****

97. *Sims to Opnav*

8 April 1918

Murmansk

Admiralty believes it desirable that a United States man-of-war be at Murmansk for three reasons. First: A force of considerable strength may be needed at any time; Second: Russians of all classes should be impressed with the unity of the Allies; Third: Russian feeling for the United States is somewhat more friendly than for Great Britain so that some difficulties might be avoided if a United States man-of-war were present.

There is no vessel in my forces suitable for this detail, unless one of the battleships be taken. I strongly recommend that no one of the battleships now in European waters be taken. ... but that a pre-dreadnought battleship or armored cruiser from home waters be sent.[1]

98. *Sims to G. A. Steel*[2]

11 May 1918

I beg to acknowledge your letter of 11 May informing me that Mrs Page[3] will attend the launching of HMS *Eagle*[4] at Armstrong's Yard at Elswick on Saturday, 8 June, and inviting me to be present upon that occasion.

Will you please be so kind as to express my thanks to the First Lord for his thoughtful kindness in this matter. I should be very glad indeed to attend this ceremony if my more or less strenuous duties will permit at that time.

99. *Sims to Franklin D. Roosevelt*

8 June 1918

****

---

[1] The old cruiser *Olympia*, Commodore Dewey's flagship at the Battle of Manila Bay (1898), was sent to Murmansk. See Trask, *Captains and Cabinets*, pp. 213–6. USS *Olympia*: cruiser, 1895; 5865 tons; 10 x 5in; 21 knots.

[2] G. A. Steel (18—-1963): Private Secretary to First Lord; Asst Private Secretary 1911–15; Asst Secretary, Ministry of Transport (under Geddes) 1919–21; Secretary, Committee on National Expenditure (the 'Geddes Axe') 1921–2; Asst Secretary, Scottish Office 1922–5; Managing Director, British Aluminium 1925–52.

[3] Mrs Alice Page was the wife of the US Ambassador.

[4] HMS *Eagle*: aircraft carrier, 1923; laid down as Chilean battleship *Almirante Cochrane*; requisitioned 1917; completed as carrier; 22790 tons; 24 knots; number of aircraft unknown but c.20–25.

Nothing but good can come from visits by our representatives to this side. In fact it would be very beneficial to all parties concerned if all of our representatives, including our senators, could come over here and see with their own eyes the condition of affairs, both military and civil, of these countries at war.

****

I have heard rumors from time to time that you were coming over to pay us a personal visit. ... I hope in this case it may turn out to be true. I am sure you would not only enjoy a visit to this side but I am quite sure it would be of benefit to us and to the Department.[1]

100. *Sims to Cone*

28 June 1918

Co-operation between U.S. Naval Aviation Forces Foreign Service, and British Government

1. The following correspondence has been exchanged with the British Admiralty:–

[Enclosures]

Sims to Murray

12 June 1918

U.S. Naval Aviation Activities in Europe

1. The U.S. Naval Aviation Forces, Foreign Service, under my command have established eight squadrons of day and night bombing aeroplanes in the Dunkirk–Calais area with the distinct mission of destroying enemy Naval Bases on the Belgian Coast. Inasmuch, therefore, as this work is purely Naval, it is proposed, with your concurrence, to place the operations of these squadrons under the command of the British Vice-Admiral at Dover as in reality they will form part of the Dover barrage.

2. With reference to the U.S. Naval Air Stations in Ireland it is proposed to place those under the command of the Admiral Com-

---

[1] Franklin Roosevelt did visit Britain, France and Italy during July, August and September 1918, See Elliott Roosevelt, ed., *FDR: His Personal Letters, 1905–1928* (New York: Duell, Sloan & Pearce, 1948), pp. 374–441. See also G. C. Ward, *A First-Class Temperament: the Emergence of Franklin Roosevelt* (New York: Harper & Row, 1989), pp. 384–408.

mander-in-Chief, Coast of Ireland, for operations in the same way that the destroyers based on Queenstown are under his command. The internal administration and maintenance of those stations will, however, remain directly in my Force. It is further proposed, with your concurrence, to place the operative command of the Air Station at Killingholme under the Admiral Commanding the East Coast when we take it over from you.

****

W. F. Nicholson[1] to Sims

26 June 1918

****

2. The views expressed by you entirely accord with those of the Board of Admiralty who wish to express their thanks for the valuable assistance already given and the generous contribution of Naval Air Forces now offered.

101. *Admiralty to Beatty*

19 July 1918

Following members of U.S. Congress Committee on Naval Affairs viz.: Padgett, the Chairman, and Messrs. Venables, Peter-mudd, Oliver, Riordan, Hicks, Browning, Hensley, Wilson and Connally[2] are on their way to Scapa in USS *Arkansas.*[3] Congressmen are coming to study naval situation and it is desirable that all possible facilities be accorded them in prosecution of their studies. It is understood USS *Arkansas* will probably arrive Scapa 25 July.

An American Naval Officer[4] and Captain Gaunt will proceed to Scapa to meet them. ...

[1] W. F. Nicholson : not traced.
[2] The Chairman, Lemuel P. Padgett (Democrat, Tenn.), was a friend of Secretary Daniels. As the Democrats controlled the House, they constituted a majority of the Committee.
[3] USS *Arkansas*: battleship, 1912; 26000 tons; 20.5 knots; 12 x 12in. She was relieving the *Delaware*, one of the US battleships serving with the Grand Fleet; see Part V.
[4] Captain F. H. Schofield, US Navy, from Sims's staff. Gaunt was the former British Naval Attaché in Washington.

102.   *Roosevelt to Daniels*

London,
27 July 1918

I got back last night late after a most interesting trip of three days with Sir Eric Geddes. He took Admiral Everett, his Naval Secretary,[1] and I took Captain McCauley.[2] We went by train to Pembroke Dockyard, an old small affair somewhat like our Portsmouth Navy Yard.[3] It has been expanded since the war from about 1,000 to nearly 4,000 employees, and does mostly repair work to patrol vessels, etc., and is also building four submarines. I was particularly interested to see over 500 women employed in various capacities, some of them even acting as molders' helpers in the foundry, and all apparently doing excellent work.

We then went on board USS *Kimberly*,[4] and ran across to Queenstown – 125 miles at 25 knots. Geddes was much interested in seeing our latest type of destroyer and made some interesting comments which I will embody in a separate memorandum.

We were met at Queenstown by Admiral Sir Lewis Bayly,[5] Captain Pringle of the *Melville* and Captain Price[6] of the *Dixie*. We spent the night with Admiral Bayly, and on Wednesday inspected everything in the neighborhood, including our flying station across the bay. We lunched on the *Melville* and visited our new base hospital, which is west from the town and on a very attractive point of land.

Personally, I think things at Queenstown are running well in every

[1] Later Admiral Sir Allan Frederic Everett (1868–1938): commanded Signals School 1900–08; Captain 1905; Flag Captain, 2nd Div., Home Fleet 1910–11; Flag Captain to CinC, Home Fleet 1911–13; Commodore and Captain of the Fleet 1913; Naval Secretary to First Lord 1916–18; Rear-Admiral April 1917; commanded 4th Light Cruiser Squadron 1918–19 and 8th Light Cruiser Squadron 1919–21; CinC China 1924–5; retired list 1925.

[2] Captain Edward McCauley, jr., US Navy: began the war as a Commander in Naval Intelligence; FDR's naval aide on this trip; later commanded troopship *George Washington*.

[3] The comparison was an apt one.

[4] USS *Kimberly*: destroyer, 1918; 1185 tons, 4 x 4in; 12 tt; 35 knots.

[5] Admiral Sir Lewis Bayly (1857–1938): Midshipman 1872; Naval Attaché, Washington 1900–02; commanded Home Fleet destroyers 1907–08; President, RN War College, Portsmouth 1908–11 and Rear-Admiral; commanded battleship and battle cruiser sqdns 1912–14; Vice-Admiral and CinC Channel Fleet December 1914 but relieved almost immediately following loss of pre-dreadnought *Formidable* to a U-boat; President, RN College, Greenwich 1915; CinC Coast of Ireland July 1915–March 1919; Admiral 1917; retired 1919. Autobiography *Pull Together!* (London: Harrap, 1939), edited and published after his death by 'the only niece', Miss Violet Voysey.

[6] Captain H. B. Price, US Navy: commanding destroyer tender *Dixie*.

particular. Sir Lewis Bayly is at first a diffident sort of man to deal with, but everybody has come to swear by him on closer acquaintance. He and his niece have been very kind to all of our officers, and have shown the kind of personal interest which counts. There is no question that he is the right man in the right place. On our second day there, Sir Eric Geddes told me that after looking over the situation, he had decided to keep Admiral Bayly in command of the Irish Station, although he has completed the usual tour of duty.

One thing at Queenstown is especially noteworthy. The American and British forces are run absolutely separately and yet in complete harmony, that is to say, although the British have a Navy Yard there, we make all our own repairs through the *Melville* and *Dixie*, and the Supply and Personnel arrangements are entirely separate at Queenstown. On shore we have put up an excellent men's club, which all the men are keen about. They run a performance in the big hall attached to it every night of the week; can get anything they want to eat there, and the soda water fountain is very popular.

The Base Hospital is to have 250 beds, and will be more than enough to take care of all the ships and Flying Bases on the Irish station for some time to come. It is unnecessarily large for normal use, but I think this is a good thing in view of the possibility of a bad accident to one of our ships or to one of the troop transports.

The Irish question has been well handled by Admiral Bayly, and I think we should trust his judgment entirely. It is quite right not to allow our men to go into Cork, as this would only be inviting trouble in view of the attitude of the Cork Authorities that the responsibility must rest wholly with us and not with them.

We left on Wednesday night on HMS *Patrol*[1] and were escorted by USS *Kimberly* to Newport in the Bristol Channel. Geddes sent a joint message from him and me to the officers of the *Kimberly* and the *Patrol*, and this I telegraphed to you today, as I think you may want to use it in the form of a Press notice.

People over here seem to think it quite unusual for the First Lord of the Admiralty to take a trip in an American destroyer in rather uncomfortable conditions, in view of the fact that he could have gone on one of his much larger vessels. As you know, British Cabinet officers are not in the habit of running around on vessels flying a foreign flag. It is probably the first case on record and should be emphasised.

On Wednesday, we inspected the new National shipyards in the

[1] HMS *Patrol*: light cruiser, 1904; 2940 tons; 25 knots; 9 x 4in; 2 tt.

Bristol Channel – three of them with a capacity of 24 ways. They are nearly completed, and will start to turn out the British standard ships within a few weeks. By the way, I did not know until I got here that all of their Government merchant shipbuilding is run by the First Lord of the Admiralty. It is just the same as if the Emergency Fleet Corporation were under you. The operating part of their system, which corresponds to our Shipping Board, is of course a separate organisation, but the Admiralty has all the shipbuilding of every kind under it, and Lord Pirrie (formerly the head of Harland and Wolff, shipbuilders of Belfast)[1] has the position which corresponds to Mr Schwab's.

We got back late last night, and this morning I have breakfasted with Geddes and Admiral Wemyss, the First Sea Lord. They brought up several questions which I am to go into further, and get all the information possible that I may report to you.

(CONFIDENTIAL. For instance, they want to discuss the possibility of dovetailing the British programme for new construction in with our programme, in order that between us we may not build too many of one type of vessel, and in order that we may have an understanding in regard to the need for new types for next year's operations. For example, Geddes is inclined to the view that between us we have enough small craft of the submarine chaser or *Eagle* boat type, or will have, when the present programme is completed.

Further, it seems a question as to whether the British or ourselves should build many additional destroyers; and they have talked about the need of a new type of Escort vessel for the convoys – a ship with less speed and better sea-going qualities than a destroyer.[2] Also we talked about the possibility of American destroyers in the North Sea in a few months, when our new lot have begun to come over in larger numbers.)

I shall be in London for four days, and expect to meet Mr Padgett and the rest of the Naval Committee on Sunday. Then I go either to the Grand Fleet or to France. This is not yet determined on.

This afternoon I spent at the Admiralty going through their

---

[1] William James Pirrie, 1st Viscount Pirrie (1847–1924): born Quebec; Chairman, Harland & Wolff; Lord Mayor of Belfast 1896–7; baron 1906; Comptroller-General, Merchant Shipbuilding, March 1918; viscount 1921.

[2] No entirely satisfactory type was evolved in this war. The 'Flower' class sloops (1916–18; originally Fleet Sweeping Vessels but some converted to Submarine Decoy Vessels and convoy escorts; 1250 tons; 15–16.5 knots; 2 x 4in; dct; 39 built) and the 'P' boats (1915–17; 613 tons; 1 x 4in; 2 tt; 2 dct; 20 knots) met the need to some extent but what was required was the destroyer escort and frigate of the next war, ships with longer ranges and higher speeds.

Intelligence Section. The thing that struck me most is that their office of Naval Intelligence is in much closer touch with operations than ours is. We must come to that, and the new building will undoubtedly help it out. There is no question that Admiral Sims has the entire confidence of the Admiralty people, besides their personal friendship; and yet it is comforting to find that he is just as good an American as he ever was, and he keeps his sense of humor through a whole lot of stuff that would turn some people's heads.

I have not been here very long as yet, but I do feel that the visit is doing good, and that eventually we must get a little closer touch between Washington and London in the naval line than we have had in the past.

****

103. *Sims to Benson*

28 July 1918

****

... [The North Sea Barrage] will at least embarrass the submarines very seriously, but only provided we can prevent them passing through Norwegian territorial waters. If we cannot prevent that it means that the barrage is a useless expenditure of money, time, energy and tonnage.

****

As you of course know, I am so thoroughly satisfied with the situation at Queenstown that I should very much regret it should the Department send a Flag Officer to command the forces based there. The situation might be very different if the personalities of Admiral Bayly and Captain Pringle were different, but they work together so perfectly and with results so eminently satisfactory that I think we could not do better than leave things as they are with Pringle in his capacity as Chief of my Staff, as least so long as Admiral Bayly remains. The First Lord of the Admiralty has recently been to Queenstown, and he was so very much impressed with the success of the cooperation there that he has announced that Admiral Bayly is to remain in command even though he has been there more than three years, and the tour of duty of a British Admiral is usually two years.

****

We are now beginning to have interests in the Mediterranean, and if any extensive mining operation is undertaken there, we shall have still further interests, and I believe it is very desirable that we have an officer of flag rank stationed with the other similar officers at Malta with the Commander-in-Chief.[1]

I am not yet prepared to say that such an officer should be in command of all of our forces in the Mediterranean. In fact at present I should not favor him having that position. Niblack[2] is doing well at Gibraltar and is working in thorough accord with the British Admiral there,[3] and I think he should not be transferred to Malta unless he were given command in the Mediterranean. I would therefore, at present, favor having a flag officer junior to Niblack sent to Malta.

Another place where we will need a rear-admiral is Plymouth, England,[4] where we expect soon to have 72 submarine chasers based, and where we are obliged to maintain a depot of stores, as well as considerable personnel. It is a distributing port for personnel coming out from the United States via England for Gibraltar and there are frequently as many as 250 men there. The whole station including the base, repair ships, stores, the chasers and personnel, make a suitable command for a rear-admiral.

As for Corfu, we have at present but a small force there. The British officer in command of the barrage, under the commander-in-chief of the Mediterranean is a Captain Kelly[5], who has what is

[1] Later Admiral of the Fleet Sir Somerset Arthur Gough-Calthorpe (1864–1937): entered RN 1878; Captain 1902; Naval Attaché, St Petersburg 1904–5; commanded *Roxburgh* 1906; Captain of the Fleet, Home Fleet 1909–10; Rear-Admiral 1911; 1st Battle Squadron 1912–13; 2nd Cruiser Squadron 1914–16; Acting Vice-Admiral March 1915; 2nd Sea Lord 1916–17; Admiral Commanding Coast Guard and Reserves December 1916; CinC Mediterranean August 1917–1919; Admiral 1919; High Commissioner, Turkey 1918–19; CinC Portsmouth 1920–23; Admiral of the Fleet 1925.

[2] Rear-Admiral Albert Parker Niblack, US Navy (1859–1929): graduated from Annapolis 1880; blockade of Cuba 1898; Boxer campaign in China 1900; Philippine insurrection 1900–02; much service as a Naval Attaché; Captain 1911; commanded *Michigan*; Naval War College 1916; General Board 1917; served with Atlantic Fleet battleships 1917; Commander, 2nd Squadron, Patrol Force, Atlantic Fleet and SNO, US Forces, Gibraltar November 1917–1919; Rear-Admiral 1918; Director of Naval Intelligence 1919; Naval Attaché, London; Vice-Admiral and Commander, US Naval Forces in European Waters; Commandant, Charleston Navy Yard and 6th Naval District; retired list 1923; President, International Hydrographic Bureau 1927.

[3] Later Admiral Sir Heathcoat Salusbury Grant (1864–1938): Captain 1904; Naval Attaché, Washington 1912–14; commanded *Canopus* 1914–16; Rear Admiral June 1916; Admiral Superintendent, Dover Dockyard January 1917; SNO Gibraltar June 1917–July 1919; retired list 1920.

[4] Captain Lyman A. Cotten, US Navy, was in command at Plymouth.

[5] Later Admiral Sir William Archibald Howard Kelly (1873–1952): Captain 1911;

called the local rank of Commodore. I have received a letter from
him speaking in the highest terms ... of the ability and tact of
Captain Leigh. ...

****

104. *Franklin D. Roosevelt: Typed Diary Letter to His Family*

London,
30 July 1918

Audience with King George V at Buckingham Palace

... we passed through several corridors lined with paintings of
naval actions that I would have given anything to stop and look at.
... We talked for a while about American war work in general and
the Navy in particular. He [the King] seemed delighted that I had
come over in a destroyer, and said his one regret was that it had been
impossible for him to do active naval service during the war.

****

He was a delightfully easy person to talk to, and we got going so
well that part of the time we were both talking at the same time. ...

****

105. *Memorandum by the Intelligence Section, U.S. Naval
Headquarters*

London,
3 August 1918

*A Brief Summary of United States Navy Activities in European
Waters with an Outline of the Organization of Admiral Sims's
Headquarters*

(Prepared for the Naval Committee of Congress on a tour of inspection abroad)

Naval Attaché, Paris 1911–14; commanded *Gloucester* 1914–16 and shadowed *Goeben* during her escape to Turkey; Admiralty for special service April 1917; Liaison
Officer, French Ministry of Marine 1916–17; Commodore, 8th LCS, Brindisi 1917;
Commodore, British Adriatic Force 1918–19; headed British Naval Mission to
Greece 1919–21; 2nd LCS 1925–7; Admiralty representative at League of Nations
1927–9; 1st Battle Squadron, Mediterranean Fleet 1929–30; CinC China 1931–3;
retired list 1936; British Naval Representative in Turkey 1940–4.

The General Organization of United States Naval Forces in European Waters

****

Admiral Sims attends the daily conference of the naval staff at the Admiralty and, in addition, each officer of the Admiral's staff keeps in close touch with the corresponding division of the Admiralty.

In order to facilitate communications between the Admiralty and U.S. Naval Headquarters and to establish a liaison service, a British naval officer assigned to Admiral Sims's staff has an office at the Admiralty and a desk at Admiral Sims's Headquarters; any division of the Admiralty desiring any information from or consultation with individual members of Admiral Sims's staff [is] enabled to do this through this officer. Similarly, officers of Admiral Sims's staff are enabled to quickly obtain information from the Admiralty.

Special telephone and telegraph wires have been installed between the Admiralty and U.S. Naval Headquarters.

****

The natural inclination of a naval service, which is a team by itself, is, of course, to operate together as a team. Admiral Sims believed from the beginning, however, that the only effective way to throw the weight of the U.S. Navy into the war without delay was to use its available units to strengthen the weak spots in the other Navies, and thus effect a more vigorous conduct of the war already so thoroughly under way in all areas.

There would have been much wasted effort and time if any attempt had been made to take over any particular area and operate it entirely with U.S. Naval Forces. Hence, as the various naval forces have been rendered available by the Navy Department, the question of the best location for them has been discussed with the representatives of the other navies and the disposition has been the result of common agreement.

Admiral Sims's Headquarters may be considered the advanced headquarters of the Navy Department in the field. The Department deals directly with Admiral Sims's Headquarters, and Admiral Sims in turn directs and coordinates the work of all of the various groups under his general command.

All the groups, wherever located, report regularly to Admiral Sims concerning their activities and operations, their condition as regards material and supplies, their needs, and their plans, together with recommendations or suggestions for changes in plans or policies. Admiral Sims in turn keeps the Department informed by general reports of the activities of all the forces under his command. Daily matters of importance or of current interest are handled by telegraph or cable.

****

United States Naval Forces in European Waters

United States Naval Forces operating in European Waters may be briefly grouped as follows:-

(a) *The force based on Queenstown* handles certain merchant convoys coming to France and to the United Kingdom and also the fast British liners carrying U.S. troops. This force is composed of 24 destroyers, 2 tenders and 3 tugs. Two additional destroyers of this force are temporarily assigned to duty at Plymouth with the submarine chasers, and one is in the United States for the renewal of her boilers.

(b) *The Force based on the French Coast* escorts the troop ships into the French ports and out to sea, assists the French in escorting Coastal Convoys up and down the French Coast and across the Channel to England and aids the French in keeping the Channel clear of mines. This force consists of 33 destroyers, 16 yachts, 9 minesweepers, 5 tugs, 4 repair ships, one break ship, 2 barges, and one tug which is temporarily assigned to duty in the Azores.

(c) *The Force based on Gibraltar* works with the British in escorting Allied trade in and out of the Mediterranean. This force consists of 2 scout cruisers, 5 destroyers, 6 coast guard cutters, 5 gunboats and 10 yachts. In addition, one destroyer and one gunboat of this force are now in the United States for a general overhaul.

(d) At Plymouth, England there are 41 submarine chasers with two destroyers and one tender. These are engaged in hunting submarines in the entrance to the English Channel. There is also one submarine from Berehaven at Plymouth on temporary duty.

(e) *At Berehaven* are six submarines with a submarine tender engaged in hunting enemy submarines off the entrance to the Irish Sea and the English Channel.

(f) *At Corfu* are 36 submarine chasers with a tender, which are engaged in hunting enemy submarines in the Adriatic Sea.

(g) *With the Grand Fleet* are five battleships operating as a battle squadron of the fleet.

(h) *The Mine Force*, based on Inverness and Invergordon, is working with the British in the laying of mines in the North Sea. This force is composed of 10 mine planters, one repair ship and two tugs.

(i) *The Force based on the Azores* is engaged in patrolling in the vicinity of the Azores to keep the route clear in order that our submarine chasers and other craft can safely use the port for coaling and obtaining supplies when en route to Europe. This force is composed of four submarines, one gunboat, one monitor, two yachts and a marine detachment on shore. There is also one tug from the Brest Force on temporary duty at the Azores.

(j) *There is a fleet of merchant ships* engaged in carrying coal for the U.S. Army from England to France, which are under Admiral Sims's general control. Seventy-three such ships have been commissioned or orders have been given for their commissioning.

(k) *There are at Southampton* four cross-channel transports engaged in carrying troops across the Channel. These are commissioned ships under Admiral Sims's command.

(l) *At Murmansk, Russia*, there is one cruiser cooperating with the Allied forces in Russia.

(m) *At Genoa* there are two tugs, which have been placed at the disposal of the Italian Government.

(n) *At Liverpool* there are two tankers.

While the United States Navy is doing its bit and doing it well, a sense of proportion must not be lost. Our effort is small compared with that of our Allies.

In this connection the following approximate percentages are of interest as giving a comparison between the naval efforts of the Allied Powers. The percentage of the various types of vessel engaged in the anti-submarine campaign in British Waters and Eastern Atlantic is about as follows:-

	Great Britain	France	United States
Destroyers	80	6	14
Submarines	78	17	5
Miscellaneous Patrol Craft	86	11	3

The following percentages give a similar comparison of the naval situation in the Mediterranean:-

	G.B.	France	Italy	Japan	U.S.
Destroyers	27	38	26	7	2
Submarines	13	37	50	0	0
Miscellaneous Patrol Craft	22	66	4	0	8

In the Grand Fleet, Great Britain has about 91% of the major fighting forces and the United States 9%.

Of the total number of all patrol craft operating against the enemy submarines in British and Eastern Atlantic Waters the American patrol forces constitute less than 5% of the total number. In the Mediterranean the United States supplies 6% of the patrol forces.

As a comparison between the naval aviation effort of Great Britain and the United States, the following data is of interest:-

Great Britain has about 4½ times as large a naval aviation personnel as the United States, and about three times as many naval aviation stations. Great Britain has approximately fourteen times as many seaplanes as the United States, and these British machines patrol eight times as many miles during a week as the American machines.

On 1 August 1918, it has been estimated that the British Navy has on active service in European waters approximately over three times as many officers and over four times as many enlisted personnel [as] the American forces operating in European Waters. This estimate must be assumed as low, because it does not include the hundreds of officers and thousands of men the British have in their so-called auxiliary patrol service.

Memorandum on Atlantic Convoy System

(As Requested by the House Naval Committee)

A further significant illustration of the relative parts being played by the U.S. Navy and the Allied Navies is given by a study of the Atlantic Convoy System and by the protection and escorting of American troop convoys to Europe.

Taking into consideration the whole Atlantic Convoy System – that is, all shipping in the Atlantic, whether French, Italian, American, British, or neutral shipping in Allied interests; also U.S. troop transports and troop convoys bound for the Mediterranean – the shipping is protected by the naval vessels of the Allies in the following proportions:

Great Britain provides the Destroyers for 70% of all convoys
United States   27%
France   3%

All convoys at sea in the Atlantic are protected by cruisers so as to guard against attack by enemy raiders. The cruisers necessary for protecting the Allied shipping in the Atlantic in this way are provided as follows:

Great Britain   61%
United States   35%
France   4%

Great Britain has organised and arranged and provides the signal codes and instructions for the entire convoy system; also the commodores and signalmen for the great majority of all convoys.

The convoy system usually carries the shipping as far as the European coast, where it is generally diverted on a coastal route as to its destination. This necessitates a great amount of coastal escorting. Great Britain provides the coastal escorts for the Irish Sea, English Channel and North Sea, and, in general, throughout all coastal waters of the United Kingdom.

There is very little coastal escort required on the French Channel coast as all shipping follows the English coast. On the French Atlantic coast, the United States furnishes three-eighths of the coastal escort and France furnishes the remaining five-eighths. The United States also furnishes about one-third of the minesweeping forces on the French Atlantic Coast.

British destroyers are now rendering the following protection to United States shipping:

U.S. Troops

(a) British destroyers escort 62% of the U.S. troops that come into England.

(b) British destroyers escort all of our troops that cross the English Channel going to France.

(c) British destroyers escort all U.S. troopships bound up or down the English Channel.

Army Store Ships

(a) British destroyers bring into the English Channel about half of the store ships that carry supplies for the U.S. Army.

(b) British destroyers escort into Scottish ports all U.S. mine carriers bringing mines for the North Sea Barrage.

U.S. Merchant Shipping

(a) British destroyers provide the coastal escort for U.S. ships along the South and East coast of England.

(b) All U.S. trade with Scandinavia is escorted by British destroyers.

(c) All U.S. trade with Holland is escorted by British destroyers.

(d) All U.S. ships bound out of the English Channel from either French or British ports are escorted to the westward by British destroyers.

106. *Sims to Opnav*

4 August 1918

****

The Naval Committee of Congress arrived at Scapa, was met by Captain Gaunt, R.N., Captain Schofield, U.S. Navy, and Paymaster Higgins. They then proceeded by train to Inverness and inspected our mining bases and the Naval Hospital at Strathpeffer.From there they proceeded to Edinburgh, inspected the Grand Fleet, being received by the Commander-in-Chief and going over British as well as American ships.

The Force Commander's staff took steps to confer with the Foreign Office and Embassy, as well as the Admiralty, before their arrival with a view of ensuring that their time while in England should be spent as profitably as possible.

They were met at the station in London by an Admiral representing the First Lord of the Admiralty, by a representative of the American Ambassador and a representative of the Force Commander and taken to the Savoy Hotel where accommodations were furnished by the Admiralty.

While in England they are being treated as guests of the Nation.

They have visited the Dover Station where Admiral Keyes had planned a most complete and interesting programme, with opportunities of inspecting all of the Dover Station activities.

They have visited and thoroughly inspected U.S. Naval Headquarters and been given every opportunity of acquainting themselves with U.S. Naval activities.

They have been entertained by the American Ambassador, the

House of Commons, and received by the King.

Yesterday afternoon, the Force Commander's Staff was assembled and the Committee given an opportunity of conducting a 'Congressional hearing', the same as in Washington, examining all members of the staff at their pleasure.

Today they are to have a conference with the Prime Minister. Tomorrow [they] will visit Harwich and on Sunday will proceed to Queenstown.

****

107. *Sims to Bayly*

8 August 1918

... All [members of the Naval Affairs Committee of the House of Representatives] say they are pleased and delighted with their trip to Queenstown is to express it but feebly. They have not talked of anything else and are grateful for everything that you were able to do for them, and they are filled with admiration over the conditions they found in Queenstown.

108. *Sims to Benson*

10 August 1918

... They [the Congressmen] are very enthusiastic in their expressions of appreciation of what the British Government has done for them, and they seem very much pleased with their observations of our bases as far as they have visited them. They are particularly pleased with the conditions they found at Queenstown. They particularly appreciated the relations that have been established with the British Authorities there, and are much impressed with Admiral Bayly. On leaving Queenstown they stopped overnight in Dublin and spent one day and one night there. They were received by Lord French[1] and shown every civility.

****

---

[1] 1st Viscount French (Field-Marshal Sir John Denton Pinkstone French) (1852–1925): CinC, BEF 1914–15; Viscount and CinC, Home Forces 1916–18; Lord Lieutenant of Ireland 1918–21; earl 1922.

109.   *Roosevelt to Daniels*

Paris,
2 August 1918

Before leaving London on Tuesday, I lunched at the Embassy and had a most delightful talk with Mr Lloyd George. I know you would enjoy meeting him. He strikes one immediately as a great leader of men. One of the things that has struck me particularly this week in England has been the absolute unanimity among all the Government people here to see this thing through to more than what they call 'a patched up peace'.

I also had another talk with Mr Balfour and with Sir Eric Geddes about the Mediterranean situation. Everybody is agreed that things as they are are not resulting in sufficient naval action. The trouble seems to be chiefly with the Italians themselves and a certain amount of jealousy of the French in regard to the Adriatic, and of the British in regard to their rather condescending attitude about things in general. I think that Geddes rather wanted to go to Italy with me, but it would have been a great mistake for us to go together, and I think I have succeeded in heading him off. The Italians may not love us, but at least they know that we have no ulterior designs in the Mediterranean. The trouble is that their Navy people at the top are thinking more about keeping their fleet intact at the end of the war than of winning the war itself. They have, of course, been very much puffed up over the exploit of the two motorboats in sinking the Austrian battleship.[1] I hope by my visit to lay the foundation for more unified action between the many Allied naval units in the Mediterranean, and also for more actual offensive work against the Austrians on the Dalmatian Coast.

On Wednesday morning we were at Dover, where we saw Admiral Keyes and went into the question of the Channel defenses and patrol. I am a little amused by the fact that they are carrying out certain operations now, which you will remember I tried to have taken up for weeks and months in the Spring and Summer of 1917. As a result, the English Channel is now fairly successfully blocked against submarines and only one, or possibly two, have got through in several months. The plans which are now being carried out ought to make the Channel wholly closed.

We crossed over to Dunkirk on a British destroyer, seeing a great

---

[1] The *Szent Istvan*, in the Adriatic on 10 June 1918 by the Italian Mas boat (MTB) no. 15.

fleet of French fishing boats as we neared the French coast. This additional food supply is one of the results of the present safety of things in the Channel.

... Proceeding to Queenstown, I had an opportunity to talk with Admiral Bayly, Captain Pringle and the other Officers who have made Queenstown a historic spot in American Naval History. All that has been written and said about our work there, since the very earliest days of the war, is still inadequate. It does one's heart good to see the splendid spirit that pervades the entire station. The same thing can be said of the spirit that has marked the American Naval operations in Scotland. Our dreadnoughts serving with the Grand Fleet are living up to the best traditions of our principal fighting forces. The new and hazardous work of the mine laying divisions, under Admiral Strauss[1] and carried out under enormous difficulties, is a great tribute to the service.

110. *Sims to Navy Department*

16 August 1918

The influence of the [U.S.] Planning Section upon the British Admiralty has been noticeable as affecting the methods of work of the Plans Division of the Admiralty and affecting the operations of the Admiralty Naval Staff. Planning Section Memorandum No. 40 which contained some recommendations capable of being construed as critical of Admiralty methods and performances was given by me unofficially to one of the members of the Naval Staff, who I felt sure would take it as it was meant, that is as a study of the situation from the German point of view and in a sense a criticism of the Admiralty. Not only was this paper highly thought of by the officer in question but it has been most favorably commented on by the First Sea Lord who has directed that a copy be sent to the Commander-in-Chief, Grand Fleet.

Great as has been the benefit to the Force Commander of the work of the Planning Section, I am disposed to believe that it's chief value has been in its tendency to establish mutual understanding as to methods of thought on military questions as between ourselves and the Admiralty.

---

[1] Rear-Admiral Joseph Strauss, US Navy: began the war as a Captain, commanding *Nevada*; Commander, Mine Force, Atlantic Fleet; responsible for laying the US portion of the North Sea mine barrage; see Part VI.

111. *Sims to Opnav*

22 August 1918

From Naval operating standpoint amalgamation Air Services [i.e., the formation of the R.A.F.] complete failure. Fact that English have already found it necessary to re-establish Naval Group in Dunkirk area as well as to operate lighter-than-air craft by the Navy is significant. Admiralty is making serious attempt to re-establish Naval Air Service. For period of about four months prior to final amalgamation serious loss of efficiency was apparent due to the fact that all departments refused to make decisions or to make plans regarding matter which would be out of their hands. Such a period of inefficiency is fatal in wartime. Youthful Generals in the Royal Air Force who have attained high rank by virtue of amalgamation are strongly in favor of it. To the best of my knowledge all officers of the Royal Naval Air Service consider it failure.

Naval Aviators must be trained in seamanship and recognition of friendly or hostile surface craft and many other matters purely naval whereas Army aviators must be able to recognise on sight different types of troops, transportation of and number of men in formations, etc.

Formation of third war making department in the middle of war and at the present moment when ready to begin operations would result in great confusion and greatly retard any progress we are making. Am therefore strongly of the opinion that operations should be kept separate under Army and Navy Commands.

****

112. *Sims to Benson*

2 October 1918

****

A couple of Sundays ago I was invited by Mr Lloyd George to spend the day with him at a country place he has near Brighton. He of course asked many questions concerning the submarine campaign and allied subjects. It was remarkable how accurate his information and understanding of these subjects are, and how well he understands their significance from a military point of view. ...

113. *Roosevelt to Daniels*

Washington,
16 October 1918

Report of Inspection Trip to Europe

1. *Operations*
    (1) Operations in the Mediterranean, Adriatic and Aegean Seas:
As you probably know, there has been a certain amount of dissatisfaction over the naval situation in the Mediterranean, Adriatic and Aegean. This dissatisfaction has been due to two causes, both somewhat connected:

(a)   The lack of a unified control of naval operations in these waters. Owing to certain causes which I have explained to you verbally it became practically impossible to have an 'Admiralissimo' for the allied navies in these waters. My visits to Paris and Rome confirmed the impossibility of this. I worked out a plan, however, in the rough, which was accepted in principle by Admiral Del Bono, the Italian Minister of Marine,[1] by M. Leygues, French Minister of Marine, and by Sir Eric Geddes, First Lord of the British Admiralty. This plan called for the appointment of a general naval staff for the Mediterranean, Adriatic and Aegean, with representatives of each nation on this staff. Frankly, this leaves the Italian Navy under an Italian Admiral, the French Battleship Fleet under a French Admiral, etc., and it does not give a clear cut supreme command, but it makes for better unity of action than exists at the present, and while in the nature of a compromise it is, in my judgment, at least a step in advance. The matter was to be taken up at the next Interallied Naval Council.

****

... I believe my visit there [Rome] was of some assistance in that

---

[1] Vice-Amiraglio Alberto Del Bono (1856–1932): CinC, Maritime Department of Spezia 1915; Secretary-General, Ministry of Marine; Minister of Marine, July 1917–June 1919; retired list 1921.

it showed the Italian Government clearly that the United States would be glad if the naval side of the war in the Adriatic could be conducted somewhat more vigorously, and the recent attack on Durazzo seems to me a proof of a more vigorous policy.

(2) *North Sea Barrage*

As you know, this has been what you might call my pet hobby since the inception of the war. You will remember that I pushed this matter as early as May, 1917; that after some time the Bureau of Ordnance indorsed the principle and worked out what it considered practicable plans. In the meanwhile, I had, with your knowledge, taken the matter up with the British and French Admiralties and with Mr Balfour. The French Navy indorsed the proposition in principle, but the British Admiralty at that time considered it impracticable. Finally, three or four months later, the plan was officially put forward by the Division of Operations, although Admiral Benson said quite frankly that he did not personally believe in its practicability. It was accepted, however, by the British Admiralty in the autumn of 1917, they undertaking to lay the English Channel Barrage, and we undertaking to lay the major part of the North Sea Barrage. This operation has been conducted under the command of Admiral Strauss, and is proceeding on the whole very satisfactorily. This is the opinion of Admiral Sims and he is wholeheartedly in favor of the completion of this North Sea Barrage. The British Admiralty stands committed to it, but Admiral Sir David Beatty, Commanding the Grand Fleet south of the barrage line, has from the beginning shown little enthusiasm, and has in fact insisted on various modifications of channels through the barrage. Admiral Sims has insisted that the barrage be made complete, i.e., from land to land without gaps. I believe and recommend that the Navy Department should back up Admiral Sims to the limit in this matter.

(3) *Co-operation with Great Britain in Building Program*

This matter I discussed in a purely tentative way with Sir Eric Geddes, as it is one of the subjects to be taken up by him when he visits this country. I shall add nothing further, except that I believe common sense requires that we should, as far as possible, seek to avoid duplication of effort in the United States and Great Britain, and in so doing should be perfectly frank in our discussions and meet Great Britain half-way.[1]

****

114.   *Sims to Opnav*

13 November 1918

... Our forces have always been small in comparison with the naval forces of the Allies. We have, however, transported 45% of the U.S. troops who have come abroad – about 900,000, and have escorted over 61% to the theatre of war without the loss of a soldier from enemy action. Our Naval forces abroad which now aggregate 368 naval ships including 128 subchasers and 85 auxiliary ships, 70,000 men and 5,000 officers have practically maintained themselves as regards supplies and nearly all repairs excepting those requiring docking. Considering the entire Atlantic Convoy system, including ships of all nationalities carrying troops, supplies, munitions, and all requirements of Allies, we have escorted 27% thereof.

The U.S. Navy has furnished twelve per cent of the battleship strength of the British Grand Fleet, the foundation of the military and naval campaign against the enemy.

All U.S. vessels have been constantly employed to the maximum of their endurance.

We have taken part in and actually laid 80% of a great mine barrage 230 miles long from Scotland to Norway. Total mines laid 56449, all of which were designed and manufactured in the United States and transported and laid by U.S. Navy.

23 Aviation Stations have been established along French Atlantic Coast, Irish Coast, in England and in Italy. All material transported from home. Bombing squadrons both day and night have been operated from bases in Flanders against enemy submarine bases all employing 18,000 enlisted men, 1,300 officers. Owing to material difficulties our principal aviation accomplishment has been the establishment of these stations in foreign countries under difficult conditions.

[1] See Part IX.

Our accomplishments are, however, principally to be judged by a comparison between the size of the Navy at the outbreak of war and its expansion since that time, the percentage of entirely new or very old material and ships and the large percentage of the personnel without previous experience with which we have worked, together with the fact that the character of the war was one for which we had not prepared, and for which there was little prewar training. The major difficulties with which we have contended are not and can hardly be made a matter of statistical or written record.

115.   *Wemyss to Sims*

16 November 1918

We recognise, with feelings of gratitude, the debt we owe to the United States Navy for its wholehearted support during the past eighteen months, not only in the anti-submarine campaign and the entensive minelaying programme, but also in sending its battleships to reinforce the Grand Fleet.

We do not forget that your destroyers came to our assistance at a moment when our small craft were feeling the severe strain of three years' continuous warfare. ...

The close co-operation between our two Services has, I venture to think, been one of the outstanding features of the war. ...

116.   *Bayly to Sims*

Admiralty House,
Queenstown,
29 November 1918

(a) Many congratulations on the coming promotion[1] which the papers foreshadow. No man has deserved it more, and the way in which you have handled the different kinds of people of all sort of different nations is a lesson, and, what is far more difficult, your head has not been turned by success. ...

(b) We had quite a successful Thanksgiving in our little way. I went to a U.S. service in the men's club at 10.00 a.m.; the parson was quite good. The niece and I went over the United States hospital in the afternoon, with Pringle. We gave a dinner to 20 (10 British, 10 United States) in the evening and then saw an amusing concert at the

---

[1] Sims, along with Benson, was about to be promoted to the rank of full Admiral in recognition of wartime services.

men's club. Probably the last big one to be given.

(c) ... What I really want, and I hope it is understood, is to remain here till about 15 January, and as much longer after that date as your people are here. I was here when your people came and would like to stay to see them off, because I know how things have been done and can decide any doubtful points. But once they are gone, I want to go and shall retire.

117. *Admiral Lord Beresford*[1] *to Sims*

25 December 1918

Many warm thanks to you for your kindly greetings on Christmas Day. I was most touched at your remembrance of me. No one has done more than yourself to bring our two great nations together and the result of your chivalrous action is now apparent. We shall never forget the good comradeship and warm sympathy expressed and shown by the American navy to our boys in blue. May the New Year bring you great happiness.

118. *Planning Section, U.S. Naval Forces in European Waters*

30 December 1918

Memorandum No. 71: Cooperation with British Plans Division

The formation of the American Planning Section followed very soon after the appointment of Admiral Wemyss as First Sea Lord of the British Admiralty and the reorganisation of the Admiralty by the new administration.

One feature of this reorganisation was the enhanced importance attached to the British Plans Division, which had previously had a very precarious existence. The Plans Division was given permanent and spacious offices and a Rear-Admiral (Keyes) made Director of Plans. Almost immediately however, Rear-Admiral Keyes was detached and succeeded by Captain C. T. M. Fuller, R.N.[2]

[1] Admiral Lord Beresford (Charles William de la Poer Beresford) (1846–1919): Rear-Admiral and 2nd-in-command, Mediterranean Fleet 1900–02; Vice-Admiral 1902; MP for Woolwich 1902–3; CinC Channel 1903–5; CinC Atlantic Fleet 1905; CinC Mediterranean 1905–7; Admiral 1906; CinC Channel Fleet 1907–9; MP for Portsmouth 1910–16; baron 1916. Beresford was Fisher's principal antagonist during the latter's reforming tenure of the First Sea Lord's office; Sims evidently managed to cultivate good relations with both men.
[2] Later Admiral Sir Cyril T. M. Fuller (1874–1942): entered RN 1887; gunnery specialist; Captain 1910; Senior Naval Officer, Cameroons operations 1914; commanded *Repulse* 1916–17; Naval Intelligence 1917; Assistant Director of Plans 1917 and Director 1918–20; Paris Peace Conference 1918–19; Chief of Staff, Atlantic Fleet

In addition to its office at the Headquarters of the Force Commander, the American Planning Section was assigned office space at the Admiralty within the British Plans Division.

Complete cordiality and freedom of informal discussion existed at all times between the two Sections. Under appropriate circumstances they submitted joint solutions to problems. Where problems were solved by one Section only, a copy of the solution was generally furnished to the other Section. Each Section kept the other generally informed of its work in hand.

Under the reorganisation instituted by Admiral Wemyss the British Plans Division was supposed to fulfill its theoretical function of a General Staff 'Thinking Department', and to initiate strategical conceptions to be carried into effect by the Operating Branches of the Staff.

The change of routine in practice proved difficult to establish in the Admiralty. The Deputy Chief of Naval Staff and Assistant Chief of Naval Staff[1] having acquired the habit of performing Plans functions themselves, or having them done by the Operations Division, were inclined to continue in the old way. Several striking examples occurred of important plans being completed without the Plans Division having been consulted or even acquainted with the fact. Plans submitted by the Plans Division frequently received apparently scant notice by the Deputy Chief of Naval Staff, Assistant Chief of Naval Staff and other high officials; being merely endorsed by them casually (and at times sarcastically) and sent to file. This attitude appeared to be partly caused by the fact of the Director of Plans having insufficient rank.

Under these circumstances the British Plans Division frankly sought the formal concurrence of the American Planning Section in many of their plans, for the sake of the greater attention given the papers on that account.

The influence which our Planning Section exerted upon British strategy is difficult to estimate. The attitude of the British higher officials toward us was apparently similar to that manifested tow-

---

1919; Rear-Admiral 1921; ACNS 1922–23; 3rd Sea Lord and Controller 1923–25; commanded Battle Cruiser Squadron 1925–27; Vice-Admiral 1926; knighted 1928; CinC, North America and West Indies 1928–30; Admiral and 2nd Sea Lord 1930–32; retired 1935.

[1] The DCNS to January 1918 was Oliver and thereafter Fremantle. The ACNS was Duff. Admiral Sir Sydney R. Fremantle (1867–1958) was descended from a long line of distinguished naval officers; Captain 1903; Acting Director of Naval Mobilisation 1910–11; President, Signalling Committee, Portsmouth 1912; Rear-Admiral 1913; at

ards the British Plans Division. Rarely were our proposals frankly accepted. From the beginning we urged constantly, both orally and in memoranda,

1. The fact that the principal naval mission was anti-submarine.
2. The great importance of completing the northern barrage.
3. The pressing need for developing and adopting offensive anti-submarine operations; if necessary at some detriment to the convoy system and to the instant readiness of the Grand Fleet to attack the High Seas Fleet.

There appeared constantly to be a strong and almost unanimous reluctance on the part of the British command to accept these doctrines. In the British Plans Division, however, they were favorably endorsed and it is believed that they gradually gained favor in other quarters and materially influenced the conduct of the campaign.

119. *Sims to Benson*

24 January 1919

****

The Admiralty are interested in the *New Mexico* and desire to send a party to visit the ship at Brest. We are still on the basis of a frank exchange of technical information and of free access to all British naval vessels and stations. I see no objection to a visit, especially in view of the fact that we have previously given them the complete specifications of the electric propelling machinery. Request we be authorized to arrange for visit of British naval representatives.

120. *Jellicoe to Sims*

5 February 1919

[I recall] ... most pleasant and delightful personal associations, which associations were of incalculable value to the Allied cause at a critical period of the war thanks to your immediate and clear perception of the naval necessities at that very critical moment.

Dardanelles 1915; 9th CS 1916; 2nd CS 1917; Aegean Squadron 1917–18; DCNS January 1918–April 1919; 1st BS 1919–21; CinC Portsmouth 1925–6; retired list 1928. See his *My Naval Career, 1880–1928* (London: Hutchinson, 1949).

121. Sims to Bayly

6 March 1919

As yours was the first command with which my forces came in contact, I believe that the success of the cooperation, which was chiefly due to you, has been of inestimable value as an example of how that sort of thing should be done between people who are fighting for a common cause.

You may be sure that as long as I live one of my pleasantest souvenirs will be my association with you and your niece.

122. Bayly to Sims

8 March 1919

On my own part I am very sorry indeed to lose you, and I most sincerely thank you for the assistance you have consistently given to me since we first met. On your part however I congratulate you on at last returning to your home and country, knowing your work to have been thoroughly and well done. And a man of your energy must feel that your work here is over, and that you can help your country better by gripping the War College[1] and teaching the coming generations the lessons of actual war, as learned at first hand.

I shall always remember with great pride and gratitude the way in which we have worked together, and the part we have taken in welding our navies into one practical body. And I shall look forward to the day when I can tell Mrs Sims face to face what a splendid friend you have been to me.[2]

The niece and I send you our heartfelt congratulations on your magnificent success, and our very real hopes for your happiness in future. The United States friends that I have made here are too numerous for me to catalogue here, but through you I send them my life long gratitude and friendship for our work together in my last command.

(PS) We met as strangers; we worked as allies; we part as friends.

---

[1] Sims was re-assigned, at his own request, to the Presidency of the Naval War College and remained there until his retirement in 1922.
[2] Bayly had his opportunities, for he visited the US in 1921 and 1934 and Sims and his wife visited Bayly and 'the only niece' at Ermington in South Devon.

123. *Geddes to Sims*

24 March 1919

I can't too warmly express to you my thanks for the never-failing assistance and co-operation which you gave the Board of Admiralty while I was First Lord,[1] and it is to you that we have to give the fullest thanks for the magnificent spirit of co-operation and unselfishness which existed between the two Navies while they were working together in the greatest crisis of our time.

You, personally, have endured yourself to the British Navy and the British Public in a way given to few distinguished Officers from foreign countries, and in leaving us now, you will be sure at all times of a hearty welcome when you are able to come back.

124. *Murray to Sims*

26 March 1919

The Board of Admiralty cannot refrain from expressing to you officially, as they have already expressed privately, their sorrow that you are relinquishing the command of the United States Naval Forces operating in European Waters. Your departure is felt as an individual loss by every Member of the Board, and will be regretted by all those Officers of the Royal Navy who have met you during your stay in this Country and who have uniformly recognised in you not only one of the outstanding personalities of the Naval profession, but also a friend and comrade in thought and feeling.

The Board are grateful for your generous appreciation of the co-operation that has existed between the Royal Navy and the Forces under your command. They are glad to believe that the Royal Navy have always given to you and the United States Ships in the fullest measure that whole-hearted support which it was our aim to accord to the United States Forces. The Board have already on other occasions expressed their high appreciation of the services rendered by the several Units under your command, but they hope that, now that you are leaving, they may also allude to the part that your own individuality has played in the achievements of the last two years. They cannot but recognise that in you was the source whence the United States Ships drew that spirit of unity which since 1917 has welded the two English-speaking Naval Forces into one service, and

[1] Geddes had left the Admiralty for the new Ministry of Transport on 11 December 1918.

which has perhaps, in addition to its far-reaching results during the war, accomplished something towards cementing the kinship of the two Nations in the future.

The Board of Admiralty in saying good-bye wish you great prosperity, and hope that you will not forget that your continued health and success will always be a matter of the greatest interest to the many friends whom you have made in the British Navy.

125.   *Winston S. Churchill to Sims*

War Office,
London,
31 March 1919

I cannot express too strongly my appreciation of the cordial terms in which, on laying down the command of the U.S. Naval forces in European waters, you convey your recognition of the sincerity and zeal with which we have endeavoured to our utmost to assist you in your momentous task.

As you say, the harmony and success of this co-operation form a new precedent, and one which is of the highest value to the future in which such vast issues hang on the unity between our two countries in ideals and in action.[1]

****

126.   *Rear-Admiral H. S. Knapp, U.S. Navy,[2] to Murray*

7 May 1919

Admiral Sir Lewis Bayly, Commander-in-Chief on the Coast of Ireland

1. The Force Commander takes great pleasure in quoting the following letter which he has received from Franklin D. Roosevelt, Acting Secretary of the U.S. Navy:-

'The Department believes that without exception the feeling tow-

---

[1] Churchill was currently Secretary of State for War and Air. The message was radioed to Sims, who was at sea on board RMS *Mauretania*, the Cunard liner taking him back home.

[2] Rear-Admiral Harry S. Knapp, US Navy: began war as a Captain and Military Governor of San Domingo City, the Caribbean republic of San Domingo being then under US Navy occupation and administration; promoted to Rear-Admiral and in February 1918 US Military Representative in Haiti, also under American control at that time; succeeded Sims as Force Commander, US Naval Forces in European Waters.

ard Admiral Bayly of all United States Naval Officers who have served during the war either ashore or afloat from the Queenstown base, is not only unusual but unprecedented in the Allied warfare.

The United States Naval Officers who have operated under Admiral Bayly's orders admired him particularly for his ability, his efficiency and his consideration for their comfort and welfare. In his requirements as to the performance of duty, he was as exacting of the United States Naval Officers as he was of British Officers, but he invariably backed them in all matters in which they were obliged to exercise independent judgment, and so arranged the details of duty that every vessel knew exactly what would be required of it.

The Department is pleased to acknowledge the tact and courtesy with which Admiral Bayly administered his command as regards United States Naval Officers and desires here to express its high appreciation for the consideration which guided Admiral Bayly in his exercise of authority over the United States Naval Officers acting under his command. The Department is of the opinion that the thorough coordination of effort which prevailed under his command is due entirely to Admiral Bayly's tact and courtesy.'

2.   The Force Commander will be greatly pleased if this letter is brought to the attention of the Lords Commissioners of the Admiralty.

PART IV

ANTI-SUBMARINE WARFARE
APRIL 1917 TO DECEMBER 1918

INTRODUCTION

American entry into the war coincided with the worst period of the submarine campaign. In April 1917, sinkings of Allied and neutral merchantmen approached 250000 tons per week, well above the German target. Moreover, the onset of longer daylight raised the prospect of yet higher losses. Most sinkings took place in the Western Approaches but there were substantial losses, too, in the Mediterranean, the English Channel, the North Sea and the Irish Sea. British food stocks were estimated at between three and ten weeks' consumption, while fuel oil was reduced to six weeks' supply. The critical level of supplies necessary to maintain the Allied armies and civilian populations was 32 million tons per annum and this mark was being approached rapidly by the end of June. The U-boats were sinking shipping far faster than it could be replaced – Allied building capacity was only 130000 tons per month. The destruction of U-boats was not increasing. Between 54 and 58 had been sunk since the war began and the current rate was about three a month – at a time when the Germans were turning out three *per week*. The morale of the crews was high and the new boats incorporated many improvements [127, 164].

In view of this dire situation, it is not surprising that Sims's first report to Washington declared that 'Control of the sea is actually imperilled' and that Page should call it 'the sharpest crisis of the war'. Sims observed that the Royal Navy was 'dangerously strained' and Page referred to 'a great depression in naval circles' [127, 129, 151, 152, 182]. Jellicoe told Carson 'we shall be very hard put to it unless the United States help us to the utmost of their ability'[1] and urged De Chair to 'keep constantly before the US Authorities the great gravity of the situation' [130]. A British correspondent of House called it 'a race against time' and British leaders from Lloyd George downwards, supported by Page and Sims, urged both the

[1] Page to Lansing, 27 April 1917, *Senate*, pp. 30–1; Page to Daniels, May 1917, Daniels Papers, box 92; Jellicoe to Carson, 27 April 1917, *Jellicoe Papers*, vol. 2, p. 162.

despatch of every available anti-submarine vessel and, more importantly, a huge emergency programme of mercantile construction,
estimated at six million tons per annum by Lloyd George. A
decrease in sinkings would not enable the target to be reduced as
even more shipping would be needed to transport and supply the
AEF.[1]

Existing anti-submarine measures, though considerable and varied, were clearly inadequate. A close surface blockade of enemy
ports being impracticable in the face of modern defences [49–51],
attempts to prevent the egress of U-boats relied on mining programmes off their exits. British mines were grossly defective until the
German pattern was copied late in 1917. Furthermore, the enemy
swept them up ceaselessly and others were dispersed by the action of
the sea. Submarine patrols in the North Sea, though intensive,
caught few victims and even more of our own boats were lost to
enemy countermeasures. Nets could be breached by bow cutters;
worse still, wave action destroyed them, so that the barrage of mines
and nets in the Dover Straits was a positive sieve. Aircraft were as
yet too few, had too short a range and carried too small a bombload
to be a serious threat to U-boats; they could only report sightings
and force surfaced boats to dive. Q-ships, the great surprise weapon
of earlier years, had been so thoroughly rumbled by the Germans
that they were suffering heavily without scoring in reply, while the
Germans had learned to treat all merchantmen as armed and thus
attacked them from under the surface. It was still important to arm
merchant ships, as otherwise the submarines could shell them or sink
them by charges, thus conserving their torpedoes, prolonging their
cruises and increasing their tonnage totals. The French were hard
put to maintain any kind of naval presence in the Bay of Biscay and
the British were constantly raiding the Grand Fleet for destroyers,
reducing its flotillas well below the requirements for fleet duty and
rendering them inferior to the destroyer strength of the High Seas
Fleet. Principal reliance was on the dispersal and varied routing of
merchant ships and on the patrol of as large an area of the Western
Approaches as available anti-submarine forces allowed. Patrol by
single ships was a frankly haphazard affair. Submarines could spot
approaching patrol craft long before their own low silhouette
became visible and thus take avoiding action. Moving surface ships
could not hear submerged submarines and would only be aware of
their presence if they spotted periscope wakes or torpedo tracks.

[1] W. H. Buckler to House, 4 May 1917, *Wilson Papers*, vol. 42, pp. 379–80; see also
vol. 43, pp. 4–7, 65–6, 142–3, 302–3.

Patrol vessels were thus little more than casual irritations in U-boat routines and though they occasionally caught the Germans napping, they had no effect on the U-boat campaign. Even worse, constant steaming to no great purpose wore out ships and crews, inflicted storm damage and drained dwindling fuel supplies. The one promising weapon thus far devised, the depth charge, was always in short supply. Furthermore, to be effective, it had to hit or explode within a few feet of a submerged submarine, which was almost impossible to locate with any precision. Little wonder, then, that by late April Jellicoe was confessing that 'There is no immediate remedy possible except the use of many more patrol craft which we do not possess' [130] and he told Carson dolefully 'our present policy is headed straight for disaster.'[1] Otherwise, he could plead only for a substantial reduction in the Royal Navy's far-flung commitments and pray for rapid and substantial reinforcement from across the Atlantic.

There was a sovereign remedy – convoy – and much ink has been spilled since the spring of 1917 on the subject of why it was not implemented earlier and more vigorously and who was responsible for its adoption. The reasons why it was not introduced until defeat stared us in the face are clear enough but the question of who made the vital decision to institute it in the eastern Atlantic, the critical area, is and will continue to be a matter of lively debate. Arthur Marder has outlined the reasons why it was not implemented before the late spring of 1917.[2] The Admiralty's arithmetic was grossly in error, positing too large a number of ocean-going ships to be defended. Even when the total was drastically reduced, there were said to be too few available escorts, and it was not simply because most of them were employed on fruitless patrols; as Nelson observed, there are never enough frigates. It was argued that the time taken to assemble and turn round convoyed shipping would cause port congestion and unacceptable delays to supplies. Large concentrations of merchantmen would present fatter targets and convoy was a purely defensive measure; it would not lead to the destruction of submarines. It was therefore a dull job and of little appeal to naval officers. Perhaps the greatest single reservation came from the Merchant Navy. Shipowners were reluctant to sanction further delays to shipping. Naval and mercantile officers alike doubted that merchant vessels could keep station at the speed of the slowest ship, in unfamiliar waters, without lights at night and with a

---

[1] Jellicoe to Carson, 27 April 1917, *Jellicoe Papers*, pp. 160–2.
[2] Marder, vol. 4, pp. 115–65.

deadly enemy lurking unseen and ready to pounce. 'The objections of merchant skippers,' Marder affirmed, 'were undoubtedly a powerful factor in the Admiralty's reluctance to adopt convoy.'[1] A more forceful, sharper and determined First Sea Lord than Jellicoe probably would have seen through these excuses and insisted upon an earlier trial. Indeed, there were already ample indications that convoy was *the* answer. The Grand Fleet itself was a living embodiment of convoy. Troopships, hospital ships (which the Germans attacked to divert destroyers to their protection) [127] and valuable individual cargoes always had escorts in the danger zone. At French insistence the cross-channel coal trade, vital to the continuation of their war effort yet subject to disastrous losses, was convoyed from late in 1916 onwards; losses fell rapidly to less than one per cent. The Dutch convoys had run equally successfully since July 1916 and in April 1917 the traffic to Scandinavia began to be convoyed, followed quickly by that along the East Coast; in all cases there was 'an extraordinary decline in losses'. Yet these striking examples were apparently ignored, either because of a lack of operational research or because they were considered irrelevant to the Atlantic problem.[2]

One of those most intimately concerned with anti-submarine warfare, Admiral Bayly, commanding on the Coast of Ireland station, commented in his memoirs, 'Considering ... the benefits we derived from the convoy system in the past, no objection to it should have been allowed to be sustained in the Great War.'[3] The objections were slowly falling away and the irreversible resumption of unrestricted submarine warfare in February 1917 hastened the process, though it was still tragically drawn out. Jellicoe, though better equipped to handle a fleet than politicians and the Admiralty, had helped by establishing an Anti-Submarine Division upon arriving at Whitehall in December 1916, under the capable Rear-Admiral Duff.[4] By February, several strands of opinion were coming to the conclusion that Atlantic convoys must be tried – Vice-Admiral Beatty, CinC Grand Fleet, Colonel Hankey, Secretary of the War Cabinet, the Ministry of Shipping, junior officers in the Royal Navy

[1] Marder, vol. 4, p. 127.
[2] Marder, vol. 4, pp. 138–44. See also Vice-Admiral Sir Peter Gretton, 'The U-boat Campaign in Two World Wars', in G. Jordan, ed., *Naval Warfare in the Twentieth Century, 1900–1945: Essays in Honour of Arthur Marder* (London: Croom Helm, 1977), pp. 130–4; Jellicoe to Sims, 6 October 1919, *Jellicoe Papers*, vol. 2, pp. 394–7.
[3] Bayly, p. 240 (but see Bayly's doubts at the time, document no. 166).
[4] Marder, vol. 4, p. 61.

and even the still neutral Woodrow Wilson.[1] The alarming figures of sinkings in April brought about the decision to try Atlantic convoys. Credit for instituting this has been claimed for or by several individuals, generally and entirely inaccurately by or for Lloyd George. Certainly he had been fed the arguments for it by Hankey, shipping officials and junior officers but it took him two months either to be convinced or to decide to act. Much play is made of the fact that on 25 April Lloyd George informed the Admiralty that he would pay it a visit on 30 April to study 'all the means at present in use in regard to anti-submarine warfare'. This has been taken to mean that the Admiralty, aware that Lloyd George was coming to force convoy upon it, resolved to forestall him by taking the decision itself on 26–27 April. In fact Jellicoe authorised a trial on 21 April, though the decisive instrument appears to have been Duff's memorandum to the First Sea Lord of 26 April, which argued for convoy in the light of current disastrous losses and in view of the additional escort forces made available by American belligerency.[2]

What part did the Americans play in the decision to institute Atlantic convoys announced by Jellicoe on 27 April? [132] Wilson had enquired about the British reluctance to adopt convoy as early as 25 February but while the General Board had mentioned it among a range of possibilities, most American opinion (supported by Browning and Grasset) was opposed to it, on grounds similar to those of the Admiralty.[3] Sims was the principal American advocate of convoy, raising the issue with Jellicoe at their first meeting [19] and declaring himself 'devoted to this convoy system since the first week I got here' [164]. No doubt Sims's advocacy assisted in its adoption but for the Admiralty the belligerency of the United States was a clinching argument, as it permitted the assembly of vessels in American ports and the opportunity to practice sailing in formation well before the submarine zone was reached and the anti-submarine

[1] E. D. Cronon, ed., *The Cabinet Diaries of Josephus Daniels, 1913–1921* (Lincoln, Neb: University of Nebraska Press, 1963), pp. 105–6.

[2] The most extravagant claim for Lloyd George is made by A. J. P. Taylor, *English History, 1914–1945* (Harmondsworth: Penguin Books, 1970), pp. 121–4; see also Gretton, pp. 131–4; Duff to Jellicoe, 26 April 1917, *Jellicoe Papers*, vol. 2, pp. 157–9; E. J. Grove, 'The Reluctant Partner: The United States and the Introduction and Extension of Convoy, 1917–18', in *Charted and Uncharted Waters: Proceedings of a Conference on the Study of British Maritime History* (Trustees of National Maritime Museum/Queen Mary College, London, 1981), p. 220.

[3] J. Daniels, *The Wilson Era*, vol. 2, *The Years of War and After, 1917–1923* (Chapel Hill, NC: University of North Carolina Press, 1946), p. 67; H. Newbolt, *Official History of the War, Naval Operations*, vol. 5 (London: Longmans Green, 1931), p. 133; Grove, pp. 218–34; Daniels to Wilson, 14 July 1917, *Wilson Papers*, vol. 43, pp. 178–9.

escort relieved the cruiser acting as anti-raider escort [188, 192, 193, 198]. The Admiralty's assumption of substantial assistance from American anti-submarine forces, though ultimately confirmed, was extremely premature. Not only was Benson reluctant to denude home waters, the US Navy had no experience of anti-submarine warfare, no depth charges and only a small force of destroyers, of which many units were unfit for immediate service. Though Marder was correct in stating that 'the small initial American contribution' of destroyers 'was enough to help tip the balance of scale in favour of convoy', it was not until 4 May that the first six arrived and not until July that most of the modern craft had arrived.[1] After the war Jellicoe and Sims asserted that the system could not 'have been established in any complete and systematic way at such an early date' without American destroyers but as Sims's biographer noted, it was not impossible without them.[2] As Sir Peter Gretton has observed, over 3,000 British and Allied escort craft were available, excluding American ships, and had the wasteful patrol system been wound up promptly sufficient ocean-going escorts would have materialised, since convoys in fact depended very little on their escorts for their safety; they were useful only to deter U-boats which met up with convoys and to mount counter-attacks once the submarines had shown their hand. The great strength of the convoy system was that it concentrated shipping in small spaces and thus 'gave enemy submarines considerably greater difficulty in finding their prey'.[3] A U-boat locating a convoy could generally expect to make only one attack; even a spread salvo of torpedoes was unlikely to sink more than two or three ships of the 16–20 in the average convoy – a far better loss rate than the one in four of independent sailings. Escorts forced U-boats to fire at longer ranges. The concentration of shipping enabled the Admiralty to order route alterations to avoid known predators with greater ease. As Bayly pointed out, 'many convoys evaded attack simply because they were never spotted.'[4] That convoying presented a vast organisational problem [151, 163, 170] is undeniable but estimates that it would increase delays by 20 per cent were unfounded; in fact, it made for more efficient use of merchant tonnage and at least merchantmen were not kept immobilised in port by rumours of prowling U-boats

[1] Marder, vol. 4, pp. 274–5; Bayly, p. 242.
[2] Jellicoe to Sims, 6 October 1919, *Jellicoe Papers*, vol. 2, pp. 394–7; Sims, pp. 111–2; Morison, p. 353.
[3] Gretton, pp. 130–4; Duff to Jellicoe, 26 April 1917, *Jellicoe Papers*, vol. 2, p. 158.
[4] Bayly, p. 240; Gretton, pp. 130–1.

outside.[1] Finally, far from being merely defensive, convoys lured submarines to them and offered the best of opportunities for offensive action [149, 150, 152, 153, 156, 184, 198]. In time, escort tactics were refined, use being made of operational experience [175, 186, 218, 224, 242].

By the end of America's first month of war, then, the Atlantic convoy system was coming into being. Its parentage remains a matter of dispute but it was certainly not the child of any one man; 'pressure was exerted by many hands.'[2] The first Atlantic convoy sailed from Gibraltar and its safe arrival on 20 May was 'one of the great turning points of the war'.[3] The extension of convoy was regrettably slow; it took, says Gretton, three months to prove itself and another three before it had a firm grip on the shipping situation. 'In the meantime, many ships and lives had been needlessly lost.'[4] In part this tardiness was the fault of the Admiralty, where officers continued to have reservations about its success to the end of the war, largely on the grounds that it was purely defensive [42] and killed few U-boats.[5] Much of the blame for the slow spread of the convoy system rests, however, with the Navy Department and with Benson in particular.

Until July 1917, the Navy Department dragged its feet on convoy [152–5, 160, 164], partly because it wished to retain anti-submarine forces to protect its own fleet and coasts from a (largely nonexistent) U-boat threat in its own waters and partly because it had naïve attitudes to modern warfare. Even after American resistance was broken, Daniels was still asking innocently whether the patrol of a single lane was a better option [167–8], while Benson doggedly maintained an unjustified faith in defensively armed merchant ships sailing alone [139, 155, 160], though both Sims and Jellicoe attempted to disabuse him [156–7]. Sims pressed tirelessly but with little success for America's wholehearted co-operation with the system [135, 150, 152–3, 156, 158, 163–4, 169] and Jellicoe, now 'convinced the convoy system is a necessity and the only method left to us' [181], urged Gaunt to impress upon the Americans the vital need for their full collaboration [149, 159]. Ultimately, it was Wilson who ordered the US Navy to co-operate fully; until his intervention early in July, the United States 'continued to play a leading role in

[1] Paxson, vol. 2, pp. 299–300.
[2] E. Morison, p. 348.
[3] Sims, p. 115.
[4] Gretton, p. 134.
[5] Marder, vol. 4, p. 291.

blocking the extension of convoy'. Even then the Americans were reluctant to integrate the AEF troop convoys into the general system, retained over 20 destroyers on their own coast and diverted the majority of those in European waters to the escort of troop convoys [149, 176, 235], while persistently attempting to take over convoy organisation in American ports from British officers, though to no avail [155, 156, 163, 203].[1]

Notwithstanding American sluggishness, the Atlantic convoy system was an immediate and unqualified success. 'Convoyed ships escape – almost all. That is the convincing actual experience', wrote Page to Wilson as early as 29 June, a view echoed by British officials. By mid-August, Sims could point to significant tonnage savings [178], cautiously confirmed a month later [182, 184], and more amply from the spring of 1918, when new construction began to exceed sinkings [221, 223, 228, 229, 231, 232]. The system was gradually extended until by the end of 1917 some 50 per cent of North Atlantic and other shipping was convoyed, rising to over 90 per cent by the Armistice. 'Sinkings fell in almost direct proportion to the increasing number of ships in convoy', less than a half of one per cent being lost. Initially, convoys had been for inbound shipping but outward-bound vessels began to be escorted from August 1917, escort groups leaving them at the outer edge of the submarine zone and picking up inward-bound convoys. Mediterranean losses remained serious, due to the Allies' inability to co-ordinate their forces [Part VII] but inshore convoys round the United Kingdom were instituted in the spring of 1918 to counter a move to shallow waters by the U-boats frustrated in their search for deep-water targets. By the Armistice, convoy had become a routine and universal practice [152, 198]. Most importantly, it was 'an unqualified success, and [one] to which the Germans discovered no counter.'[2]

The principal weight of the anti-submarine campaign fell upon the shoulders of the Commander-in-Chief, Coast of Ireland, Admiral Sir Lewis Bayly, whose headquarters were at Queenstown. An able if brusque man, Bayly was a fine organiser, experienced in the handling of destroyers and had been at his post for some eighteen months before the Germans resumed unrestricted submarine warfare. He was not, however, a man of great vision, for he was sceptical about

[1] Grove, pp. 218–34; H. & M. Sprout, *The Rise of American Naval Power* (Princeton, NJ: Princeton University Press, 1946), pp. 359–68; Daniels to Wilson, 14 July 1917, *Wilson Papers*, vol. 43, pp. 178–9.

[2] Page to Wilson, 29 June 1917, *Wilson Papers*, vol. 43, p. 47; see also pp. 65–6, 141–2, 172–3, 464; Marder, vol. 4, pp. 277, 282; vol. 5, p. 85; Newbolt, vol. 5, p. 337; Bayly, pp. 244, 248.

convoy [166] but he put it into practice with great efficiency and fashioned a formidable escort from an amalgam of British sloops and American destroyers. Escort groups were formed from both navies, both defensive and offensive tactics were devised and, drawing upon operational experience, revised, and a joint (if somewhat unofficial and unorthodox) command structure supervised operations [172, 175, 179, 185, 186, 189, 193, 227, 234, 336–7, 242, 243]. Harmony, dedication, skill and good fellowship marked the Queenstown command, yet it could so easily have been a disastrous relationship, given Bayly's gruff and irascible nature. That his better side was displayed in 1917–18 was due largely to American tact, efficiency, determination and good organisation. For this, the principal credit is attributable to Admiral Sims, Captain Pringle and Commander Taussig,[1] who led the first destroyers to Queenstown [128, 134, 140–3]. These vessels, excellent boats for Atlantic convoy duty, were reinforced by successive flotillas until by July 37 ships were on station [137], serviced by well-equipped depot ships [147], and were quickly in action. Within a few weeks, Sims was able to report absolute smoothness in Anglo-American relations at the base [146] and he himself struck up a close and lasting friendship with the previously reserved Bayly.[2] He visited Queenstown on several occasions, even taking command for a week [147–8, 166, 170, 206, 236]. The excellence of the joint operation at Queenstown was widely recognised [211, 213, 220, 234, and Part III]; wisely, the unusual command arrangements were not disturbed, for it was the touchstone of Anglo-American naval co-operation.

Though overall U-boat strength increased from 120 in February 1917 to 180 in November 1918, boats at sea never exceeded 50 at any one time. There was no great drive to expand production and there was a severe decline in efficiency. As Allied countermeasures improved, more boats were lost (though construction consistently exceeded losses), morale shrank, the best commanders (responsible for a disproportionately large amount of sunken tonnage) were killed or captured, while expansion compelled dilution of crews, and there was little attempt to devise new tactics (such as wolf packs) to

[1] Cdr. (later Rear-Admiral) Joseph Knefler Taussig, US Navy (1877–1947): graduated from Annapolis 1899; severely wounded and mentioned in despatches Boxer Rising 1900; commander, 8th Div, Destroyer Force, Atlantic Fleet 1917; Bureau of Navigation, Navy Dept. 1918; Naval War College 1919; dispute with F. D. Roosevelt over return of offenders to naval service 1919–20; commanded *Maryland*; Rear-Admiral 1931; Asst. CNO 1933–6; Commandant, 5th Naval District 1938; retired 1941; Chairman, Naval Clemency Board 1943; notable writer on naval subjects.
[2] See Simpson, 'Sims and Bayly'.

outwit the convoys. The only real variation adopted was the U-cruiser. In 1915 Germany had built several large cargo-carrying submarines which made a number of trips to America in a bid to overcome the British blockade. After America came into the war, these were converted to carry two 5.9in guns and torpedo tubes. With their great radius of action, they were able to operate far beyond the 500-mile line west of Ireland, the limit for conventional boats. The Allies feared these craft inordinately, especially when they learned that several purpose-built vessels were under construction. Some operated round the Azores and others paid visits to the American coast but they accomplished little, owing to effective countermeasures, ineffective operational direction, and the clumsy characteristics of the type.[1] The principal defences against them were patrols by Allied submarines and the provision of cruiser escorts of superior gun-power outside the destroyer zone. Empty threat or not, cruiser submarines caused the coalition high command a disproportionate amount of anxiety [177, 183, 196, 198, 210, 216, 217, 231].

Both British and American officers and the First Lord, Geddes, persisted in regarding convoy as a purely defensive measure (even if it did allow opportunities for counter-attack) and as a temporary expedient. Their constant intent was to go over to the offensive and hunt enemy submarines by various means. Direct assaults on their bases either being rejected or proving to be costly if heroic failures, the submarines had to be harried at sea before they reached the open ocean. One method, mining them into confined bodies of water, was attempted in the Dover and Otranto Straits and between Scotland and Norway [Parts VI and VII], in conjunction with surface and air patrols and other devices.[2] A second means was intensive air patrols by flights of heavily armed flying-boats or land-based machines. The Royal Naval Air Service (absorbed into the new Royal Air Force early in 1918) already did a good deal of anti-submarine work, supplemented by airships and shipborne kite balloons. The American naval air contribution was intended to focus on bombing submarine bases and reinforcing British anti-submarine patrols, though it hardly got under way before the war ended [194–5, 197–8, 202, 204, 225, 231–4, 236]. The Americans also reinforced a further British measure, the employment of their own submarines in a 'hunter–killer' capacity. From the beginning of American partici-

[1] Trask, *Captains and Cabinets*, pp. 186–7, 218–20.
[2] Marder, vol. 4, pp. 229–54; vol. 5, pp. 66, 97–109; House to Wilson, 21 November 1917, *House Papers*, vol. 3, p. 236.

pation in the war, Jellicoe had urged the Navy Department to use their submarines in this way [14] and in due course small flotillas operated from Berehaven in Ireland and in the Azores. Though Allied submarines achieved a number of successes, they were less prominent than surface craft and mines as a means of destroying U-boats[1] and appear to have exercised little influence on U-boat behaviour, other than inducing greater wariness and perhaps a shift to other waters [158, 160, 177, 183, 187, 193, 215, 216, 236, 237, 243].

Jellicoe in particular found himself under regular pressure to act offensively against the U-boats [Part III], both from the home and American press, Wilson, Lloyd George, the British Churchill and retired officers like Lord Fisher. He told Beatty of the 'six-monthly agitation' for an offensive and that the Americans 'keep harping on about an offensive', but assured Benson that he was always looking for opportunities to act aggressively; overwhelming defensive commitments and the impracticability of most suggestions prevented this until 1918.[2] By that time Jellicoe had gone and while overall resources were still inadequate the British and American planning staffs were now in active collaboration and producing offensive plans like rabbits out of a hat. To their disgust, but fortunately for the Allied cause, the Sea Lords shelved most of their proposals. The planners, who had no direct responsibility for directing men and ships or ensuring the safe arrival of vital supplies [214, 218], blithely proposed to denude convoys of their already slim escorts and 'hunt hornets all over the farm'. They placed their faith in mine barrages but also in hunting groups of hydrophone-equipped light craft. A number of these groups were organised in the North and Irish Seas and in the English Channel. They consisted either of old British destroyers working with trawlers or of an American destroyer teamed with submarine chasers.[3] The object was to patrol likely submarine-infested areas, and when contact was made with a submerged U-boat, to track it, and either destroy it with depth charges or force it to the surface and finish it off by gunfire. Some use was made of aircraft and kite balloons. Late in the war, similar groups were organised in the Straits of Otranto [Part VII].

Hunting depended on both visual and aural contact. Aircraft and kite balloons extended visibility at bridge level but special devices

---

[1] Eighteen U-boats appear to have been destroyed by Allied submarines; see Marder, vol. 4, pp. 118–20; R. M. Grant, *U-Boats Destroyed: The Effect of Anti-Submarine Warfare, 1914–1918* (London: Putnam, 1964), p. 74.

[2] Jellicoe to Beatty, 8 June and 31 July 1917; to Sims, 6 October 1919; to Benson, September 1917, *Jellicoe Papers*, pp. 168, 191, 209–10, 394–7.

[3] Bayly, p. 247.

were necessary to locate submerged U-boats under way. The Royal Navy, rather half-heartedly, had established a research unit to develop listening apparatus and the Americans, always eager to apply advanced technology to problems, were pursuing similar lines.[1] By the time they joined the war, both navies had a variety of devices which could detect underwater noises and these were installed in anti-submarine craft, either towed or affixed to their hulls. Operators were trained to pick up electric motor sounds with these devices [145]. Among the ships fitted with them were destroyers and trawlers, but a new type of vessel seemed eminently suitable for the listening and hunting function: the American submarine chaser, 110 feet in length, 60 tons displacement, 18 knots, one six-pounder or three-inch gun, and several depth charges. Designed originally for coastal patrol work off America's eastern seaboard, they were offered to the European theatre [161, 180] when the U-boat assault on the American coast failed to materialise. America's partners, desperate for anything that could sail and fight, accepted them gratefully, though, apart from 40 for the French Navy, they remained under the American flag; over 300 were built, of which about 170 served abroad [162]. The brainchild of the effervescent Franklin D. Roosevelt, these little craft were regarded with some scepticism by Sims and other US and Allied officers, as they were unable to function in any kind of seaway, were unsuitable for convoy work, gobbled scarce fuel and lacked sufficient gun armament [171, 181, 226]. Great hopes were placed on the efficacy of the hydrophones, the American type being regarded as superior to the British, and even Sims was converted to the chaser listening/hunting concept [194, 210] and allocated staff and destroyers to the work [195]. The British seemed equally enthusiastic [198] and co-operation was close [205–10, 212, 214–5, 222, 230–2, 236–7, 240, 241, 243].

Results, however, were extremely disappointing [210, 212, 226–7, 230–1, 235], though both navies remained optimistic that further development of the devices, better training and more groups would yield dividends. The hydrophone, unfortunately, was a dead-end, suffering from a number of deficiencies. It was difficult to separate underwater electric motors from other sounds, it could only be used when surface craft in the vicinity were stationary or drifting, and it was in fact far more useful to submerged submarines equipped with it than to their surface pursuers. After the war, the hydrophone was discarded in favour of the asdic or sonar system, the basis of

[1] See Hackmann, *Seek and Strike, passim.*

listening gear in World War II. Like the submarine chasers, hydrophones were 'No great factor in the anti-U-boat fight'.[1] Convoys
well
protected by powerful escort groups, with sufficient vessels to mount
counter-attacks without depriving the convoy of adequate defence,
offered the best hope of defeating the submarine campaign. Until a
reliable listening device, able to distinguish between underwater
sounds and usable at reasonable speed, was available, escorts could
only attack when submarines revealed themselves, by which time
one or two merchantmen might have gone down.

While the Royal Navy shouldered by far the greater part of the
anti-submarine role in 1917–18, the American contribution in men,
materiel, morale and mechanical devices was far from negligible.
Both navies underwent painful learning processes and followed false
leads before adopting the best means of trade protection. Neither
high command was unanimous about the measures to be adopted
but the convoy system, introduced as a final gamble, forced the
policymakers to develop it by its total and instant success. Though
younger officers on planning staffs and some of their seniors han-
kered after an offensive approach, no undeniably successful attacking scheme was discovered. More importantly, though some scarce
resources were misused chasing ultimately unsound options. those
who held the final responsibility spotted the flaws in these schemes
and maintained the integrity of the convoy system – the saviour of
the whole coalition cause.

---

[1] Frothingham, vol. 3, p. 120.

127. *Sims to Daniels*

London,
14 April 1917

The submarine issue is very much more serious than people in America realise. The recent success of operations and the rapidity of construction constitute the real crisis of the war. The *morale* of the enemy submarines is not broken, only about fifty-four[1] are known to have been captured or sunk and no voluntary surrenders have been recorded. The reports of our press are greatly in error. Recent reports circulated concerning surrenders are simply to depreciate enemy *morale* and results are not very satisfactory.

Supplies and communications of forces all fronts, including the Russians, are threatened and control of the sea actually imperilled.

German submarines are constantly expanding their operations into the Atlantic, increasing areas and the difficulty of patrolling. Russian situation critical. Baltic fleet mutiny, eighty-five admirals, captains and commanders murdered, and in some armies there is insubordination.

The amount of British, neutral and Allied shipping lost in February was 536,000 tons, in March 517,000 tons, and in the first ten days of April 205,000 tons.[2] With short nights and better weather these losses are increasing.

The British forces could not effectively prevent the escape of some raiders during the long nights, but the chances are better now.

The Allies were notified that hospital ships will continue to be sunk, this in order to draw destroyers away from operations against submarines to convoy hospital ships; in this way causing a large demand for large convoy forces in all areas not before necessary, and also partially immobilizing the main fleet.

[1] Marder, vol. 4, p. 106, notes 58 U-boats lost to this point.
[2] Marder, vol. 4, p. 102, lists monthly tonnage losses in 1917 (British, Allied and neutral) as follows:

	By submarine	By all forms of enemy action
January	291,459	357,299
February	464,599	532,856
March	507,001	599,854
April	834,549	869,103

On account of the immense theatre and the length and number of lines of communication, and the material deterioration resulting from three years' continuous operation in distant fields with inadequate base facilities, the strength of the naval forces is dangerously strained. This applies to all of the sea forces outside of the Grand Fleet. The enemy has six large and sixty-four small submarine minelayers; the latter carry eighteen mines and the former thirty-four, also torpedoes and guns. All classes submarines for actual commission completed at a rate approaching three per week. To accelerate and insure defeat of the submarine campaign, immediate active cooperation absolutely necessary.

The issue is and must inevitably be decided at the focus of all lines of communications in the Eastern Atlantic, therefore I very urgently recommend the following immediate naval cooperation:

Maximum number of destroyers to be sent, accompanied by small anti-submarine craft, former to patrol designated high seas area westward of Ireland based on Queenstown with an advance base at Bantry Bay to be an inshore patrol for destroyers [;] small craft should be of light draft with as high speed as possible but low speed also useful. Also repair ships and staff for base. Oil and docks available, but advise sending continuous supply of fuel. German main fleet must be contained maximum conservation of the British main fleet. South of Scotland no base is so far available for this force.

At present our battleships can serve no useful purpose in this area except that two divisions of dreadnoughts might be based on Brest for moral effect against anticipated raids by heavy enemy ships in the Channel out of reach of the British main fleet.

The chief other and urgent practical cooperation is merchant tonnage and a continuous augmentation of anti-submarine craft to reinforce our advanced forces. There is a serious shortage of the latter craft. For towing the present large amount of sailing tonnage through dangerous areas, seagoing tugs would be of great use.

The cooperation outlined above should be expedited with the utmost despatch in order to break the enemy submarine morale and accelerate the accomplishment of the chief American objective.

It is very likely that the enemy will make submarine mine laying raids on our coast or in the Caribbean to divert attention and to keep our forces from the critical areas in the Eastern Atlantic through effect upon public opinion. The difficulty of maintaining submarine bases and the focus of shipping on this side will restrict operations to minor importance, although they should be effectively opposed principally by keeping the Channel swept on soundings. Enemy submarine mines have been anchored as deep as ninety fathoms but majority at not over fifty fathoms. Mines do not rise from the bottom to set depth until from twenty-four to forty-eight hours after they have been laid.

So far all experience shows that submarines never lay mines out of sight of landmarks or lights on account of danger to themselves if location is not known. Maximum augmentation merchant tonnage and anti-submarine work where most effective constitute the paramount immediate necessity.

Mr Hoover[1] informs [me] that there is only sufficient grain supply in this country for three weeks. This does not include the supply in retail stores. In a few days Mr Hoover will sail for the United States.

128. Daniels to Commander J. K. Taussig, U.S. Navy[2]

14 April 1917

Protection of Commerce near the coasts of Great Britain and Ireland

1. The British Admiralty have requested the cooperation of a division of American destroyers in the protection of commerce near the coasts of Great Britain and France.
2. Your mission is to assist naval operations of Entente Powers in every way possible.
3. Proceed to Queenstown, Ireland. Report to senior British naval officer present, and thereafter cooperate fully with the British navy. Should it be desired that your force act in cooperation with French naval forces your mission and method of cooperation under French Admiralty remain unchanged.

Route to Queenstown.

Boston to latitude 50°N – long. 20°W to arrive at daybreak then to latitude 50°N – long. 12°W thence to Queenstown.

When within radio communication of the British Naval forces off Ireland, call G-CK and inform the Vice-Admiral at Queenstown in British general code of your position, course, and speed. You will be met outside of Queenstown.

[1] Herbert Clark Hoover (1874–1964): at this time US War Food Administrator; a self-made millionaire mining engineer and company promoter; based in London in 1914 and made high reputation as organizer of Belgian relief; after war attended peace conference; later organized relief for Russia in civil war; Secretary of Commerce in Republican administrations, 1921–28; President, 1929–33.
[2] Commander, 8th Div, Destroyer Force, Atlantic Fleet.

4. Base facilities will be provided by the British Admiralty.

5. Communicate your orders and operations to Rear-Admiral Sims at London and be guided by such instructions as he may give you. Make no reports of arrival to Navy Department direct.

129.   *Sims to Daniels*

18 April 1917

Complete blockade of German and Belgian coasts against egress and ingress of submarines has been found wholly impracticable. Every practicable means [has] already been attempted and numerous nets and mine-fields have been and will continue to be laid, also submarine destroyers and other craft will be used in an endeavor to prevent the exit of German submarines and also to prevent mines and nets being dragged out by the enemy.

There is naturally considerable danger to vessels operating in such close proximity to the bases of the enemy and several have been torpedoed and mined.

Even the maintenance of an effective patrol against submarines between Scotland and Norway has been found impracticable as too many vessels have been torpedoed. A patrol is now maintained on lines between Scotland and Iceland and also between Scotland and Greenland icefloes. In order to maintain these lines and prevent torpedoing it is necessary to change their location after each contact with the enemy as there are no vessels available to screen the cruisers against submarine attack. The destroyer has proved to be by far the most efficient weapon against enemy submarines operating against commerce and consequently the enemy uses every means at his command to force their employment for other duty and has for this purpose adopted a policy of sinking hospital ships. All destroyers are now so employed except the minimum required by the Grand Fleet and those necessary for convoying troops and their supplies. Every effort is being made to build destroyers as rapidly as possible but numbers are wholly inadequate to meet the present submarine issue particularly against merchant shipping.

The situation is so serious that I urgently repeat my recommendations that we send immediately every destroyer capable of reaching Ireland and also all light draft vessels of whatever speed capable of performing any patrol duty. It is impracticable for our battleships to take any part in the war [,] neither do they need destroyer protection unless operating in the critical war theater on this side.

The British are willing to try any anti-submarine methods which have not already proved inefficient. Present developments are the result of exhaustive trials of many methods which have often been carried out at great expense.

It would seem most advantageous that we should adopt existing British methods and base further developments only upon actual experience in co-operation with them. This is to the best of my knowledge the policy that we should pursue.

130.   *Jellicoe to De Chair*

26 April 1917

You must emphasise most strongly to the United States authorities the very serious nature of the shipping position. We lost 55 British ships last week, approximately 180,000 tons and rate of loss is not diminishing.

There is no immediate remedy possible except the use of many more patrol craft which we do not possess. Press most strongly that the number of Destroyers sent to Ireland should be increased to 24 at once if this number is available.

Battleships are not required but concentration on the vital question of defeat of submarine menace is essential.

Urge on the Authorities that everything should give way to the submarine menace and that by far the most important place on which to concentrate patrols is the S.W. of Ireland.

It would be a fatal step to disperse the U.S. Destroyers amongst different nations from every point of view. If the U.S. concentrate vessels on one route we can release ships to assist other Allies and the work would be much facilitated by all U.S. vessels working together.

You must keep constantly before the U.S. Authorities the great gravity of the situation and the need that exists for immediate action.

Our new methods will not be effective till July and the critical period is April to July.

131.   *De Chair to Admiralty*

Washington,
27 April 1917

With regard to destroyers sent from U.S.A. to operate in European waters Admiral Benson appears to be nervous that British and French Admiralties might not be agreed as to their base of operations and he fears any friction might reflect on Navy Department here if it was [thought?] by France that undue favour was shown British. Could I be informed confidentially of base to which other destroyers may be sent in near future [?]

132. *Jellicoe to De Chair*

27 April 1917

The situation shows no improvement.

I am organising a system of convoy for all inward and outward trade.

The arrangements will probably be that a cruiser will escort a convoy of about 20 merchant ships to positions westward of Ireland clear of submarine activity where convoy will be met and escorted to port by destroyers. But the system necessitates first a considerable increase in number of destroyers and therefore the assistance of USA in provision of as many more as possible is very urgently needed.

133. *De Chair to Jellicoe*

28 April 1917

I have pressed continuously very serious condition shipping position. United States authorities realise it now. Admiral Benson informs me twelve additional destroyers will leave shortly for Southwest coast Ireland. I am encouraging establishment American flag command at Berehaven, thirty or forty destroyers and other craft, Sims in command. This is only way to keep destroyers from being dispersed. Sims should not be told this as matter is now before President and not settled. I have rubbed it in how fatal it would be to disperse United States destroyers amongst different nations but there is a strong party who are anxious to conciliate French. Navy Department are pressing forward all measures for supply of small craft.

It is possible four United States cruisers now in Pacific will be directed to proceed through Panama Canal for service off Coast of Brazil where *Kaiser Wilhelm* and *Prinz Eitel Friedrich* will join them when ready. This is also before President now.[1]

---

[1] These were German liners, interned in American ports in 1914, sabotaged by their crews when America joined the war, subsequently repaired and put into service under new names transporting troops across Atlantic.

134. *Sims to Taussig*

29 April 1917

I am delighted to know that you are in command of the advance guard of the destroyer force. Needless to say your command will receive a most hearty welcome by this country both for sentimental and military reasons, for the submarines are becoming more and more successful with longer daylight and better weather, in spite of all the destroyers and patrol boats the British are able to send against them. In the week ending 22 April they destroyed 237,000 tons of shipping. Manifestly if this is not checked the Allies cannot win.

Besides the welcome which your force will receive you will find an equally warm personal welcome. When I informed the Admiralty of the name of the Commander of the 8th Division I was at once asked, 'Is he the Taussig who was with Admiral Seymour in China?' You will probably receive a message from Admiral Jellicoe, the First Sea Lord, who of course remembers you well.[1]

As soon as I was informed that the Division was coming over, I asked the Admiralty to detail an experienced destroyer commander to meet you at Queenstown and give you and your gang all the points, tricks, and stunts, that the British have learned during nearly three years of actual warfare. You will be supplied with 'depth charges' and other appliances now employed, and will be informed as to the best known methods of using them. Also as to the various methods that have been tried and found less efficient.

The Officer selected is Commander Evans, who was second in command of the Scott Antarctic Expedition, and now in command of the Torpedo Leader *Broke*, at present repairing the damage she received in the recent (20 April) destroyer fight off Dover.[2] ... He can also give you some very useful points on keeping your men

[1] Jellicoe had also been wounded during the Boxer Rising and had met Taussig in hospital.

[2] Later Admiral Lord Mountevans (Edward Ratcliffe Garth Russell Evans, 1st Baron, 1881–1957): polar explorer and mountaineer; second-in-command of Scott's last expedition 1910–13; Commander July 1912; commanded flotilla leader *Broke*, December 1916, and always known as 'Evans of the *Broke*' following the encounter between the *Broke* and *Swift* (Cdr. A. M. Peck) and six German destroyers in the Straits of Dover, 20–21 April 1917; promoted to Captain and served as Flag Captain to Admiral Sir Reginald Bacon at Dover; on Gibraltar convoy run 1918; SNO Ostend 1919; Captain of *Carlisle*; China station 1920–22, where he rescued survivors from wrecked passenger steamer; Captain of *Repulse* 1926; Rear-Admiral 1928 and commanded Australian squadron until 1931; Vice-Admiral 1932; CinC Africa 1933; CinC Nore 1935–39; Civil Defence 1939–45; barony 1945. See his *Adventurous Life* (London: Hutchinson, 1946) and *Happy Adventurer* (London: Lutterworth Press, 1951).

contented while doing work which is necessarily largely monotonous.

****

Evans will explain the use of the 'depth charges', the most effective weapon against the subs, and from his explanation and the nature and use of the weapon you will recognise the absolute necessity of practically instant action in carrying out a prearranged plan of attack.

I have just been placed in command of all U.S. destroyers operating on this side including twelve more destroyers with tenders and auxiliaries to be sent later, but as the active command will of course be exercised by the senior officer on the spot, under orders of the Vice-Admiral of the Port, I want to warn you as to certain difficulties that may arise.

This relates to possible friction with the British Naval authorities. You will, I am sure, recognise the necessity of avoiding this as long as it is practically possible.

I would not consider this warning so necessary were it not for two facts, namely (1) there has been more or less serious friction of this nature between the Allies, as has been more or less the case throughout the history of Allied warfare, and (2) I have been informed by the Admiralty that the Vice-Admiral (Bayly) in command at Queenstown is a peculiarly difficult man to deal with.[1] You will make no new discoveries as to his manner or character. We have heard it all and more. His outstanding good qualities are that he is capable and is as unsparing of himself as he is of his subordinates.

He was recently called to the Admiralty for consultation as to cooperation between our forces, and when I was introduced to him he was very rude, as he was also to some very high Admiralty officials present. It was evidently one of Admiral Bayly's bad days. Of course I treated it as an amusing incident and declined to make any trouble over it. However the Admiral was taken very severely to task, in the presence of the First Lord (our Secretary) and very distinctly informed that there should be no friction of any kind.

In view of the above explanations of the peculiarities of Admiral Bayly, who is very able and valuable in other respects, I am sure you will be able to make things go smoothly.

[1] For the story of Sims's relations with Bayly, see my article 'Admiral William S. Sims, US Navy, and Admiral Sir Lewis Bayly, Royal Navy: An Unlikely Friendship and Anglo-American Relations, 1917–1919', *Naval War College Review*, vol. XLI, no. 2, spring 1988, pp. 66–80.

However if you find that friction does arise which interferes with the efficiency of your command, I want you to report the instances to me at once, and if it cannot be abated the cause will at once be removed.

There is one other feature of such a condition which is of importance, and that is the necessity of keeping your own counsel. If anything disagreeable occurs in your own intercourse with the naval authorities do not mention it to any of your own people, not even your own executive, and do not permit the officers to discuss any differences which they may observe. Otherwise they will get about among the crews and be sent home in private letters and may cause serious trouble through leakage into the press.

Require all officers not only to refrain from all criticism of British methods, manners and custom, and ask them to refrain from mentioning them in their letters. Also give attention to bringing about friendly relations between our enlisted men and the British. This is very important.

Criticism can do no good, it may do much harm. Let us set a record among the Allies for cooperation and show what can be done in a common cause.

I have received an invitation to spend the night at Windsor Castle and meet the King Tuesday the 1st, and so may not be able to meet you at Queenstown on arrival, but I will be there in the course of the next few days, probably on the third. Report to the Vice-Admiral, commanding, tell him that I have been placed in command of our forces in these waters, explain why I will be delayed, and tell him that you will report with me again as soon as I arrive.

I hope you will be able to shake your gang down and get on the job with as little delay as possible, and thereby make a good first impression, which counts for a good deal. To that extent, and perhaps more, you have the reputation of the service in your hands, as far as the British go. Whatever you accomplish is liable to have pretty wide circulation in their service. Paymaster Tobey,[1] who is thoroughly in touch with his end of the game over here, is going over with Evans and will assist you in arranging for supplies, repairs, etc.

I am sure your people will be intensely interested in this work. Of course you and they will understand that it will be no picnic. It will not only be hard but may prove very monotonous. Its success will be largely in keeping the subs below the surface or chasing them away from a certain area.

[1] Paymaster E. C. Tobey, US Navy, of Sims's staff.

I may be able to assign you to more interesting work later, as a change if nothing else. In the meantime I am sure I need not warn you not to allow the monotony of the present duty to cause the least relaxation of extreme vigilance upon which success in such work alone depends.

I am sending an operational order specifying the manner in which the operations of your force are to be coordinated with those of the British.

I have no doubt that, no matter how arduous the duty may prove to be, you will not only remain cheerful, but will keep all hands same.

135. *Sims to Daniels*

30 April 1917

Question of convoy system for shipping is being studied by Admiralty. Tentative plan contemplates two general rendezvous American Coast for assembly every 4 days for all ships under 15 knots speed. Similar action at Gibraltar and on other trade routes. One war vessel to act as escort against raiders, destroyers to meet convoys at war zone. Two escort ships will rest at each end about eight days. This plan would require us to furnish some escort vessels and additional vessels on this side and would necessitate abandonment of present patrol against raiders. Admiralty have not yet fully decided upon plan.

Foregoing is for Department's consideration as advance information.

136. *Admiralty Memorandum*

1 May 1917

Outline Proposals for Convoys from New York and Ports to the North including the Gulf of St Lawrence

The proposal is to form a convoy of 16 to 20 vessels every 4 days, vessels of 12 knots sea-going speed and above being excluded from the convoy. With this exclusion the volume of traffic for June is as follows:-

Canada to East Coast Ports	22
Canada to West Coast Ports	30
Canada to Havre	16

New York, Boston, Portland to East Coast	40
New York, Boston, Portland to West Coast	50
Total	158

or a daily average of approximately 5 per day.

It is proposed to assemble this North American and Canadian convoy at two ports, New York being the assembly port for Boston, Portland, etc., Louisberg or Sydney (Cape Breton) for the Gulf of St Lawrence trade.

The New York convoy to be considered the main convoy and port from which the escort ship capable of dealing with a raider will start.

The Louisberg or Cape Breton convoy to be called the subsidiary convoy, and escorted by local vessels to a rendezvous south of parallel 40 North, and between the meridians of 50 and 60 West, where they would rendezvous with the main convoy and both be escorted together by the Ocean escort vessel to a secret United Kingdom rendezvous, there to be met by 6 destroyers, who would take them into port.

It is proposed to arrange that the convoys should be alternately East and West [coasts of Britain] convoys, in which case, generally speaking, the West going convoy would enter via the North of Ireland, and the East bound convoy through the English Channel.

****

It is expected that the average speed of the convoy will be approximately 9 knots.

To institute this route every 4 days, both for vessels bound to the United Kingdom and those bound for America and Canada, 14 escort vessels will be required, as well as 18 destroyers, which it is suggested should be taken from the American vessels now at Queenstown.

137. *De Chair to Jellicoe*

2 May 1917

Six destroyers leave for Berehaven this week six next and eighteen are now being ordered to [Seattle?] to get ready to proceed as soon as possible. This will make total of 36. Two destroyer tenders *Melville* and *Dixie* sail with them one of which will act as flagship of Admiral Sims. It is hoped six trawlers will start over as soon as they can get them. French Commission much disgruntled at these concessions to us.

138.   *Admiralty to Gaunt*

3 May 1917

It is proposed if Navy Department concur and if speed of convoy is not too slow for fuel consumpton of U.S. Destroyers to assemble a convoy of not more than 16 to 20 British or Allied vessels. Convoy to assemble at Sandy Hook and to consist of vessels of under 12 knots sea-going speed from Ports of New York, Boston, Portland.

Convoy to be escorted to United Kingdom by United States Destroyers leaving for this country and definite date for assembling convoy will be wired when date of Destroyers leaving is known.

Vice-Admiral North America will order a cruiser to Sandy Hook to assist in assembly. This ship will not form part of the escort but will detail an officer to take passage in one of the Merchant Vessels and act as Commodore of convoy under the directions of Senior Naval Officer of Escort. The Senior Officer of Escort and Commander of Convoy are to be provided with G.S. Code and Memorandum C. Call sign will be allocated later.

Ask Navy Department if they will detail one signalman to each vessel in the convoy and arrange for a few simple manoeuvering signals so that convoy may be under control.

When East of Meridian of 30° West Convoy should be in 4 columns.

Cask fog buoys for night and fog station keeping should be provided. Stern lights to be shaded and to show over arc of 8 points. Bow lights dimmed. No steaming lights.

When East of meridian of 20° West ships to be darkened at night and no lights shown except when absolutely necessary. Slowest ships should lead columns.

Masters should be interviewed and carefully instructed before sailing. Convoy to be so arranged that trade for West Coast are in Northern columns, London and East Coast Trade Southern columns.

Rendezvous off British coast will be wired later and additional destroyer escort will be provided through danger zone.

It is essential to allow 2 days margin over time on passage of slowest vessels so that there will be no doubt that convoy will be at the rendezvous on the date arranged by Navy Department.

Consult Navy Department as to these arrangements and wire if they are considered feasible by Department. Captain Lionel Wells[1]

---

[1] Captain Lionel de Vere Wells: a retired officer serving at this time under the Director of Naval Equipment; later based at Norfolk, Va.

is being appointed to organise Convoys sailing from Hampton
Roads. This message is to be communicated to him.

139.   *Gaunt to Admiralty*

Washington,
5 May 1917

Navy Department [were?] very strongly against convoy scheme
and I put forward an alternative of small separate convoys not
exceeding four and accompanied by two Destroyers. They held long
conference and have handed me a Memo. making following points.
1. Navy Department fully appreciates advantage of utilising Destroyers on passage.
2. Does not consider it desirable to attempt to carry out convoy
outlined for various reasons.
3. Suggests instead as an experiment sending groups of four of equal
speed convoyed by two Destroyers.
4. Will assist Admiralty every possible way to carry out Admiralty
plan as an experiment if Admiralty so desires.
5. Halifax is suggested as a rendezvous on account of cruising
radius of Destroyers to be employed.
   They are sincerely keen to help and will undoubtedly support any
scheme to full extent of their power if Admiralty [wish?]

140.   *Sims to Bayly*

8 May 1917

****

You will, I am sure, find our officers more than willing to carry
out your orders and instructions and to cooperate with your forces
as completely as their present inexperience in this peculiar warfare
will permit.
   My aide, Lieutenant Commander Babcock,[1] reports them
enthusiastically grateful over the reception you have given them and
anxious to be of the maximum service to the common cause. As they
will doubtless make mistakes which will need correction, I hope you
will not hesitate to let me know if I can be of assistance in such
matters.

---

[1] Commander J. V. Babcock, US Navy: began war as a Lt-Cdr and assistant to
Commandant, 2nd Naval District (Newport, RI); travelled to London with Sims
March 1917 and was for several months his only assistant.

141.   *Bayly to Sims*

11 May 1917

****

[The work here is] different from what it is elsewhere. But our fellows pick it up in a very short time, and I see no reason whatever why your people should not do the same. In fact they have already shown that they can do it. I do not consider that I am in charge of two different kinds of destroyers, or that there is any reason to make a difference. We are all one here, and an order is sent out to such destroyer as is in any particular place, whether she is American or English. I have told the Captains of your destroyers, as I tell ours, that the way to prevent misunderstandings, doubts, etc., is, when they come in here to come and see me. It is an old plan of mine that I have always found useful, whether with Captains or Lieutenants in command. I am always here and my business is to help them. Should you come here, please come to Admiralty House and bring your aide. I do not entertain, but can make you comfortable.

142.   *Sims to Daniels*

8 May 1917

Berehaven now established, defended for use as an advanced base. It is suitable for our purposes against present area of main activity of submarines. Queenstown will be used for docking or dock yard repairs. The British and French agree that our destroyer force should remain concentrated upon its own supply and repair ships and if it be essential to have the mobile forces ready to follow shifting of main submarine activity, we will be given by the British any necessary supplies and assistance but their vessels for supply and repair are strained nearly to the limit. I therefore urge that our force should be as self-sustaining as possible. Both *Melville* and *Dixie* should be provided with complete stores as for extended West Indian cruise. There should also be supply ships with meat, stores and provisions to replenish repair ships. We should send in addition to usual stores carried by our repair ships such stores in supply ships as our experience indicates will be necessary, such as boiler and condenser tubes, piping, separate parts and repair material, etc. As many depth charges, as per drawing forwarded about 8 April, should be made and forwarded as soon as practicable to relieve present drain on British supply for their patrol craft and destroyers.

Oil will be supplied by small oilers from British oil stations to our destroyers' relief bases. As the oil [situation] is becoming critical we should maintain a continuous supply from our large oil tankers discharging into their main tank stations so as not to detain large tankers at advanced bases.

In as much as it is essential that our force should be not only self-sustaining but also as mobile as possible it is not necessary for us to have special equipment for our housing stores on shore.

143.   *Sims to Secretary of the Navy (Operations)*

11 May 1917

Concerning Military Situation and Arrival of 8th Destroyer Division in British Waters

1. The 8th Destroyer Division, under command of Commander J. K. Taussig, arrived Queenstown in excellent condition. They had attempted a sea speed of 15 knots, but during about half of the passage were forced to slow to 12 on account of heavy beam seas and water coming aboard. The division stopped en route for a total of ten hours for repairs to maintain condenser of *Wainwright*.[1]

2. An interesting feature in connection with their arrival is the report that their sailing appeared in Berlin newspapers about four days before they arrived, and also that a field of mines was planted immediately off entrance to Queenstown the day before their arrival. These were the first mines in the immediate vicinity of Queenstown during the previous three months.

3. The Division was met, as per previous arrangement, by British Destroyer[2] and escorted into the harbour through a swept channel.

4. In view of the historical nature of the arrival of the first American Naval Force, an official moving picture photographer was sent from the War Office General Staff, London, and photographs taken of their arrival and the reception of the officers on shore, as a matter of official record. I shall endeavour to obtain a copy of this film for the Department's official records.[3]

5. On arrival in harbour, our Destroyers commenced oiling immediately and the Commanding Officers went ashore and paid official

---

[1] USS *Wainwright*: destroyer, 1915; 1050 tons; 4 × 4in; 8tt; 29 knots.

[2] HMS *Mary Rose*. She was sunk, together with HMS *Strongbow* and 9 merchantmen of a Scandinavian convoy, on 17 October 1917 by the German cruisers *Brummer* and *Bremse*.

[3] The most famous record of the 8th Division's arrival was the painting 'Return of the *Mayflower*' by the British marine artist Bernard Gribble.

calls to Vice-Admiral Sir Lewis Bayly, Commanding British Naval Forces, the General Commanding Military Forces, and the American Consul. At the Consulate they were welcomed by the Lord Mayors of Cork and Queenstown. On the following day, the Commanding Officers returned the call of the Lord Mayor of Cork in that city.

6. I am pleased to be able to report the excellent impression given by our officers and the ships and crews under their command. Contact with British Officers made it evident that owing to their system of specialization, their officers were not as familiar as our officers, with all details of the material with which they work. This apparently results in their being much more dependent upon Navy Yard assistance. Our ships made no demands of consequence upon the Navy Yard facilities after arrival, in spite of the length of their passage under adverse conditions. The Commander of the Division, when questioned by the Vice-Admiral as to when his vessels would be ready for duty, reported that he should be ready that night, as soon as the ships were refueled. This apparently was a considerable surprise to the Vice-Admiral, who then gave them four days before taking up active work.

7. The vessels themselves caused a great deal of complimentary comment, and, contrary to expectations, were found to be well equipped for their prospective duty, with the single exception of 'depth charges'. The Dockyard authorities immediately commenced installation of the latter.

****

10. Speaking generally, the impression made by our officers and our ships has caused very favourable comment both at their base and in the Admiralty.

11. The Naval Dockyard at Queenstown had practically been abandoned for Naval purposes for some years prior to the outbreak of War. Its equipment and facilities are therefore very limited. It has a dry dock for destroyers, but Liverpool and other repair stations are within easy striking distance. The British use Berehaven as an advanced base, as it saves a round trip of approximately 150 miles to Queenstown from the destroyer operating area. This is a very important consideration for forces operating to the Westward and Southward of Ireland, not only on account of fuel saved, but also affording more time for rest by the personnel and more opportunity for overhauling. The harbour of Berehaven is defended by nets and shore fortifications and the Admiralty will keep small oilers there,

supplied with oil from the main tanks at Queenstown and other locations. All vessels, of course, periodically return to Queenstown for more extended rest and necessary dockyard repairs. A hospital ship will be placed at our disposal at Berehaven.

12. I have considered it vitally important, and in this decision am in complete agreement with both the French and British Admiralties that our destroyer forces should not only remain concentrated and operate together but, what is more important, that they should remain essentially mobile. The destroyer is by far the greatest enemy of the submarine; and I am particularly anxious that our forces should be used to the greatest possible effect in assisting in putting down the enemy submarine campaign. I am prompted in this decision not only because it is manifestly the most effective assistance which we can render at this time to the common cause, but also the secondary reason that such a course is certain to be productive of the greatest distinction for the U.S. Naval Service.

It is therefore my aim, as reported to the Department, to keep our forces, to the extreme possible degree, independent of any shore station, in order that the entire force with its mobile base can be moved at will and follow the centre of enemy submarine pressure.

13. As reported by cable dispatch, the situation remains critical owing primarily to the enemy submarine campaign. The question at issue is, and must remain, the control of our lines of communication. It is of course true that the primary naval mission should always be the destruction of the enemy's fleet, but this must not blind us to the fact that its destruction may often not be an effective form of pressure in itself, but merely a means to an end.

****

The only apparent solution to the submarine issue lies in numbers of anti-submarine craft with a view to sufficiently dispersing the enemy submarine effort so that shipping losses will be reduced below the critical point.

14. From the point of view as seen here, and not being fully aware of the Department situation, it is strongly recommended that all of our heavy naval forces, not actually operating against the enemy, be kept in the highest possible state of material repair for distant service, in order that their use, if the opportunity should occur, will not in any way be delayed.

This opportunity may offer at a comparatively early date if negotiations now under way with reference to Norway should result in the entry of that country into the war on the side of the Allies (with the neutrality of Sweden assured), and the consequent establishment of a base on the southern coast of Norway with a view to holding the straits and denying their use to German raiders and submarines, and also facilitating allied operations in the Baltic.

The undesirability, from our own point of view, in breaking up the organisation of our fleet is fully realised. It seems absolutely necessary however, not to view our forces as an entity in themselves but rather as an integral part of the combined Allied naval forces. From this point of view it would seem essential that we should be prepared to so divide and dispose our forces that they will furnish the maximum possible effect upon the actual situation as a whole.

****

144. *Lieut. R. C. Grady,*[1] *US Navy, to Sims*

American Embassy,
London,
16 May 1917

Copy of Report to Chief of Naval Operations

****

8. Most of the German submarines and especially the large ones after clearing the mine field off the German coast head directly for Fair Island between the Orkneys and the Shetland Islands and do not hesitate to pass through to the Atlantic. The British have found it wholly impracticable to net this passage. The submarines usually make a landfall at St Kilda west of the Hebrides and thence down to the vicinity of Fastnet and the Scillys. They are usually out twenty days, eight of which are required for passage to and fro. Submarines usually spend two-fifths of their time away from base. As the Admiralty believe that the Germans have 150 submarines there are sixty submarines always out. The Germans are turning out about two submarines a week.

****

---

[1] Lieut. Ronan C. Grady, US Navy: attached to Office of Naval Operations, Washington; Lieut.-Cdr., February 1918; at end of war Commander and CO, Submarine Division 5.

145. *Gaunt to Admiralty*

23 May 1917

The Scientific Commission[1] which is investigating the method of combating submarines has asked me following questions. I will be glad of as early and [?comprehensive] an answer as possible.
1. Has any method been tried of placing [?listening] devices in quantity at bottom of North Sea?
2. Has any workable magnetic detector been developed?
3. Has a mine been developed for use in large numbers which is dangerous to submarines and not to surface craft?
4. How effective are seaplanes as offensive instruments against submarines both for detection and offensive?
5. Can you [?inform] us status Bragg Scientific sound devices?
6. What is most effective method of destroying a submerged submarine once it is discovered?
7. Do Germans use non-magnetic steel in submarine construction?

146. *Sims to Daniels*

Admiralty House,
Queenstown,
26 May 1917

... this letter is to inform you that everything is proceding *most* satisfactorily. Indeed, I could not possibly have imagined anything more satisfactory as regards our relations, both personal and official, with the British naval service, both here at Queenstown and in London. The same applies to our relations with the French Ministry of Marine.

The Vice-Admiral commanding at Queenstown, Sir Lewis Bayly, is one of the wisest, ablest men of my acquaintance, as well as one of the most admirable characters, and it is a positive pleasure to serve under him. I am aware that I have his confidence. Our young commanding officers characterise him as 'hot stuff', 'the real thing', 'the finest whatever', etc., and he is open in his admiration of them and their boats and the way they are equipped and handled – also of the service they are performing.

You need have no fear that there will arise any of the differences and difficulties that are so common between allies.

[1] The Commission, headed by the inventor Thomas Alva Edison, had been set up in 1915. For a discussion of US technical contributions to anti-submarine warfare, see Hackmann, *Seek and Strike*.

147. *Bayly to Sims*

Admiralty House,
Queenstown,
30 May 1917

I have a suggestion. If I should go on leave from 18 to 23 June, would you like to run the show in my absence[?] I should like it (and you are the only man of whom I could truthfully say that), your fellows would like it, and it would have a good effect all round. If you agree go and see the First Sea Lord and we will arrange it between us without any frills. And if the Admiralty during my absence 'regret that you should have', etc., I will take the blame. If they give you a DSO keep it.

148. *Sims to Bayly*

1 June 1917

Your letter reached me yesterday evening. It was the surprise of my life. I will not attempt to express my appreciation of the honour you have done me, or my gratification for the confidence your suggestion implies.

****

Under the circumstances I shall be more than glad to act as your representative, particularly as I assume that in case of an unforeseen problem of a serious nature I can fall back on your mature experience.

So, if it can be arranged with the Admiralty, I believe, as you say, that 'our fellows would like it, and that it would have a good effect all round'.

I will take the matter up at once and let you know the result.

****

149. *Benson to Sims*

?June 1917

One of the most important future cross water operations in which our naval forces will be involved concerns the safe transportation of American troops to French soil. Every guarantee has been given the War Department that the Navy Department would do its utmost to safeguard the lives of the troops in transit under complete naval control. [Liners] will be commissioned in the Navy and used to transport troops. It is imperative that these ships should receive the utmost destroyer protection possible on the passage in and it is desirable on account of the valuable character of the ships and the difficulty of adequately replacing them if lost to guard them on the passage out. ...

150. *Sims to Benson*

13 June 1917

Convoy operations in submarine danger zone

****

6. If the greatest possible degree of safety for convoys is to be insured, it is entirely necessary that their movements should be under control of one source, and therefore as all enemy is concentrated on this side of the Atlantic, and his main effort must necessarily remain in its present zone, it follows that selection of rendezvous, routes and other directions in regard to movements of convoys should be controlled and directed from this side, that is, in the Admiralty itself. It is for this reason that the Admiralty has requested, and I strongly recommend, the immediate detail of a competent and tactful officer whose duties in the Admiralty under my general direction will be confined to those above indicated.

7. The following procedure in relation to convoys is therefore recommended:-

   (1) Early advance information regarding prospective sailing of convoys and their character.
   (2) Immediate information as soon as definite hours of sailings can be foreseen.

As soon as this information is received, and after consultation with the Admiralty, a rendezvous and route to be included in sailing orders will be selected and given. Definite information should then be given when convoy sails, as to its prospective speed and time of passing through rendezvous designated.

****

10. Ships of convoy should zigzag together from two to four points irregularly. Organised irregularity is one of the principal requirements in opposing submarine attack.

11. Escorting destroyers should be allowed the maximum independence of movement and the exercise of initiative. They should not be

held to strict formations in reference to bearings and distances from the convoy. This procedure is necessary in order that full advantage may be taken of their experience in operating against submarines and their later information in regard to enemy methods, which are continually changing.

****

14. Up to 1 April there is no evidence to indicate that any German submarine carried beam tubes, and this is one of the principal reasons why they have never attempted attacking a formation from ahead, – that is approaching from ahead and firing as they pass through the formation. With bow tubes they would be forced to use the helm before reaching the formation, with considerable danger to themselves, which they seldom if ever incur. Hence the principal arc for destroyer protection is on the bows and wings of formations.

15. The two principal requirements of formations of a considerable number of ships for defensive purposes against submarines, are:-

(1) Minimum depth of formation, – that is minimum length of formation in the direction of course. This in order to reduce the arcs on the bows and beams, which must be protected by destroyers.

(2) The second consideration is to concentrate the formation as much as possible, – that is, it is also necessary to reduce the dimension of the formation at right angles to the course.

This not only reduces the range of visibility of the force, but it also restricts the advantageous positions of attack which the submarine desires to attain.

It is for the above reasons that line of divisions formation is generally adopted, with the distance between columns as small as consistent with zigzagging evolutions.

151. *Sims to Benson*

14 June 1917

Total losses week ending 12 June 193,975 tons. Pressure during latter part of week greatly increased, and estimated number of submarines now operating corresponds to greatest number during worst fortnight in April. Twenty-four submarines are known to be operating round United Kingdom the majority of which left their bases in comparatively short time which is new practice. Irregularity of enemy operations prevents accurate estimations of his plans. Principal area of activity still remains on Atlantic approach routes to south westward of Ireland and England. Five or six apparently working in White Sea and one or more to West of Gibraltar and a large number in addition operating in Mediterranean. Forty-three encounters with submarines during week ... Minelaying about average concentrated south-east and west coasts British Islands. Ten ships lost in one day. Defeat of campaign can only be effected by increasing number of anti-submarine craft immediately. If safety of oil and other valuable and urgently needed supplies for Allied Forces is to be insured greatly increased numbers of anti-submarine craft are necessary.

152.   *Sims to Benson*

14 June 1917

General situation and prospects for immediate future very grave. ...

... Whatever is done to meet the situation must be done immediately. British are in process of changing from previous methods of handling shipping to the convoy system. The first convoy from Hampton Roads has arrived safely, two more are en route and convoys from Gibraltar and across the North Sea have proved successful. Every indication points to the desirability of adopting the convoy system for all traffic and particularly from our North Atlantic ports, ... I cannot lay too much stress upon the urgent necessity of increasing the destroyer and other patrol forces here with utmost dispatch. Cannot other craft be sent also [?] Anything armed which can make above twelve knots and keep the sea will relieve the situation. Our shipping and our coast is better protected in the field of enemy activity than in any other place. It is doubtful if the enemy will send any submarines on our coast, but it is a certainty that if they do it can only be a movement of diversion calculated to influence us in withholding our forces from critical area. Submarines cannot work efficiently or in numbers for any length of time on our coast. In any case the submarine campaign can never be effective if not concentrated at the focus of all lines of communication. ... The Admiralty informs me that the present prospect is that if oil supplies are protected food supplies cannot be. I again urgently recommend that all destroyers that can be brought to the Coast of Ireland be sent at once.

153.   *Sims to Daniels*

16 June 1917

****

I strongly urge that we put convoy system into effect from Philadelphia, Boston, New York, and North Atlantic Ports as previously recommended, immediately. British propose assembling Canadian Convoy to join ours. This convoy system is looked upon as an offensive measure, as at present our machinery is being strained and fuel expended in looking for an enemy whose primary object has always been to attack merchant shipping and avoid action. Similarly we are necessarily enforced to combine escort duty with independent offensive operations, escorting such individual ships as the situation permits, combined with our limited number of vessels. If shipping were grouped in convoys the enemy would be forced to seek us, thereby imposing upon him the necessity of dispersing his forces, [so] as to locate us, while on the other hand, we obtain the benefit of the principle of concentrated attack on his dispersed line. Even if a few ships were sunk, a study of the convoy system shows that our losses would not be so great as at present. Among the marked difficulties of the enemy are his distance from bases and limited offensive power and ammunition. It is manifest that the enemy cannot afford to expend much effort against our antisubmarine craft. All our experience shows that the reason the submarines have not attempted to attack in number is due to the difficulty of coordination and the danger to themselves. Such attacks, if defunct, would facilitate the defensive operations of escorting destroyers. If diverted from attacks on shipping the whole objective of the enemy campaign is lost. Request that the Department consult the British Commodore in charge of assembling convoys at Hampton Roads. If the proposed plan is to be adopted at all it is absolutely necessary that it be put into force immediately and without delay while the campaign is most severe. I request information as to the Department's action. ...

154. *Daniels to Sims*

20 June 1917

There will be no additional movements before August of troops. You will be furnished fully with information as to sailing of Army Supply ships as far as possible in advance and the actual sailing intended route and probable dates of arrival will be reported. We hope to sail four Army supply ships now fitting out in about ten days' time. The 32 destroyers which are all that there are available have sailed. 110 feet [submarine] chasers which are to be sent to France should begin to deliver in August. Fishing vessels twelve in number will sail in August for France. There are no other small craft available at present though work on yachts is being pushed probably ready 15 July. In regard to convoy I consider that American vessels having armed guards are safer when sailing independently.

155. *Daniels to Sims*

24 June 1917

****

... the Department recognises ... the necessity of sending all anti-submarine craft which can be spared from the home waters into active European waters, and when such craft become available will send them. In making the local assignments abroad of such forces, the Department requests and will be guided by your advice, which should be given after consultation with the various Admiralties concerned as to priority of requirements.

The Department is strongly of the opinion – based on recent experience – that the question of supplying adequate guns and trained gun crews to merchant ships is one which can – in no wise – be treated as a minor issue. Coupled with a rigid system of inspection, this method is believed to constitute one of the most effective defensive submarine measures.

It announces, moreover, as its policy its willingness to co-operate in every way, and will consider the question of supplying additional naval forces of types other than anti-submarine craft, when the advisability of doing so is justified. The Department is also considering the outline of a scheme which it is hoped will allow of a greater degree of cooperation and ability to supply escort to vessels through the danger zone, without interfering with the destroyers' other duties as much as does the present system of individual escort, and it will not displace the present method of handling merchant shipping from U.S. Ports. Details when [available] will be cabled.

In the matter of construction, the Department recognises the necessity of pushing to the utmost the type of destroyer of the general specifications recommended by you, and this it will do.

156.   *Sims to Daniels*

Queenstown,
28 June 1917

Referring to Department's opinion, reported in last two cables, to the effect that adequate armament and trained crews constitute one of the most effective defensive anti-submarine measures, I again submit with all possible stress, the following based on extended British war experience. The measures demanded if enemy defeat in time is to be assured, are not defensive but offensive–defensive. The merchantman's inherent weakness is a lack of speed and protection. Guns are no defense against torpedo attack, without warning, which is necessarily the enemy method of attack against armed ships. In this area alone, during the last six weeks, thirty armed ships were sunk by torpedoes without submarine being seen, although three of these were escorted each by a single destroyer. The result would have been of course the same no matter how many guns these ships carried or what their calibre. Three mystery ships, heavily armed, manned by expert naval crews, with much previous experience with submarine attack, have recently been torpedoed without warning. Another case within the month of mystery ship engaging submarine with gunfire at six thousand yards, but submarine submerged and approached unseen and torpedoed ship at close range. The ineffectiveness of heaviest batteries against submarine attack, is conclusively shown by Admiralty's practice [of] always sending destroyers to escort their men-of-war. The comparative immunity of the relatively small number [of] American ships, especially liners, is believed here to be due to the enemy hopes that the pacifist movement will succeed. Cases are on record of submarines making successful gun attacks, from advantageous sun position, against armed ships without ship being able to see submarine. I submit that if submarine campaign is to be defeated, it must be by offensive measures. The enemy submarine mission must be [one] of destruction of shipping and avoidance of anti-submarine craft. Enemy submarines are now using, for their final approach, an auxiliary periscope less than two inches in diameter. This information just acquired. All of the experience in this submarine campaign to date demonstrates that it would be a seriously dangerous misapprehension to base our action on the assumption that any armament on merchantmen is any protection against submarines which are willing to use their torpedoes. The British have now definitely decided the adoption, to the maximum possible extent, [of] convoys from sixteen to twenty ships. This is an offensive measure against submarines, as the latter will be subject to the attack of our anti-submarine craft whenever they come within torpedoing distance of convoyed merchantmen. Moreover it permits of concentrated attack by our forces, and obliges the enemy to disperse his forces to cover the various routes of approach.

Concerning the Department's reference to a scheme for protection of merchant shipping, which will not interfere with present escort duties, I submit that the time element alone prevents utilization of any new anti-submarine invention. The campaign may easily be lost before any such schemes can come into effective operation. The enemy is certainly counting on maximum effort being exerted before long nights and bad weather of autumn, that is, in next three months. Heaviest effort may be anticipated in July and August. I again submit that protection of our coast lines and of allied shipping must necessarily be carried out in field of enemy activity if it is to be effective. The mission of the allies must be to force submarines to give battle. Hence no operations in home waters should take precedence over, or be allowed to diminish, the maximum effort we can exert in area in which enemy is operating, and must continue to operate to succeed.

157.   *Jellicoe to Gaunt*

30 June 1917

Am informed idea is prevalent in United States that good look out combined with gun armament is adequate defence against submerged submarine.

Following instance coming under my own observation is best disproof of theory.

I had all submarine look out men of 6 ships of 4th Light Cruiser Squadron on board flagship of squadron steaming across Scapa Flow at high speed with submarine ordered to attack. She was torpedoed four times running without a periscope being seen on any single occasion.

Make use of this information with Admiral Benson.

158. Sims to Daniels

28 June 1917

Protection of all Allied shipping in time – I repeat in time – is present mission. Whatever efforts we can exert must be put into operation at once if they are to be effective. Reliable submarines would be of great use to strengthen British submarine patrols, and also as scouts ahead of convoys. All submarines we send to Irish Coast in time will therefore be invaluable in insuring success of convoy system, and hence success of war, provided these submarines are supplied from America and based upon their own mother ships.

159. Jellicoe to Gaunt

29 June 1917

I am convinced convoy system is a necessity and only method left to us. Absence of cruisers and destroyers prevented earlier adoption and still presents great difficulties unless we can rely on help from U.S.A. in both classes of vessel. System of partial convoy combined with system of partial patrols is very bad but unavoidable until complete convoy system introduced. Complete convoy system for all but very fast and very slow vessels is necessary and even these should be included in system when number of vessels permits. This system however requires about 50 cruisers and 80 destroyers permanently earmarked for the work. Cruisers absolutely necessary to keep convoy together up to rendezvous, practice them zig-zagging and maintain W/T communication with us so as to ensure destroyers meeting convoy. We cannot start complete convoy system from even North America ports unless U.S.A. can guarantee 7 cruisers for weekly New York convoy and constant use of 11 destroyers this end from the U.S. force now at Queenstown. To include ships from South American ports in system would necessitate guarantee of a second batch of 11 USA destroyers this end. If Admiral Benson could undertake convoy from New York both as regards cruisers and the eleven destroyers at this end I should be most grateful and this would greatly relieve situation. Convoys would be organized at once on hearing of his consent.

160. *Gaunt to Jellicoe*

1 July 1917

Have just discussed your and Sims's cables of last three days with Admiral Benson. He is still opposed to convoys and strongly in favour of armed merchant vessels despite Admiralty's 154 of 28 June. He, however, is prepared to do anything he possibly can. He has [?] given orders to send 5 destroyers from China to Admiral Sims's flag. They are small vessels and will probably take a long time. He sent out orders to try and send 5 submarines to operate in Mediterranean but says, and United States submarine Admiral agreed with him, that these vessels are so bad that he doubts even their being able to leave coast of United States.[1] Admiral Benson is undoubted[ly] influenced by Naval Attachés who play their country individually and not for Allies. I think they consider their own personal credit first. For instance, when talking of small craft this morning he said Prince Udine[2] had just been in and complained there was no protection on south of Spain and Admiral Benson had a fixed idea that he should send there small craft which I considered suitable for Atlantic. The French promised to safeguard the *Neptune*[3] yet she has been delayed in French port and only just has sailed with American escort. The French Naval Attaché[4] apparently hinted that, as everything was going to us, and nothing to France it was difficult to carry out their promises above all things under Admiral Sims who was equally in London and Paris and would delegate their station. Captain Pratt has temporarily taken Chief of Staff post. He is a strong man and I should think most capable. After leaving Admiral Benson I talked practically the whole of [morning?] privately with him and he entirely agreed. When I left him he decided to put forward:

(a) some of destroyers in Canal Zone could be spared

(b) some of larger tugs in Canal Zone could be spared for sea duty releasing big tugs. The *Des Moines, Sacramento* class of cruiser might be sent over (I urged this but I should like your opinion, he thought they were too slow).[5] ...

---

[1] On destroyers from Manila, see Part VII. On US submarines, see note 2 on p. 32.

[2] Prince Udine was Italian Naval Attaché in Washington.

[3] USS *Neptune*: collier, 1911; 19480 tons; coal capacity 10500 tons; 4 × 4in; 13 knots.

[4] Commander Blanpre.

[5] USS *Des Moines* class: light cruisers, 1901–03; 3200 tons; 8 × 5in; 16.5 knots. USS *Sacramento*: gunboat, 1914; 1425 tons; 3 × 4in; 12.8 knots.

The first 12 destroyers will not be ready before [?] 1 August. Under requisitioning bill just passed we made out there were 30 yachts [corrupt group] available and Captain Pratt was putting this forward at once. When quarrel between Shipping Board and Navy Dept is adjusted Admiral Benson hopes to employ heavily armed merchant vessels as transport escort thereby relieving cruisers.

161.   Gaunt to Jellicoe

3 July 1917

Ships mentioned have sufficient radius.[1] There is decided change at Navy Department this morning. CONFIDENTIAL, I saw the subject for discussion by Navy [General] Board today and hope to telegraph that there will be considerable speeding up during course of week. I suggested more Destroyers might leave before their reliefs came from Panama and Captain Pratt promised to try and do it. Pratt and I discussed Admiral Sims's request for him on that side. I am sure he is more valuable here and he says himself he can do better work for Admiral Sims where he is. Are 110-foot chasers of any use?

162.   Jellicoe to Gaunt

4 July 1917

Consider *Des Moines* class sufficiently fast for convoy of vessels of less speed than twelve knots.
110-foot chasers would certainly be of use.

163.   Sims to Daniels

c. 3 July 1917

With reference to the convoy system.[2] Modification of the convoy system, and Admiralty suggestion thereto, has been fully discussed. The disadvantages of the Department's proposals which have already been the subject of partial trial and considerable previous study are as follows:
1. It is almost an impossibility and causes great difficulty to

[1] *Des Moines* and *Sacramento*.
[2] On 2 July, Daniels had informed Sims of the despatch of 5 destroyers from Manila and promised 7 US cruisers for convoy escort. He had suggested modifications to the convoy system which would have given the US much more control. Daniels to Sims, 2 July 1917, UP file, Navy Subject File, National Archives, Washington, DC.

assemble merchant convoys on the high seas at a distant rendezvous. When convoys are operating on a decided schedule, and have even been assembled for departure, their arrival at one time is very doubtful, and a forecast cannot be made within from thirty to forty hours.

2. In assembling convoys there is necessity for an excessive amount of wireless communication on the high seas. This is a vital objection.

3. Where convoys in formation have had no previous drill experience there is difficulty in handling them. It is most necessary that the escorting cruiser, besides its principal duty as a protection against raiders, should act as convoy flagship, exercising them in zig-zagging, and all evolutions that may become necessary if attacked, from the day of sailing. It is unsafe to use all merchant wireless codes. Escorting cruisers should therefore send in the most recent secret code all communications, and the wireless should not be used by merchant ships at all.

Before the escorting destroyers join, it is desirable to divert convoys if necessary. This is now done by broadcasting Poldhu[1] on high power to cruisers, to which no reply is given, and in fact even beyond four convoys, aggregating 350,000 tons. Loading and grouping of convoys is now being effected according to their destination at European ports, for instance, where cargoes are bound for Eastern British ports, they are grouped in one convoy. Cargoes from Baltimore and Philadelphia, Chile and Panama Gulf are included in convoys from Hampton Roads. One convoy a week now starts from Cape Breton Island, Canada, and two a week from Hampton Roads. At this stage of development of the convoy system, and in view of all the available information here, I am strongly of opinion that we should for some time at least, co-operate to the maximum extent of our resources. Would it be possible for cruisers escorting convoys to leave them outside the submarine zone and return to their base without refuelling? Plans for the future as regards outgoing ships are to escort them until clear of submarine zone, and after that to disperse them. The presence of cruisers with convoys should be avoided in the submarine zone.[2] Immediate information is desired by the Admiralty as to whether the first New York convoy can be started by 8 July. In connection with convoy duties I

[1] Poldhu, Cornwall was an Admiralty long-range radio station.

[2] In October 1917, HMS *Drake*, a cruiser, and HMSs *Bostonian* and *Orama*, armed merchant cruisers, were lost in the submarine zone during or just after convoying merchantmen to British waters. On 1 March 1918, another AMC, HMS *Calgarian*, was sunk in the same area. See H. Newbolt, *History of the Great War, Naval Operations*, vol. 5 (London: Longmans Green, 1931), pp. 162–3, 227.

urgently recommend that a carefully selected commander may be sent me immediately for duty at the British Admiralty. If Captain Pratt can be sent as Chief of Staff, the Admiralty particularly desires this.

Please inform me if Captain Twining is available.[1]

164.   *Sims to Pratt*

3 July 1917

****

It would be very funny, if it were not so tragic, the spectacle of many dozens of ships, destroyers, yachts and so forth parading up and down the American Coast three thousand miles away from where the vital battle of the war is going on. How is it that they cannot see that this is as wrong as it possibly can be from a military point of view. In other words, why does not America send her forces *to the front* instead of keeping them three thousand miles in the rear? If there were any danger on our coast, or if dangers should develop later, you could send the forces back again, or such as were needed, before any considerable number of the enemy could get over there.

If you have been reading my recent cables you will realize, that at least I believe, that this situation over here is a very dangerous one. To understand this you need only to be in possession of some very simple arithmetical facts. They are as follows:- The Allies are losing about 500,000 tons of shipping a month. The building capacity of the available yards within the next year are not more than 130,000 tons a month. This means that when the available shipping is reduced below the amount of tonnage that will land a certain amount of freight in England and France the war will be lost. The necessities are about 32,000,000 tons of imports a year. It requires a certain amount of tonnage to accomplish this. When it falls below it, it will be wholly impossible to maintain this population and to maintain the armies in the Front. It would be impossible to import the wholly essential ore that is necessary for munitions and to export the tremendous quantities of coal that are required for both France and Italy. In order to find out how soon the pinch will come all you have to do is to make the arithmetical calculation as to when the available shipping will be reduced to the point indicated. I have seen a study of this made out by the appropriate department of the

---

[1] Captain Twining, at that time in the USA, was to become Sims's Chief of Staff.

British Government and it shows that the pinch will come in December if a certain rate of destruction is assumed, something like 300,000 tons a month, and by September if a certain greater rate of destruction is assumed, a little over 400,000 tons a month.

These incontrovertible facts show what I mean when I state in my messages that the situation is very critical. The truth about the matter is that the enemy is *winning the war*, and all of the help that we will be able to give in the way of increased shipping facilities, money and so forth, a year or even six months from now, will be of no value. When the pinch comes on the Western Front, it would be impossible to provide reinforcements because you cannot feed them, and the end will then be very near. This opinion is founded upon absolutely reliable information, and it is held by all the responsible British officials that I know. ...

****

There is only one way in which disaster can be avoided, and that is by diminishing the effectiveness of the campaign which is necessarily influencing all others, that is to say, the submarine campaign. God knows I have said everything which I could say in official communications on this subject – so has the American Ambassador. I therefore went to him the other day and told him that in my opinion our statements, which cannot be successfully disputed, should be verified *directly* by the *British Government*. He agreed that this was so, and therefore took me to call upon Mr Balfour. I explained the whole situation to him and he agreed with me that an acknowledgement of the seriousness of the situation should be made by their Government. He therefore requested me to go to Admiral Jellicoe and between us draw up the despatch which we would suggest that he send. We did so and it was sent practically in the same words. I assume that this will be brought to the attention of the Navy Department. You will note, of course, that the language of the despatch is not as energetic as I have been sending in. The reason [for] this is the fear that it might leak out and do damage. But you can read between the lines and see that it is a very strong statement and very frank acknowledgment of the necessity for help sent by one great Government to another.

There is one thing that I would like you to understand and that is the embarrassment and the delay which is caused by the insistence of our people on the other side trying to advise these people over here in the *direct lines in which they have had the most experience*. My last letter, concerning the convoy business, indicates what I mean.[1] ...

A most flagrant example of this was the astonishing statement received from the other side to the effect that the best protection of the merchant ships was a thoroughly trained and efficient gun crew. ...

I do not know, but I suspect that this estimate of the situation has been the cause of holding up the introduction of the convoy system, particularly from New York. If this is true it has cost the Allies some hundreds of thousands of tons of shipping, assuming that the convoy system is going to prove effective. That it will probably prove effective, at least against the present tactics of the submarines, seems to be sufficiently proven by the fact that it has been successful up to date. I have been devoted to this convoy system since the first week I got here in London. I have been putting it up to our Navy Department as strongly as I know how and supported it with all the arguments that there were, and not until yesterday was there any reply on the subject. I leave you to imagine what sort of a position this places me in and how seriously it affects my relations with the people over here. I am happy to say that our government has now expressed its willingness to help out with the convoy. I really believe that this will have the desired effect on the submarine campaign, that is, that it will at least reduce the losses well below the rate of building.

But in order to put this generally into operation, it will be absolutely necessary to have more anti-submarine craft both for the purposes of handling the large convoys in question as well as for the purpose of convoying specially valuable cargo ships, that make over 12 knots, through the dangerous part of the submarine zone. This is why I have been so insistent that America should get a move on. ...

165.   *Gaunt to Jellicoe*

5 July 1917

Your 183,[2] following scheme is not signed yet but will undoubtedly get through. Eight cruisers of U.S. *Des Moines* and U.S. *Albany*[3] Class have 4500 miles [radius] at 10 knots to be ready for convoy duty. Six practically ready now, three of these to be available

---

[1] No. 163.

[2] See No. 157 and subsequent Jellicoe–Gaunt communications.

[3] USS *Albany*: light cruiser, 1900; 3430 tons; 8 × 5 in; 20 knots.

to leave New York 8 July and seventh ready 10 July, eighth will be about 30 days. Sincerely hope Sims will leave Captain Pratt in present post, he is excellent and fully alive to the urgency of speed.

166. *Bayly to Sims*

6 July 1917

As regards convoy; if all our merchant ships had W/T, a gun, and at least 12 knots: and if we had enough Destroyers to patrol from Tuskar to 16° West constantly, leaving enough at sea to spare so that all valuable ships could be escorted in addition to patrols, then I am against convoys: and I would have a line of shipping, of which the line itself was continually patrolled, and in which every valuable ship would be escorted; and where the line could be shifted every four or five days or on any exceptional pressure by W/T. But allowing for the number of German submarines and the number of our merchant ships, and remembering that many of the latter are very slow though carrying valuable cargoes, and seeing that the number of destroyers must be limited, I am reluctantly compelled to allow that the present situation calls for convoy. But it will require very careful handling, for though a well worked, well escorted convoy is the best thing at present; so a badly escorted convoy will be the worst.

As soon as the Germans are awake to the fact that we are using convoys along this track, they will work their submarines in pairs or threes and I shall counter by asking to be allowed to accompany our convoys with our own submarines, between 17° and 11° West. ...

Don't forget that this is your real home from home; your stick is always in the hall.

167. *Daniels to Sims*

7 July 1917

Is it not practicable to thoroughly patrol a single lane through the danger zone, by having sufficient number of anti-submarine vessels constantly passing back and forth, thus guarding a constant stream of vessels through the lane[?]

168. *Sims to Daniels*

11 July 1917

The plan has been fully considered in the past by the British Admiralty, but not adopted for primary reason that the number of patrol craft available have been, and will continue to be, inadequate. Another vital objection is that no matter how much, or how often the lane can be shifted, its western end would always be clearly defined. Submarines have operated to a maximum distance from Ireland of four hundred miles, and sinkings are frequent up to two hundred miles. Even if the submarines did not attempt to attack through the patrol line [itself], it could always attack to the westward, and the patrol line would afford excellent information as to the proper areas for attack. As experience shows that a vessel, even when zig-zagging and accompanied by a single zig-zagging destroyer close ahead, is not always immune to attack, it is apparent that, unless such a proposed patrol line was very dense, the submarine could undoubtedly attack successfully at any point along it. As more than one lane would have to be established, and as at least one third of all patrol craft would always be resting, refuelling or repairing, it seems manifest that the number of ships required for such a plan would never be available.

169. *Sims to Daniels*

8 July 1917

Replying Department's cablegrams received 4 July my despatches and letters have covered plans of operations in force or under consideration. To date the only assistance which we could effectively offer has been in anti-submarine campaign particularly patrol craft and in connection with convoy system. Have forwarded today complete exposition of British naval policy. Determined efforts are being made by Grand Fleet destroyers and submarines to intercept enemy submarines to North of Scotland. Every effort now being concentrated towards insuring success of Merchant Convoys. I recommend that all coal burning dreadnoughts be kept in readiness for distant service in case future developments should render their juncture with Grand Fleet advisable. Shortage of oil and difficulty of protecting

lines of communication would prohibit use of oil burning heavy
ships at present. Anti-submarine patrol craft are needed in vicinity
of Gibraltar, in French coastal waters, in North Sea and in all areas.
They will be particularly necessary as convoy system gradually
comes into force. Recommend *Birmingham, Chester,* and *Salem*
joint Grand Fleet Light Cruiser Squadron now. In consideration of
sea keeping qualities of *Sacramento, Yankton, Machias, Castine,
Paducah, Wheeling, Marietta* recommend they be based on Gibraltar for assisting in escorting convoys clear of the coast. They will
also release some British Destroyers from that area for convoy duty.
In general however I recommend that the majority of our available
forces should be concentrated in area of maximum enemy activity,
that is on approach routes to Channel and Irish Sea. The majority of
the shipping essential to Allied success must use these vital
approaches and hence the enemy submarine campaign will probably
be won or lost in those areas. Effort exerted in those areas is
therefore best assistance which can be afforded to all Allies. It is true
that there is an urgent need for Patrol Craft on French Coast, in
Mediterranean and in all areas but the most important routes of
supplies to Allied Forces must be selected for maximum protection.
Our forces are now well established based at Queenstown with
Berehaven as advanced base. This area is closest to our coast and
hence easiest reached by our supply ships. Revenue cutters and tugs
would be of extreme value on patrol duty in this area and in reinforcing merchant convoy protection. They would also be invaluable for
salvage work. Next to destroyers consider revenue cutters and tugs
most useful anti-submarine craft which could be sent particularly
when bad weather and winter comes on. Cannot following destroyers come immediately: *Worden, MacDonough, Terry, McCall,
Balch, Duncan, Aywin, Downes, Jouett, Beale, Henley, Monaghan*[1]
and all west coast destroyers. Also all torpedo boats under tow of
fleet or other tugs and revenue cutters. If above forces can be sent in
time there is every reason to believe that convoy system can be
sufficiently extended to defeat submarine campaign. Recommend
that coal burning destroyers of *Preston* type join Queenstown forces
instead of basing on Azores.[2] Coal can be supplied here. As
number of coal burning ships increases however would recommend

[1] USS *Monaghan, Terry, Beale, Henley, Jouett, McCall*: destroyers, 1910–12; 742
tons; 5 × 3 in; 6 tt; 30 knots. USS *Aylwin, Duncan, Balch, Downes*: destroyers, 1913;
1036 tons; 4 × 4in; 8 tt; 29 knots. USS *Worden*: destroyer, 1902; 433 tons; 2 × 3in; 4
× 18in tt; 28 knots. USS *MacDonough*: destroyer, 1900; 400 tons; 7 × 6pdr; 2 tt; 28
knots.
[2] USS *Preston* class: destroyers, 1909; 700 tons; 5 × 3in; 6 tt; 28 knots.

periodical trips by our fleet colliers. Oil is however the critical feature and should be sent in maximum possible quantities. All such forces sent should base on Queenstown with Berehaven as advance base. All ships sent should be equipped with depth charges similar to latest British design and all with liferafts.

170.   *Jellicoe to Sims*

11 July 1917

I am very much disturbed about the convoy question. As you know, we are making great efforts to get it going, but it is quite impossible to organise the system unless we know absolutely what vessels are available as escorts through the submarine zone, and we cannot know this unless the whole system of sailings from ports abroad to British and French waters is organised some way ahead, and, by some way ahead, I mean that we should know at least a fortnight before ships requiring escort leave ports on the other side, the reason being that convoys have to be arranged about three weeks ahead.

At the present time we have arranged four distinct convoys, namely, two from Hampton Roads every 8 days, one from Canadian waters every 8 days and one from New York every eight days.

The first three of these convoys are escorted through the submarine zone by British sloops or destroyers, but we are absolutely dependent upon U.S. destroyers for the convoy coming from New York. Therefore, we must be certain of having 11 U.S. Destroyers for this sole duty. Do you think you can guarantee that we shall have these destroyers, and that you can inform your Government that you have given the guarantee [?]

The next step that will be necessary will be to make it perfectly clear to the U.S. Navy Board that they must give a fortnight's notice before it is proposed to sail ships requiring escort in anything but the smallest numbers. We have, for instance, been informed within the last few days of troops being sent over in two White Star liners, of a hospital unit coming over in another vessel and of 4 ships with valuable Government cargoes – all requiring escort; and we received the notice as the ships were sailing. As it happens we also have troop convoys arriving at about the same time, and there will be the very greatest difficulty, I am sure, in providing adequate escorts for all these vessels, whereas, if a little notice were given, we could suggest the possibility of deferring the sailing of some of the ships, perhaps for a few days, so that escorts would be available when they arrived.

I think the matter is so important that I would suggest to you the desirability of wiring at once to say that it is essential that you should be given notice immediately of any proposed sailings within the next fortnight. Otherwise, I fear that we may be faced with great difficulties. If we know that we are pretty clear for about a fortnight, we should be able to decide definitely whether the 4 destroyers could be taken for the service which I mentioned to you this morning.

171.   Sims to Lieut-Cdr C. C. Belknap, U.S. Navy[1]

11 July 1917

****

I am sorry that so much emphasis has been put on building 110 foot boats. These are not able to keep the sea if there is any weather on and it would be much better to expend our energies on boats which would be really useful in these waters.

172.   Bayly to Sims

16 July 1917

In view of the closeness together with which Captain Pringle and I must work; of the necessity of our relative positions being understood; and of his knowing exactly where he stands; I strongly suggest that he be put on my staff.[2] It will help him and help me, and will strengthen the bonds that hold us all together. Of course Captain Pringle would remain in command of *Melville*.

P.S. I will be grateful if you will show this letter to Jellicoe.

173.   Gaunt to Jellicoe

20 July 1917

A.   Suggest some [idea?] be given of where the Torpedo Boat Destroyers from Manila are to be based. They have only small radius and Gibraltar is suggested here. B.   The coal and oil fuel burning Destroyers temporarily despatched to the Azores are to have *Panther*[3] as Mother Ship. The idea is that they will be on the line of communication [when?] American troops go over. Privately, there is a good deal of feeling at the French failing to properly convoy

---

[1] Lt-Cdr Charles C. Belknap, US Navy: Office of Naval Operations; later a Commander, serving aboard USS *North Carolina*.

[2] This was done. In effect, Pringle became Bayly's Chief of Staff.

[3] USS *Panther*: depot ship, 1889; 3 380 tons; 4 × 3in; 13.5 knots.

vessels on their coasts. There are a number of complaints in the Navy Department on [the] subject, and it thought these destroyers having a radius of 2000 miles, may help to fill the gap. C. The strikes in New York are delaying other small craft, such as Yachts and Trawlers. D. I have tried [to obtain] two German ships as Minelayers. The difficulty is not with the Navy, and I suggest the only way of getting them, if it were urged strongly through [diplomatic?] channels, that these ships would be more valuable as minelayers than for carrying supplies, the Navy would support it, and it would carry weight with the civilian board who are blocking it. E. It is again suggested how valuable gunnery and torpedo Officers would be attached to this office, and lent as necessary to the United States, provided that they have come from the Grand Fleet and have acquired War experience.

174.   *Jellicoe to Gaunt*

22 July 1917

A and B. Admiral Sims and I both think that the Torpedo Boat Destroyers from Manila would be best based at present on Gibraltar. We think that those sent to the Azores would be better at Brest, where they would lie in a safe harbour and would have dockyard facilities and whence they could be sent out to meet United States transports carrying troops. D. I understand matter is now in train. E is somewhat dependent upon the decision as to whether a strong body of officers will be sent to work at the Admiralty and it depends also on the possibility of being able to supply the officers required to the United States. Our shortage of officers is now exceedingly serious.

175.   *Orders to a Convoy Escort Group*

Admiral's Office,
Queenstown,
25 July 1917

US Ships *Wadsworth* (a), *Jacob Jones* (b), *Wainwright* (b), *McDougall* (b), *Shaw* (b), *Ericsson* (b), *Trippe* (a), *Walke* (a) are detailed to escort a mercantile convoy in accordance with Admiralty letter M.09119/17 of 18 July 1917, an extract from which is herewith [attached]. They will sail in accordance with orders to be issued by Commander Taussig of USS *Wadsworth*.

Those marked (a) are at Queenstown, those marked (b) are at Berehaven.

2. HMS *Adventure*[1] is due to leave Queenstown on 25 July to relieve USS *Albany* and will escort the convoy until destroyer escort is met, when she has orders to return to Queenstown.

3. The rescue tugs *Paladin II* (from Queenstown) and *Flying Foam* (from Berehaven) will, if weather permits, be ordered to meet the convoy in Lat.50° 4′ N., Long.9° 35′ W. at 4.0 a.m. (GMT) on Monday, 30 July. When the convoy separates, *Paladin II* is to accompany ships for the West Coast ports as far as the Smalls and then return to Queenstown; *Flying Foam* is to accompany the East Coast convoy as far as the Lizard and then return to Berehaven.

Wadsworth will be furnished with a copy of orders given to the tugs.

4. The Commander of *Wadsworth* is to communicate to the Commodore of the convoy (in SS *Tennyson*) the changes in ports of destination notified in Paragraph 3 of the Admiralty letter, and is to arrange also for each ship concerned to be informed by one of the escorting destroyers.

5. When the convoy separates (see Paragraph 7 of the Admiralty letter), *Jacob Jones* and *Ericsson* are to escort the oiler *Norman Bridge* to Queenstown. The six other destroyers are to escort the West Coast convoy as far as the Smalls.

****

(Enclosure)

Extract from Admiralty Letter M.09119/17 of 18 July 1917

1. USS *Albany* escorting a convoy of 19 vessels left New York on 14 July and is due at the Destroyer Rendezvous Latitude 48° 36′ North, Longitude 15° 37′ West, on Saturday, 28 July at 10.0 p.m. (GMT), estimated speed 8½ knots, where they should be met by 8 destroyers of the U.S. Flotilla. The orders for the Convoy are, to pass through position Latitude 47° 00′ North, Longitude 22° 00′ West, and steer for position Latitude 51° 10′ North, Longitude 5° 00′ West.

****

7. When the track of the Convoy crosses the Meridian of 8° 00′ W.

---

[1] HMS *Adventure*; cruiser, 1904; 2670 tons; 2 × 6in; 6 × 4in; 2 tt; 25.5 knots. USS *Wadsworth* class: destroyers, 1915; 1050 tons; 4 × 4in; 8 tt; 29 knots: *Jacob Jones* torpedoed in English Channel, 6 December 1917.

the Convoy is to be met by four Destroyers of the Fourth Flotilla who will take over and escort the 5 vessels bound for the [English] Channel. Six of the U.S. Destroyers are to escort the 13 vessels for West Coast Ports; the remaining two U.S. Destroyers are to escort the Admiralty oiler *Norman Bridge* to Queenstown.

8. The West Coast Convoy should steer for the Smalls and, provided there is no submarine activity in the Irish Sea or Bristol Channel, the ships for Avonmouth should be detached on making the South Wales Coast, the remaining ships being dispersed on reaching the Smalls, the latest routes in force being transmitted to them by the Escort. In the event of submarine activitiy in the Irish Sea, the West Coast Convoy is to be escorted to Dale Roads, the necessary orders being issued by the Vice-Admiral at Milford Haven.

The Vice-Admiral, Milford, is to arrange escort of 2 'P' boats[1] to escort Admiralty oiler *Astrakhan* to the Clyde.

The safe navigation of the West Coast Convoy remains in the hands of the Commodore of the convoy until it is finally dispersed.

176.   *Daniels to Sims*

28 July 1917

The paramount duty of the destroyers in European waters is principally the proper protection of the transports with American troops. Be certain to detail an adequate convoy of destroyers and in making the detail bear in mind always that everything is secondary to having a sufficient number to ensure protection to American troops.

177.   *Sims to Benson*

30 July 1917

Naval and Military Conferences at Paris, 24 to 27 July

At the request of the French and British Admiralties, I attended certain naval and military conferences in Paris between 24 and 27 July.

****

A general discussion followed concerning various questions in

---

[1] 'P' boats: war emergency patrol vessels; 1915–17; 613 tons; 1 × 4in; 2 tt; 2 dct; 20 knots.

connection with the anti-submarine campaign. The first point considered was the problem presented by the use by the enemy of large type submarines of the nature of the *Deutschland* class carrying two 5.9" guns and a large number of torpedoes – perhaps thirty. It is understood that a number of this class are under construction and that four will be ready for sea toward the last of this year. As reported to the Department, one vessel, something of this type, has been operating in the general vicinity of the Azores for some time, using captured neutral or other merchant vessels as a floating base.[1] It is believed that the only answer to such a move on the part of the enemy (which could not be an extensive one for some time) is the convoy system of escorting each convoy by a cruiser which would prevent the above type of submarine from using their guns, and hence force them to a restricted role with torpedoes only.

The available destroyers of the Allied powers are wholly insufficient to attempt any more extensive high sea escort work than that now, or soon to be, in operation. Even the extent to which this duty is being carried on now greatly restricts all contemplated strictly offensive plans. That is, against submarines themselves at, or near, their bases, and to the exclusion of immediate protection of trade.

Concerning this new type of submarine, we only need consider their operations outside of the areas which are now commonly termed the submarine zone, because within that zone the destroyer escorts will prove effective, *providing* the convoy system can be put into full operation.

The relatively small numbers of the new type and the large areas over which they must operate outside of the submarine zone, will greatly restrict the menace which they will present.

If shipping is concentrated in convoys, the routes of which the submarine can determine only by scouting, it is believed that success on their part will occur only in isolated instance, and, in the presence of a cruiser (which will prevent the use of the submarine's guns) it is not believed that the losses they can inflict will be critical. For example: a submarine of this nature might be able to approach a convoy during daylight and fire two or three torpedoes, but the cruiser which would immediately proceed in that direction on a widely zig-zagging course, would prevent succeeding attacks in the same arc of approach. At night fall, if the cruiser has thoroughly kept the submarine under in the direction of its approach and if the convoy makes a radical change of course for some hours, it is

[1] The vessel off the Azores was U-155 (Lt-Cdr Meusel); see Newbolt, vol. 5, pp. 128–9.

doubted whether a second torpedo attack could be carried out the same day or night.

England has sent a Mystery Ship and two submarines to the Azores, and it is hoped that the United States will also send two submarines and a mystery ship to this locality at least for the time being.

The advisability of the United States sending one of her older battleships with perhaps one or two small auxiliary craft to the Azores to prevent the use of those islands as a base during the coming winter should be considered. The needs of the situation in more vital areas however should be given full weight.

It is believed that no destroyers should be kept in the Azores as their operations are much more seriously needed closer to the European coast from whence they can be sent out for important escort duty.

England has at present four convoys every eight days across the Atlantic. In order to cover all trade it will require at least eight convoys each eight days, but this extension cannot be realized for some time. There is no prospect in sight of ability to convoy outgoing ships.

****

178.   *Sims to Bayly*

14 August 1917

****

I understand from a conversation with the convoy people in the Admiralty that they now believe they can convoy outgoing vessels without any appreciable loss of time. I understand that for the last month the amount of tonnage coming into the United Kingdom was 600,000 more than the average during the last few months. These figures may not be quite correct but the point is that the convoy method, notwithstanding delays in assembling vessels, and so forth, is working successfully. ...

179.   *Sims to Pratt*

30 August 1917

****

During my recent visit to Queenstown I found everything as satisfactory as it could possibly be imagined in so far as concerns our relations with the British Authorities there. It is not too much to say that they are delighted both with our destroyers and with their personnel. The destroyer people swear by Admiral Bayly and he admires and likes them all. He sees them very often as they go to the Admiralty House frequently for dinner or to play tennis or a kind of cricket in which he and his niece[1] always join. Incidentally, the latter is one of the most attractive young ladies of my acquaintance. She runs the house for him and pretty much runs him as well and about all of the relief activities of Queenstown and its neighbourhood.

I rather anticipated that the work of patrolling and convoying would become monotonous and that our fellows would grow a bit stale. This has not been the case in any degree. On the contrary I should say that they are now more enthusiastic than they have been. They do not find the work at all monotonous. This is shown by the fact that officers on the *Dixie* and *Melville* are always asking for opportunities to go out and the fellows on the destroyers decline to give them this opportunity at the expense of remaining in port.

****

When I first arrived, and it was decided that a destroyer force would be sent over here, Admiral Jellicoe expressed to me grave concern as to whether we would be able to get along with the Vice-Admiral in command at Queenstown. He had, and still has, a reputation of being very difficult, and was supposed to have it in for all Americans because, when he was Naval Attaché in Washington, he was practically fired out at the request of our people. Before I had visited Queenstown he was ordered down to the Admiralty to talk over the matter of coordination.

For a long time he had been at outs with the Admiralty. It is not necessary to go into reasons why, but this had gotten to such a stage that the anti-submarine people in the Admiralty no longer corresponded with him nor he with them, though he had vastly more experience in this line than the people in the Admiralty who came in with the advent of Admiral Jellicoe.

Moreover, the estrangement was such that Admiral Bayly would not ask for the men he needed at Queenstown and would not ask for the detachment of men who were totally unsuited to the work.

[1] Miss Violet Voysey: 'the only niece' as Bayly called her; she was related to the distinguished British architect Charles F. A. Voysey.

He did not tell me anything of this. He never even mentioned it.
But I learned it from the remarkable young woman whom Admiral
Bayly calls 'the niece'. When Admiral Bayly came to the Admiralty I
was invited of course to meet him in Admiral Jellicoe's office. On
that occasion he was as rude to me as one man can well be to
another. He was apparently deeply incensed at having been sent for.
I do not know what they had been saying to him. When he had gone
Admiral Jellicoe apologised to me, and said that he would remove
the Admiral if I thought it was necessary. Of course I said that I was
quite sure that it would not be necessary, that I did not know what
the cause of the friction was but I believed I could find it out and
indicate how it could be corrected.

Shortly afterwards I went to Queenstown. The Admiral received
me very nicely but without enthusiasm. After about three days it
became apparent that he quite approved of me. The niece told me
subsequently that he had 'walked around me' for three days and
finally told her 'that man is on the square'. Directly afterwards it is
not too much to say that we became really sincere friends and this
friendship has been increased as time goes on.

When I returned from this visit I went to Admiral Jellicoe with the
full knowledge of all the causes of friction and I said that it would be
impossible for us to successfully co-operate with the British Admiralty unless they could be removed. At my instigation, Admiral
Jellicoe, who is an old friend of Admiral Bayly's, wrote him a nice
personal letter in which he wondered that the Admiral had not been
on leave in two years and suggested that he seek an early opportunity to go. I said that I thought it essential that the Rear-Admiral
who had the direction at the Admiralty of the anti-submarine
campaign[1] should write the Admiral a letter requesting permission
to visit him for the purpose of benefitting by his experience. The
Admiral in question strongly objected at first but upon my insisting
that this was war and that personal feelings should have no place in
its conduct, he consented to go and did go. I explained to Admiral
Jellicoe that the Flag Captain at Queenstown[2] had always been a
thorn in Admiral Bayly's side and he should be exchanged. Also that
two officers of his staff were quite useless and should also be
removed. This was done and the officers that Admiral Bayly wanted
were sent to him.

I also invited attention to the fact that officers serving in other
similar stations, and who were junior to Admiral Bayly had been

[1] Rear-Admiral Duff.
[2] Unidentified.

made Commanders-in-Chief while he had received no recognition for his valuable services at Queenstown. Admiral Jellicoe said that he would be glad to see him made Commander-in-Chief (this is not a rank but a distinction which carries greater pay and allowances with it) but that when he had proposed it to the Board of the Admiralty they were unanimous against it. I asked permission to see the First Lord, Sir Edward Carson, on the subject. When I explained it to the latter he agreed that it should be done and he did it the same day. Since that time there has been no trouble on either side.

I regard Admiral Bayly as one of the ablest naval officers with whom I am acquainted in any Navy. The experience that he has had in handling the forces at Queenstown is wholly invaluable. I recognise that he has a peculiar character. He is peculiar in this respect that he has difficulty in doing business with people that he does not like. With those he does like he is one of the most agreeable men to serve with.

... I am apprehensive lest anything should be done to disturb the relations which now exist.

... such an organization in time of peace [the U.S. forces at Queenstown] would be commanded by a Rear-Admiral ... The situation is a peculiar one and it is so eminently satisfactory and so efficient that it would not be well to interfere with it.[1]

****

180.   *Gaunt to Admiralty*

31 August 1917

Navy Department informs me they will shortly be in a position to accept contracts for their 110 foot submarine chasers. Will Admiralty require any of this class of boat [?]

181.   *Gaunt to Admiralty*

2 September 1917

Length over all 110 feet, beam 15 feet 4¾ inches, draught 4 feet 10 inches ... cruising radius 12 knots 1500 miles speed 18 knots ... 6 pounder [gun]. Admiral Sims has full details of these boats. The

---

[1] There were rumours from time to time that a Rear-Admiral would be sent to Queenstown; the name most frequently mentioned was Rear-Admiral Edward Walter Eberle, US Navy (1864-1929), then Superintendent of the Naval Academy; later

American scheme is to use them in conjunction with a kite [balloon] three to a destroyer. They carry depth charges. Some success has been obtained by using them for listening and then following submarines and calling up the destroyer.

Memorandum by the Director of the Anti-Submarine Division[1]

4 September 1917

With our experience of Motor Launches it is not considered that the proposed submarine chasers are worth getting over here,

They should, however, be better sea boats as they are 25 feet longer and considerably more powerful, but they would at best be suitable for coastal work and could not be looked on as suitable for escorting convoys.

The fuel question must also be considered – they would be very heavy petrol consumers.

It would be of value if we could get one or two for trial purposes, but it is not recommended to place an order for them until one has been seen and tried.

Further Memorandum by DASD

8 September 1917

My Minute was largely influenced by the unofficial remarks of U.S. Officers over here who think little of these craft. They were built, I understand, as an answer to any popular demand that might arise as a result of submarines operating on American Coasts, in the event [of] most of their craft being [on] our side of the Atlantic. Now they can point to a large number of Chasers ready to deal with the

commanded a battleship division; CinC Pacific; and (1923–27) Chief of Naval Operations. See R. W. Turk, 'Edward Walter Eberle' in R. W. Love, ed., *The Chiefs of Naval Operations* (Annapolis, Md.: Naval Institute Press, 1980).
   [1] Captain, later Admiral Sir, William Wordsworth Fisher (1875–1937): entered RN 1880; Flag Commander to CinC, Home Fleet 1909–11 and to CinC Devonport 1911—12; War Staff Office 1912; Captain 1912; commanded dreadnought *St Vincent* 1916–17; succeeded Duff as DASD June 1917; Chief of Staff to CinC Mediterranean 1919; Rear-Admiral 1922; Chief of Staff, Atlantic Fleet and commanded 1st Battle Squadron 1922–24; 4th Battle Squadron 1924–5; DNI 1926; 4th Sea Lord 1927; Vice-Admiral and DCNS 1928; 2nd-in-command, Mediterranean Fleet and Admiral 1930; CinC Mediterranean 1932–35; CinC Portsmouth 1936. One of the RN's outstanding figures, known as 'Big Bill Fisher'.

U-boat when he appears, though they are not sanguine as regards the actual effectiveness of the measure.

Most certainly these craft can be useful in the Mediterranean and West Indies, but I do not think their qualities warrant large supplies of personnel (officers, mechanics, W/T operators, etc.) or Petrol. If U.S. are ready to man these craft the case is different.

Otherwise I would prefer to see our men reserved for craft that can keep the sea in any weather and can remain out a long time. (This implies accommodation as well as fuel capacity).

Anti-Submarine Craft fall in one of three categories:-

(1) Escorting
(2) Patrolling
(3) Hunting

These Chasers cannot carry out (1); can only do (2) near the coast and in good weather, and as regards (3), a successful hunt may be protracted and the issue may call for a good gun, and in these respects the 110-foot Chaser does not meet requirements.

182. *Page to Daniels*

Knebworth House,[1]
Knebworth,
Hertfordshire,
September 1917

You see that these last two weeks the number of British vessels sunk by German submarines is less; so far [so] good. And of course you know the hearty approbation the British have of our service, which is a great service. For if we hadn't added to their convoys our fleet of destroyers, God knows what would have happened by this time. The submarines are afraid of destroyers. We've proved that and that is a great service.

The trouble is that we and the British haven't enough, not half enough yet. If the Germans are still building submarines and if they continue to get raw material to build them, another year even at the present rate of destruction and in spite of our vast shipbuilding activity will hardly see the situation improved. We can't build faster than they are now sinking – say, of all ships, about 500,000 tons a

---

[1] Knebworth House was the home of the Earl of Lytton.

month. Mr Asquith[1] told me a few days ago that this is about the present rate – of ships of all nationalities.

Now the point is, the public on this side [of] the water doesn't know nor believe that this high rate of destruction is still going on. The Government and the politicians minimize it. … But don't let *them* fool *you*. The situation is still hazardous.

For instance – our army in France has bought coal in England, but it can't get ships to carry it. The French and Italians will again suffer for coal this winter – not enough ships. Practically every problem of the war turns on ships. If the Allies had the ships that have gone down, they could pretty quickly win the war. The Germans are able to continue only because of their submarines.

I see that the American papers accept the British political minimizing of the present destruction. Everybody who accepts this fools himself.

Of course I'm not predicting that the old high rate of destruction will be renewed. I know nothing about the German ability to go on, and of course the season and the weather will soon be less good for them. All I say is, we've not yet got out of the wood even with our great help. But for that help, the Allies would by this time have been lost. The Germans are yet winning in this activity of the war.

183.   *Benson to Sims*

5 September 1917

1. There is quoted for your information and guidance the following cable received from Admiral Mayo with the Department's answer to the same:

'After discussion with Admiral Jellicoe, Admiral Beatty, and Vice-Admiral Sims, recommend sending one division submarines operate against enemy submarines vicinity Azores Islands with monitor tender base of supplies Fayal Azores where monitor guns furnish local base defense, tender should be prepared to lay net in Horta harbor entrance from breakwater and following 20 fathoms towards signal station, submarines and tender should be attached to Naval Forces in European Waters. After arrival submarines in Azores Islands destroyer Division One proceed operate for base Brest France stop Queenstown en route for

[1] Herbert Henry Asquith, later 1st Earl of Oxford and Asquith (1852–1928): Liberal MP and minister from 1885; Prime Minister 1908–15 and of Coalition government 1915–16; lost Commons seat 1924; earldom 1925.

instructions, etc., etc.'

2. Department's reply to above is as follows:

'For Admiral Mayo. Disposition recommended in your cable approved. USS *Tonopah*[1] will be assigned to division of submarines operating Azores. State reasons for selecting as submarine base Horta instead of Ponta del Gada where our forces are now based and where we have established a coal pile.'

3. In view of the above it will be necessary for you to make arrangements whereby one division of submarines operates in British waters and the other in the Azores. ...

184.   *Sims to Navy Department*

11 September 1917

With reference to the anti-submarine campaign, generally speaking, the losses since April have not increased but, on the contrary, appear to be on the decrease. This, coupled with the fact that the number of submarines operating has, if anything, increased, is difficult to explain. There is considerable difference of opinion as to the causes for the above. The most reasonable opinion as to the decrease in submarine losses [i.e., sinking of merchant ships by submarines] and upon which there is the greatest degree of unanimity is as follows:

(a) The gradual extension of the convoy system together with increasing experience of both the merchant shipping and escorting craft.

(b) Increase of anti-submarine craft and constant increase of experience thereof, coupled with the more extensive use of the depth charge.

(c) Effect on enemy submarine morale from the above, and particularly, from the more extensive use of depth charges. It is wholly impossible to estimate the number of actual submarine losses caused by depth charges, but the fact that depth charges are used liberally whenever a submarine is encountered, unquestionably has a marked effect upon morale.

(d) Difficulty the enemy must be experiencing in maintaining an adequate supply of efficient torpedoes.

[1] USS *Tonopah*: monitor, 1901; 3235 tons; 2 × 12in, 4 × 4in; 12 knots.

185. *Memorandum by Bayly to Commanding Officers U.S. ships Melville and Dixie, HMS Adventure and all US Destroyers and HM Sloops based on Queenstown*

Admiral's Office,
Queenstown,
11 September 1917

The Commander-in-Chief wishes to congratulate Commanding Officers on the ability, quickness of decision and willingness which they have shown in their duties of attacking submarines and protecting trade. These duties have been new to all and have had to be learned from the beginning and the greatest credit is due for the results.

The winter is approaching with storms and thick weather; the enemy shows an intention to strike harder and more often, but I feel perfect confidence in those who are working with me that we shall wear him down and utterly defeat him in the face of all difficulties. It has been an asset of the greatest value that the two Navies have worked together with such perfect confidence in each other and with that friendship which mutual respect alone can produce.

186. *Sims to Commander, Patrol Squadrons based on Gibraltar[1]*

12 September 1917

The following is a copy of the confidential orders issued by the Vice-Admiral commanding the Irish Station:-

'There will be a meeting of Commanding Officers of sloops, destroyers and special service ships about once a month when the greatest number of ships are present in the port for those who wish to give suggestions for the best means of sinking submarines and protecting the trade based on actual experiences, either personal or what has been gained by others.'

****

I should be pleased if similar meetings could be arranged with the local authorities so as to provide for closer cooperation and a mutual understanding of methods, particularly where Allied forces are operating together. This conference should be, of course, under the senior allied officer, and is suggested merely as a means of

[1] Rear-Admiral Henry B. Wilson, US Navy.

indoctrinating all our forces, and in making progress in anti-sub-marine operations.

The conclusions of the conference held in Queenstown [on] 8 September are as follows. They have been laid before the Admiralty for consideration:-

****

(b)   It would be useful to have a special service vessel in a convoy, and when submarines are reported in the vicinity for her to drop astern as if unable to keep up, thus acting as bait. (This will be tried when I have a special service vessel available).[1]

(c)   Twenty ships is considered the limit for a convoy to be properly guarded in all weathers.

****

(k)   The following scheme is proposed as formation for escort with destroyers: see figure, below.

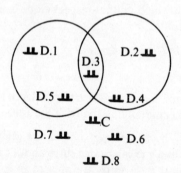

C = Convoy. D = Destroyers.

Radius of circle is visibility from deck of destroyer.

The relative bearing of D.1, D.2 from C is such that their circles of visibility interlock, and well ahead of C, thus greatly increasing their chance of seeing a submarine before the submarine sees C.

D.3, D.4, D.5 should be visible from D.1 or D.2 and about 2000 yards from C.

D.6, D.7, D.8 would be about 2000 yards from C.

D.1, D.2 should move out before daylight and close in at dark.

[1] A 'special service vessel' was a 'Q' or 'mystery' ship.

187.   *Bayly to Admiralty*

16 November 1917

[United States] Submarines should be sent to Queenstown which is the best strategical and tactical position under present conditions. If however submarines or supply ship are too big they will have to work from Berehaven owing to congestion in Queenstown Harbour.

Please send dimensions of supply ship and displacement and length of submarines as soon as known.[1]

188.   *Benson to Opnav*

London,
19 November 1917

Charleston, St. Louis, Colorado and *Minnesota*[2] should be utilised for convoy duty in addition to vessels already being so used. Additional precautions are being taken to prevent egress of raiders from North Sea but due to long nights and bad weather [in] winter considerable apprehension is felt that some may get out and attack convoys. British will increase their North Sea cruiser patrol and we must do everything possible to assist in convoy.

189.   *Charles Walker, Assistant Secretary of the Admiralty[3] to Foreign Office*

3 December 1917

I am commanded by My Lords Commissioners of the Admiralty to request that you will inform the Secretary of State for Foreign Affairs that the United States Destroyer *Fanning*[4] on 17 November, while operating within the Queenstown Command, engaged and sank a German submarine.

2. It appears from the report of the Commander-in-Chief, Coast of

---

[1] Five US submarines of the 'L' class worked from Berehaven.

[2] USS *Charleston*: cruiser, 1905–06; 9700 tons; 12 × 6in; 21.5 knots. USS *St Louis*: sister ship. USS *Colorado*: armoured cruiser, 1905; 16000 tons; 4 × 12in, 8 × 8in; 18 knots. USS *Minnesota*: sister ship.

[3] Later Sir Charles Walker (1871–1940): Private Secretary to Admiral Sir John Fisher when he was 1st Sea Lord 1904–09; became Assistant Secretary of Admiralty during the war.

[4] USS *Fanning*: destroyer, 1912; 742 tons; 5 × 3in; 6 × 18in tt; 30 knots. With USS *Nicholson* assisting, she sank U-58 on 17 November, the first American 'kill'; all but one of the crew were saved. See Admiral W. S. Sims, *The Victory at Sea* (London: John Murray, 1920), pp129–34.

Ireland, on this engagement that the *Fanning* was worked with great ability, and that her action probably saved two ships in a Convoy which the submarine was in a good position to attack. Credit is given to Lieut. A. S. Carpender, U.S. Navy,[1] commanding the *Fanning*, for the excellent discipline and organisation of the *Fanning*; to Lieut. W. O. Henry, U.S. Navy,[2] for his quick and correct decision as Officer of the Deck when the submarine was sighted; and to Coxwain David D. Loomis, who sighted the periscope, for the alertness of his lookout.

3. It further appears that the United States Destroyer *Nicholson* assisted in the action with excellent results, and that her Commanding Officer acted with good judgment in continuing with the convoy when he saw that *Fanning* needed no further assistance.

4. The whole engagement in Their Lordships' opinion reflects great credit on the discipline and training of the United States Flotilla, and I am to request that the Secretary of State will be good enough to convey, through the appropriate channel, to the United States Government, the high appreciation of the Admiralty of the services rendered by the two vessels, and particularly to the *Fanning*.

5. I am to add that had it not been for the recently conveyed decision of the United States Government that the United States Naval Forces are not allowed to accept decorations, My Lords would have desired to submit to the King the names of the United States Officers and men engaged on this occasion for appropriate recognition.

190.   *Sims to Bayly*

10 December 1917

... Everything which we have recommended since the month of April has now been recommended by the [House–Benson] Mission, or will be pushed there as soon as they arrive in Washington, which will be about 16 or 17 [December].

Admiral Benson is so thoroughly convinced of our necessities on this side that he declares that he will send over every destroyer that can get across the ocean under her own power or by being towed. He will also send over all the other vessels that we have asked for as soon as they can possibly be despatched. This includes, I believe, 18 powerful sea-going tugs.

All the members of the Commission have expressed themselves as

[1] Lieut. Arthur S. Carpender, US Navy: later Lieut.-Cdr. and CO, USS *Radford*.
[2] Lieut. (j.g.) W. O. Henry, US Navy: later served aboard USS *Breeze*.

very satisfied with the activities they found on this side, and all are determined to give us all the help they can in all respects.

191. *Jellicoe to Benson*

17 December 1917

We are anxious to provide more effective protection for Troop Convoys from Halifax against possible enemy surface vessels or raiders of light cruiser type.

We propose [to] use *King Alfred*[1] for this purpose and possibly *Leviathan* but this will exhaust our resources and I venture to suggest that as American troops are concerned U.S. Naval Authorities may be disposed to detail four pre-Dreadnought Battleships[2] for this duty.

Estimate such vessels can do journey to Destroyer rendezvous and back without coaling, round journey occupying about fortnight at sea.

192. *Gaunt to Jellicoe*

19 December 1917

Admiral Benson expressed himself as hostile to suggestion in Admiralty message, his point being that while he had knowledge of German Battle Cruisers building, he did not think they would be used for this sort of work. Captain Pratt supported the cable and [said that?] the ships were available. Admiral Benson told me to leave it for 24 hours and he would consider.

****

193. *Sailing Orders to an Escort Group*

Admiral's Office,
Queenstown,
2 January 1918

You are to leave Queenstown at 4.00 p.m. on Thursday, 3 January, and proceed to meet and escort a Mercantile Convoy (H.E. 3) of 14 ships, due in position Latitude 46° 30′ North, Longitude 9°

---

[1] HMS *King Alfred*: cruiser, 1901; 14100 tons; 2 × 9.2 in, up to 14 × 6in; 2 tt; 23.7 knots. *Leviathan* was a sister ship.

[2] American pre-dreadnoughts and cruisers were formed into an escort force under Rear-Admiral Albert Gleaves, US Navy.

30' West at 9.30 a.m., on 5 January, ...
2. Having met the convoy you are to escort it as far as a position
Latitude 52° 00' North, Longitude 6° 00' West (unless you receive
orders to proceed further), and then return to Queenstown. ...

****

7. British submarine *L-1*[1] is operating in [area] 'F' until 5 January 1918, and then returns to Berehaven.
Additional Orders from Escort Commander

****

3. When clear of swept channel form in following cruising formation, ships 1000 yards apart.

Jessamine

Ericsson   Benham

Parker   Burrows

Heather   Jenkins

Accurate station keeping not necessary but ships must keep in
touch, especially at night.
4. While escort is steaming alone in close formation, escort will zigzag as a unit as follows:-

Base course 10 minutes
25° right 8 minutes.
25° left 8 minutes.
Base course 10 minutes.

****

10. When with convoy all vessels of escort must see that vessels of
convoy nearest them keep in position.
11. In case of a raider, *Jessamine, Ericsson, Heather* with convoy,

[1] 'L' class submarines: 1917–20; 890/1070 tons; 17.3/10.5 knots; 4–6 tt.

Benham trail raider, remainder attack. Use smoke screen if conditions favourable.

12. On meeting convoy following positions to be taken up:-

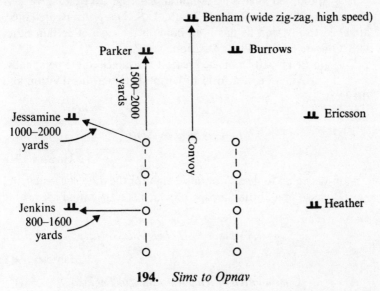

194.   *Sims to Opnav*

9 January 1918

Captain Leigh returned from two weeks with listening division in Channel. His reports very favorable to American devices. All American equipment used throughout the test without damage and without necessity of using spare parts. All English Fish hydrophones were out of commission before end of period of operations. Detection by American devices superior to that by English devices. The maximum number of submarine chasers equipped with listening devices and manned by personnel trained for this work should be placed in service [in the] war zone without delay. This is a matter of the highest importance warranting extraordinary effort. Admiralty attitude towards listening operations is not entirely satisfactory, as some lukewarmness is exhibited and indisposition to perceive superiority of American devices over the Fish Hydrophones. This feeling not shared by officers at sea directly charged with work, but in view of existence in Admiralty I deem it most important that Captain Leigh remain here to inject the necessary energy into the operations. ... I earnestly request that the Department insist on the most energetic action in the matter of dispatching the one hundred and ten footers to this side, allowing no difficulties to stand in the way.

195. *Minute by Captain W. W. Fisher*

10 January 1918

It is submitted that Vice-Admiral Sims be asked to give permission for Captain Richard Leigh, U.S. Navy, to be definitely attached to my staff as has been done in the case of certain other U.S. Officers and the Plans Division.

Captain Leigh will be of the greatest assistance to me personally, and will provide the best form of liaison between this division and the U.S.

Endorsement by Sims

12 January 1918

I am very glad to detail Captain Leigh for the duty suggested and have done so in an order, a copy of which is transmitted herewith.

Sims to Captain R. H. Leigh, U.S. Navy

12 January 1918

Continuation of temporary duty in England

1. You are hereby assigned to temporary duty as Liaison Officer between the Force Commander and the Anti-Submarine Division of the British Admiralty.

2. At such time as the Admiralty is ready to take up the activities below enumerated you will aid them in every way possible by your assistance and advice:

(a) Organisation and training of hunting units.

(b) Establishment of schools for the training of personnel in the use of sound detection devices of American design.

(c) Superintending the installation of all sound detection devices coming from the United States.

(d) The development of devices, signals, and manoeuvers, based on information obtained from Officers engaged on hunting patrols.

(e) The development of towing 'K' tube and trailing wire devices.

(f) The development of off-shore directional stations, using anchored tubes.

(g) The development of improved methods for patrolling English Channel and other similar bodies of water.

3.   You will also hold yourself available for any outside work such as:

   (a) Witnessing tests of new or improved devices.

   (b) The application of sound detection devices to various types of vessels.

   (c) Superintending manufacture of devices of American design.

   (d) Performance of any special work in connection with sound detection devices not herein specifically mentioned, and which may be proposed by the Force Commander or by the Admiralty.

****

196.   *Bayly to Sims*

10 January 1918

... I am afraid that the situation will be very serious for the yachts and trawlers at the end of this month when the big submarines come out* as they will not dive and risk depth charges but will use their surface speed and 6″ guns and attack our weak patrols and trawler escorts. Destroyers will not be able to go about singly, and we shall want all the light cruisers that can carry fuel enough (not *Adventures*) out here so as to assist.[1]

*you should talk to Wemyss about this.

197.   *Admiralty Memorandum of Discussion with Captain Cone, U.S. Navy, on Aerial Operations*

11 January 1918

[The United States Navy] Hope to have Lighters, Pilots and Personnel ready at Killingholme by 1 May. 40 Pilots to be trained at Felixstowe, and 40 in the U.S.A., from which they hope to obtain the requisite 60. It is understood that the Air Council are giving all facilities so that the numbers required may be obtained.

The present 1918 programme consists of 4 Stations in Ireland and a number of Stations on the West Coast of France. These should be working by July or August. The present scheme of patrol is to work in flights of three machines, 2 Bombers and one of the Cannon. It is proposed also to have some fast bombing machines to deal with

---

[1] The *Adventure* class of British light cruisers carried at most 455 tons of coal, which severely limited their radius of action compared with other light cruisers, which carried 750–1000 tons.

S.O.S. work. They have no plans yet for 1919, but almost unlimited output. At present there is no Ministry of Munitions centralizing productive facilities in U.S.A. A large machine capable of carrying 9,000 lbs. of bombs and a wireless controlled machine, are being experimented with.

The Central Depot of distributing American Air Stores, and also the Factory, is being established at Pauillac up the Gironde River, with a large Pier and Railway facilities.

198.   *Allied Naval Council: First Meeting Report of Sub-
Committee on Ocean Convoys and Escorts*

22–23 January 1918

German Submarine Cruisers
(Memorandum by Great Britain)

****

Theatres of Operation – The advantages of the unrestricted war on sea-borne commerce are so great from the German standpoint, that it seems probable that the operations of the submarine cruisers will for the present be confined mainly to the so-called 'barred zones' within which no distinction need be drawn between neutral and enemy ships. For the moment, in the instructions issued to submarines a sharp distinction is drawn between the methods to be employed outside the barred zones round the Azores and the Cape Verde Islands. The recent extension of these zones indicates that the Germans consider they now have sufficient cruiser submarines to maintain continuous operations in this part of the world.

The next theatre of operations to be reached by the widening circle of submarine warfare may perhaps be off the East Coast of Central or South America, and there is evidence of the Gulf of Mexico having recently been considered in this connection. It may be taken for granted that during the coming summer a determined effort will be made to interrupt communications from the United States of America and Canada, and that for this purpose some of the submarine cruisers will be employed in the Western Atlantic. The extensions of submarine action may or may not be preceded by the announcement of a new barred zone.

****

It is unlikely that more than six cruiser submarines, that is, one-third of 19, will be operating simultaneously in distant waters at any time up to the end of the coming summer.

****

Employment of Patrol Vessels against Submarines, formation of
Submarine Hunting Groups, and utilisation of Vessels fitted with
Listening Apparatus
(British Remarks)

The only purely offensive measures are those of the Special Hunting Flotillas. In 12 of the 22 areas round the coast of the United Kingdom, Special Hunting Flotillas of four trawlers working with aircraft from the coast have been created. These trawlers are fitted with the latest pattern hydrophones and with wireless of the best kind at present available. ...

****

Up till quite recently it was possible to have hunting patrols of destroyers or P-boats, but the creation of an elaborate system of convoy, both oversea and coastal, has made such calls on these craft for escort work that it is only occasionally that fast vessels of these kinds can be employed on hunting work. This is a very great drawback to any system of hunting, since the trawlers, whose speed seldom exceeds 10 knots, generally take a long time to reach the spot where the submarine was last reported, and this naturally makes the subsequent search for the submarine more difficult.

****

The convoy system, although designed primarily as a protective measure to shipping, brings in its train a useful degree of offence. Whether the escort consists of sloops, destroyers, or trawlers, the submarine attacking the convoy or showing herself in the vicinity of a convoy is attacked in return, and so long as a reasonable possibility of success remains she is hunted; and since a convoy will always be an attraction to the enemy submarine, the possibilities of successful offensive action by the escort are great.

****

The Desirability of an Extension of the Existing Ocean Escort
System throughout the World
(Great Britain)

ADMIRAL WEMYSS stated that this item is to a certain extent a concrete proposal, but it is not put forward as one which should be taken in hand and brought into force immediately, but rather as one on which the British Admiralty would like a discussion and the provisional acceptance of the principles, so that arrangements might be made to be in readiness to put the organisation in force if, and when, it becomes necessary. The Memorandum giving the proposals has been circulated to everybody, and it is hoped in the discussion to obtain the various views of the general principles. It may be added that if the proposals be accepted it is considered that the details of the organisation will probably have to be settled in London, and the procedure operated from London, since there is already at the Admiralty much of the necessary machinery in existence. Under these conditions the best method would appear to be that representatives of the Allies should work here with the British Admiralty in drawing up and operating the system.

VICE-ADMIRAL DE BON expressed the opinion that a system of convoys with cruiser protection would improve the transportation difficulties, but so far as France is concerned the position is rendered difficult by the fact that though the cruisers are ready there are no crews available, and for this reason several have been paid off. At present the organisation of convoys results in very great delays, the result being practically the loss of a large proportion of tonnage in any given time, and this at a time when France is already short of means of transport and the whole question of supply to the population is involved. The first thing to be done is to take steps to reduce and avoid, as far as possible, the delays now incurred in convoys, otherwise the situation may become critical. If a system of convoys is generalised as is here proposed, and the suggestion seems to be a happy one, something should be done to group the ships in each convoy according to speeds at the earliest possible moment. So far as the crews for the French cruisers are concerned, it has been proposed that these ships should be put at the disposal of the United States of America if they can find the men to man them. On a former occasion when the suggestion was made the reply was that the United States of America could not provide the crews.

VICE-ADMIRAL SIMS stated that he was of opinion that probably there had never been any logical reason for the use of a patrol system except while the convoy system was being brought into operation, and he was entirely in favour of doing everything possible to put all merchant shipping under convoy, under such methods as to obviate any avoidable delays.

With reference to manning the French cruisers, although the previous reply was that the proposal was not practicable, the circumstances may have altered and it may be practicable now, and further enquiry would be made from the authorities in the United States of America.

VICE-ADMIRAL DI REVEL remarked that several of the Italian cruisers named in the Memorandum had recently been disarmed and turned to various uses, such as repair ships, etc., but that everything possible would be done to find other ships that might be available. He desired again to emphasise the point that the utilisation of convoys should not result in delays to shipping, and consequently delay in the receipt of the necessary supplies. Everything possible should be done to reduce delays to convoys. Another point worthy of consideration was whether the escorting craft might not carry seaplanes or kite balloons to assist in the protection of the convoy.

REAR-ADMIRAL FUNAKOSHI[1] observed that generally speaking he was in accord with the British proposals. Although these apply to the escort system throughout the whole world, it is evident that attacks by submarines or surface raiders are more probable in certain oceans than in others, and in some parts of the world there is very little real probability of such attacks, as, for example, in the vicinity of Australian waters. It is therefore more necessary to have a system of this sort ready in places where attacks are probable than where they are not likely to occur, and though it is advisable to be prepared in advance everywhere, it would not be desirable to put the system into actual operation in Eastern waters and elsewhere unless actual necessity arises.

VICE-ADMIRAL DUFF stated that he desired to make it clear that the proposal was only intended to be brought into force in case of necessity. Experience of convoys has clearly shown that there must be some delay due to any system of convoy, no matter how well organised, unless the convoys can sail daily, and that, of course, is impossible. With the system of convoy in force in the Atlantic it has been found – and especially with French ships, as Admiral de Bon has remarked – that there are considerable delays owing to the intervals we are forced to make between successive convoys. The further off the convoy is collected and consequently the longer its voyage, the greater will necessarily be the delays. This proposed extension of the convoy system is really a matter of urgency only so far as the preparation of a detailed organisation is concerned, and it is not proposed to put it into force until necessity arises, and then

[1] Japanese Naval Attaché in London.

only in the case of the particular area in which enemy submarines are known to be operating.

Conclusion

General agreement was expressed in the principles enunciated in the British Memorandum on this subject,[1] it being understood that the arrangements proposed therein were only intended to be put in operation in any particular area or on any special route as necessity arose, but the desirability of making the fullest possible preparation beforehand was concurred in.

As regards the provision of cruisers by France, it was stated that the ships proposed to be employed had been paid off for lack of personnel, and for this reason could not again be commissioned. On a previous occasion it had not been found practicable for the United States of America to man these cruisers as had been proposed, but Vice-Admiral Sims undertook to make enquiry as to whether in the altered circumstances it might now be possible for the United States of America to man the cruisers if necessity arises. The four Italian ships specifically mentioned in the British Memorandum cannot be provided for this purpose, as they are already partially disarmed or employed as workshops, etc.

The general principles ... being agreed upon, it was decided to appoint a Sub-Committee, consisting of a representative of each country to consider in detail the proposals regarding the extension of the existing convoy escort system contained in the Memorandum ... and also all other questions relating to ocean convoys and their operation ... this Sub-Committee to be constituted as follows, and to meet as soon as practicable for the purpose of forwarding a report on these matters to the Council:–

France .... Captain H. Violette.[2]
Great Britain .... Vice-Admiral Sir A. L. Duff.
Italy .... Commander di Villarey.[3]

---

[1] On U-cruisers, see 177, 183, 196, 210, 216, 217.
[2] Capitaine de vaisseau Louis-Hippolyte Violette, French Navy: in 1916–17 he commanded patrols in the eastern Mediterranean. See Halpern, *Naval War in the Mediterranean*; pp. 258, 340.
[3] Capitano di fregata Count Carlo Rey di Villarey, Royal Italian Navy: Italian Naval Attaché in London. See Halpern, *The Royal Navy in the Mediterranean*, p. 284.

Japan............................ Rear-Admiral K. Funakoshi.
U.S.A. .... Captain F. H. Schofield.

****

199. *Bayly to Murray*

26 January 1918

Recommendations of United States Officers

In continuation of former letters on this subject, I desire to bring
to the notice of the Lords Commissioners of the Admiralty the very
excellent work done by the United States' destroyers based on
Queenstown during the period 1 July to 31 December 1917.

The Officers and men of these destroyers have worked continuously and successfully to protect troop convoys and commerce.
The Commanding Officers have displayed high qualities of leadership and exceptionally good judgment. These destroyers work in an
area where they are exposed to the full force of the Atlantic gales;
they have to escort ships to ports on the West Coast of France and
South coast of Ireland where fog and driving mists are exceptionally
prevalent. Despite this high trial of efficiency, they have never failed
to pick up their convoys and escort them safely to harbour.

The work of the repair ships *Melville* and *Dixie* in keeping the
destroyers always ready for sea has been in all respects admirable; I
cannot speak too highly of the expeditious way in which they deal
with defects. This is due principally to the tact, energy and ability of
Captain Pringle.

****

200. *Sims to Bayly*

31 January 1918

****

I am sorry to say that our destroyer program is not going to be up
to expectations. I know that this is usually the case with promises
that concern construction of vessels, but I had hoped that under the
present special circumstances this might have been avoided. I believe
that we will not be able to count upon having more than fifteen of
the new destroyers by the middle of May. I am, however, doing
everything I can to hurry matters up on the other side.

201.   *Memorandum by the Director of Plans*[1]

11 February 1918

The Anti-Submarine Campaign in 1918

****

54. ... The seizure of a Norwegian base primarily concerns this country but the U.S.A. would have to supply the additional battleships for the Grand Fleet, and the few troops that would be necessary might be supplied by her in order to accentuate the temporary nature of the occupation.

55. If Norway is presented with a *fait accompli*, she will no doubt protest very vigorously; but, taking into consideration her sufferings from the submarine campaign and her dependence on this country and the U.S.A. for food and coal, she will probably be inclined to accept the inevitable with a good grace.

****

67. ****

One thing is certain: that without a Norwegian base, the Northern barrage will be in the air, like some great girder supported only at one end.

202.   *Planning Section, U.S. Naval Forces in European Waters:*
Memorandum No. 18

19 February 1918

Mission: To determine the best employment of our present forces to defeat the enemy submarine campaign.

Decisions:

1. To indoctrinate our command with the necessity for offensive anti-submarine effort wherever possible.

2. To make the principal mission of the Grand Fleet that of combatting enemy submarine activity.

3. To immediately thin the destroyer escorts for off-shore convoy, and thicken them in coastal waters.

4. To indoctrinate the destroyer escorts so as to make their primary mission the counter-attack and hunt of all submarines which may attack convoys.

5. To substitute trawlers, sloops, yachts, etc., for destroyers in

[1] Captain Cyril Fuller.

escorting slow convoys, as practicable.

203.   *Benson to Sims*

20 February 1918

... the lack of a Central Controlling British Authority on shore in Washington, D.C., leads sometimes to a confusion of requests and a certain lack of thorough cooperation in any plan which affects our joint forces operating on this side [of] the Atlanctic.

****

A. The Controlling British Authority representing Admiralty should be stationed in Washington, D.C.
B. That a convoy officer representing Admiralty be stationed here as part of this office.

Take this up with Admiralty for a decision. This matter should be brought to an early settlement because were a submarine to operate off our coast undoubtedly the Department would immediately take some sort of action into its hands, especially as regards routing for incoming vessels and it is desired that we not only have full information on subject but also take no separate action which the present lack of centralization would force us to do.

204.   *Memorandum by Planning Section, US Naval Forces in European Waters*

25 February 1918

The English Channel

****

Special Situation
The Allies and the United States decide to deny passage through the Channel to enemy submarines, and to render the Channel safe for merchant ships.

****

Decisions
1. To unify the Channel command.
2. To man with American crews the present French anti-submarine Channel forces, exclusive of Harbor defense craft.
3. When practicable to augment the present anti-submarine effort at

Dover by:-
(a) A mine barrage (deep and surface) from Kentish Knock to Dunkerque.
(b) A deep-mine barrage from Hastings to Touquet Point.
(c) A system of ground listening devices operated from the shore, located about 20 miles eastward of Dover Straits.

4. To organise immediately a continuous surface patrol east of line Start Point-Sept Isles, with a total force of 30 destroyers or P-boats, the patrol to be assisted by ground listening devices operated from shore, by air patrols and by kite balloons.

5. To augment the above patrol by a series of deep minefields; planting continuously in the usual areas of enemy operation until he abandons the Channel.

6. Until extensive minefields can be laid, to employ a few hunting groups in the eastern Channel in conjunction with the patrols, and to develop tactics for 'mining in' a bottomed submarine with deep mines.

7. To concentrate the hunting effort west of the line Start Point-Sept Isles; and to assist this effort by deep minefields and patrols in waters favorable to bottoming, off both Cornwall coasts.

8. To place orders immediately for 70,000 additional mines.

9. To increase the efficiency of the Channel convoy system by the following measures:
(a) Carrying a kite balloon on one ship of each escort.
(b) Placing convoys in a formation of wide front which decreases as the depth increases.
(c) Adopting a policy of determined depth charge attack by several escorts against every attacking submarine.
(d) Arranging convoy sailings so as to avoid passage at night during moonlight.

205.   *Sims to Murray*

23 February 1918

1. I forward herewith copy of memorandum of the Planning Section regarding the use of K-tubes for the establishment of a Sound Barrage to the northward of the Dover–Calais line.

The object of the proposed barrage is to provide warning to the Dover and Dunkirk forces in case of an attempted raid on the part of the enemy so that the enemy may be met by superior force.[1] Our experiments with the K-tube justify fully the claims made for it in the attached memorandum.

I have cabled to the Navy Department requesting that 12 K-Tube Units complete be shipped immediately, in case it should be found desirable to establish the barrage as suggested.[2]

206. *Sims to Benson*

28 February 1918

****

It cannot be said that the submarine situation is encouraging. Very considerable progress has been made in rendering the Channel difficult of passage. A much smaller number of submarines have passed through recently than heretofore. The passages that have been dug out through the minefield surrounding Heligoland are pretty well blocked. The enemy has lost so severely there in torpedo boats, sweepers and submarines, that he is now very chary. Last night (28 February) he lost 4 out of 9 vessels escorting some submarines on the way out. The mining of the various passages is going on continuously, and the corresponding dragging on the other side. Within the last two or three weeks the submarines have been concentrating their efforts in the Irish Sea and in the Channel. Measures are now being taken to increase as rapidly as possible the hunting squadrons for diminishing this danger. Two hunting squadrons, composed of four 30-knot destroyers each are to be transferred for service, based on a port of Ireland about half way up the Irish Sea. A number of trawlers will also be employed. Two hunting squadrons are now working the Channel and two more are about ready to operate. Leigh is co-operating with the Admiralty officials in this matter. This morning I had a long talk with the 1st. Sea Lord on this

---

[1] Raids by enemy destroyers on the Dover barrage had occurred on several occasions, the latest just a few days before this letter (14–15 February 1918). See Marder, vol. 5, pp. 42–45.

[2] It is not known whether these were installed.

276 ANGLO-AMERICAN NAVAL RELATIONS 1917–1919

subject and expressed the opinion that radical and even somewhat risky measures were justified to render this channel of the Irish Sea practically untenable to submarines. At the same time I presented to him for discussion by the Admiralty Planning Staff, an estimate of this particular situation that was drawn up by our Planning Staff.

These two bodies are working together continuously and, I believe, with very good results. Our people have certainly drawn up a number of very able estimates and Admiral Wemyss has gladly placed these before his people so that eventually the two planning bodies can get together and make a joint decision for the benefit of the Admiralty.

****

A day or two ago, Mr Pollen called upon me and told me of his experiences at Queenstown, from whence he has just returned from a visit. He is most enthusiastic about conditions that he found there. He is, as you know, a man who has been well acquainted with the personnel of the British Navy for many years. He, as well as many other people, expressed their surprise that we have been able to get on with the Admiral who has such a reputation for being difficult in intercourse with his fellows. This is due to a certain extent to the relations which I was able to establish there on my first visit, and maintained on subsequent visits. This very able Admiral apparently took a shine at me and we have been fast friends ever since.

But the continuance of our good relations without friction of any kind though it has often been threatened, are due exclusively to the very remarkable ability in this line, of Captain Pringle. The situation is a very curious one and remains at all times a rather delicate one. It is very fortunate indeed for us to have the services of a man like Pringle. It would take pages to explain to you just how he has been able to do so in a very masterly manner. He is really one of the ablest officers in this respect that I have ever had to do with. He has ingratiated himself with Admiral Bayly to such an extent, and has been such a material help to him, that I sometimes wonder whether the Admiral could continue to hold down the position without such assistance. The trouble is that Admiral Bayly has been under a continuous strain since nearly the beginning of the war. It is one of those strains that never let up. He never knows at what hour of day or night there may come an S.O.S. call that will need immediate attention. He also has on his back the responsibility of taking prompt and drastic *political action* in case the troubles of Ireland break out. It is this latter feature which is so worrying.

I am telling you all this to try and make it clear that it would be a very grave mistake to make any change in conditions as they now exist at Queenstown. I do not know that any such changes are contemplated, but I always assume that there are a number of people that are applicants for duty over here.[1]

****

207. *Minute by Director of Plans*

1 March 1918

The tentative programme for the arrival of American submarine chasers in European waters is: [144 to arrive between March and October].

One Tender is also being allocated to every 36 submarine chasers.

2. (a) D.1 S.L.[2] has a proposition for allocating the first 36 submarine chasers to the Eastern Mediterranean, where the fuel difficulties could be met.

(b) A.C.N.S.[3] proposes that of the remaining submarine chasers, as they arrive in European waters, 72 should be distributed between

Gibraltar	18
Holyhead or Kingstown	18
Penzance	18
Plymouth	18

in the order named.

(c) If these allocations are effected, there will still be 36 submarine chasers to allocate in the autumn.

3. With reference to the above

(a) The U.S. Officers concur in sending the first 36 submarine chasers to the Mediterranean, unless a radical change in the general situation should develop before they arrive.

(b) They consider that the allocation of submarine chasers subsequent to the first 36 should not be decided on until nearer the date of their arrival in European waters, in case the situation should have altered in the meantime.

(c) They do *not* consider the submarine chasers suitable for North Sea work, or for escorts for minelayers, men-of-war, or convoys.

---

[1] See 179, above.
[2] Rear-Admiral George Hope.
[3] Rear-Admiral Duff.

(d) They consider that submarine chasers *are* suitable for submarine hunting work in the Irish and English Channels, and for inshore work on the French Coast.

4. In view of par. 3 (c), D.C.N.S.[1] has stated he will not require any submarine chasers.

208. *Murray to Sims*

25 March 1918

****

2. ... the Allied Naval Council has met[2] and, as you are aware, it was decided by the Allied Council to recommend to the United States Government that the first two squadrons of submarine chasers to be completed and despatched from the United States of America to European waters should be allocated for service in the Mediterranean, with the exception of six or eight boats, as may be found necessary, which you desire to be stationed in Northern waters, in order that experimental work and the trial of certain new devices in these new boats might be continued.

3. It was also agreed that the above two squadrons of submarine chasers should be employed, if possible and convenient, in the service of the Otranto Mobile Barrage, with the definite proviso that they are not to be used for escort work.

4. We are informing the British Commander-in-Chief, Mediterranean,[3] that he is to consult with the United States Senior Naval Officer of the Squadrons on their arrival, in regard to the best arrangements it will be possible to make for supporting ships for units of four chasers in the system on which the squadrons are trained to operate.

5. As the question of the employment of the remaining 112 submarine chasers under construction will be considered by the Allied Naval Council at a later date, it is recognised that the provisional allocation ... must be regarded as purely tentative.

6. The Admiralty would have wished to arrange at once tentatively the allocation of the new U.S. Destroyers and Ford Destroyers,[4] in order that the fuelling, refitting and repairing arrangements for them

---

[1] Rear-Admiral Sydney Fremantle.
[2] On 12–13 March 1918.
[3] Vice-Admiral Gough-Calthorpe.
[4] The 'Ford destroyers', otherwise known as 'Eagle' boats, were built by the Ford Motor Co.: 500 tons; 2 × 4in; 18 knots. The first of these ungainly production line-war emergency escort vessels was commissioned only on 28 October 1918.

might then be put in train. It appears, however, that the Allied Naval
Council contemplate this question coming before them for decision
in the same way as the Submarine Chasers. The Admiralty would be
glad to know whether you consider it possible nevertheless to make
some provisional arrangement as to the dispositions which would be
a sufficiently reliable basis for the preliminary action as to supplies
and maintenance which is very desirable.

209.   *Sims to Murray*

28 March 1918

Employment of United States submarine chasers in the
Mediterranean

1. Captain R. H. Leigh, U.S. Navy, of the Force Commander's
staff, is leaving London today for Brindisi, Italy, to confer with
Commodore Kelly[1] in the matter of the employment of United
States submarine chasers which it is proposed to allocate to the
Otranto barrage.
2. Captain Leigh will also discuss with Commodore Kelly the subject of the best port upon which to base these vessels, and he will, if
necessary, continue on to Malta to confer with Admiral Calthorpe.
3. Captain Leigh will probably arrive at Brindisi on 3 April.
4. The recommendation of the Allied Naval Council as to the allocation of thirty-six submarine chasers to the Mediterranean was
duly communicated to the United States Navy Department, which
has not as yet given its approval to the plan, but will doubtless do so
at an early date.
5. Assuming that the thirty-six chasers are allocated to the Otranto
barrage as planned, it seems probable that the remaining 108 of the
total of 144 of vessels of this type will be allocated to the waters
contiguous to the Irish Sea and Channel, the English Channel, and
the North Sea, and that the Ford destroyers of which a maximum of
one hundred may be expected, will be allocated in part to the same
locations and part to the Atlantic coast of France, and in part to the
Mediterranean with base at Gibraltar. While this assignment cannot
be considered as more than provisional at the present time, it is
thought that dispositions should be made for taking care of 108
submarine chasers of the 110-foot class and 50 Ford destroyers in
the ports of the United Kingdom, and of about 20 of the Ford
destroyers at Gibraltar.

[1] Commodore W. A. Howard Kelly.

6. With respect to the new large destroyers which are to be added to the United States Naval Forces in Europe: It may be said that approximately 50 such vessels may arrive during the present calendar year, and it is safe to assume that of these 50 at least 30 will be assigned to such operative areas as will involve their being supplied from bases in the United Kingdom.

210.   *Sims to Benson*

7 March 1918

In the first place let me say that our Planning Section, combined with that of the British Admiralty, is I am convinced, having a very beneficial effect. Of course this is a matter that has to be handled very cautiously. You will understand this when I explain that the officers of our Planning Section have had a very much more thorough training than the corresponding British officers have had. They have taken the initiative in making a number of estimates of situations on various problems. They are now taking these up with the Planning Section of the British Admiralty so that the final conclusion of the combined sections will be the only one presented to the governing officials of the Admiralty.

****

There is nothing particularly new in the tactics of the submarine. Some time ago there were an unusual number of submarines that came out and they are now on the way back. No less than ten of them were bound in towards Skaggerack last night. Very few of them have attempted to use the Channel lately (a UB submarine was blown up on 10 March, in the mine barrage in the Dover Straits. No survivors. Her log book was recovered from the wreckage[1]), and all of the passages through the Heligoland Bight are now either blocked or considered by the enemy too dangerous to risk submarines therein.

They have been making very determined efforts to break through this barrage, as it is much more advantageous for them to use it than the Skaggerack. This is for the reason that they cannot go out through the Skaggerack without being seen as they pass through the Belt, and they must pass the minefield off the Skaw coming out. They probably know the minefields are there, but if they go out on the surface they are reported and chased and if they go out sub-

[1] UB-58. An insert by Sims, after original letter typed.

merged they run the risk of the mines. To show how much they desire to clear the passages out through the Heligoland Bight, I may say that during the last week or so they have been attempting to drag a passage with barrier breakers, sweepers, destroyers, trawlers, and so forth, backed up by the 4th Battle Squadron, and accompanied by all of the battle cruisers. Yesterday, they came out from Heligoland with this force and a vessel carrying aeroplanes. The latter [was] for the purpose of searching for the position of mines. The British sent a force to oppose them, and this might have brought on a very considerable action, had it not been that bad weather and fog obliged the enemy to abandon the enterprise and retreat behind Heligoland.

Generally speaking, the submarines have been operating lately in the Irish Sea and the passages leading thereto and in the Channel. Their tactics seem to be to wait until convoys split up at the entrance of the Channel, and then attack the sections, or any ship which may have become separated or which branches off to go into a port. This would seem to be a demonstration that they cannot hope for an equal amount of success by attacking the convoys in the open sea. Heavy weather does not seem to prevent them making successful attacks, so that they can carry out operations against convoys whenever they choose to. As showing that they are not particularly embarrassed by heavy weather, I may state that the *Calgarian*[1] was torpedoed at the northern entrance to the Irish Sea while it was blowing between [force] 7 or 8.

... Convoys of many ships are now being brought in with, in some cases, but five or six destroyers, which is manifestly insufficient to give reasonable protection. There have, of course, been propositions to let the convoys come in without any escort and send all the destroyers to attack the submarines. This of course would be a dangerous procedure because it frequently happens that there are many submarines that are known to be out but whose positions are not known. So while we might chase those whose positions are known, those that are still free might do a great deal of damage in the way of destroying ships. As an example of this state of affairs, I may mention that three or four days ago, when there were a considerable number of submarines out, there were seven of them that were known out in the Atlantic that had not been located within the last thirty hours. Today there are only six or seven submarines in the Atlantic and two UB boats.

[1] HMS *Calgarian*: armed merchant cruiser, sunk by a U-boat on 1 March; see Newbolt, vol. 5, p. 227.

It is thoroughly realized that what is needed, indeed more than anything else, is war against the submarine. It is hoped that this will be successful when there are enough vessels to carry it out and when they are fitted with the latest listening devices. In the meantime, however, a number of 30-knot destroyers are being transferred from several stations on the east coast of England and Scotland in order to constitute two hunting squadrons in the Irish Sea, which is the most serious danger point. These two squadrons will be based on ports [on] opposite sides of the sea and about halfway up its length. They will coordinate their work with that of four American destroyers that are now engaged in this same work and they will, of course, be under the command of one man. When efforts like this can be increased we will then have high hopes, not perhaps of destroying all the submarines, but of destroying enough of them to break down their morale.

There is evidence already that this morale is very considerably shaken. As the 1st Lord stated in the House the other day, every submarine commander who goes out on a cruise, knows that the chance of his being destroyed is about one in five.

One of the danger points is, of course, the Mediterranean. This will become very serious indeed if the extensively advertised blow at the Western Front is nothing but camouflage to conceal a blow that is to be struck either in Italy or in the Balkans. If the latter should prove the case, the submarine menace in the Mediterranean would be very serious indeed. This whole matter will be discussed before the Allied Naval Council and it is very probable that the discussion will result in the recommendation to very considerably increase hunting operations against the submarine in the Mediterranean. This decision will include some of our submarine chasers, which are particularly adapted for work in the lower end of the Adriatic.

****

As far as we can see we have nothing in particular to fear from the present type of cruising submarines that are out. These are the ones of the *Deutschland* class, which have a relatively slow speed. They are not nearly so efficient as the ordinary U-boats. I have enquired particularly as to the record of the operations of these boats, and I can find almost no instance where they have attacked vessels with their torpedoes. It is certain that there is no instance in which they have even approached and tried to attack a convoy. I think this is readily understood when we consider that these boats are very slow and very poor divers and that they keep away from a convoy for fear she may be accompanied by a high speed vessel that can attack them with depth charges – either a destroyer or a PQ boat, that they could not see until they had made a tolerably close approach. (Note: a PQ boat is a P-boat that has her upper works built up to resemble a small coast steamer. They have 18 knots speed, a very strong ramming bow, and a considerable number of depth charges. They have been very successful in both ramming and bombing submarines).

Of course the tactics of a cruising submarine that has a higher speed on the surface, and that may be presumed to be a more rapid diver, might be more dangerous to convoys, but I must say that I have never been able to work up any serious apprehension in this regard.

Our destroyers are now being fitted, as fast as they come up for overhaul, to carry all the way from twenty-four to forty depth charges, dependent upon the position of the after gun. This will enable us to very seriously menace any submarine that is sighted within a mile or so, by encircling him with a very considerable number of depth charges, so that he will have to have very good luck indeed if some of these do not explode very near to him.

As you know the 110 ft. boats have turned out to be better sea boats than anybody believed they would be. This means only that they are apparently able to stand any kind of a sea, but it does not mean that they are able to make any progress in a sea that is at all considerable. This makes them very useful as patrol boats or as members of hunting squadrons, but their limitations are such as regards speed, in any considerable weather, that they could not be used for convoys.

As a result of the conference that was held in Rome it was decided to ask the Allied Naval Council at its next meeting, which will be 12 and 13 March, to recommend the dispositions that should be made of these chasers that are coming over. It was pointed out that as one of the greatest danger points in submarines is now in the Mediterranean, that it would probably be well to send a certain number there of those which first arrive. I was asked if I would agree to this, and I replied that I understood that both Great Britain, France and Italy were agreed to this, and that personally I was also in agreement, but that I thought that in all such cases the recommendation should come from the Allied Council, if there was time to place the question before that body. I took this attitude because it is my understanding that this is one of the important functions of the Inter-Allied Naval Council, that is, to recommend the distribution of the Allied anti-submarine forces that, in the opinion of the Council, will have the maximum effect in opposition to submarines.

Of course I know that in the past, and I suspect even at present, pressure is frequently brought to bear through diplomatic channels to have anti-submarine vessels of various types assigned to this or that country. Of course, it might be dangerous for any particular government to decide upon the employment of these boats in accordance with such recommendations. It therefore seems to me that the best possible resistance to such recommendations is the statement that one of the principal duties of the Inter-Allied Naval Council is to advise the respective governments upon just this particular point.

****

There is nothing very definite that can be said about the Russian situation either at Petrograd or at Mourmansk. The Admiralty was very desirous that the British, French and American flags should be represented there for the influence that it might have in that part of Russia. I do not think it would require the services of one of our vessels for a long time, but of course that is more or less conjecture.

In regard to your telegram about protecting the vessels laying the mines in the barrage, it, of course, goes without saying that all of the vessels engaged in this work must be protected against the possible interference by enemy forces. This is now the common practice on both sides.

Referring to your telegram about the desirability of keeping the Russian battleships, in the Baltic and Black Sea, from falling into the hands of the enemy, this has been the subject of continuous preoccupation on the part of the Admiralty. They have agents on the spot who have been standing by to perform this service, either through 'agreement' with the Russian officials or through the action of their own people. Just what the method employed would be, will depend upon circumstances; but you may be sure that they will not pass into the hands of the enemy in a condition to perform service if it can possibly be prevented.

Great difficulty has been experienced in the North Sea, and particularly in the Dover Straits, in keeping mines in position. More or less continuous and very heavy weather has dragged some mines out of place and worn out the fastenings of others, so that a very considerable number have become adrift. This applies to the German mines as well as the British, in that neighbourhood and in the south end of the North Sea. This is simply an illustration as to the difficulty of maintaining an effective minefield in these areas.

It is an interesting fact that about the beginning of the intensive submarine campaign, the Germans habitually reported the amount of tonnage sunk as about 15% greater than the actual sinkings. This excess has been gradually increasing until they are now reporting the sinkings 75% in excess of what they actually are.

This is undoubtedly for the effect it will have in keeping up the morale of the German people, who are beginning to get impatient because the promises as to the finishing of the war by the submarine campaign have not been carried out.

211.   Bayly to Sims

10 March 1918

I have just had Jellicoe here for two days. He was fascinated with *Melville* and the destroyers; made a very neat little speech at the men's club, said just the right thing in the right way and enjoyed his visit.

212.   Director of Admiralty Intelligence: Endorsement on Prawle Point Hunt

10 March 1918

1. The impressions left after the perusal of the hydrophone observations off Prawle Point and many similar hunts are that the chances are so enormously in favour of the quarry as hardly to justify the employment of the large number of craft and personnel at present engaged on this duty.

2. As a 'detector' the hydrophone appears to be most useful, but when it is claimed that by means of it the hunter can locate the submarine with sufficeint exactitude to justify the expenditure of his depth charges, it presupposes a very highly trained and intelligent personnel that would take a very long time and patient organizing to create.

3. The following qualifications and conditions appear to be essential:-

(1)   A very delicate sense of hearing in hydrophone listeners.

(2)   The power to deduce correctly and rapidly.

(3)   An intimate knowledge on the part of the Commanding Officers of drifters, trawlers, etc., of methods and capabilities of enemy submarines.

(4)   The capability of the flotilla leaders to direct the hunt which

includes the possession of qualifications (2) and (3) in a very high degree.

(5) The warning off of all surface craft from area of hunting field.

(6) Knowledge of the correct method of delivery of an attack by depth charges.

4. When it is considered that the distant approach of a single surface craft, as in the case quoted, can lead the hunt away from the quarry on a false track; also that the quarry can detect the approach of the hunters in the same degree that his motors are available to them, and if necessary remain motionless on the bottom till dark, the disadvantages under which even a perfectly trained 'field' has to work can be realised.

5. The above considerations have been suggested after the perusal of many hydrophone reports. In none of these cases has the submarine been either destroyed or forced to come to the surface, and in some of them chart evidence has shown the improbability of the presence of a submarine in the locality.

6. It seems therefore very much open to question whether the time and energy expended in training hydrophone flotillas to the degree of efficiency at present reached has been justified by the results obtained, and whether further results are likely to justify an extension of the flotillas on the same line.

7. The degree of efficiency to be reached before hydrophone hunting can be considered likely to produce results commensurate with the personnel employed must be very high indeed, and apart from the organization and system and training required, the careful selection of personnel is bound to be a most important consideration. Can officers and ratings possessing the requisite qualities be spared from other duties in sufficient numbers [?]

8. Considered as detectors however it would appear very desirable to have fixed hydrophones in localities much frequented by minelaying or other submarines, such as off Lerwick, Fair Island Channels, Kirkwall, Aberdeen, Firth of Forth, Harwich–Yarmouth area, Straits of Dover, Beachy Head, Royal Sovereign, Owers, the area bounded by Scillies and Lands' End, etc.

9. Submarine hunting appears from results up to date to be preeminently the work of the high speed surface craft. There is no doubt from observation obtained from prisoners of war that the enemy has a wholesome dread of attack by these craft, and it is doubtful whether an equal moral effect, apart from actual results, would ever be obtained from hunting by slow craft fitted with hydrophones, except in narrow waters.

213. *Wemyss to Sims*

26 March 1918

I have just come back from Queenstown, where I spent a most profitable and enjoyable day amongst your officers and men.

Our relations have always been so cordial that I am going to allow myself to make remarks to you which otherwise might seem an impertinence; but under the circumstances I cannot refrain from telling you how pleased I was with everything I saw.

Quite apart from the personal pleasure it gave me to meet your officers and see them and your men at work, I came away with a feeling that the organisation, discipline and general effectiveness of your squadron are of a very high degree. One and all, from the highest to the lowest, struck me as being so extraordinarily keen, smart and efficient, and the state of the ships appeared to me to leave absolutely nothing to be desired.

Captain Pringle's organising powers must be very great, and the good feeling which so evidently prevails all through your squadron can but be due very greatly to him.

As to personal relationships between the two services I will say nothing, as we have so often discussed them; but an actual sight as to what was going on brought home to me more than ever the magnificent way in which the officers and men of your service have entered into a partnership with ours. I know that the feeling is entirely reciprocated and that the co-operation between the two services can lead to nothing but good, both during the war and after it.

The cordiality with which I was received made a very deep impression upon me, and I would like to take this opportunity of thanking you and all your officers and men for that heartiness which is characteristic of our brotherhood in arms.

214. *Joint Appreciation by the British and American Plans Divisions*

28 March 1918

Anti-Submarine Policy in the Immediate Future

****

6. It is clear that the vast majority of anti-submarine forces in the vicinity of the United Kingdom are spread over a wide field, and are not concentrated to attack submarines. We try to be strong everywhere and are strong nowhere.

7. Part of the protective system, viz., the escort of convoys by fast vessels, has, however, the great advantage of forcing the submarine to attack in the vicinity of the escort, and gives it a chance of counter-attack. In practice, however, only a few submarines are destroyed under these circumstances. This may be due to the fact that the forces on the spot are insufficient to bring about results.

8. It may also be due to faulty tactics, and in order that full advantage may be taken of these contacts, it appears essential that the escorting destroyers should drop the defensive role, and assume a vigorous offensive, which should not only include an immediate depth charge attack, but also a persistent hunt during the remainder of the day by a large proportion of the escort. The question whether any destroyers should remain with the convoy would depend on the locality and probability of further attacks.

****

Proposed Modifications to the Present Policy

10. Instead of the above system of dispersion of force, it is urged that we should eventually aim at closing the Northern exit by a great offensive effort in that area.

11. Decisive results will not be obtained until a very strong mine barrage is completed, and it would be inexpedient to abandon the local protection of trade until the hydrophone is more fully developed. It is urged, however, that a concentrated offensive effort, covering the reported track of submarines be instituted in the Northern area as soon as possible.

12. In February, about 70% of the submarines operating outside the North Sea passed North about, and the number will tend to increase. ...

13. At the present time, submarines passing North about confine themselves almost exclusively to the Fair Island Channel, the passages averaging about one a day during February 1918. ...

14. An intensive patrol in this area could be quickly moved to another track, and would be flexible in its dispositions, enabling the utmost use to be made of any information available, which, at present, is certainly not utilised to its fullest extent.

15 It is most strongly urged that *the success of the above policy rests on allotting certain definite anti-submarine functions to the Grand Fleet, for unless its present functions are modified, neither sufficient destroyers nor the necessary standard of organisation will be forthcoming.*

16. So long as the movements and dispositions of the Grand Fleet are based on the idea that the High Seas Fleet is likely to be inveigled into action by any other means than the defeat of the submarine, the most efficient part of the British Navy must play a comparatively minor part in defeating the enemy's primary line of attack. It must stand aside and leave the real battle to the militia of the sea – the trawlers, mercantile marine, etc.

17. On the other hand, if the primary function of the Grand Fleet during the summer months is defined as the barring of the Northern exit to submarines, the High Seas Fleet will only become an object of immediate attack if it threatens the barrage.

****

19. By assembling the whole Grand Fleet at one base, and freeing it from the responsibility of dashing after the High Seas Fleet *at short notice*, except in the support of anti-submarine operations, a flotilla of destroyers could probably be released for hunting submarines, but the Commander-in-Chief might allocate more or less according to circumstances.

20. In order to provide the remainder of the anti-submarine destroyers and patrol craft, it is proposed to reduce the escort destroyers, sloops and P-boats by approximately 30%, and the trawlers round the coast on patrol duties by about 50%.

21. The withdrawal of trawlers from coastal patrol will probably not influence shipping losses one way or the other. The effect of reducing the convoy destroyers cannot be exactly foreseen, but no appreciable increase in sinkings is expected. The great initial success of the convoy system was due more to the concentration of shipping in a comparatively small space, and the consequent difficulty of locating it than to the protective power of the escort. ... the enemy attempted to meet the convoy system by transferring his attack to the coastal and terminal areas, where his submarines would have a better chance of finding the convoys; ...

22. The proposed reduction in destroyer escorts must be compensated by increasing the destroyers in the dangerous zones at the expense of the comparatively safe areas. For example, whilst the submarine campaign is mainly confined to the coastal areas of the United Kingdom, the escorts to the Westward of say 10°W, might be greatly reduced.

23. ... Under the present system of scattered coastal Commands, it is most noticeable that submarines frequently operate for days in very limited areas without any large forces being brought to the spot,

although they might be concentrated in a comparatively short time.
24. The foregoing may be summarised by saying that *the principal
factor in the solution of the submarine problem is a new orientation of
the functions of the Grand Fleet and that if the Commander-in-Chief is
allotted the primary task of preventing submarines from passing North
about, and is freed from responsibilities which interfere with that duty,
everything else will follow in due course. A consolidation and reorganisation of the coastal Commands are also required.*[1]

215. *Joint Memorandum by the British and American Plans
Divisions*

1 April 1918

*Suggested Plans for Offensive Anti-Submarine Operations in
Northern Waters*

****

2. The object of the patrol is to destroy outward and homeward
bound submarines.
  To effect this the submarine must be *brought to the surface* by
exhausting her battery.
  (a) By extending the patrol over a considerable distance.
  (b) By locating and hunting her with special groups of vessels.
  Depth charges are an invaluable auxiliary and should be used
freely but cannot be relied upon to effect the desired result.

****

7. The suggested patrol consists of:-
  (1) Kite balloon groups, consisting of one Torpedo Boat Des-
       troyer towing the balloon, and two others.   Their function is
       to drive submarines under, or to attack them if opportunity
       offers, and to report the position of any sighted.
  (2) A supporting force of T.B.D.'s.
  (3) Hunting groups, each consisting of 3 trawlers, which should
       be fitted with Hydrophones, and one sloop or P-boat to
       support them.
       Their functions are to take up the hunt of any submarine
       which comes within reach.
  (4) Submarines, disposed well in rear of the Hunting groups.
       Their functions are to attack any submarine which gets

---

[1] It seems that practically none of these recommendations were accepted.

clear of the patrol and is endeavouring to re-charge her battery.

(5) Aeroplanes should patrol areas within their reach and assist the work of the Kite Balloon Groups.

****

216. *Benson to Sims*

5 April 1918

Presence of hostile cruiser submarine around Canary Isles and Cape Verde[1] operating as indicated in the estimate by your planning section, coupled with recent requests to run sailing vessels to African Coast through the zone for lumber leads the Department to look with favor upon the establishment [of] minor bases of our own at Madeira Islands and Cape Verde. As base from which a few of our submarines might operate assisted by heavily armed cruising craft of 'P' or 'Q' type these Islands seem to present possibilities. Matter has been taken up with British authorities through our State Department but has not progressed to a decision. What is opinion of Admiralty as regards feasibility of such a scheme and if considered feasible what pressure can Admiralty bring to bear to further it provided United States agrees to furnish operating craft to make scheme merely an extension of Azores Islands operations.

217. *Sims to Opnav*

7 April 1918

Upon preliminary consideration of plan opinion of Admiralty in which I concur is that submarines based as suggested would probably have the effect of denying the adjacent waters to cruising submarines. Admiralty experience is that hostile submarines have almost invariably moved their hunting ground when they have discovered the presence of Allied submarines. It is not thought that vessels of the 'P' type would be useful for operating with submarines, but vessels of the 'Q' type probably would be. The examination of charts of available harbors will be made to determine possibility of using them as bases. Admiralty will at once take up with British Government the matter of obtaining permission to establish bases in Portuguese Islands.

[1] U-157 (Lt-Cdr Max Valentiner). Newbolt, vol. 5, p. 283.

218. *Joint Memorandum by the British and American Planning Divisions*

15 April 1918

Anti-Submarine Attack by Convoy Escorts

****

3. ... It is therefore recommended that the following principles and general instructions be promulgated for the guidance of all commanding officers of submarine hunting and zone escort vessels.

4. *Guiding Principles and general instructions for Anti-Submarine attack by Convoy Escort Vessels*

(1) *The enemy's submarine campaign cannot be defeated by* defensive measures which consist mainly in *warding off his blows.*

(2) The enemy must be brought to have a wholesome fear of coming within the reach of our ships. It has been proved that *depth charges* exploded even within a radius of 1,000 yards *have an effect on enemy submarine morale, the effect of which cannot be over-estimated.*

(3) *The best method of defending a convoy from submarine attack is to destroy the submarine in its vicinity.* It is therefore imperative that the maximum possible advantage should be taken of every close tactical contact with an enemy submarine to *pursue it to destruction.*

(4) The practice of escorting convoys serves to draw more hostile submarines into close tactical contact with concentrated forces of our anti-submarine vessels than is possible by any other means. *It rests with the escorts to see that the trap is set.*

(5) Apparently the *defensive* role of anti-submarine vessels *should only be assumed while awaiting an opportunity for decisive offensive action.*

(6) Escort vessels will therefore automatically pass from the defensive to the offensive whenever close contact is established and will prosecute a vigorous and persistent attack. *The mission of protecting the convoy then becomes secondary to the vital necessity of destroying the submarine.* [*Note:* Every submarine destroyed saves approximately 50,000 tons of shipping per year.)

(7) *The pursuit and attack should be made by as large a proportion*

of the escorting force as circumstances admit, and should be continued until there is no longer a reasonable hope of destroying the submarine, or of sighting it again before dark.

(8) *The actual proportion of the escorting force which should carry out the attack will depend on the nature of the convoy and the probable degree of submarine activity in the zone through which it has to pass before reaching its destination.* In the case of a troopship convoy the need for saving life may limit the number of escorts sent to attack. On the other hand when steaming westward away from the zones of intense submarine activity, a larger proportion of the vessels can proceed to the attack.

(9) It is not intended to lay down hard and fast rules, but generally speaking, every close contact with an enemy submarine should be construed as an order *to attack* as heavily and persistently as possible *and with a very lavish use of depth charges. Even if the position of the submarine is not exactly known* there is always a chance of damaging her by a free use of depth charges.

Minute by Duff

This question is best left in the hands of practical experts who, while fully alive to the necessity for offensive action on the part of Convoy Escorts, are best able to judge how far the offensive can be carried with due regard to the safe conduct of the convoy through many miles of submarine infested waters. Escorts are not only provided, as assumed by Plans in paragraph 8, for saving life, but primarily to assure supplies vital to our needs reaching this Country.

219.   *Sims to Keyes*

23 April 1918

Referring to your letter of 10 April, the members of my Planning Section have now returned from Queenstown and the following are the only suggestions they have to make concerning possible operations in the Dover Straits:-

1. A sound barrage established somewhere between Dover and Ostend. This is by means of what is known as the K-tube, the object of which is to notify the approach of submarines through these appliances. They have worked out rather successfully on the other

side and I believe they have been considerably improved since then. We are also going to install them in the Otranto Straits.

2. It is thought a surface barrage would of course be very useful, providing a mine can be devised that will ensure that it will stay at a constant depth below the surface during all states of the tide and currents. The problem of developing such a mine and gear was suggested for solution by our own Bureau of Ordnance, but I do not know what progress has been made. I realise of course, that this is a difficult proposition; that any appliance that is supposed to work automatically month after month under water must be a very good one indeed.

Needless to say we are all rejoicing over the success of the gallant operation that was carried out last night against Zeebrugge and Ostend.[1] This should have a marked deterrent effect upon the small submarines and will surely have a very great moral effect upon all of the Allies.

220. *Pringle to Sims*

USS *Melville*,
Queenstown,
24 April 1918

****

In connection with any contemplated change down here, I do not recollect whether I have ever informed you in previous letters of the principal result of Admiral Wemyss's visit to Queenstown, which was that Admiral Bayly received assurances that it was the intention to retain him in command of this Station and not to disturb him at the end of his three years of office which expires in July next. Of course, there is no telling what may happen in the future, but at present it is the intention to retain Admiral Bayly here. In my judgment and entirely apart from any consideration of the personalities that may be involved in this matter, it would be wholly impossible to conduct affairs at this Base on any other general system than the system upon which they are at present conducted; that is to say, the Commander-in-Chief must control the movements of the ships, and the senior officer of our own ships must look out for the internal administration, discipline, supply, etc.

[1] See Marder, vol. 5, pp. 45–66.

221. *Sims to Bayly*

5 May 1918

... I saw while in Paris figures compiled by the International Maritime Transport Council. These show that the curve of destruction and the curve of construction will cross each other before the middle of summer; that construction will thereafter remain ahead of destruction, but not very much ahead until the month of December, when it will be 100,000 tons ahead, but that after that the excess will increase with great rapidity.[1]

222. *Sims to Murray*

6 May 1918

Duty of Submarine Chasers ordered to Portsmouth, England

1. On the 4th instant, six U.S. Submarine Chasers manned by U.S. Naval personnel arrived at Brest en route for duty in British Waters.
2. These chasers have been ordered to proceed to Portsmouth as soon as practicable.
3. As the USS *Aylwin*[2] before leaving the United States Waters was employed on experimental duty with the same type of chasers, and in order to give the American listening devices with which these vessels are equipped a thorough test, it is desired that they be operated as a hunting unit under the direction of the Commanding Officer of the *Aylwin*.
4. The Commanding Officer of the *Aylwin* has been directed to take charge of these vessels upon their arrival and prepare them for service as a hunting unit as soon as possible.
5. The U.S. Navy Department has expressed a desire that if practicable these vessels be used exclusively as a hunting group with a view of thoroughly testing out the devices which they carry and gaining experience which will assist in preparing other vessels of the type for similar service.

223. *Sims to Rear-Admiral H. O. Dunn, U.S. Navy*[3]

7 May 1918

****

[1] See Marder, vol. 5, pp. 77–81.
[2] USS *Aylwin*: destroyer: 1913; 1036 tons; 4 × 4in; 8 tt; 29 knots.
[3] Commander, US Naval Forces, Azores Islands.

We are using every destroyer to the limit in order to bring in and take out the greatly increased troop transports and mercantile transports and as it is many vessels must go unescorted in the Channel and Irish Sea, particularly on their way to the rendezvous where the convoys are formed. It is in these areas that we are losing nearly all the vessels that are now being sunk. That is to say, the convoy system has practically defeated the submarine but we have not enough destroyers to do the necessary escorting in inclosed waters let alone enough to organise hunting squadrons which are the sole hope of putting the submarine out of business for all time.

224. *Report of an Admiralty Conference on Offensive Action against Enemy Submarines*

31 May 1918

****

2. General agreement was reached on the following points:-

(a) In open waters, if a submarine is sighted ahead of a convoy, i.e., inside the probable danger angle, at any distance up to about 4 miles, at least half the escort force (if composed of T.B.D.'s) should immediately proceed to the attack. The number of depth charges to be expended should vary from a large proportion of those carried when submarine leaves any definite traces, to a small proportion if there is nothing to indicate the position of a submarine, the action in the latter case being a general deterrent as opposed to a vigorous attack.

(b) The nearest destroyer, probably in most cases the destroyer which sights the submarine, should in addition to bombarding the probable area, drop a mark buoy to indicate where submarine was sighted. Other T.B.D.'s as they arrive should bombard the 'likely area'. This area can only be guessed, but the assumption can be made that the submarine, after being sighted or after firing her torpedo, will probably turn away from the convoy and will proceed at an average speed of about 200 yards a minute.

****

(d) It was considered inadvisable that any ship of the convoy should use a gun as a means of drawing attention to a submarine, as this leads to much indiscriminate shooting, which may sometimes be dangerous to the escort, and in any case leads to confusion.

(e) At night time when the first information of the presence of a submarine is the explosion of a torpedo, the general feeling of the conference was that some organised bombardment of an area astern of the position where the steamer was torpedoed should be carried out.

(f) *Disposition of escorts.* The general opinion of the conference[1] was that on account of the great increase in the number of depth charges carried by the escort and the deterioration of the enemy's morale, it was permissible to try the effect of modifying the disposition of the escorts in favour of the offensive positions. This was not to be taken to mean that the usual escorts ahead of the convoy should be reduced, but that the wing escorts might be stationed further aft. In cases where the strength of the escort permitted, one destroyer should be stationed astern zigzagging across the rear of the convoy.

****

225.   *Lieut. W. A. Edwards, U.S. Navy[2], to Murray*

6 June 1918

Arrival of the First United States Navy Aerial Detachment for Killingholme

1. The Force Commander takes pleasure in informing you that the first detachment of the U.S. Naval aeronautical material has arrived at Killingholme. This detachment consists of 23 H-16 Seaplanes, 8 Towing Lighters, and approximately 150 officers and enlisted personnel of the U.S. navy.

2. A second detachment of approximately the same material is expected at Killingholme within the next month. You will be duly informed of its arrival.

226.   *Geddes to Sims*

12 June 1918

I have a note dated 5 June from Commander-in-Chief at Malta, and I give you, for your personal information, an extract which he has written to me on the subject of Chasers. Where criticism is

---

[1] British and US escort vessel officers and Merchant Navy captains attended.

[2] Lieut. Walter A. Edwards, US Navy: began the war as a Lieut. (j.g.) aboard the

implied in what he says, I feel quite sure that you will not take it amiss, and will treat it as a personal and private communication from me.
(Enclosure)

Vice-Admiral Sir S. A. Gough-Calthorpe to Geddes

Mediterranean
Naval Staff Offices,
Malta,
5 June 1918

****

The whole 30 American Submarine Chasers have been docked here (10 in dock at a time). Nine arrived at Corfu yesterday and the remaining 21 sail this afternoon for Corfu with Commander Nelson, U.S. Navy.[1]

I went out in one of them to see her fire 'depth charges' and to try her Hydrophones. The Chasers are good sea boats and well fitted, but some are built of green wood, and I doubt if they will last long without a good deal of nursing.

They are at present overloaded with stores, etc., for the voyage which affects their speed, but this will no longer be the case when they work from Corfu Base.

The officers and men impressed me most favourably, and they are all as keen as possible.

The Chasers are well fitted with Hydrophone gear, but the gun armament is poor and the depth charges barely sufficient.

227. *Pringle to Sims*

8 July 1918

Davis and Allen – Attack on Submarine, 29 June 1918

Report of Commanding Officer [USS] *Davis* (Commander W. V. Tomb)[2] is quoted herewith:

destroyer *Cushing*; later joined Sims as his aide for aviation and ultimately promoted to Lieut.-Cdr.

[1] Cdr. Charles P. Nelson, US Navy: on outbreak of war stationed at Navy Yard, Philadelphia; in February 1918 commanded USS *Leonidas*; commanded submarine chaser squadron based on Corfu in later stages of war.

[2] Cdr W. V. Tomb, US Navy: began war as executive and gunnery officer and Lt-Cdr, USS *Louisiana*; at end of war commanded USS *Upshur*.

'*Davis* (S.O.), *Allen, Caldwell, Sampson, Wilkes, Beale, Ammen* and HMS *Heather* were escorting H.S. 44, consisting of HMS *Coronado*[1] and 38 merchant ships. Position, – Latitude 49° 04' North, Longitude 9° 25' West; speed 7 knots; course 109° magnetic; sea smooth; wind E.N.E. force 1; depth of water 55 fathoms.

At 1531 B.S.T., *Allen*, on port front, blew six blasts of whistle, increased speed, put marker buoy overboard, and began dropping depth charges. *Davis*, on starboard front, made full speed, 24 knots, and headed for marker buoy. When about 250 yards from buoy fired 'Y' gun, followed 9 seconds later by both Thorneycroft throwers. Put rudder over 20 right and dropped seven more depth charges at intervals of 9 seconds.

All depth charges set at 150 feet, and functioned properly. No apparent results.'

Report of *Allen* (Commander L. C. Farley)[2] is quoted herewith:

'At 3.25 p.m. B.S.T., 29 June, 1918, in Latitude 50° 03' North, Longitude 9° 15' West, while patrolling ahead of left front of convoy H.S. 44 of 40 ships, sighted periscope and feather about 1500 yards distant about 2 points abaft of starboard beam and about 1200 yards directly ahead of center of convoy. Periscope was moving in same general direction as convoy, and judging from the large feather and wake made, was making about 5 to 6 knots. It was seen twice by the Commanding Officer, once for the interval of about six seconds, again for about five seconds. *Allen* was making about 15 knots at the time and was swinging away from the periscope. Full speed, hard right, and general quarters were immediately given. Owing to the fact that *Allen* was then swinging to the left, she was somewhat slow in turning, it taking 2½ minutes to swing through some 160°. The position where the periscope disappeared was marked as accurately as possible. It was assumed that the submarine was going 200 yards a minute.

'A barrage of fifteen depth charges and buoy, including two from 'Y' gun were dropped ... The first four charges were set at 100 feet, the rest at 150 feet. All charges functioned, except the charge from the port leg of the 'Y' gun, which went off prematurely at a depth of approximately 40 feet, giving the ship considerable shock.

[1] HMS *Coronado*: convoy escort, ex-merchantman; 6939 tons; 4 × 6 in, 2 × 4 in; 15 knots.
[2] Cdr Louis C. Farley, US Navy: began war as Lt-Cdr, Bureau of Navigation, Navy Dept; at end of war commanded USS *Ammen*.

The *Davis* joined in the attack and also dropped an unknown number of depth charges. *Allen* continued circling at high speed, while convoy split. *Allen* remained in vicinity of buoy until convoy disappeared over the horizon, when she rejoined the convoy. There were no apparent results from the attack.'

****

228. *Sims to President Wilson*

13 July 1918

****

I am also glad to say that we now believe that we have the submarine campaign well in hand. It will doubtless be continued to the end, and we will doubtless suffer more or less serious losses, but it is perfectly apparent that the means of offence are gradually being improved, and the number of anti-submarine vessels increased, while the submarines are decreasing in number and in efficiency, so that there would appear no possibility of the enemy ever succeeding in destroying enough commerce to bring the Allies to terms.

229. *Admiralty Memorandum*

17 July 1918

Enemy Attacks on Merchant Shipping: Sailings and Losses

Nearly 93% of the Oversea traffic to and from the United Kingdom is now convoyed: the losses in convoy during the month representing 0.59% of the convoyed sailings, while those sunk before joining or after dispersal from convoy represent 0.16% of these sailings, making a total of 0.75% as against 0.97% in May. 6.2% of the non-convoyed sailings in Overseas trade were sunk.

230. *Sims to Captain N. A. McCully, U.S. Navy*[1]

4 August 1918

Employment of Submarine Chasers

****

---

[1] Captain Newton A. McCully, US Navy: commanded US Naval forces in Russia at end of war.

3. The special usefulness of submarine chasers depends upon their listening equipment, and upon the fitness of their personnel. Sea service in these chasers is extremely arduous when the sea is at all rough and listening equipment is entirely useless in rough weather. There are at present about seventy-seven American submarine chasers in the war zone. So far experience indicates that chasers should hunt in comparatively smooth deep waters which submarines frequent, such as the south coast of England, the Irish Sea and the Straits of Otranto. It has been found that when submarine chasers are in the vicinity – 10 to 12 miles – of surface vessels, the noise made by the latter interferes very seriously with the ability of the submarine chasers to hear submerged submarines.

4. In order to bring the chasers most frequently into contact with enemy submarines, it has been found desirable to station them either in a drifting or a listening patrol across the probable routes of submarines. The tendency of the submarine is to operate amongst vessels sailing singly rather than amongst convoys, since the latter are usually well protected by anti-submarine vessels and difficult to get at.

5. So far the difficulty has not been in getting contact with the enemy submarines but rather in attacking them successfully once contact is established. There have been repeated instances of chases, lasting from a brief period to several hours, in which the submarine has finally escaped through being able to conceal its movements by silent running or by remaining submerged.

6. The dropping of a large number of depth charges in the vicinity of a submarine is a policy which has received my approval but which so far has not been very productive of results. The average requirements of depth charges for the Queenstown Force alone is about 1,000 per month, and yet in spite of their very prodigal use of depth charges, no destroyer of the Queenstown Force is known to have sunk or seriously damaged an enemy submarine recently.

****

231.   *Memorandum by Admiralty Plans Division*

28 August 1918

Measures Required to meet the Submarine Situation in the Future

****

(Extract)

Minutes of the Operations Committee, 27 August 1918
Losses of Merchant Ships by Submarines

97. ... statistics of losses indicated that the enemy is directing his attack against the larger size of ship ...

The statistics also showed that the monthly losses of tonnage were not decreasing but were remaining fairly constant and that the distance from land at which ships were attacked and sunk showed a tendency to increase. ...

... It was generally agreed that the escorting of convoys far from land by destroyers was the most effective means of protection, but in this connection it was recognised that an escort of Destroyers could only be supplied to a very limited extent owing to the difficulty of providing the necessary number of this Class of Vessel and complements of men required. As an alternative escorting vessel the Patrol Gunboat was considered the best, though its utility for attacking submarines was necessarily inferior to that of the Destroyer by reason of its limited speed.

It was agreed that Mr Roosevelt should be asked to consider what assistance the United States Government could give in the direction of providing vessels of the Patrol Gunboat Class, and for the purposes of a discussion with Mr Roosevelt A.C.N.S. was asked to check the accuracy of the statements in the memorandum and the Director of Plans[1] was instructed to prepare an appreciation of the whole situation with suggestions as to the steps which might be taken to improve the effectiveness of the methods of combatting submarine attacks.

(Plans Division Memorandum)

****

3. The only new factor in this respect is the advent of the cruiser submarine, which has a surface speed of 18 knots and will probably remain at sea for six months, and be able to visit any part of the world. Twelve are believed to be on order, and six should be in commission before the end of the year.[2]

****

5. These vessels were probably designed with the primary role of attacking trade on the surface by gunfire. The reply is the extension

---

[1] Captain Cyril Fuller.
[2] Only two of these vessels got to sea before the war's end; see Trask, *Captains and Cabinets*, p. 220.

of the ocean escort system to the South Atlantic and to the outward trade in the North Atlantic. If certain British cruisers are withdrawn from patrol duties on distant stations and, together with the United States pre-dreadnought battleships and [armoured] cruisers, are used for ocean escorts, it is considered there should be sufficient ships for the purpose.

6. The United States are arranging for a percentage of their merchant ships to be equipped with a special armament[1] which will enable them to strengthen the ocean escorts, and the application of this system to the British Mercantile Marine is under consideration.

7. The ocean escort system is also a protection from the submarine cruiser's torpedo attack, for by concentrating shipping in a small space, it is more difficult to find. The only other possible countermeasure, on the North American Atlantic Coast, is the provision of anti-submarine escorts on similar lines to those in the British submarine zone, but the number of vessels required would be out of all proportion to the very limited enemy submarine force in that area. It is considered that such vessels would be better employed in preventing the enemy submarines proceeding into the Atlantic.

****

10. With regard to the present stationary position of monthly losses of tonnage, this is due to the fact that we are not destroying sufficient submarines to reduce it, and that, neglecting losses amongst vessels not in convoy, the present rate of sinking is a measure of the limitations of the convoy system's defensive power.

11. In order to reach the present situation and reduce the loss of merchant tonnage, the rate of destroying submarines must be accelerated, and that is the factor which dominates every other aspect of the situation. Up to the present the vast majority of fast anti-submarine forces have been employed on escort duty, and this is more particularly true of destroyers, which are the only vessels with sufficient speed for hunting purposes.

12. The enemy has maintained the initiative in the submarine campaign from the beginning, and we have never felt sufficiently safe to withdraw destroyers from escort work for purely hunting operations. Also the fact that he has a free passage through the North Sea, and passes backwards and forwards without interruption, makes us scatter our forces over a wide field, and, under these circumstances, the destruction of the submarines becomes largely a matter of chance.

[1] Six 5-in guns.

13. It is much more important to consider the destruction of the submarine in the narrow waters of the North Sea than the extension of anti-submarine escorts across the Atlantic. The latter measure is not only impracticable but would be opposed to every sound principle of concentration. The minimum number of small craft likely to be required for the purpose would be about 1000, and a small proportion of these operating in the North Sea should be able to destroy enemy submarines.

14. It is considered that the progress made with submarine listening devices makes it almost certain that hunting by a combination of sound and sight will eventually prove effective if suitable vessels, such as destroyers, are used in sufficient numbers, together with personnel well trained in the tactics required and the listening devices employed. The geographical position of the East Coast, right on the flank of the inward and outward submarine tracks, is a factor of which full advantage has not yet been taken.

15. If a sufficient number of suitable craft are continuously and systematically employed in offensive anti-submarine operations in the North Sea, they will, in conjunction with the Northern Barrage and other obstacles, destroy and damage a percentage of the submarines en route between their bases and their operating areas, and this percentage will increase as the personnel and instruments improve, so that eventually it should only be possible for a small proportion of submarines to succeed in reaching the Atlantic.

****

19. The measures suggested to meet the submarine situation are:-
   (a) Completion of the Northern Barrage from the Norwegian Coast to the Orkneys.
   (b) The provision of strong hunting forces in the North Sea composed of destroyers or similar vessels with listening apparatus and personnel to work it. It is considered that at least 50 are required to have any effect on the submarines.
   (c) The augmentation to a suitable establishment of anti-submarine craft for ocean escort duties up to 500 miles from British and French Atlantic ports. These craft to be suitable for working with the hunting forces if required.

Note: With regard to the above, the requirements of (b) should be met before those for (c).

Minute by ACNS

****

The actual fact is that experience has proved that until we have discovered a really effective listening apparatus for high speed craft, and possibly not even then, there is no more futile offensive measure than that of employing Destroyers in so called hunting operations.

...

Convoy is a bait which must attract enemy submarines. ...

232. *Memoranda by British and American Planning Sections on Submarine Situation in general, Anti-Submarine measures, and manner in which American shipyards could assist British construction of anti-submarine vessels*

30 August 1918

****

Memorandum by U.S. Planning Section

****

2. Our principal and most successful reply to the submarine has been the convoy system. By means of it we have been enabled to keep losses within bounds and to continue the war.

3. One of the enemy's anti-convoy measures has been to extend submarining further into the Atlantic and, to a small extent to the North American coast.

****

5. ... We have reached approximately the limit of protection which a practicable convoy escort system is able to afford.

6. We adopted the convoy system originally because at that time there was no other alternative. The enemy had the initiative and has maintained it. At no time have we felt sufficiently secure to assign forces, at the expense of the convoy system, to operations more offensive in character.

7. Our losses will not be reduced much below the present figures until we succeed in developing an offensive support to the convoy system. The inevitable effect of success in this form will be a reduction in escort requirements.

8. The most important anti-submarine measure which can be effected at present is the speedy completion of the North Sea and Adriatic Mine Barrages; complete in length from coast to coast, and in depth from the surface to about 300 feet.

9. The support of the barrages by surface craft and aircraft will render them more effective. In fact the barrage will furnish a nucleus of effort about which we may assemble with safety our main anti-submarine effort, and ultimately conform to the principle of concentration; which the enemy's advantage of the initiative has heretofore denied us.

10. Another important offensive measure which should be further developed is submarine hunting. It should be most useful when used to support the mine barrages.

11. Our experience to date with hunting by sound has been disappointing. Undoubtedly to some extent [this was] due to inexperienced personnel and to the necessity for operating with material which was still in the development stage. The lack of success has been due also to the lack of development of hunting tactics.

12. Large groups hunting by sight during long nights is worthy of trial; and a combination of sight and sound hunting should prove effective with vessels of proper type and personnel trained in the special tactics required. While no untried effort should be put into effect on a large scale, still we are justified at this time in allotting a sufficient number of vessels to demonstrate whether an offensive method of such apparently promising value is in reality worth further effort.

13. With barrages properly completed and properly supported by hunting groups and other craft, it is very probable that convoy requirements will be reduced materially. But we cannot afford to rely wholly upon such an assumption; and it is possible that a greater number of anti-submarine vessels, suitable for high seas work, than are now projected will be required.[1]

****

In the original draft of the British paper, insufficient emphasis was laid upon the Northern Barrage and its support to satisfy the American representatives and since time forbade further discussion, the two memoranda were then submitted separately.

Subsequently the British memorandum was altered to emphasize more strongly the importance of completing and supporting the Northern Barrage.

[1] For the most part the Admiralty memorandum echoes that of US Planning Section.

Memorandum by Admiralty Plans Division

1. The fact that the percentage of sinkings beyond fifty miles from the coast has risen during the last few months, does not, so far as the ordinary U-boat is concerned, indicate any radical change in the enemy's submarine policy now or in the future. There does not appear to be any ground for the assumption that as our anti-submarine measures improve, the submarines will work further out. Outside narrow areas, such as the North Sea, Irish Sea and English Channel, the space involved is so large that counter-measures must be more or less limited to the immediate vicinity of the convoys, and these are much the same whether the convoy is 30 miles or 300 miles from the coast.

****

4. It is physically impossible for us to counter this move by extending the convoy system throughout the Atlantic route. About 1200 escorting vessels of sea-going anti-submarine type would be required for such a convoy system. The most complete defensive reply which we are able to make is to duplicate approximately on the North American coast the convoy escort system now in effect in Europe.
5. But it should be specially noted that such measures alone will not reduce materially the mercantile losses below present figures.

233. *Notes by Admiralty Plans Division on Proposed Agenda for Conference on American Naval Air Operations*

11 September 1918

1. (a) It is considered that American Naval Air Forces should co-operate with Allied Forces on anti-submarine, enemy coast, long [range] reconnaissance and bombing operations, assuming responsibility for these operations in certain defined areas within which they should operate as complete units.
   (b) Proposed that the following areas, involving operations as stated, be taken over by American Forces as early as can be arranged, British or other Allied Forces now operating in these areas to be diverted as requisite:

(1) *Adriatic Sea and Gulf of Taranto*
Operations against Austrian naval bases, fighting, reconnaissance, patrol of Otranto Barrage and anti-submarine intensive patrols.

(2) *Irish Coast*
Anti-submarine patrols, convoy escorts and reconnaissance. Americans to be requested to allocate one squadron for surveillance of West Coast of Ireland to prevent possible attempts to land arms and ammunition.

(3) *Dunkirk*
Bombing operations on Flanders coast and naval bases.

(4) *Bay of Biscay*
Anti-submarine operations and escort of convoys as arranged with French Naval Authorities.

(5) *Killingholme*
Patrol of British minefields in North Sea, long distance reconnaissance, and bombing of naval bases on German Coast.

British Naval Air Forces to carry out anti-submarine operations on coast of Great Britain, together with operations in the Mediterranean area, with the exception of the Adriatic Sea and Gulf of Taranto, but including operations in the Aegean Sea.

2. (a) British forces to be developed in accordance with present approved policy.

(b) Fighting, torpedo, bombing and reconnaissance aeroplanes, and flying-boat seaplanes.

(c) Present approved programme to be completed. Requirements in Adriatic and Aegean to be assessed upon a basis of resources of material and personnel available. A statement of priority to be established.

****

6. The policy of long-distance bombing included in 1918 policy for Killingholme Base to be modified to include patrol of minefields and to admit of the development of bombing aeroplanes from lighters should the results of tests to be carried out show this to be a preferable method of attacking German North Sea bases.

234. *Sims to Bayly*

21 September 1918

****

[quoting Admiral Mayo][1]

'...After spending sufficient time at the Queenstown Base to see something of each one of the activities covered by the United States Naval Forces at that point I desire to heartily congratulate you and all concerned in carrying on these activities, upon the manifestly thorough organisation, system, and general efficiency. The spirit and high sense of duty maintained by the entire personnel of these activities is to be congratulated and the harmony and spirit of cooperation maintained between the American and British personnel at that point was most apparent.

The above remarks may also be applied to our Air Stations on the Irish Coast although due to regrettable difficulties these stations are not yet in full operating condition.'

235. *Sims to Bayly*

24 September 1918

****

... You may be sure that I realise that there should be a greater force at Queenstown, but I am sure also that you can readily see that the first new destroyers that come out must be utilised to increase the protection of not only the troop transports but also of the vessels that are supplying them.

I think I mentioned that some of our quite valuable supply ships are going through the Mediterranean two at a time escorted by one destroyer and sometimes not escorted at all. We must also face the fact that the number of supply ships coming in to the western ports of France are continually on the increase, and this makes it quite impossible to give adequate protection to the empty transports going westward. It is also a fact that our troop transports are not as strongly escorted as they probably should be. This is particularly true of the ones that pass in through the Channel and up the Thames. There is no doubt at all that the principal dignitiaries at home are very nervous lest some of our troop transports be torpe-

---

[1] Mayo had recently visited the European theatre for a second time.

doed. Of course you will understand that this nervousness is largely of a political kind. It is therefore apparent that the first reinforcements will have to be devoted to the services above indicated. These necessities, as I have said, are largely political.[1] Personally, I cannot persuade myself that the Germans have any intention of concentrating their submarine efforts against our troop transports. There was an explanation published in the German papers explaining to the German people why it was that they were not successful in stopping the arrival of troop transports. It seems to me that this explanation is perfectly sound from a military point of view. It pointed out that transports may arrive anywhere from the north of Scotland to the south of France; that it was exceedingly difficult to intercept them; that they were heavily escorted; and that a greater effect could be produced upon the enemy by attacking merchant vessels bringing in supplies of all kinds. This is exactly my opinion. It seems to me that if I were a Hun and in complete command of the Hun submarine campaign I would give the submarines orders not to attack loaded transports. This for the reason that the submarine runs a very considerably greater danger in attacking through the escort of a troop transport than through the escort of a much larger merchant convoy.

Moreover, the torpedoing of an occasional troop transport would not sensibly decrease the number of men flowing into Europe while the torpedoing of a number of merchant vessels will eventually limit the number of troops that we can maintain in Europe. There is a commission over here now earnestly looking for more ships than our shipyards will be able to supply in the coming year. If they cannot find these ships the flow of troops will have to be decreased.

236. *Bayly to Sims*

30 September 1918

I have been away to Kingstown and Wexford or I would have written earlier. So very many thanks for getting Pringle off and helping him to cross over with a reasonable certainty of his return.[2] When   he   returns   safely   you   must   go   over,   and   get

---

[1] See Admiral W. V. Pratt, *Autobiography* (unpublished typescript, 1939, in Operational Archives, Naval Historical Center, Navy Yard, Washington, D.C.), p. 219: 'Imagine what the effect would have been upon [Americans] had a few troop laden transports been sunk at the beginning of this vast movement. It might have stopped the flow. Certainly it would have impeded it. We couldn't afford to take the risk.'

[2] Pringle made a brief visit to the USA.

refreshed for the spring offensive. I shall be very glad to get the *Hannibal*;[1] the chasers are well under weigh now and I have hopes of them, but am not very certain that the best work is to be got out of them where a Warrant Officer is in charge of a unit and Hepburn[2] I think agrees. What they want more than anything else is a quick brain; they will soon learn seamanship, and these young university boys are just the youngsters to succeed. The seaplane stations are getting under way and beginning to patrol, and altogether your people are beginning to feel that they are now really helping; just as your destroyers were after they had got through their apprenticeship. Herbster[3] at Wexford is a great boy; as keen as he can be, and very knowledgeable.... I have been able to give Rodgers[4] an escort for sub calibre in Bantry Bay, but have told him I cannot take the responsibility of escorting him outside to do heavy gun practice with submarines passing nearly every day. I like him very much, he showed me the triple turrets the other day; they may be good but at present I prefer the double ones. But I like very much the blast screen between the guns inside the double turrets; we ought to have it.

I did not mean the other day to worry you for more destroyers because you know the situation as well as I do. What I want now is three of our 'K' submarines[5] to operate against these new German submarines from now on between about 47° and 51°, and 7° to 15°. The Admiralty refusal seemed to me very weak.

I agree with your argument showing why the German s/ms do not attack your transports; I want the 'K' s/ms as an offensive weapon against the enemy, and the Atlantic is well suited for them.

... your room is ready for you, you had better come in October before the November rains begin.

[1] USS *Hannibal*: tender to submarine chasers, formerly fuel ship and surveying vessel; 1898; 4000 tons; 1 × 6 in, 2 × 3 in; 9 knots.

[2] Captain Arthur J. Hepburn, US Navy: began war as Lt-Cdr and executive officer of *South Carolina*; in February 1918 a Cdr and CO of *Chicago*; at this time in command of submarine chasers based at Queenstown.

[3] Lt-Cdr Victor O. Herbster, US Navy: began war as Lieut, receiving ship, New York; in February 1918, aboard *Huron*; at this time commanding US Naval Air Station, Wexford.

[4] Rear-Admiral Thomas S. Rodgers, US Navy: formerly commanded Battleship Division 5, Atlantic Fleet; arrived at Berehaven summer 1918 in command of Division 6 (3 dreadnoughts), intended to deal with a feared German battle cruiser raid on convoy routes.

[5] 'K' class submarines: 1916–18; 1880/2650 tons; 24/9.5 knots; 6 tt. First steam powered fleet submarines, intended to operate with Grand Fleet, therefore designed to make same surface speed as battleships. They were not a success and suffered several accidents.

****

237. *Sims to Bayly*

2 October 1918

****

I have telegraphed to Washington explaining how useful some additional submarines of our 'O' and 'R' classes would be.[1] I am assured by Constructor Land,[2] who has recently come over from the other side, and who makes a speciality of submarines, that these boats are really efficient. I think the more submarines we can send out after the Hun submarines the better. There is nothing they fear more than the presence of enemy submarines in their operating area. Today there are no less than seven submarines in the latitude of Brest and between longitudes 9° and 12°. The Admiralty intends to base six submarines on Falmouth and keep three in the area of this concentration until it is broken up. They are only waiting to make an agreement with the French, as these submarines were allocated by agreement to a certain position in the Channel.

****

238. *U.S. Office of Naval Intelligence: Prolonged Submarine Hunt with Hydrophone*

17 October 1918

While returning from escort duty, 1100, 17 October 1918, the USS *Kimberly*[3] received a dispatch from the Commander-in-Chief, Coast of Ireland, stating that an enemy submarine, homeward bound, was due off Fastnet about 4.0 p.m.

The estimated hourly positions of the submarine were plotted, both for his making Fastnet and for the contingency of his making straight for Bull Rock Light. The *Kimberly's* courses were steered to pass through his probable positions for the second contingency, but

[1] US 'O' class submarines: 1916–18; 485/630 tons; 14/10 knots; 4 tt.US 'R' class submarines: 1917–20; 569/680 tons; 13.5/10 knots; 4 tt.
[2] Constructor Commander Emory S. Land, US Navy (Construction Corps): Bureau of Construction and Repair, Navy Dept., Washington; a distinguished naval architect.
[3] USS *Kimberly*: destroyer; see note to 102, Part III.

yet so as to arrive by 1600 at his 1500 position near Fastnet.

At 1600 arrived at submarine's assumed 1500 position off Fastnet and laid down a base course for Bull Rock. Primary zigzags of 60° from the base course were established; proceeded to hunt with 'K' tube and 'S' tube, superimposing a zigzag on the primary zigzag. Speed 15 knots. Visibility good. Sea northwesterly and moderate. Wind northwest – 3 to 4. Several trawlers and one British destroyer hull down in the vicinity.

Stopped to listen 28 times. The periods during which the ship was stopped and all auxiliaries shut down (including time for stopping and getting away again) was fixed at five minutes. Two listeners always were employed at the 'K' tube, and the bearings announced by each were considered before deciding on the next course and run. During the latter half of the search neither 'K' tube listener was permitted to communicate his bearings to the other – a matter which is considered important. The two listeners – an officer and an enlisted man – gave readings that practically agreed, throughout the search, from 1600, 17 October, to 0200, 18 October. The 'S' tube got no sound contact at any time.

Sound contact was made at 1710. Zigzag was employed in most cases in running down successive contacts, calculating the necessary advances and time at which the next observation should be made. The intervals between observations were varied widely, in order that the submarine might not anticipate the destroyer's listening time, and be quiet. Observations showed the submarine to be making wide and irregular zizags. He was approximately 4 miles northwest when first detected. Successive observations showed that he came southwest and then northwest, then southwest again. *Kimberly* then used two 60° legs to westward of a base course approximately south and forced him back again to the eastward. Again employed two westward zigzags legs on the northerly course, to keep him from getting out to the westward and at 1856 had him close abroad, evidently trying to escape by going east and north. Went ahead full speed and laid a straight barrage, on a northeast course, of seven charges – 4 from depth charge racks, 2 from 'Y' gun, and 1 from Thorneycroft thrower.

Stood on for several minutes, parallel to course of barrage, then ran back over barrage. Much oil was visible on the water, but, of course, may have been the oil from ship's old wake. Maneuvered to get to westward of oil patch (so as not to be silhouetted against the moon), when it was reported that a depth charge was in danger of being released. Was compelled to stand on various courses in the vicinity, as stopping would have endangered the ship. The sea made work with the cockbilled charges, at releasing position, very difficult. All that could be done was to let go the charge, having previously placed it on safety. Shifted depth charges from starboard to port rack, as releasing gear of former was jammed, and could not be repaired during hunting operations.

It is regretted that listening was not possible immediately after laying the barrage. A larger barrage would have been laid, but it was expected that Kimberly could keep close enough to submarine to force him to surface, and it was accordingly concluded that the supply of charges should be conserved for that event.

At 2035 could make no sound contact, after running to northwestward. Stood southeast, and at 2107 heard submarine about 1 mile to westward. Then stood north and west and at 2124 picked submarine up again slightly to eastward, at a distance estimated to be about one-half mile. It was concluded that he was again attempting to get away by curving to eastward, northward and westward. Such proved to be the case as shown by observation at 2137, when he was heard fairly close aboard about one-fourth mile northeast. It was concluded that he would now change course to the southward, and accordingly stood east and heard him very close aboard at 2150, immediately after which a second straight barrage of three depth charges were laid.

The locality of the second barrage was swept and at 2219 found by observation that he had stood almost due west. At 2245 again found him to the westward. It was concluded that he would try to make to the northward, and after two legs of zigzag to the westward end of a northwest base course, heard the submarine at 2258 about 2 miles to the northward.

Contact was maintained until 0128, 18 October, when difficulties were experienced in getting bearings. At 0140, off the mouth of the Kenmare River, the sounds were faint and could not be centered. Contact was considered lost at 0200.

In listening the ship was headed to the sea to eliminate water noises. During the latter part of the search the wind and sea had increased somewhat and made listening more difficult. It will be noted that contact was maintained for practically seven hours.

239. *Bayly to Sims*

20 October 1918

... I sincerely trust that you men of action in London will not allow the kid-gloved politicians to let us down.[1]

There are two matters I want to draw to your notice. One is the number of collisions and accidents that are happening, and which (in my opinion) are closely related to the untrained youngsters in command of the destroyers. A man may be Executive Officer of a destroyer for years, and never handle one, and although you want good men in your new destroyers, we want good and experienced men over here. And the winter is only beginning.

Another is that when a destroyer such as the *Caldwell*[2] is sent for a week to Devonport, it means a serious loss to us. We lose her during the time going there, there and returning, and if away during full moon she (our best listening ship) is a serious loss to me in the Irish Sea if she is not used in an escort. It hardly seems fair on us here, especially with *Davis*, *Shaw*, *Balch*, *Paulding* all out of action in collisions.

****

240. *Captain R. H. Leigh, US Navy, to Sims*

30 November 1918

****

2. The Director of the Anti-Submarine Division of the Admiralty[3] has at all times shown the greatest interest in American Listening Devices and given us every encouragement and most cheerful and hearty assistance in their development. All information of the development of British devices has been most freely and fully

---

[1] The Armistice was in course of negotiation. Bayly and Sims shared the general antipathy of serving officers everywhere to politicians.

[2] USS *Caldwell*: destroyer, 1917; 1125 tons; 4 × 4in; 12 tt; 31 knots. She was a hydrophone-equipped vessel and had been detached to the Plymouth command to work with US submarine chasers in U-boat hunts.

[3] Captain W. W. Fisher.

placed at our disposal and been of greatest value to us; in this connection we have been given every opportunity to visit the Experimental Stations of the Admiralty and to witness all tests conducted. On all occasions of such visits we have been treated with more than courtesy; we have been made to feel that we were on the same status as the British officers with whom we have been associated in this work, the one object being to develop with energy those devices which appeared to give promise of greatest effectiveness against the enemy submarines without regard [to] whether the principle involved was based on American or British initiative.

****

4. Every effort has been made to see that all trials and tests of the various devices, whether American or British, were conducted in standard conditions in order that fair comparison might be had of the devices. ...

****

241.   *Murray to Sims*

17 December 1918

****

...Captain Fisher has from time to time represented the value of the assistance and advice so constantly and generously accorded to him by Captain R. H. Leigh, US Navy, and the officers associated with him.

It is fully recognised that in America a large band of experts in specially equipped stations have for months past been engaged in devising apparatus to meet the submarine menace, and it is owing to the close liaison that has existed between your staff and the Admiralty Naval Staff that there has not only been complete knowledge of developments in your Country but that a large quantity of apparatus designed in America and in part made in America is actually, at the present moment, carried by British vessels that have been engaged in the anti-submarine campaign.

Their Lordships would ask you to record the fact that this happy result is mainly owing to the personality of [Captain Leigh] and they would be grateful if an expression of the thanks of the Admiralty could be conveyed to Captain Leigh for the unvarying tact and courtesy he has shown and for the special technical knowledge that he has placed so unreservedly at the service of the Admiralty.

242. *Gunnery Department, United States Destroyer Flotillas based on Queenstown, Ireland*

24 December 1918

****

5. *Policy*

... Immediately upon our arrival a complete and careful study was made of British methods and practices and, for a time these were adopted. The British Authorities furnished us with all information at their disposal covering the question of anti-submarine warfare. As the experience of the force grew, these policies were modified as good judgment dictated and before long the Queenstown Force was able to draw up and put into effect the policies and instructions which remained in use until the end. In the preparation of such policies we were constantly assisted and advised by the British Authorities. The experience of the sea-going element was the deciding critic. Conferences of Commanding Officers were often held and useful information was mimeographed and sent out to the Forces as soon as received. In this way complete harmony and co-operation was effected. The policies developed covered all questions of patrol, convoy escort, anti submarine warfare, various types of gun and torpedo practices, and also provided for major ship action should we be called upon to operate as Flotillas with the British Grand Fleet or our own fleet. ...

Organization of Base Facilities

... The British Authorities placed at our disposal such material and weapons as they had and at all times assisted us with their excellent advice. Before long the Base had accumulated sufficient spare parts and spare guns to answer the ordinary requirements of the service and of any probable action.

****

6. *Antisubmarine Warfare and Methods, Depth Charge Policy*

In the development of this warfare a careful study was made of British methods. Officers visited British ships as often as opportunity permitted. Representatives were sent to attend conferences at the British Admiralty in London. Conferences of Commanding Officers were frequently held and all data possible was collected and compiled, and from this information concrete plans covering methods of attack on submarines under various conditions were drawn up and issued.

****

10. *General*

The work accomplished by this Force would have been impossible had it not been for the cordial relations which existed between the officers of the British vessels attached to this Base, the officers of the staff of the Commander-in-Chief, Coast of Ireland and those attached to the Dockyard at Haulbowline. Every effort was made by them to supply us with the latest information in use in the British Forces and to procure material for us for our work and to advise us as to its installation and use. All British publications which could have been of the slightest benefit to us were procured for us. All plans of any consequence which were developed by this Force were sent to the British Authorities for comment and suggestion. In this way the most complete unity of ideas at all times prevailed.

It is interesting to know that a depth charge attack instrument designed, developed and constructed on board the USS *Allen* was submitted to the British Admiralty for comment and this instrument has been universally adopted by order of the Admiralty on all destroyer forces of the British Navy.

During this entire period of activities, the Ordnance Department attempted to maintain the destroyers and the USS *Dixie* and USS *Melville* in such a state that all of them could proceed at 24 hours notice on distant service. They carried sufficient reserve ammunition, torpedoes, warheads, and spare parts to make them self-sustaining during a considerable period of time.

243.   *Bayly to the Admiralty*

Commander-in-Chief's Office,
Queenstown,
31 December 1918

Be pleased to lay the following letter before Their Lordships, with a view (should they agree) to its being forwarded to the Navy Department, Washington, D.C., U.S.A., through Admiral W. S. Sims, US Navy.

2. Sea fighting having ceased on this station on the signing of the Armistice; and the fighting units of the U.S.A. that were stationed on the Coast of Ireland having completed their work, and been withdrawn; it appears to me opportune to make a few remarks as a record of what is probably a unique situation, viz., US Navy forces operating entirely under a British Admiral in British waters.

3. When each of the various units arrived here, they found themselves confronted by an entirely new situation. They were faced by an unprecedented kind of warfare, and new methods of attack and found themselves operating in waters which were strange to them and in unfamiliar types of weather.

4. They at once set to work with all their energies to learn the new methods; there was no foreign feeling about them, not a sign of jealousy, no impatience at receiving their orders from a foreign Admiral, they were single minded in their endeavours to do their utmost for the common cause, and in consequence they proved to be a most valuable asset to the Allies, and assisted magnificently to save a very dangerous situation.

5. It is hard to express in words the singleness of purpose which animated them; the eagerness with which they set themselves to learn all the methods which had been tried, and to improve these methods so as not lose any possible chance of success. It should be remembered that success in this submarine war is not only measured by the number of submarines sunk (except in the case of Mystery Ships and other craft whose sole duty is to sink them) but by the number of ships, crews, and cargoes preserved from attack, and in this they have every reason to be most proud of their success, though the actual numbers can never be known as we can never know the number of attacks that were prevented by their constant vigilance and ability.

6. It appears to me reasonable to make a few remarks on each type that came over:-

(1) *Destroyers*

They were at once sent out to patrol certain areas, mostly west of the Fastnet; later on they were formed into escorts for convoys, and when a chance came they were formed into hunting squadrons.

Frequently they were under the orders of British Officers such as when they were in an escort whose senior officer was a British Commander or Lieutenant Commander in a sloop, frequently they had British Officers under them, and it is very greatly to the credit of both that there never was a question, a doubt, or any sign of anything but perfect co-operation.

When in harbour for the usual rest, they were always ready to be called on for an emergency, and more than once they proved their readiness when necessity arose.

(2) *Submarines*

They were handed over to Captain H. H. Nesmith in the
Ambrose at Berehaven[1] to learn the new method of warfare.
Thanks to his infinite tact and well proved ability, and to their
keenness and eagerness to learn, they were soon able to take
up the duties of a sea patrol, and under Captain T. S. Hart, US
Navy, and Commander W. L. Friedell, US Navy,[2] who
relieved him, they were able to keep their patrols in any
weather and to be relied on to keep their patrol waters clear.

(3) *Seaplanes and Kite Balloons*

They proved to be a very valuable asset to the station; their
difficulties in the matter of being housed in a foreign country
and operating in unfamiliar weather over strange lands were
considerable. They soon grappled with the situation and
proved to be most useful. Commander F. E. McCrary, US
Navy[3] took infinite trouble to get the greatest value out of
them, and for the short time during which they operated, they
were most useful.

(4) *Chasers*

The chasers came in at a late season, September, and before
starting to operate had to learn the appearance of the coast,
and the navigational necessities such as tides, currents,
appearance of headlands, etc. They were untried being a new
type of craft, and commanded by officers who had no previous
fighting training. But thanks to their plucky energy which
declined to see difficulties, and owing to the great ability and
tact of Captain A. J. Hepburn, US Navy, who was in charge
of them, they soon grasped an unfamiliar situation and would
soon have become a great asset in working with the sea-planes
off the coast.

[1] Captain H. H. Nesmith: not identified. Probably a misprint for Captain M. E.
Nasmith (later Admiral Sir Martin Dunbar-Nasmith) VC; a Dardanelles submarine
hero; at that time commanding HM submarines at Berehaven. HMS *Ambrose*:
submarine depot ship, 1915; 6480 tons; 14.5 knots.
[2] Captain Thomas S. Hart, US Navy: began war as Lieut-Cdr commanding Division 3 of Submarine Force, aboard the tender USS *Alert* of the Pacific Fleet; in
February 1918 a Commander in charge of Division 5; later a Captain in Office of
Naval Operations, following a spell with his submarines at Berehaven. In December
1941, Admiral Hart was in command of the Asiatic Fleet in the Philippines. Cdr
Wilhelm L. Friedell, US Navy: began war as a Lieut commanding submarine tender
Bushnell; Lieut-Cdr by February 1918; succeeded Hart as CO, Submarine Division 5
at Berehaven.
[3] Cdr Frank E. McCrary, US Navy: begun war as a Lieut-Cdr and instructor at the
Naval Air Station, Pensacola, Fla., the US Navy's principal aircrew training base; at
this time commanding the US Naval Air Station at Queenstown.

(5) *Repair Ships*
Without these the work could never have been done. Working complete 24 hours in three shifts of eight hours each; sleeping among the noise of machinery; always ready for extra work when an unexpected accident happened, or an unforeseen call was made on a destroyer that was being dealt with; they never failed me. Captain J. R. P. Pringle of the *Melville* and Captain H. B. Price of the *Dixie* were not only always ready to do the expected but used their utmost endeavours to be prepared for the unforeseen, and the result was such as their country has reason to be proud of.

(6) *Battleships at Berehaven*
Although the battleships were not directly under my operative orders, Admiral T. S. Rodgers laid himself out to meet my wishes in every way, and did all that was possible to help at Berehaven whenever he had an opportunity to do so. He worked with me when his squadron was ordered to sea, and always showed that his intention was to be an integral part of the U.S. Forces operating off the Coast of Ireland as long as it was in time with his other orders to do so.

7. It is proper to place on record the behaviour of the men on shore, which was excellent. A Men's Club was built for their entertainment, and thanks to Captain J. R. P. Pringle's discipline (he being the Senior U.S. Officer in the port) there was practically no trouble on shore. Even when, owing to the hostile attitude of certain of the inhabitants of Cork, it was necessary to put the city and a radius of three miles outside, out of bounds to British and U.S. Officers and men, the situation was accepted and no trouble ensued.

8. Finally I wish to acknowledge the generous, broad-minded help which I have always received from Admiral W. S. Sims, US Navy. From first to last he has worked with me for the Allied cause in a way which has compelled the admiration of all concerned.

PART V

THE GRAND FLEET
JUNE 1917 TO DECEMBER 1918

INTRODUCTION

By the summer of 1917, Britain was beginning to run short of manpower. Sustaining for the first time a mass conscript army of millions, subject to enormous casualties, Britain was also building up incomparably the world's greatest air force and at the same time functioning as the principal arsenal, coal supplier and industrial base of the Entente. In these circumstances, the Royal Navy was finding it difficult to man new ships, by this time largely light cruisers and flotilla craft. It was proposed that several pre-dreadnoughts of the Channel Fleet should be paid off and replaced by four of the older dreadnoughts from the Grand Fleet, themselves to be superseded by four American battleships [244]. The Navy Department declined the request on several grounds. American admirals (Sims being the notable exception) remained faithful to the rigid Mahanite 'fetish'[1] of battlefleet concentration and were resolved not to dribble it away in penny packets. They feared that the United States might have to meet an undiminished German fleet alone should the shaky Entente collapse. Even if this were not the case, the untrustworthy Japanese might take advantage of the scattering of American naval power to switch sides and stab the United States in the back. The US Navy had a paranoid fear of such a strike but even more so of a two-ocean conflict with both Germany and Japan.[2] Furthermore, the British had given little indication of the use to which they intended to put the American dreadnoughts and certainly nothing of an offensive nature.[3] The US Navy was equally short of trained personnel and four battleships with full war complements would drain the pool still further. Daniels believed the British supply system would be put under unacceptable pressure by their demands. In any case, he observed to Wilson, the British already enjoyed a capital ship superiority over the Germans of 2.5:1 and therefore required no reinforcement.[4] Sims, exasperated, pointed

[1] R. F. Weigley. *The American Way of War* (New York: Macmillan, 1973), p. 187.
[2] Allard, p. 77.
[3] Trask, *Captains and Cabinets*, p. 136
[4] Daniels to Wilson, 14 July 1917, *Wilson Papers*, vol. 43, pp. 178–9.

out that, since the United States was fighting alongside the United Kingdom, the Grand Fleet represented the concentrated battlefleet and thus America was at liberty to strengthen it without rejecting Mahan's doctrine.

Washington remained adamant in its refusal until Benson himself visited the war zone and was impressed with the awesome might of the Grand Fleet and the warmth of his reception. Junior officers led by his deputy, Captain Pratt, seem to have persuaded him out of his inflexible adherence to the Mahanite gospel. In November 1917, therefore, Benson executed an abrupt change of course and discovered several reasons to justify the despatch of an American battleship division to Scapa Flow. Their presence would assist his general aim of increasing American influence on British strategy. The US Navy would gain in prestige, the morale of the ships' crews would rise with the prospect of purposeful activity and they would obtain invaluable war experience (which could be maximised by the rotation of ships from the Atlantic Fleet). At Scapa Flow, Benson was made aware of the generally foul weather in the North Sea (which had helped to rob the Grand Fleet of a decisive victory over the High Seas Fleet at Jutland); a substantial addition to the Grand Fleet's broadside might clinch victory on a future occasion. He had evidence already [245, 248] of the value of the interchange of information between the two navies and an American unit in the Grand Fleet would materially facilitate that traffic. Perhaps the strongest argument in Benson's mind was that if America's large, expensive and growing battlefleet remained entirely idle throughout the conflict it would be difficult, if not impossible, to secure funds for further dreadnoughts. Wilson had already expressed scepticism about the value of capital ships. Finally, relations with Japan had improved following the signing of the Lansing-Ishii agreement, relieving the Navy at least temporarily of its nightmare.[1] Benson therefore recommended, and Daniels approved, compliance with the Admiralty's request [249–51].

Four coal-burning battleships accordingly left America within a few days of Benson's recommendation and joined the Grand Fleet in mid-December 1917 [253]. They were formed into the Sixth Battle Squadron and, in order to retain a constant strength of four ships,

[1] Allard, p. 77.

allowing for one absent refitting, a fifth ship was added shortly thereafter. The idea of rotation was quickly abandoned and continuity of training was thus ensured. Absorption into the British command, operational and communications structure was complete. Relations with the British, from Beatty downwards, were excellent throughout their stay.[1] The American division's commander, Rear-Admiral Hugh Rodman,[2] a cheery, pugnacious man noted for his affability and sense of humour, made an immediate hit with his hosts [255, 258, 261]. His squadron took its place in the Grand Fleet's formidable line of battle, most memorably when the German fleet was escorted to internment following the Armistice. Though the hoped-for decisive clash with the enemy was denied them, the squadron also acted independently, chiefly as distant cover for the Scandinavian convoys and the minelayers laying the North Sea Barrage [255, 260, 271]. Mayo, visiting the division at the end of the war, believed it had attained a high state of efficiency but Beatty, though acknowledging the Americans' keenness and quickness in learning, was less convinced [268]. According to Admiral Fremantle, Beatty regarded the American ships as late as June 1918 'rather as an incubus to the Grand Fleet than otherwise. They have not even yet been assimilated to a sufficient degree to be considered equivalent to British Dreadnoughts, yet for political reasons he does not care that the Grand Fleet should go to sea without them'. They were 'distinctly poor and disappointing' in gunnery and their signalling was equally weak (this was a defect in the Grand Fleet, too).[3]

Comparisons between the British and American capital ships were made long before Rodman's ships arrived. British ships seemed to enjoy advantages in construction, fire control, and the concentration of fire, and in equipment rendered necessary by wartime experience, such as paravanes. British squadron organisation and staff work also seemed superior, while Royal Navy officers were far more specialised than their American counterparts, who displayed all-round competence. American shipboard organisation was said to be better and they were undoubtedly more habitable and supplied with

[1] Marder, vol. 5, p. 126.
[2] Rear-Admiral Hugh Rodman, US Navy (1859–1940): began war as a Captain on General Board; Rear-Admiral March 1917; commanded Battleship Div 9, Atlantic Fleet; after war commanded Pacific Fleet. Rodman had a reputation for amiability, an earthy humour, high professional standards and plain speaking. See his *Yarns of a Kentucky Admiral*, (Indianapolis: Bobbs-Merrill, 1928).
[3] Marder, vol. 5, pp. 124–6.

many more amenities than British ships. Where American ships really scored was in their capacity to maintain themselves independently of dockyards, to which the British were inordinately tied. The British greatly appreciated the visit of a US Navy team demonstrating photographic analysis of target practice and Mayo noted the British pioneering achievements in naval aviation [245, 248, 254, 255, 268, 270].

Discussion of further American reinforcements took place at intervals. Admiralty planners coveted the remaining ten American coal-burners to enable British dreadnoughts to be stationed further south to guard against possible German raids in the southern North Sea, or to take advantage of a Norwegian base, should that materialise [252]. Alarm at the possibility of the four Russian Baltic Fleet dreadnoughts being acquired by the Germans led to another call for American capital ships [256] but these eventualities were too remote to justify the despatch of further ships. The only additional battleships to serve in European waters were the three commanded by Rear-Admiral T. S. Rodgers, US Navy, based on Berehaven from August 1918. It was always possible, following the evident failure of the U-boat campaign by early 1918, that the German high command would seek to disrupt shipping in the North Atlantic by using their otherwise redundant battle cruisers. A break-out would be difficult to discover and there was little prospect of hunting them down in the open ocean; the only hope was to despatch British battle cruisers to intercept their return passage. US battleships were maintained in a state of readiness at their Hampton Roads, Virginia, anchorage, and others were sent to Halifax, Nova Scotia. After months of discussion, the British and American high commands finally agreed on 'Plan BCR', with its division of responsibility between Washington and London and its elaborate arrangement for the protection of convoys. There is little sign that the Germans contemplated such a raid but the Americans willingness to dole out their battleships so readily and in small groups demonstrated how far the US Navy had departed from Mahanite concepts of battlefleet integrity within a few short months [259, 262–269].

The service of Rodman's and Rodgers's divisions with British forces, though uneventful, is of interest in displaying the Navy Department's initial inflexibility in strategic doctrine and how this collapsed rapidly under the stress of actual warfare. It reveals also the amicable relationship forged between the two navies at operational level, the distinct differences between the ships and their organisation and the opposed points of view of their officer corps. Finally, it indicates the massive reserve of capital ship strength available to the coalition and more than sufficient to be deployed effectively to meet any threat, actual or potential, posed by the enemy.

244. *Sims to Opnav*

21 July 1917

U.S. Battleships for Grand Fleet

Visited Grand Fleet nineteenth with Admiral Jellicoe for consultation with Commander-in-Chief. The result is that Admiralty request that the four strongest coal burning battleships with six destroyers be sent [to] join Grand Fleet now Firth of Forth. Also that our submarines could be very usefully employed in anti-submarine [capacity].

The reason for this request is that five *King Edward* class[1] must be put out of commission and their places taken by four dreadnoughts to provide officers and gunnery and torpedo ratings for light cruisers, destroyers, submarines, etc., to be commissioned. Shortage of officers will be four thousand after advancing reserves from motorboats, etc., to Fleet. Our oil burning battleships could not be supplied, and more than four would unduly increase burden on coal supply, and would necessitate additional screening vessels not now available.

The conference agreed that moral effect would be very great also mutual benefit of exchange of ideas and methods. The intelligence service thereby created between the two Fleets would be superior to any service which exists or could be established. Carefully selected expert staff should be sent. Also recommend temporary detail representative our Commander-in-Chief on Admiral Beatty's staff.

245. *Sims to Pringle*

31 July 1917

[Lieut.-Cdrs. Castle[2] and Robinson[3], US Navy returned from a visit to the Grand Fleet] and told me that in their opinion they should get back to America as soon as possible, and tell our people about the number of things they found in the Grand Fleet in which we are very distinctly inferior. This includes such fundamentally

---

[1] Predreadnought battleships.
[2] Lieut-Cdr Guy W. S. Castle, US Navy: attached to Bureau of Steam Engineering, Navy Department; later a Commander aboard receiving ship, New York.
[3] Lieut-Cdr Samuel M. Robinson, US Navy: attached to Bureau of Steam Engineering; later promoted to Commander.

important things as fire control, concentration [of fire] and so forth. To their astonishment, they found that the British are very distinctly in advance of us in the application of electricity to fire control. They were so much concerned about it that they insisted that they should return at once, and, of course, I ordered them [to do so].

246. *Benson to Sims*

20 August 1917

United States believes that the strategic situation necessitates keeping battleship force concentrated, and cannot therefore consider the suggestion of sending a part of it across. The logistics of the situation would prevent the entire force going over, except in case of extreme necessity. The Department desires that you discuss situation with Admiral Mayo upon arrival.

247. *Sims to Benson*

1 September 1917

****

Admiral Mayo's visit will, I believe, prove of great benefit to the Department and to the Fleet.[1] He is going into things very thoroughly and will be able to give you a much better idea of the situation when he returns.

There is one thing about which I am really anxious and that is as to the final decision of the Navy Department in sending to this side the battleship reinforcements which the situation in the Grand Fleet requires. As you know, I do not understand what is really meant by the disintegration of our Fleet. I do not see how it will ever be possible for it to engage in a combined operation as a unit with the naval forces of the Allies. For example, in all of the schemes that I have seen proposed for aggression against the enemy, the naval forces of the Allies have been distributed according to types. The scheme proposed by Winston Churchill[2] required the organization of two fleets each composed of certain types of British, French and American vessels. Another proposal for blocking the enemy Fleet in

---

[1] Admiral Mayo's first visit to Britain is dealt with in Part III.
[2] This seems to have been the British Churchill, who from time to time bombarded the Admiralty with schemes for bold frontal assaults on German bases on the North Sea and Baltic coasts. See Marder, vol. 4, pp. 168–9, 229–30.

port would require the sacrifice of certain of the older battleships and cruisers of all three nations, to block the channels leading to German ports.

I have explained in my cables and letters why it is that the British Fleet needs a reinforcement of some of our dreadnoughts. I cannot see that the sending of this division of ships would be any disintegration of our fleet, but merely an advance force interposed between us and the enemy fleet. [*Marginal note, presumably by Benson*: 'But this is a division of the main force which is always faulty if not fatal. Show us the plan and we will make our decision.']

No man can tell what the outcome of this war will be. But whatever the outcome proves to be we must at the end find ourselves in a position which can be justified on sound military principles. Can we afford to have history record that the Allies asked for reinforcements and that we declined to send them?

****

248. *Sims to Beatty*

30 October 1917

I have just been informed that Lieut.-Cdr. H. E. Kimmel, US Navy,[1] is to be sent up to the Fleet in a few days. At the request of the Admiralty, following the visit of Admiral Mayo, Lieut.-Cdr. Kimmel has been sent over by our Navy Department to explain our Camera methods of recording and analysing results of target practice. He has brought with him a complete camera outfit as used in our Fleet. I have also cabled to the Department asking that they send over cinematograph films of recent practices in our fleet which will probably be of interest to you and your officers.

Lieut.-Cdr. Kimmel is an assistant of our Director of Target Practice and is thoroughly in touch with all target practice information and development in our Service. I am well acquainted with this officer's work and ability and am in hopes that in some little way he may prove of value to you.

I hope you will look upon Kimmel while he is with you as an officer under your command and will not hesitate to make use of him in any way that you may see fit.

---

[1] Lieut-Cdr (later Admiral) Husband E. Kimmel, US Navy: fated to be C in C, US Fleet at Pearl Harbor at the time of the Japanese air strike, 7 December 1941.

249. *Memorandum by Benson*

London,
November 1917

Having given this subject considerable thought since the war began, I would like to add something to what has been said in favor of sending a division of battleships to join the Grand Fleet. Besides the reasons given by Captains Pratt and Schofield and Commander Pye,[1] there are some points that have not been covered.

In connection with the great gain to be had in training, by acquiring in actual first hand experience what now we can get only by more or less complete reports, it should be noted that the United States Navy is the only great navy that has had no experience in war since 1900.

As to the adequacy of the Grand Fleet to cope with the German Fleet without our assistance, it is true that in numbers the British are in great superiority. In all engagements hitherto, however, weather of low visibility has had a considerable influence, according to reports; and there might easily be situations where a still greater superiority would be important. If, in any encounter, it should be indicated that the outcome would have been more favourable or decisive had more allied forces been available, it would be difficult to satisfactorily explain the absence of our ships, in the face of the present request to send them. In the event of a reversal to the Grand Fleet, a refusal could never be defended.

The fact that we are asked now to send a battleship division across will come up for public explanation sooner or later, in any event, and it will be extremely difficult to justify a refusal to the great majority of lay minds, which will weigh the situation against the broad principle that the battleships' place is at the front, to strike at the enemy whenever he comes out. This has an important bearing on the Navy's future.

As to the influence on our own morale, in my opinion the effect has been understated. The stimulation would go through not only the battleship force but through every branch of the service. We have only to consider how widespread and deep the interest was when our destroyers entered in. We have put in our destroyers, our cruisers, our small patrol vessels armed largely by partly trained reserves; our submarines are on the way across, our colliers are regular carriers across, and we are now contemplating sending a

[1] Commander William S. Pye, US Navy: began war as a Lieut-Cdr and Fleet Intelligence Officer, Atlantic Fleet.

mining force, – every branch represented but the battleship force. The morale of the battleship force needs the stimulus of the real thing to replace artificial conditions and a cramped, defensive atmosphere. Under present conditions it is impossible to cultivate a bold and watchful spirit; but to enter a division at the front would change the whole aspect. Considering our great need of training and the very large number of new officers and men being taken into the Navy, it is more than ever important that training and experience should be the best. But it is not only the immediate effect that would be beneficial. There would be a most important influence on the whole future development of the Navy.

Whatever may be the present situation, the future of the United States will depend in large measure upon the strength, the training, the spirit, and the prestige of the Navy. A decision now averse to sending any of our battleships to the front will be invoked in future against the building of large vessels. But the major consideration is prestige. This must be based upon sound training and high spirit, but it will be fundamentally affected by our employment in the present war. There should be no possibility of an impression, at home or abroad, among the hostile, allied or neutral, that we are performing an auxiliary or secondary part in the military prosecution of the war. We should be well represented in every major employment. It is of the first importance to our present and future prestige that the Navy of the United States shall act in a principal role in every prominent event.

The principle not to divide the fleet does not apply to this matter, in my opinion. It would apply to the portion of the fleet necessarily kept in American waters by logistic considerations, rather than to a division sent to join the Grand Fleet.

250.   Benson to Opnav

London,
9 November 1917

After further discussion with Admiral Jellicoe recommend sending one division coal burning dreadnoughts *Utah* class[1] to join British Grand Fleet and to be relieved later by another until all of fleet has had experience or until conditions change. Recommend division be sent as soon as practicable to get ships off. Request to be informed about when they may be expected to start.

[1] USS *Utah* and *Florida*: battleships, 1911, 21 825 tons; 10 × 12in; 20.75 knots.

Everything progressing satisfactorily.

251. *Daniels to Benson*

13 November 1917

After consultation with Admiral Mayo the following coal-burning dreadnoughts were selected to form division to be dispatched to England: USS *New York, Florida, Delaware, Wyoming.*[1]

These ships after docking should be ready to sail about 25 November. Rear-Admiral Rodman[2] will command this division.

252. *Memorandum by Director of Plans*[3]

19 November 1917

Co-operation of the British and American Battlefleets and suggested redistribution of Forces

1. *Possible future developments in the Naval Situation*

Next year there may be considerable development in the naval situation, and various contingencies may arise rendering the presence of the U.S.A. dreadnought battlefleet urgently necessary in the North Sea.

The American Fleet cannot co-operate satisfactorily with the British, either in a strategical or a tactical sense if they have not worked together for some time previously. Unless therefore the U.S.A. battlefleet is sent here some months before it is actually required, its value as a fighting force will be greatly discounted.

2. *Possible objections to use of American Fleet in North Sea*

... it is difficult to see arguments which keep the American battle-fleet immobilised on the other side of the Atlantic. There might be difficulty in supplying the four latest battleships with oil, but they have ten coal-burning 'Dreadnoughts' which might be sent over now whilst for docking and re-fitting, two could be continually detached to the United States.

If it is fear of attack from Japan which prevents a fuller degree of co-operation, the despatch of Japanese battle-cruisers to Europe

---

[1] USS *New York*: battleship, 1914; 27000 tons; 10 × 14in; 21 knots; sister ship *Texas*. USS *Delaware*: battleship, 1910; 20000 tons; 10 × 12in; 21 knots; sister ship *North Dakota*. USS *Wyoming*: battleship, 1912; 26000 tons; 12 × 12in; 20.5 knots; sister ship *Arkansas*.

[2] Rear-Admiral Hugh Rodman, US Navy, flying flag in *New York*.

[3] Rear-Admiral Roger Keyes.

would remove that objection, and this might be urged on the Japanese Government with a promise to return one or more of our own battle-cruisers if any of theirs are lost from enemy action.

3. *Situations which may arise*

Some of the situations in which the U.S.A. battlefleet might be required will now be considered:

Future policy against the enemy attack on trade, both by surface and submarine raiders, is directed towards securing a more effective and intensive control over the North Sea exits, and that outside these all forces should be employed in escorting convoys. This idea has already taken shape in the proposed mine barrage, and the entry of Norway into the war on the side of the Allies would greatly increase the efficiency of the support which can be given to the vessels patrolling the Eastern end of the barrage.

Also with a base in Norway the problem of intercepting surface Raiders would be considerably simplified. ...

****

11. *Suggested Re-distribution*

... If a U.S.A. Battle Squadron of ten ships were sent to the Grand Fleet and eight of the older British and American dreadnoughts were based on the Humber in combination with the light cruisers and destroyers now stationed at Harwich, the East Coast would be equally well protected and control of the Southern area strengthened. ...

Minute by DCNS[1]

24 November 1917

... there is probably now no suspicion of Japan since the Japanese Naval Mission has been to the U.S.A. ... Concur that a portion of U.S.A. battlefleet (not the oil burners) should jo:n the Grand Fleet.

Minute by Commander Dewar[2]

28 November 1917

If as suggested 8 or 10 of the American Battlefleet were used to replace 8 of the older Dreadnoughts in the Grand Fleet and the latter were based on the Humber or Swin with the Harwich force,

[1] Acting Vice-Admiral Sir Henry Oliver.
[2] Commander (later Vice-Admiral) Kenneth G. B. Dewar (1879–1964): Commander 1911; War College Staff 1911; War Staff Officer 1912; commanded monitor *Roberts*; joined Operations Div May 1917; Asst Director of Pla ıs 1918; commanded

more destroyers would be available for escort, because the Battle
Cruiser Force with its attendant destroyers and light cruisers could
then be concentrated with the battlefleet. ...

It is not clear why the inclusion of eight U.S.A. battleships in the
Grand Fleet should lead to any greater difficulties with regard to
escorts than exist at present.

With reference to U.S.A. views:

The British Admiralty is in the same relative position with regard
to the naval war as the German General Staff with regard to the land
war. The responsibility for asking for the co-operation of the U.S.A.
battlefleet in the North Sea rests with the Admiralty and if we do not
ask for it in clear and definite terms the U.S.A. will naturally assume
that it is not required. It is probable that the U.S.A. would send their
fleet over if the necessity were explained. If they refuse to do so the
responsibility will be theirs.

****

If it is desirable to get the U.S.A. fleet over here, is it not advisable
to inform the U.S.A. and then let them put forward any objections?
If the U.S.A. Fleet were embodied in the Grand Fleet would not the
present Grand Fleet destroyer force suffice as a screen?

Final summing up

The Plans Division's contention that various contingencies may
arise next year necessitates the use of the American Fleet in the
North Sea is accepted.

The question then is 'Will the proposed arrangement of sending
one division over at a time' meet the case:-

It takes some months to obtain the necessary co-operation
between Allied ships.

It is doubtful whether the proposed arrangement will be a satisfactory one from the C. in C.'s point of view.

As long as there is only one division of American ships on this side
the force available will be insufficient to carry out the various contingencies we have referred to and if we have to wait until more ships
are brought over the delay may prevent us seizing the opportunity.

battleship *Royal Oak* 1928–9 but there was discontent aboard and he was retired in
1929 with the rank of Rear-Admiral; Vice-Admiral on retired list 1934; assisted in
Naval Historical Branch in 2nd World War. Dewar was one of the 'Young Turks',
offensive-minded and more intellectual than the general run of naval officers; see
Marder, vols. 4 & 5, *passim*.

Another argument, and a powerful one, for bringing the American ships over *now* is the small number of destroyers available for the Grand Fleet at the present time.

There can be little doubt that the Germans could muster many more destroyers, at *their* selected moment, for a Fleet action than we could.

Is it not then all the more necessary to make up for this possible inferiority in destroyers by bringing the maximum battleship strength to bear?

Difficulties of Supply

More supply ships would certainly be required for 8 or 10 ships than for 4 but the increase would not be very great and the advantages to be gained appear to warrant the necessary use of extra tonnage.

Escort

****

Should the C. in C. however ask for additional destroyers for the American ships the question of escort has to be considered as the extra destroyers must be taken away from convoy or anti-submarine work.

… From the remarks of D.C.N.S. it appears that the Japanese question is not likely to prove an obstacle.

This being the case it is doubtful if the U.S.A. would have any more reluctance to the suggested use of their ships than they have in sending their Army to France.

If we proved the necessity for their ships coming over and state definitely what we required the ships would almost certainly be forthcoming.

****

253. *Gaunt to Jellicoe*

New York,
15 November 1917

Admiral Rodman expects to sail with 4 ships not later than 24 November. They have 6 months' stores and provisions some of which they will want to land and expect to arrive with sufficient coal to last for some time. He has completed all ships with British Signal Flags and as he expresses it hopes he will be 'absorbed into the Grand Fleet at once'.

254. *Beatty to Sims*

5 December 1917

I must write a line to thank you for the services of Lieut.-Cdr. Kimmel, Mr Jamison and party.

They showed us the use of the American Triangulation Camera and its advantages, and no trouble was ever too great for them. We were very sorry when they had to leave us and we certainly hope to have the pleasure of seeing them back again.

We are all ready for the U.S. Squadron and hope that all will go [well] with them.

It will be a great day when we have the larger units of the two great Services working together.

255. *Sims to Benson*

20 December 1917

I have just returned this morning from a visit to a part of the Grand Fleet, and our division of battleships, that arrived yesterday at Rosyth. I called on the Commander-in-Chief and Admiral Rodman and went to see the people on each one of our ships, except the *Utah*[1] which had a few cases of mumps.

I need hardly say, I am sure, that our ships and our people have created a very favorable impression. It would be difficult to imagine better relations than exist between the two services. Admiral Rodman, as you know, is a good mixer and is already very popular with everybody. He has been assigned to one wing of the Fleet, a sort of independent division that corresponds to Admiral Evan Thomas's[2] division on the other wing. According to the present battle plans, which I assume you will be acquainted with, these two divisions have a certain freedom of action which is comprised in what might be called a battle doctrine. It is thoroughly understood by our people and they are very well satisfied with it indeed.

Four days before the ships arrived at Rosyth, the British codes and signals were given to our ships and they were used with perfect success on the way down. A signal officer has been assigned to the *New York* and a signalman placed aboard each ship until our people are entirely familiar with the British system and can handle them with the necessary rapidity.

[1] Surely *Florida*.
[2] Vice-Admiral (later Admiral) Sir Hugh Evan-Thomas (1862–1928): entered RN 1876; Captain 1902; Rear-Admiral 1912; commanded 5th BS (*Queen Elizabeth* class) at Jutland; Vice-Admiral 1917; Admiral and CinC Nore 1920; retired list 1924.

A liaison officer, a commander, has also been assigned to the *New York* in order to facilitate business between the two services. Whether this is to be permanent, or temporary, I do not know.

We talked over with the British officers concerned all questions of supply, repairs and so forth, and the division paymaster came to London with me last night and completed arrangements with Tobey.

Admiral Beatty expressed considerable anxiety because our ships are not supplied with paravanes. When they came into Rosyth he had our ships follow as exactly as possible in the wake of the *Queen Elizabeth*.[1] An examination of her paravanes showed that she had probably cut down two or three mines on the way in, although the channel had of course been swept. This was probably one of their delayed action mines which come up after being on the bottom a certain length of time. I understood from Rodman that before he left he asked to have the castings of the paravanes made and sent over as soon as possible. Of course these could be made here, but in the absence of sufficiently detailed drawings, it would be necessary to dock the ships, take the measurements, make the castings, and then redock them to put the castings in place. For this reason I telegraphed expressing the opinion that the castings could be obtained more rapidly on the other side and sent over.

As you doubtless know, all vessels of the Grand Fleet are kept ready to go to sea at four hours' notice as a maximum and sometimes much less. This does not make it possible to do any considerable repairs and overhauling of machinery. This is done periodically by the vessels of the Fleet going into a yard in the same manner as our destroyers do now after steaming about 500 hours. As this will necessitate one of the vessels being absent overhauling during the greater part of the time, it would leave but three to balance the Evan Thomas squadron at the other end of the line. This latter squadron has a powerful battery of 15″ guns. For these reasons it would seem very desirable that the *Texas* should be added to our squadron, and perhaps it would be well to add another vessel so that there may at all times be five to balance the Evan Thomas squadron.

Our officers have of course visited the British ships and have found a number of things of very considerable interest. They are particularly struck with the fact that the *Warspite* came through the Jutland Battle with water over her berth deck and still got into port. As our vessels do not have water tight hatches on this deck, it is apparent that similar injuries would sink them. It would seem really

[1] HMS *Queen Elizabeth*: battleship 1915; 27000 tons; 8 × 15in; 25 knots. Beatty's flagship and most up-to-date British battleship. *Warspite* same class.

imperative that water-tight hatches be fitted on this deck.

British experience has also shown that water tight hatches in the protected deck, and elsewhere, should have the manhole placed in them. These should also be fitted in ours.

****

Our vessels did not understand until I told them that it was the intention to send over another division to relieve them. In view of the information they have collected as to the number of things to be done upon our vessels and as to the amount of training they will have to do to put themselves in coordination with the British methods, all of our officers are of the opinion that these vessels should remain here and should not be relieved by another division. They say that in effect it would be to make use of the British Fleet for the training of all of our fleet in their methods and would therefore to that extent diminish the effectiveness of our vessels in case they have to be used in battle. I wish to make my meaning quite clear in this matter, and may do so by saying that the vessels that have recently arrived here will not have reached their maximum ability for service in battle earlier than, say, two or three months. The changes will have to be made in their hatches, paravanes will have to be rigged and so forth.

Having reached this condition of increased battle efficiency, the increase would immediately be lost if they were withdrawn and another division substituted which would have to undergo the same changes and the same amount of training.

It seems to me that this is a matter that is worthy of very serious consideration. If our vessels are to be used in action with the British, it would seem that this cannot be later than next spring at the outside. This opinion is based upon the assumption that if the Germans intend to come out they will not wait until further reinforcements arrive and can be trained and coordinated.

****

I hope that you had a pleasant voyage on the way back, and escaped the gales that prevailed on this side. I am afraid that we cannot expect to avoid some damage to our destroyers during the gales to be expected in January, February and March. As you know, there are not enough destroyers at any of the bases where they are now employed and I therefore hope that you can see your way clear to sending over additional ones at the earliest practicable time.

****

256.   *Memorandum by Director of Plans*[1]

13 January 1918

The Naval Situation and Russia

****

5. As there appears to be no certain method of preventing the Russian Baltic ships falling into enemy hands, it is considered necessary the 'Grand Fleet should be reinforced with an additional four U.S.A. coal-burning dreadnoughts as soon as possible. This admits of 8 of the 10 U.S.A. coal-burning Dreadnoughts being continuously in co-operation with the Grand Fleet. This suggestion is made in spite of the fact that it may not be possible to make any corresponding increase in the number of Grand Fleet destroyers, as battle power depends on the combined effect of various types of vessels and a shortage of destroyers can to a certain extent be redressed by a surplus of battleship force.

****

257.   *Rodman to Benson*

19 January 1918

General report, week ending 19 January 1918

1. *North Sea Weather*

It is not that it blows any harder in the North Sea than in many other parts of the world, but that it seems to be almost continually blowing, shifting rapidly from one point of the compass to another, and kicking up a rough cross sea, which has again demonstrated the disadvantage of having our 5 inch guns mounted too low. Our gun deck was flooded in our last run, to such an extent that not only were the guns useless, but the ports had to be kept closed to keep the water from flooding the gun deck.

In addition to the wind and sea, there is a great deal of precipitation in the form of snow, hail, sleet, and rain, often coupled with fog and mist. Owing to the above causes, much difficulty was experienced in keeping in formation during our last passage at sea; the *Delaware* got separated, thus depriving her of the benefit of the paravanes of the British ship leading the column, and exposing her to the danger of the mine fields, about whose exact locality and

[1] Captain Cyril Fuller had succeeded Keyes on 1 January 1918.

limits some doubt existed.

2. *Paravanes*

Assuming that the *Texas* will have been fitted with the clamp casting on her stem before sailing, the remainder of the gear, including the paravanes, will be installed on her arrival, by divers, and if, as requested, she brings the castings for the remainder of these ships, they will go at once, one at a time, to our docking base, and have them fitted. The Commander-in-Chief considers it essential that all ships be equipped with paravanes at the very earliest possible date; they will undoubtedly add much to our security, particularly since the enemy is very active in mine laying in these waters.

****

5. *Entrance into Scapa Flow*

On entering the Pentland Firth in column, with the British battleships leading, a strong spring tide running against the wind, the upper or main decks of the leading ships were repeatedly smothered and submerged, due to local conditions, and not to the intensity of the wind. It would have been dangerous for men to remain on their decks. Our ships, with higher free boards, made better weather of it.

6. *Heavy Snows*

Unusually heavy snows, with temperature much below normal have prevailed at the northern base, in consequence of which there has been much suffering amongst the inhabitants ashore, and a shortage of food.[1]

****

258.   *Sims to Benson*

15 February 1918

****

I wish to say that Rodman's handling of the situation seems to me to have been admirable. He is certainly persona grata with everybody and is spoken of in the highest terms not only by the British but by all of our people who come in contact with him.

****

---

[1] As Rodman recorded elsewhere in this report, the weather had been so severe that two British destroyers were driven ashore and wrecked; only one man survived, and that by a miracle.

259. *Admiralty Plans Division Memorandum*

6 May 1918

Proposed Measures to be taken if Enemy Battle Cruisers enter Atlantic

1. The *Derfflinger*[1] could operate for three days in the [Atlantic] ... and return to Germany, leaving a margin of 1000 tons of fuel for emergencies. ... The endurance of later battle cruisers is not known, but it is not likely to be less than this; that of earlier battle cruisers is considerably less, and as far as is known they carry very little oil.

2. The *Derfflinger* carries about 1000 tons of oil, in addition to her coal, and the capture of an oiler in one of the East bound convoys would greatly increase her period on the trade routes, oiling at sea presenting no serious difficulty in fine weather. She might also be accompanied by a fast collier, or capture one in a South bound convoy, and coal, for example, in the Canary Islands. Between July and September she might also coal on the Greenland coast.

3. As the chances of hunting down a battle cruiser in the open Atlantic are negligible, our main battle cruiser force should co-operate with the Grand Fleet in the endeavour to intercept the enemy on his return journey. For the protection of trade, dependence should primarily be placed on the immediate diversion of convoys. In certain cases, battleship escorts might be used (vide paragraph 13).

****

5. In the event of a battle cruiser attacking a convoy escorted by a cruiser, a large proportion of the convoy would probably be saved by scattering as widely and rapidly as possible. Instructions on this point are being issued in the Allied Signal Manual. It is also important that destroyer escorts sighting a powerful raider should understand that their duty by day is to watch and report, rather than to attack.

****

13. Unless battleship escorts can be provided, convoys must either be exposed to some degree of risk or be delayed by detaining them at Halifax or other port of refuge, diverting them to Lisbon and detaining them there until the enemy withdraws. Delays would become dangerous if the enemy succeeded in maintaining himself in the

---

[1] SMS *Derfflinger*: German battle cruiser, 1914; 26000 tons; 8 × 12 in; 26.5 knots.

Atlantic with the help of a collier.

14. In the case of troop transports or important convoys detained at or recalled to Halifax or other American ports, it is suggested that U.S.A. should be asked to provide battleship escorts. Re-fueling in Great Britain will not be necessary, except in the case of coal burning ships should the latter have to exceed east of Long. 25° W. In such a case they could be screened in through the danger zone by the TBD convoy escort and re-fuel at Plymouth or the Clyde. It is therefore proposed that a general scheme should be agreed upon for the provision of USA battleship escorts from their battleships in America either at Halifax or at a sea rendezvous to be arranged by W/T, on warning being given that a raiding battle cruiser is out; the battleships to be recalled by W/T as soon as she is known to have withdrawn. Details to be arranged according to the circumstances of the moment.

****

260. *Rodman to Sims*

23 May 1918

Statement of Naval accomplishments for publicity purposes

1. ****

Communication

Immediately after our arrival the British system of communication was adopted and put into effect, and in a very short while we were able to manoeuver and cooperate efficiently with the Grand Fleet.

General Duties

Since our arrival we have taken part in all operations with the Grand Fleet in the North Sea; taken our turn at escorting Norwegian Convoys, and have done our share in the work ashore at Scapa Flow, which consisted of building an Air Station, and were complimented by the British upon the amount of work accomplished on the latter.

****

Refitting

****

We have been complimented by the Admiralty for the small amount of work required at the yard from the yard workmen during our refit periods, due largely to the excellent upkeep maintained by the different Commanding Officers with the ship's forces.

Theater of Operations

The areas in which these vessels operate is in the North Sea, and extends from the Shetland Islands, North, to the Heligoland Bight, South.

Operations

31 January to 2 February

In Grand Fleet manoeuvers in the North Sea.

6 to 10 February.

On Convoy duty (Norwegian Convoy); 33 vessels outbound and 27 vessels on return voyage.

16–17 February.

Operating with Grand Fleet in the North Sea, with a view to intercepting the German Battle Cruisers which we had information were out. This operation was in a very heavy gale. On this trip we had one casualty – the *New York* lost an enlisted man overboard.

8–12 March.

On Convoy duty (Norwegian Convoy); 28 vessels outbound and 25 vessels on return voyage.

17–20 April.

On Convoy duty (Norwegian Convoy); 28 vessels on outbound and 27 vessels on return voyage.

24–26 April.

Operating in North Sea with Grand Fleet; with the object of intercepting the German High Seas Fleet. We had information that they were out, and just missed making contact by 30 miles.[1]

All the above operations were carried out without mishap and on scheduled time. One or more enemy submarines were sighted on each operation and torpedoes were fired at us on several of them. Many floating mines were sighted and destroyed by Destroyer Screens.

****

261.   *Report of Captain D. W. Knox,[2] US Navy, on visit to*
Rosyth and Mine Bases

24 May 1918

****

[1] The operation is described in Marder, vol. 5, pp. 143–56.

[2] Later Commodore Dudley Wright Knox (1877–1960): graduated from Annapolis 1896; Cuba blockade 1898; Naval War College 1912; Sims's staff 1913, Atlantic Fleet Destroyer Force; Commandant, Guantanamo Naval Base 1917; Sims's staff

It is very apparent that the Grand Fleet, including the American battleships, is thoroughly indoctrinated with the single mission of destroying the High Seas Fleet at the earliest possible moment. So far are the minds of personnel impregnated with this idea, that they seldom think of anti-submarine warfare or other questions in connection with the war.

****

It is very evident that extremely cordial relations exist between our officers and the British in the Fleet, and there is a very highly developed spirit of co-operation among them. Vice-Admiral Evan Thomas remarked to me, 'We all belong to the same fraternity here'. Admiral Beatty, in speaking to me of the Commander of the Sixth Battle Squadron, referred to him as 'Hugh Rodman'.

The manner in which our ships are kept up, both as regards their cleanliness and mechanical efficiency, is the object of much comment among the British. The *New York* has been inspected by practically every Admiral in the British Fleet, and each one of them (following his inspection) has sent the Captains of his squadron over at odd times to inspect the *New York*

Admiral Beatty's concern principally seemed to be the lack of a sufficient number of destroyers attached to the Grand Fleet; he complained that he could spare none whatever for anti-submarine work. He enquired as to the availability of submarine chasers, stating it to be desirable that some high speed supporting anti-submarine vessels be detailed to assist the present patrol operations round the Fair Isle passage.

****

262. *Benson to Sims*

2 July 1918

As last hope, German battle cruisers may be sent out to completely destroy one of our large troop convoys. We depend upon you to gain and give information on this point, and Grand Fleet to take necessary action until United States could act.

November 1917–1919; Naval War College staff 1919; Captain and commanded *Brooklyn* and *Charleston*; retired due to ill health 1921; officer in charge of Office of Naval Records and library 1921–46, undertaking extensive reorganisation, research and publication.

263.   *Sims to Benson*

3 August 1918

I believe it extremely dangerous to base a plan on assumption that information of enemy's escape will be obtained otherwise than through news of an attack. There is certainly a small chance that this information will be available and in long nights of winter chances will be very much against this information. I believe that safety requires plan should be based on assumption that one or more battle cruisers will be at large in Atlantic with ample fuel supply and in a position to attack convoys before we have any knowledge of their exit from home ports. Only possible protection against this danger is battleship escort of convoys inaugurated before the danger arises. This would subject the battleships to a relatively small risk of being torpedoed as compared with the great risk of one or more convoys of many thousand troops being destroyed before measures could be taken to protect them. I have consistently advocated this plan and am convinced that no other can offer the same certainty of protection to troop and other convoys.

The following comments are submitted on the Department's plan as set forth in its cable. Assembly of a large number of merchant vessels at Azores dangerous because possibility [of] submarine attack and extraordinary submarine risk due to assembly so many vessels. Think general principle of action should be to keep all convoys moving towards destination. To turn back shipping or to deflect it towards other terminal ports would make anti-submarine escort impossible in many cases and would introduce re-fuelling difficulties that would tie up many vessels until fuel could be sent to them.

Battleships based upon Irish ports as proposed would be available for escort to safe position [of] such troop convoys as might be in danger area when alarm was given and this is deemed a safer plan than to have such vessels proceed to destination unescorted or have them proceed to Azores. If Department should decide to adhere to its plan of having battleships go to the Azores to furnish escort to the shipping assembled there, it is suggested that the Tagus River would be a better base than an Irish port, being 300 miles nearer the Azores. When the Department has decided on general principles of plan I will take up whole question with British Admiralty. Final plans must be joint plan taking cognizance of all Allied shipping.

264.   *Memorandum by US Planning Section*

10 August 1918

The Navy Department's plan for protecting Convoys against raiders from the North Sea or Mediterranean is as follows:-

Battleship Division 6
Utah
Nevada
Oklahoma

To be based at Brest or vicinity of Queenstown, preferably the latter (Berehaven).

Battleship Division 8
Arizona
Mississippi
New Mexico
Pennsylvania

also a division of 4 Japanese battle-cruisers.

These to be based apparently on Hampton Roads or some port on our Atlantic coast.

Battleship Divisions 2,3,4 & 5 plus *Delaware* and *North Dakota* to escort troop convoys. This makes a force of 18 battleships, and together with the two Divisions above mentioned includes all battleships except the *Kentucky* and *Illinois* classes. The use of the Japanese battle-cruisers depends upon getting Japan to send them to our Atlantic coast and securing her consent to using them as proposed.[1]

****

265.   *Sims to Bayly*

20 August 1918

I am enclosing you herewith a copy of the letter of instructions prepared for issue to Rear-Admiral Rodgers. ...

---

[1] USS *Nevada* and *Oklahoma*: battleships, 1916; 27500 tons; 10 × 14in; 20.5 knots. USS *Arizona* and *Pennsylvania*: battleships, 1916; 31400 tons; 12 × 14in; 21 knots. USS *Mississippi*: battleship, 1917; 32000 tons; 12 × 14in; 21.3 knots. USS *New Mexico*: battleship, 1918; 32000 tons; 12 × 14in; 21.3 knots; 2 turbine-driven generating units; 4 propelling motors. The turbo-electric drive was invented by Professor R. A. Fessenden; see note 3, p. 49. The *Kentucky* and *Illinois* classes were pre-dreadnoughts, 1898; 11500 tons; 4 × 13in, 4 × 8in or 8 × 6in; 16 knots. The Japanese refused to send their battle cruisers.

****

Enclosure

Letter of Instructions No. 1

Forces

(a) Battleship Division Six. Rear-Admiral T. S. Rodgers, US Navy.

(b) Destroyer Flotillas based on Queenstown.

1. Possibility exists that enemy battle-cruisers or heavily armed raiding vessels may enter the Atlantic from the North Sea for the purpose of attacking convoys of troop ships, store ships, or other vessels. Information of such vessels being at large may be obtained by Allied intelligence service or it may be obtained first by report of an attack or a sighting at sea.

2. (a) Battleship Division Six, consisting of the *Nevada, Oklahoma,* and *Utah,* is stationed at Berehaven, Ireland, for the purpose of affording protection to convoys which, being on passage in the Atlantic when the presence of any enemy raider becomes known, are diverted to the Azores Islands to await escort.

    (b) Two divisions of destroyers from the Flotillas based on Queenstown will operate with Battleship Division Six when the situation contemplated in these instructions arises.

    (c) The general plan as prescribed by the Navy Department is applicable to the following convoys:

Designation of convoy	Speed (knots)	Character	Destination
1. US	12 or more	US Troops	French Atlantic Ports
		,, ,,	Alternately London &
2. HX	13	,, ,,	West British Ports
3. HC	11½	,, ,,	,, ,, ,,
4. HB	9	Stores	Biscay Ports

and to corresponding west bound convoys or ships moving singly.

****

3. (a) Battleship Division Six shall, upon receiving notice of the

escape of an enemy raider, and unless otherwise ordered, proceed at top speed towards San Miguel, Azores Islands, to furnish escort thence to European destinations to convoys and other shipping there assembled.[1]

(b) Destroyer Flotillas based on Queenstown. Upon receiving notice of the escape of an enemy raider or upon receiving definite orders, all available destroyers from this force, not exceeding twelve in number, shall be dispatched immediately to Berehaven, to act as escort for the vessels of Battleship Division Six. Suitable arrangements must be adopted to ensure that, at any time when the services of this force become necessary, destroyers can be made available with the least possible delay whether they are at sea or in port. Destroyers actually engaged in troop escort work shall not be diverted therefrom until the particular service upon which they are engaged has been completed.

(c) Notice of the escape of any enemy raider or orders to proceed in accordance with these instructions may be received either from the Force Commander, or from the British Admiralty, or from some source subordinate to one or other of these. Owing to the necessity for prompt action officers commanding the forces will take action on any information or orders which they believe to be authentic, regardless of the immediate source.

****

5. (c) The Commander Battleship Division Six shall keep the British Commander-in-Chief, Coast of Ireland, informed of his movements, actual and prospective.

****

(f) The Commander Battleship Division Six shall not exercise command over any British naval forces afloat or ashore at Berehaven nor shall any command over his force be exercised by any British naval officer except as provided in paragraph 3(c).

****

[1] It was proposed to hold eastbound convoys for France and the Mediterranean at the Azores when news of a raider's entry into the Atlantic was confirmed.

266.   *Opnav to Sims*

3 September 1918

Take the necessary steps to inform the forces under and cooperating with you to put the plan as modified into execution. ... The disinclination of the Admiralty to divert the HX and HC convoys in accordance with our plan naturally weakens it. Since protection must be afforded the HX and HC convoys as they carry our troops your plan to use Division Six for the protection of HX and HC convoys ... [is] approved but the United States troop convoys diverted to Azores according to our plan must receive the protection of at least one of our dreadnoughts from Division Six. Therefore until joint agreement is reached we will expect the United States troop convoys and the HB to be diverted and the HX and HC to proceed. If the Department finds that according to this arrangement which scatters our forces we will be unable to adequately protect all troop convoys it may be necessary to urge upon the War Department the advisability of discontinuing sending troops in the HC convoy. As no joint agreement has been reached convoys at sea are not familiar with our plans and United States convoys must be given diverting instructions, but on receipt of this issue instructions to all transports, US men-of-war, and escort ships in European waters making them familiar with necessary detail. Also furnish all American merchant ships with sealed orders to be broken in case of receipt of operating signal as prescribed whereby westbound ships may avail themselves of protection if desired. The operating signal will be sent in a US code to American ships only. Beginning with 9 September it is the Department's plan to furnish pre-dreadnought escort to the HX and HC convoys whose Captains will be familiar with our plan but will not use it unless the Admiralty so desire. The Commander, Cruiser Force, will issue similar instructions to ships on this coast. Finally this plan is only a temporary expedient and does not solve the problem of continued activities of an enemy battle cruiser in the northern Atlantic. Escort by old battleships will protect convoys against the ordinary raider but the cargo convoys will still be lightly protected. Our dreadnoughts are too slow for an efficient pursuit division and no answer has been received from the Japanese on our request that they send four battle cruisers to base with our Fleet. The Department desires to know what will be the Admiralty's policy as to the use of their battle cruisers for pursuit in case of the escape of an enemy battle cruiser.

267. *Sims to Opnav*

10 September 1918

... Admiralty propose to use their battle cruisers to bar the return of enemy raiders, and do not propose to use them for pursuit of raiders in the Atlantic.

I recommend the adoption of the following joint plan which has been prepared jointly by my staff and Admiralty Plans Division, and has the approval of the Admiralty:-

The following Plan shall govern all vessels and convoys at sea after they have received warning of a raid.

Plan

1. Raider warning shall not be sent out without mutual consent of Navy Department and Admiralty, unless evidence is conclusive that raider is out.
2. As a rule convoys and supporting forces will be handled by radio from the Navy Department or the Admiralty.
3. The aim will be to continue all voyages and to provide all convoys that are in danger with battleship escort by sending battleships from Halifax and Berehaven to overtake or to meet convoys not already escorted by battleships; and by combining convoys of approximately equal speed.
4. Battleship escorts will leave eastbound convoys and join west-bound convoys as indicated by the situation, getting all their fuel in American ports.
5. During a raid all operations West of longitude forty shall be controlled by the Navy Department, in consultation with British C-in-C North America and West Indies, and all operations East of longitude forty shall be controlled by the Admiralty in consultation with Commander, US Naval Forces, Europe, with complete inter-

change of information received and orders issued.

6. The ordinary machinery for routing shall continue in operation except that orders to convoys and escorts at sea to avoid raiders shall be sent direct from the Navy Department and the Admiralty to save time. Base commanders concerned shall be informed of orders issued.

7. Special rendezvous routes to be used in the case of a raid in the absence of radio instructions will be given each convoy unescorted by battleships before sailing, and battleships will be sent out from Berehaven to join the convoys.

8. Commanders of battleships at Halifax and at Berehaven, and all Commodores of Convoys and Commanders of Escorts, shall be given the routes of convoys sailed or about to sail, together with the latest information on the submarine and raider situation.

9. Destroyer escorts will accompany Berehaven battleships when practicable.

****

268. *Mayo to Opnav*

1 November 1918

Inspection of Battleship Division Nine

1. The Commander-in-Chief, accompanied by his Staff, inspected the ships of Battleship Division Nine (Sixth Battle Squadron of British Grand Fleet), beginning on 21 September 1918. ...

2. The inspection consisted of an inspection of both personnel and material of the division at anchor in the Firth of Forth, together with two days at sea in a Fleet Exercise. ... At Rosyth the usual exchange of calls was made between the Commander-in-Chief and the Commander-in-Chief and other Flag Officers of the Grand Fleet.

3. The inspection of the five US ships showed them to be in a highly satisfactory condition, both as regards material and personnel. It was apparent that the ships have reached such a condition now that the personnel is not subjected to hardships or unusual conditions, excepting when at sea at maneuvers. Ships are underway very little, but when underway are required to steam at high speeds – in fact it was noted that during the [exercise] problem while the Fleet was shifting base, the Sixth Battle Squadron was required to steam at speeds equal to those of their acceptance trials. The conditions of the

engine and fire rooms was particularly noticeable, on account of being so excellent, which, taking into consideration that ships have been under short steaming notice at all times, speaks most highly for the efficiency of the division in this respect.

****

11. Upon them reporting to the Commander-in-Chief of the Grand Fleet, the division immediately took its place in the battle line and was placed on the same status as the other units of the Grand Fleet. The same opportunities for gunnery exercises were allowed the division as were allowed other divisions, and in due course of time, five to six months, the gunnery efficiency had reached a fairly satis-factory state and continues to improve.[1] No special provisions were made for the division, ...

****

38. While the morale is still quite high, it is naturally not at the pitch which existed during the first few months following the arrival of the division in the Grand Fleet. This seems to be due to the difficulty in keeping up enthusiasm incident to the expectation of early action with the enemy fleet. The very limited facilities for liberty, the unusual weather conditions and the fact that, although occasional short furloughs are given, they do not result in seeing any of the 'home folks' appears to have resulted in a mild 'home-sickness'. At present there is nothing for the men to look forward to in the matter of getting home, but the expiration of their enlistments and, of course, the younger officers have not even this.

****

43. It was noted that the British have undertaken in earnest the very important task of developing the Fleet Air Service. It is of immediate necessity to take up the question of development of airplane carriers and the installation of airplanes on battleships. The subject will be discussed at length in separate papers.[2]

---

[1] But see Marder, vol. 5, pp. 124–6.
[2] On British developments in naval aviation, see S. W. Roskill, ed., *Documents relating to the Royal Naval Air Service* (London: for Navy Records Society, 1969) and Marder, vol. 4, pp. 3–24.

269. *Instructions as to Action to be taken in regard to North Atlantic Convoys in the event of a Raid in the North Atlantic by an Enemy Battle Cruiser. To be known as Plan B.C.R.*

4 November 1918

1. The following plan of action in the event of a raid by enemy Battle Cruiser in the North Atlantic has been agreed upon by US Navy Department and the Admiralty and is communicated for the information and guidance of all concerned.[1]

Should it be decided to put the plan in action, a warning will be sent out from the Admiralty and also from the US Navy Department, Washington, in the convoy cypher in the words 'Battle Cruiser Raider Action' followed by the time (GMT) indicating the hour at which the plan would be regarded as having been brought into force. The latest reported position of the enemy Battle Cruiser will be added to this message, if possible, and later reports of the enemy's position will be broadcasted in the Convoy Cypher by Shore Stations.

2. On issue of this warning, the Navy Department, Washington, in consultation with the C-in-C North America and West Indies, will take all the action which they consider desirable as regards Eastbound Convoys whose time 'A' (GMT) is later than the time (GMT) given in the raider warning. This time 'A' (GMT) is the estimated time at which the Convoy would cross Longitude 40° West and will be fixed for each Convoy before the Convoy sails and be included in the sailing telegram sent to London. The Admiralty, London, in consultation with the Force Commander, US Navy, will take all the action as regards Eastbound Convoys whose time 'A' (GMT) is earlier than the time (GMT) given in the raider warning.

(Note – This division by form of a sphere of action is necessary as it is not possible to know exactly the actual position of each convoy at the time when the raider warning is issued, and it is necessary that it should be quite clear as to whether Washington or London is to take action in regard to each particular convoy.)

3. Dreadnought Battleships have been based on Berehaven and will be detailed under orders to be issued from London to proceed to meet troop convoys whose time 'A' (GMT) is earlier than the time (GMT) given in the raider warning; if there are any Dreadnought Battleships at Berehaven in excess of the requirements of the troop convoys they will be utilized to meet cargo convoys. On making

---

[1] This plan was drawn up by the Admiralty mission to the United States (led by Geddes), which visited Washington in October 1918.

contact the Dreadnought Battleship should report the fact by W/T to the Admiralty, London, and should accompany the convoy until further instructions are received.

4. Dreadnought Battleships will also be based on Halifax or [an]other North American Port and will be detailed by orders to be issued from Washington to reinforce troop or other convoys whose time 'A' (GMT) is later than the time (GMT) given in the raider warning. On making the contact the Dreadnought Battleship will report the fact by W/T to Washington and will accompany the convoy on instructions being received from Washington but will not go to the Eastward of 20° West unless so ordered.

5. Apart from the Dreadnought Battleships mentioned above, it is intended that eventually each convoy, whether troop or cargo, should have either a Pre-Dreadnought Battleship or an Armoured Cruiser as Ocean Escort. In normal times, this escort if acting as an additional Ocean Escort would return to North America on reaching the British Islands Submarine Danger Zone, but after the raider warning is issued, the Pre-Dreadnought Battleship or Armoured Cruiser should continue with the convoy unless and until orders are received except in the case of a convoy being met by the Dreadnought Battleship, when the Pre-Dreadnought Battleship or Armoured Cruiser should return to her North American Port. When, however, an Armoured Cruiser is acting as Ocean Escort and in charge of the convoy, she will under normal conditions and when met by a Dreadnought Battleship, continue with the convoy as at present.

6. Each convoy routed by the North of Ireland is also to be given an alternative by the South of Ireland; in the event of a raider warning being issued and when time admits of the Destroyer escort being diverted to the South, such convoys may be directed from London to proceed by the South-about route, and London will then inform Berehaven accordingly.

7. All convoys to be given as at present ocean route showing where they will cross Longitudes 60, 50, 40 and 30° West, so that their course may be known approximately at any moment.

8. Washington and London to keep each other closely informed of action taken in regard to various convoys.

9. Convoy Cypher to be issued as at present to all Escorts and Commodores of Convoy and also to the ships in the fast US troop convoys and to the 'Monster Ships'[1] which sail independently.

---

[1] The great Atlantic liners such as RMS *Mauretania*.

10. Officers Commanding the Battleships or Cruisers mentioned above, all Officers in charge of Convoys and Commodores of Convoy to be instructed in the sense of this plan and also to be informed that on receipt of the raider warning they should listen in for radio instructions, but in their absence, the following general principles should govern their action in the event of immediate danger.

   (a) Notwithstanding the general instructions that follow, special vessels and convoys are given full discretion as to action taken to evade the enemy when danger is imminent.

   (b) When practicable convoys should seek to escape in the general direction of their destination.

   (c) As a final resort Convoy Commanders when insufficiently protected may disperse their convoys.

   (d) Maintain radio silence except that the Senior Officer's Ship shall:

     (1) Report position and movements of raiding force if sighted.

     (2) Relay to shore stations such reports if deemed necessary.

     (3) Answer calls from a Dreadnought Battleship endeavouring to make contact, unless the safety of Convoy is thereby endangered.

11. No special plan will be adopted at present for West bound traffic and such traffic will proceed independently after dispersal from Outward Convoy. In default of other instructions the aim of each ship should be to continue her voyage, but ships should be guided by warning received by them and also by any instructions which may be broadcasted.

270. *Report of Committee of US Officers on Comparison between British and American Warships*

10 December 1918

****

2. (e) ... it is indisputable and cannot be gainsaid that the living conditions of the crews of the US ships are above comparison with those which obtain in the British Service, and are second to none whatever. It is considered that we have nothing to learn from anyone in the question of sanitation, cleanliness, ventilation, or in the installation of what are in most services conceived to be luxuries for the men.

****

4. In general, it would seem that our ships have carried during this

war, more men, type for type, than the British ships. This seems to be due to two things: first, we conduct more activities aboard ship by manpower than the British do in their ships; the second consideration is that a large number of our men are not men but unseasoned boys, and consequently it takes more of them to do manual work than would be the case with fully developed men. Furthermore, we attempt and actually accomplish very much more repair work and upkeep work in our ships than any of the British ships attempt.

The general impression of the Committee is that the British, at least theoretically, lay more emphasis upon the fighting qualities of their ships, while we lay an added stress upon the daily life of the ship.

****

6. Fundamentally, in so far as organization for battle is concerned, the British and American standards are much the same, and the organizations are not dissimilar. Both services attempt to accomplish the same purpose, and the fundamental principles striven for by the British are the same in general as those for which we strive, except that there is a slight difference in the method of approaching them, due to a difference in personnel, equipment, and the building up of the system. But for other activities which concern the business of the ship for other than battle conditions – that is, for her daily work – the organization in the two services is quite different. In our service the division officers are usually responsible for the personnel in their divisions and the activities of the personnel, including their instruction, drill, and cleaning of the ship. The division officer is also responsible for the upkeep of all material in his division and the equipment which is assigned him for use in action and in daily work. This is not true in the British service, where these activities are divided under departmental heads who are specialists in the particular activity concerned. It is not considered that we need make any change in this respect.

7. In regards to plans and schedules it would seem to be the general custom in the British service, to attempt the same things in very much the same way. It is the impression of the Committee, however, that British schedules which have come under observation have been carried out with more certainty and promptness and push than are our schedules.

****

8. It would appear that there is a very considerable difference in the administration of the higher command of the fleet in regard to the activities of flag officers and their staffs. The British officer holds in

high esteem estimation a position on the staff of a flag officer, and knows that if he does well in this position his reward will be forthcoming. In our service the staff duty is not highly considered, and as a net result the staff work in the British service is better than that staff work in our service, because they place a premium on getting the best possible personnel on the staff. This in turn is dependent upon the fact that the flag officers themselves are assigned definite tasks and have more authority in command and freedom in minor matters than is usually the case in our service. A flag officer is expected to have personal ideas and knowledge in regard to gunnery, engineering, and everything that affects the tactical and strategical qualities of his command. In other words, each flag officer is given a job and is expected to carry it out, and is let alone to a very considerable extent in carrying it out. As a consequence, he wishes the best possible personnel to help him, and the selection of the best available personnel is therefore forced upon the flag officer and becomes automatic. This general doctrine may be said to emanate and flow directly from the Admiralty which permits and expects the C-in-C to administer his command, and furnishes him a command to administer. The difference seems to be that there is a definite sphere of authority which is invariably accorded dignified respect; rather than a system which is largely controlled by immediate considerations of expediency.

9. ****

The organization and administration in the individual ships of our fleet is believed superior in most respects to that of the organization and administration in the individual ships of the British Fleet. The organization and administration of units larger than that of individual ships is much below the standard obtaining in the British Fleet. This is very largely due to the fact that our fleet has never operated as a fleet under a single command; and as the flag officers have not been expected to assume responsibilities commensurate with such operations nor given a status corresponding thereto.

Report submitted by Engineer Officer of Arkansas

****

2. Under [upkeep] it is found that a distinct difference exists. In our service the manufacturing facilities aboard ship are developed to the highest possible degree. Shops are utilized for casting, machining, welding, acetylene welding, forging and wood-working. A broken

part, whether it comes under one department or another is replaced by manufacture on board. In this manufacture several departments are often involved but it is customary to make everything except large items beyond the capacity of the installation. In the British service the upkeep is carried on by liberal allowance of spares. Broken parts are renewed with spares from the stores carried aboard or at a base, and the spare stock is replenished by demand of a dockyard. Of course the British ships do use their shops but not to the extent customary on our ships. It is not believed that their shops are allowed to run down any more than ours, but the method of keeping them up is different. In one case renewals are made by manufacture aboard ship, in the other spares on hand.

Another difference in upkeep is in the matter of dockyard work. Owing to the fact that during the war the dockyard period is the only one in which it is possible to spare men for necessary leave, it is the custom to turn the ship over to the dockyard and release the ship's force for leave. The fact that the ship's mechanics are not accustomed to doing manufacturing work aboard ship makes it less necessary for them to remain and assist. All the big work then is done by the dockyard employees. The average period is about two or three weeks. When a ship requires extensive refit it is customary to pay off and turn her over to the dockyard completely. A few shipkeepers remain, but the officers and crew are detached to other duty and the ship recommissioned afresh on completion. It is obvious in the light of our own experience in the days of overhaul with reduced complement that this practice is bad. The officers with whom I talked agreed on this point.

... It is believed that their upkeep is equal to ours as far as results are concerned but that our method is superior in that better training is obtained, we are better able to meet emergencies, and are more nearly self sustaining away from a base.

3. ****

... British ships are notoriously too cold for the comfort of men brought up in American homes. They are likewise poorly ventilated by comparison with our standards. They do not go in for laundries and the other labor saving appliances such as a motor driven dough mixer, potato peelers, etc., nor do they use as much power for workshops or turrets. Where we drill full main battery daily, it is customary with them to drill once a week. All these things and others [which] are too numerous to mention, reduce the generator loads by the amount of power necessary to run fan and other motors. This reduces the coal expenditure correspondingly.

Now, whereas the average British sailor is not used to these refinements at home and does not miss them, our men are so accustomed to them that their removal would work a serious hardship and militate against efficiency. The superior British economy in port then is not due to better engineering practice but to conditions outside the engineer's department which are matters of policy.

In the matter of operating at sea, our ships have been fully as satisfactory as theirs in so far as maintaining speed is concerned. ...

****

5. Under the head of personnel there is one important difference to be noted, namely that the British ships are all operated by officers restricted to engineering duty only, whereas ours are not. It is difficult for them to understand our lack of specialization.[1]...

271. *Rear-Admiral Rodman's Final Report*

[after the Armistice]

Convoy Operation of Battleships

US Battleships comprising the Sixth Battle Squadron took their turn with other units of the Grand Fleet at convoy work escorting convoys to and from the Norwegian Coast. Their performance of this duty is shown by the following table:

Date left Base	Date arrived at Norwegian Coast	Date left Norwegian Coast with return convoys	Date returned to Base
February 2	February 8	February 8	February 10
March 8	March 10	March 11	March 12
April 17	April 19	April 19	April 20
June 30*	July 1	July 1	July 2
August 8§			August 10

* Supported Mine Force from base 18 on outbound trip.
§ Supported Mine Force on both out and inbound trips.

[1] The US Navy had amalgamated line and engineer officers in 1899.

The chief mission of US Battleships in European Waters was, of course, to reinforce the British Grand Fleet and engage the German High Seas Fleet. For this purpose they were kept at the highest possible state of battle efficiency and were habitually kept on a 4 hours' notice. On several occasions they were put on 2½ hours' notice, and twice put to sea with the expectation of meeting the enemy. The following is a brief statement of these operations:

(1) On 23 April the Division (less *Wyoming*) was put on 2½ hours' notice. Sailed with the Grand Fleet at 3.0 p.m. 24 April for active service against the enemy, it being understood that a large German Force was operating in the North Sea. They reached a strategic centre at 5.00 a.m. 25 April and occupied [it] until orders were given to return to base. During the operation several floating mines were destroyed by gunfire; one of the British flagships was attacked by submarine, 2 torpedoes being fired at her; the submarine was attacked by destroyer with depth charges. The enemy [fleet] was missed by about 4 hours. It was believed that he was out in force to attack the Norwegian convoy and supporting force. Grand Fleet returned to base, arriving at 7.45 a.m. 26 April; recoaled and remained on 2½ hours' notice.

(2) In the evening of 12 October report was received that 3 large enemy vessels had been sighted at 6.0 p.m. on Lat. 58° 08' N., Long. 2° 43' E steering in a northwesterly direction. A convoy standing to the northward along the west coast of Scotland was warned to look out for an attack about 10.00 p.m. The Sixth Battle Squadron, a Battle Cruiser Squadron and a Light Cruiser Squadron, accompanied by destroyer screens, left port shortly after midnight for assigned positions to the northward and westward of the Orkneys to scout and patrol the passage between the Orkneys and the Shetlands with the hope of intercepting and engaging the enemy. Weather was threatening, storm warning flying, blowing moderately; visibility decreasing until at daylight it was low and continued to decrease until noon, when it was reduced to about 2 miles. On account of rough sea speed had to be gradually reduced from 18 to 12 knots owing to the inability of the destroyers to make more speed.

From assigned 5.00 a.m. position (55° 59' N., 4° 30' W.) the force scouted toward Fair Island Passage until noon when it was directed to return to port. Arrived at 7.00 p.m. 14 October without having sighted the enemy.[1]

---

[1] No enemy surface warships appear to have left German waters at this time. The report was therefore false.

During the night of 20–21 November, the Grand Fleet got under way and proceeded to sea to meet and escort the German High Seas Fleet to an anchorage for internment. The American Battleship Force occupied a position in the middle of the North line between 2 British Battleship Squadrons.[1]

****

---

[1] The Grand Fleet was disposed either side of the High Seas Fleet to make it impossible for the Germans to open fire with anything other than suicidal intent.

PART VI

THE NORTH SEA BARRAGE
APRIL 1917 TO NOVEMBER 1918

INTRODUCTION

Before 1914, the Royal Navy, confident of its supremacy at sea, gave little consideration to either the production and laying of mines or to sweeping minefields. Serious losses of warships and merchantmen to enemy mines forced the hasty organisation of sweeping flotillas of converted trawlers, paddle steamers and tugs, reinforced later by purpose-built vessels. As close blockade of enemy ports by surface warships was impossible, in part because of enemy minefields, the British resorted to sowing their own mines around Heligoland and off the Jade and Ems, initially to inhibit sorties by the High Seas Fleet but, after the introduction of submarine warfare against shipping, increasingly to block the exits of U-boats. In addition to mining by submarines and converted minelayers in the Bight, the British sought also to close the Straits of Dover and Otranto to the U-boats, using nets and surface and air patrols as well as mines. Despite prodigious efforts, none of these measures met with much success. At best they represented an inconvenience to the enemy.[1] The Germans swept marked channels regularly and natural forces swept away other mines. Moreover, the standard British mine was notoriously ineffective, though by the time the Americans came into the war, the Admiralty had begun to copy the much more reliable German pattern [272].

The Americans, imbued with an offensive spirit, a desire for instant solutions and an unquenchable faith in the ability of modern technology to solve any question, at once pressed for the whole-hearted introduction of mine and net barrages at every narrow point, especially the northern outlet of the North Sea. Their somewhat accidental discovery of a wonder mine and ingenious proposals emanating from the Coast and Geodetic Survey of the Department of Commerce were seized upon by the zealous Assistant Secretary of the Navy, Franklin D. Roosevelt.[2] Stressing the high potential

[1] Newbolt, vol. 4, pp. 343, 379–81; vol. 5, pp. 119, 131–2, 178–9, 207, 209–10, 337.
[2] Daniels, *Wilson Era*, vol. 2, p. 83; W. C. Redfield (Secretary of Commerce) to

efficacy of barriers across the Straits of Dover and Otranto and, most importantly, between Scotland and Norway, he urged Wilson, the Navy Department and the visiting Balfour mission to adopt the scheme and the American antenna mine. A North Sea Barrage would lie nearer British bases than German and therefore it could be patrolled and defended without undue difficulty and would pose the Germans an intractable and demoralising problem. Roosevelt presented the idea with all the zest and imagination for which he was noted. Furthermore, he was insistent on the urgency of the proposal, advocating the organisation of an immediate joint operation to take advantage of coming good weather [273–4, 276, 278–9, 281, 288].

The Admiralty, disappointed with its own mining campaign, was unimpressed by the Americans' grand idea. It was sceptical about the claims made for the new antenna mine and only too well aware of the natural hazards to be overcome in the North Sea: strong currents, frequent storms, great depths and the unprecedented distance involved (about 250 miles). The barrage would require possibly hundreds of patrol craft to force U-boats down onto the mines and since the priority was the defence of trade these were not available. The enemy could punch holes in the line with raiding groups and sweepers. In any case, in no class of vessel was the Royal Navy more deficient than minelayers. The initial American approach, made in May, was therefore rejected [275, 277, 280, 282]. Sims, who accepted the Admiralty's arguments, remarked later that 'convoy ... was the one sure method of salvation for the Allied cause. To have started the North Sea barrage in the spring and summer of 1917 would have meant abandoning the convoy system'.[1]

A few months later, the Admiralty intimated to Admiral Mayo during his visit in August and September that it was prepared to discuss the North Sea and other mining projects. This did not represent a totally genuine conversion, for the British were anxious to conciliate the Americans with a view to extracting more naval assistance in general. However, there was growing domestic pressure for more aggressive action against the U-boats and the new pattern of British mine was now in production. Jellicoe therefore told Benson in September that 'now for the first time' the North Sea Barrage 'becomes, I think, a feasible proposition'.[2] Roosevelt seized on this

Wilson, 19 May 1917, and Roosevelt to Wilson, 5 June 1917, *Wilson Papers*, vol. 42, pp. 348, 457.
[1] Sims, p. 291.
[2] Jellicoe to Benson, September 1917, *Jellicoe Papers*, vol. 2, p. 210; Klachko, p. 93.

opening to agitate once again for prompt action, lamenting the loss of valuable time. 'By degrees,' writes Trask, 'he had made the barrage his special project'[1] and he sent Daniels and Wilson a detailed memorandum on it [272]. Even his chief and Sims, originally among the sceptics, now supported him and in the autumn of 1917 preparations at last got under way [281–91].

Implementation proved difficult. There were delays in the production of the American mines and a halt when the minelaying sloop *Gaillardia* was blown up.[2] The area between Scotland and Norway had to be divided into British and American zones, the depths and positions of the lines of mines agreed, depots set up and a vast quantity of equipment delivered, most of it from America, which also provided most of the mines and minelayers. There were problems, never resolved, on the margins. On the east, Norway was still neutral and failed to prevent U-boats using her territorial waters; the British were unable to secure either Norway's belligerency or her agreement to close the coastal route, or to allow the coalition to mine it. Naval proposals to force the issue were vetoed by the diplomats and politicians. Even more difficulty was encountered at the western end where Beatty, always hostile to the scheme, insisted on a clear passage for his heavy ships and the Scandinavian convoys, much to the Americans' disgust. The Admiralty, too, never shared the Americans' evangelical faith in the plan's prospects. The surface patrols never materialised, so additional mines were planted close to the surface [292–4, 296–9]. Minelaying finally got under way in March 1918. By the end of the war, some 70,000 mines had been sown, of which 57,000 were American, in 15 lines at varying depths and 30 miles in width and 230 miles in length, at a cost of $40 million.[3] The operation was very much a joint mission and the co-operation was excellent [295, 296, 300].

After the war, the Americans claimed that the barrage was 'among the outstanding effective contributions to the allied success'.[4] It was said to have destroyed several U-boats, damaged others, delayed the passages of some and sapped morale throughout the submarine service, as well as handicapping surface raiders [301]. The best estimate is that three U-boats were definitely lost in it and

---

[1] Trask, *Captains and Cabinets*, pp. 154–6; Roosevelt to Wilson, 29 October 1917, *Wilson Papers*, vol. 44, p. 464; F. B. Freidel, *Franklin D. Roosevelt*, vol. 1, *The Apprenticeship* (Boston: Little Brown, 1952), p. 312.

[2] Marder, vol. 5, pp. 66–76. HMS *Gaillardia*, a 'Flower' class sloop, was lost on the minefield on 22 March 1918.

[3] Trask, *Captains and Cabinets*, pp. 216–18.

[4] *Annual Report of the Secretary of the Navy, 1919*, p. 47.

three certainly damaged, while possibly three more were sunk there and perhaps a further one damaged. It is arguable whether this striking rate justified the enormous effort expended, as the barrage was still incomplete at the war's end and thus the effect of the completed scheme cannot be assessed. Grant, perhaps best placed to judge, declared that 'It can hardly be claimed that the Northern Barrage was as successful as the one in the Straits of Dover', where the barrier was formidable by early 1918. Grant concludes that the barrage was dangerous by October 1918 but, though passage was unpleasant, it was far from impossible.[1] The Admiralty, sceptical to the last, deplored 'the large proportion of premature explosions' in the American sector and remarked that, though the general conception was sound, the barrage was not 'a serious obstacle' [302].

[1] Grant, *U-Boats Destroyed*, pp. 98, 106, 107.

272. Sims to Navintel

16 April 1917

Admiralty reports Vickers Elia mine as originally designed very unsatisfactory, and that necessary service improvements, since war began, are essential to efficiency. Particular trouble with depth taking and pistol. Distance weight now not released until mine and anchor sink about ten feet. New design pawl on mooring line reel, and elimination shearing pins and modification firing pin sleeve release. All are Admiralty improvements and war secrets. Am sending drawings next dispatch bag, and British expert mine officer, as soon as possible. Admiralty now building German mine similar Carbonit, with changes; see Babcock intelligence reports 1912 and 13.[1] Please send me latest torpedo war nose and anti-circular run device, both drawing and sample. Advise sending McBride,[2] also engineer and gunnery officer. All information now wide open.

273. Daniels to Sims

17 April 1917

Is it not practicable to blockade the German coast efficiently and completely thus making practically impossible egress and ingress of submarines?

Steps attempted or accomplished in this direction to be reported at once.

274. Daniels to Sims

11 May 1917

Consult with British Admiralty in regard to following:-

Much opinion is in favor of concerted efforts by the Allies to establish a complete barrier across the North Sea – Scotland to Norway, either direct or via the Shetlands to prevent the egress of German submarines.

---

[1] On the inefficiency of British mines, see Marder, vol. 4, pp. 87–8.
[2] Constructor Commander Lewis B. McBride, US Navy: then assistant to Naval Attaché, London; later on Sims's staff.

This plan would involve the use of various forms of mines, nets, patrols, and the release for this purpose of all ships upon American coast patrol as well as many vessels of the Allies now employed elsewhere.

The plan also involves regulations for the commerce of Holland and Scandinavian neutrals to pass barriers and definite controlled gates. It also includes closing Norway's territorial waters with her consent or over her protest.

The difficulty and size of the problem is recognized but if it possible of accomplishment the situation would warrant the effort.

If this plan is not feasible could not the same plan be carried out between Denmark and Norway *across* the Skaggerack?

Make a full report.

275. *Sims to Opnav*

11 May 1917

****

21. There has been great difficulty in maintaining nets and mines in place. Gales frequently sweep out both, and the enemy mine sweepers are constantly at work destroying them.

22. In some places neither mines nor nets are effective on account of the strong tides. This is particularly the case between the Orkney and Shetland Islands.

23. Mines and nets are very extensively used in the attempt to prevent the ingress and egress of submarines from German Ports and to embarrass their movements, and also in attempting to prevent their passage through the Channel. I have been shown the working charts and have had the various efforts explained to me by Admiral Jellicoe.

24. Generally speaking, the area enclosed within a line running first NNW, then North, from Texel Island, thence in a curve to the Eastward to a point North of Horns Reef, contains numerous lines and fields of mines. Within this area there are at least thirty thousand mines, and additional ones are being laid at the rate of three thousand a month. The field is now being extended to the Westward and Northward from Texel Island to Broken Bank. Some submarines are known to have been destroyed in the Channel; but the difficulty of the problem will be recognised from the fact that the comparatively narrow Dover Strait is not now completely closed to the passage of submarines.

25. This latter illustrates the difficulty of closing such a wide gap as

the Northern entrance of the North Sea from Kinnaird's Head to
Norway. On this line of about 230 miles there is 30 to over 100
fathoms of water. The number of patrol boats necessary to *watch*
these nets would be very great.

26. As for *protecting* such a long line, or any line of considerable
length, it is of course, physically impossible to do so effectively, and
this for the fundamental reason that the defence is stretched out in a
long and locally weak line, while the enemy can concentrate an
attack at any point of it, destroy the patrol vessels and drag out
some sections of the mines or net, thus permitting the passage of any
number of submarines.

27. This can be done in as many places as desired and as often as
may be necessary, whether the barrier is nets or mines; and it is
because of this fundamental principle of a concentrated attack
against a point of a necessarily dispersed force that no such barrier
can ever be sufficiently effective to prevent the passage of all the
submarines the enemy wishes to send out.

28. This is the gist of the whole matter – the physical impossibility of
a dispersed force successfully resisting a locally concentrated attack.

(a)   Enemy cruiser of considerable gun power can make a hole in
      any patrol of a barrier.

(b)   The patrol vessels must retire before such a force, thus
      permitting a section of mines or nets to be dragged out, and
      thus defeating the object of the barrier.

(c)   It has, of course, been proposed to guard the barrier with
      heavy vessels. This is what Germany hopes Great Britain will
      do, thus exposing them to torpedo attack and permitting
      their policy of attrition to be carried out. The German vessels
      would also be exposed to similar attack, but the British
      cannot successfully compete with Germany in torpedo war-
      fare particularly near the bases of the latter.

I cannot too strongly emphasize the fact that during nearly three
years of actual warfare this whole question has been the most serious
subject of consideration by the British Admiralty, and that many
schemes of the nature of those in question have been thoroughly
discussed, and those considered practicable – those which do not
violate a fundamental principle – have been, or are now being, tried
and extended; but the point is that no barrier can be completely
effective; and, unfortunately, a barrier or system of barriers, such as
mines, etc., needs only to be slightly ineffective to permit continuous
passage without much loss of submarines.

29. It is in view of the above and of the large amount of supporting

evidence obtained that I have urgently recommended the primary military effort should be concentrated in getting the maximum number of anti-submarine craft of all descriptions into the enemy's main area of activity.

Nets, barriers, and similar methods can never be entirely effective but only palliative. The submarine must always be opposed in its field of action. and the most effective opposition discovered to date is numbers of anti-submarine craft.

The difficulty at the present time is lack of such craft.

276. *De Chair to Admiralty*

Washington, D.C.
10 May 1917

United States Navy Department seriously contemplate a scheme for confining submarines in the North Sea by means of nets and mines extending from North of Shetland to Norwegian coast South of Bergen. If this is considered possible they are prepared to bear the cost and maintain the barrier with necessary small craft, etc., in fact they would send over all suitable small craft which otherwise would be protecting their shores. This scheme involves the violation of Norwegian territorial waters concerning which F. O. could express an opinion. A formal protest by Norwegian Govt. is probable but there is a strong feeling here that it should be overridden.

277. *Admiralty[1] to De Chair*

14 May 1917

From all experience Admiralty consider project of attempting to close exit to North Sea to enemy submarines by the method suggested to be quite impracticable. Project has previously been considered and abandoned. The difficulty will be appreciated when total distance, depths, material and patrols required and distance from base of operations are considered. Even were it practicable to lay, maintain and protect such a barrier it would not owing to want of resilience prove effective against the passage of submarines fitted with cutters.

Special memorandum with drawings sent to Washington deals fully with limitations of barrage as result of experience.

Although this particular project is not considered practicable the

[1] Probably from Rear-Admiral Duff, formerly DASD and now ACNS.

proposal to send over all small craft suitable for patrol work would if adopted prove of the very greatest value.

Vessels should have good sea-keeping qualities.

278. *Memorandum by Asst. Secretary Roosevelt on Submarine Situation*

24 May 1917

****

Problem

In view of the fact that the British have been practically successful in closing the Straits of Dover, it is obvious that if a complete barrier could be extended from Scotland to Norway and another complete barrier across the Straits of Otranto from Italy to Albania, German submarines would operate only in the North Sea and in the Adriatic. It would be impossible for them to operate in the Atlantic Ocean or in the Mediterranean, as their sole means of exit would be closed. To solve this problem by the creation of successful submarine barriers at these two points would at the same time stop one hundred per cent of the losses of merchant shipping by submarine attack and would bring with it a speedy termination of the war.

Proposed Plan

It is felt that no single new invention or development of a particular device in the nature of mines or nets can be relied upon as a *sole* means of closing the North Sea. The plan proposes the use of *several* types of nets and mines and may be set down roughly as follows:

First, the North Sea Barrier.

(a) *Location*: Either a line from a point on the coast of Scotland, near Buchan Ness, to the coast of Norway near Obrestad, or a line from the North of Scotland to the Orkneys, thence to the Shetlands, and hence by the shortest line to the coast of Norway. The location of the barrier must be determined after careful investigation of physical conditions and military advantages.

(b) *Form of Barrier*: The barrier to consist of a number of lines of net each complete in itself and also a number of lines of mines. It is impossible to specify the most desirable type of net or the most desirable type of mine. Probably different types of each should be used and experience will show which proves the most satisfactory under the varying conditions existing on the barrier. For instance, if the heavy net intended to stop submarines does not give the best results the nets with bomb attachments may be better. Also, some nets may be superior in shallow water and others in the deep waters near the Norwegian coast. In the same way the individual anchored mines may be best part of the way and in other localities the suspended mine may be found better.

(c) *Patrol*: The question of patrol of the barrier is of the utmost importance. It is suggested that in order to establish this patrol the entire coast patrol of the United States, and of the western coast of France, England, Scotland and Ireland may, of necessity, be concentrated at the barrier. If, for instance, the barrier is from 225 to 250 miles in length a proper patrol may call for 4,000 vessels. It is submitted that it is entirely feasible by a concentration of all of the resources of the Allies to obtain this number of vessels. In the operation of the patrol the smaller vessels would obviously be used when the water is smooth and the larger vessels in rough water. The object would be, of course, to cover every mile of the barrier at all times and prevent raids, to prevent night operations against the barrier by enemy submarines or ships, and to drag with depth bombs and nets in case the nets or mines of the barrier itself were disturbed by enemy submarines.

(d) *British Grand Fleet*: The mission of the British Grand Fleet would remain much what it is today. It should base south of the barrier and the present system of scouting should be continued so as to disclose immediately any attempt by the German High Seas Fleet to leave their base in an attempt to cut the barrier by an attack in force. It is obvious that the barrier itself would be closer to the British fleet base than to the German fleet base, and further consideration of such military importance is not necessary.

Practicability

Investigations as to material have been conducted far enough to prove that the requisite amount of net and the necessary number of mines can, without question, be turned out by the factories of England and the United States. For example, it is physically quite possible to construct 1,000 miles of net 200 feet in depth. It is also perfectly possible to construct 500,000 mines, and it is possible further to provide one hundred per cent of replacements of nets and mines by the time they will be needed. The cost of manufacturing, transporting, installing, etc., 1,000 miles of net and 500,000 mines has been variously estimated at from $200,000,000 to $500,000,000. Even if the greater figure is taken, the Allied governments can well afford the expenditure if only in comparison with the value of the merchant tonnage which has been sunk during the first five months of the present year.

Conclusion

This is a problem which has been discussed in the United States and Great Britain in Admiralty and civilian circles for nearly three years. Experiments have been made along individual lines and without a conception of the task as a whole. Experiments have been made in small areas and with small amounts of material. Many officers are convinced that the present defense against submarines is fundamentally wrong and can never accomplish the ultimate result. Nearly all officers believe in the fundamental soundness of the theory of closing the north end of the North Sea. Most officers with whom I have talked believe that the time has come when the attempt to carry this out must be made, not half-heartedly, but on the greatest possible scale and with the resources of England and the United States combined. It goes without saying, of course, that all of these remarks apply to a lesser extent to the closing of the Adriatic. If the North Sea proposal is feasible it is also feasible to close the Straits of Otranto. The two proposals march hand in hand. To carry out the attempt requires naval and industrial cooperation of the highest type, but the important thing is to prevent this subject from being discussed for six or eight months and to have it accepted or rejected immediately.[1]

279. *Roosevelt to President Wilson*

5 June 1917

In confirmation of what I said to you about the North Sea question, I have thought over the composition of a Board or Commission to make speedy report on the advisability of making the attempt to carry out this plan on a large scale. ...

---

[1] Roosevelt was a young man in a hurry and had a reputation for 'action, and action now'. In the event, the subject was discussed for another six months.

****

... time is of the essence of the plan, especially because during the next three or four months the weather conditions will be good for carrying out the preliminary work.

I am showing this to Mr Daniels, and I feel sure that the whole Department will approve the initiation of the project. ... in the execution of the work the usual department routine and red tape should be cut to a minimum, and that outside of the actual patrol of such a barrier the work to be done has a distinctly civilian and industrial character.

280. *De Chair to Roosevelt*

Washington,
12 July 1917

... [The Admiralty] are of the opinion that though the placing of such a net is practicable the difficulties attending its maintenance, and the prevention of submarines from passing through it or over it are so great as to render it of secondary value compared to the present methods of dealing with the submarine menace. ...

281. *Benson to Sims*

18 August 1917

Bureau of Ordance has developed mine which [it] is hoped may have decisive influence upon operations against submarine. Utmost secrecy considered necessary. Request that officer representing Admiralty, clothed with power to decide, be sent here to inspect and thoroughly test mine. If found satisfactory arrange for cooperation in mine operation.

282. *Sims to Rear-Admiral Ralph Earle, US Navy*

25 September 1917

... it is hardly possible to do anything efficient in the way of manufacturing or laying mines without taking full advantage of all of the experience which has been gained on this side in actual warfare. It is by reason of the very bitter experience which the English and French have had in this particular respect that they are so reluctant to accept a mine which is believed by those having no war experience to be superior to theirs instead of going ahead with the manufacture of a mine which has been tried out in actual experience until it has proved satisfactory.

... this is a good scheme if it works but a very expensive one if it does not. ...

283. *Jellicoe to Benson*

17 October 1917

Should there be any difficulty in using the lower antennae of US mines for first supplies it will be necessary to increase the number of lines of US mines in each system in the North Sea Barrage from two to three. Can you please give an approximate date when supply of complete mines and sinkers will commence and state at what rate the supply will be maintained?

As all British Minelayers will be fully occupied in laying the British portions of the barrage will you please say how many American Minelayers will be available to deal with the output of US mines. It is estimated that each ship could make 5 minelaying trips a month. It is proposed to use Cromarty as a base for the US mines and minelayers. Question of facilities for assembling ready use storage, and embarkation is being looked into on the spot. Suggest desirable that US Officers should confer with ours on this question and examine proposed arrangements as to suitability for dealing with US mines and sinkers; also to ascertain whether our depot system will be suitable for application to US mines. It is proposed that the necessary assembling and testing of US mines and sinkers on receipt and before issue to minelayers should be dealt with by Depot staffs provided by you if possible. It is hoped that you will be able to agree with this. US officers if sent over can report numbers required. Should be grateful if you would inform me as soon as possible whether you can supply sinkers for US mines.

284. *Benson to Sims*

21 October 1917

Department requires to be informed whether plan for placing mine barrage across North Sea on Aberdeen–Egersund line has approval of Admiralty. It is believed that great experience of British naval forces, in North Sea operations and their experience in naval mining during present war, put them in best position to decide whether in opinion of Admiralty it is best scheme in sight for limiting operations of enemy submarines provided that Strait of Dover can be effectively closed to passage of submarines which if possible in opinion of Department should be done at earliest possible date.

285.   *Navy Department to Sims*

21 October 1917

****

6. Contract has been let for one hundred thousand mines of American type. The United States has offered to commandeer, for British Admiralty, three vessels suitable for mine laying, and in addition can probably commandeer two or three more vessels suitable for minelaying, to be manned by United States, for employment in cooperation with British minelaying force, in joint plan which may be finally agreed upon.
7. Question of proposed mine barrage. Scotland to Norway, as presented to Navy Department, is not definitely concurred in, but careful consideration is being given to this particular subject, with a view to arrive at a definite conclusion in regard to employment of the mine barrage, which measure is considered in principle to promise good results.

286.   *Jellicoe to Benson*

22 October 1917

Admiralty has approved mine barrier and now confirms approval. Preparations proceeding rapidly. Assistance desired from United States of America is indicated in my telegram No. 513 of 17 October.[1] Admiralty consider this is best scheme to carry out at a distance from enemy bases. Admiralty is working on supplementary scheme for operations closer in shore, but any such inshore operation has defect that enemy can eventually clear a passage through for submarines therefore North Sea Barrage also necessary. No scheme yet tried has effectively closed Dover Straits to submarines, but measures are being constantly improved and they are at least always a considerable deterrent.[2] Extensive mining operations in

---

[1] See document 283.
[2] The CinC Dover, Admiral Sir Reginald Bacon, had been unable to close the Straits to U-boats and lost the confidence of the Admiralty, being replaced immediately after Jellicoe's dismissal in December 1917. See Marder, vol. 4, pp. 347–8.

Dover Straits against submarines commence in November. Hitherto delayed from lack of effective anti-submarine mine.

287.   *Senior Member, General Board,*[1] *to Daniels*

24 October 1917

****

21. The further advantages [of the North Sea Barrage over other possible barrages] are: (1) one end of the barrier rests on England, close to British naval bases; (2) the entire barrier is much nearer to British fleet bases than to any German submarine or surface craft base; (3) the discouragement of the Germans that will follow if the rate of tonnage destroyed decreases more rapidly than the allied merchant tonnage construction increases; (4) the corresponding encouragement to our allies.

22. The difficulties in the way of laying and maintaining an efficient barrier across the North Sea are such that the British have, until recently, considered them insurmountable. With the use of the American mine, and with full American cooperation, the barrier promises sufficient success to warrant undertaking it. The disadvantages are: (1) the difficulty of supplying the material on the spot and laying the barrier; (2) the constant danger of interruption by the enemy while in progress of construction and concentration of German effort upon the barrier when completed; (3) supplying the patrol craft necessary to protect the construction while in progress, and patrol the barrier afterwards. If the barrier is pushed out in successive sections from the British coast, a small patrol will be required at first, then constantly increasing in numbers as the work progresses.

23. The necessity to close the Dover Strait is imperative. Whatever other measures to control submarines are employed, it is self-evident that no single measure would do as much to prevent merchant ship destruction as to deny a passage for submarines to the Atlantic by this route. Closing this Strait would compel the smaller submarines to pass round Scotland to the Atlantic, thus very materially reducing their season of active operations against commerce. In the heavy weather to be encountered on this route in the winter months, probably none but larger submarines would attempt to operate in the Atlantic.

[1] Rear-Admiral C. J. Badger, US Navy.

24. *Conclusions*: ... the best chances of success [lie in the schemes] ... to close the North Sea by the Aberdeen-Egersund barrier approved by the British Admiralty, and to similarly close the Dover Strait.
25. The General Board does not underestimate the practical difficulties that must be overcome in providing the necessary material and transporting, placing and maintaining it in the face of the determined efforts of the Germans to render the barrier abortive. Further, the barrier even when placed cannot be effective without an adequate patrol. The General Board is, however, encouraged to give its endorsement to this plan because it has the approval of the British Admiralty; it is proposed by it as the best practicable plan to meet present war conditions; the Chief of Bureau of Ordnance states the material, mines, anchors, moorings, etc., can be surely supplied; and the accompanying memorandum of Captain R. R. Belknap, US Navy,[1] who has been actively engaged in conducting mining operations, points the way to handling the details of transporting and planting.

288.   *Roosevelt to Daniels*

29 October 1917

Proposed Measures to close English Channel and North Sea against submarines by mine barrage

1. This is, of course, nothing more nor less than a resurrection of my proposition, which, with all earnestness possible, I called to the attention of the President, the Secretary of the Navy, the Chief of [Naval] Operations, the General Board, Admiral Sims (and through him the British Admiralty), Admiral de Chair (and through him also the British Admiralty) and Admiral Chocheprat (and through him the French Ministry of Marine) during the months of May and June past.
2. While I have never claimed that the proposed plan was an infallible one, and while, quite properly, I have never attempted to lay down the exact location or the exact type of mines, etc., to be used in the barrage, I did state, and still state, that every consideration of common sense requires that the attempt be made, first in the English Channel and then in the North Sea.
3. But above all, starting when the Balfour and Viviani missions were here in May, I reiterated the need for haste. I know how

[1] Captain Reginald R. Belknap, US Navy, in charge of minelaying operations in the US sectors.

unseemly it is to seem to say 'I told you so', but is is a literal fact that, while the British Admiralty may be blamed in part, our own Navy Department is at least largely responsible for failing to consider this proposition seriously during all of these months ...

4. Now, this is the milk in the coconut: The powers that be seem at last willing to take up this proposition seriously. Unless we are willing to throw up our hands and say it is too late, we must admit that the same need for immediate haste exists today as existed last May. We have done altogether too much amiable 'consideration' of this matter. If it is to be carried out at all it must be carried out with a different spirit from any of the operations up to now. It will require prompt decision all along the line and an immediate carrying out of the procurement of the material – mines and ships.

5. To accomplish the above it should be placed in the hands of one man on our part and one man on the part of the British. These two men should receive orders from their governments, not as to details, but simply orders to carry out the plan. *And most important of all, these men should have all the authority requisite to do this.* This is a bigger matter than sending destroyers abroad or a division of batt-leships, or building a bunch of new destroyers – it is vital to the winning of the war. Its success cannot be guaranteed. No military or naval operation can be guaranteed. But if it works it will be the biggest single factor in winning the war. I have seen something during the past four and a half years of how our present Navy Department organization works and it so happens that I am also fairly familiar with the way the British Admiralty works.[1] If the suggested plan is carried out solely under the present organizations its chances of success will, in my judgment, be seriously diminished. You need somebody with imagination and authority to make the try.

6. I know you will not mind my sending a copy of this to the President, as I have discussed it with him several times.

289. *Navy Department to Sims*

2 November 1917

Inform Admiralty that Department concurs in project for mine barriers, Scotland to Norway, and has already taken steps to fit out eight mine planters, to sail 1 February; also expediting completion

---

[1] No doubt from his conversations with Gaunt, De Chair, Pollen and the American Churchill.

twelve mine-sweeping tugs. Expect begin shipment of mines 15 January. Will send Officers to confer and arrange details within a few days.

290. *Benson to Daniels*

London,
9 November 1917

Called on Geddes, had long conference with Jellicoe. All fully convinced practicable and desirable to lay North Sea Barrier if shipping for handling material can be spared. Have assured them we will do our part. Officer who is to actually supervise our part should be sent over as soon as convenient.
****

291. *Memorandum by the Rear-Admiral (Mining)*[1]

10 December 1917

Northern Mine Barrage: Dates for the Establishment of Bases and the commencement of Minelaying

The following dates are proposed and should, if possible, be kept to:-
United States of America – General
1. American personnel to commence arriving in England – 1 February 1918
2. The first of the weekly cargoes of 3500 mines and sinkers to leave the United States of America on – 1 February 1918
3. American Minelayers to arrive Inverness and Invergordon – 15 March 1918
4. Commence laying Area A – 1 April 1918
5. One system of A should be completed by – 1 May 1918

292. *Planning Section, US Naval Forces in European Waters*

31 December 1917

The North Sea Barrage

Position: [Original Aberdeen-Egersund line modified to meet Admiralty wishes]
... The new position is deemed best by the Grand Fleet upon

---

[1] Rear-Admiral Lewis Clinton-Baker: Captain 1908; commanded *Benbow* 1916; Rear-Admiral August 1917; HQ at Grangemouth on the Forth.

which will rest the responsibility for the support and patrol of the barrage.

****

It will be noted that the original line extended from mainland to mainland, while the new line extends from island to island and has in it passages completely navigable to submarines. This condition is, in our opinion, undesirable. We believe it wrong to accept a plan that provides in advance a way by which the plan may be defeated.
Character of the Barrage: The proposed character of the barrage does not provide for the full accomplishment of the mission. ... The submarine must be taught to fear all Norwegian territorial waters. ...

****

Memorandum by Admiralty Plans Division

****

C. The stopping power of a mine barrage such as we propose to lay should not be over-rated. ...
... It is patrol craft, armed with anti-submarine devices, on which we must rely to actually kill the submarines. ... Assuming that we are correct in considering the minefield only as an accessory to the patrol we must arrange the minefields to that end. ... Until we have proved the efficiency of the American Minefield we must look upon it as a bluff. ...

293. *Joint Memorandum by British and American Planning Staffs*

12 January 1918

As a result of conference, the Plans Division of the Admiralty and the American Planning Section are agreed on the plan of barrage and on the division of responsibility in establishing the barrage. ...

****

2. The barrage shall be laid as nearly as may be in the following positions:-

Section A
Section B
Section C.

3. The barrage in all sections shall consist of not less than three rows

of mines at each level and shall be thickened as necessary to make the hazard of its passage prohibitive.

****

5. The vertical distance between successive rows of mines in the same vertical system shall be such as to render the barrage complete.
6. The barrage in Section A shall be complete from a point about eight feet below the surface to 200 feet below the surface plus a sufficient distance to prohibit the passage of submarines except they incur the hazard of mines.
7. The barrage in Sections B and C shall be complete from a point about sixty-five feet below the surface to 200 feet below the surface plus a sufficient distance to prohibit the passage of submarines, except they incur the hazard of mines.
8. The American navy shall be charged with furnishing the mines and sinkers and laying the barrage, above described, in Section A.

The British Navy shall be charged with furnishing the mines and sinkers and laying the barrage, above described, in Section B and in Section C.
9. The British navy is charged with the responsibility of preventing the passage of enemy vessels across Section B and Section C, through Norwegian territorial waters adjacent to the barrage and through unmined exits from the North Sea to the westward of Section B.
10. The British Navy is charged with the escort and support of all mine laying operations.
11. The British Admiralty accepts the principle of surface mining in Areas B and C should experience indicate that the surface barrage is more effective in preventing the passage of submarines than the surface patrol.
12. The British Admiralty will extend Area B westward or southward to the coast should this be found necessary to prevent the passage of enemy submarines.
13. The American Navy will provide sufficient surplus mines and sinkers to lay two rows of mines throughout the length of Areas B and C in order to anticipate the decision to surface mine those areas. Responsibility for the actual laying of these mines shall be determined by future agreement.
14. The British Navy will furnish all buoys and moorings for buoys

and all navigational aids needed in Sections A, B and C.

15. The general direction of barrage operations shall be with the British Navy but complete technical and tactical freedom in mine laying shall reside with the American mine laying Force.

16. No changes in the characteristics of the barrage, as above outlined, shall be made without further conference and agreement.

17. The plan of the barrage shall be subject to review at any time, on the request of either the British Admiralty or of the American Navy Department.

294. *Memorandum by US Planning Section*

12 March 1918

Present and Future Mining Policy: A Joint estimate of the Situation by the British and American Planning Divisions

****

... the continuance of the present rate of tonnage losses cannot be permitted without ultimate defeat. The next six months will present the gravest tonnage difficulties.[1]

... It is almost certain that the Northern Barrage, as at present designed, will not fulfil its purpose. ...

Admiralty Plans Division Appreciation of the Anti-Submarine Campaign in 1918

... success will depend entirely on the possibility of supporting the patrols in Area C. ... like a girder supported at one end, the plan will collapse unless a base is established in Norwegian waters. ... The part which the Grand Fleet plays in the control of the Northern Barrage is the crucial question in the 1918 anti-submarine campaign. ... It is suggested that the primary function of the Grand Fleet should be defined as the support of the barrage and the prevention of submarines passing out of the Northern exit. ...

[1] In fact at this point new construction was just beginning to outstrip losses, though this only became really clear in May. See Newbolt, vol. 5, pp. 1, 277, 336–7. Demands on the increasing tonnage were, however rising, especially as the flow of American troops and their supplies to France swelled from the spring of 1918.

388   ANGLO-AMERICAN NAVAL RELATIONS 1917–1919

295. *Memorandum by Beatty*

Grand Fleet,
5 June 1918

Operation 'M.1'

1. Object:

A. ... To lay British deep mines between approximate positions latitude 59° 47' North, longitude 4° 00' East and 59° 39' North and 4° 59' East.

****

B. ... To lay American mines fifty miles in a direction 249° from approximate position latitude 59° 43' North, longitude 3° 10' East.

****

2. Forces Employed:

Force A. ... First Minelaying Squadron, consisting of *Princess Margaret, Amphitrite, Angora* and *London*[1] screened by a leader, or half leader, *Nimrod* and 6 destroyers as detailed by the Commodore (F).[2] The Rear-Admiral (M)[3] will fly his flag in *Princess Margaret*.

Force B. ... Second Minelaying Squadron, consisting of USS *San Francisco, Baltimore, Canandaigua, Quinnebaug, Housatonic, Canonicus* and *Roanoke*[4] screened by *Vampire* and 9 destroyers of the 14th Flotilla.[5]

Force C. ... Fifth Battle Squadron screened by 6 destroyers as detailed by Commodore (F), *Blanche*.[6]

Second Battle Cruiser Squadron screened by 6 destroyers of the 13th Flotilla.[7]

Fourth Light Cruiser Squadron.[8]

[1] HMS *Princess Margaret*: merchant vessel, 1913–14; converted to minelayer; 5440 tons; 2 × 4.7in; 22.5 knots. HMS *Amphitrite*: 1898; converted to minelayer 1917; 11000 tons; 4 × 6 in; 21 knots. HMS *Angora*: minelayer; unidentified. HMS *London*: pre-dreadnought, 1899; converted 1918; 15000 tons; 3 × 6in; 18 knots.
[2] Commodore (F), commanding Grand Fleet destroyers: from December 1917, Commodore Hugh J. Tweedie; flag in light cruiser *Castor*.
[3] Rear-Admiral Clinton-Baker.
[4] American minelayers, all but the first two converted merchantmen. *San Francisco* and *Baltimore* were old cruisers.
[5] HMS *Vampire*: flotilla leader, 1917; 1316 tons; 4 × 4in; 6 tt; 34 knots.
[6] HMS *Blanche*: light cruiser, 1910; 3350 tons; 8 × 4in; 2 tt; 26 knots. 5th BS (Vice-Admiral Evan-Thomas), *Queen Elizabeth* class.
[7] 2nd BCS (Rear-Admiral Arthur C. Leveson, *Australia*, flag).
[8] 4th LCS (Commodore Rudolf W. Bentinck, *Calliope*, flag), of war-built 'C' class cruisers: 3750–4190 tons; 4–5 × 6in; 28–29 knots; 8 tt in some. Squadron included *Caroline, Comus, Constance* and generally two others.

****

296. *Memorandum by Admiralty Plans Division*

24 July 1918

History of the Northern Barrage

1. In September 1917, the question of our future policy with regard to the enemy submarine campaign was under review. This question dominated every other consideration, for, if the sinking of the mercantile marine had continued at the then existing rate, it would probably have brought about an unsatisfactory peace. The enemy were producing submarines at a greater rate than the Allies could destroy them and destroying shipping quicker than we could build. The policy of coping with the submarines after reaching the trade routes was not sufficiently effective, and everything pointed to the necessity of a more effective control in the areas between the enemy's ports and the vital communications.

2. It was finally decided to lay a mine barrage between the Orkneys and the Norwegian Coast, consisting of a large area of deep and shallow mines in the centre, to be provided by the United States, flanked by British deep minefields on its West side, to within a few miles of the Orkney Islands, and on its east side to the Norwegian territorial waters. The British were to provide sufficient patrol craft for their deep minefields, with a view to driving the submarines onto their mines. It was fully appreciated that the effective patrol of Norwegian Waters would be extremely difficult without a Norwegian base to work from, and, at this stage of the plan, it was assumed that there would be a very good chance of obtaining such a base. It was considered that the central, or American, area was to be regarded as not requiring patrols, in view of the shallow minefield.

3. The original date for commencing to lay the minefield was delayed, owing to :-

(a) The lack of British minelayers ...

(b) The American production of mines being delayed;

(c) The delay in the collection of the patrol craft.

4. Eventually, on 2 March 1918, the British commenced to lay a line of deep mines for the deep minefield between the Orkneys and the American area; but after the fourth laying the *Gaillardia*[1] was blown up on a surface mine, and laying operations in this area were deferred pending trials being carried out with regard to the reliability

[1] HMS *Gaillardia*, a 'Flower' class sloop.

of deep mines, and so far these trials have not been completed.

5. On 26 April 1918, the area embracing the American field and the British field to the Eastward of it was published as a proclaimed area, and on 8 June 1918, the British commenced mining in the Eastern area, and so far have laid the following lines of mines:-

2 lines at 65 feet
2 lines at 95 feet
2 half lines at 125 feet

As the maintaining of a surface patrol in this field could not be efficiently carried out without a base on the adjacent Norwegian Coast, and there being no hope of obtaining such a base, it was decided not to establish a surface patrol in this area, but to mine the area up to the surface. To meet this, two lines of American mines with 70 foot antennae have been laid to the Southward of the British deep mines, and a further two lines of British mines are about to be laid 10 feet below the surface. The Americans have also on order two more shallow lines of American mines with 35 foot antennae for this area. Besides this, it is proposed to complete the two British half lines at 125 feet, and further to lay two lines at 55 feet and two at 185 feet.

6. With regard to the American area, the first minelaying operated consisted in laying three lines of mines with 70 foot antennae from the Eastern limit to longitude 1° 40' East. They then laid two lines off the Norwegian Coast, as mentioned in par. 5 above, by which time sufficient minelayers had arrived from America to enable them to lay three lines of mines in one operation from 1° 40' E to the Western limit of their area in longitude 0° 50' W. It was, however, decided at the last moment prior to their laying these mines, that they should not proceed further West than the Meridian of Greenwich, in consequence of which it is understood they have laid three lines of antennae mines 80 feet below the surface, and two lines of mines with 70 foot antennae, one of which is 160 feet deep, and one at 240 feet deep. The result of this is that, as the mines are at present laid, there is a clear gap of 30 miles at the Western end of the proclaimed area.

7. This gap was left on the strong representation of the Commander-in-Chief, Grand Fleet, in order to allow a clear passage some 25 miles wide, for supporting forces to the Scandinavian Convoy. Although the line of mines between the proclaimed area and the Orkneys has been swept to 30 feet he does not consider it safe for his heavy ships to pass over it.

A surface patrol for this area has never been established, as sufficient mines have not been laid to make it worthwhile. The vessels originally designated for this duty are at present being used with the Northern Patrol.

297.   *Sims to Captain R. R. Belknap, US Navy*

25 July 1918

I have recently taken up with the principal dignitaries the whole question of the Northern barrage, and I believe the ultimate result will be that we will plant our mines all the way from Norway to the Orkneys, a solid barrier that all submarines passing out or passing in will have to cross. This is not entirely confirmed yet, but it is the opinion of the Admiralty and the matter will be taken up immediately with the Commander-in-Chief.

298.   *Memorandum by Wemyss for War Cabinet*

31 July 1918

****

The steps which have been taken by the Allies to refuse the passage of the enemy's submarines round the North of Scotland into the Atlantic are locally stultified by the persistent use of Norwegian Territorial Waters by these vessels. Of this fact we have ocular proof from our submarine patrols.

Under these circumstances, the Admiralty consider that it should be brought to the notice of the Norwegian Government that ... [it is] committing an unneutral act by allowing the enemy's submarine forces to pass through their waters in order to reach their hunting grounds ...

This communication should be accompanied by an offer of assistance on the part of the Allies to Norway to close the passage through her Territorial Waters by Mines; and in default of her accepting such an offer, she should be informed that in the interest of the World's shipping it is necessary for them to undertake this work themselves.

...

****

The United States Naval Authorities are whole-hearted advocates of this measure, realising that the results of their exertions in producing and laying a vast quantity of mines are largely reduced by the inertia of Norway.

... Norway should be given a time limit of three days in which to decide on her action. ...

299. *Sims to Benson*

30 August 1918

****

... The Chief of Operations[1] was sent to consult the Commander-in-Chief [about the American desire for a coast-to-coast
North Sea Barrage]. ... The result was that an agreement has now
been reached to mine Area B to within ten miles of the Orkneys, to
send the convoys hereafter through West Way Firth and Pentland
Firth and thence across the north of the barrage; to declare Area B
mined all the way to the Orkneys and then if it was found that any
submarines passed through the ten mile gap, that this was to be
mined with both surface and deep mines, thus closing the whole of
the North Sea between Norway and the Orkneys. Of course this is
on the assumption that the neutral waters along the Norwegian
coast will be effectively closed. This proposition seemed to me fair
and I accordingly withdrew my objection.

As for Norwegian neutral waters, negotiations between the British
Government and Norway are now proceeding and it looks as
though the matter would be settled very soon, perhaps before this
letter reaches you.

The British take the attitude that their experience shows that it is
quite futile to attempt to stop the passage of submarines through all
these neutral waters by patrol vessels and that therefore Norway
should put down mines. I think it would be well if our Government
took the same attitude.

****

300. *Captain R. R. Belknap to Sims*

22 September 1918

There was never any friction with the British Mining people and
the way Captain Marshall[2] got on with them had a good deal to do
with starting things on a proper basis. While always perfectly willing
to hear all they had to say and suggest, and let their people come on
board – and in brief while perfectly acquiescent in everything –

[1] Probably Captain Dudley Pound, DOD (Home).
[2] Captain Albert W. Marshall, US Navy: CO of 'mine planter' USS *Baltimore*.

Marshall showed them that the training and standard that his ship (*Baltimore*) was accustomed to were so high that no apprehension need be felt as to the squadron as a whole being able to fulfil its part. The British were unaware that we had been working towards an operation of this kind for three years and the *Baltimore's* showing convinced them that we had the necessary qualifications.

301. *Captain R. R. Belknap, US Navy: Submarine Mines in War*

undated typescript

[quoting Sims]:

'There is no doubt that this barrier had a considerable moral effect on the German naval crews, for it is known that several submarines hesitated some time before crossing. Also, reports from German sources are that the barrier caused no small amount of panic in some of the submarine flotillas.

It is also probable that the barrier played a part in preventing raids on Allied commerce by fast enemy cruisers.'

302. *Memorandum by Admiralty Plans Division*

1 November 1918

Future Anti-Submarine Policy with Special Reference to Hunting Tactics

****

Increase of Anti-Submarine Mining Efficiency

10. *The Northern Barrage is undoubtedly the only sound strategical method of intensifying the killing power of the mine on a large scale.* Unfortunately, the USA mines, on which its efficiency mainly depends, have not come up to expectations owing to the large proportion of premature explosions, and because the floats, which actuate the shallower mines, are very liable to be washed away by surface wave action. Also, even if they function, the mines are so deep that they are not likely to destroy submarines on the surface. *As at present designed, the Northern Barrage does not appear to be a serious obstacle to submarines on the surface.*

11. These remarks are, however, no reflection on the soundness of the general conception, but they are arguments for improving the

394   ANGLO-AMERICAN NAVAL RELATIONS 1917–1919

material. *In order to intensify and develop the killing-power of the mine, it will be necessary to improve the USA mines or replace them by British, and to arrange that submarines on the surface come in contact with actual mines.*

The Barrage may then be expected to account for a fair number of submarines, but its factor of probability will always be uncertain, owing to mines breaking away and the possibility of the enemy sweeping passages unobserved. In other words, it cannot, by itself, be accepted as a complete solution of the submarine problem.

PART VII

THE MEDITERRANEAN
JULY 1917 TO FEBRUARY 1919

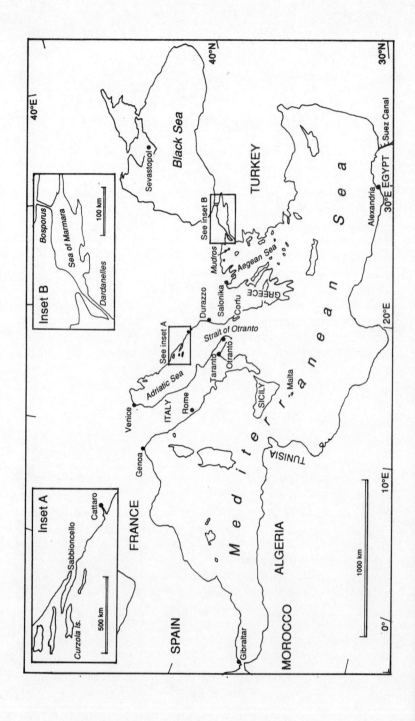

Inset A

Curzola Is.

Sabbioncello

Cattaro

500 km

Inset B

Bosporus

Sea of Marmara

Dardanelles

100 km

40°E

40°N

30°N

Black Sea

Sevastopol

TURKEY

See inset B

Mudros

Aegean Sea

Salonika

Corfu

Durazzo

GREECE

See inset A

Strait of Otranto

Adriatic Sea

Taranto

Otranto

Venice

ITALY

Rome

SICILY

Malta

Genoa

FRANCE

SPAIN

Alexandria

Suez Canal

EGYPT

30°E

Mediterranean Sea

20°E

10°E

TUNISIA

ALGERIA

MOROCCO

Gibraltar

0°

1000 km

INTRODUCTION

The Mediterranean was a perennial problem for the Allies, yet there was no good reason why this should have been the case, as their combined navies enjoyed a substantial numerical superiority in practically all classes of warship over the Central Powers and an infinitely better strategic position. Even after the disconcerting episode of the escape of the *Goeben* and *Breslau* and Turkey's subsequent entry into the war, there was little to fear from enemy surface forces, as they could be confined to the Dardanelles and the Adriatic.[1] The chief threat arose from the German and Austrian U-boats, of which there were ultimately about 50. They roamed the whole Mediterranean and caused heavy losses. The Allies failed to contain them, despite possessing numerous anti-submarine craft, extensive sea and air patrols and mine and net barrages, notably that across the Straits of Otranto. Though convoys were instituted in 1917, escorts were generally weak and losses continued at a depressingly high rate until the end of the war. In many ways, the Allies' problems were of their own making, for they failed utterly to co-ordinate their naval activities and thus nullified their paper and geographical superiority. Mutual jealousies and suspicions, often of ancient lineage, combined with ambitions to be satisfied at the peace conference to frustrate genuine Allied co-operation at the highest levels. The British and French agreed that the Italians were only in the war for what they could get out of it (a charge of which they, too, were not innocent), and considered that the Italians were therefore determined to maintain their fleet in idleness, and thus intact. The Americans prided themselves on having no territorial or other material designs on the Mediterranean; it was a distinctly secondary theatre for them and their military commitment remained small, though the Italians in particular agitated for more assistance from the US Navy. The Italians remained sceptical about American protestations of clean hands and felt that Wilson intended to deprive

---

[1] Marder, vol. 5, pp. 20–8.

them of the gains promised to them by the Treaty of London (1915). When American vessels arrived in the Mediterranean, they joined a veritable league of nations fighting the Central Powers there: Britain, France, Italy, Portugal, Greece, Serbia, Romania and Japan. America found herself in some difficulty, for she had declared war against Germany alone and she never went to war with Bulgaria or Turkey. Only with reluctance, and chiefly to bolster Italian morale after Caporetto and to weaken Germany, did she declare war on Austria-Hungary (7 December 1918).[1]

In July 1917, the British were offered a handful of old and weak American warships and these were accepted gratefully by the hard-pressed Jellicoe, who suggested that they should be based on Gibraltar where they could assist in local escort duties. By August the orginal eleven ships had risen to 22 and the first of them arrived towards the end of the month. Apart from six smart and efficient Coast Guard cutters, they represented 'a heterogenous collection of antiques',[2] slow and often defective [303–5]. Their first commander was Rear-Admiral Henry B. Wilson, though in fact the force came under the orders of the Senior British Naval Officer at Gibraltar, Rear-Admiral H. S. Grant. To Sims's delight, Wilson pledged the utmost co-operation with the Allied forces [306, 307] and this was maintained when Rear-Admiral Albert P. Niblack replaced Wilson in November 1917, following the latter's posting to Brest [309]. Second-rate though the American ships were, they were distinctly better than the ancient relics sailing under the White Ensign and were employed on the more arduous duties – convoys to east and west of the Rock and convoys to and from the United Kingdom. Niblack complained constantly about the antiquated forces left to Gibraltar, apparently after all other stations had been satisfied. Nevertheless, he and Grant, as fine a team as one could wish, kept up a vigorous programme of patrols, convoys and hunts, earning the plaudits of the British C-in-C Mediterranean, Admiral Gough-Calthorpe.[3] Unfortunately, Gibraltar remained 'the poor relation' throughout the war [308, 318, 320, 326].

Most of the action, actual and potential, took place further east, in the Adriatic. The Austrians had a substantial and well-handled fleet based on good harbours, and they harried the Italian coast,

[1] Trask, *Captains and Cabinets*, pp. 225–9, 231–5; Parsons, pp. 83–103; P. G. Halpern, *The Naval War in the Mediterranean, 1914–1918* (Annapolis, Md: NIP, 1987), pp. 377–9.
[2] Halpern, *Naval War*, p. 446.
[3] P. G. Halpern, ed., *The Royal Navy in the Mediterranean, 1915–1918* (London; Temple Smith for Navy Records Society, 1987), document no. 246.

communications and the Otranto barrage. Much more damage was done, however, by the Austro-German submarine force, which passed the barrage at will and ravaged Allied shipping. The immunity of the Austro-German surface and sub-surface forces and the impunity with which they interdicted Allied communications, bombarded the coast and raided the barrage displeased the British and infuriated the Americans. Here, surely, was a 'hornet's nest' which must be wiped out. Almost immediately following the establishment of the Allied Naval Council at the end of 1917, the American planners offered the Council (which spent the bulk of its time wrestling with the increasingly intractable Mediterranean problems) a scheme for an amphibious operation against the Dalmatian coast. In part a commando raid and in part an attempt to seize offshore islands commanding the exits from mainland enemy ports, it was to be supplemented by a mine barrage and bombing raids.[1] The British planners gave enthusiastic support, for the principle embraced was that of attacking the enemy at one of his weaker points, the traditional British strategy of peripheral combined operations. The operation demanded substantial land, air and naval forces, always difficult to obtain but impossible following the German offensive on the Western Front in March 1918 [310, 312–6].

After the grand design in the Adriatic had been frustrated, the Americans developed another characteristically bold and technically demanding scheme, a network of mine barrages criss-crossing the Mediterranean. They had already agreed to send two squadrons of submarine chasers to act in conjunction with the Franco-Italian-British Otranto barrage [311] and in the summer persuaded the Allied Naval Council to endorse their comprehensive plan of mine barrages elsewhere.[2] This system would compartmentalise the Mediterranean, thus making it easier to control and defend shipping and to hunt U-boats [319, 324–5]. The war came to an end too swiftly for these proposals to be put into effect.

Allied approval for raids in the Adriatic, anti-submarine offensives off Corfu and a plethora of mine barrages was obtained much more easily than an agreement to pool all naval forces and establish an integrated coalition naval command in the Mediterranean. The nominal Allied commander in the Mediterranean was a senior French admiral but essentially he commanded only the French

[1] Halpern, *Naval War*, pp. 434–41, 473–6; Trask, *Captains and Cabinets*, pp. 236, 240–9.
[2] Halpern, *Naval War*, pp. 508–13, 518–21; *RN in Mediterranean*, documents 235, 238.

battlefleet. The Italians paid the slightest of lip service to his authority and went their own way. The minor powers, Portugal, Greece and Japan, had little say in naval policy-making and even the British were junior partners, for they had only token or obsolescent forces in the Mediterranean and the primary responsibility of the British C-in-C at Malta was the defence of shipping. The refusal of the Italians to prosecute any kind of offensive in the Adriatic galled the British, who also had little confidence in the French Navy. Geddes welcomed the arrival of the Americans, for their well advertised proclivity for operations of derring-do would reinforce his arguments for aggressive action. This would require the co-ordination of coalition forces and the appointment of a supreme commander, an 'Admiralissimo'. Of particular concern to Geddes, and to Sims, was a possible foray of the *Goeben* and *Breslau*, supported by Turkish units, Russian dreadnoughts and powerful modern destroyers manned by Germans, in conjunction with a sally by the Austrian fleet, which would leave the Franco-Italian heavy forces facing strong enemy forces ahead and astern. It was in fact a most unlikely scenario but it encouraged the Anglo-American leaders to press for an Admiralissimo. Jellicoe was proposed for the post and agreement was almost reached on 1 June 1918 when, as so often occurred the Italians sabotaged it; they would not serve under any foreign commander, however minimal his powers.[1] Everyone was exasperated by this latest example of wilful non-co-operation by the Italians [317, 321–3].

It was at this point that a young knight in shining armour, Franklin D. Roosevelt, attempted to come to the rescue. Visiting American naval units in Europe in July and August, Roosevelt had talks with British and French naval leaders and offered, when he visited Rome, to make a further attempt to secure Italian agreement to some form of supreme naval command. Roosevelt's formula was necessarily vague and would have changed little. He was aware of its shortcomings but thought it better than nothing and perhaps capable of enhancement. He persuaded himself that he had charmed the Italians into an agreement. However, not only did he fail to do so but he also upset the French with his breezy personal diplomacy and angered President Wilson by appearing to speak for the United States Government. With the departure from Rome, somewhat chastened, of the energetic Assistant Secretary went the last vain attempt to co-ordinate Allied naval forces and make positive and decisive use of their undoubted superiority. The Mediterranean remained a naval headache until the enemy collapsed in October 1918 [327–30].[1]

At the Armistice the Americans had 75 ships in the Mediterranean and over 5500 men. Most of their effort was centered on Gibraltar and they constituted about a third of the Allied force there, all of it under British command. The Americans undertook a substantial share of the escort work from the Rock.[2] Further east, the submarine chasers based on Corfu arrived only in the final months of the conflict and, despite intensive hydrophone patrols, accomplished nothing other than zealous participation in a modest operation against the Austrian base at Durazzo. As on other stations, Anglo-American operational co-operation was exemplary [331–3].

[1] Freidel, vol. 1, pp. 363–4; Halpern, *RN in Mediterranean*, documents 237, 239, 242–5.

[2] Halpern, *Naval War*, pp. 503–8; *RN in Mediterranean*, document no. 229; Grove, pp. 232, 235.

303. Gaunt to Jellicoe

6 July 1917

The following ships have been put forward with a view to being [? sent at once]. Pratt is in favour, Admiral Benson told me he thought it a waste of ships but Admiral Mayo implied that he would support it. I told Admiral Benson I thought that they would be of great use: USS *Birmingham, Chester, Salem, Sacramento, Yankton, Nashville, Marietta, Machias, Castine, Wheeling, Paducah*.

304. Jellicoe to Gaunt

6 July 1917

Should be very grateful if Gunboats *Sacramento, Yankton, Nashville, Marietta, Machias, Castine, Wheeling* and *Paducah* could be sent to Gibraltar where they would be invaluable for seeing convoys clear of the submarine area off the coast. Admiral Sims concurs.

305. Duff to Rear-Admiral Heathcoat Grant[1]

9 August 1917

Details of US Ships to be based at Gibraltar[2]

Ship	Displcmt. (tons)	Radius (mls.)	Draught (Feet)	Speed (knots)	Remarks	Date due
Birmingham	3500	4000	18	24	Lt. cruisers,	1 Sept.
Chester					2 × 5 in.	1 Sept.
Salem[3]					6 × 3in.	indefinite
Sacramento	1100	7000	12	12	new gunboat, good ship, 3 × 4 in.	8–10 Aug.
Nashville	1000	3000	12	10	old gunboats,	15–20 Aug.

[1] Duff was ACNS.
[2] Some details given here differ from those in *Jane's*. The cruiser displacements are listed there as 3750 tons and *Sacramento* (1914) as 1425 tons. Other gunboat displacements ranged from 990 to 1177 tons and armament from 2 to 4 × 4in. *Yankton* (1893) carried 2 × 3in. *Nahma* is listed at 1800 tons and her speed as 15 knots.
[3] USS *Salem* did not in the end go to Gibraltar.

Castine	„	„	„	„	speed reduced	„
Machias	„	„	„	„	in seaway	„
Wheeling	„	„	„	„		30 Aug.
Marietta	„	„	„	„		indefinite
Paducah	„	„	„	„		30 Aug.
Yankton	900	2500	15	9	yacht	5 Sept.
Nahma	900	2500	16	10	yacht	15 Sept.
					fitting out,	
					Glasgow,	
					1 × 4in,	
					4 × 3in	
Tampa	1000	3000	13	12	4 × 3in, Coast	10 Sept.
Algonquin	800	„	„	„	Guard gunboats,	
Seneca	1000	„	„	„	good sea boats,	
Manning	1300	„	„	„	good crews,	
Ossipee	1000	„	„	„	much better than	
Yamacraw	1000	„	„	„	old gunboats.	
Chauncey	450	1500	10	23	old destroyers,	1 Oct.
Barry	„	„	„	„	coal burning.	
Bainbridge	„	„	„	„		
Decatur	„	„	„	„		

306.   *Rear-Admiral Henry B. Wilson, US Navy, to Sims*

USS *Birmingham*,
Gibraltar,
20 August 1917

Upon arrival I received the Campaign order and immediately got in touch with the Senior Naval Officer and told him we were ready to do our 'bit', and that I meant by this that we were here for any work that would bring about the best results. I understand what you want, and will do my best to co-operate in every way with the Senior Naval Officer and recognize his command.

****

I have just had a conference with the Senior Naval Officer, and he is sending a memorandum to the Admiralty regarding how our Force is to be utilized. He proposed to have us on convoy work, generally, both east and west of here. My instructions, as given by you, were merely to direct me to co-operate. I have told him that the memorandum meets with my approval. Of course, if it does not meet with yours, I trust you will take it up at the Admiralty and straighten me out. Without definite instructions it is to be my endeavour to do *something* in *each case*, and I trust you will not hesitate to check me if you think I am doing wrong.

307. *Sims to Wilson*

5 September 1917

Your letter of 20 August, just received. It is the real stuff. It expressed just exactly how I believe we should co-operate in doing our best to end this beastly war.

****

Please present my best respects to Admiral Grant, and say that I should like a frank opinion from him, through you, indicating in what way we can help you out.

308. *Grant to Murray*

20 August 1917

****

2. The force which will be under my command is understood to comprise the following USA vessels:-

3 Light cruisers, 14 Gunboats, 5 Torpedo Boat Destroyers
and the British force already based on Gibraltar consists of

7 Yachts, 5 Sloops, 10 Torpedo Boats, 4 Armed Boarding Vessels, 9 Trawlers, 18 Motor Launches, 2 Torpedo Boat Destroyers.

3. Generally speaking it is proposed to employ the USA Force, being the better armed and having the larger radius of action, as the escort for both East and West convoys, and to retain the British force at my disposal for the necessary patrols, escorts of Western convoy in the Straits as far as Cape Spartel, and the occasional strengthening of Eastern escort of convoys as far as Malta.
4. *Western Convoy*: The ocean escort for this convoy will consist of six USA vessels which will include the three light cruisers. The escort through the Gibraltar danger zone to consist of seven USA gunboats. The six vessels detailed for ocean escort should enable one of them to leave every four days and to return in time from the Home Port to keep this duty continuous and allow for refit.
The seven Gunboats detailed for danger zone escorts should allow

of continuous duty and of at least three Gunboats to each convoy. These latter will be reinforced through the Straits of Gibraltar, and as far as 30' West of Spartel by British Torpedo Boats, Trawlers or Motor Launches.

5. *Eastern Convoy to Malta*: Taking an approximate time of six days to Malta at seven knots and four and a half days for return, this will absorb the remaining nine units of the USA Squadron, consisting of four Gunboats and five Torpedo Boat Destroyers. This will allow of four USA units to each convoy. It is hoped that with the additional two British Torpedo Boat Destroyers which have been allocated to Gibraltar each of these escorts can be reinforced by one British Torpedo Boat Destroyer and one Trawler and so give a total escort of six vessels to each convoy, which it is understood should leave every 10 days.

****

9. It is proposed to take full advantage of any of the USA Squadron ready for sea who may be waiting for their turn for escort duties, as extra patrols in the waters in the vicity of Gibraltar according to the activity of the enemy's submarines.

309. *Rear-Admiral Albert P. Niblack, US Navy to Sims*

US Patrol Squadron,
Gibraltar,
USS *Decatur*,
19 January 1918

****

Craven[1] showed up today. I want to talk aviation to him because Admiral Grant is keen to establish a number of stations at points other than Gib (which on account of the Rock is full of air pockets) because the absence of destroyers and any form of new construction down here makes it necessary to hunt subs with aircraft and audions[2], to give the slow moving offensive vessels a chance to pinch them in these narrow and deep waters. I understand that all of our new destroyers are liable to be assigned anywhere else than here. That makes the importance of getting some of the sea-planes here all the more important. There are roundly here about two-thirds the

---

[1] Commander (later Captain) T. T. Craven, US Navy: in 1917 commanded *Sacramento*; at this time attached to Naval Aviation HQ, Paris.
[2] 'Audions' presumably refers to hydrophones.

number of ships really necessary to furnish escorts for convoys. Nevertheless it is astonishing what a strong offensive Admiral Grant is keeping going. He is an extremely able man and our relations could not be more satisfactory. If there should be a sudden lot of sinking around Gibraltar it would raise an interesting question as to who is responsible because every morning at 10 o'clock the British, American, Italian and French representatives gather around a table and plan for the day. It is the ALLIED Conference really working with all the material available at the moment. Angels could do no more. Possibly devils could, but it is hard to be a devil with a back numbered type of ships we have here, most of which are on their last legs.

****

310.   Minutes of the Allied Naval Council

30 January 1918

Paper by US Planning Section on Possible Allied Operations in the Adriatic

Decisions[1]

1. To seize and secure a base between Curzola Island and Sabbioncello Peninsula.
2. Simultaneously with the seizure of the base to raid the railroad in its vicinity, destroying tunnels and bridge and occupying a position astride the road as long as possible. When compelled to retire from this position the forces to retire in Sabbioncello Peninsula and thereafter hold it permanently.
3. To place sufficient naval forces at Curzola Island to interrupt completely all traffic of surface vessels between Northern Adriatic bases and Cattaro.
4. When troops and transports become available to seize and hold the islands of Lissa, Brazza, Lesina, Lagosta, Meleda, Gazza, Pelagosa.
5. To fortify Lagosta Island, Gazza Island, Pelagosa Island, so that light vessels patrolling in this region may find refuge from attack under the guns of these islands.
6. To lay a mine barrage from the Italian coast to Curzola Island, and to support this barrage by vessels based on Curzola Island and Brindisi.

---

[1] That is, those reached in the Planning Section's paper.

7. To organise and carry out as a surprise attack a raid on Cattaro which shall have for its mission the sinking of all enemy vessels in the harbour, provided subsequent information indicates conditions to be such as to warrant the effort.

8. To assign immediately areas of operation for the patrol of the Southern Adriatic, the mission of the patrol being to make it increasingly difficult for the exit and entrance of enemy submarines in the Adriatic.

9. To equip the maximum number of patrol vessels with efficient listening devices, and to arm them in a manner suitable to their employment.

10. To assign the general command of all of these operations to a single Naval Officer of one of the co-operating Powers.

11. To assign the task of the raid on Cattaro to the American battleships, supported by such sweepers and destroyers of other nations as are best suited to the task.

13. To carry on a continuous air attack on Cattaro and the vessels based there. For this purpose to concentrate a maximum possible number of suitable aircraft.

13. To hold a force of surface vessels in readiness at Corfu sufficient in strength to prevent the escape of enemy cruisers from the Adriatic.

14. In directing the air offensive, to concentrate first on Cattaro and then successively on the ports at which most enemy submarines may be building or may be harboured.

15. To augment patrol effort by all available aircraft not specially suited to the attack of enemy bases. To select mining bases after consultation with the Italian authorities.

16. To plant special minefields as submarine traps in the vicinity of Cattaro, but to do this subsequent to the raid.

Note – The above decisions, if executed, require the execution of plans for simultaneously closing the Dardanelles to enemy submarines.

311. *Memorandum by Admiralty Director of Plans*[1]

18 February 1918

The Reinforcement of the Commander-in-Chief Mediterranean by Small Craft for use on the Otranto Barrage

****

---

[1] Captain Cyril Fuller.

2. Under these circumstances, it is proposed that a complete unit of 36 American submarine chasers, with their tender, should be sent to the Mediterranean by April for the Otranto Barrage. Although these craft are inferior in sea-keeping qualities to trawlers, it is believed that they will be capable of the work required in the Mediterranean during the summer months. By midsummer the Ford submarine chasers will, according to programme, be becoming available; and as they commission, they should relieve the early type of submarine chasers.
3. Submarine chasers are equipped with a 3-inch gun, four 300lb. depth charges and a thrower, and listening devices; thus, except for the 4-inch gun, they should fulfil requirements satisfactorily as to armament and equipment. Ford submarine chasers are larger and better armed, and should be excellent for this service.
4. If the allocation of the American chasers to this service is approved, it is suggested that 6 US destroyers should work with them and that a definite area or areas should be assigned to them. In this case one of the two Yachts would probably be required by the US Officer in charge, and could be provided from the American Yachts at Gibraltar or on the French coast.
5. The other yacht required – and more if necessary – could also, it is understood, be supplied from the American yachts on the French coast; but if a British yacht is required, it is suggested that one of the yachts from Gibraltar should be transferred.
6. As 6 new US destroyers will not be available in time to start the Otranto barrage in April, it is suggested 6 US destroyers, drawn from Queenstown, the French coast or Gibraltar, should be allocated to the Otranto barrage for duty with the chasers.
7. The above proposals have been drawn up in conjunction with the United States Officers in the Plans Department, who concur generally in the proposals.

[Minute by Captain Pound][1]

19 February 1918

****

Assuming that the Chasers go to the Adriatic, it seems desirable that US Destroyers should work with them, and possibly the four small Destroyers now at Gibraltar might be suitable. They, in turn,

[1] Captain Dudley Pound, DOD (H).

could be relieved by four British Destroyers when the US can provide screening Destroyers for the 6th Battle Squadron.

In view of the large number of US troops to be sent across the Atlantic this summer, I think that it would be most unwise to make any reduction in the Queenstown escort force on whom will fall the brunt of the work.

[Note]   25 February 1918

The Commander-in-Chief has replied that for various reasons he does not consider the submarine chasers suitable for the Otranto Straits, but the principal objection is the difficulty of the petrol supply.

The Commander-in-Chief can, however, make use of them on the Palestine Coast where the petrol supply is simpler.[1]

312. *Memorandum by US Planning Section on Adriatic Project*

7 March 1918

The British and American Planning sections are in agreement on the essential features of the Adriatic project. These are:-

(a) The seizure of a base at Sabbioncello.
(b) The laying of a mine barrage, Gorgona–Curzola.
(b) The denial of Cattaro to enemy submarines.

****

The resources that will be required of each nation are roughly:-

Italy
Naval Forces in Adriatic.
Mines.
Mine Layers.
Use of ports as bases.

France
Naval Forces in or near Adriatic.

Great Britain
Troops and Transports.
Light Cruisers.

---

[1] They were in fact stationed at Corfu and employed in the Straits of Otranto. They did not arrive until June. See 226, 331.

Destroyers.
Harbour Defence Nets.

United States
Pre-dreadnoughts.
Destroyers.
Mines.
Mine Layers.
Troops and Transports.

****

As the operations after seizing the base will include a vigorous offensive patrol of the Adriatic to prevent the movement of enemy surface craft, the vessels for this duty should be in adequate force.

The Planning Section is constrained to believe that, unless the Allies are able to inaugurate offensive operations in contra-distinction to purely defensive operations, the outlook as to our success in this war is extremely dubious.

****

27.   The shipping losses by enemy action in the Mediterranean are 30% of the total. This area, therefore, is second to the North Sea in importance [as an area to be mined].
****

313.   *Memorandum by Admiralty Plans Division on Proposed Operations in the Adriatic*

7 March 1918

In judging the soundness of the conclusions arrived at in the [US Planning Section's Memorandum] ... it is urged that the following points receive consideration:-
1. The value of an offensive attitude whenever such offensive attitude is possible.
2. The soundness of the principle of concentration of effort.
3. The great importance of unity of command, and, in the case of Allied operations, the extreme importance of deciding beforehand upon spheres of activity.
4. The principle of attacking the enemy where he is weakest. Enemy morale in Austria and Turkey is weaker than in Germany. The attack of the morale in either of these Countries is a flank attack upon German morale; this we cannot afford to neglect.

5. The weakened morale of Italy due to recent reverses requires of the Allies that an extraordinary effort be made to build that morale up again to its former high standard.

6. That success in the Adriatic would release large forces for other important operations and make possible a still greater concentration of effort in the areas which finally must be the areas of critical importance.

****

314. *Sims to Opnav*

8 March 1918

... I suggest that immediate steps be taken to provide a force of twenty thousand marines with all necessary armament and equipment, including artillery, signal forces, aeroplanes, engineers and infantry. Since early and rapid action will be essential elements in the execution of the plan it is recommended that the mobilization and equipment of the marines be undertaken immediately without waiting for the definite adoption of the plan.

315. *Sims to Wemyss*

10 March 1918

As you of course know, the question of aggressive action against the submarine bases in the Adriatic is on the agenda [of the forthcoming Allied Naval Council meeting]. My recent advices from America indicate that our Navy Department is very earnestly in favor of some aggressive action of this kind, particularly for the effect it will have on morale.

****

316. *Benson to Sims*

12 March 1918

Before Department takes any action in the matter [Adriatic operations] it desires to know has this plan been presented to the Inter-Allied War Council and to British War Council[1] for expression of opinion[?] The logistic demands now to supply the needs on the Western Front are so great that no eccentric move regardless how

---

[1] Presumably the Supreme War Council and the British War Cabinet.

attractive its local aspect may be can be contemplated without full discussion by all parties concerned. Shipping is now working to its full capacity. In addition to troops under Pershing the Army is obliged in the next few months to supply six divisions to the British Forces on the Western Front. As the plan contemplates a landing force of 20,000 additional men plus a division of our old battleships the various War Councils concerned must be consulted and a joint opinion given as to the desirability and practicability of such an assignment and location of fighting force as contemplated in the suggested plan. The Department must not be committed to any plan until full details are submitted and our decision rendered.

317. *Sims to Opnav*

13 May 1918

The situation in the Eastern Mediterranean taking into consideration a possible offensive movement by Turkish and former Russian vessels now in possession of Germans demands that the Allied forces be sufficient and that their dispositions be such that they could successfully oppose any such movement. In the opinion of the Allied Naval Council the forces are sufficient, but their present disposition is not satisfactory, and owing to lack of training of Italian battleships the efficiency of a combined French–Italian force is doubtful. The Italians now appear to be determined not to send their dreadnoughts to Corfu unless all French forces withdraw from that base, except those French ships that are to join the Italian ships as a Corfu Force, and this force be under an Italian Admiral and not subject to the French Commander-in-Chief in the Mediterranean. Both the British Admiralty and myself fear that an impossible situation would be created by such disposition, and that a disaster might easily occur should the enemy issue from the Black Sea in considerable force and the Austrians cooperate from the Adriatic.

Allied Naval Council will hold emergency meeting London 15 May at which this subject will be discussed. I give this advance information in order that the Department may be prepared for a possible request that a division of oil burning American Dreadnoughts be sent to the Mediterranean. Oil burning vessels preferred as they can be more readily supplied with oil via Suez than coal from England.

318.   *Sims to Niblack*

23 May 1918

Your recent letter just received and I note what you say concerning the difficulties at Gibraltar. I can assure you that I realize them very thoroughly and they will be rectified just as soon as it is possible to do so.

The Navy Department has supplied me with a paper alibi which prevented me from sending three destroyers to the Mediterranean to cooperate with the chasers in hunting the submarines at the neck of the bottle where they come in and out. The destroyer program is dreadfully behind time. According to really official predictions, we should have actually over here between thirty and forty destroyers now, and we will probably not get more than sixty or seventy before the end of the year. We were to have twenty Ford boats per month after June, and now we are informed that we will get twenty only before the end of the year.

The necessity for faster destroyers in the Mediterranean to assist the convoys is painfully apparent, but they are simply not available. The fifty-odd troop ships that are now coming in, not counting the great number of supply ships, or the four or five big vessels that are running independently, inside a month for the round trip, are straining all our destroyers up here to the utmost. Actually vessels ready to sail for America have to lose time in port waiting for escorts to take them through the zone. The number of destroyers escorting merchant convoys have been cut down way below the safety mark, so much so that the submarines no longer fear to attack them. When the convoys were much less numerous we were able to supply enough destroyers to make it so dangerous that the submarines practically abandoned attacks on convoys, and vessels bound for rendezvous ports. It is since we have been obliged to reduce these escorts that the submarines have now moved out and are attacking the convoys. Of three of them that came in in one day all were successfully attacked. On top of this I am informed that the Department expects me to further reduce the escorts supplied [to] merchant vessels in order to make the safety of the troops absolute. This is what I call a paper alibi. We all know that it is not possible to make any convoy safe.

The above to show you what we are up against.

****

As for chasers, we know from experience that they are very unsafe as escorts for convoys. They are all right as long as the sea remains smooth, but when it comes on a bit of a blow, although the chasers are perfectly safe as regards sea worthiness, they cannot make speed enough to keep up with even a slow convoy, and this places the convoy in great danger. We have therefore forbidden anybody to use them for this purpose. Moreover, they have been specially designed for hunting submarines in connection with destroyers, and naturally, they should be so employed in those waters where all of the submarines must pass in order to get at their prey. It may be that when all of the chasers are over, it will be advantageous to assign some of them to Gibraltar for hunting purposes.

319. Benson to Sims

27 May 1918

****

3. *General strategy of the Adriatic Sea barrage plans.*

Without approval or disapproval of the present suggested plan in its entirety but merely to bring forward the particular United States interest in the matter the following points are offered. If the Western Mediterranean Sea were made safe by barrage from Sicily to Cape Bon, and the Straits of Messina control scheme were made practicable the Eastern Mediterranean Sea situation would be no worse than it is at present, while the liability of the United States to transport both men and supplies particularly to French and Italian Western Mediterranean ports would be greatly facilitated. The length of convoys would be shortened, the number of necessary escorts in the safe section reduced, the water area in which our hunting groups based at Corfu would operate would be reduced from its present size, both ends of the barrage would rest in friendly soil eliminating the necessity for the military operations at one end, the project could be pushed through now or as soon as mines could be provided without waiting on military events on the Western Front. The Bureau of Ordnance has studied the conditions and is of the opinion that the depth of water between the points indicated offers no bar to our form of mines. If the original plan is adhered to it will still require the further closing of the Dardanelles by separate barrage. Especially does this latter operation seem necessary in view of the present Russian situation.[1]

Finally the Department will agree to furnish the mines necessary for any barrage project in the Mediterranean Sea or Adriatic Sea, and it is willing to furnish whatever fast minelaying ships it can find, if fast ships are required but in this matter it expects Italy or France to contribute any ships that are idle and may be so used, the entire mine laying project to be handled by our personnel. The Department is also willing to discuss this or any other similar plan further but is inclined from an estimate of the general military situation to the opinion that the Cape Bon to Sicily project if practicable should come first, in which case it would attempt to handle the mine portions of the operation and that this operation should be undertaken as early as practicable. Second that the Adriatic Sea project can only be put into effect later, must wait on Military events on Western Front, and is to some extent a dissipation of military effort. Third, that the Adriatic Sea project alone without blocking the Dardanelles is not a complete project. Fourth, that the value of both Adriatic Sea and Dardanelles projects are largely dependent upon the military situation on Macedonian Front.

320. *Niblack to Sims*

28 May 1918

I have never met anyone who thinks along the same lines I do as agreeably as Admiral Grant, and you can rest assured that there will be no friction here between us. There is, however, a very lamentable lack of similarity in views between here and Malta, much, in my opinion, to the disadvantage of Malta, where this Station is regarded as an adjunct to be stripped to furnish the means to carry on operations in that region. Certainly Gibraltar is simply a 'poor relation' in this war.

[1] That is, the possible acquisition by the Germans of Russian Black Sea Fleet warships and their use in the Mediterranean with the Turkish/German battle cruiser *Goeben*.

321. *Supreme War Council*

Paris,
1 June 1918

Resolution by Sir Eric Geddes

The Supreme War Council, having heard the views of Admiral di Revel[1], Admiral De Bon,[2] and Admiral Wemyss, and having studied the Report of the Allied Naval Council, are agreed that the new naval situation created in the Mediterranean by the German seizure of the Russian Black Sea Fleet, can be met by a proper distribution and co-ordination of the existing Allied Naval Forces in the Mediterranean, Adriatic and Aegean. They are further agreed that this object can best be secured by applying to the Allied Fleets in the Mediterranean the unity of command already adopted on land. They have, therefore, decided to appoint Admiral Lord Jellicoe to co-ordinate the movements of the Allied Naval Forces in the Mediterranean, Adriatic and Aegean, as well as to arrange for the preparation and conduct of naval operations in those waters. Admiral Jellicoe will make his general dispositions subject to the approval of the Allied Naval Council, but each Commander-in-Chief will have the right of appeal to his Government, if, in his opinion, the safety of his Fleet is compromised by these general dispositions. The details as to Admiral Jellicoe's duties and powers are to be laid down forthwith by the Allied Naval Council on the basis that it is the intention of the Supreme War Council that Admiral Jellicoe shall be in effective strategic command in the Mediterranean, Adriatic and Aegean.

322. *Memorandum by Geddes for War Cabinet*

8 June 1918

Command in the Mediterranean

I think it desirable, in view of the failure of the proposal to co-ordinate the Naval efforts of the Allies in the Mediterranean, to put before the War Cabinet the present situation.

---

[1] Admiral Paolo Thaon di Revel (1859–1948): Chief of Italian Naval Staff and Chief of Mobilized Naval Forces, 1917–19; later served as Mussolini's first Navy Minister, 1922–25.
[2] Vice-Amiral Ferdinand-Jean-Jacques De Bon (1861–1923): Chef d'Etat major-general 1916–18; CinC 1ere Armeé Navale 1919; chief technical adviser, French delegation, Washington Naval Conference 1921; retired 1923.

The Cabinet will realise that the Command of the Mediterranean and Aegean today is French, and the responsibility for holding the enemy in these Seas is French, with such Allied forces as are allocated to them to assist. Similarly the Italians are responsible in the Adriatic, and the British in all three Seas play a subordinate role with subsidiary responsibility only. The particular responsibility of the British Commander-in-Chief, Malta, is anti-submarine and escort work, but everything he does is under the Command of the French Admiral at Corfu. The Board of Admiralty therefore can only bring the present unsatisfactory state of affairs to the notice of the War Cabinet, and has neither the right nor the means of taking any active steps to improve matters, except in the manner which we have already done, viz., by advocating co-ordination of the Allied effort and better use of our Forces in those Seas.

It is the opinion of the Allied Naval Council that the capital ships at the disposal of the Allies in the Mediterranean are amply sufficient to deal with those of the enemy, but a redistribution of Forces has recently become necessary in order to meet the menace caused by the possibility of Germany commissioning the Battleships of the Russian Black Sea Fleet, which either have already fallen into their hands or may so fall in the near future. At present six Russian Battleships of the Pre-Dreadnought Class from the Black Sea Fleet are in the hands of Germany, and unless destroyed by the Russians it is probable that the two Russian Dreadnoughts will shortly also be captured. To meet the threat of action of these ex-Russian ships it is necessary to increase the number of Allied Battleships in the Aegean, which is at present two British Pre-Dreadnoughts,[1] and consequently the Allied Commander-in-Chief, Admiral Gauchet,[2] has ordered a reinforcement of four French Battleships to Mudros from Corfu, and this has carried with it a transference of the Command of the heavy forces in the Aegean from a British Admiral to a French Admiral. The Cabinet and Secretary of State for Foreign Affairs[3] may wish to consider whether this has any political import.

To compensate for this reduction in the strength of the French main Fleet based on Corfu, it was proposed by the French and British Naval Authorities that Italy should send a Squadron of Battleships from Taranto to Corfu to work as a Squadron of the

[1] *Lord Nelson* and *Agamemnon*: semi-dreadnoughts.
[2] Vice-Amiral Dominique-Marie Gauchet (1857–1931): commanded 1ere Armeé Navale (the French Fleet) December 1916–May 1919; also official Allied CinC Mediterranean; retired 1919.
[3] Mr A. J. Balfour.

main French Fleet under the direct orders of the French Commander-in-Chief. Such a combined Fleet at Corfu, *trained to work
under one Command*, ought to be certain of defeating the Austrian
Fleet should the latter attempt to leave the Adriatic.

This redistribution of Forces was discussed by the Allied Naval
Council, and although all the representatives of the Allied Navies
agreed that the proposal was right in principle, Italy declined to
place any of her Battleships under French orders. It will be noted
particularly that Admiral di Revel 'Agreed in principle with what
had been proposed and thought it might be a useful and prudent
measure to remove some Italian Battleships from Taranto to Corfu'.
Also it was minuted that the Members representing Italy 'considered
that in principle, and apart from the question of maintenance of
supplies, the transfer to Corfu of Italian Dreadnoughts would be
desirable'. The subsequent discussions at Abbeville and Paris at the
Meetings of the Supreme War Council I will not recapitulate, but the
fact remains today that the French Force at Corfu is weaker than we
have all agreed in principle it should be, and that even with the
reinforcements sent to the Aegean it is conceivable that in the future
the ships there may be outclassed by the ships which the enemy can
bring against them, and, it will be noted, quite unnecessarily outclassed because there is ample Force belonging the the Allies in the
Mediterranean to do what is necessary, and it would be sheer waste
to send more Battleships there if the Allies are to retain in commission and fuel the existing Forces.

The situation consequently as it is today is unsatisfactory, and the
Admiralty cannot regard it otherwise than with misgiving. As will
have been noticed from the proceedings of the Supreme War
Council which took place on the first days of this month at Versailles, Admiral di Revel put forward the contention that Battleships
must be kept at their bases safe from submarine attack, and as far as
possible also from aerial raids, only actually being required to
engage the enemy's Battleships.[1] This theory, if carried out – and it
is being carried out – must logically result in the Italian Fleet putting
to sea to meet the enemy in an untrained and consequently inefficient state, and the valour of the Italian personnel combined with
the excellent material of their Ships cannot make up for the lack of
training that is entailed by a Fleet remaining constantly in harbour.
For effective co-operation my Naval Advisors are unanimous that

---

[1] The Italian battlefleet swung gently at anchor in Taranto harbour for almost the
entire war. The comment on safety from air attack is ironic in view of the successful
raid by British carrier-borne aircraft against the same fleet in the same port in 1940.

combined training is absolutely essential, and the testimony of Admiral Sims from his own experience with American Battleships joined with the Grand Fleet is of great importance. It is thus recorded in the minutes of the Allied Naval Council. His opinion was 'that when the five United States Battleships joined the Grand Fleet they were not a real addition of strength, but possibly even the reverse. They have now become a source of strength'. In Admiral Sims's opinion at least six months' training is required, and in that case no large difficulty existed. Admiral De Bon, in whose opinion we have great confidence, entirely concurs with Admiral Sims.

As long as the whole French Fleet was at Corfu its excess of strength over the Austrian Fleet was sufficiently great to enable it to act without the efficient co-operation of the Italian Fleet, but now that it has become necessary to detach a French Battle Squadron to the Aegean, the efficient co-operation of at least one Italian Battle Squadron is under the circumstances essential, and this efficient co-operation cannot be obtained without combined training under one Command.

It is certain that the only way in which unity of action of the Allied Fleets in the Mediterreanean, Aegean and Adriatic, and the most economical and efficient use of those Forces can be obtained, is by uniting them under the strategic Command of one Admiralissimo, and the Admiralty therefore suggest to the War Cabinet the advisability of making further efforts to obtain the adhesion of the Italian Government to the resolution agreed to in principle by the Supreme War Council on 1 June, but subsequently cancelled owing to its emasculation by the objections put forward by Admiral di Revel.

323. *Memorandum by Geddes for War Cabinet*

13 June 1918

Command in the Mediterranean

It was apparent during the discussions at the Allied Naval Council that Admiral Triangi[1] had come with instructions to agree to no co-operation which he could avoid, and that the whole attitude of the Italian Navy, as represented by him, was that it should be kept in a water-tight compartment, prepared to seek all the help that the Allies could give, but not prepared to share or co-operate in any

---

[1] Contrammiraglio (later Ammiraglio di Squadra) Arturo Conte Triangi di Maderno (1864–1935): Sotto Capo di Stato Maggiore March–June 1917 and March–November 1918; Minister of Marine June–July 1917.

way. This attitude was undoubtedly, in our opinion, the outcome of and sequel to the tactics adopted by Admiral di Revel in blocking the question of the appointment of an Admiralissimo in the Mediterranean at the Meetings of the Supreme War Council at Versailles last week. ...

After the Allied Naval Council had concluded its deliberations, I held a Meeting with Admiral De Bon (France), Admiral Sims (United States of America), and the First Sea Lord, and we discussed the situation. As an outcome of that discussion we agreed that the three Admirals should make representations to their Governments on the lines of this Memorandum. It was considered better not to submit a joint Memorandum, nor indeed to compare Memoranda, before submission. In our opinion the time has arrived when judicious pressure might be brought to bear in order to bring about a reasonable spirit of co-operation in the Italian Navy.

I regret to have to bring a personal note of adverse comment into this Memorandum but the attitude of Admiral di Revel at Versailles, the information we have as to his attitude upon his return to Rome, and the instructions he gave Admiral Triangi before the latter left Rome to attend this Council, force me to the conclusion – which is shared by the First Sea Lord, Admiral De Bon and Admiral Sims – that Admiral di Revel, and he alone, is responsible for the present state of affairs and for the inactivity of the Italian Light Naval Forces, who do nothing to co-operate with those of Great Britain, France, and the United States of America in anti-submarine work, and also for the general policy of which we complain.

324.   *Sims to Rear-Admiral Joseph Strauss, US Navy*[1]

July 1918

****

12. I do not consider the mine barrage around the Dardanelles close in to enemy territory as being worth very much, owing to the ease with which the enemy can sweep a passage through it, and I would not agree to accept it as a substitute for the Euboea–Cape Kanapitza Barrage.

13. I do not consider that the mine-net barrage which is being laid across the Otranto Straits will be effective in preventing exit of submarines from the Adriatic. At the very least it should be supple-

[1] Rear-Admiral Joseph Strauss, US Navy: began the war as Captain of the new dreadnought *Nevada*; later commanded Mine Force, Atlantic Fleet, and responsible for US sections of North Sea Barrage from March 1918.

mented by mines, and I believe it would be better to put all of our time, money and energy into a mine barrage, abandoning the proposed net barrage. It would not be necessary to insist on this, however, if the other Allies are keen for the nets. It is plain, however, that the nets alone cannot be entirely effective since they neither stop surface passage nor very deep passage of submarines.

****

17. I do not wish to make any binding promise that the United States will furnish all of the mines, or all of the mine layers for any project adopted. The most I am willing to agree is that if a project which the United States deems sound is adopted, it will supply material and equipment to the limit of its ability, and will expect the other Allies to do the same. You are perfectly advised as to the capabilities of the mine laying force under your command, and you will know what portion of it, if any, will probably have to be retained in Northern Waters and what portion will be available for Mediterranean operations. France and Italy both have some mine layers which should be made available for this work, but it is not probable that Great Britain could furnish any.

****

19. With regard to mines that can be successfully laid in deep water: It may be stated that our Bureau of Ordnance has been requested to develop such a mine, and has stated that experiments are now in progress with hope of success.

325.   Sims to Opnav

26 July 1918

Referring to Opnav 6489[1] in which the Department stated:
'The Department will agree to furnish the mines necessary for any barrage project in the Mediterranean Sea or Adriatic Sea, and it is willing to furnish whatever fast minelaying ships it can find, etc.'

At a Committee Meeting of Allied Naval Council in London 23 July, the subject of Mine Barrages in the Mediterranean was discussed on the basis of the plans suggested in Planning Section Memorandum thirty-seven forwarded to Department 11 July. Committee accepted certain general fundamental principles regarding mine barrages in Mediterranean suggested by me, which are briefly

[1] See 319.

as follows:
  (a) Both ends should rest in territorial waters to be under military control from shore.
  (b) Both ends should be secure against raiding operations.
  (c) They should be as short as possible and should exclude submarines from operating areas.
  (d) No enemy submarines should be able to gain sea except via hazard of Barrage.
  (e) Barrage extending to surface is more effective than patrol.
  (f) Deep barrage not effective unless patrolled.
  (g) Surface portion of barrage should be densest.
  (h) Surface barrage should always be superposed upon deep barrage.
  (i) Secure harbor in advance of barrage necessary as base for counter raiding force.
Foregoing comprises Conclusion Number One of Committee.

Conclusion Number Two subsequently as follows:

Effective plan of anti-submarine barrages should be developed. When developed, United States together with Allied Countries will endeavor to supply mines and mine layers.

Conclusion Number Three was that if physical difficulty of mining in very deep water can be surmounted, first effort in Mediterranean should be to complete Otranto Barrage and establish Aegean Barrage while studying Cape Bon-Sicily Barrage. If delay would result from experimenting with deep water mines, mines of existing type might be used on Barrages other than those found most important but temporarily impracticable account depth water.

Conclusion Number Four is textually as follows:

The Commission now studying at Malta various matters in connection Mediterranean Mining Operations is therefore requested to examine in detail the various proposals which have been brought before the Council and to recommend where the necessary mine bases could best be established, so that a definite policy can be settled and the necessary preparations put in hand. It may be assumed that ample materials will be available for any of the schemes which are outlined in Memorandum Number One Six Eight or for any reasonable alternatives.

Memorandum Number One Six Eight was prepared by me and favors following complete barrages:

First: Otranto to Corfu via Fane Island.

Second: Euboea to Cape Kanapitza via Andros, Tinos, Mykoni, Nikaria, Furnia and Samos.

Third: Sicily to Cape Bon, provided the latter can be made a complete surface and deep minefield with exception necessary gate for traffic.

First Barrage would require nine thousand mines present type and eleven thousand for deep water.

Second Barrage would require twelve thousand present type and five thousand for deep water.

Requirements of third barrage not estimated, but present types of mines would serve for entire barrage. This barrage although important as stated by Department in cable 6489, does not strike at the root of the difficulty by blocking exits from present submarine bases and is, therefore, not considered as of primary importance.

Shall send Rear-Admiral Joseph Strauss to Malta to discuss project with representatives of other Governments now there.

I propose to hold out for complete and effective barrage against exit of enemy submarines from Adriatic and from Dardanelles with the Cape Bon–Sicily project as secondary although possibly executed first on account of availability of material.

I request Department's specific approval in order to strengthen my hands in this matter, as I think there may be some dispositions to favor use of our mine layers for other purposes less important strategically. Exact location of barrages must depend somewhat on tactical considerations presented by Allied Commanders in Mediterranean.

326. *Niblack to Sims*

29 July 1918

Vessels of the Gibraltar Patrol Force

****

3. ... the so-called 'Ford Destroyers' would be well adapted for service on the Gibraltar station. The British torpedo boats are of a very unseaworthy and dangerous type in bad weather, and the motor launches are too small for the rough weather encountered in the Straits. The policy here is to undertake whatever is entered, and the equipment is so far below what could be utilized that almost

anything is welcomed.

****

6. The British are assigning more and more ships to the Ocean Escort, thereby affording an opportunity of withdrawing our ships for service in the Mediterranean. Up to recently our nine ships did all the Ocean escort work. Two British ships have recently been added, and several more are to be assigned. My own preference in withdrawing ships from the Ocean Escort would be in the following order: *Sacramento, Seneca, Tampa* and *Ossipee*. This is based entirely upon their comparative speeds, as they can only make less than thirteen knots but their speeds would be adequate for the Mediterranean patrol. With regard to reliefs for ships sent away from here, no request is made because it is assumed that the disposition of forces has been the best that can be made under the circumstances, and this disposition has been accepted in that spirit. No suggestion is therefore made for the assignment of any other ships to this station.

327. *Benson to Sims*

7 August 1918

Referring to your letter 4 July regarding Admiralissimo Mediterranean Sea following letter from the State Department quoted for your information and action ...

'You express the view in the opinion of the Navy Department [that] a unity of naval command in the Mediterranean Sea during the war is just as essential as is the unity of military command on the Western Front to which we have already agreed and inquire whether the foregoing is consistent with the policy of the Department of State. In reply I desire to inform you that this department shares your view and is glad to note that you are ready to instruct Vice-Admiral Sims to give his support to the proposal that the allied governments agree upon a single naval commander for the force in the Mediterranean Sea.

In accordance with your suggestion I am advising the United States Ambassador at Rome, Italy, that this Government is in entire agreement with the British and French Governments that the naval force operating in the Mediterranean Sea should be under the command of a single Admiralissimo.'[1]

[1] Probably from Robert Lansing, Secretary of State.

328. *Roosevelt to Daniels*

Paris,
2 August 1918

Before leaving London on Tuesday, I lunched at the Embassy and had a most delightful talk with Mr Lloyd George. I know you would enjoy meeting him. He strikes one immediately as a great leader of men. One of the things that has struck me particularly this week in England has been the absolute unanimity among all the Government people here to see this thing through to more than what they call 'a patched up peace'.

I also had another talk with Mr Balfour and with Sir Eric Geddes about the Mediterranean situation. Everybody is agreed that things as they are are not resulting in sufficient naval action. The trouble seems to be chiefly with the Italians themselves and a certain amount of jealousy of the French in regard to the Adriatic, of Britain in regard to their rather condescending attitude about things in general. I think that Geddes rather wanted to go to Italy with me, but it would be a great mistake for us to go together, and I think I have succeeded in heading him off. The Italians may not love us, but at least they know that we have no ulterior designs in the Mediterranean. The trouble is that their Navy people at the top are thinking more about keeping their fleet intact at the end of the war than of winning the war itself. ... I hope by my visit to lay the foundation for more unified action between the many Allied naval units in the Mediterranean, and also for more actual offensive work against the Austrians on the Dalmatian Coast.

****

329. *Franklin D. Roosevelt to his family*

Paris,
2 August 1918

... I am convinced that this [Geddes accompanying him to Rome] would be just the wrong move, as the whole situation is deadlocked between the British and the Italians, and my business is to find a way out or a compromise. I can't do this if the Italians think the British are bringing me along as 'Exhibit 1' to prove that America takes wholly the British position.

****

Rome,
10 August 1918

... they [Italian senior naval officials and officers] are more anxious to know what we are going to do than to speak of their own work. This whole Italian situation is difficult. I hope my visit will really help, and that this continued pressure and especially a fresh viewpoint from the United States will result in closer naval co-operation and more activity in the Mediterranean and Adriatic.

****

We went over the whole naval situation and I insisted on keeping to the main point, the enormous superiority of the combined French, Italian, British, Japanese and American naval strength in these waters over Austria, and the lack of practically any offensive operations. ...

Rome,
11 August 1918

... Things have worked out all right. I have proposed a plan for the creation of a General Naval Staff in Mediterranean, Adriatic and Aegean waters, to be composed of a Britisher, probably Jellicoe, as senior member or chairman, and one member each from the French, Italian, American and Japanese Navies. This obviates the Italian and French objections to a British Commander-in-Chief, and while it does not give complete unity of command it would be a distinct step toward unity of action and a policy directed more along the lines of an offensive. I also told the Italians that if in any new operations against islands on the Dalmatian Coast, a land force of fifteen to twenty thousand men were needed, the American Navy could undoubtedly supply them before the close of the year. All of this will be taken up at the next Inter-allied Naval Council.

****

330. *Roosevelt to Daniels*

Paris,
13 August 1918

****

After I got there [Rome] on Friday, I held interesting conferences
with Admiral del Bono, the Minister of Marine, with his Chief of
Staff, Admiral Thaon di Revel, with Baron Sonnino, the Minister
for Foreign Affairs, and with the Prime Minister, Signor Orlando.[1]
    The situation developed somewhat as follows: They finally agreed
to the proposition of a commander-in-chief for the naval forces in
the Mediterranean, and they seemed anxious to cooperate in every
way possible (that is, as far as the Italian Navy can cooperate with
anybody). There was, however, one reservation, and after talking
the situation over I think it is a reservation which in my opinion we
cannot escape and which in a sense is entirely proper: this reservation in a nutshell is that the actual conduct of operations in the
Adriatic shall continue to be under the leadership and command of
the Italian Naval Commander-in-Chief.
    The Italians make the point of the fact that there are almost daily
active naval operations in the Adriatic Sea, and while it is true that
the Italian battleship fleet is locked up in the harbor of Taranto,
their smaller craft, aeroplanes, etc., are taking every opportunity to
harrass the Austrians. The Italians do not want to give up the
direction of these daily operations, nor to put these operations
directly under the Allied commander-in-chief who probably would
have his headquarters at Malta, a long way off, but under the Italian
plan the Italian commander-in-chief in the Adriatic would work *with*
the inter-allied commander-in-chief at Malta.
    Personally, I feel that the main point has been gained, i.e., the
right point of an inter-allied commander-in-chief for the Mediterra-

---

[1] Baron Sidney Sonnino (1847–1922): held numerous ministries and the Premier-
ship twice (February–May 1906 and December 1909–March 1910); Foreign Minister
November 1914–June 1919. Vittorio Emmanuele Orlando (1860–1952): held several
ministries before becoming Prime Minister following catastrophe at Caporetto
(October 1917) and held it until end of Versailles Peace Conference (June 1919), at
which he was one of the 'Big Four' with Wilson, Lloyd George and Clemenceau;
reemerged in 1944, after fall of Mussolini, to help restore Italian democratic politics.

nean. The fact that one section of the Mediterranean is under the actual command of an Italian as far as the actual operations go will work out all right if it is handled with a little judicious common sense.

****

I should get back to Paris next week, and go straight to London thence to the Grand Fleet, the Mine Laying Division, the Scotch Base Hospital and be ready to sail home 5 September.

2.   *Operations*

I discussed questions of operations in London, Paris, and Rome, and it is probably not necessary to give any detailed description of these conferences. The subjects come under three heads:

(1)   *Operations in the Mediterranean, Adriatic and Aegean Seas*:

(a)   The lack of a unified control of naval operations in these waters. Owing to certain causes which I have explained to you verbally it became practically impossible to have an 'Admiralissimo' for the Allied navies in these waters. My visits to Paris and Rome confirmed the impossibility of this. I worked out a plan, however, in the rough, which was accepted in principle by Admiral del Bono, the Italian Minister of Marine, by M. Leygues, the French Minister of Marine, and by Sir Eric Geddes, First Lord of the British Admiralty. This plan called for the appointment of a general naval staff for the Mediterranean, Adriatic and Aegean, with representatives of each nation on this staff. Frankly, this leaves the Italian Navy under an Italian Admiral, the French Battleship Fleet under a French Admiral, etc., and it does not give a clear cut supreme command, but it makes for better unity of action than exists at the present, and while in the nature of a compromise it is, in my judgement, at least a step in advance. The matter was to be taken up at the next Inter-allied Naval Council.

(b)   There was general feeling in England and France, and shared in by Admiral Sims that the Italian Battleship Fleet should be more employed in offensive operations against Austria. I will give you verbally a report of my conferences in Rome on this subject with the Prime Minister, the Foreign Minister, and the Minister of Marine. It is sufficient to say that I believe my visit there was of some assistance in that it showed the Italian government clearly that the United States would be glad if the naval side of the war in the Adriatic could be conducted

somewhat more vigorously and the recent attack on Durazzo
seems to me a proof of a more vigorous policy.[1]

****

331. *US Naval Command, Gibraltar*

c. November 1918

The American Effort in the Mediterranean

On 18 August 1917, the USS *Birmingham*, a scout cruiser and
flagship of the patrol force of the United States Atlantic Fleet,
steamed into Gibraltar. On 20 August, Vice-Admiral Sims sent
Rear-Admiral Wilson, whose flag the *Birmingham* was flying, a cable
instructing him to cooperate wherever possible with the British
forces at Gibraltar. These instructions were in accordance with the
policy adopted by Vice-Admiral Sims upon the arrival of the first
United States Naval Forces in European Waters in May: viz., in
order that the American Navy might render the greatest service to
the Allied cause, it should supplement the activities of the British
Navy. In other words, the forces of the US Navy were to strengthen
the weaker spots of the British Navy. Rear-Admiral Wilson showed
his comprehension of this policy by despatching the USS *Sacramento* as escort to an English convoy on 22 August; the *Sacramento*
had arrived from the United States only four days before. On the
other hand the British Naval authorities under Rear-Admiral Grant,
RN, showed their willingness to help the United States Naval Forces
by offering them the use of their supplies of all kinds: food, fuel, coal
and repair facilities. Thus began the activities of the US Navy in the
Mediterranean in August 1917.

In March 1918, the American forces at Gibraltar had increased
from the original three ships to twenty-eight; by the middle of June,
seventy American Naval vessels were in operation in the Mediterranean with a personnel totaling 5,542 men. Thirty-five of these vessels
have been stationed at Gibraltar, while forty have made the Island
of Corfu their base.

The vessels based at Gibraltar are actually a part of the British
forces as far as operations are concerned; they constitute about 35%
of the vessels operating from that base. The American ships are
under the command of the British Admiral and their employment

[1] The attack on Durazzo took place on 2 October; see Halpern, *Naval War in the
Mediterranean*, pp. 556–8, and *Royal Navy in the Mediterranean*, pp. 557–66.

[is] at his disposal. They are of course entirely manned and officered by American personnel, as all the US Naval vessels in European Waters are, but in order to make their services of the greatest value, they operate with the British under one command. An American Admiral, Rear-Admiral A. P. Niblack, who commands the American ships as a unit of the whole, is on the spot. He has placed the forces under his command at the disposal of the British Admiral. The American and the British vessels operate as one navy.

The duties of the American vessels vary greatly, partly so because of the variety of the types of vessels. These consist of cruisers, destroyers, gunboats, and coast guard cutters, and yachts converted into warships. The larger vessels, cruisers, destroyers and coast guard cutters, are continually on duty at sea with convoys between Gibraltar and England or between many points in the Mediterranean; they also escort large merchant convoys to and from the United States or South American ports. In this duty it is not unusual for a vessel to be absent at sea for ten days or even weeks and then to return to port for four days, only to be despatched again on similar duty. The smaller craft, that is, gunboats and yachts, come in for their share of hard work by acting as escorts to many local Mediterranean convoys and to those bound for the Azores. Their lot is perhaps more difficult than that of the larger vessels in that they are less seaworthy, while the yachts were never designed to serve as war vessels. Patrol duty forms no small part of their curriculum, as a constant watch at the mouth of the Mediterranean is always kept. Their work has at all times been satisfactory and they have filled the demands made upon them, a condition rendered possible only by their efficient upkeep.

The volume of work actually done by the American vessels at Gibraltar is best seen in a few figures of a statistical nature. During July and August 1918, for instance, the average time at sea for all the vessels was 57%. This means roughly that each ship was at sea six days out of ten; of the 4 days in port, at least 2 or perhaps 3 were essential for repairs, refueling, taking on provisions, etc. During these 2 months they steamed 170,000 miles or 6 times around the world and were at sea 17,000 hours. They furnished 25% of the escorts for local Mediterranean convoys and over 70% of the escorts for the ocean and deep sea convoys.

In the offensive war against the submarine, these vessels have also played their part and suffered their losses. The action of the USS *Lydonia*, a yacht which had assumed a belligerent aspect, stands out conspicuously. On 11 May, while she was proceeding as an escort, along with British warships, to a convoy of merchant vessels in the Mediterranean, a submarine was sighted. It appeared that the submarine was manouevering to get into position to fire a torpedo, but by skillful co-operation of HMS [*Basilisk*] and the USS *Lydonia*, a net work of depth charges was laid around the submarine. The submarine was not seen again: three months later it was discovered that it had been sunk.[1]

The loss of the USS *Tampa*, a former coast guard vessel, is the subject of one of the greatest tragedies of the sea in the history of the war. On 26 September, she was proceeding with an English convoy from Gibraltar to Milford Haven. When in sight of the English coast she detached herself from the convoy and stood in towards the coast. She was sighted from some of the shore stations for a few moments; a slight mist then descended and hid her from view. A loud explosion was heard from the shore stations and the *Tampa* was never seen again. American destroyers searched the area for 2 days in hopes of finding some survivors, but the only traces found were the floating body of an American sailor and some wreckage marked *Tampa*.[2]

The incident which perhaps stands out above all other experiences of the US Navy in European Waters, is that of the USS *Seneca* based at Gibraltar. On 16 September 1918, she was proceeding from England to Gibraltar with a convoy, when the British SS *Wellington* was struck by a torpedo. The *Seneca* dropped enough depth charges in the direction whence the torpedo came, to prevent the submarine attempting more damage. Shortly after the *Wellington* was torpedoed, her merchant crew deserted her and came alongside the *Seneca* in their boats. The master of the *Wellington* told the Commanding Officer of the *Seneca* that with the help of about 30 men, he thought the *Wellington* could be kept afloat until she reached port. Ten of the *Wellington's crew* volunteered to go back to try and save the ship; about 35 refused. Lieutenant Brown of the *Seneca* asked permission to go with the Master of the *Wellington* and picked 16 of the *Seneca's* crew to help him. The *Seneca* in the meantime was ordered to proceed with the remainder of the convoy and so left her eighteen volunteers to be of what service they could. It seemed at first as if they would be able to keep the *Wellington* afloat, but a heavy wind and sea made their task impossible. An SOS call was sent out and answered by the USS *Warrington*, a destroyer based at Brest. The *Warrington* came to the rescue at full speed and arrived at the scene a

---

[1] Sims, *Victory at Sea*, p. 136.
[2] Cause unknown.

few minutes before the *Wellington* sank. In the heavy seas and the unusually dark night, the task of rescuing the men was difficult. Eight of the *Seneca's* crew were rescued while 10 went down with the ship they had volunteered to save.[1]

So much for the work and story of the 35 American vessels at Gibraltar. There are 40 more vessels at the Island of Corfu, 39 of which are Sub-chasers, the other, their mother ship. The American sub-chaser is a craft of 110 feet in length and only 65 tons displacement. In spite of their limited size they came across the Atlantic under their own power, passed through the Straits of Gibraltar and made their home at the Island of Corfu, in the mouth of the Adriatic Sea.

The American sub-chaser is a very vicious looking little war vessel for its size. Forward there is mounted a 3″ gun, and aft the necessary and elaborate paraphernalia for launching depth charges. A small pilot-house stands just forward of amidships and behind it a mast, at the top of which is a lookout's nest; a wireless is rigged from the top of the mast also. With the help of 3 high powered gasolene engines the chaser has more speed at its disposal than it can often use. Each is manned by a crew of 2 officers and about 22 men.[2]

It had always been the intention of the Navy Department in Washington to use these chasers in European Waters, but through delays of one kind or another, they did not arrive at their destination, the Island of Corfu, until about the first of June 1918.[3] This island at the mouth of the Adriatic, had never been occupied as a naval base, although its location for hunting submarines was ideal.[4] Accordingly, the Americans were confronted with the task of converting a barren and uncivilized cove into a modern naval base. This work was accomplished by the 1,444 officers and men of the crews in a remarkably short time. Shacks for staff officers, repair shops, barracks, hospital space, etc., all had to be erected, but before the end of June, the job was complete and the forces were ready for operations.

The tactical employment of the submarine chaser is hunting submarines in limited areas by means of hydrophones and listening devices, and by these means ascertaining the submarine's course,

---

[1] USS *Seneca* was a Coast Guard cutter.

[2] Some 400 were built, of which about 170 served overseas. Sims, *Victory at Sea*, p. 168.

[3] See document no. 226.

[4] The French Fleet had used it as an anchorage throughout the war, even during the period of Greek neutrality (August 1914–July 1917). Halpern, *Naval War in the Mediterranean*, pp. 31, 33, 180, 367, 503–8.

speed and position. When it is definitely located, it is attacked with depth charges according to certain doctrines. The mere methods of hunting present many difficulties. Listening for submarines requires a trained ear on the part of the listener; he must be able to distinguish the peculiar sound of a 'submarine beat' from that of surface craft; learn how to ascertain its speed, course, etc. Furthermore one chaser alone cannot accurately fix the position of a submarine; to do this, it is necessary to have cross-bearings from other chasers also. Accordingly the training of the personnel in their particular duties was one of the first tasks to be accomplished. It can be easily seen that close co-operation between the various chasers or units is imperative; they had to learn to listen together and to report or communicate the results of their listening to each other and thereby establish the information to govern their attack. While chasers are hunting it is also necessary that their listeners should not be hampered by other craft in the vicinity. Accordingly listening periods were established during which all vessels in the vicinity must stop their engines to give the chaser a chance. In order to prevent the submarine from learning the interim of the listening period during which he would stop his engines and between which he could run them, these periods were different every day. The personnel of the sub-chasers then had a great deal to learn but they took to their work enthusiastically and soon attained great efficiency.

The first hunt at the Island of Corfu took place in the latter part of June 1918. All [enemy] submarines in the Mediterranean have their bases in the Adriatic Sea and as the Island of Corfu is at its mouth, the chasers shouldered a tremendous responsibility. Since the latter part of June at least 3 units, usually 4 or 5 (3 vessels in a unit) have been out hunting day and night. A hunt ordinarily lasts from 4 to 6 days, during which time the chances of at least hearing a submarine or of perhaps getting one are always good. ...

****

Thus with 75 ships and 5,542 men in the Mediterranean, the American Navy has endeavoured to contribute its share to the joint cause. The contribution it has made has been the outcome of the whole-hearted co-operation between the Americans and the Allies. The British requested aid at Gibraltar; the American Navy answered the request to the extent of 35 ships and over 4,000 men. The British and Italians wanted forces at the Straits of Otranto at the mouth of the Adriatic; the Americans sent their little 110' chasers across the Atlantic under their own power, to be of what service they could.

The close co-operation has proved its value.

332.   *Grant to Murray*

4 February 1919

*General report on the Employment of Allied Forces based at Gibraltar,
July 1917 to December 1918*

****

2. Though this force was composed of a collection of every description of vessel, for the greater part of low speed, they undoubtedly did
excellent work in the protection of Convoys from Enemy submarine
attack. ...

****

5. Of the British Special Service Vessels, Sloops, and US Sloops and
Yachts, few vessels have been called on for more continuous work,
and at one time, owing to shortage of vessels for Escorts, it was
found necessary to keep them at Sea for 5 days out of 7, the 48 hours
off being employed in coaling and making good defects. ...

****

10. The keenness displayed by British and Allied forces under my
command was deserving of all praise.

The US force acted in every way as part and parcel of the British
force, sharing all the risks and hard work in the fine spirit of
comradeship. ...

333.   *Grant to Murray*

4 February 1919

*Report on the Disposition of, and Work done by, vessels of the Gibral-
tar Command between July 1917 and December 1918*

****

As each US vessel arrived on the station she was taken in hand by
the Dockyard and fitted out, with the utmost dispatch, for service in
the Mediterranean. At first the Gunboats and Coast Guard Cutters
were employed as Danger Zone Escorts, but later, as more vessels
arrived and became available, they were employed on escort duties,
first with Oran Convoys and later with Bizerta and Genoa Convoys.

The US Destroyers were employed, almost exclusively, on Danger Zone escort duty, and for detached operations against submarines. It was not considered that the two US Cruisers were suitable for service in the Mediterranean, and therefore they remained inactive until October 1917, when it was decided that convoys between Gibraltar and the United Kingdom should be accompanied by an ocean escort throughout the voyage, and after this date these two vessels were employed exclusively on this duty until the cessation of hostilities. All the US Coast Guard Cutters were also employed on this duty as were for a time US Ships *Sacramento* and *Nahma*, they being later transferred to Mediterranean Escort work.

****

During October 1917, ... further reinforcements in the shape of five US Destroyers and four US Gunboats also arrived. On 23 October, Rear-Admiral H. B. Wilson, US Navy, relinquished the Command of the US patrol force based on Gibraltar and was relieved on 25 November by Rear-Admiral A. P. Niblack, US Navy.

****

All the new United States Destroyers, as they arrived on the station, were employed on escort duty, between Gibraltar and Marseilles, with US Army Supply Ships until the anti-submarine barrage was established in the Straits at the end of October, when all the available US Destroyers, Submarine chasers, and such Yachts as were available for this duty, operated on the various lines of the Barrage.[1]

****

---

[1] Grant set a series of patrol lines across the Straits in October to try to trap German U-boats on their way home from the Adriatic following Austria–Hungary's collapse. USS *Dyer* and *Gregory*, new destroyers, went to Gibraltar in the summer and two further new vessels, *Luce* and *Stribling*, were allocated in October. *Dyer*, commissioned in July, sailed for England a few days later, carrying Franklin D. Roosevelt. Halpern, *Naval War in the Mediterranean*, pp. 514–5.

PART VIII
THE WESTERN HEMISPHERE
MAY 1917 TO JANUARY 1919

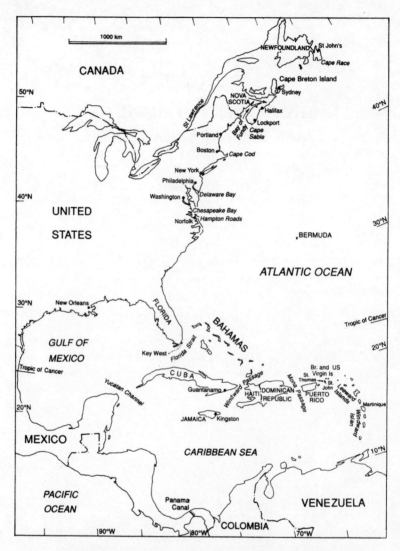

The Eastern Seabord of the USA and the Caribbean

INTRODUCTION

The British naval presence in the Western Hemisphere in 1917 was almost minimal. British strength had been run down following the general rapprochement with the United States between 1895 and 1903 and as a result of Admiral Fisher's policy of concentrating the Royal Navy's strength in the North Sea.[1] Further slimming had taken place under the pressure of war and the C-in-C North America and West Indies, Vice-Admiral Browning, was left with a handful of superannuated cruisers and armed merchant cruisers. The South American squadron was similarly stretched and diluted. Attempts had been made, with little success, to persuade the Canadian Government to raise substantial naval forces for general imperial defence and Browning doubled as Naval Advisor to Ottawa. Despite this token presence, the British nevertheless sought to control all neutral and Allied shipping sailing from eastern seaboard and Caribbean ports, British naval officers installed in these ports acting as routing, and later as convoy, controllers. When the United States entered the war, the Navy Department was naturally desirous of controlling all shipping emanating from US ports and made approaches of this kind to the Admiralty at intervals. All were resisted by the Admiralty, supported by Sims, on the grounds that the British organisation was complete, experienced, efficient and effectively co-ordinated with that of the Admiralty itself [334, 335, 338, 413]. The Americans did not help their cause by resisting the introduction of convoy, thereby compelling the British to establish their own organisation (based on existing routing offices) in North American ports [338]. More palatable to the Admiralty was the American request for a British convoy officer to be attached to the Navy Department; with this, the Admiralty happily conformed [349–50, 353–4].

Most of the early contact between the British, French and American navies was entirely without friction and devoted initially to the

[1] See, for example, B. Perkins, *The Great Rapprochement: England and the United States, 1895–1914* (New York: Atheneum Press, 1968).

439

solution of the surface raider problem (though unknown to the coalition, this was a declining problem as Germany channelled its resources increasingly into the U-boat campaign). Local commanders came to amicable agreements and friendly working · arrangements on patrols and zones of responsibility, as well as the control of shipping should U-boats appear in these waters [336, 337], 345–6, 348, 355, 361].

The extent of the U-boat threat in the Western Hemisphere was for some months a matter of dispute between Benson and the Admiralty and Sims. The Chief of Naval Operations, like most Americans, seems to have anticipated the sudden arrival of a whole flotilla of self-sustaining submarines. US Navy vessels engaged in fruitless searches of remote inlets for U-boat bases or depot ships and many patrol craft were held at home to safeguard local shipping and to screen the Atlantic Fleet. Sims insisted that the Germans had neither the desire nor the capacity to mount a substantial and sustained submarine campaign in American waters [343]. The Germans (who never declared war against the United States) hoped that their magnanimous abstention from sinkings off American shores would encourage pacifist and other anti-war groups in America and at the very least lead to a desultory prosecution of the war. The German high command seems to have been divided on the wisdom of attacking shipping in the western Atlantic and only in the spring and summer of 1918 did it at last make any sizeable effort to take the war to the Americans. Even this was of little consequence. On seven cruises, the U-cruisers employed sank 110000 tons of shipping, by mine, gunfire and charges, their victims being so small as not to be worth a torpedo.[1] When no threat materialised by July 1917, Benson released flotilla craft for service in the much more crucial European theatre and, to his credit, when the submarines did appear in the following spring, he was not panicked into holding back new craft or recalling others. Indeed, it was Browning's successor, Vice-Admiral Sir William L. Grant, who raised the alarm signals and argued for the retention of new US destroyers in home waters, a view in which he was supported by the Canadians [355, 358–9, 367]. Sims and the Admiralty rejected these suggestions firmly, insisting, rightly, that the focus of the submarine campaign was in the Western Approaches and that it was there that the Anglo-American anti-submarine strength must be concentrated. As they divined correctly, any U-boat presence in the western Atlantic would be intermittent,

---

[1] Herwig, pp. 142–3; Trask, *Captains and Cabinets*, pp. 220–3; Klachko, p. 108.

the shipping losses insignificant, and it would have as its object the diversion of Anglo-American escort forces from the real danger zone [360, 368]. The Admiralty intelligence service, renowned for its ability to identify, locate and track U-boats, kept Grant and the Navy Department fully informed of their progress across the Atlantic [362]. This gave Benson and Grant ample time to institute route diversions and local protection schemes, which largely frustrated the Germans' hopes of sinking a substantial tonnage [356, 357, 360, 363–5, 369, 370].

It was natural that proposals should be put forward for a British equivalent to the Sims mission in London, thus making permanent the contacts made by Rear-Admiral de Chair, Naval Advisor with the Balfour mission in the spring of 1917. Indeed, de Chair himself was proposed as the head of a suggested permanent British naval mission. The proposal was supported by the Ambassador, Sir Cecil Spring-Rice, the head of the British War Mission, Lord Northcliffe, Browning and de Chair himself but Jellicoe preferred a strengthening of Sims's team in London, for the very sound reason that the locus of the naval war was in the eastern Atlantic. The whole notion was rejected equally firmly by Benson, who liked and respected the indefatigable, thoroughly integrated and cheerful Gaunt [339–41]. However, when Browning was replaced by Grant early in 1918 [347], Benson appeared to change his mind and pressed for the new C-in-C to base himself in Washington, where he could become as intimate a member of the American naval high command as Sims was of the Admiralty. The fuller and closer naval co-operation resulting from Benson's visit to Europe in the late autumn of 1917 and the increased traffic across the Atlantic arising from the rapid build-up of the AEF, together with experience of some hiccups in previous months, indicated to the CNO that a more efficient structure for naval co-operation was required than the one furnished by the ever-willing but peripatetic Gaunt, who, according to his racy memoirs, had fingers in several pies.[1] Grant, who had large responsibilities and scant resources, was understandably reluctant to tie himself largely to Washington. In effect, he would be transformed from a station commander into a superior liaison officer. However, Wemyss was evidently willing to meet Benson's request and for the last six months of the war, Grant headed Britain's naval representation in the American capital. Benson clearly felt more comfortable with this arrangement and Grant, despite wry criticisms of American organi-

[1] Gaunt, *The Yield of the Years*, pp. 134–264.

sation and pretensions, enjoyed good relations with his American hosts (349, 351, 352, 358, 370, 371]. At the war's end, Grant recorded his appreciation of his American colleagues [374]. Once again, at the operational level and in joint strategic work, relations between the two navies were uniformly excellent. The curious episode of the American article sounding out the possibility of a major US base in the Caribbean (other than Guantanamo Bay, Cuba) led to no further action, but it caused the British some concern [342] and indicates that the young giant's ambitions were growing at a rate commensurate with its developing strength, confidence and world role.[1]

---

[1] See, for example, Rear-Admiral H. O. Dunn, US Navy (US Naval commander in Azores) to Sims, 29 December 1918, and Sims to Dunn, 31 December 1918, box 55, *Sims Papers*. Dunn thought the US should purchase the Azores and Bermuda, especially if the British re-acquired Heligoland. Sims wrote back, 'I believe that when the final settlement comes the islands will naturally fall into our hands'.

334. *Gaunt to Admiralty*

8 May 1917

Navy Department are asking

A   That all routing from American Ports be done by American Officers.

B. All routing from Allied Ports be done by Allied Officers.

C. All routing of American vessels from neutral ports by American Consuls in close touch with Allied Consuls.

D. British Officers now routing vessels from United States Ports [to] get in touch with local Naval Commandants and do the work jointly until such time as all arrangements regarding exchange of information regarding routes have been perfected.

E. In order that the work may be done efficiently to gain the advantage of our experience the Navy Department ask for details of our present procedure.

335. *W. Graham Greene to Gaunt*

18 May 1917

****

2. I am to request that you will inform the Navy Department that Their Lordships see no inherent objection to the issue of instructions in each allied country being carried out by Officers of that country, but that as a matter of fact the British organisation for doing this work in the United States is now very complete and the change suggested would be certain to lead to some difficulty and overlapping, at any rate at first. The important matter, however, is that there should be one common system of control for Ocean Routes. It will be essential that no organisation shall be adopted which could result in contradictory instructions being issued by the Authorities of the different countries. At the present time, by agreement with the French, instructions as to the routes to be followed are issued from the British Admiralty.

3. Their Lordships suggest that the United States should send an Officer to confer with the Admiralty Department responsible for carrying out this work, with a view to studying the system. It will be

443

desirable, if possible, that this Officer should be given full authority to settle the principles which shall be adopted.

4. It is observed that the French would have to be consulted as to any change in the present arrangements.

336. *Commanding Officer, USS Chattanooga, to Commander, Third Squadron, Patrol Force, US Atlantic Fleet*[1]

28 May 1917

1. Kingston, Jamaica is the headquarters of a branch of the British Naval General Staff. The General Staff Officer in charge is Major E. T. N. Farmer, RMLI.[2]

****

3. Major Farmer's organization is the clearing house of all naval information from ports on the Gulf of Mexico, Caribbean Sea, West Indies, and South American Coast as far as Pernambuco, movements of British men-of-war in the Western North Atlantic and French information from the French Admiral at Martinique.[3]

****

4. Major Farmer is most anxious that at the earliest moment communication be established between his organization and the US Forces in his area, as well as the French Forces. A mutual exchange of information would then be available that would be most valuable to the Third and Fourth Squadrons of the Patrol Force.

I cannot too strongly recommend this.

The Commandant, Naval Station, Guantanamo [Cuba] would be the logical clearing house for our Forces.

****

---

[1] Captain Arthur MacArthur, US Navy, commanding the cruiser *Chattanooga*; brother of Douglas MacArthur, the General. Commander, 3rd Sqdn, Patrol Force was Captain Henry B. Wilson, US Navy.

[2] Major E. T. N. Farmer, RMLI: Lieut 1905; Captain 1915; Temporary Major and GSO, 2nd grade; on Vice-Admiral Browning's staff; HMS *Exmouth* November 1918.

[3] Rear-Admiral Grasset.

337. *Procedure agreed upon by Commander-in-Chief, US Pacific
Fleet, and the Commodore commanding the British Forces on the
East Coast of South America at a conference held on board the USS
Pittsburgh*[1]

Rio de Janeiro,
Brazil,
29 June 1917

At a conference held on board the USS *Pittsburgh* on 25 June, it
was decided that as soon as circumstances admit, the following
arrangements will be made for patrolling the East Coast of South
America.

The United States Squadron to have two ships based on Bahia
which will patrol the United States designated area north of Bahia,
extending the patrol to cover the Allied Traffic Lane as far North as
Fernando Naronha and as far East as Long. 20° West. Also two
ships based on Rio de Janeiro which will patrol the United States
designated area from Bahia South to the latitude of Rio de Janeiro,
extending the patrol to cover the Allied Traffic Lane.

The British Squadron to have, if available, two ships based on Rio
de Janeiro South to Lat. 30° S., extending the patrol to cover the
Allied Traffic Lane. Also, if available, two ships based on the Plata
which will patrol the United States designated area from Lat. 30° S.,
to the latitude of English Bank, extending the patrol to cover the
Allied Traffic Lane.

Circumstances permitting, ships will patrol two-thirds of the time,
the remainder being spent coaling and refitting; the intention being
always to have one ship in the specified area.

Should a reliable report be received of recent date of the presence
of a raider, and circumstances are favorable, a combined search will
be carried out.

The United States and British Naval Attaches will pool all information and decide what intelligence shall be broadcasted. The message will be sent by BKW Code (AFR Signal Book) through the
Wireless Stations at Ascension and Falklands and the United States
Man-of-War which happens to be in harbor. Each message to be
reported at least twice.

The Naval Attachés will keep each other mutually informed of the

---

[1] Admiral W. B. Caperton, US Navy, commanded the Pacific Fleet, at this time
serving on the Atlantic side of the Panama Canal. The armoured cruiser *Pittsburgh*
was his flagship: 1903; 13 680 tons; 4 × 8in, 4 × 6in; 2tt; 22 knots. The commander of
the British squadron was Commodore Aubrey Smith: Captain 1910; commanded
Glasgow October 1916; Commodore 2nd class.

movements of their respective Squadrons.

Wireless silence is of the first importance and every effort will be made to maintain it.

The ships of the British Squadron have been instructed as follows:

'From information received, in at least one instance an enemy raider steamed up to a ship at night and suddenly switched searchlights on to her. Ships of the Squadron are not to burn searchlights at night, and if any vessel acts as described above, fire should be opened on her.'

The foregoing agreement is tentative and will not be considered to come into force until the US Commander-in-Chief signals to the Senior British Officer 'Patrol orders in force, (date), (time)'.

Mutual arrangements have been concluded for communication by visual signals and by wireless telegraph.

338.   Admiralty to Captain Keppel Wade[1]

5 July 1917

It is anticipated that the first convoy from New York will sail for United Kingdom one day next week. For the present all arrangements for organisation and sailings of convoys from New York are to be made by Captain Wade and he is therefore to proceed to Norfolk as soon as possible to confer with Commodore Wells[2] and obtain all information concerning the routing of convoys from him.

339.   Jellicoe to Browning

3 August 1917

Should like you to see Benson. I am convinced that strong US Naval Mission here is a necessity. US Navy Board cannot keep in close touch with changing aspects of war in any other way.

Please press strongly for this if opportunity occurs. Need is immediate.

If US Mission comes here I hardly think complete British Naval Mission in US is required. Such a mission cannot keep in touch with operations here and would become merely technical after a time. We are also very short indeed of Officers and should find greatest difficulty in sending any. Please discuss this aspect with Benson without

[1] Captain Keppel Wade: British Naval Vice-Consul, New York; a retired officer.

[2] Commodore Lionel de Vere Wells: a retired captain recalled to serve under Director of Naval Equipment; later in charge of routing and convoy operations from US ports.

committing us at all to sending mission.

340. *Browning to Jellicoe*

Halifax,
3 August 1917

Both De Chair and I formed opinion in June that a Naval Mission to United States would be advisable also Ambassador. I understood De Chair would explain situation to you.

Gaunt has no war and little sea experience and therefore cannot speak with authority though he does all he can.

I recommend mission should be reciprocal and believe ours would be welcome on this side.

They would of course be advisory and consultative only.

During my visit to Hampton Roads next week I could go to Washington if desired and see Benson who apparently wished to see me on last occasion.

If you concur, please reply before I sail p.m. tomorrow Friday and authorize me to tell him as you decide.

341. *Gaunt to Hall*

7 August 1917

I had not seen Ambassador's telegrams on the [?matter] until today. Had a conference with Pratt and asked him to tell me honestly America's wishes. I told him I would wire you and he said I might in strictest confidence. 'The Admiral [Benson] does not want any change, does not want any higher Officer, not even De Chair. What he does want is that you [Gaunt] should be kept more fully informed as to Admiralty wishes so as to be able to speak with greater authority at our conferences.'

... I urge that some reply be sent to me as difficulties increase and there is no one to organise or give necessary orders promptly.

342. *Memorandum by Geddes for War Cabinet*

4 September 1917

In an Article entitled 'Our Gibraltar', published in the July Number of *The World's Work*, Mr George Marvin[1] discusses the necessity of establishing an American Naval Base of the first magni-

---

[1] George Marvin: Asst Editor, *The World's Work* (a Page publication); former schoolmaster at Groton, Massachusetts, where he had taught Franklin D. Roosevelt;

448 ANGLO-AMERICAN NAVAL RELATIONS 1917–1919

tude in Caribbean Waters for the protection of American interests in the West Indies and the Canal Zone. He discusses the relative value of various sites in Cuba, Haiti, San Domingo, Puerto Rico, and the Virgin Islands recently acquired from Denmark, and decides in favour of forming a Base by building breakwaters enclosing the area between the newly acquired Virgin Islands of St Thomas and St John.[1] He points out that the only objections which can be made to the selection of this site for the Naval Base are (1) difficulties as regards water supply, which, however, can be surmounted, and (2) the close proximity of the British Islands of Jost Van Dyke, Tortola, and Virgin Gorda, which Islands dominate the approach from the Atlantic to St Thomas and St John. Mr Marvin says that Great Britain might possibly be willing to hand over these Islands to USA or, if not, might agree by Treaty to leave them, as at present, unfortified, and he points out that the latter course might best serve the purposes of the United States as in the event of War between America and a Third Power the existence of neutral British waters in this region would be a distinct gain to America.

If Mr Marvin's article is to be considered as officially inspired, it would seem that USA are considering the advisability of approaching Great Britain on the matter.[2] It would become necessary, therefore, to consider what quid pro quo should be asked for, if such a suggestion should come from the United States and the British Government decide to negotiate. It should be borne in mind, however, that the United States have already obtained very considerable interests in the Greater and Lesser Antilles extending from the coast of Florida eastward to the Virgin Islands and at various times suggestions have been made unofficially for the acquisition of French, Dutch and Venezuelan possessions in the Lesser Antilles, the transfer of which to the United States would give them a preponderating influence in the Caribbean Sea.

the two remained close friends.
[1] The US had purchased the Danish West Indies in 1916 (now the US Virgin Isles). See C. C. Tansill, *The Purchase of the Danish West Indies* (Baltimore: Johns Hopkins UP, 1932).
[2] Marvin may have picked up the idea from a recent trip to the Caribbean in the company of FDR. This visit (January and February 1917), as much a joyride as an inspection, took in Cuba, Haiti and Santo Domingo, all to a greater or lesser extent US protectorates, the last two occupied by the Marines and hence practically ruled by the Navy Dept. It is unlikely that the cautious State Dept. inspired the article and it was certainly not the anti-imperialist Daniels (who was acutely uncomfortable with his responsibility for the administration of the island of Hispaniola), but young FDR was then a carefree expansionist and a strident jingo. See Ward, *A First-Class Temperament*, pp. 325–35.

Sir Alex. Swettenham[1] makes the suggestion that some Territorial concessions should be sought in proximity to the Strait of Juan de Fuca, Haro and Georgia, in order to improve the access to the Canadian Ports of Esquimault, Victoria and Vancouver. The boundary between British Columbia and the United States at this point was fixed by the German Emperor in 1872 which put an end to a period of strained relations which had for some years existed between Great Britain and the United States in connection with this boundary.

Admiral Parry, Hydrographer,[2] points out that it would be extremely unlikely that the United States would entertain the giving up of any territory in this region, nor does he think any useful object would be attained by a transfer to Great Britain of any Islands in the Straits in question, as the proximity of other Islands would obviously militate against the possibility of any superiority on gun protection being effected. Admiral Parry states that the only two portions of the Globe where the USA have possessions contiguous to British possessions which appear worthy of consideration in this connection are:-

(1) The Eastern portion of the Samoan Group in the Pacific, the Western portion of this Group being formerly German possessions and now in British occupation, and

(2) The islands including the Sulu Archipelago extending from Mindanao (which is the Southernmost of the larger islands in the Philippine group) in a South Westerly direction towards British North Borneo.

Captain Nugent, for DID,[3] emphasises undesirability of permitting the Caribbean Sea to come under USA control and possibly become a 'mare clausum' to European Nations, and points out in reference to the American Pacific possessions that all these had a definite place in the American strategic scheme against Japan's antebellum position in the Pacific and that the possibility of Japan retaining some of the Islands she has captured, tends to weaken the American position. He concludes that USA would not, therefore, be likely to abandon any Pacific Island position that has a potential

[1] Sir Alexander Swettenham: colonial administrator, initially in Ceylon (now Sri Lanka) and later Governor of Jamaica.

[2] Rear-Admiral John Franklin Parry: surveying on Australian coast 1895–1900; Chief Asst to Hydrographer of the Navy 1900–03; Captain 1905; Asst Hydrographer 1910; Hydrographer of the Navy 1914; Rear-Admiral June 1916.

[3] Captain Raymond A. Nugent: NID 1908–10; Commander 1910; Captain and command of 12th Destroyer Flotilla 1912; a Flag Captain 1912–14; invalided home; asst to DID.

value against the Japanese menace. Both American Samoa and the Sulu Archipelago are in this category.

Captain Nugent agrees with Admiral Parry's objections to the territorial exchange in the Strait of Fuca suggested by Sir Alexander Swettenham.

Admiral Hope, DOD,[1] concurs with Captain Nugent and points out that it does not appear likely that the United States would suggest, or agree to, any exchange of territory, but that any engagement on our part not to fortify the British Virgin islands should receive a quid pro quo.

343. *Sims to Navy Department*

9 October 1917

Reports of Submarine Activity in Western Atlantic

With reference to the information which has reached the Department recently from various sources concerning the possibility of a force of large enemy submarines operating off the Atlantic coast or in the West Indies, the Force Commander's despatches have given practically all information available here. The Force Commander is strongly of the personal opinion that no extensive oversea campaign of this nature will be initiated by the enemy. He is further of the personal opinion that such a campaign is a practical impossibility.

****

It is always, of course, quite possible that the enemy may send a small number of submarines to operate temporarily on our coast or in distant fields, with the object of affecting the disposition of our forces. It would be greatly to the interest of the enemy to force the removal of our anti-submarine force from the critical areas, that is, near to the enemy bases and in the focal areas of allied trade, upon which the war is largely dependent.

It has been a source of more or less surprise that such an operation as this has not been undertaken before, and the only theory offered to explain the fact that it has not been undertaken has been that the enemy apparently did not consider it to their interests to arouse the American public unnecessarily.

It has been believed that the enemy hopes that peace will arrive before the military pressure of the United States has become at all serious. The population of the allied countries, now in the fourth

[1] Rear-Admiral George Hope.

year of the war, has reached what might be called a 'bitter stage' which will react upon the enemy following the war during the reconstruction period. The theory is therefore advanced that it will be greatly to the enemy's advantage during the reconstruction period if the American public at large has not been given any cause to reach the so-called 'bitter stage'.

On the other hand, it may be urged that a few submarines sent to operate temporarily on the American coast, or on the trade routes from South America particularly in the vicinity of the Canal, might result in sufficient popular agitation to force the Department into withdrawing either all or part of its forces from European waters. The possibility of this contingency must therefore, of course, receive serious consideration.

344. *Commander American Patrol Detachment to Commander-in-Chief*[1]

10 November 1917

Proposed Plan of Cooperation between British and United States Naval Force

1. I forward herewith for your consideration copies of a proposed plan of combined operation between United States and British Naval Forces in the event of a hostile submarine appearing in the Western Atlantic, as agreed upon by the Commander of the American Patrol Detachment and the British Naval General Staff Officer at Kingston, Jamaica.

****

3. The proposed plan for the safeguarding of shipping is the result of much thought and mature deliberation and if the Commander-in-Chief has not a better plan, based upon a fuller and more complete knowledge of the situation and our resources, I strongly recommend that this plan be given his formal approval as soon as possible so that that fact can be communicated to the British General Staff Officer in Jamaica and through him to Vice-Admiral Browning, Royal Navy, on whose staff he is serving.

****

[1] The Commander of the US Patrol Detachment was Captain E. A. Anderson, US Navy; Rear-Admiral 1918 and CO Patrol Sqdn 1. The CinC is almost certainly Admiral Mayo, CinC Atlantic Fleet,

5. It is my intention to proceed to St Thomas, West Indies, as soon as my flagship, *Dolphin*[1] is relieved from duty of affording passage to the Military Governor of Santo Domingo between Santo Domingo City, Santo Domingo, and Pau Pau, Haiti, and acting as residence for him during his stay in the latter city.[2] I consider that this visit is highly desirable in case the plan is approved as it is very necessary for me to ascertain conditions at that place as I would rather turn [?] immediate base there in case of approval of the plan and in the event of a submarine appearing in the Western Atlantic.

****

[Enclosure]

Proposed Plan of Combined Operations Agreed upon by Representatives of the Royal and United States Navies, at Kingston, Jamaica

9 November 1917

1. In the event of hostile submarines appearing in the Western Atlantic the following measures will be taken to safeguard Allied shipping to and from the Gulf of Mexico and the Caribbean Sea.

(a) The British Naval General Staff Officer at Jamaica will order all British Naval Vice-Consuls to hold all Allied shipping in port. He will then, after sufficient time has elapsed to develop the situation, order all shipping from the Gulf of Mexico to be routed through the Yucatan Channel. That portion of this shipping which is to be formed into convoys will be concentrated at St Thomas, West Indies. Shipping not to enter convoys will be routed through the Windward and Mona Passages.

(b) The Commander, American Patrol Detachment, United States Atlantic Fleet, will concentrate at St Thomas as much as possible of his present forces. Any additional forces assigned him will be concentrated at the same place until sufficient forces have been assembled to clear a considerable area around St Thomas of hostile submarines. Any further forces assigned to him will patrol the Windward and Mona Passages.

(c) The British Naval Officer, Commanding Auxiliary Patrols,

---

[1] USS *Dolphin*: despatch vessel, 1884; 1486 tons; 2 × 3in; 15.5 knots.
[2] Usually a US Rear-Admiral.

West Indies,[1] will be requested to send any forces he can spare to St Thomas until sufficient United States forces can be assembled there. The Commander-in-Chief of British Naval Forces in the Western Atlantic will be required to furnish armoured cruisers as raider guards for convoys after they have left St Thomas.

(d) The United States Navy is to make every effort to keep sufficient coal on hand at St Thomas for bunkering merchantmen. Should there be a shortage there, merchantmen will call at San Juan, Puerto Rico, Kingston, Jamaica, or Guantanamo Bay, Cuba.

(e) The United States Navy will make all arrangements for the efficient protection of merchant shipping when passing through the Florida Straits, including a seaplane patrol.

(f) When in the opinion of the Commander of the American Patrol Detachment, he can afford safe conduct to merchant ships in the Florida Straits all Gulf shipping will be so routed, the Senior Naval Officer at Key West being responsible for all arrangements. In case it is considered desirable to send shipping through the Straits in convoys, all Allied merchantmen leaving Gulf ports will be given certain rendezvous in the eastern part of the Gulf of Mexico, these rendezvous being changed from time to time, blank days being allotted on which there will be no convoys. The Senior Naval Officer at Key West will be informed by cipher telegram whenever ships leave Gulf ports, giving the approximate times at which they will arrive at the rendezvous, and will have the escorting vessels ready to meet them there.

2. It is understood that the above general plan is to be carried out intelligently, that many minor variations may be necessary, and that important changes may possibly be required by exceptional situations.

3. It is further understood that to be binding this agreement must be ratified by both Commanders-in-Chief.

345. *Commander, American Patrol Detachment, to Commandant, Seventh Naval District, Key West Florida*[2]

30 November 1917

[Enclosure]

---

[1] Unidentified.

[2] Captain Anderson. Commandant of 7th Naval District was Cdr W. J. Terhune,

ANGLO-AMERICAN NAVAL RELATIONS 1917–1919

From Opnav to Commander, Squadron One, Patrol Force

The Navy Department has approved the plan submitted by Commander Patrol Detachment for cooperation between British and American Naval Forces in event that hostile submarines appear in the Western Atlantic. Convoy escorts in the Straits of Florida to be undertaken by Patrol Detachment increased as practicable by District craft. Plans should be based upon present force only, pending a redistribution of other forces if circumstances warrant. Report if British authorities concur and as soon as practicable the requirements for coal at St Thomas, W.I.

346. *Benson to Sims*

28 November 1917

Following is agreement entered into by Admiral Caperton and Commodore Smith (referring paragraphs 2 and 3 of confidential agreement with British Commodore dated 29 June above paragraphs modified to read 'United States to have two ships based on Bahia, Brazil, which will patrol United States designated area north of Abrolhos Islands, extending patrol to cover allied traffic path as far north as Fernando, Noronha, and as far east as Longitude 20° West. Also one vessel, Flagship, based on Rio de Janeiro to preserve freedom of action, to proceed where her presence may seem most needed.

British forces to have one ship based on Bahia, Brazil, to assist in patrol above described for area north of Abrolhos Islands. One vessel based on Montevideo, Uruguay, to cover approach to La Plata River. One vessel, flagship, based on Rio de Janeiro to preserve freedom of action, to proceed where her presence may seem most necessary.

Remainder original agreement unaltered. Request approval.'

Navy Department approves and requests information of Admiralty's opinion.

347. *Admiralty to Gaunt*

20 December 1917

Convey to US Navy Department that it is proposed to appoint Vice-Admiral Sir Montague Browning to command our 4th Battle Squadron and while fully sensible of the very happy relations which

US Navy; HQ, Key West, Florida.

exist between them and him First Lord has every confidence that in his successor – Vice-Admiral W. L. Grant – the same satisfactory co-operation will continue.

348. *Admiral Caperton, US Navy, to Daniels*

US Pacific Fleet,
USS *Pittsburgh*,
Flagship,
14 January 1918

1. After six months of working in cooperation with a British Naval force in South Atlantic waters, it seems fitting that I should report to the department the unusually excellent good feeling and the perfect coordination which has existed between these two forces. Numerous friendships between the officers of the squadrons have developed, and the mutual relations have been in every way pleasant, in personal as well as in official matters.

2. That the manner of cooperation leaves nothing to be desired is due to the ever readiness of Commodore Aubrey Smith to do all in his power toward a successful combination of effort. I am unable to express too strongly my admiration for his delightful personality as well as for his professional ability and the excellent manner in which he conducts the affairs of his squadron.

3. That he was able, during the long-period when South American ports were closed to British men-of-war, to maintain a high morale in his force while every vessel was remaining almost continuously at sea, and anchoring in uninhabited spots for overhaul of machinery, is particularly worthy of note. The proportion of time which he has kept his vessels at sea is remarkable even from the viewpoint of our service.

4. Specific instances of his readiness to cooperate in the fullest sense of the word are shown by his proceeding from southern waters to maintain the patrol of our assigned sea area off the Brazilian coast while the vessels of my squadron were visiting Uruguay under departmental orders, upon the occasion of that country's breaking relations with Germany; and again today when he has proceeded with the *Newcastle* to maintain the patrol off Bahia while it is necessary for the *Raleigh* to be withdrawn temporarily to Rio.[1]

5. If not inconsistent with the Department's views, it would seem to

---

[1] HMS *Newcastle*: cruiser, 1910; 4800 tons; 2 × 6in, 10 × 4in; 2 tt; 25 knots. USS *Raleigh*: light cruiser, 1894; 3183 tons; 9 × 5in; 18 knots.

be proper to inform the British Admiralty of my sincere appreciation
of his perfect cooperation.

349. *Benson to Sims*

20 February 1918

After discussing subject with Commodore Gaunt and Lieut-Commander J. V. Babcock who both thoroughly agree with following conclusions. It is consensus of opinion that centralization of control and organisation for handling convoys is not as efficient as it could be. Department is of opinion that if British method of handling affairs was more in accord with our organisation in London situation would be simplified and we would be in closer touch with Admiralty than we are at present. In matters connected with operations abroad touching Department you are naturally medium through which most information and consequently action flows, but there are certain matters mostly connected with operations and affairs on this side which do not pass through you. Under these circumstances lack of a Central Controlling British Authority on shore in Washington D.C., leads sometimes to a confusion of requests and a certain lack of thorough cooperation in any plan which affects our joint forces operating on this side [of the] Atlantic. This is especially true of convoy situation now and would immediately [be]come acute involving all joint plans and operations of any sort instant a single cruising submarine were to appear on our Coast. To forestall any such confusion in joint plans and operations Department believes that:

A. Controlling British Authority representing Admiralty should be stationed in Washington, D.C.

B. That a convoy officer representing Admiralty be stationed here as part [of] this office. Take this matter up with Admiralty for a decision. This matter should be brought to an early settlement because were a submarine to operate off our coast undoubtedly Department would immediately take some form of action into its hands, especially as regards routing for incoming vessels and it is desired that we not only have full information on this subject but also take no separate action where present lack of centralization would force us to go.

350. *Sims to Benson*

25 February 1918

Admiralty is in complete accord with recommendations of Department. Details will be made without delay.

351. *Sims to Benson*

1 March 1918

First Sea Lord has requested me to convey to you following information.

Vice-Admiral Grant is ultimate convoy authority as well as commander British Naval Forces in America.

In view of above Admiral Wemyss requests that you would be kind enough to advise him as to whether you consider it advisable that Admiral Grant's headquarters should be in Washington in order to insure immediate action be taken in case of an emergency as to employment of combined British and American Naval Forces to operate against submarine menace on American side and route convoys in accordance therewith.

352. *Benson to Sims*

3 March 1918

Chief of Naval Operations desires you convey to First Sea Lord his appreciation of message. It is thought wise here and desirable that Vice-Admiral Grant should at least be temporarily stationed in Washington, D.C., and probably permanently after conference is held with Chief of Naval Operations and Admiral Grant's view obtained. Space has been assigned him in connection with operations.

458   ANGLO-AMERICAN NAVAL RELATIONS 1917–1919

353.   *Sims to Murray*

16 March 1918

British Naval Officer for detail in Convoy Section of US Navy Department

1. US Navy Department has recently established a Convoy Section that will deal not only with the question of convoys, but also of routes of shipping, especially approach routes to the Atlantic seaboard of North America, including the Panama Canal.
2. The Navy Department intends to provide approach routes to all the principal ports on the Atlantic seaboard, so that in the event of submarine activities ships or convoys en route to the westward can be instructed as to the safest route of approach to their destinations.
3. In order that the Navy Department may have the advantage of the experience of the Admiralty, as well as to provide for cooperation in the protection to shipping, I am directed to request that the Admiralty detail a suitable officer for duty in the Convoy Section of the Navy Department.

354.   *Murray to Sims*

3 April 1918

With reference to your letter ... requesting that a British Naval Officer might be appointed for duty in the Convoy Section of the Navy Department, I have to inform you that the Admiralty have appointed Acting Captain Hugh B. Mulleneux, RN,[1] for this duty. He will spend a week or so at the Admiralty in order to get in touch with the latest changes in Routeing and Convoy work and will then proceed to Washington.

355.   *Grant to Admiralty*

Washington,
18 March 1918

Just received report which recommends if submarines be located in Western Atlantic
(A) Immediately close Florida Strait to traffic until measures for its defence are assured.

[1] Acting Captain Hugh B. Mulleneux: Commander 1910; at this time attached to Trade Div, Admiralty.

(B) Trade from Gulf for European Ports which now joins convoys to be diverted through Yucatan Channel to St Thomas
and proceed thence in one fast and one slow convoy per week
under protection of French and United States Cruisers.

(C) Anchorage at St Thomas to be prepared and protected by
United States with aid of such patrol forces [as] French
Admiral and British Commodore can spare; coal stock to be
provided by United States.

(D) When defence of Florida Strait is assured present convoy
arrangements to be reverted to.

I have had no opportunity yet to study volume and importance of
trade through Florida Straits but understand that half the ships in
Hampton Roads convoys and some in New York would be affected.
United States Admiral[1] was the moving spirit in these proposals.
Advantages appear to be smaller convoys, spreading of routes and
increase in number of escort ships available. I would be glad to be
informed if Admiralty and Shipping Controller are prepared to
consider this.

356. *Gaunt to Wemyss*

23 March 1918

Admiral Benson says that from [source] which he describes as
absolutely reliable he has information that four German submarines
will shortly be operating on this Coast. One of the points will be
Cape Race and he asks me whether we are satisfied as to Intelligence
Service there and if not suggests sending two American submarines
to that vicinity.

357. *Deputy First Sea Lord[2] to Gaunt*

26 March 1918

We have no information to confirm that received by Admiral
Benson.

Matter should be referred to C.-in-C. North America and West
Indies who should advise as to local intelligence service.

As far as experience goes submarine cruisers do not require to use
coastal waters. Weather and ice conditions appear adverse to submarine operating in vicinity of Cape Race for the present.

[1] Presumably Caperton.
[2] Rear-Admiral Hope, formerly DOD, became D1SL on 14 January 1918.

358.   *Grant to Murray*

1 April 1918

Location at Washington

****

2. *Visit of Commander-in-Chief to Washington and New York*

In accordance with instructions ... I, on 4 March, proceeded by train from Halifax to Washington to discuss with US Navy Department various points which needed consideration.

It became evident that the question raised as to the establishment at Washington of the central Admiralty Convoy Authority ... and the supply of information in connection therewith was merely subsidiary, and that the location of the British Commander-in-Chief, as the central Naval Authority in the West, at Washington, was the ultimate desire.

In view of the increasing weight of the United States in the War and the comparative lack of touch between the naval forces [on] this side both as regards defence measures and convoy work, it had to be conceded that the view taken was reasonable and I accordingly sent the following to the Admiralty:-

> 'US Navy Department lay great stress on executive authority over British naval forces and the convoy system in North America being present at Washington and have provided office. I demurred suggesting Halifax as my Headquarters with frequent visits and intimate touch with Washington, but in view of large number of matters requiring close conference and settlement it seems advisable and practicable to bring *Warrior*[1] and office to Washington. This meets US naval views ... I would visit Ottawa when advisable and will make clear to them that my location at Washington for the time being will not in any way affect my duties as C.-in-C. as they affect Canada. If you concur, the Ambassador[2] will also do what is necessary to regularise matters with higher authorities. I will wire a detailed proposal for arrangement of Station duties later.'

which was concurred in.

---

[1] HMS *Warrior*: a yacht lent to the British Government by her American owner, a Mr Cochrane.

[2] Spring-Rice, having become ill, had retired at the beginning of 1918 and was succeeded by the Marquis of Reading, formerly the leading KC Sir Rufus Isaacs; Attorney General 1915–17; Lord Chief Justice 1917.

****

The ship [*Warrior*] is connected by telephone and the closest possible touch is being established between myself and staff and Admiral Benson and the Navy Department from which valuable results will I trust be achieved. I cannot speak too highly of the very cordial and wholly unreserved attitude of the US Naval Authorities.

****

4. *Co-operation with United States for Protection against Powerful Submarine Cruisers and Raiders*

This question was raised in my telegram No. 594,[1] given in the last general letter, and in reply I was directed to discuss the matter with US Navy Department.

Before doing this, however, it was necessary to ascertain whether Admiralty considered the menace sufficient to justify the retention of US Destroyers in these waters. I accordingly sent the following:-

'If you concur that menace against shipping on this side in the immediate future is very grave and justifies the retention of destroyers, a telegram to that effect to the US Authorities would be very advisable having in view that their present policy is to send as fast as possible and without question practically all destroyers to your side.'

I received in reply the following:-

'There is no intention to propose any alteration in policy of US authorities.'[2]

****

I cannot but concur in the view generally expressed this side that we are very open to a sudden attack and sinkings possibly of large troop transports and am afraid that this would very probably cause great popular emotion in Canada and the United States. At the same time the US are fully prepared to accept the home ruling as to the relative degree of menace and the consequent most expedient appropriation of the destroyers and small craft at our disposal.

The Admiralty Telegrams above quoted are somewhat conflicting but I read them as meaning that the policy of getting all possible destroyers into European Waters with as little delay as possible will

[1] Not reproduced.
[2] Grant's telegam was sent on 8 March and the Admiralty's reply (by Hope) on 10 March.

not be waived in any degree, but that if US, Canada and myself concur in the necessity of keeping a minimum, we will keep them; this reading I propose to act upon so far as I am myself concerned.

****

359. Benson to Sims

7 April 1918

The question of allocating some of our new destroyers to the port of Halifax, Nova Scotia, for protection of that area and of convoys sailing from there is one that is being pushed by Canadian authority and British Commander-in-Chief [in] these waters. Minimum number of destroyers wanted for this duty five. We are sending our destroyers abroad as fast as they can be made available; reserves only 12 speed 10 knots on entire coast, most of which are either crippled, under repair or engaged on important experimental work. To allocate five additional destroyers to Halifax, Nova Scotia, will cripple our efforts abroad and in our opinion that is not justified now. The department desires a definite statement from you backed up by the Admiralty as to correctness of our present policy or whether they advise yielding to the Canadian desires. It is further desired that advance information be furnished us when it may be considered desirable to increase the reserve on our own coast due to the prospect of submarine operations here. This information requested not from any desire on our part to hold back destroyers but is dictated by the necessity which would naturally arise from protecting adequately the numerous convoys sailing from our ports. In case of attack on Canadian Coast we naturally would go [to their] assistance with such force as could be spared from imminent attack on our own coast.

360. Sims to Benson

11 April 1918

After consultation with Admiralty I can say unreservedly that they are in entire agreement with me in regarding as correct the Department's present policy and in recommending against yielding to the Canadian desires. This same subject was broached some months ago before Vice-Admiral Browning came home and it was decided at that time that there was no necessity for allocating destroyers to the port of Halifax, Nova Scotia, and furthermore that if such allocation were made there would be an immediate demand for similar allocation to United States ports such as New York and Hampton Roads. Such dispersion of force would be contrary to sound military principles and should be avoided at all costs.

The Department will be kept supplied with all information obtainable here as to probability of hostile operations on home coasts.

361.   *Commandant, First Naval District[1] to Opnav*

Boston, Mass.,
25 April 1918

Recommendations of conference held at Boston 22 April 1918, discussing measures for obtaining co-operation between United States and Canadian Patrol Forces

1. The Commandant, First US Naval District to take over Coastal Patrols, sea-patrols, protection of traffic and offensive action taken against submarines, as far east as the 65th meridian (Lockport, N. S.) including the outer part of the Bay of Fundy.

2. Squared charts on the same system to be prepared for the adjacent areas and mutually communicated and used for reference in all patrol operations.

3. Current edition of Auxiliary Code to be used for directing operations of patrols in the United States and Canadian adjacent areas, to insure each knowing what is going on by interception. All important movements to be communicated by land wire in addition.

4. Local inter-allied recognition signals to be arranged and used whenever patrols meet at sea. Signals being issued to vessels for period on patrol.

5. Procedure for entering defended ports of each country to be communicated to the other and adhered to.

6. Detailed organization and changes in procedure to be mutually communicated.

7. All communications to be made between Admiral Superintendent Navy Yard, Halifax and the Commandant, First US Naval District using the current edition of the Allied code and cipher.[2]

[signed by]

C. C. Marsh, Captain US Navy, Chief of Staff, First Naval District.

V. H. Haggard, Captain RN, Chief of Staff to British C-in-C.

---

[1] Rear-Admiral Spencer S. Wood, US Navy.
[2] Rear-Admiral Charles E. Kingsmill commanded at Halifax.

Walter Hose, Captain RCN, Captain of Patrols.[1]

****

362. *Hall to Grant*

15 May 1918

The following information has been handed to Admiral Sims.

From the report of sightings there would appear to be reasonable probability that a *Deutschland* class submarine may arrive off the American coast any date after 20 May, she will probably carry mines. From experience of our own coasts the favourite spot for laying mines is the position in which Merchant Ships stop to pick up pilots for instance for Delaware bay pilots for large ships are picked up south of the five fathom bank light vessel. This is considered one of the most likely spots where submarine will lay mines.

Germans have information that there is a patrol off most harbours and especially Chesapeake Bay where a neutral has reported that the patrol extends as far as Cape Skerry.

It is again emphasised that except for minelaying these *Deutschland* class submarines always work in deep water, mines have been laid by Germans in depths up to 70 fathoms, as far as is known there is no reason why they should not lay mines in depths up to 90 fathoms.[2]

363. *Benson to Sims*

5 June 1918

Enemy submarine commenced operations 60 miles SE Barnegat 2 June 3 pm. Sunk by bomb Schooner *Edward H. Cole*. Sunk by method not yet known *Jacob Haskell* lat. 39° 30' N., long. 73° 30' W. Noon 3 June. USS *Preble*[3] reports now engaging submarine. Captain of *Cole* reports sighting periscope of second submarine. Characteristics of submarine actually [?] about 200 feet long, mounting two large guns forward one aft one small gun amidships. It is not intended to allow this to interrupt Eastbound convoys.

---

[1] Captain Walter Hose was the 'father' of the RCN.
[2] The U-cruiser was U-151 (Lt-Cdr Kophamel), previously active off Azores. She did lay mines in Delaware Bay; see Sims, *Victory at Sea*, p. 273.
[3] USS *Preble*: destroyer; 1903; 480 tons; 2 × 3 in; 2 tt; 29 knots.

364. *Grant to Admiralty*

Washington,
6 June 1918

Probably only 1 submarine *Deutschland* class last seen definitely 37° 38' N., 42° [00'?] W. 1330 4 June. Has been in American waters since 25 May, has sunk by gunfire several coasting vessels, 1 passenger steamer, 1 oiler by mine off Overfalls Light Vessel since salved. All above mentioned American ships.

Probably laid mines elsewhere. No torpedoes yet used.

Am maintaining ship and convoy programme subject necessary modifications and utmost feasible precautions by US who eagerly co-operate. Counter measures improving.

365. *Grant to Admiralty*

15 June 1918

We do not consider it wise to operate 'Q' boats this side because

(A) U-151 has so far operated with humanity. Military value of ships sunk small.

(B) 'Q' ships valuable only in initial stage; value later small; their use would be met by reprisals which might induce public to bring to bear pressure to hold forces here.

(C) Navy Department feels measures being taken will in short time have situation well in hand.[1]

366. *Grant to Senior British Naval Officer, New York*[2]

14 June 1918

Submarine Menace: Defence of Shipping in the United States

With reference to my telegram 1820 of 3 June,[3] the responsibility for the defence of shipping in the approaches to New York and other United States ports must of course necessarily rest with the United States. It must be remembered however that owing to the submarine situation on the British and European coasts the United States have retained on this side a comparatively weak force of anti-submarine craft and that in consequence the anti-submarine protection it is possible to afford troopers, large liners, convoys, and other shipping

---

[1] Sims had suggested that a British Q-ship should be sent to the US coast.
[2] Commodore Wells.
[3] Not reproduced.

may not always be as adequate as might in other circumstances be
desirable, also that the situation [on] the other side is such as to
render the holding up of troops and supplies and the ships that carry
them little short of disastrous.

2. At the same time though troops and supplies if lost may be
replaced, the ships, according to their relative importance, cannot
and it behoves us to take every possible precaution and, weighing in
true proportion the conflicting arguments, to judge in each case as to
the justifiability of permitting transit through a danger area with the
protection it is possible at the time to afford.

3. You should be in the closest touch with the United States Naval
Authorities at New York and, having full regard to the above
factors, you should maintain British traffic at its maximum
efficiency so long as in your opinion the protection afforded, taking
into consideration the resources available and the war importance of
the vessels affected, is such as to warrant the risk taken.

****

367. *Grant to Admiralty*

21 July 1918

Having regard to present Military and Food position in France
and England and the increasing relative importance to Germany of
checking vast movement of troops, munitions and supplies from
North America also increased difficulties and losses to submarines
operating in home waters am of opinion that present inadequate
anti-submarine forces on this side can no longer be justified and that
they should be gradually increased by detention of US destroyers as
completed for sea if they can possibly be spared from Home forces.

I have of course not mentioned this in any way to United States
nor has point been raised by them.

368. *Admiralty to Grant*

22 July 1918

As you are not in a position to form a true appreciation of the
Submarine situation generally it is essential that you should not
express any opinion to the US Authorities on the subject of retention
or otherwise of US destroyers in American Waters.

369. *Admiralty to Grant*

24 August 1918

Admiralty would be glad to have full information with regard to measures in force or contemplated by US Navy Department for action against submarines operating on East Coast of North America, Gulf of Mexico and West Indies.

Request you will forward report dealing fully with these matters, including statement of vessels and aircraft employed or to be employed on these duties, and details of any arrangements made for co-operating with Canadian Navy.

US Navy Department has been provided with all details of the British dispositions in European waters and the Admiralty would welcome corresponding information with regard to the Western Atlantic in order to be able to deal with any problems arising in Canadian waters or in the West Indies.

370. *Grant to Murray*

16 September 1918

The Distribution of United States Naval Forces, Western Atlantic Waters, applying in Anti-Submarine Warfare

With reference to the attached report, I wish to offer the following remarks:-

In addition to the ocean escort of convoys, the United States are now giving battleship escort to troop convoys except HC, for which battleships are not at present available and as they carry few US troops, but it is thought that these and the slower cargo convoys require reinforcement of the escort quite as much as the faster troop convoys. Escorts are also provided at request when considered necessary for portions of convoys meeting at sea and for groups of ships proceeding from one port to another to join convoys, as for instance, ships proceeding from New York and Hampton Roads to join HS Convoys at Sydney [Nova Scotia], also in special cases for individual ships.

2. Arrangements have been made for the institution of convoys in the Gulf of Mexico at short notice should it become necessary.

3. Up to date only one torpedo boat destroyer has been sent with each troop convoy.

4. Efforts are being made to escort the *Mauretania*, *Aquitania* and *Olympic* in and out of New York with a destroyer or destroyers, and

it is hoped in future to be more successful in meeting these ships now that their Approach Route and time of arrival at initial position is known in advance. My report No. 278/42 of 19 June 1918[1] gives the principles upon which our local officers are acting re destroyer, etc., escorts for convoys.

5. *Naval District Craft*

Local patrol and escort services are under the supervision of local Section Commanders and vary with their idiosyncracies; they appear to act on no very clearly defined system and are subject to impulse.

6. A proper organisation for minesweeping or of minesweepers appears to be lacking, and a determined attempt to mine any portion of the coast would probably meet with considerable success – from the enemy's point of view.

7. The Navy Department favour the coastal route for all inter-port US and Canadian traffic, however far apart the ports might be; this is the best course on the assumption of efficient patrol and minesweeping services, but failing this, I regard the open route, at any rate so far as fairly fast and well armed ships are concerned, as preferable, and to this opinion I fancy the Navy Department are slowly coming round.

8. The submarines available for anti-submarine patrol are a source of danger to themselves and of annoyance to shipping in general, while they cause great anxiety to the Navy Department; there is always the doubt when a submarine is reported off the coast whether she may not be American. They have been fired on by merchant ships in several cases and one came in with a 7.5 inch unexploded howitzer shell on board.

9. The efforts with decoy ships have so far been ingenuous; a schooner *with wireless*, generally stationary, with a submarine *on the surface* in attendance. The only result up to date has been to scare considerably various merchant vessels.

10. Aircraft, destroyers, and chasers are very inexperienced and cause much trouble by their continuous reports of attacks on and destruction of non-existent submarines.

11. In general it must be confessed that little reliance can as yet be placed on the anti-submarine defences, and greater importance attaches therefore to the full development and employment by merchant ships of their own resources, to the protection afforded by the variation of Approach Routes used in conjunction with the Diver-

[1] Not reproduced.

sion Code and to the utilization to the fullest extent possible of the experience gained by the British.

****

[Enclosure]

Navy Department to Admiralty

5 September 1918

Distribution of United States Naval Forces Employed against Enemy Submarines in Western Atlantic Waters, 1 September 1918

The forces are being employed in two categories:-
Convoy and escort duty and in anti-submarine patrol – the latter including also some short range escort work, rescue work and minesweeping.

Ocean Escort of Convoys
Detailed to this duty are:-

Seven Armored Cruisers
Three First class cruisers
Two Second ,,   ,,
Eight Third ,,   ,,
Two large auxiliary cruisers
Thirty ocean going destroyers

Escort work of large ships is usual. Present plan is to send two destroyers with each troop convoy; they are to go all the way to port of destination and perform a similar service for westbound convoys.

Naval District Craft
The Atlantic coast of United States is divided into Districts as shown by the accompanying charts.[1] These Districts extend seawards along the parallels of their boundaries. They have for hunting, patrol, rescue and minesweeping the craft shown below.[2] Each District cares for all activities within its area under the general

---

[1] Not reproduced.
[2] Not reproduced.

direction of Navy Department and cooperates with deep-sea and special forces working into or from it.

371.   *Grant to Murray*

1 October 1918

****

6. *Transfer of HB Convoys to United States Control*
In reply to Admiralty telegram 475[1] urging that the arrangements for routing, etc., of HB Convoys should continue to be made between Commodore Wells and the Admiralty as heretofore and as in the case of all other homeward convoys, I sent the following–

> 'Entirely agree present centralization best but fear nothing gained and harm done by re-opening question of HB which is a matter of amour propre. Navy Department determined [to] keep them in US hands all arrangements being made between Naval Department and Sims direct. Question arose with France but Navy Department insisted as US Army in France vitally dependent on HB Convoys, US must be entirely responsible for them and would eventually undertake whole escort, running them every four days. New York Authorities will be largely dependent on Wells's help in their organisation for present. Many signs point to growing US restlessness under British control and they will desire to control this side as you do yours when they feel able. It was officially mooted US should control all convoys carrying their troops but this received no Headquarters support and was easily met. Generally speaking I would suggest we should be clear what is essential to retain in our hands and what is not, giving way on latter when necessary while not placing more of our shipping under United States control than absolutely necessary so that we may hold the reins.'

I quote this as it states fairly clearly what is the position and what are the difficulties we may expect to encounter.
The Navy Department are out to help to the fullest extent in their power and the country is behind them, but the country has an overweening sense of its power and efficiency and is, generally speaking, quite unconscious of the extent to which it depends upon the

---

[1] Not reproduced.

Allies, and British especially, for support, instruction, and guidance. The fact of their dependence is fully recognised by some at the Navy Department, but at the same time it can hardly be expected that they should desire this to become more apparent, and especially known, than can be avoided and it follows also that directly they feel able to shake themselves free of such guidance or leading strings they will wish to do so. Many think the time has now come, some, and the abler, do not, but at any rate we must expect a continuously increasing assertion. I see no reason whatever to anticipate trouble but great care will be needed in order to maintain our influence and leadership, and at the same time to meet their desire for a greater equality in council and control.

In the present instance they were in no way capable of undertaking the HB convoys and Commodore Wells is still, much to his disgust, really doing the work, the United States Navy getting the credit.

****

372. *Admiralty to all Commanders-in-Chief and Senior Officers*

11 November 1918

The armistice is signed. Hostilities are to be suspended forthwith. All anti-submarine defensive measures in force to secure the security of men of war at sea or in harbour are to remain in force until further orders. Submarines on the surface are not to be attacked unless their hostile intention is obvious.

373. *Grant to Admiralty*

3 December 1918

Most urgent representations from Philadelphia for retention of HMS *Cumberland*[1] there over Saturday 7 December Great Britain's Day. Extensive arrangements have been made to celebrate part taken in war by Great Britain and to promote good feeling between the two nations in which HMS *Cumberland* forms principal feature. Have authorised *Cumberland* to remain and trust that you will endorse.

These visits at present juncture are of utmost importance.

[1] HMS *Cumberland*: cruiser, 1904; 9800 tons; 14 × 6 in; 24 knots.

374.   *Grant to Daniels*

Washington,
1 January 1919

On giving up my command as British Commander-in-Chief of the North America and West Indies Station and returning to England, I desire to express the deep thanks and gratitude of myself and the Officers of my staff for the great kindness which has invariably been extended to us by the United States Navy during our stay in Washington.

We shall ever regard it as the greatest honour to have had the privilege of coming to Washington and joining with your Officers in the work of the war and I venture to think that the professional understanding and co-ordination which has been the outcome, and the sincere personal friendships made, will be a lasting symbol of the future relations of our two services acting together in the great work which lies before them.

2. While so many US Naval Officers have been met, one and all showing a great sympathy and anxiety to make our lot a pleasant one, I should fail in my duty were I not to specially mention the consideration and courtesy extended to me at all times by

Admiral W. S. Benson whose sympathetic and genial collaboration has made it a real pleasure to work with him, also

Captain W. V. Pratt with whom perhaps I have had more to do than any other Officer and whose frank and warm nature coupled with his very great ability have aroused in me feelings of the greatest affection and admiration.

3. I should also like to mention the following Officers with whom I and the Officers of my staff have had much work in common.

Rear-Admiral Roger Welles, who at all times has gone out of his way to make my work easy and pleasant.

Commander R. S. Crenshaw, matters relating to Routeing and Convoys, Diversion of traffic, etc.

Lieut-Commander C. E. Gilpin, information regarding submarines and mines and plotting of same.

Captain Waldo Evans, Tactical matters, War Warnings.

Commander C. Belknap, Coaling matters and general questions.

Commander W. B. Woodson, Movements, Provision of United States Escorts.

Lieutenant E. G. Adams, Assistant to Commander Woodson.

4. I should be glad too if the following officers could be informed

how grateful we are to them:-
Captain A. L. Willard, Commandant US Navy Yard [Washington],
and *Lieutenant J. E. Reed (PC)*, for their assistance at all times
especially in matters relating to *Warrior* and our accommodation at
Seventh Street Wharves, which has done so much to add to the
personal comfort of those living on board.[1]

[1] Rear-Admiral Roger Welles, US Navy: DNI. Lt-Cdr Russell S. Crenshaw, US
Navy: ONO. Lt-Cdr C. E. Gilpin, US Navy Reserve: ONO. Captain Waldo Evans,
US Navy: ONO. Cdr Charles C. Belknap, Jr., US Navy: began war as Lt-Cdr, ONO;
later a Cdr aboard armoured cruiser *North Carolina*. Cdr Walter B. Woodson, US
Navy: ONO. Lieut Ernest G. Adams, US Navy Reserve: Navy Dept. Captain A. L.
Willard, US Navy: Commandant, Washington Navy Yard and Superintendent,
Naval Gun Factory. Lieut J. E. Reed, Paymaster Corps, US Navy: Navy Yard,
Washington.

PART IX

BRITANNIA, COLUMBIA AND THE STRUGGLE FOR NEPTUNE'S TRIDENT
APRIL 1917 TO MAY 1919

INTRODUCTION

Since the 1890's British naval policy had been based on a two-power standard, a navy equal to the two next largest fleets, though the scale of the German challenge had reduced the standard to a sixty per cent superiority in capital ships over the High Seas Fleet. The United States Navy, in third place in 1914, was not seen as a threat by the Royal Navy, as its strength was in seas only lightly tenanted by British sea power, and since 1895 there had been a developing *rapprochement* between the two powers which led to a British policy decision, arrived at around 1900, that war with the United States was unthinkable. Under the Roosevelt and Taft administrations (1901–13), the Americans seemed content with local supremacy in the Western Pacific, Caribbean and Western Atlantic; they offered no challenge to the Royal Navy's global predominance. That supremacy was an article of faith among British statesmen, seamen and citizens. The imperative needs of Imperial defence, the security of the home base, the flow of trade, the blockade of enemies and distant water operations on their flanks, as well as deeply-ingrained national tradition and pride, seemed to dictate resolute adherence to British naval supremacy, however small the margin.

When Woodrow Wilson came to power in 1913, the Panama Canal was about to open. American naval strategy centred round this artery, now firmly under Washington's control, for it permitted the United States to maintain a single powerful battlefleet which could be switched from one ocean to another almost overnight.[1] In normal peacetime conditions, the American public would not sanction a naval budget for mighty fleets in both oceans. Wilson, essentially a domestic reformer, was 'Uninterested in military matters'[2] and his nomination of Daniels as Secretary of the Navy underlined the fact, as 'the Right Hon. Josephus', as his critics delighted in calling him, was at least as pacifically inclined as the President. For two years the Wilson administration's naval policy permitted only modest appropriations for new ships and Daniels offered immediate

[1] As Franklin Roosevelt recognised; see document no. 439.
[2] Coletta, *Naval Heritage*, p. 220.

support for Winston Churchill's call in 1913 for a naval holiday. The outbreak of World War I produced no significant increase in the naval budget.

Other Americans, however, were disturbed by the outbreak of · global warfare and America's comparative defencelessness. Well-to-do business, professional and rentier groups on the eastern seaboard formed America's 'Establishment'. Largely conservative and Republican in politics, well-educated and acquainted with the international scene, they began to agitate for 'Preparedness' in the autumn of 1914. Pro-Allied in sentiment (though few of them called for American belligerency at this stage), they demanded a substantial naval programme to enable the United States to fight powerful enemies simultaneously in both oceans. Should an enemy contrive a landing on American shores, a trained conscript army at least a million strong would repel the invaders. Ex-President Theodore Roosevelt led the band, supported by his old friend Senator Henry Cabot Lodge, the latter's son-in-law Representative Augustus P. Gardner, Roosevelt's former Secretary of War and State, Senator Elihu Root, Colonel Robert M. Thompson, President of the Navy League, the aviation propagandist Henry A. Wise Wood, and General Leonard Wood, a former Army Chief of Staff who had founded volunteer training camps. Young Franklin Roosevelt clandestinely supplied ammunition for the group to use against his chief, Daniels.[1]

As the war in Europe settled into stalemate and the U-boats began their campaign against merchantmen, notably with the sinking of the *Lusitania* in May 1915, the Preparedness movement reached proportions formidable enough for Wilson to heed its demands and political significance. In July 1915 he instructed his Secretaries of War and the Navy to prepare major expansion plans. 'Wilson's sudden shift from apathy to all-out support constitutes a landmark in naval policy,' wrote Albion.[2] The President's adoption of Preparedness was an attempt to regain the political initiative and to serve notice on the warring powers that the United States would not only defend its rights and interests but also demand a major voice in the eventual peace settlement. A navy 'equal to the most powerful' would act as both a deterrent and a big stick to support American diplomacy. If the new military and naval power could not be available for this war, then it would serve as an insurance in the event of a

[1] Ward, pp. 300–02.
[2] R. G. Albion, *Makers of Naval Policy, 1798–1947* (Annapolis, Md: NIP 1980), p. 221.

challenge to American security by the war's victors.[1] Wilson also took steps to revive America's moribund merchant marine.[2] At St Louis on 3 February 1916, he declared, 'There is no other navy in the world that has to cover so great an area of defense as the American navy, and it ought, in my judgement, to be incomparably the greatest in the world.'[3] Here was a direct challenge to British naval supremacy, though one understandably ignored at the time by the British. Moreover, while the General Board of the Navy thought in terms of a five-year programme, looking to equality with the Royal Navy by 1925, Wilson wanted the programme completed in three years. This was a far more credible challenge than that of the Germans, for Tirpitz knew that Germany could never sustain simultaneously the most powerful army in Europe and effectively equal British naval strength. The Americans could outbuild the British and the alarmist climate produced by the war gave Wilson the public support to do so. Most of the Navy's senior officers were either anti-British or advocates of ultimate superiority.[4] Passage of the three-year programme in 1916 launched the United States on a voyage to at least parity with the Royal Navy. The programme envisaged ten battleships and six battle cruisers, together with 140 other craft. By 1921 the US Navy was likely to have 27 battleships and six battle-cruisers, in addition to 350 other warships; in modernity and weight of broadside, the American battlefleet would be superior to the Grand Fleet [457].[5] This unprecedented programme had scarcely got under way, however, when the United States was plunged into a maritime war for which her existing fleet was 'peculiarly ill-suited', lacking sufficient flotilla craft and deficient in anti-submarine equipment and training.[6]

It was, of course, the little ships that were so desperately needed in

[1] Daniels to Wilson, 20 August 1915, *Wilson Papers*, vol. 34, p. 267; G. T. Davis, *A Navy Second to None* (New York: Harcourt Brace, 1940), pp. 212, 220–2.
[2] J. J. Safford, *Wilsonian Maritime Diplomacy, 1913–1921* (New Brunswick, NJ: Rutgers UP, 1978); Davis, p. 223; Daniels, *Wilson Era*, vol. 1, p. 416.
[3] Woodrow Wilson, address at St Louis, Mo., 3 February 1916, *Wilson Papers*, vol. 36, pp. 119–20. The President admitted almost immediately that the call for supremacy was an indiscretion; see Wilson to Senator B. R. Tillman (Chairman of the Senate Naval Affairs Committee), 14 February 1916, *Wilson Papers*, vol. 36, p. 174.
[4] G. E. Wheeler, *Admiral W. V. Pratt, US Navy: A Sailor's Life* (Washington: Naval History Division, Navy Dept., 1974), p. 128; Woodrow Wilson, Annual Message, 7 December 1915, *Wilson Papers*, vol. 35, pp. 299–301; Coletta, 'Daniels', pp. 558–63.
[5] Braisted, pp. 200–1.
[6] J. A. S. Grenville & G. B. Young, *Politics, Strategy and American Diplomacy: Studies in Foreign Policy, 1873–1917* (New Haven, Conn: Yale UP, 1969), pp. 297–336, esp. p. 334.

the spring of 1917 and the British pressed the Americans incessantly not only to send across all those they possessed or could commandeer but also to abandon dreadnought construction in favour of light craft. The Americans stolidly refused to amend their 1916 programme. The General Board expressed the official fear that the US Navy might shortly have to meet alone the combined forces of the German and Japanese navies [375, 377, 378, 380]. When the administration was approached about a suspension of dreadnought construction, it took refuge in the constitutional argument that Congress alone could alter the programme. Given that Congressmen displayed 'an occult fascination' with battleships, such amendment was unlikely but the administation could have taken other initiatives.[1] Its refusal to do so was founded upon a belief that the situation was not as bad as the hysterical Allies (and Sims and Page) painted it and, if it was, all the more reason for the United States pressing on with dreadnoughts.

Nevertheless, the British continued to call for a switch to light craft. Gaunt, Balfour, de Chair, Spring-Rice, Page and Sims all conveyed the sense of crisis and urged the supply of merchantmen and escorts in great numbers. Jellicoe requested cheap, quickly-built sloops, de Chair appeared before the House Naval Committee and the War Cabinet pointed out the US Navy's existing superiority over the Japanese in capital ships, both built and projected; what the Americans would need in a war against Japan, the Admiralty advised, were more flotilla craft. The coalition certainly had no need of further capital ships and it was in any case unlikely that any of the planned American vessels would be ready before the end of the war [376–81]. The most remarkable attempt to bring about the cessation of dreadnought construction in favour of destroyers was in fact an American initiative. The ever resourceful House, prone to stray beyond his remit, proposed on his own responsibility a secret treaty whereby the British would afford the United States assistance if the latter were attacked by Japan. In return for the Americans halting work on their capital ships in favour of destroyers, the British would transfer an appropriate number of battleships to the United States in the event of the latter experiencing trouble with Japan. Balfour, though intrigued by House's suggestions, shrewdly pointed out the problems involved. Not only was Britain allied to Japan and would therefore find it difficult to explain the purpose of the treaty but also

[1] H. C. Bywater, *Sea-Power in the Pacific: A Study of the American-Japanese Naval Problem* (Boston: Houghton Mifflin, 1921), p. 122; B. J. Hendrick, 'Hurry Up the Destroyers!', *World's Work*, November 1917, pp. 18–24.

the American diplomatic tradition excluded military alliances. House had not consulted the President, who was a declared opponent of secret diplomacy. Balfour attempted to overcome these hurdles by internationalizing the proposed treaty. The United States, he suggested, should have the right to call upon the Allies for naval assistance for up to four years after the war, the period taken to build a dreadnought; the Japanese would be included in the treaty [380–3]. Page took the lead in presenting the proposal to Wilson.[1] The President rejected the idea flatly as impractical and unpalatable to the American people. He told Wiseman that Japan offered no serious threat to American security and that in any case the war had proved that capital ships were of little value. He proposed to ask Congress for a separate appropriation for new destroyers. This did not, however, settle the question of the priorities in the existing programme and it took a decisive recommendation from Pratt on 20 July 1917 to persuade Daniels to slow down battleship construction and order additional destroyers. Even this was not finally approved until 14 August, by which time the Navy had on order 266 destroyers. The Americans had at last realised that their battleships on the stocks would play no part in this war and that if they did not throw their full weight into the defeat of the U-boat campaign, they might well be faced by the very combination they feared.[2] The delay of four months in going over to an anti-submarine priority aroused disappointment among the Allies and criticism in America. 'We have not played a part which is worthy of the nation and its naval traditions,' complained *World's Work* (a Page periodical) in October 1917.[3]

By the spring of 1918, if the end of the war was not yet in sight, victory over the submarines was at hand. The convoy system was a proven antidote and was rapidly becoming universal; under it, mercantile sinkings were minimal and new construction was about to outstrip losses. It is not surprising, therefore, that Pratt should seek Sims's advice on 2 April as to when the United States could safely resume dreadnought construction. Sims's Planning Section recommended the resumption when the shipping situation eased or when the issue on the Western Front had been settled. It reiterated the 1916 policy, a navy 'more powerful than any Navy that may oppose

[1] Page to Wilson, 6 July and 14 August 1917, *Wilson Papers*, vol. 43, pp. 112, 463–5.
[2] Sir William Wiseman, Memorandum of Conversation with President, 13 July 1917, vol. 43, pp. 172–3; House diary, 9 September 1917, vol. 44, p. 178, *Wilson Papers*; Wheeler, p. 109; Parsons, p. 66; Klachko, pp. 72–3.
[3] *World's Work*, October 1917, pp. 589–91.

it', enjoying a 'commanding superiority' in the Pacific and a 'defensive superiority' in the Atlantic. The American planners expressed
doubts about Britain's benevolence and still counted on the United
States having to face alone the combined fleets of Germany, Japan
and Austria [386, 387]. Even as late as October 1918, the Office of
Naval Operations still saw these three as the likely combined enemy,
but far more significant was its remark that its proposed crash
programme of battleship construction would 'incidentally' bring
about equality with the Royal Navy. In four years, the United States
should build 27 capital ships (the General Board had called for 12
battleships and 16 battle cruisers) [409]. American naval planners
were throwing down the gauntlet and asserting a claim to parity on
the high seas which had lain dormant during the submarine crisis of
1917–18.

The British were engaged in a parallel campaign to maintain their
naval and mercantile supremacy. By the summer of 1918 Geddes
had come to certain broad conclusions. The war was expected to last
for at least another year and in the course of it the Germans were
expected to redouble their U-boat effort.[1] Far more anti-submarine vessels were required, not simply to reinforce convoy escorts but
primarily to hunt and kill U-boats. Geddes intended that most of the
new construction should be provided by the Americans. This would
permit the British to switch shipbuilding resources from naval to
merchant construction. Between July and October 1918, therefore,
much of Geddes's considerable energy was devoted to securing the
'dovetailing' of British and American shipbuilding programmes. He
seized on the visits to Britain of Franklin Roosevelt and the House
Naval Committee[2] to paint a stark contrast between the mighty
British naval effort and the puny contribution of the United States.
Moreover, while the British merchant fleet had lost millions of tons
of shipping, the US merchant marine was enjoying a mushroom
growth. The Americans might now be turning out a vast new tonnage in merchant bottoms but their naval construction was lamentable – eleven vessels in five months compared with over 200 from
British yards. It was likely that the American merchant navy would
surpass Britain's in 1920–21, an event Geddes was determined to
prevent, just as he was committed to ensuring that henceforth the
United States shared equal responsibility for the naval war [388, 391,
395–6]. Discovering that neither Roosevelt nor the Congressmen
could satisfy his requests, he engineered an invitation to visit Daniels

[1] Trask, *Captains and Cabinets*, pp. 301–5.
[2] Freidel, vol. 1, p. 349.

in Washington, hoping thereby to convince the administration of the justice of Britain's case [392–4]. The British delegation arrived in Washington in early October with a sizeable shopping list [397–401]. Apart from 128 destroyers and sundry small craft, the British also demanded compensation in merchant vessels for the repair of American ships in British yards (which naturally reduced British output).[1] Geddes pursued the negotiations with his customary vigour, Daniels with his characteristic langour. The discussions were amicable and both British and American observers commented on the successful nature of the mission. Geddes was more reserved. The United States either could not or would not meet all the British demands. However, their output of warships, hitherto disappointing to the British and embarrassing to themselves, was just coming on stream and they did make considerable promises for 1919.[2] Geddes obtained 'all that can reasonably be expected' but noted that 'the United States will continue to be a naval liability', that is, she would require more naval assistance than she could provide [390, 402–8]. Geddes's relative disappointment was due to several factors. Exposing so bluntly America's tiny share of naval duties was hardly calculated to win from Washington the hearty co-operation he demanded. Furthermore, though the Americans entered into the talks genuinely enough and met the British as far as their capacity permitted, they were unlikely to be anything but indifferent to British wails about the state of the Empire's merchant fleet and the need to restore it to its pre-war level. Moreover, the mission was ill-timed. Its arrival coincided with the onset of armistice negotiations and Geddes angered Wilson by demanding harsh terms for Germany.[3] As his visit coincided with the war's dying coda, Geddes's hard-won if imperfect agreement quickly became redundant.

The sudden, unexpected and total collapse of the Central Powers in the autumn of 1918 caught the coalition unprepared for either an armistice or a peace treaty and the subsequent post-war world. The only agendas for peace, very different from one another in both philosophy and content, were the 'secret treaties' of the Allies, with their promises of enemy territories and loot for the victors, and Woodrow Wilson's lofty Fourteen Points of January 1918, a charter of international self-denial issued originally to induce the Russians

[1] Trask, *Captains and Cabinets*, p. 295. An attempt by Sims to prepare the ground for compensation was slapped down by the Navy Dept in no uncertain terms.

[2] *House Papers*, vol. 3, p. 74, records that only 44 destroyers were completed during the American period of war; Davis, p. 223, asserts that 267 were built by 1922.

[3] Trask, *Captains and Cabinets*, p. 305.

to remain in the war and now proposed by the Germans themselves as the basis for an armistice. To the chagrin of his coalition partners, Wilson conducted the preliminary negotiations from Washington without consulting them; it was the first ominous sign of transatlantic differences on the mode and meaning of diplomacy. The New and Old Worlds were aptly named when sides were taken on the concept and conduct of international relations. Naval issues – the maritime terms of the armistice and peace treaty, the surrender and subsequent disposal of the enemy fleets, the naval side of a League of Nations (Wilson's Fourteenth and greatest point), postwar maritime law and naval strengths after 'a war to end all wars' – exposed major differences between the United Kingdom and the United States.

Mutual resentment had begun to appear before the Armistice. The Americans, for example, were angered by the British de Bunson mission to Latin America, intent on recovering Britain's pre-war economic predominance there (undermined by the Americans during the war) and the British were irritated by American probes in the oil-rich Middle East. The American shipping chief, Edward N. Hurley, claimed that 'The British are fearful that under a League of Nations the United States, with its present wealth and commercial power, may get the jump on the markets of the world'.[1] The sailors were as suspicious of one another's intentions as were the diplomats and the politicians. Their view of international relations, perhaps understandably, was almost universally based upon perpetual confrontation. American naval chiefs were determined to relaunch and complete their 1916 programme and scarcely any senior American officer was prepared to settle for less than equality with the Royal Navy. With the German Navy's future in considerable doubt, the British and American navies were free to nurture suspicions about each other's plans, associations and behaviour.

Anglo-American naval differences surfaced first over the treatment proposed for the German Navy. Both navies were adamant that Germany must surrender a substantial proportion, perhaps all, of her submarines so that she could not resume the campaign after a respite [415]. It was over the fate of the surface fleet that they differed. The British demanded its total destruction and proposed to leave Germany with only a coast defence capability [411, 418, 433],

---

[1] On the oil issue, see F. M. Venn, *Oil Diplomacy in the Twentieth Century* (London; Macmillan, 1986). L. Ambrosius, *Woodrow Wilson and the American Diplomatic Tradition: The Treaty Fight in Perspective* (Cambridge: UP, 1987) pp. 52–3; S. W. Roskill, *Naval policy between the Wars*, vol. 1, *The Period of Anglo-American Antagonism, 1919–1929* (London: Collins, 1968), pp. 22–3.

in which aim they were supported, not surprisingly, by Sims [412].
Wilson, Benson and the London Planning Section desired to leave
Germany with a major fleet, including about ten capital ships. They
envisioned it as a curb on British naval ambitions. If the British had
to take account of a powerful fleet in their rear, they would think
twice about launching aggressive policies elsewhere, such as interfering with American neutral and maritime rights. A Royal Navy with
no European rival could be the instrument of a global dictatorship.
The sinking of the German fleet would be bad enough but even
worse would be its distribution among the victors. The Americans
assumed it would be on the basis of war losses, in which case the
Allies would obtain the whole fleet, leaving the Americans with little
more than a couple of destroyers. The disparity between British and
American naval strength would then be colossal (3:1 in capital ships
alone) – and that was without taking into account Britain's allies.
The Americans predictably opposed distribution. That, though, was
not an issue between the two navies, for on grounds of cost, difficulty of assimilation and superfluity the British had no desire for
German ships (American naval planners nevertheless chose to
ignore this disclaimer) [410–13, 418, 448].

The United States consistently opposed harsh naval armistice and
peace terms, in part to retain Germany as a check on Britain but also
to avoid the creation of revanchism in Germany. As Wilson's Secretary of War, Newton D. Baker, explained, 'The terms of the armistice should be rigid enough to secure us against the renewal of
hostilities by Germany but not humiliating beyond that necessity.'[1]
While the Allied Naval Council demanded stringent armistice conditions, Benson and his staff stood for moderation, a stance supported by the Supreme War Council, which softened the ANC's
proposals, requiring the surrender of all U-boats but only internment for selected surface vessels [417–8]. In line with American
demands, the final disposition of enemy vessels was left to the peace
conference [411]. At the end of the conference the Germans took
matters into their own hands and scuttled the greater part of their
fleet at Scapa Flow. By that time, the British and Americans were 'in
full agreement in their basic objective of eliminating Germany as a
sea power' and both were relieved at the timely disappearance of the
problem.[2] The Americans had come to place greater reliance on the

[1] Trask, *Captains and Cabinets*, p. 327; *House Papers*, vol. 4, pp. 117–36; Marder,
vol. 5, pp. 175–89.
[2] S. P. Tillman, *Anglo-American Relations at the Paris Peace Conference of 1919*
(Princeton, NJ: Princeton UP, 1961), p. 175; Klachko, p. 127.

League of Nations as the guarantor of world peace; the German Navy thus seemed less relevant.

For a time, the Americans toyed with a League of Nations Navy, which inevitably would be under the control of its two largest components, the Royal Navy and the United States Navy. Wilson and Pratt seem to have thought it a viable proposition but Benson and most other seamen considered it impracticable.[1] Pratt championed it as a device to compel parity between the two fleets, while Benson was insistent that the League, with or without its own Navy, must not be dominated by one power; it must have at least two navies of equal strength [422–4, 428, 429, 442, 443]. The British were almost universally sceptical about a League Navy, and indeed about the efficacy of collective security [414, 431, 449]. Churchill was adamant that the League could not replace the Royal Navy as the guarantor of imperial security.[2]

From the outset of peace talks, Wilson had insisted 'I cannot consent to take part in the negotiation of a peace which does not include freedom of the seas.'[3] This was more than a ritual reiteration of a traditional American policy, it was the principle for which the United States had gone to war. Moreover, the Americans had almost as strong a grievance against Britain, since her interference with American trade was more extensive than Germany's; the single crucial difference was that the British method did not cost lives. American anger at British blockade policy and the stopping, searching and seizure of US merchantmen had reached boiling point on several occasions, Wilson exclaiming to House on 24 September 1916, 'Let us build a bigger navy than hers and do what we please!'[4] Though America perforce supported the Allied blockade during her belligerency, the Wilson administration never abandoned its underlying belief. As the head of British intelligence in the United States, Sir William Wiseman, remarked to Sir Eric Drummond on 25 January 1918, 'I think trade rivalry after the war and freedom of the seas are going to be the two dangerous rocks for Anglo-American relations.' Thus it proved, for at Paris there was 'a bruising diplomatic clash' between the two nations.[5] Wilson had told Geddes as

[1] Marder, vol. 5, pp. 244–7; Klachko, pp. 137–8.

[2] A. Walworth, *America's Moment: 1918: American Diplomacy at the End of World War I* (New York: Norton, 1977), p. 151.

[3] Trask, *Captains and Cabinets*, pp. 337–8.

[4] C. Seymour, *American Diplomacy During the World War* (Baltimore: Johns Hopkins UP, 1934), p. 77.

[5] W. B. Fowler, *British-American Relations, 1917–1918: The Role of Sir William Wiseman* (Princeton, NJ: Princeton UP, 1969), p. 198; Tillman, p. 39.

early as October 1918 that the world was no longer willing to tolerate British naval mastery and the Naval Advisory Staff reiterated his demand for the absolute freedom of the seas in peace and war [413, 414, 448]. As the American planners observed, the British did not believe in freedom of the seas in wartime [416]; indeed, the British felt that belligerents must fight for control of the seas in wartime, albeit with as little interference to neutral shipping as was consistent with the prosecution of their cause[414].

The airing of this issue at Paris brought about a direct confrontation between Lloyd George and Wilson which, if it had persisted, might have wrecked the conference. Lloyd George insisted that Britain could not abandon its historic and virtually sole strategic weapon, the blockade of enemy coasts; Wilson stood by his Second Point. The impasse was resolved by Wilson's retreat. When Lloyd George offered to discuss the issue at the Peace Conference proper, Wilson accepted the olive branch, though he knew that Lloyd George would not shift his ground on the vital importance to Britain of the strategy of blockade. Wilson covered his retreat by announcing that 'Under the League of Nations there are no neutrals'. In fact, Wilson had little leverage, for Britain had accepted the other thirteen points and her support for the League of Nations was a prerequisite for the adherence of the other powers. Further argument on this one point, House advised Wilson, would result in 'serious friction and delay', a loss of time which the President could not afford. Wilson, as with so many other cherished points, had to leave Point Two for the League of Nations to sort out, an outcome which suited Lloyd George.[1] As Tillman concludes, 'the issue was thus settled on the basis of a major American concession as an issue which, in the strongest possible terms, had been declared to be beyond compromise'; the Americans thus conceded the very principle for which they had gone to war.[2]

The most intractable Anglo-American problem arose from the American demand for parity, signalled by the 1916 programme, latent until victory was assured but then reaffirmed by the US Navy's planners [386, 387, 434, 435]. The Germans and Austrians being now at the mercy of the peacemakers, a new antagonist had to be found to justify so huge a peacetime programme. The memoranda thus began to explore America's differences with Britain and to

[1] Trask, *Captains and Cabinets*, pp. 341-2; Parsons, p. 172; Walworth, pp. 59, 62, 63, 65; Trask, 'Benson', p. 18; Klachko, pp. 124, 138.
[2] Tillman, p. 51; E. N. Hurley, *The Bridge to France* (Philadelphia: Lippincott, 1927), pp. 260-1. Hurley said that the British 'never were quite able to comprehend

discuss the possibility of hostilities between them [410, 435]. The planners took an adversarial view of international relations, based upon inevitable economic competition, resolvable only by war.[1] Benson in particular made much of Britain's alliances, her exclusive trade and communications policies, her history of crushing her rivals and her determination to cling to her superiority. He warned Wilson and Daniels of the 'great danger' to the United States posed by a malicious and perfidious Albion [417, 429, 446, 447, 450, 455]. Always darkly suspicious of British intentions, he noted their unease about America's naval and mercantile programmes [417, 446]. He was supported by the London Planning Section (which became his Naval Advisory Staff in Paris), a cabal whose world picture was as bleak and unalterably confrontational as that of any prophet of doom [410, 435]. Moreover, the United States was now undeniably the world's greatest power and 'professional logic demanded that her navy reflect this superiority'.[2]

American fears and ambitions were rationalised in a new three-year programme launched by Daniels in the autumn of 1918. Naked confrontation was not the influence behind the Secretary's 'carbon copy' of the 1916 programme; rather, his purpose was to ensure perpetual peace [421, 435-8]. This '1919 programme' had two objects in view. It served notice to the American people that failure to endorse the League of Nations would compel the adoption of a costly 'Fortress America' policy. Secondly, the largely unenthusiastic Europeans would be cowed into joining the League; with them and the United States safely in the bag, the new programme could be quietly dropped. In addition to intimidating the Allies at the peace table, the Americans, who 'meant business', were determined not to yield to a British blockade in a future war in which the United States was again neutral. Furthermore, as Roosevelt explained to the anxious British, the United States had to defend lengthy coastlines, distant possessions and a burgeoning trade [439]. This zeal for headlong naval expansion in peacetime was astonishing, 'a manifestation of militarism by an Administration which has been distinguished above all in recent American history by pacifistic tendencies'.[3] However, equality on the seas enjoyed broad political support, at least as a long-term policy aim. The 1916 programme,

[Wilson's] meaning, or just what significance "freedom of the seas" had for them'.
[1] Trask, *Captains and Cabinets*, p. 289.
[2] Westcott, p. 336; Klachko, pp. 158-60.
[3] F. P. Stockbridge, 'Our Navy and a League of Nations', *World's Work*, February 1919, pp. 436-7; *World's Work*, July 1919, pp. 239-40; Marder, vol. 5, p. 226.

when completed, would endow the United States with qualitative parity by 1923–24, as the US capital ships would be more modern and muster heavier broadsides than most of the British vessels [434, 457]. The carrying out of the 1919 'repeat order' would ensure for America 'substantial superiority'.[1]

The British (and Sims) were alarmed, angered and puzzled by this display of American aggressiveness. 'The whole business of Anglo-Saxon brotherhood and hands across the sea underwent a sharp deflation.'[2] How could the Americans speak simultaneously of a League of Nations and disarmament and also of 'a navy second to none'? [421] The British sought desperately for explanations other than hostility to the British Empire. It was 'inconceivable' that enmity fuelled the demand for parity, though it was difficult to predict the future and the challenge of the US Navy 'must be a matter of great concern to us', as it was now the only possible rival. The Admiralty speculated that the 1919 programme was designed either to give the United States a substantial voice in the League or to deter the Japanese, 'for the belief in an eventual struggle with that country is deeply rooted in the minds of many Americans' [422, 423, 440].

Tradition and pride, as much as strategic calculations, impelled Britain to defend its superiority [441]. The Americans remained unconvinced of the British case for continued supremacy. 'Neither side could understand the point of view of the other,' wrote Marder.[3] Lloyd George led the British defence. The Prime Minister exhibited 'a pugnacious determination to maintain British naval supremacy', affirming in November 1918 that Britain 'would spend her last guinea to keep a navy superior to that of the United States or any other Power, and that no Cabinet official could continue in Government in England who took a different position'. When House reminded him that 'We had more money, we had more men, our national resources were greater', he moderated his line: 'If the League of Nations is a reality, I am willing to discuss the matter.' House, a natural conciliator, assured him that 'it was not our purpose to go into a naval building rivalry with Great Britain' but he also reflected the President's view that 'It was our purpose to have our rights at sea safeguarded, and that we did not intend to have our commerce regulated by Great Britain whenever she was at war.'[4]

[1] Coletta, *Naval Heritage*, p. 220; Roskill, vol. 1, pp. 71–2.
[2] Davis, p. 254.
[3] Marder, vol. 5, p. 232.
[4] J. K. McDonald, 'Lloyd George and the Search for a Postwar Naval Policy, 1919',

By the spring of 1919 'tension between the United States and Great Britain reached formidable proportions'. British naval supremacy was likened to Prussian militarism and Daniels was dubbed 'a resurrected Tirpitz'. The climax came in 'the naval battle of Paris' between Wemyss and Benson in March 1919 [445, 446]. 'The sailors arrived at the conference breathing fire', reported Wiseman. While Benson was thoroughly chauvinistic, Wemyss seems to have forgotten his aristocratic breeding and diplomatic protocol on two occasions. Lloyd George deployed all of his formidable political skills to secure another American retreat. He resurrected the possibility of the distribution of the German fleet, intimated that he might oppose the inclusion of the Monroe Doctrine in the League Covenant and even sowed doubt about British membership of the League.[1] Other British leaders were less eager to challenge the Americans. Jellicoe expressed a desire not to build against them but warned that Imperial security could not rest upon the good will of another power. Furthermore, it 'would be unwise to depend on US naval co-operation in the event of trouble arising between the British Empire and Japan.' The King, Grey, Bonar Law and other British and Canadian statesmen urged that Britain should not respond aggressively to the American policy but seek instead naval co-operation.[2] Talk turned to the likelihood of Daniels carrying his programme. Admiral Grant, lately CinC North America and West Indies, thought he would fail to do so, provided the British did not adopt a bellicose stance. The Republicans were opposed to the scheme, chiefly on grounds of cost. Their elder statesman Theodore Roosevelt had told the British that Congress would not support the programme. The Republicans also aimed to curb Presidential power after its wartime dominance and they seemed content to leave Britain with the responsibility of policing the world's seas. Prominent Republican Senators such as Lodge, Borah, La Follette and Norris, already plotting Wilson's downfall over the League, remarked that the United States had fought militarism apparently only to become militant herself. Moreover, battleships were useless in modern conditions, there were no enemies on the horizon, and the United States

in A. J. P. Taylor, ed., *Lloyd George: Twelve Essays* (London: Hamish Hamilton, 1971), p. 191; *House Papers*, vol. 4, pp. 160–4, 180–1.

[1] Tillman, p. 37; *House Papers*, vol. 4, p. 179; Klachko, pp. 144–51; M. G. Fry, *Illusions of Security: North Atlantic Diplomacy*, 1918–22 (Toronto: University of Toronto Press, 1972), pp. 37–8; Braisted, p. 434.

[2] Jellicoe to Long, 3 March 1919 and 3 February 1920, *Jellicoe Papers*, vol. 2, pp. 293, 393; Fry, pp. 7, 10, 17, 30.

should take the lead in preventing another arms race.[1] Grant concluded that the better educated Americans were well disposed towards Britain; only the Irish and German immigrant blocs were hostile and the general public seemed indifferent to a big navy [436, 441]. Wilson's political strength ebbed daily as the untreated problems of post-war readjustment burgeoned; his party had been all but repudiated by the electorate in November 1918. The President's attempt to frighten the Allies (and the US Senate) into acceding to his demands began to appear absurd. 'If the threat of a great American naval program was designed as a club to compel adherence to Wilson's peace program,' wrote Tillman, 'then it was indeed a stuffed club.'[2]

Nevertheless, tempers needed to be cooled and a solution found. Long and Daniels, old political hands and amiable men of common sense, though worried by their professional advisors' dogged refusal to compromise, did not openly oppose them. The naval officers were quietly shunted away from the negotiations. The dispute was referred to 'two men of good will', House and Lord Robert Cecil, and in April 1919 they patched up a compromise which held until the Washington Conference of December 1921 effected a more permanent solution. The British had wanted the cessation of all American building beyond those ships already well advanced [447] and Cecil began by reaffirming Lloyd George's commitment to superiority. House, while echoing Wilson's assurance that the United States had 'no idea ... of building a fleet in competition with Great Britain', was equally determined to seek parity. It seemed that the impasse might continue but both men were committed to the League of Nations and a permanent Anglo-American accord and 'agreed that the point of view of the fighting services made any accommodation between the nations very difficult'; they were resolved to find one. In return for the abandonment of much of the 1916 programme and the whole of that of 1919, the United Kingdom would confirm her membership of the League, support the inclusion of the Monroe Doctrine in the Covenant and agree to the destruction of the German ships. House replied that only Congress could cancel the 1916 ships but the administration would consider postponing the 1919 programme until after the Peace Conference and would abandon it once the League of Nations got safely under way. Cecil accepted the American assurances. The House–Cecil agreement was something of an anti-climax to an absurd episode. According parity to the United

[1] Coletta, 'Daniels', pp. 558–63; Davis, pp. 264–6; Parsons, p. 179.
[2] Tillman, p. 294.

States was unlikely to affect Imperial security and, as House had pointed out, the United States could achieve parity or even superiority whenever she chose to do so; a war-ravaged British economy could not fund competitive building. When the Washington Conference took place, the British settled gladly for parity. However, in 1919 the British held the firmer ground, for taxpayers in all the warring countries were unlikely to sanction a further arms race [456].[1]

By May 1919 the situation was beginning to clarify. Daniels, fundamentally pacific and conciliatory, sought to reassure the British of America's good will. He reiterated America's need of a large navy but also acknowledged the British Empire's dependence upon sea power. Calling for the continuation of wartime co-operation, he hinted clearly that the 1919 programme would be withdrawn as soon as the League of Nations was established. His visit to London in May found both sides still holding their positions but both also determined to preserve the transatlantic accord [451–4]. Benson continued to insist on the untrustworthiness of the British [455] but Pratt believed that the future of the world rested upon Anglo-American co-operation [407, 424, 429]. The most percipient statesmen of the day – House, Grey, Cecil, Churchill and even Fisher [432] – realised that quarrels of this kind 'obscured the identity of interests' between the two nations. The naval confrontation had evaporated by the time the Peace Conference proper met in May and the Peace Treaty was signed amicably in June 1919. Daniels's parting from Long was as cordial as could be wished [458] and the 1919 programme died quietly, yet nothing had been resolved. If 'everything remained to be played for in the field of maritime supremacy', this was a brief illusion, for as Paul Kennedy has pointed out, only a truce was possible, since Britain had few cards to play.[2]

In assessing the impact of the proposed 1919 programme, *World's Work* observed correctly that 'it is not clear precisely what this manoeuvre has accomplished, except to arouse ill feeling in Great Britain and cause distrust throughout the world concerning the pacific intentions of the United States.' American demands for equality or supremacy had little to do with defence requirements and a great deal more to do with ham-fisted diplomacy and 'spreadeagleism'. The British adopted a die-hard commitment to supremacy for no good strategic reason. There were major diplomatic and

---

[1] Marder, vol. 5, pp. 233–4; *House Papers*, vol. 4, pp. 418–23; Braisted, pp. 435–7.
[2] Marder, vol. 5, p. 236; Roskill, vol. 1, p. 100; P. M. Kennedy, *The Rise and Fall of British Naval Mastery* (London: Macmillan, 1983), p. 263.

commercial differences between the two nations but more severe crises had passed off peacefully and the British were almost alone among the great powers in manifesting enthusiasm for Wilson's ideals. 'For their own sakes and that of the world,' concluded *World's Work*, the United Kingdom and the United States 'should cultivate the spirit of the most amicable co-operation.'[1] An artificial naval rivalry, which persisted for another decade, helped to preclude an intimate relationship which, had it flowered, might have prevented a second global catastrophe.

In the two years from 1917 to 1919, two navies which had hitherto enjoyed little official contact were forced into an intimate relationship by the hostile actions of a third navy. Before the US declared war in April 1917, explorations of possible co-operation were furtive and unofficial. Even when the Americans adopted belligerency, it took them many months to galvanize their people, industries and armed services and it was not until the House mission of November 1917 that the US can be said to have entered wholeheartedly into the prosecution of the war. Doubts about Allied prospects, Admiralty strategy and conduct, and fears of a future hostile combination of East and West, were only dissipated fully when Benson came over with House. The final twelve months of hostilities saw co-operation at its most intense, productive and harmonious. Success in the war, however, sowed fresh doubt, distrust and disharmony, as each power began to lay plans for the post-war world. The absence of other competitors and enemies and the headlong growth of American power, together with the increasingly perceptible decline of British strength, brought the two navies face to face in the famous but rather discreditable 'Sea Battle of Paris' (March 1919). Chauvinism, ambition, naval logic and personal inadequacies brought about the confrontation, and though an open break was averted, it took hard argument to restore a temporary amicability; at that time, in the confused aftermath of the most chastening and traumatic bloodbath in modern history, no more was possible than a tenuous truce. The right to Neptune's trident was still a matter of contention and only in the economy-driven atmosphere of late 1921 was a more permanent solution forthcoming. By the Washington Naval Treaty of December 1921 the two nations agreed, rather gracelessly on the part of the professional advisors, to share the trident. The attempt to extend arms limitation at sea foundered in 'the naval battle of Geneva' in 1927 and it took personal discussions between two pro-

---

[1] *World's Work*, July 1919, pp. 239–40.

fessed pacific statesmen, President Herbert Hoover and the British Prime Minister, Ramsay MacDonald, to bring about final accord at London in 1930, an agreement amicably extended in 1934–36, also at London.

In 1938, as the clouds of war rumbled once more, covert naval discussions between the two great navies began again. This was the first step on the way to a formidable combination of maritime strength, sufficient to overcome enemies in all corners of the globe, though many catastrophes were suffered before the final triumphs. The co-operation of World War II surpassed that of World War I not only in extent but also in genuine integration of strategic and tactical doctrine and, despite prickly personalities on both sides, in deep personal friendships at all levels.

375. *Memorandum by the General Board of the US Navy*[1]

20 April 1917

Types of vessels required for present and future conditions

In making preparations to meet the emergencies of the present war as they arise, it is the part of wisdom to keep constantly in view the possibilities of the future. One of these possibilities is a war resulting from the present one in which the United States may be confronted by Germany and Japan operating conjointly in the Atlantic and Pacific; it is also possible that we may have to meet these two powerful navies without allies to restrict the operations of the German fleet; and while the contingency outlined above may appear remote because of the entente now established, the experience of warring nations is that the apparently impossible in war should receive the most careful consideration.

2. Our procedure so far has been the normal one of an unprepared people confronted by war with powerful nations. ...

3. ... to be ready, the United States must hasten the development of a symmetrical fleet equipped with the fighting units in the proportions which experience in this and other wars has proved to be imperatively necessary for its successful operation, ...

****

7. ... the United States fleet is so deficient in screening vessels, battle cruisers, scouts and destroyers, that it could not logically leave the shelter of a protected port to seek and fight the enemy on the high seas except at great disadvantage. The total available United States scouting force, cruisers and destroyers, could not break through the British or German screen such as employed in the battle of Jutland, and against the above assumed United States force operating in the Pacific, the Japanese would have the advantage of a greater number of screening vessels, assisted by four powerful battle cruisers of 28 knots speed.[2]

[1] Rear-Admiral Charles J. Badger, Senior Member Present.

[2] The General Board estimated that in 1920 Japan would have 8 battleships and 5 battle cruisers in service, with 3 further battleships and 2 battle cruisers authorised, as against an American strength of 21 battleships and 5 battle cruisers completed, with 6 battleships and 1 battle cruiser authorised. The US would have a slight preponderance of cruisers and destroyers but this would be more than offset if she had to face Germany (estimated to have 26 battleships and 10 battle cruisers plus numerous lighter craft in 1920) simultaneously with Japan. To meet these combined forces the US Navy would require a further 23 capital ships by 1920!

****

9. The General Board considers that the most urgent need of the fleet today is to provide a screen for the fleet; that every possible effort should be made, beginning now, to increase (1) scouts and cruisers, (2) destroyers, (3) battle cruisers, in accordance with the requirements indicated by the above comparison; and that, further, the construction of battleships and submarines should be continued and expedited, using the full resources of the nation to do so.

376. *Jellicoe to de Chair*

7 May 1917

The type of ship desired by Admiralty is sloop of *Viola* class.[1] We do not now desire to build ships of ordinary mercantile type for Admiralty work but only patrol craft of which *Viola* type is best for rapid construction.

377. *de Chair to Jellicoe*

Washington,
9 May 1917

I attended Naval Committee of Congress[2] on Friday last and strongly urged commandeering of all necessary small craft in US harbours and suspension of work on capital ships. Am informed that impression on Committee was favourable and Bill for appropriation of shipping was much advanced thereby. Question of suspending work on new construction capital ships is not however settled and present capacity of shipyards and slips is fully taken up. Navy Department is nervous about Japan after war.[3] They fear she may threaten US. Am finding great difficulty in placing orders for small craft due to Navy Dept. controlling all Shipyards. Shipbuilders are compelled to obtain permission of Navy Dept. before undertaking any work.

[1] The wartime 'Flower' class sloops displaced 1250 tons and carried 2 × 4in guns and depth charge throwers; they made about 16 knots. *Viola* herself was torpedoed off Northern Ireland but salved.

[2] Probably the Naval Affairs Committee of the House of Representatives.

[3] This nervousness was pervasive in Washington and had persisted for over a decade. See T. A Bailey, *Theodore Roosevelt and the Japanese–American Crises* (Stanford, Calif.: Stanford UP, 1934) and W. R. Braisted, *The United States Navy in the Pacific, 1909–1922* (Austin, Texas: University of Texas Press, 1971).

378. *de Chair to Admiralty*

10 May 1917

United States Navy Department have not yet dropped capital ship programme as they fear supremacy of Japanese Navy after the war. The suggestion has been made though not by responsible heads of Departments that if capital ship programme is dropped British Government should guarantee assistance to United States after the war in case of trouble with Japan. Can any information be given as to extent and progress of new construction for Japanese Navy as I am continually being asked if Japan is continuing work on new capital ships.

379. *Head of M Branch, Admiralty Intelligence Division,[1] to de Chair*

16 May 1917

Suggestion referred to in second sentence is receiving consideration. Present plans of Japanese Navy Department are limited to maintenance of a main fleet of 8 battleships and 4 battle cruisers all not more than 8 years' old. Battleships now under construction: *Ise* completes Decr. 1917; *Hyuga* completes July 1918; *Nagato* delayed but will be laid down this year. Future programme to lay down 1 battleship in 1917–18, 1 battleship and 1 battle cruiser in 1918–19, 1 battleship and 1 battle cruiser in 1920–21.[2] It is anticipated this programme will be in the main adhered to.

380. *Balfour to Lord Robert Cecil[3]*

British Embassy,
Washington,
14 May 1917

Large United States programme for capital ships makes construction of any considerable number of additional destroyers impossible. We have suggested the abandonment for the present of capital

---

[1] The head of M Branch was not identified.

[2] *Ise* (1917), *Hyuga* (1918): 31 260 tons; 12 × 14in, 20 × 5in; 6 tt; 23 knots. *Nagato*: 1920; 32 000 tons; 8 × 16in; 24 knots.

[3] Lord [Algernon] Robert Cecil (later 1st Viscount Chelwood) (1864–1958): Under Secretary, Foreign Office (Balfour's deputy); Minister of Blockade (later Economic Warfare); a man of peace and probably the keenest British advocate of the League of Nations.

ships, but the fear of Japan is so great, both in the Navy Department and elsewhere, that we have made no progress. In discussion with Colonel House yesterday latter suggested that programme might be modified in direction we desire if United States could receive a guarantee from us that if necessity arose they could call on us for assistance in capital ships to a not less extent than number which would have been completed under present programme. Danger to which United Kingdom might be exposed in such conditions from German fleet was pointed out to him. He then developed the idea, and suggested arrangement might take a wider form and be mutual; in short a defensive alliance on the sea between United States and ourselves. He was in favour of a secret agreement on these lines, but I doubt whether this is consistent with United States constitution, and, in any case, it is a violent departure from United States practice.

If, however, you agree to general principle, I would consult him as to the best method of carrying it out. Personally I consider that, apart from all-important need for more destroyers, there would be quite an advantage in obtaining anything in the nature of a defensive alliance with United States. Of course Japan's susceptibilities will have to be spared, but this should not be difficult to manage.[1]

381.   *Cecil to Spring-Rice*

4 June 1917

Question of future naval co-operation with the United States has now been carefully considered by War Cabinet who are in general agreement with the views which I expressed in above telegram,[2] but, much as they would like to be in a position to give forthwith a formal guarantee of naval aid to the United States for the future and out of that to develop a definite naval alliance, they are of opinion that its announcement at Tokio, which could not justifiably be withheld, must inevitably raise in a highly dangerous form the whole extent of Anglo-Japanese relations and would certainly be interpreted by Japan as primarily aimed at blocking her ambitions in China, the Pacific and the Far East generally.

The United States Government must, however, be aware that,

---

[1] Balfour was being unduly optimistic; Japan would have demanded a substantial *quid pro quo*.
[2] Not reproduced.

quite independently of any diplomatic agreements that might be concluded, this country would be unable to refrain from going to America's assistance in case of need, and they can hardly feel that they are incurring any serious risk in shaping their naval policy on that assumption and foregoing the formal guarantee which, as stated, the present international situation makes it difficult for His Majesty's Government to give, short of a general recasting of existing agreements.

His Majesty's Government have indeed been primarily impressed by the prospect of the possible development of Anglo-American naval co-operation in the future, but they have also given their attention to the technical considerations which gave rise to the larger question, namely the reluctance of the United States Government to alter their naval programme in favour of the construction of additional destroyers.

With some important exceptions, the American fleet is much superior to the Japanese numerically and otherwise. Of the larger capital ships, both constructed and under construction, with the exception of battle cruisers, the United States have already a considerable preponderance. On the other hand, their number of fast light cruisers is, in the opinion of our Naval authorities, quite inadequate for the operations of a fleet of the dimensions of that of the United States, while their superiority in destroyers over Japan is also insufficient.

The most urgent requirements of the American navy as against Japan are in fact for light cruisers, destroyers and anti-submarine craft, and, with the exception of the battle cruisers, it would be a waste of resources for the United States Government to build more capital ships. The same requirements apply to the present war, and it seems essential that the United States Government should concentrate on building the classes of vessels required even at the cost of postponing the completion of the dreadnought battleships.

Your Excellency should take an early opportunity of resuming the discussion begun by Mr Balfour with Colonel House, or elsewhere, and developing agreements in favour of the United States modifying their naval programme as desired by us, and, with regard to the ultimate question of a naval guarantee from us or an Alliance you should, while explaining our difficulties, make it clear that we are extemely disappointed at being unable at once to surmount them and that only the sensitiveness of the Far Eastern situation under present circumstances prevents us from tackling the problem immediately.

382. *Memorandum by Balfour*

22 June 1917

Future Naval Construction in the United States

I gather from the Minutes of the War Cabinet that I am supposed to have promised to prepare a statement about a suggestion, which I have put forward in order to enable the American Navy Department to divert all their energies from the task of building capital ships – which would be useless during the present war – to the construction of destroyers and other anti-submarine craft – which are urgently required.

The reason, and the only reason so far as I am aware, which prevents the Navy Department from carrying out this policy – which they admit to be desirable so far as the present war is concerned – is that, when the present war is over, they may find themselves, with a much smaller fleet of capital ships than they had originally designed to build, in the face of a German fleet (which will still be powerful, because it does not come out to fight its enemy) and a Japanese fleet (which has no enemy to fight). This, say the Navy Department, is too great a risk for America to run, and therefore, however reluctant, we are compelled to employ money, labour, and dockyard space on building ships which are admittedly useless for the war on which we are engaged.

My suggestion is that for four years, *i.e.*, for the time required to build new capital ships, America should have a right to call other fleets to her assistance, in case of maritime attack.

****

383. *Gaunt to Jellicoe*

10 July 1917

While discussing situation with Captain Pratt who is very keen to help me in every way possible I asked him plainly if they could not do better on the building programme. He told me confidentially 'if their future was assured' after the war, in other words if they could make certain that any alteration in their building programme of capital ships would be fully made up to them he was certain 'the Admiral [Benson] would do a great deal more'. I am sure there is quite a strong feeling amongst some of the leading men along this line. I realise the foregoing is a diplomatic question but thought I ought to let you know privately of what might be a practicable way of speeding up construction of class of vessels required.

384. *Gaunt to Admiralty*

12 February 1918

Bureau of Ordnance are asking me for general opinion as to thickness and dispositions of armour for Battle Cruisers and are temporarily holding up their designs to see if we could render them any advice or assistance which would be much appreciated.[1]

385. *Third Sea Lord[2] to Gaunt*

13 February 1918

Full particulars of *Hood* class[3] have been furnished both to US Constructor McBride[4] and to our Constructor Goodall[5] who is now in Washington.

Armour protection of *Hood* design was most carefully considered and was increased after the first design was made in view of lessons learnt during War.[6] It is considered that design now embodies best form of protection compatible with the weight which can be allowed for this item in the design.

Goodall is in a position to discuss general question.

386. *Pratt to Sims*

2 April 1918

****

I would like an estimate from your point-of-view of the time when we should begin to change our present building policy (which you

---

[1] The six battle cruisers of the 1916 programme.

[2] Rear-Admiral (later Admiral Sir) Lionel Halsey (1872–1949): at siege of Lady-smith 1899–1900; Captain 1905; commanded battle cruiser *New Zealand* 1912–June 1915; Commodore 1st Class and Captain of Fleet 1915–16; 4th Sea Lord 1916; Rear-Admiral April 1917; 3rd Sea Lord 1916–June 1918; 2nd Battle Cruiser Squadron October 1918; Chief of Staff to Prince of Wales on visit to North America 1919 and Australia and New Zealand 1920; Vice-Admiral and lent to RAN 1921; retired list 1922; Admiral 1926.

[3] HMS *Hood*: battle cruiser, 1920; 42000 tons; 8 × 15in; 30.5 knots. One of four projected (*Rodney, Anson, Howe* all suspended March 1917, later cancelled). Pre-Jutland design but plans revised in light of battle.

[4] Constructor Commander Lewis B. McBride, US Navy: assistant to Naval Attaché, London; later on Sims's staff.

[5] Acting Constructor S. V. Goodall.

[6] *Hood*: armour: lower belt 12in; lower bow and stern 5–6in; mid-belt 7in; mid-belt (bow) 5in; upper belt 5in; gunhouses 11–15in; conning tower 9–11in; improved bulges

know is a drive on the destroyers, submarine chasers , submarines and merchant ship program) and return to the big ship program. ... You people are in a wonderful position to get a world point-of-view which will never happen again.

387. *Memorandum by US Planning Section*

May 1918

National Policy

****

The basic national policies of the United States may then be summarised as follows:-

1. Self preservation.
2. Defensive self-interest as required for political and economic self-preservation.
3. The Monroe Doctrine, including the responsibilities which it entails.
4. Non-interference with political affairs, and non-acquisition of territory in the Eastern Hemisphere.
5. No entangling alliances.
6. Equality of trade opportunity, and freedom of the seas.
7. Control of the Panama Canal and of the Caribbean Sea.
8. Exclusion of Asiatics from United States territory.[1]

****

... our sole means of fighting alone a Great Power is by naval force. Aircraft may in time present another method of attack, provided our national morality will permit us to make war on the unarmed.

From the above we conclude that our primary weapon, either for offense or defense, must be the Navy; and that our Navy must be more powerful than any Navy that may oppose it.

In a political survey of the world at present, it is obvious that there are but three great aggressive Powers, Great Britain, Germany and Japan. The possibility that Great Britain will ever be an ally of either

and double internal HT screens.
  [1] The list omits the Open Door policy with respect to China. In notes issued in 1899 and 1900, the US supported diplomatically (though not militarily) the political independence and territorial integrity of China and free trade for all comers in China, special privileges for none. The Japanese increasingly opposed this policy and it was a major cause of friction with the US and contributed to the war between them in 1941.

Germany or Japan against us is too small to merit consideration. On the other hand, the motives that will keep Great Britain from siding against us cannot be counted upon to bring her to our support.

****

The most powerful combination against us that we may expect is therefore Germany, Austria and Japan in alliance. *Considering national temperaments, interests and tendencies we cannot assume we have a due degree of security unless we are prepared to fight at sea the German, Austrian and Japanese Navies simultaneously.*

****

Basic Naval Policy of United States

The Navy of the United States shall be a self-contained organisation designed to exercise, in the Pacific, a commanding superiority of naval power, and, in the Atlantic, a defensive superiority of naval power against all potential enemies who may seek to extend their sphere of influence over, or to impose their sovereignty on, any portion of the American Continent or Islands contiguous thereto, not now in their possession, or who may unjustly interfere with our international rights or our trade expansion.[1]

****

... our basic naval policy should not be modified, but that we should for the present bend all our energies towards winning the present war by completing our Destroyer and Chaser programmes as soon as possible, and by increasing in every possible way the output of our merchant tonnage.

When to take up new Naval Programme

Whenever the military situation in France reaches a decision, or when the need for shipping is no longer a controlling factor in the present war, the shipbuilding resources of the country should turn their efforts sharply to the Naval programme. In order to determine what this programme should be, we have to consider present relative strengths of the navies which, either singly or collectively, may be opposed to us.[2]

---

[1] This policy was revised several times in the 1920s but remained substantially the same.
[2] The paper goes into elaborate detail on ships, bases and areas of operation. The date when the two requirements were satisfied was August 1918.

****

388.   *Memorandum by Geddes for War Cabinet*

2 August 1918

Naval Effort – Great Britain and the United States of America

... As the Cabinet knows, the relationship and co-operation between the British and US Navies is as cordial and close as could be wished; I submit this memorandum merely so that these important questions may be raised for discussion.

Naval

There is no doubt that broadly speaking the burden of the Allies in naval warfare is mainly borne by Great Britain. ...

The following is a general comparison of the Fleets of Great Britain and the United States into three main classes:-

	Great Britain	United States Total Forces	Forces in European Waters
Warships	1,250	286	109
Auxiliary Patrol Vessels	3,350	417	105
Non-Combatant Auxiliaries, Colliers, Oilers, etc.	760	293*	9
Totals	5,360	996	223

*A number of Auxiliary Vessels will be employed on Trans-Atlantic Service; in fact it includes all the US Troop and Storeships and unlike our corresponding figure is not ships on Fleet Service.

During the *five* months ended 31 May last only 11 Warships and Auxiliary Vessels (excluding the small Submarine Chasers) were actually completed in the United States, of the following descriptions:-

Battleship	1
Destroyers	6
Submarines	3
Minesweepers	1
Submarine Chasers	Number not known.

The last named is merely a Motor Launch which we do not count in our figures but of which we have several hundreds.

During the same period there were completed in Great Britain the following:-

Light Cruisers	2
TBD Leaders	2
TBD's	28
Submarines	14
Sloops	16
Patrol Boats	5
Minesweepers	18
Fleet Oilers	10
Boom Defence Vessels	10
Trawlers (Spl. Anti-Sub. design)	70
Patrol Gunboats	9
Drifters (Spl. Naval)	13
Tugs (Naval)	2
Seaplane Towing Lighters	4
Total	203

****

If the war continues for a few years we shall probably be left with a large fleet of Warships and Auxiliary Vessels, and a large effort in Merchant ship repair to our credit. On the other hand, the Americans will have built up a Mercantile Fleet approaching that of Great Britain, whereas before the War they only owned one-fourth of our tonnage.

****

... I feel that it is not impossible for the representatives of the two Nations to meet and agree roughly on the Naval effort due from each. If that be done, it would not be very difficult to agree that Great Britain should be allowed to acquire in the United States merchant tonnage equivalent to the labour involved in the excess effort now put forward in Warship construction, and the labour engaged on repairs to Warships and Merchantmen for the Allies. If such a discussion were entered into it would, of course, be one for the Admiralty and the Shipping Ministry jointly. Unless some arrangement of this character is come to the position of Great Britain as the Carrier of the World is seriously threatened as well as her position as the premier Shipbuilding Country.

From a Naval point of view the question is one of high policy; but there is also a most important economic aspect to it both during and after the war. The main questions it raises are:-

(1) Is this Country to continue its policy of accepting the responsibility for the whole burden of Naval warfare, less such contributions as our Allies feel disposed to make, to the sacrifice of other vital demands on our resources?

(2) Are we to go on losing ships in our Allies' immediate interest, and repairing ships for them while they overtake us in their Mercantile Marine?

This question is only part of a much larger one, including the provision of many articles to our Allies, e.g., Guns, Equipment, Clothing, Machines and Engines, Material, Coal, Steel, etc., to the detriment of the size of our Army.

The first question is one upon which I would like to have the guidance of the War Cabinet after discussion, as it essentially affects the programme of construction for 1920 delivery which we are now preparing and which I must discuss with Mr Roosevelt before he goes back to America.

389. *Pratt to Sims*

15 August 1918

****

... As you know, I am an American first and last, but I also feel that the best work of America lies in the very close relation now and in the future with England. ... the war won't kill [anti-British feeling in the United States], unless those of us who really aim for the betterment of both countries strive to prevent such a [rift] from broadening. ... I have sounded the warning on every possible occasion [that Germany would try to exploit Anglo-American differences] and I have talked most frankly with every Englishman that I think has a grain of sense along just these lines. ...
****

390. *Daniels to Geddes*

20 August 1918

****

I beg to thank you for expressing the hope that in the near future I may be able to come over. ... We had ordinarily built only a handful

of destroyers a year, and practically no other small craft for the
Navy, and when we undertook to build three or four hundred
submarine chasers, three or four hundred destroyers and perhaps as
many more of the *Eagle* type, and to continue the construction of
other naval craft in addition to the large programme of merchant
shipping, which is so essential to all of us, it demanded the reconstruction of our facilities. To that task we of the Navy and the
Shipping Board have addressed ourselves, and I may say daily and
hourly seeking 'with full steam ahead' to secure the delivery of the
ships that we first saw in our budget. As soon as this work is so far
advanced that we can be certain that our contribution will be the
largest possible one for our country to make, I will feel free to follow
my inclinations to come to Great Britain, France and Italy.

****

391.   *Geddes to Lloyd George*

26 August 1918

I have been looking into the question of the American share in
Naval war. Owing to the fact that that Naval effort takes so much
longer to produce than Military effort – e.g., a destroyer takes 18
months to build – the problem of the American ultimate contribution in European Waters which was faced in Military matters a year
ago is only now becoming pressing. The American output of destroyers has been greatly disappointing, and we are still month by
month having most disastrous retardations in the forecast of completions. At the same time having regard to what undoubtedly they
are trying to do, and to our experience that after undue optimism
has been written off the United States do in fact accomplish a great
deal, and also having regard to the fact that the will of the United
States Nation for war has become stronger and stronger, there is no
doubt that at a certain date they should be contributing very largely
to the Naval war. Up to now they have done very little. I have
quoted figures before, but I now quote two which Admiral Sims
gave me today – that of the number of craft in the waters around the
British Isles they have only 3%, and in the Mediterranean only 6%.
The time is coming, however, when their effort will undoubtedly be
felt.[1]

You are familiar with, and I will not recapitulate, the National

[1] See no. 105.

disadvantages which we have suffered through taking up to now practically the whole burden of augmentation of the Naval programme of the Allies, and of the disadvantages which we are suffering to an increasing extent in repairing Allied merchant tonnage and in refitting Allied naval craft. I have been going into the question of our programme of deliveries of craft after January 1919. If the Americans put into the war in European waters a reasonable number of the craft they have forecast to be commissioned, it is possible for the British Navy to decrease materially their Naval construction effort, making the men available either for the Army or for what I contemplate will be the destiny approved by the Cabinet – for Merchant shipbuilding. This can have an almost immediate effect. Supposing the Americans agree to the proposals which we have to make to them that they should undertake to place at the disposal of the Naval authorities in European waters certain numbers of craft by certain dates – and those proposals are within the bounds of probability having regard to their ability to produce – I see no reason why we should not be able to release progressively up to 20,000 men from the Shipyards towards the end of the year. Rising eventually to a figure directly and indirectly materially greater than this. The mere fact also that we would be commissioning fewer ships after 1 January would reduce the Naval demands for enlisted personnel.

Now it is imperative that we should come to an understanding with the United States on this most important matter, and it must be a binding understanding. There is also the question of compensation on a reasonable basis for the refitting work which we are doing for the United States Navy. We have undertaken to do certain refitting up to the end of this year and for a year beyond, of their destroyers. Up to the end of the year, upon the basis of man-power effort involved, we asked them to compensate us with 5 Admiralty Oilers. This they have refused to do and you will have seen in a Paper I have sent to the Cabinet Admiral Sims's letter on the subject.[1]

There is the further general matter of compensation for Merchant tonnage lost in their service, which was considered by a Committee presided over by Mr Balfour, resulting in a recommendation that I should discuss the matter with Mr Roosevelt just now, but taking no further action. As to this latter point, discussion with Mr Roosevelt will have little effect because he is in no way concerned with Merchant tonnage production,[2] and the matter is obviously one of high

---

[1] Trask, *Captains and Cabinets*, p. 295.
[2] This was a matter for the US Shipping Board and Emergency Fleet Corporation.

THE STRUGGLE FOR NEPTUNE'S TRIDENT 509

policy which will, I think, have to be discussed with the President. Dealing however with the two points which are strictly Naval. Firstly the joint Naval programme of ships to be sent to European Waters in which the British Navy is chiefly concerned, I must come to an understanding with the United States Naval Authorities and at once.

I find that Mr Roosevelt is not, as we thought, in a position similar to a Deputy or Assistant to the First Lord of the British Admiralty, but is concerned only in the production of Naval material and has no say at all in the use made of that material when it has been produced. In fact he is more like the Admiralty Controller than I first supposed.[1] I also find that Mr Roosevelt, like all capable men, while his energy is much admired, is not without his own difficulties, and I am told that any agreement come to with him, or any agreement which he went back and recommended as a result of a conference here, would start prejudiced.[2] At the same time, as far as I can learn, there would be great hope of arriving at a satisfactory conclusion with the United States Navy Department if one could put the matter before the president, get his general blessing, and then proceed to a detail discussion with the Navy Department.

The matter is one of really prime importance to the Country's interest, and I have somewhat reluctantly come to the conclusion that, subject to your better judgement, and to a reference to Lord Reading[3] which I have made, it would be desirable for me, with a Naval Advisor, to pay a flying visit to Washington and to endeavour to get the thing settled as soon as possible after Mr Roosevelt's return. I am told it would be unwise for me to go back with him, but that he would undoubtedly be a help if my coming had no appearance of collusion with him. If Lord Reading is returning promptly to the United States I would make my plans either to go with him or to time my visit so that he would be there when I arrived, as his presence would be of inestimable value. If, however, his return is to be long delayed it would probably be best that I should go at an

[1] Roosevelt, like his cousin Theodore 20 years earlier, got his 'fingers into about everything' but his chief responsibilities were for navy yards, their labour and supplies; most of the Admiralty Controller's duties were in fact retained firmly by Daniels.
[2] Roosevelt had been openly pro-Allied since the outbreak of the Great War and had many friends in Britain; he was still rather immature and impetuous; he was an active promoter of his own political interests, regardless of those of the Wilson administration or of his own chief; and, like his cousin, he was regarded as a dangerous maverick.
[3] Lord Reading, Ambassador in Washington, was then on leave in Britain.

early date.

You will realise that what I am proposing is in fact what in Military matters you have to work through Foch[1] as Generalissimo. There is no Admiralissimo and no Supreme Naval Council which can speak with the authority with which Foch speaks, and if we are not going to waste our man-power effort in Naval production which is not absolutely essential, I am convinced that we ought now to come to grips with this at the earliest possible date, and in a more definite way than is possible by the exchange of diplomatic communications by wire. It would of course be better (although it is not all one way) if we could settle the matter with an American representative over here, but from the investigations I have made I am quite clear that to endeavour to do so with Mr Roosevelt would in fact prejudice a satisfactory settlement, and even with the disadvantage of going to Washington to make a request, I have come to the conclusion on the whole that probably it would be better for me to go, and to go very soon. Will you please let me know your views?

The second point is compensation for refits of their Naval Craft undertaken by us in this Country, and on that I have great hopes that after discussion they would adopt our view.

I have sent a copy of this letter to Lord Reading, the Chancellor of the Exchequer,[2] and to Mr Balfour.

392. *Balfour to Geddes*

Foreign Office,
27 August 1918

... my general impression is that such a visit to the United States as you suggest would be very useful.

The three points with which you propose to deal may however require somewhat varying treatment. Questions of the naval construction, the amount of American Naval shipping to be put into European waters and the dates of such operation should clearly be discussed and definitely decided as soon as possible.

I do not think you ought to experience much difficulty in coming to an agreement for the determination of a joint naval programme, as you have the military precedent to appeal to.

---

[1] Marshal Ferdinand Foch, nominally Allied CinC on the Western Front since April 1918. Geddes exaggerated substantially the extent of Foch's authority.
[2] Andrew Bonar Law.

The second question, although naval, falls in a somewhat different category. We are, I gather, to ask the United States for compensation for work which we are doing for their navy. I quite agree with you that the request is just, and that probably in the end the United States Government will assent to it, but it is important to choose the right moment to put it forward.

The third problem is of a somewhat similar kind and like considerations seem to me to apply. In this connection I rather fear that you have misunderstood the recommendations of the Conference over which I presided. The meeting was very definitely of opinion that it was useless to approach the United States with any proposal for compensation for merchant tonnage lost since it was quite certain that the request would be refused. If this were the result, and both Lord Reading and Sir Joseph Maclay[1] held strongly that it would be – to make the request will only irritate the Americans and do us no good, rather the reverse. I hope you will assent to this view.

****

I am afraid from reports that have reached us that we are for various causes not at the height of our popularity in the highest quarters in the United States. This attitude is of course reflected lower down and I am therefore doubtful whether it would be wise to raise at the moment, questions involving compensation. I understand that Lord Reading proposes to return to the United States about the middle of next month and unless the first question is so pressing as to brook no delay would it not be better to wait till he has had an opportunity of testing the ground with regard to the other two? He would then be able to advise you when you arrive of the chances. We should not like the First Lord to meet with a blank refusal such as Admiral Sims seems to have received recently.

I am sending a copy of this letter to the Prime Minister.

393. *Roosevelt to Daniels*

London,
28 August 1918

[Geddes wishes to visit Washington] ... partly to make future plans with you. Their visit would be very short. I think it would be nice if you would cable Sir Eric Geddes expressing the hope that he'll come.

---

[1] Shipping Controller.

394.   *Sims to Geddes*

30 August 1918

I take pleasure in transmitting to you the following cablegram which has just been received from Mr Daniels, the Secretary of the Navy:

'It would give me the greatest satisfaction and pleasure to have you and such of the British Navy as you desire to have accompany you visit this country. I sincerely trust you will be able to arrange for this visit. I am sure your coming would be of mutual benefit to our respective countries. A warm welcome to you as head of the powerful Navy of Great Britain and to you personally awaits you from all America.'

395.   *Admiralty Memorandum for the War Cabinet*

31 August 1918

The Battlecruiser Position and the Shipbuilding Programme

****

In order to make our position secure in the future with regard to battlecruisers it is recommended that in addition to the *Hood*, two of these ships[1] should be progressed at the normal rate.

With the object of effecting this and at the same time assisting in the construction of Merchant Shipbuilding, the Board of Admiralty have given most serious consideration generally to the Warship Building Programmes which have been authorised by the War Cabinet, with a view to seeing how far it is possible for them to cut down or retard numbers of vessels, the construction of which has been authorised, and thus enable men who are now engaged on naval construction to be transferred to merchant ship building.

Such are the exigencies of naval warfare, and particularly of anti-submarine warfare, that the War Cabinet will appreciate that the Board of Admiralty are powerless to effect economies in naval construction unless they can look with confidence to the United States Government to render material assistance by supplementing, out of the resources now at their disposal, the classes of vessels of which the Allies stand most in need, but the Board have every reason

---

[1] *Hood's* 3 intended sisters had been halted in March 1917 to release labour for anti-submarine craft and merchant vessels.

to believe that it is within the power of the United States Government to render the assistance in this direction which is required.

Statements are attached[1] which indicate clearly the economy in ships which the Board of Admiralty feel justified in accepting and the nature of the assistance which is desired of the United States Government; but the War Cabinet will appreciate that this programme of economy is entirely dependent upon the required contribution to the Allied forces in the waters concerned being forthcoming from the United States. Assuming, however, that the War Cabinet approve of the cutting down and retardation of the Naval Building Programme to the extent which will effect these economies, and that an arrangement which can be relied upon can be made with the United States Government to provide the assistance indicated, it will be possible to gradually release to merchant shipbuilding a large number of men now engaged on naval construction, and it is anticipated that the number so released will rise by the second quarter of 1919 to an aggregate of about 22,000 men.[2]

****

It is desired that the War Cabinet should approve of these proposals and steps will be taken to obtain their adoption by the United States Government so far as the United States of America are concerned.

396. *Geddes to Roosevelt*

31 August 1918

****

... I venture to suggest to the United States Navy Department that so long as there is a deficiency in essential craft, it is a matter for their most serious consideration whether they are justified in continuing to build capital ships, which I understand they are still doing in accordance with the instructions of the Congress. I hope that I shall not be accused of presumption, nor of interference with matters that do not concern me, in referring to this point, but with the general shortage of skilled labour and the serious shortage of skilled ratings which I understand the United States, in common with ourselves experience, we have not felt justified in building capital ships because of the other great demands upon our resources; and

[1] Not reproduced.
[2] Britain was facing an acute manpower shortage. See J. M. Winter, pp. 39–48.

we have in addition had to sacrifice very greatly our merchant shipping output in order to meet the imperative demands of the Naval war.

Coming to Battle Cruisers, the situation is different. In no particular naval arm are the Allies so unfavourably placed as in Battle Cruisers. The *Goeben*[1] is a menace to which there is no entirely satisfactory reply, because Battle Cruisers cannot be spared to prevent a raiding exit from the Dardanelles. In the North Sea the position as regards Battle Cruisers between the Grand Fleet and the High Seas Fleet is by no means one of complete satisfaction. The only other Battle Cruisers which exist are in the Japanese Navy, and repeated efforts have been made, without effect, to obtain their co-operation in European Waters. In these circumstances, and having regard to the German Battle Cruiser building programme, we have felt obliged to go ahead with one Battle Cruiser, and it is a matter of high policy, having regard to the probable duration of the war, whether we should now undertake the completion of one or more of the three which are partially built in this Country.[2]

Turning now to the craft of smaller size than Battle Cruisers and dealing only with the war demands of the waters which I have called the British waters, we would suggest that you frame your destroyer programme upon a basis of allotting to these Waters between now and 31 August 1919 a minimum of 128 additional destroyers permanently in commission. Thereafter, unless the Naval situation changes, it would in the opinion of my Naval advisors, be adequate if that number were maintained and not necessarily increased.

As regards Minesweepers, you will be aware that the British minesweeping is a very formidable task, and we actually sweep some 45,000 square miles of water every month. It is suggested that the United States might wish to undertake a proportion of this Naval service, taking over definite areas to sweep, and we suggest for your consideration that you should arrange a programme of building to commission 3 Mine-sweepers per month from 1 January next year.

Then as regards Trawlers, it is suggested that the United States might make a contribution to the trawler fleet in the areas concerned from 1 July next year and complete and commission at the rate of 4.5

---

[1] The German battle cruiser, nominally a unit of the Turkish Navy, had been damaged by mines and grounding during a brief Mediterranean sortie on 19–20 January 1918 and was effectively inoperative for the rest of the war, having to go to Sebastopol for extensive repairs. The extent of her damage, however, was unknown to the Allies.

[2] See Marder, vol. 5, pp. 137–40.

per month for service in these waters

... We are ... preparing to embark upon a programme of fast Mine-layers for this offensive work in the North Sea, and we have two vessels of suitable character at present under construction and propose to go on with an improved type as soon as slips become available.[1] We suggest, however, that the United States might desire to contribute to this offensive mine laying and that the Navy Department might consider laying down at once two or more fast Mine-layers to carry 200 mines with a minimum speed of 30 knots. Should you desire it we should be glad to place at the disposal of the Navy Department any further information on the subject, together with designs if required.

A further direction in which we would invite the United States' co-operation is in the construction of craft suitable for ocean escort work. As you are aware, last summer and again this summer the sinking of merchant ships by submarines has been undertaken much further out in the Atlantic than during the intervening months. Whether this fluctuation as between in-shore sinking and ocean sinking is caused entirely by the weather, or is due – in part at any rate – to the offensive measures of the Allies, we are unable to say. But the fact is undoubted that at the present time and during the last 6 months there has been a very noticeable tendency for a large proportion of submarines, other than those of the 'Cruiser' type, to operate further out in the Atlantic. We think that although our methods for dealing with the submarines on passage and in-shore are by no means perfect, they are proceeding on lines calculated to give the most satisfactory results as the efficiency of material and personnel improves, but we are not satisfied that we have got the appropriate reply to the actions of the submarine far out at sea, say between the 250 mile and 500 mile belt from the coast. Admiral Sims and his Officers have been considering this matter with the British Naval Staff, and whatever type of craft might be considered most desirable by our Naval advisors, I suggest to you that the time has arrived when we should lay our plans to have a more suitable type of escort craft for ocean work than exists today in adequate numbers. We have developed a comparatively slow ocean escort craft called the 'patrol gun boat',[2] and if more heavily armed with say 5.5″ guns this craft may be very useful for ocean escort, but it is generally admitted that it does not combine all the qualities desired. It must be

---

[1] Possibly one was HMS *Adventure*, not completed until well after the war.
[2] *Kil-* class: 890 tons; 1 × 4 or 4.7in; 13 knots.

a good sea boat; its radius of turning must be small; it must have the capability of quickly attaining high speed; it must have a long radius of action; it must be mechanically simple and capable of being manned by a less experienced and less highly trained crew; a patrol gun boat is being used with great satisfaction in the medium ten-knot through convoys to Port Said, and we have a considerable number of these under construction. Experience has shown that when all is said and done the destroyer is the most satisfactory known type of vessel for this work but it has certain drawbacks, the chief of which are the time occupied in construction and the diffi-culty in finding the necessary skilled personnel to man them, and I venture to suggest that the matter is one deserving the most careful consideration of the United States Navy Department as it is receiv-ing ours.

You will of course understand that the allotments out of your total future resources which I have outlined, are put forward as minimum allotment.

In concluding this letter I would like to reiterate that I would not presume to write in this sense had you not invited me to give the matter some consideration, and I feel sure that my action will therefore not be misunderstood.

397. *Memorandum by the Director of Plans*[1]

[September 1918]

*American Assistance desired and proposed allocation thereof
Destroyers: USA Assistance Desired*

****

Note – It is not anticipated that any US Destroyers will be available for the relief of the British building programme until 1 January 1919, as the Admiralty understand that the American output of destroyers up to that date are already allocated for specific US requirements.
Explanatory Statement
Additions are required under three headings:-
(i) *Replacements of Casualties*
The average is not less than 24 a year, and as the number of destroyers increases the number of casualties may also be expected to rise. It will consequently not be safe to allow for less than 30 a

---

[1] Captain Cyril Fuller.

year, or 20 for the eight months ending 1 September 1919.

(ii) *Relief of Obsolete types*

There are in commission 60 of the 30-knot Class and 28 *River Class*.[1] The latter may be of use for another year but the former, except for limited purposes, are overdue for relief. Fourteen are to be relieved this year and six might be retained for minor services but the remaining 40 should be replaced by more modern boats.

(iii) *Additions to existing forces*

The requirements formulated at the present amount to 94 for 1919. Of this 94 -

(a) 36 are required to initiate a system of hunting flotillas for which it has not been possible to spare more than a few destroyers, hitherto, without weakening to a dangerous extent the Fleet and escort flotillas. With the institution of these forces, it is hoped to operate on the lines of communications of the enemy submarines and to render their ingress and egress more hazardous.

(b) 30 are required to augment the escort flotillas, which at present are worked almost beyond the limit of their capacity.

Convoy escorts were originally on the basis of one escort unit per convoy. A unit consists of 11 vessels of which 3 were estimated to be resting and refitting; and they would take out and bring in a convoy every eight days, the unit being at sea about six days.

Convoys were then dispersed at the approaches to the Irish Sea and English Channel but they have now to be escorted to and from their ports.

Other factors which have thrown extra work on the escort flotillas are:-

(1) The increased distance that Convoys have to be escorted owing to the extended area of operations of enemy submarines in European waters.

(2) The augmented cross-Channel traffic of US troops amounting at present to 6,000 a night.[2]

(3) The enormously increased American troop movements consisting of two convoys every eight days.

(4) Escorts for the Archangel Expeditionary Force.

(5) The monster transports necessitating separate escorts.

---

[1] 30-knot class: 1895–1904; 340–470 tons; 1 × 12 pdr; 2 × 18in tt; 30 knots. *River* class: 1902–05; 540–590 tons; 4 × 12 pdrs; 2 × 18in tt; 25.5 knots.

[2] Many US troops were disembarked initially at Liverpool and other British ports because of congestion at Brest and other French ports and the lack of berths and fuel for the great liners there.

(6)   Escorts for armed merchant cruisers to their ports after they leave their convoys.

(7)   Escorts for all oilers.

(8)   Special escorts for cable ships, special missions, etc.

Generally speaking, there is no doubt that escort craft have been worked to their maximum, and that personnel and material will require some relief if this effort is to be maintained in the future.

(c)   12 are required to reinforce the Grand Fleet Flotillas so that each flotilla may be maintained at a strength of 4 divisions, the division being the tactical unit.

(d)   10 are required for augmenting the Flotillas in the Mediterranean, and 6 for the Halifax anti-submarine patrol and escorts. It has not been possible to meet these requirements hitherto while more vital needs were unfulfilled.

****

... it is proposed to ask the USA to contribute 128 at the rate of 16 per month and British construction will provide 32 at the rate of 4 a month making a total of 160 (approximately the number required) by 1 September 1919.

Proposed Allocation of US Destroyers

In order that the US Destroyers should operate together and in co-operation with their own forces, it is proposed that they should, as they become available, relieve the 2nd and 4th British Escort Flotillas at Buncrana, and Devonport, the British Destroyers on the Otranto Barrage, and constitute a small force at Halifax for escort and patrol duties.

The total of 128 destroyers would thus be allocated as follows:-

Devonport Escort Flotilla	56
Buncrana Escort Force	30
Otranto Barrage Patrol	36
Halifax Patrol	6

Total	128

Statement of Estimated Establishment of Destroyers at the end of 1918 compared with Required Establishment[1]

	Establishment 31 December 1918	Increase Required	Required Establishment
Grand Fleet	111	12	123
Harwich and Dover	57	–	57
Mine Laying	12	–	12
Escorts	105	30	135
Mediterranean	57	10	67
Hunting Flotillas	21	36	57
Local Flotillas, etc.	41	–	41
Halifax	–	6	6
Totals	404	94	498

****

398. *Conference between First Lord and Naval Members of the Board*

5 September 1918

[Draft letter to Prime Minister]:
'With reference to what passed at our Conference on Merchant Shipbuilding today, and to cabinet consideration of the Naval Shipbuilding programme, I am writing so that the decisions you wished to take should be duly recorded.

****

(b) the men released by the reduction be kept as shipyard workers in the Yards on merchant shipbuilding work, and not being put into the Navy, Army or Air Force. This provision being

[1] A following table details more precisely the proposed allocation of the 94 listed here under 'Increase Required'.

made so that in the event of a Fleet action or serious losses they will be available for retransfer to Naval work with Cabinet approval.

****

[Minutes of Meeting of Board]

The Prime Minister thought it best to save the four or five weeks which it would take before we can get the American allocation, and there was every reason to think we could get that allocation from America. It was thought desirable to take a somewhat more strong line with America in asking for that allocation, and to tell her that if she did not agree we should be unable to do as much escorting work for her transports in the future. This means that we start reducing our building programme exactly as we mean to reduce it when we reach an agreement with America. If we fail to get an agreement we have really taken no irrevocable step which we cannot go back upon. We have only deferred on certain craft which will be delivered in 1919 and we will have only deferred their completion by say a month. If it was necessary when we came back from America, we could ask the firms to go full speed ahead and say we cannot have them deferred.

The First Lord remarked that ... there was every reason to think we could come to an agreement with America in the matter.

399.   *British Naval Mission to the USA: Special Operations Committee to Consider Matters for Discussion Memorandum by the Director of Statistics*[1]

22 September 1918

Comparison of British and American Naval Effort

... with the exception of Destroyers the greater part of the United States Fleet is employed outside European Waters. In the case of Destroyers, 66 out of a total of 81 are operating in European Waters, 24 of these being based on Queenstown, 32 on Brest and 7 on Gibraltar.

[1] Lieut-Colonel (later Sir) John George Beharrell (1873–1959): like Geddes a North Eastern Railway executive; commissioned in the Army; Director of Statistics and Requirements, Ministry of Munitions; Assistant Director of Transportation, BEF; Assistant Inspector General of Transportation; lent to Admiralty 1917 to serve as Director of Statistics; Director-General, Finance and Statistics, Ministry of Transport (under Geddes again) 1919–22; Managing Director, Chairman and President, Dunlop Rubber Co. 1923–57; President, Federation of British Industry 1932–33.

The total displacement tonnage of all United States Vessels in European Waters amounts to 363,321. This tonnage is nearly 50,000 tons below the displacement of British Naval Vessels in the Mediterranean, and the Mediterranean Forces represent less than 10% of the tonnage of the British Fleet.

Grand Fleet

The United States Navy has five Battleships operating as a Battle Squadron with the Grand Fleet; but these ships must be provided with attendant Destroyers and other small craft. If a comparison on the basis of displacement tonnage is made it is found that the British tonnage represents 94% of the total tonnage of the Grand Fleet.

Naval Construction

The completion of Warships and Auxiliary Naval Vessels by the British and United States Navies during the first half of the current year is set out in Table 3 attached.[1] It will be seen that during the six months 300 vessels having a displacement tonnage of 219,272 were completed for the British Navy. During the same period the United States Navy completed 24 vessels having a displacement of 51,861 tons.

The forecast of completions for the six months ending 31 December next (Table 4)[2] indicates a greatly increased effort of production by the United States, but considerably below the British effort as the following figures show:-

	Numbers	Displacement Tonnage
British forecast	441	279,391
United States forecast	153	180,497

It should be pointed out, however, that the British figures are based on the actual output in July and August, and the latest forecast made on 3 September which, unless unforeseen circumstances arise, will probably be realised; whereas the United States forecast was made on 30 June. Previous experience, however, shows that forecasts of United States completions have not been realised. For example, on 31 January last 23 Destroyers were forecast for completion during the months of March, April, May and June. The completions, however, only amounted to ten during those months, and eight of the ten were completed during the last two months of the period.

[1] Not reproduced.
[2] Not reproduced.

Anti-Submarine Campaign

The following table of the percentage of vessels engaged in the Anti-Submarine campaign in British Waters and the Eastern Atlantic, is extracted from a paper prepared by the Intelligence Section of Admiral Sims's Staff in August last. The figures may be accepted as approximately correct:-

	Destroyers	Submarines	Miscellaneous Patrol Craft
Great Britain	80%	78%	86%
France	6%	17%	11%
United States	14%	5%	3%

The following percentages from the same source give a comparison of the Naval situation in the Mediterranean.

	Destroyers	Submarines	Miscellaneous Patrol Craft
Great Britain	27	13	22
France	38	37	66
Italy	26	50	4
Japan	7	0	0
United States	2	0	8

Escort Work

The escorting forces of the United States Navy in European Waters are based on Queenstown and Gibraltar where they work in common with the British forces; and also on the French coast escorting US Troopships into French ports and assisting in Escort along the French coast.

From the figures available it is clear that the individual Destroyers of the United States Navy perform very good work. A comparison has been made between the work of the Destroyers of the United States Navy and the Destroyers of the Second and Fourth Flotillas which are engaged largely in similar work; and it is found that over a period of six months the average mileage per vessel per month is as follows:-

United States Destroyers	4,694 miles.
British Destroyers	3,648 miles.

This may be accounted for to some extent by the fact that some of the British boats are engaged on a number of shorter journeys, for example, Cross-Channel.

The convoy work of the United States Destroyers in European Waters is limited to the Atlantic.[1] The whole of the convoy work in the North Sea, Cross-Channel and [?most of that] in the Irish Sea is performed by British Destroyers, which are also responsible for the whole of the escort work round the shores of Great Britain.

Information as to the comparative mileage performed whilst on escort duty during the month of August by the craft of the two Navies has been compiled and is attached, Table 5.[2] The total mileage steamed by British craft is 1,442,800; the United States figure being 229,000, or 13.7% of the total. The mileage of the United States Destroyers based on Gibraltar is not known but making full allowance for them the United States mileage will not exceed 250,000, or say 14.5% of the total. The United States figures are of course exclusive of any Escort work done by Destroyers on the American coast.

Minelaying

The United States has made considerable provision of Minelaying craft, and at the present time they have

2 Light Cruisers fitted for Minelaying
8 Merchant Vessels converted into Minelayers
4 Tugs similarly converted

engaged in European Waters.

The British have 9 Minelayers at present available, including one Battleship and one Flotilla Leader. One Cruiser and two Merchant Ships are in course of conversion. Mines can also be laid from certain Light Cruisers, Destroyers, Trawlers, etc. but the Cruisers are not set apart for this work.

The number of Mines laid by the American Minelayers in European Waters during the six weeks ended 7 September averaged 3,447 per week. During the same period the number of Mines laid by British Minelayers averaged 1,801 per week.

Repairs and Refits

A comparison of the work of the two Navies under this heading is not possible. The repair of British Warships and Auxiliary Naval Vessels places a great strain on the facilities and Man-power of the Country. The number repaired and refitted per quarter is over 3,000

[1] This failed to take account of the 6 US destroyers at Gibraltar, employed on patrols and as convoy escorts in the Western Mediterranean.
[2] Not reproduced.

involving the employment of 43,000 men. Having regard to the fact that United States Vessels in European Waters are operating so far from their own ports, the work of repairing and refitting is largely carried out in British Yards. During the first eight months of this year 151 War Vessels of various kinds were repaired and refitted in British Yards. This number is relatively small having regard to the British figure, but even then considerable Man-power is involved.

Aircraft for Naval Purposes

A comparison between the Air Service efforts of the two Navies is almost impossible as the forces of the United States Navy are still exceedingly small.

British aircraft engaged on Naval duties as at 31 August 1918 were as under: –

Airships – Rigid	5
– Non-Rigid	99
Aeroplanes and Seaplanes	1699
Kite Balloons	253

The only [air] forces of the United States Navy at present in British Waters are three or four machines operating from Killingholme and three Kite Balloons at Berehaven. Certain Stations in Ireland are being taken over by the United States Navy; but their machines are not yet operating. Arrangements have also been made for the United States Navy to supply eight bombing squadrons for Dunkirk; but these are not yet in operation.

400.   *Wemyss to Geddes*

3 October 1918

****

I hope you have had a good trip across. I am looking forward enormously to receiving a telegram from you to say that the main object of your visit has been successful. Such a lot lies in that, because if you get what is wanted, doubts which have arisen in my mind as to the bona fides of our friends will be removed.

401.   *Notes for Guidance as to the Line to be adopted in*
Conferences with United States Navy Department and in Informal
Conversations

[October 1918]

****

When the United States came into the war the immediate result –
and a very welcome result – was the addition of their destroyers to
European waters. As the American Army began to appear in
France, however, and more particularly in the second quarter of this
year when the numbers leaped up very considerably, instead of the
United States' advent into the war causing a nett augmentation to
the Naval forces of the Alliance, the demands for safeguarding
American seaborne traffic increased so enormously that, looking at
the matter purely from a Naval point of view, they have become a
tax on the Alliance. That tax has entirely fallen upon the British with
the result that we have had to utilise essential forces, intended for
hunting the submarine, in order to escort the American Armies and
supplies across the seas, and although it was a quite unavoidable
development, the figures of enemy submarines sunk and submarines
in commission at the present moment are a striking commentary on
this subject.

****

During the last quarter of 1917 and the first quarter of 1918, the
British Navy was able, by a great effort, effectively to hold the
submarine menace, and there is every reason to believe that the
destruction of submarines would have continued had the demand
for defensive escorts not been so vast and imperative. The anti-
submarine campaign for 1918 in a great measure had to be, and was,
abandoned and we must now look to 1919 and lay our plans so that
we allocate and organise our forces which will again enable us to feel
that the submarine campaign is under control, and that the number
of submarines is decreasing.[1]

---

[1] May, with 14 U-boats sunk, was an exceptional month; the monthly average for
1918 was half that. The numbers fluctuated wildly from month to month. See Marder,
vol. 5, pp. 81–82.

****

Of the five zones mentioned above the two in which the British
Admiralty is particularly concerned are[1]

1. The Anglo-American zone, ... where the forces under Admiral
   Sims work in the closest co-operation with the British Admiralty
   and Navy; and
2. the Mediterranean, where the Otranto Barrage and the patrol
   and escort work for the Mediterranean is entrusted by the French
   Commander-in-Chief to the British Commander-in-Chief at
   Malta. As regards these two zones it is essential that we should
   confer and arrive at some understanding, if possible, as to what
   contribution each country can give to the total forces necessary.
   The types of craft which mainly come into this consideration are
   destroyers, trawlers, patrol gunboats and minesweepers. Mines
   and minelaying can be treated as a separate subject. It is suggested that the other zones in which the British Admiralty has no
   direct and participating interest should be dealt with separately.

****

If the United States Government is able to contribute to the war
at sea a force equivalent to the quota necessary to screen its own
capital ships and minelayers, and to escort its own cross-Atlantic
traffic, and will then fix a percentage of the minesweeping, patrol,
and hunting work which it is prepared to undertake progressively by
certain dates, this will enable the British Admiralty to lay its plans
accordingly. It is hoped that the result of this visit will be to arrive at
an understanding on the lines indicated.

Mines and Minelaying

The American minelaying contribution to the Northern barrage
has been immense. The way in which this work was tackled by the
United States Navy has been the admiration of all of us who have
come into contact with it. There appears to be, however, no phase of
Naval warfare more beset with difficulties and more fraught with the
elements of disappointment than minelaying, disappointments
which Great Britain has felt in no small degree. There appear to be
great difficulties, not only of a physical kind such as designing mines
capable of being laid at the required depth, but also in striking the
happy medium between premature detonation and a lack of sensiti-

[1] The others were the 'Franco-American Zone' (French Atlantic coast); 'American
Atlantic coastal zone'; 'the rest of the globe'.

vity in the mine which amounts almost to rendering it inert.[1] It is thought that good might result from a conference with the Mining experts of the United States on the subject of prematures, and from a comparison of the experience of the two countries in this connexion. The United States Navy Department will have heard of the proposals which were discussed and adopted by the Inter-Allied Naval Council for the laying of extensive Mine Barrages in the Mediterranean and the Aegean, and of the great difficulties, some of which have so far baffled the experts, of the maintenance of these barrages in position. It is thought that the opportunity of this visit might be taken for a discussion and an understanding as to the provision of suitable material for this extensive system of anti-submarine mining in the Mediterranean, the burden of which will, to a great extent, fall upon, and has it is believed been accepted by the United States. This kind of minelaying, however, is of a special type. It consists in laying Mine barriers in waters controlled by the Allied Navies, the minelayers themselves being defenceless craft covered by light forces against enemy attack.

The other kind of minelaying, however, is of the more offensive type. It is carried out in enemy waters by fast craft of the very highest quality and efficiency, and manned by picked Officers and crews. This minelaying is conducted at present by a destroyer flotilla, and we have on occasion used Cruisers for the work, but it would be of inestimable benefit, the particular aspects of which can best be explained by Admiral Duff, if we had the addition of fast minelayers for offensive work in the Bight and in the Cattegat. The risks of the work are considerable; the losses in craft may be comparatively heavy. The British at the present time have 27 destroyers specially fitted for this purpose, and excellent and most effective results are obtained.[2] We are providing two fast Minelayers, however, in the meantime, and would be glad to know if the United States would be prepared to provide two or even three of such craft; to take them in hand and build and commission them with the least possible delay. It is not known whether the United States have so far had need for building or designing such craft, but if they have not the British Admiralty would be glad to place their designs and drawings at the disposal of the United States Navy Department.

[1] Until the British copied Germany's successful contact mine late in 1917, their mines tended to be 'inert'. The much-vaunted American mine produced a high percentage of premature explosions.
[2] Few sinkings, of U-boats or surface craft, were obtained. For a vast expenditure of effort, all that could be claimed was considerable inconvenience to the enemy. See Newbolt, vol. 5, pp. 207–8, 337–8, 343, 344.

Appendix 'A'
German Submarines

	U	UB	UC	Long-range	Total
Position at 31 August 1918 (No. available)	60	62	28	11	161
New Boats Forecasted deliveries, 1 September to 31 December 1918	13	16	15	5	49
Total	73	78	43	16	210
Estimated losses based on the rate of losses during the six months ended 30 June 1918, which is considered optimistic	8	14	6	1	29
Estimated position at 31 December 1918, of numbers available	65	64	37	15	181

Memorandum on the Establishment of the US Destroyers necessary to afford protection to US Naval Forces Operating in European Waters and to US Traffic to and from UK Ports

The requirements may be divided under two headings –
(I)   Screen for Forces
(II) Escort

****

Total requirements set out above –
(I)   Screen for Forces   32[1]
(II) Escort   98[2]

130

[1] Eight destroyers were required for the 3 US battleships at Berehaven and 12 for the 5 battleships with the Grand Fleet. A further 12 were needed to escort the US minelayers sowing the North Sea Barrage.
[2] Thirty were required for Atlantic convoys, 12 for the 'monster' transports (RMS *Olympic, Mauretania, Aquitania*), 12 for US Cross-Channel troop convoys, 12 for US Bristol Channel–Bay of Biscay stores convoys, 14 for extension of escort limit to 500 miles W. of Ireland, and 18 for UK–Gibraltar convoys.

Numbers now based
on Queenstown   24

106

It will be observed that no assistance is asked in connection with escort of American ships to and from Archangel or Coastwise round the United Kingdom.

There is a third class of work towards which it is hoped the Americans will be able to make a substantial contribution, viz:-

(III) Offensive Hunting Flotillas.

Owing to the insistent demands for escort, the methods adopted to meet the submarine menace have had to be largely defensive, but the development of Offensive operations by means of Hunting Destroyer Flotillas is a matter of great urgency. This policy must, however, wait until urgent escort needs are met. The request for 128 Destroyers which has been put forward leaves a balance of 22 after the needs under (I) and (II) have been fully met. These and any others which can be provided, beyond the 106 asked for, could be most profitably employed as Hunting Craft.

****

402. *Memorandum of a Conference held at the Navy Department to discuss the Naval Situation*

8 October 1918

The proceedings were opened by Sir Eric Geddes with a general appreciation of the Naval Situation from the point of view of the British Admiralty.

As regards surface craft, it was pointed out that the position in the North Sea, where the Anglo-American Fleet is containing the German High Seas Fleet, can be regarded as satisfactory and that no reason for anxiety can be foreseen until 1920 when the German preponderance in Battle Cruisers will become serious.[1] It was pointed out that to meet this situation, the British Admiralty are completing one Battle Cruiser which will be ready for service about the middle of 1919, and if, on reconsideration of the question at the

---

[1] The Germans were expected to have the *Hindenburg* and *Mackensen* in service by 1920. This would give them 7 ships to 9 British but with an edge in speed, possibly in broadside (the new ships were reputed to be armed with 15in or even 17in guns) and certainly in protection. See Ranft, ed., *Beatty Papers*, vol. 1, pp. 284–93; Marder, vol. 5, pp. 133, 137–40.

end of this year, it is considered that a further effort in this direction must be made, the British Admiralty will then proceed with the completion of two more Battle Cruisers. These, however, could not be completed before the Spring of 1921.[1]

Passing to the Mediterranean, it was agreed that the total Allied force in these Waters is sufficient to deal with any enemy force that can be brought against us but that difficulties exist with regard to the co-ordination and joint action of the Allied forces. Reference was made to the question of a unified command in the Mediterranean and the difficulties raised by Italy to the appointment of an Admiralissimo.[2]

In this connection Mr Daniels stated that representations have been made to Italy through the State Department, which it is hoped may prove beneficial in reaching a decision on this question.

The situation in the Eastern Mediterranean as it is affected by German action in the Black Sea and the *Goeben* having recently undergone a complete refit at Sebastopol was considered and the conclusion reached that, should the situation in the Black Sea develop, the necessary steps can be taken to counter any enemy action in the Eastern Mediterranean.[3]

The submarine situation was next taken into consideration and discussed at length. The following figures were given to illustrate the growth and progress of German submarine policy and effort:-

At the outbreak of war the number of submarines the Germans had available was 28. Allowing for losses, this number steadily increased until 1 January 1918 when it stood at 160. The number then showed a gradual decrease until 31 May 1918 when it stood at 145. From that date up to the present there has been a gradual increase, and on 1 August 1918 the number of German submarines available again stood at 160. A careful estimate of the submarine situation, based on reliable information as regards the German rate of construction and allowing for losses on the average of the first six months of 1918, shows that on 31 December 1918, the Germans will have available 181 submarines. Of this total it may be accepted that a maximum of 20% operate in the Mediterranean.

From these figures it is noticeable that in May 1918, the anti-submarine campaign was meeting with great success, the number of enemy submarines destroyed considerably exceeding the monthly

[1] *Hood*, though proceeded with, did not enter service until 1920. None of the other 3 made any further progress and were shortly cancelled.
[2] See Part VII.
[3] See Marder, vol. 5, pp. 29–30.

output. It was agreed that the unsatisfactory change in the situation was a matter of serious concern. Sir Eric Geddes pointed out that the reduced destruction of enemy submarines might be accounted for in several ways. A change of enemy tactics was made last May when the submarines changed their operating grounds from the Coastal routes to areas from 200 to 300 miles from the Coast. To whatever causes this change may have been due, the result was to make the detection and destruction of the submarine a matter of much greater difficulty. He further pointed out that the events in France last March which led to the transport of large American forces across the Atlantic had had a very serious and detrimental effect on British anti-submarine policy. It had long been realised that defensive measures and offensive-defensive measures, such as the convoy system, although affording a great measure of safety to the mercantile marine and resulting in the destruction of some submarines, were quite inadequate by themselves to counter the submarine menace. The British Admiralty had, therefore, decided to add to the other measures some purely offensive units for hunting submarines. The safety of American troops crossing the Atlantic was, however, necessarily the first consideration, and thus the destroyers and other fast craft which were to have been allocated to the offensive were instead required for the escort of troop convoys through the Atlantic danger zone and also across the English Channel. It was considered that, for the reasons given, the falling off in destruction of German submarines since last May is fully accounted for and the safe conduct of troop transports must remain the first consideration until sufficient forces are available to enable hunting units to be organised.

It was agreed that what is described as the Anglo-American Zone, including as it does all the Home Bases for German submarines and their exits into the Atlantic, is the one important theatre of operations against the submarine and that combined and co-ordinated effort on the part of the United States and Great Britain is essential for future success against the submarine menace, and that to insure the most efficient use of all available forces it is necessary, in preparing our plans, to look well ahead and definitely decide the number of destroyers and fast craft that each Nation will allocate to the work. No definite decision as regards the relative effort to be made by the two Countries was reached, but certain proposals of the British Admiralty were put before the Conference and reserved for further consideration at another Conference.

Some discussion took place as to the best type of craft to be employed for hunting operations, and while it was generally agreed that taken all round the destroyer is probably the best type in existence, it was thought that, in view of the large skilled personnel they require and the time occupied in their construction, consideration might well be given to other types of fast craft less costly in material and personnel. It was pointed out by the Secretary of the US Navy Department that it was hoped that the 'Eagle' type of destroyer would be found to supply this need but as yet they had no exact data to go on as the first of the Class was only now undergoing trial.[1]

Mention was also made of the British Patrol Gunboat as a very useful type of vessel for coastal and cross-channel mercantile convoy escort escort, and Sir Eric Geddes promised to supply the plans of this type of craft for examination by the US Technical Authorities.

Minelaying policy was next considered and the British weakness in fast minelaying vessels was pointed out. The great utility of such vessels and the necessity for very high speed was fully concurred in, and the suggestion was made that the US Navy Board might wish, in view of the importance of these vessels and the peculiarly interesting nature of the service, to build two or possibly three for duty in the North Sea. The Secretary of the US Navy asked that plans of this type of vessel might be handed over to the Navy Department for examination.

The vast extent of the daily routine Minesweeping carried out in British Waters was also touched upon, and it was suggested that the US Navy might allocate some fast Minesweeping craft for this service.

Finally it was decided that the points raised at this Conference should be considered in detail by Officers representing the US and British Navies and a Memorandum drawn up embodying definite proposals for the joint and co-ordinated Naval effort of the two Countries.[2]

403. *Memorandum of a Meeting between US and British Naval Officers*[3]

Washington,
8 October 1918

****

---

[1] The *Eagle* boats, built by Ford, never saw action.
[2] These officers met on 8, 9 and 10 October. The results are in no. 408.
[3] The meeting discussed the whole range of craft required by the British. This table was submitted by the British side.

Naval Forces in Anglo-American Zone, 1 September 1918[1]

	British	United States
Battleships	37	8
Battle Cruisers	9	–
Cruisers (Special)	2	–
Seaplane Carriers large	3	–
Cruisers	5	–
Light Cruisers	50	–
Armed Merchant Cruisers	29	–
Flotilla Leaders	28	–
Destroyers	348	26
Torpedo Boats	71	–
Submarines	121	7
Monitors	20	–
Gunboats	14	–
Seaplane Carriers small	3	–
Kite Balloon Ship	1	–
Minelayers	7	10
Sloops	56	–
Patrol Gunboats	10	–
Trawlers	1038	–
Drifters	997	–
Motor Drifters	62	–
Boom Defence Vessels	316	–
Minesweepers	153	–
Yachts	44	14
Whalers	14	–
P. Boats	61	–
Armed Boarding Steamers	7	–
Motor Launches	360	41*
Motor Boats	3	–
Depot Ships	39	5
Repair Ships	2	1

*Submarine Chasers.

[1] This does not take into account the US battleships and cruisers, based on US East Coast ports, which escorted convoys as far as the submarine zone, or the destroyers, minesweepers and patrol craft based on French Atlantic ports. The aged but substantial collection of US warships working from Gibraltar are also omitted, as are the 39 submarine chasers recently arrived at Corfu.

534 ANGLO-AMERICAN NAVAL RELATIONS 1917–1919

404. *Geddes to Daniels*

British Embassy,
Washington,
10 October 1918

****

I suggest ... that the United States Navy Department should undertake to build for the Admiralty in exchange vessels to an extent representing as nearly as one can calculate, the man power effort involved in the repair and refitting of United States vessels. ...
****

405. *House to Balfour*

13 October 1918

I would like to congratulate your Government on the success of Sir Eric Geddes's mission to this country. No mission has produced a more favorable impression both among the members of the Administration and the people generally. Apart from any practical results achieved, the visit of Sir Eric Geddes has undoubtedly helped us all to understand and appreciate the great work of the British Navy during the war.

Sir Eric had a most cordial interview with the President this morning, and the President tells me that he is delighted with Sir Eric and the members of his mission, and the manner in which he has conducted his business with our Navy Department.[1]

406. *Geddes to Lloyd George*

British Embassy,
Washington,
13 October 1918

****

My own visit has only been partially successful owing to the really serious failure of their Destroyer building programme upon which they have been very unduly optimistic, but Admiral Duff is of the opinion that they have met us as far as their limited production capacity at present permits. The negotiations and intercourse

[1] Wilson disliked Geddes's harshness towards Germany; see Trask, *Captains and Cabinets*, pp. 308–9.

throughout have been of a most satisfactory and cordial nature.

407. *Pratt to Sims*

15 October 1918

... I think the British Mission was a success over here, if for no other reason than that it established a closer relation and gave us a little better [?insight] into the Admiralty's way of working. ... I think one of the things Sir Eric was most interested in was our merchant shipping. Naturally, that will be the matter of greatest interest with them after this war is over but I can see no reason why we can't arrange things openly and frankly on a share and share alike basis.

****

408. *Admiralty Memorandum for War Cabinet*

October 1918

Shipbuilding Programme

... The British Naval Mission to the United States discussed most fully, during the week 7–12 October, with the United States Navy Department at Washington, the programme of assistance which it was desired the United States should provide. ... As a result of these discussions, the following agreements were come to:-

Type	Assistance Desired	Agreement come to
Destroyers	128, to be provided at the rate of 16 per month between 1 January and 31 August 1919.	(a) That the provision by the United States of 94 Destroyers by 31 August 1919 can be looked to with certainty and that not less than this number will be allocated by the United States to the Anglo-American Zone. In view, however, of delays in the constructional yards which cannot be overcome, the supply of a greater number than 94 cannot be relied upon, although it will

be made if possible.

(b) That the United States will, as a temporary measure and as soon as possible, allocate 34 *Eagle* boats, as a substitute for the deficiency on the 128 Destroyers.

(c) That although the United States are unable to supply, by 31 August 1919, 128 Destroyers which it is agreed are essential for the Anglo-American Zone, they will use their best endeavours to supply the deficiency later in 1919, and accordingly as the war situation develops, will continue to supply such additional Destroyers as may be agreed to be necessary.

Minesweepers	45, to be provided in 15 months at the rate of 3 per month from 1 January 1919 or earlier if possible.	(a) That 45 Minesweepers are necessary in 1919, but that owing to the difficulties in constructing in the United States a new type of Minesweeper with which the United States are not familiar, the best alternative is to substitute Minesweepers of the United States Trawler design.

(b) That the United States will provide 45 Minesweepers as early as possible, it being anticipated that delivery of this number can be given between June and December 1919, the first instalment reaching Europe

		in July 1919.
Trawlers (Patrol Gunboats)	4.5 per month until cessation of hostilities.	(a) That the provision of 54 vessels of this type in 1919 is essential, but that owing to difficulties involved in constructing in the United States a new type of boat with which the United States are not familiar, the best alternative is to substitute 54 *Eagle* boats.
		(b) That the United States will provide 54 *Eagle* boats and will put them into the Anglo-American Zone in 1919 and as early as possible in that year.
Minelayers	3	That owing to the situation in the United States constructional yards, it is not possible for the United States to build the fast minelayers desired by the British Admiralty and the best alternative is to fit out 8 large Destroyers as Minelayers, and that the United States will take them in hand as soon as the full Destroyer programme (128) up to 31 August 1919, is completed if the demand for Minelayers still continues and will complete them as soon as possible.

It will be seen from the above that the Mission has not been wholly successful in obtaining from the United States Government the assistance desired, but they are satisfied that the agreements come to fairly represent all that can reasonably be expected of the United

States in the circumstances which obtain in that Country. The proposals put forward by the Mission received sympathetic consideration by Mr Daniels and the Staff of the United States Navy Department.

The most important respect in which British requirements cannot be met by the United States is in the number of Destroyers to be provided by 31 August 1919, the deficiency being 34, and although the US have undertaken to make up for this deficiency by the supply of 34 vessels of the *Eagle* type, it must be remembered that the efficiency of this type of ship is as yet unproved and in any case they cannot be accepted as a satisfactory replacement of Destroyers.

The Naval situation may, therefore, be summarised as follows:-

An intensive renewal of the submarine effort on the enemy's part is in preparation which, when it materialises, will, it is anticipated, be far in advance of any previous effort.

The US will continue to be a naval liability on the Alliance until the end of 1919, that is to say, her demands for transport protection will exceed the contribution she makes in light craft for escort purposes.

Since April last our anti-submarine effort has been sacrificed in favour of the war on land, the British provision of light craft having been diverted from offensive to defensive purposes.

The War Cabinet, therefore, has to consider whether it will:-

(a)   Retain, in part or whole, the authorised building programme of Destroyers to the detriment of merchant shipbuilding, thus sacrificing, correspondingly, the economy in Destroyers ... to be effected in 1919, or

(b)   ... reduce the obligations of the British Navy as regards escorting American troops, thereby releasing British light craft for submarine hunting. This can be effected either:

(i)   by a reduction in the number of transports escorted; or

(ii)   by a reduction in the distance from land at which the vessels are escorted; or

(c)   Act on the assumption that a military decision will be reached in 1919 and accept, in the meantime, a growing and formidable submarine menace which may, and probably will, have serious results in the latter half of that year.

The Admiralty hold very strongly the view that the submarine menace will probably not be controlled, and certainly will not be overcome, without the aid of listening appliances which are now in an advanced state of development, and that the effective use of these appliances necessitates the employment of a strong force of Destroyers for hunting operations over and above those employed on escort duties.

The War Cabinet are asked to decide at the earliest possible date which of the three alternatives mentioned above is to be adopted, but it is not proposed to ask them to express any opinion until the end of the year as to whether the completion of the two Battle Cruisers *Rodney* and *Anson* should be proceeded with at the normal rate.

409. *Planning Committee, Office of Naval Operations,*[1] *to Benson*

Navy Department,
Washington,
7 October 1918

Building Policy

1. In any future war in which the US may be engaged, the most probable combination against us would be Germany, Austria and Japan in alliance. It therefore seems advisable that our Navy should be prepared to meet such a combination and our building policy should be such as to insure us against such a combination. Incidentally, this would also provide for us a Navy equal to that of the greatest Naval power (England).
2. The following table shows the strength of the United States as compared to other powers:

---

[1] This was a separate body from the General Board, though rather duplicating its functions.

	Dread-noughts		Battle Cruisers		Light Cruisers		Destroyers		Submarines	
	Blt	Bldg	Blt	Bldg	Blt	Bldg	Blt	Bldg	Blt	Bldg
Great Britain	33	0	11	4	62	24	398	121	130	86
Germany	19	6	5	4	18	14	228	38	186	172
Austria	3	4	0	0	4	3	9	1	25	10
Japan	8	2	4	0	3	7	22	23	9	27
Total	30	12	9	4	25	24	259	62	220	209
United States	14	13*	0	6	3	10	328			

*To No. 54, inc.[1]

Capital Ships

The General Board recommends in its Building program for 1920 12 battleships and 16 battle cruisers, specifications for which it has recommended in previous papers. These battleships have a speed of 23 knots and the battle cruisers a speed of 35 knots.
****

Summary

The Committee's recommendations are, in brief,:
1. Complete the development of all home yards, bases, stations, etc., as above, *at once.*
2. Undertake the development of main and secondary bases in the Atlantic, *at once.*
3. Undertake the development of main bases in Hawaii and Guam *at once.*
4. Urge the development of intra-coastal canals on the Atlantic, for Fleet use, *at once.*
5. Build the following vessels as soon as the three-year program is complete, in the order recommended above, all to be completed and in commission by 1 July 1923.

[1] US battleships were given numbers during construction.

Battleships	27	(30-knot type 'C')	(4 to begin with)
Destroyer Scouts	18		(no)
Destroyer Flotilla			(12 or 15 of a type)
Leaders	36		(no)
Scout submarines	54		
Tenders			
Destroyer	18		(no)
Submarine	6		(no)
Airplane carriers	2		
Patrol vessels	200	(*Eagle* type)	
Mine sweepers	54		
Mine layers (fast)	2		

Aircraft –covered in a separate paper.[1]

410. *Memorandum by Planning Section, US Naval Forces in European Waters*

October [?] 1918

United States Naval interests in the armistice terms

****

3. In view of the readiness with which France and Italy agreed to the taking over of German and Austrian vessels there can be little doubt that an understanding exists between France, Italy and Great Britain as to the distribution of these vessels. In other words there have been councils on this subject of vital importance to us from which we have been excluded.

4. It should not be forgotten that we have strong evidence of an agreement between Great Britain and Japan by which not less than five British deadnoughts are to be transferred to Japan after the Peace. Therefore, it becomes of special interest that we study the probable strength of the Fleets of the principal Naval Powers after the war under the most reasonable assumptions which we can now make. Table 1 gives the present strength of those Powers in dreadnoughts, battle-cruisers, and destroyers and submarines:

---

[1] Marginal notes by Benson.

Table 1
Present Built

	Dreadnoughts	Battle-cruisers	Destroyers	Submarines
Great Britain	33	10	425	136
France	7	0	43	64
Italy	5	0	33	41
Japan	6	7	67	17
United States	17	0	172	55
Germany	21	6	218	177

****

6. By combining Tables 1 and 2[1] we get the probable postwar strength of the six greatest Naval Powers, as follows:

Table 2
Probable Post War Strength

	Dreadnoughts	Battle-cruisers	Destroyers	Submarines
Great Britain	35	16	449	206
United States	17	0	172	55
France	11	0	55	99
Japan	9	7	78	52
Italy	9	0	45	76
Germany	11	0	168	17

****

8. Assuming the distribution [of enemy ships] made as indicated the United States with seventeen modern capital ships would be faced at once with an alliance between Great Britain and Japan controlling a total of sixty-seven capital ships. Even with Japan left out Great Britain would face us with *three* times the number of capital ships that we have. This in itself is an intolerable situation, but if we join to the mere recital of figures political considerations which we know has governed in the past, we shall see more clearly that our national interest demands that this distribution of vessels shall not take place.
9. Four Great Powers have arisen in the world to compete with Great Britain for commercial supremacy on the seas – Spain, Holland, France, Germany. Each one of those powers in succession have been defeated by Great Britain and her fugitive Allies. A fifth

---

[1] Table 2 not reproduced; it was entitled 'Assumed Distribution' of German and Austrian vessels, under which the British would receive the lion's share and the US precisely nothing.

commercial power, the greatest one yet, is now arising to compete for at least commercial equality with Great Britain. Already the signs of jealousy are visible. Historical precedent warns us to watch closely the moves we make or permit to be made.

****

Conclusions

1. All German and Austrian submarines should be destroyed.
2. No German or Austrian Naval vessel should be used to increase the Naval armament of any power whatever.
3. The German Navy should remain after this war sufficiently strong to exercise a distinctly conservative influence on the application of British Sea Power. To this end not more than ten German capital ships should be taken from Germany.
4. The United States should never permit the transfer of British capital ships to Japan, as the move would be distinctly hostile to American interests.

411. *Memorandum by Rear-Admiral Sir Sydney Fremantle and Comments by US Planning Section*

October 1918

Rear-Admiral Fremantle: A case for the Surrender of the German Fleet as an Article of the Terms of the Armistice

****

... if the surface command of the sea were lost, or even for a time in dispute, or if we allowed the submarine campaign to get out of control our main lines of communication would be interrupted, and the land war as at present being carried on be rendered impossible.

The naval war is therefore the foundation of the strategical plan of the Allies, and since it is the British Navy which bears the brunt of the naval war, and which maintains by far the largest part of the naval effort of the Allies, the voice of Great Britain, and in Great Britain of her Naval Representatives, has a dominating claim to be heard in the determination of such of the terms of the armistice as are more distinctly naval.

We must determine the terms of the armistice with two principal objects in view:-

(1) They must be such that, should the armistice not result in peace, the enemy will, at the recommencement of warlike

operations, be in a position not more favourable than that in which he finds himself at this moment.

(2) Since there will be every tendency once an Armistice has been declared not to revive war, the armistice terms must be substantially the eventual peace terms, or must at any rate be such as to afford no means to the enemy of refusing compliance with the Peace terms which the Allies will impose upon him.

****

As regards the eventual peace terms, our security for the future depends upon that of our sea communications. The German Fleet is the only enemy asset which can interfere with them. The surrender of the German Fleet is the only compensation we can accept as the consequence of our great and successful naval efforts in the war. It is our only guarantee for security in the future if we are not to recommence an [era] of bloated navy estimates and of a navy constantly on a war footing.

****

It is essential in order that the fruits of the present situation shall be garnered, to demand the surrender of the whole German Fleet, located though it may be for the moment in German ports, as to demand the disarmament of the German Army.

****

These requirements can be met only by demanding as the terms of the armistice, the surrender into Allied hands of every unit of the German Navy, to be subsequently disposed of in accordance with the terms of peace.

Comments by the US Planning Section

18 October 1918

****

The Armistice terms and Peace terms may be viewed from many different points. The proposal of Admiral Fremantle is the strictly British idea: the safety of the British Empire and the Sea communications of the British Empire are the sole considerations which govern him in his contention.

As for the terms of the Armistice, those terms which have already been tentatively agreed upon in Paris, and which are now about to be submitted in a somewhat modified form to the Allied Naval

Council, furnish sufficient guarantee that the enemy shall not benefit in a naval way by the Armistice, no matter how long it may be prolonged, since he is required by the terms of the Armistice to deliver into Allied hands to be interned for the period of the war, a minimum of 60 and possibly all of his submarines, thereby taking from him his sole naval weapon that has influenced the conduct of the Allies' land campaign during the latter years of the war.

We may conclude, therefore, that for the purpose of the Armistice alone, the surrender of the German Fleet to the Allies is not an essential condition.

****

If the fleet were distributed among the powers now at war with Germany, it would have the effect of immediately increasing the naval armaments of all the Powers concerned, and therefore operating against the desired tendency toward the reduction of armaments. If the German Fleet were, by the terms of the Peace, destroyed, the effect would be to leave Great Britain the absolute naval master of Europe, without a single threat from any European source whatever. Such a commanding position is contrary to the idea of a League of Nations in which equality of opportunity is supposed to be a dominant factor.

Viewing the position from a strictly American view point, if the German Fleet were destroyed, Great Britain would be at liberty to do with our new merchant marine as she thought fit, since her naval power would so far outbalance our own as to make it practically impossible for us to oppose her, no matter how arbitrary her methods might be. It is not for a moment suggested that the German Fleet could ever be an ally of the American Fleet against Great Britain, but it is suggested that the presence in Europe of the German Fleet is a balance wheel governing any undue or arbitrary ambition on the part of those who may temporarily be in power in Great Britain.

It may be right and proper that Great Britain should have a greater naval force than other European Powers, since she must, by the very nature of her insular position, assure to herself the opportunity to live by the importation of food. It is not, however, right for Great Britain to occupy as commanding a naval position that she may by the mere exercise of her will and the employment of her Fleet, stop the importation of food equally necessary to all the countries of Europe. This she could do if the German Fleet were annihilated. She would be, without a German Fleet, the dictator of

Europe, since she herself would be absolutely safe from invasion, and at the same time would be able to control every sea line of communication across the Atlantic or from the Indian Ocean.

****

Admiral Fremantle's contention that, since the brunt of the naval war has been borne by the British Navy, the British Navy should dictate the naval terms of the peace, is not consistent with any of the proposals regarding the League of Nations, freedom of the seas or with the principle of equality of sovereignties. As we understand it, the aim now is a permanent peace based on justice and not a peace in the interest of any power.

We therefore recommend that the entire question of the disposition of the German Fleet be left to the Peace Conference. We venture to express the opinion now that the German Fleet should remain after the Peace, German property, but that it should be subjected to whatever form of international demobilization may be decided upon by the Peace Conference. We have already recommended the delivery to the Allies and internment of German submarines for the duration of the war. In making this recommendation, we were actuated by two motives. First that the submarines had been used illegally and contrary to all maritime practice up to the present war, and that this weapon should be taken away from those who had thus used it illegally. Second, that the terms of Peace should include a proviso either for the total abolition of submarines as a weapon of naval war or for the abolition of submarine warfare against merchant ships of all nations, both friend, neutral and enemy.

412. *Sims to Bayly*

15 October 1918

****

... I have just seen a telegraphic report of the President's reply to the last German proposal. This has not yet appeared in the Press but probably will this evening. It seems to be everything that could be desired. In a word it indicates that we are to beat the Germans to their knees and get an absolutely unconditional surrender.[1] I will

---

[1] As the Germans requested and obtained the armistice on the basis of Wilson's Fourteen Points, their surrender was not unconditional, a point seized upon by Hitler and, in 1943, by Franklin Roosevelt, who insisted on an unconditional German surrender in the Second World War.

not be satisfied unless this includes the High Seas Fleet. We must make an end of barbarism for all time.

****

I can imagine your indignation over the sinking of the *Leinster*.[1] You know that we were particularly unfortunate in having such a valuable man as Captain Cone[2] so severely injured. ...

****

There is no accounting for the psychology of the Germans. It is incredible that they should have committed this outrage at the same time that they are negotiating for terms of peace. However, this time we will finish with them for all time, and fix things so that the world may remain in peace.

****

413. *Memorandum by Geddes*

16 October 1918

Notes of an Interview with the President at the White House[3]

****

The Fourteen Points – 2: The Freedom of the Seas

This was a question which would naturally interest Great Britain more than any other country on account of the preponderance of her Navy and her position as a world-wide Empire. He admitted that the British Navy had in the past acted as a sort of naval police for the world – in fact for civilisation. For his part he would be willing to leave this power to the discretion of the British people, who had never abused it, but he wondered whether [the] rest of the world would be willing to go on doing so indefinitely. Many nations, great and small, chafed under the feeling that their sea-borne trade and maritime development proceeded only with the permission and under the shadow of the British Navy. He had always felt that the deepest rooted cause of the present war was this feeling in Germany – an unjust fear and jealousy of the British Navy, but a feeling none the less real. I gathered that the President was searching for a remedy

---

[1] The *Leinster*, an Irish Sea packet, was sunk earlier in the month by two torpedoes fired by a U-boat.
[2] Captain H. I. Cone, US Navy, in command of US naval aviation in Europe. He suffered a broken leg and other injuries but happily made a complete recovery.
[3] See document no. 405.

which he might suggest, but that he had found none; in his mind there is an idea that the great power of the British Navy might in some way be used in conjunction with the League of Nations and thereby cease to be a cause of jealousy and irritation.

It would be necessary, the President observed, soon after peace to have a Conference to revise international law, and particularly International Maritime Laws.

Since the beginning of the war he had recognised that submarines introduced a new element in naval warfare which must modify existing international law. That was why, in his neutral days he had not insisted more strongly on the strict observance of international law in his dealings with the British Government. The old American theory was that the highways of the sea should be free in war as in peace. It remained to be seen how far this must be modified.

The extent of territorial waters would also have to be enlarged owing to the greater range of modern guns, and the old-fashioned definition of 'blockade' must be revised.
****

414. *Memorandum by Wemyss*

17 October 1918

An Inquiry into the Meaning and Effect of the Demand for 'Freedom of the Seas'

The proposal as stated by President Wilson on 8 January 1918 is:-

'Absolute freedom of Navigation upon the seas outside territorial waters alike in peace *and in war*, except as the seas may be closed in whole or in part by international action for the enforcement of international covenants.'

****

(1) *What is meant by 'Freedom of the Seas'?* As far as the seas *in time of peace* are concerned, they have been free for centuries and their freedom has been maintained by the British Navy. Nothing further need therefore be said on this point.

As regards the seas *in time of war*, ... the President must have in mind freedom, both to belligerents and neutrals, to carry on overseas trade in spite of the existence of a state of war.

Further, not only will neutrals be free to carry contraband, but belligerents and neutrals alike will be free to carry food stuffs and raw materials of every description and apparently also troops and munitions.

In these circumstances there will be no right of capture or detention at sea, except of warships by each other, and no object will be served by the exercise of the right of search.

If these assumptions are correct, blockade will be impossible, and it will be possible for a belligerent to transport and maintain expeditions overseas, subject only to interference on the territorial waters of his enemy. Purely naval operations will be hampered, in spheres in which they are being conducted, by the presence of uncontrolled merchant shipping.

If this is not a correct interpretation of the meaning of the phrase 'Freedom of the Seas', it is necessary that the meaning shall be made clear before the subject can be further discussed.

(2) *Overseas Communications in war*

It is a truism to say that unless communications can be maintained warfare is impossible. Neither naval nor military forces can act unless they are reasonably secure. If a belligerent can cut the lines for a sufficient length of time the enemy is defeated, and in war it is always an object – often the principal object – to do this. In the present war we have succeeded in cutting almost entirely Germany's overseas communications; she is trying by means of submarine warfare to cut ours. The proposal to make the seas free in wartime is in the nature of a step to prevent sealanes of communication being cut.

At first sight it may be thought that as the sea is practically our only line of communication, while to any other nation it is but one of their lines, we have more to gain by the proposal than anyone else. It must be remembered, however, that the need for maintaining our oversea communications has forced us to provide for their protection, and that this has given us the power to interfere with the communications of the enemy. If, therefore, our lines are secured by freedom of the seas in war, so are those of anyone opposed to us. The same lines are used by both, and the freeing of them from attack acts both ways. It would prevent us from using our strongest weapon and place in the hands of our enemy a power which he does not possess. The value of military power, both for attack and defence, would be enhanced, and its radius of action increased, while the value of naval power for attack and defence and its radius of action would be correspondingly diminished.

Further, the establishment of the principle of 'Freedom of the Seas' in time of war would act as an incentive rather than a deterrent of war.

(3) *The German object in originally making the proposal*

From the foregoing the German object in making the proposal is evident. Germany, a strong land Power making a bid for world supremacy, found her efforts baffled by the sea-power of the British Empire. She was suffering from shortage of food, munitions, and raw materials, and saw her enemy supplied with all of them by sea. Could she carry an army safely over the sea she could hope to destroy us; could she use her merchant ships or import in neutral bottoms her shortage would disappear. These objects were denied to her by our sea-power. If the use of sea-power could thus be restrained, she could achieve her desires. The demand for 'Freedom of the Seas' was therefore revived and put forward as an aim for which all nations should strive, in the interests of the world's peace. Germany, whose industry is war, saw a military advantage in the proposal. Napoleon constantly raised a similar cry.

(4) *International control*

It is observed that President Wilson contemplates international action in emergency, and it is said that the activities of the various countries would henceforth be controlled by a League of Nations, which would keep the peace by exercising a dominating influence over any recalcitrant member and determine the extent of the force which each member of the League would require to maintain in order to provide by joint force for this purpose. The conditions of the British Empire, however, are so unique and its dependence on sea communications so vital, that it is impossible even to contemplate committing its whole destinies at sea to any League or combination of nations.

The British idea of the freedom of the seas is free and unfettered access in time of *peace* to all the seas by all who wish to cross them 'upon their lawful occasions', in time of *war* this privilege must be fought for by belligerent navies, causing as little inconvenience as possible to neutrals, but maintaining the rights of capture of belligerent merchant ships and of searching neutral merchant ships in order to verify their nationality and prevent their aiding a belligerent.

(5) *Conclusions*

(i) Acceptance of the proposal would result in making sea-power of little value to a nation *dependent upon it* for existence whilst providing a Military Power with free lines of oversea communication.

(ii) The right to decide for ourselves questions which concern such

vital interests, could not be surrendered to any League or combination of nations for by assenting to the proposal we should give up
by a stroke of the pen the sea-power we have for centuries maintained and have never yet misused. On this basis the British Empire
has been founded, and on no other can it be upheld.

415.   *Benson to Daniels*

Paris,[1]
3 November 1918

****

The only armistice [the Allied Naval Council] would feel justified
in submitting for consideration would be one which would leave the
United States and the Powers associated with her in position to
enforce any agreement that may be entered into and make the
renewal [of] hostilities on part of Germany impossible. ...

416.   *Memorandum by US Planning Section*

7 November 1918

The Freedom of the Seas

****

4. *The American conception of the freedom of the seas* in the past has
been that the merchant vessels of all friendly and neutral nationalities shall be permitted to use the high seas freely and unhindered on
their lawful occasions and that the following employments are
unlawful:

(a)   Carriage of contraband.
(b)   Blockade running.
(c)   Unneutral service.

and that the following acts are unlawful:

(a)   Attempts to avoid visit and search by flight.
(b)   Resistance by force.
(c)   Presentation of fraudulent papers.
(d)   Acceptance of belligerent convoy.

In the application of the above the governing principle is that a

---

[1] Benson had gone to Paris to help arrange the naval armistice and the subsequent
peace conference.

neutral shall suffer the minimum dislocation of his normal maritime activities. The American Government has from time to time contended for the immunity of private property, even though it be enemy property, from capture on the high seas unless it be contraband of war. This contention has never received international assent.

The British conception of freedom of the seas is not freedom of the seas at all but the freedom of the belligerent to adjust his maritime action to the necessities of the military and naval situations. As sea power is necessarily the basis of all British activities on land Britain contended for the greatest possible freedom of action of belligerents on the high seas. Their contention in this respect is emphasised and enlarged by the fact of their great naval superiority and the consequent military advantage that will accrue to them from the increased freedom of action at sea even though the rights of neutrals may thereby be infringed upon. The actual rules of maritime warfare which are accepted by the British Government coincide in most respects with American practice but the liberality of interpretation of those rules which a great navy permits to Great Britain operates to the greater restriction of freedom of commerce.

Great Britain may be more willing to accede by international agreement to increase rights to belligerents because of a belief that should she be neutral the power of her navy will enable her to require an interpretation of those rules favorable to neutrals. In other words the influence of her naval power will sway the interpretation of the rules for maritime warfare to her advantage whether she be belligerent or neutral.

****

Summary of Conclusions

From the above considerations we conclude:

1. That absolute freedom of the seas is at present impracticable.
2. That a belligerent's right to capture or to destroy combatant ships of the enemy on the high seas cannot be questioned.
3. That the right to capture enemy merchant ships should not be denied.
4. That the liability for the exportation and carriage of contraband should become a national liability instead of a private liability.
5. That the nature of contraband should be determined during peace by universal agreement and that these agreements should be unalterable during war.
6. That no merchant ships, either belligerent or neutral, should be

destroyed in war.

7. That the right of visit and search should be granted for the sole purpose of identification and to determine the guilt for unneutral service and breach of blockade.

8. That the permissible limits of blockade areas should be determined precisely during the peace and the corresponding freedom of belligerents to determine the extent of blockade areas restricted.

9. That strategic areas should be limited in extent as much as possible and that the discretion of belligerents in declaring such areas should be defined during peace.

10. That the underlying principle of belligerent and neutral rights on the high seas should be that a neutral shall not aid a belligerent nor shall a belligerent interfere with a neutral except in accordance with precise rules determined during peace and unalterable during war.

11. That the changes or modifications in International law suggested above should not be put forward for adoption except in principle until they have received the closest scrutiny by the International jurists of the nations concerned.

417.   *Benson to Daniels*

10 November 1918

... the collapse [of the Central Powers] has been so complete that it is much worse than anyone apparently had anticipated.

****

... the Inter-Allied Naval Council convened and immediately took up the question of the naval terms to be proposed for the armistice. I consider it extremely fortunate that I was able to be present at these meetings. It was evident from the very first that the other members of the meeting were determined to impose terms that were most exacting and almost impossible of acceptance. The stand that I took was that the terms of the armistice should fully meet the conditions laid down by the President, but they should be neither humiliating in expression nor impossible of acceptance because of their severity. This attitude practically isolated me from the rest of the group at once. The feeling was such that I could not escape the impression that an agreement had been entered into by some of the other representatives as to the final disposition of the various vessels to be taken over, and I felt strongly, if such a thing were true, that every effort should be made to thwart it. I have cabled you the result of my interview with Sir Eric Geddes on this subject,[1] and so far, have been unable to get any definite information along these lines.

No doubt many will think that the terms as finally drawn up were pretty severe, and they undoubtedly were, and possibly had not the governments concerned completely collapsed, would not have been accepted.

There is a marked feeling of anxiety, if not one of uneasiness, on the part particularly of our English friends in regard to our building program, both naval and commercial. I finally succeeded in making my position clearly understood and the personal relations have very much improved. ...

418. *British Admiralty Draft of Naval Armistice Terms and Comments by United States Naval Advisory Staff*[2]

November 1918

Admiralty Staff Draft

Comments by US Naval Advisory Staff

(a)   All German, Austrian, Turkish and Bulgarian submarines built or building should be sunk or broken up.

Agreed to. If submarines are broken up, no part of such submarines to be used again in connection with other submarines.

(b)   All German surface warships interned under the terms of the Armistice, the eight other 'Dreadnought' battleships, and all warships interned in neutral ports should be sunk. The vessels remaining will leave Germany with sufficient vessels for self-protection and police duties, while not giving her naval predominance in the Baltic.

The proposal to sink all vessels interned under the terms of the Armistice is agreed to. The proposal to sink eight other dreadnoughts is not agreed to. The proposal to sink all German warships interned in neutral ports is agreed to. To demand the surrender of and to sink eight additional dreadnoughts which were not required to be turned over to the Allies and the United States by the terms of the Armistice, will produce an unnecessarily bitter and hostile

---

[1] Not reproduced.
[2] This was the Planning Section from Sims's HQ, now transferred to Paris to serve as Benson's staff.

attitude on the part of Germany, which would be prolonged into the future. So far as the interests of the United States are concerned, we see no objection to these vessels except the reasons given above. The question appears to us to be almost wholly a political one in which the results to be gained by the act have to be balanced against the probable adverse political effects. If Germany is to survive as a nation, we cannot expect to deny her the right to maintain a Navy.

****

(g) All German, Austrian and Turkish vessels being built (torpedo boats and above) should be surrendered, and sunk or destroyed. The sinking or destruction of the above vessels should be carried out within three months of delivery in the case of those which are interned in neutral ports.

Not agreed to. It is assumed that the proposal refers to naval vessels, although it is not so stated. We believe it unwise, for reasons already given, to prohibit Germany from building or possessing a Navy.[1]

(h) The fortifications and harbor works at Heligoland should be destroyed by German labor and at German expense within a definite period. The future ownership of the island should be left to the decision of the Peace Conference.

Not agreed to. The island of Heligoland is a defensive position for Germany. Its defenses and its harbor works are the same nature as other defensive measures taken on the German mainland to control approaches to harbors. We believe that the future ownership of Heligoland

---

[1]Naval vessels only are referred to here; merchant vessels were dealt with in clauses (f) and (o).

556 ANGLO-AMERICAN NAVAL RELATIONS 1917-1919

(i) All fortifications or batteries which command the routes into the Baltic should be dismantled, and an undertaking should be given by Germany not to rearm them, or to establish any fortifications or batteries commanding these routes.

should remain with Germany.[1] There should be freedom of passage between the Baltic and North Seas in peace and war. The neutralization of the passage between these two seas should be handled as one question, in which Germany, Denmark and Sweden are all interested. We refrain from any specific recommendations as to the method of neutralization of these passages, as this is a political question.

(j) The Kiel Canal should be opened at all times to the commerce and war vessels of all nations on equal terms.

The Kiel Canal is distinctly a German canal, wholly within German boundaries, connecting German waters, and as such should remain in the complete control of Germany.

(k) Germany should be excluded from her former colonies. This is necessary to the future security of the world's trade routes.

The German islands in the Pacific should be distributed by the Peace Conference, under the following restrictions of the sovereignty of the Powers to which they are awarded, said restrictions to be guaranteed by all the Powers signatory to the Treaty of Peace: (1) each and every island shall be administered in the interests of its inhabitants – especially of its native inhabitants. (2) no fortifications shall be created or maintained, or material for fortifications or defenses, or military stores be accumulated on any one of the islands

---

[1]Heligoland gave Germany control of the German Bight. As Sims recognised, it would have been a strategic liability in Allied hands, as it was only 30 miles from the German mainland. This note of disagreement is probably a further instance of the American desire to preserve a strong Germany as a counterweight to Britain. See Sims to Bayly, 9 November 1918, box 145, *Sims Papers*.

during the time when the
Power which owns the island is
at peace. (3) there shall be perpetual equality of trade opportunity for all nations, with no
discrimination whatever in
favor of the commercial or
shipping interests of the sovereign power. (4) there shall be
no closed ports or closed areas
during the time when the
sovereign power is at peace.[1]
The United States should not
seek nor accept the award of
any of these islands. The German colonies in Africa should
not be returned to Germany,
and the same provisions should
apply as in the case of the German islands in the Pacific.

****

(m)   Submarine cables should
not be returned to their former
owners. Compensations should
be refused. The present division of cables between France
and Great Britain should be
made permanent.

Not agreed to. There were in
1914 three German cables
across the Atlantic, two in the
North Atlantic and one in the
South Atlantic. The two in the
North Atlantic were laid from
New York via the Azores and
Emden. The British have
assumed control of one of
these cables and the French the
other. ...[2] It is distinctly in the
interests of the United States

[1]These conditions were characteristic American demands: freer trade, anti-colonia-
lism, no fortification. They resurfaced at the Washington Conference of 1921–22 and
appeared in its various treaties and agreements. Article XIX of the Five-Power Treaty
on naval limitation, for example, declared that there should be no further fortification
of most of the Pacific islands.

[2]The Americans and the British were engaged in a global struggle for the control of
cable and wireless communications. Daniels and Roosevelt believed in a government-
owned international communications network. The Navy had general oversight at
this time because of the need to contact ships in distant waters. See Jonathan Daniels,
The End of Innocence (Philadelphia: Lippincott, 1954), p. 313.

that these cables be re-established at the termination of the war, in order that commercial messages may flow directly between Germany and the United States. Further, it is not in the interests of an equitable distribution of trade that all cable communications should be in the hands of any single Power. The effort should be toward either an internationalization of cable and radio communications, or a distribution of control of such communication facilities, so that no one Power may monopolize them and thereby gain undue trade advantage. We believe it to be unsound in principle not to recognize the inviolability of private property, and for this reason, do not agree, even if the cables be seized, that their private owners should not be reimbursed.

(n)   With reference to mine clearing, the decision of the Allied Naval Council should be included in the Terms of Peace. The Allies should indicate to Germany any priority necessary to sweep clear channels of importance to the Allies.

Agreed to.

****

419.   *Minutes of the Allied Naval Council*

Paris,
11 November 1918

Appendix K
Naval Conditions of Arrmistice with Germany, as amended and
approved by the. Supreme War Council[1]

****

XX.   Immediate cessation of all hosilities at sea and definite
information to be given as to the location and movements of all German ships.
Notification to be given to Neutrals that freedom of
navigation in all territorial waters is given to the Naval
and Mercantile Marines of the Allied and Associated
Powers, all questions of neutrality being waived.

XXI.   All Naval and Mercantile prisoners of war of the Allied
and Associated Powers in German hands to be returned
without reciprocity.

XXII.   Handing over to the Allies and the United States of all
submarines (including all submarine cruisers and minelayers) which are at present at the moment with full
complement in the ports specified by the Allies and the
United States. Those that cannot put to sea to be
deprived of crews and supplies, and shall remain under
the supervision of the Allies and the United States.
Submarines ready to put to sea shall be prepared to
leave German Ports immediately on receipt of wireless
order to sail to the port of surrender, the remainder to
follow as early as possible. The conditions of this article
shall be carried out within fourteen days after the signing of the Armistice.

XXIII.   The following German surface warships, which shall be
designated by the Allies and the United States of America, shall forthwith be disarmed and thereafter interned

[1] Trask, *Captains and Cabinets*, pp. 343–9.

in Neutral Ports, or failing them Allied Ports, to be designated by the Allies and the United States of America, and placed under the surveillance of the Allies and the United States of America, only caretakers being left · on board, namely:–

6 Battle Cruisers.
10 Battleships.
8 Light Cruisers, including 2 Minelayers.
50 Destroyers of the most modern types.[1]

All other surface warships (including river craft) are to be concentrated in German naval bases to be designated by the Allies and the United States of America, and are to be paid off and completely disarmed and placed under the supervision of the Allies and the United States of America. All vessels of the auxiliary fleet (trawlers, motor vessels, etc.) are to be disarmed. All vessels specified for internment shall be ready to leave German ports seven days after the signing of the Armistice. Directions of the voyage will be given by wireless.

Note. – A declaration has been signed by the Allied Delegates and handed to the German Delegates to the effect that in the event of ships not being handed over owing to the mutinous state of the Fleet the Allies reserve the right to occupy Heligoland as an advanced base to enable them to enforce the terms of Armistice. The German Delegates have on their part signed a declaration that they will recommend the Chancellor to accept this.

XXIV. The Allies and the United States of America shall have the right to sweep up all minefields and obstructions laid by Germany outside German territorial waters, and the positions of these are to be indicated.

XXV. Freedom of access to and from the Baltic to be given to the Naval and Mercantile Marines of the Allied and Associated Powers. To secure this the Allies and the United States of America shall be empowered to occupy all German forts, fortifications, batteries, and defence

[1] Neutral countries having refused to accept them, the German ships ended up at Scapa Flow.

works of all kinds in the entrances from the Cattegat into the Baltic, and to sweep up all mines and obstructions within and without German territorial waters without any questions of neutrality being raised, and the positions of all such mines and obstructions are to be indicated.

XXVI. The existing Blockade conditions set up by the Allied and Associated Powers are to remain unchanged, and all German merchant ships found at sea are to remain liable to capture. The Allies and the United States contemplate the provisioning of Germany during the Armistice as shall be found necessary.

XXVII. All Naval Aircaft are to be concentrated and immobilised in German bases to be specified by the Allies and the United States of America.

XXVIII. In evacuating the Belgian Coasts and Ports, Germany shall abandon all merchant ships, tugs, lighters, cranes, and all other harbour materials, all materials for inland navigation, all aircraft and air materials and stores, all arms and armaments, and all stores and apparatus of all kinds.

XXIX. All Black Sea Ports are to be evacuated by Germany; *all Russian Warships of all descriptions seized by Germany in the Black Sea are to be handed over to the Allies and the United States of America*; ...

****

420. *Office of Naval Operations to Benson*

25 October 1918

The proposed ship-building program of the United States he [Pratt] believes will throw a bomb shell into the British camp. He has talked with Admiral Grant and has received their point of view. They believe it does not coincide with our talk of disarmament. Captain Pratt told Admiral Grant that we were like a family, the son had grown up and wished equal representation with the father. He wished the English Government would look at it that way and realize that we have considerable interests that need this construction. Furthermore, it will lighten the burden of England in the maintenance of her huge fleet if the United States will carry this out.

421.   *Grant to Murray*

HMS *Warrior*,
Washington,
1 November 1918

****

3. *United States [Post-] War Programme*

One of the most interesting events of the month has been the publication of the United States 'after the war' programme of capital warship construction. This is the result of careful deliberation and represents the views of those concerned from the President down.

It seems amazing that such an enormous proposed increase of naval strength after the war is hardly recognised as being illogical or inconsistent when advanced with the concomitant advocation of a league of nations and general reduction of armaments: as a published programme it may I think be fairly taken as representing the Governmental view, in this country as to the standard of naval strength to be adhered to *equally* by the United States and Great Britain after the war, and very considerable influence and pressure will be necessary in order to obtain any modification if such is deemed desirable.

422.   *Memorandum by Geddes for War Cabinet*

7 November 1918

United States Naval Policy

The Cabinet may remember that as a sequence of my recent visit to the United States, I gave verbally as my view that the President was looking to the exercise of sea power to enforce, in the ultimate resort, anything which the League of Nations, as he sees it, wish to enforce.

I also drew attention to the fact that America was continuing to build capital ships, at a time when the whole of her energies ought to have been thrown into building destroyers for convoying and escorting her own Army across the Atlantic.

In Paris, the one outstanding feature, which I detected in the American Naval Representatives' attitude at our Meetings, was that nothing we did there should in any way prejudice or have any influence upon the disposition of any warships of which Germany may ultimately be deprived after Peace.[1]

My sequence of thought in observing these various happenings, has been that President Wilson wishes to create a sea power other than ours.

(a) By building in the United States at the present time.

(b) By the allocation of the ships of which Germany is to be deprived at the Peace Conference; and

(c) By combining with other nations, jealous of our sea power, which will, in combination, be the equivalent of, or greater than, the sea power of the British Empire.

In other words, he is pursuing the 'Balance of Power' theory, which has hitherto so much influenced European politics, and is applying it in sea power only to world politics.

I called to say good-bye to Colonel House before I left Paris, after the conclusion of all the Meetings, and I got an interesting but rather unaccountable confirmation of this view. Colonel House told me that the President had realised how sea-power had built up and maintained the British Empire, and how the absolutely essential importance of it had been demonstrated by the present War, and that the League of Nations would control recalcitrant members in the future by the exercise of sea-power.

I can hardly think why Colonel House made this statement to me. He is the last man to suspect of thoughtlessly indiscreet utterances, but I am convinced that by the methods I have set out above, it is the aim and purpose of the President to reduce comparatively the preponderance in sea-power of the British Empire.[2]

423.   *Memorandum by Admiralty Plans Division*

11 November 1918

Remarks on the USA Building Programme

[Copy of] Note from the First Lord to the First Sea Lord, DNI, Controller and DP[3]

24 October 1918

---

[1] Geddes is referring to the meetings of the Allied Naval Council hurriedly arranged to draw up the naval terms of the Armistice.

[2] House sometimes acted on his own initiative but here he seems to be conveying the President's own views.

[3] I.e., Geddes to Wemyss, Hall, de Bartoleme and Fuller. Commodore (later Admiral Sir) Charles Martin de Bartoleme (1871–1941): Commander and Asst. to Director of Naval Ordnance 1905–07; Captain 1907; Flag Captain, Home Fleet 1911;

With reference to the attached copy of a dispatch from Washington which appears in today's *Globe*,[1] I think it might be useful – having regard to the important questions relating to the ideal of the freedom of the seas which may arise – that we should consider at the Board a report from DNI on the probable strength in let us say 3 years' time of the various Navies of the world, including Germany and United States.

It is a remarkable thing that the United States, with no need for larger ships in this war, are building heavily on the type of vessels which we cannot afford to build. No doubt they have problems of their own, specific and otherwise, but the idea of the League of Nations does not comprise increased armament but decreased armament.

If a study of the question by DNI and the Naval Staff produces any interesting matters for discussion you might consider bringing it up at the Board.

Paragraph from the Globe, 24 October 1918

Bigger US Navy

Washington, Wednesday – Mr Daniels, Secretary of the Navy, speaking today before the Naval Committee of the House of Representatives, urged the adoption of a second three-year naval construction programme, providing for ten additional Dreadnoughts, six battlecruisers, and 140 smaller vessels, at a cost of £120,000,000. – Reuter.

Minute by DCNS[2]

12 November 1918

****

The magnitude of this fleet, now the only fleet which is a potential rival, and consequently menace, to ours, must be a matter of great concern to us, as it must govern our future building programmes.

... it will certainly require to be taken into consideration before the decision is made respecting proceeding with battle cruisers now

---

Naval Asst. to 1st Sea Lord 1911–16; Commodore and 3rd Sea Lord June 1918 and also Controller from November 1918.

[1] Presumably the London *Globe*.

[2] Rear-Admiral Sydney Fremantle.

building, or respecting laying down of new battleships.

(Memorandum)

1. If the increase proposed by Mr Secretary Daniels is adopted, the number of vessels building or projected will be as follows.

Type	Already building or projected	Increase	Total
Dreadnought battleships	13	10	23
Battle Cruisers	6	6	12
Light cruisers	10 } 258	140	398
Destroyers	248		

2. The probable reasons for the proposed expansion of the USA Navy may be examined under two headings:

(a) Protection of USA interests.

(b) The provision of a fleet for upholding a League of Nations.

Protection of USA Interests

3. The USA are practically independent of overseas for the necessaries of life and their existence as a Nation is not therefore dependent on sea power to the same extent as this country. They have, however, a very extensive coastline, colonial possessions in the Philippines, a valuable oversea trade and since the war, a large mercantile marine, each of which can only be safeguarded by naval forces.

4. If the expansion of the USA fleet is being undertaken to safeguard their own interests, it is probably aimed at Japan, for the belief in an eventual struggle with that country is deeply rooted in the minds of many Americans and their interests are certainly liable to clash at several points.

5. Japan aims at occupying a predominant position in the Far East both in a military and a commercial sense and the war has certainly increased her financial and industrial power; America stands for the 'open door' in China whilst Japan has adopted a directly opposite policy in Korea, Formosa and Southern Manchuria. The Philippines, the immigration question in California and an aggressive Japanese policy towards China or Siberia are viewed as possible sources of an American-Japanese war in the future.

6. Although it would appear to the unprejudiced onlooker that the danger of Japanese aggression is very much exaggerated and that that country could not face a war with the USA, it must be

remembered that the military party has possessed great power in Japan and that the Government and the general state policy of the country are run on very much the same lines as Germany.

7.   By the end of 1924 it is possible that Japan's fleet will consist of:–

8 Dreadnought battleships
8 Battlecruisers
7 Modern light cruisers

and a number of destroyers which cannot be accurately forecasted. She is also making every effort to increase the capacity of her dockyards.

8.   So far as the national interests of the USA are concerned, no other reason for the expansion of their Navy can be suggested. In the event of trouble with Mexico or any of the Central or South American Republics, an increased number of Dreadnought battleships would serve no useful purpose, unless another European Power was involved and that appears to be most improbable.[1]

9.   Any attempt on the part of another power to build up a great Navy must always be viewed with suspicion in this country, but it is inconceivable that the proposed expansion of the USA Fleet is in any way aimed at this country. The future however cannot be foreseen and it may become a danger to us later on.

League of Nations

With regard to (b), it is generally agreed that any practical plan for a League of Nations and the abolition of war are dependent on a super-national force consisting of the armies and navies of the contracting Powers. A desire to possess a voice in such a League commensurate with her size and wealth may account for the proposed expansion of the USA Navy.

Conclusion

The army and navy of a democratically governed country are seldom developed in accordance with any clearly defined policy, except a general idea of self-defence.

It is probable that President Wilson and his advisors have in the back of their minds the idea of Japanese aggression combined with a strong Navy to assist in supporting a future League of Nations.

---

[1] The Atlantic Fleet battleships had been employed on a rather aimless and debilitating blockade of Mexico's Caribbean coast in 1913–14, leading to the bloody assault on Vera Cruz in April 1914.

424.   *Pratt to Benson*

12 November 1918

I am sending you a copy of the fundamental plan of the proposed League of Nations Navy, with explanations. ...

****

... as you will see by looking in the explanations the percentage of representation is such that England and the United States practically control, and with France will have the controlling voice in the directorate. Our idea is based on the fact that there should be about seven states represented to begin with. While a theoretical League might naturally take in all of the countries of the world, we feel that the practical application of it does not permit of such a proposition, and that at the outside the number will be limited to seven. Furthermore, it would seem wise that those nations, meaning of course ourselves and Great Britian, who have the means and the ability to properly police the seas, should control. At least for the present, and so long as the present state of affairs exists, I was very strong in advocating equal representaion for the United States and Great Britain. While we may not have the number of ships that Great Britain has at present, our future development is going to put us on a par with her, so far as ships are concerned. On the other hand she has the colonies while we have the money and a prospective future for expansion.

From all I can learn I believe Great Britain would be very glad to have some sort of alliance with us, and I think come to an agreement in the matter of naval armament. I feel very strongly that this is a most wise thing to do for if we don't, I believe that we will have other countries attempting to sow the seed of discord between [us] and thus to profit by the results of such discord. If we each attempt singly to create Navies of our own, along the old established lines, it will immediately put us in competition with her. I think without the slightest doubt we can very readily surpass her in the matter of building, for we have the means and we have not been so hard hit by this war. However, were we to do this the same old causes for friction in the way of trade competitions, tariffs, etc., would remain, and there would be no ultimate Court of Appeals, with its corresponding international police force, to remedy matters. Again, if we compete openly for the supremacy of the seas it will surely cause this discord, because, without reasoning as to the justice in the latter, the British are bound to wince at their loss of prestige on the sea, and will compete with us to the best of their ability in the matter of building ships. This means practically that for many years to come the balance of power will be established between the United States and Great Britain, which will ebb and flow as our resources are greater than hers or less, and which may later turn against us as Canada, Australia, New Zealand, India and all of her colonies develop to the extent that we have developed and come to the assistance of the Mother country. Such competition extended over a number of years is bound to result in the same state of feeling which existed during our War of 1812, and up to and including the War of the Rebellion. This would be a regrettable state of affairs, and it would be directly against the interests of humanity to have the two great Anglo-Saxon speaking nations, who should be closely tied together and who of all nations are the only ones capable of effecting the work of reconstruction which must go on, pitted against each other. For these reasons I feel that there is a great deal to be said in favor of a League Navy and I feel that it is a way in which Great Britain may gracefully yield her prestige without causing too much dissention within her own boundaries, and, at the same time, unite with us in effectively policing the seas. We feel very strongly that such a scheme as outlined will probably tend to draw Great Britain and ourselves somewhat closer together and that it will remove the competitive feature between the only two great powers now able to compete with each other, and that it will tend in the course of time toward a general decrease of Naval armament.

****

425. *Sims to Benson*

14 November 1918

Types of Capital Ships

****

3. My conclusions, the reasons for which are set forth at length hereafter, are:

(a) For the present we should concentrate on a single type of capital ship.

(b) Its characteristics should be about as follows:

Not less than eight 16-inch guns, (Note: Any increase in battery desired should be obtained by increased displacement and not by sacrifice of other characteristics.)

12-inch armor for the side belts, barbettes, and turrets.

Corresponding deck protection.

Complete torpedo protection.

The highest speed attainable with the machinery installation already designed for the Battle Cruisers, which is understood to be of the maximum power which is considered practicable in the present stage of engineering development. This speed should, if possible be 32 knots, and in any case, not less than 30 knots.[1]

(c)   The policy outlined in (a) and (b) should be applied to the six Battleships and the six Battle Cruisers of the 1916 Program which have not yet been laid down, even though some delay in their construction may be caused thereby.

9.   ****

... the following letter from Rear-Admiral Hugh Rodman, US Navy, who has had exceptional opportunities to gage opinion in the British Service, is quoted:

'1. From the best sources of information available, and after discussion, I am very much of the opinion that Battle*ship* and Battle *Cruiser* types have a strong tendency to merge in the British *Hood* Class; characteristics as follows:

Speed 30.5 knots; Eight 15-inch guns; 12-inch armor.

2. Without having our own data at hand, I believe that our new Battle Cruisers would be far more valuable and efficient if they were modified to conform to the above mentioned principle, with the following tentative characterisation:

Displacement 45,000 tons; Speed 32,5 knots; Eight 16-inch guns; 12-inch armor.

If 14-inch guns were used, more might be installed with same displacement.

3. It is undertsood that 7.5" guns are contemplated on future British Light Cruisers, such being the case, 5-inch armor on a Battle Cruiser would have mighty little chance.'[2]

10.   It is known that the decision of our General Board to adhere to our original Battle Cruiser Design has been the subject of official discussion in the British Admiralty, and the unanimous opinion recorded is that we are making a grave mistake.[3] This has natur-

---

[1] British naval architects believed 144000 s.h.p. was the current maximum. *Hood* was originally designed for 32 knots, as were *Repulse* and *Renown*. After Jutland, additional armour protection brought *Hood* down to 30.5 knots and the other two to 29 knots.

[2] The *Effingham* class: cruisers, 1919–25; 9750 tons; 7 × 7.5in; 6 tt; 30 knots.

[3] Sims had taken it upon himself to write this memorandum of dissent from the General Board's decision to ignore the apparent lessons of Jutland and the paper

ally never been brought to my attention officially, and it has been mentioned to me personally and to a member of my Staff with the greatest diffidence, as it is felt to be entirely a matter for our own determination. It has therefore only been on my request that several of the Admiralty Officials have discussed the matter personally as one of professional interest, and it is evident that they feel that we have not fully grasped what they consider as the outstanding lesson of the Battle of Jutland, viz: The necessity for added protection of Battle Cruisers, a characteristic in which they are frank in admitting that the German ships of this Class are superior.

14.   ****

(a) As regards existing Fleets, a vessel of Americanised *Hood* type, with a battery of eight 16-inch guns, will be capable of meeting, on at least equal terms offensively, any ship afloat.

(b) Its 12-inch armor arrangement will be as efficient as that of any existing Battleship with the possible exception of United States Battleships Nos. 43 to 48, and the German *Bayerns*,[1] and the probable disposition of the latter should permit them to be disregarded. (Note: Whereas the *Hood* is slightly inferior in vertical armor to the *Royal Sovereign* and *Queen Elizabeth* Classes, it is superior in horizontal protection to any existing British Battleship.) The torpedo protection is more complete than any existing Battleship, with the exception of the United States Battleships Nos. 43 to 48.

(c) In view of (a) and (b), it appears that the *Hood*, due to its great speed, is superior as a fighting unit to any existing Battleship, and with the exception of United States Battleships Nos. 43 to 48, could meet on equal terms, in a stand-up fight, where speed did not figure, any existing Battleship.

(d) If, therefore, the six Battleships (Nos. 49 to 54)[2] of the 1916 Program, as well as the six Battle Cruisers of the same Program, were laid down of this type (Americanised *Hood*), it would give the United States a homogenous squadron of 12 vessels, capable of taking their place in the line of battle, and thereby strengthening our present Fleet by the addition of 12 units, and at the same time,

includes extensive discussion of British ships and design policy and quotations from senior British officers.

[1] SMS *Bayern*: battleship, 1917; 28000 tons; 8 × 15in; 18 × 5.9in; 23.5 knots.

[2] US battleship numbers and names: 43 *Tennessee*, 44 *California*, 45 [?], 46 *Colorado*, 47 *Maryland*, 48 *Washington*, 49 *South Dakota*, 50 *Indiana*, 51 *Montana*, 52 *North Carolina*, 53 *Iowa*, 54 *Massachusetts*. Some of these were not built, others not until World War II.

give us a Battle Cruiser Squadron far more powerful in offence and defence and far more speedy than anything now contemplated by any Naval Power. If armaments are to be limited in the future (and our proposed new three-year Program would probably be eliminated thereby), the present strength of existing Fleets will be of far greater importance as new units, if any, will be added [at] a slower rate. . . .

426.   *Benson to Daniels*

20 November 1918

Further knowledge of situation over here convinces me that unless peace is secured in accordance with principles laid down by President, this war will have been fought in vain. Allied propaganda amongst our people more dangerous than German. Apparent efforts being made at home to have peace terms in accordance [with] views and wishes [of] Great Britain, France and Italy most injurious and dangerous. If press could, without arousing bitterness on this side, reveal to our people the true conditions, such as efforts to minimize what we have done, exacting high prices and illiberal conditions wherever possible, our people would be indignant rather than morbidly sentimental.

While we should stop thinking and arguing in terms of force, we should face the situation. No one thing will serve more to help in carrying through President's views, particularly freedom of the sea, than decided evidence that we are going to build up our Navy as soon as possible. This should be done even if considered desirable to ease up later.

427.   *Sims to Bayly*

25 November 1918

I find it difficult to believe that sixty or seventy German vessels steamed quietly in between the two lines of the Grand Fleet and surrendered. There is every official evidence that this was accomplished, and I was present on the *New York*[1] and witnessed the astonishing spectacle, but even now at times it is difficult to believe that it has really happened.

This is certainly an astonishing war. Some of our people have visited the submarines that are being surrendered to Admiral Tyr-

---

[1] Flagship of the American squadron serving with the Grand Fleet.

whitt[1] at Harwich. In most cases the Captains to the submarines did not come with them, but the rest of the people did not seem to be particularly depressed.

It was curious to hear the expressions of opinion in the Grand Fleet and on our vessels on the morning of the 21st before the German vessels came in sight. Many expressed the doubt as to whether we would find them at the rendezvous, saying that they would probably sink the vessels rather than surrender them. Some wondered whether the arrangement for sending in the vessels did not conceal a trick by which the power of the Grand Fleet might be seriously reduced. It was probably for this reason that the distance between the two lines of battleships was six miles, with the Germans three miles from either line. This would have enabled fire to be maintained from both lines without much danger of hitting the other. It was a dramatic moment when the British cruiser's[2] kite balloon was first seen, followed later by the outlines of the leading German ships. For a great wonder the weather was entirely clear overhead with bright sunshine and very little wind, so that all the vessels could be seen with great distinctness. I do not know yet much about any details of incidents that occurred on board the German vessels when they were inspected each by a designated British mate, but doubtless we will get this information later.

428.   *Benson to Daniels*

27 November 1918

I have noticed with great concern press quotations from United States indicating discussions at home regarding the distribution [of] surrendered German ships. Naval terms of armistice with Germany practically complied with. This leaves Great Britain with only Navy stronger than our own. Any distribution of German ships would have to be made in proportion to those parts of the several navies which were instrumental in forcing surrender of German ships and keeping them blockaded in port. Sims has stated publicly in London that percentage of United States has been very small.[3] According to these figures our proportion of German

---

[1] Later Admiral of the Fleet Sir Reginald Yorke Tyrwhitt (1870–1951): entered RN 1883; Captain 1908; Commodore of Harwich Force 1914–18; Rear-Admiral 1918; 3rd Light Cruiser Sqdn, Mediterranean Fleet 1921; Flag Officer Scotland 1923–5; CinC China Station 1927–9; Admiral 1929; CinC Nore 1930–33; Admiral of the Fleet 1934.
[2] HMS *Cardiff*: light cruiser, 1917; 4190 tons; 5 × 6in; 8 tt: 29 knots.
[3] See document no. 387.

men-of-war would be very little whereas British proportion would be such that practically entire strength of German captured vessels would go to British. If there is no definite limitation to naval armaments, my observations confirm my previous opinion that we must eventually have a navy equal to or superior to that of any other country. By dividing surrendered German men-of-war proportionately we consent to tremendous increases in British Navy thereby necessitating our building just that many more vessels of equal or superior strength thus augmenting our expense at least to the extent to which Great Britain should profit. On the other hand we have fought for the avowed purpose of destroying a military autocracy. To use or to consent to the use of the captured instruments of this autocracy would weaken our purpose while to insist upon their destruction would greatly strengthen it. For these reasons I am opposed to division of German men-of-war and believe our best interests as well as best interests of all mankind will be served by disposing of surrendered German men-of-war without their actually coming into the possession of any power as potential fighting weapons.

Memo for Secretary [by Captain Pratt]

I concur in the above and believe that:

1. Until settlement, they should be held in trust.

2. That if a League Navy be formed they be turned over to that international body and distributed in that body in proportion to representation.

3. That under no circumstances they be portioned out to national navies, but failing to form League Navy, they be destroyed to avoid friction.

429.   *Memorandum by Pratt on League of Nations*

28 November 1918

****

The prime difficulties will center about freedom of the seas, and the details to be agreed upon to make that freedom possible. Essentially this is the problem between the United States and Great Britain. If these two powers whose aims should be similar, whose paths lie side by side, will enter into a just sea compact, sharing like and like the burdens and giving of their plenty to others, the first and most essential agreement is reached. The complete League of Nations is a natural consequence.

430.   *Grant to Murray*

1 December 1918

****

United States Postwar Naval Programme

As regards the new naval programme, Secretary Daniels informed me he will be tied to Washington till he got his bill through and must at any rate defer his visit to England for that reason until February.[1] How far he really hopes to carry his immense programme I am unable to say; he implies determination but the feeling among a very large number of influential men in and out of Senate and Congress is undoubtedly crystallizing against it and holds to the justice of England's claim for a predominant fleet, to a proportionate reduction of armament, and against the so-called freedom of the seas; these latter points are freely discussed everywhere by politicians, and the Republicans especially, who will shortly be in power, appear prepared to back up the British point of view.[2]

The relative strength in the future of the two fleets, British and United States, has at different times been advanced to me at all numbers from two to one to five to four, as opposed to the Government professed point of view of equality.

431.   *Memorandum by Wemyss for War Cabinet*

18 December 1918

The Naval Aspects of a League of Nations

****

10. ... a League of Nations, however efficient it might seem for the prevention of war, would not alter the fact that it is vital to the existence of the British Empire to maintain a fleet strong enough to ensure its oversea communications in war time. It is, therefore, essential that, in entering such a League, Great Britain should make it a condition that the predominating fleet shall be furnished by itself, unless it can share its predominance with some power or

---

[1] Daniels eventually visited Europe in March, April and May 1919.
[2] Theodore Roosevelt was prepared to accord Britain naval supremacy as he believed her interests were broadly in accord with those of the US and that her control of the Atlantic was to the advantage of America.

powers on whose good faith it can place implicit and unwavering reliance. The fleet or fleets concerned must moreover be qualified to co-operate with the British Fleet in general fleet work.

11. The co-ordination of naval action in these circumstances could be simplified to a great extent. If the British Empire and the United States furnish the bulk of the naval forces of the League the organisation to direct their activities and those of the smaller contributions of other powers would naturally fall mainly into their hands. The question of supreme command would in these circumstances be a matter of arrangement between the two powers.

432. *Admiral of the Fleet Lord Fisher to Sims*

29 December 1918

****

What President Wilson has to do is to establish a Great Federation of Free Nations who speak our Common Tongue! A Big Commonwealth of Free Republics! *That* would ensure Peace! Yours till hell freezes.

All kings and all secret diplomacy must be swept away! This is vital!!

433. *Memorandum by Wemyss for War Cabinet*

6 January 1919

Proposed Disposal of Enemy Ships of War

Enemy Submarines

All German, Austrian and Turkish submarines surrendered under the terms of the Armistice are to be sunk within three months of the signing of the Peace Treaty. All Bulgarian submarines are to be surrendered within the same period and sunk.

All submarines building, or unfit for Sea, in Germany and Austria, to be destroyed under Allied supervision within 3 months of the signing of the Peace Treaty. German submarines interned in neutral countries are to be surrendered to the Allies and sunk.

The above action will be taken in order to prevent the Central Powers commencing another submarine campaign in the near future; and while removing the possibility of any disagreement among the Allies and Associated Powers as to the distribution of the submarines it will be a judgement on the enemy for the outrages committed by his submarines during the war.

Enemy Surface Warships

Note – In all cases where it is laid down that enemy vessels, built or building, should be destroyed the following reasons have dictated the policy:–

(i)   To reduce the Naval power of the enemy.

(ii)   To prevent the enemy again acquiring the ships.

(iii) To avoid disagreement among the Allies and Associated Powers as regards the distribution of the Ships.

Germany

All vessels interned under the terms of the Armistice, and the nine other remaining 'Dreadnought' battleships are to be surrendered to the Allied and Associated Powers, and are to be sunk in deep water within 3 months of the signing of the Peace Treaty.

In addition, warships interned in neutral ports are to be surrendered and sunk within 3 months of delivery.

The vessels remaining, which are for the most part obsolescent, will leave Germany with sufficient vessels for self-protection and police duties, while not giving her a predominance in the Baltic.

****

434.   *US Navy Department Memorandum*

[probably early 1919]

British and American Naval Strength

****

... It will be noted from the list[1]:–

1. That if Great Britain built no more battleships, and if the American programme of battleship construction were completed, that the battleship strength of the two Navies would be approximately equal.

2. That if Great Britain built no more battle cruisers and if America completed her battle cruiser programme, she would still lack 4 battle cruisers to have a battle cruiser squadron equal in strength to that of Great Britain.

3. That some emphasis has been placed on the relative strengths of the batteries of ships, the claim being put forward that the 16-inch battery is a much more powerful battery than the 15-inch battery.

---

[1] Not reproduced, but listing capital ships of the two navies – existing, building and projected.

This claim is largely a matter of opinion; either shell is capable of penetrating the heaviest armor afloat or likely to be afloat. The 15-inch gun is capable of making up by rapidity of fire a large part of whatever advantage the 16-inch gun may have over it in the matter of weight of shell.

4. That those American ships which have 12 16-inch guns carry them in four turrets, which necessarily is a disadvantage compared with two guns in the turret from the standpoint both of rapidity of fire and general handiness.

5. That an examination of our new battle cruiser programme as compared with the latest type (*Hood*) of British battle cruiser will show our own vessels to be inferior in protection, and consequently not so fit for action.

In discussing relative naval strengths we must keep constantly in mind the object of the exercise of naval power – that is, control of sea communications, which in simpler language means the control of merchant ships of your enemy and of other merchant ships which assist your enemy. This kind of control requires cruisers capable of driving hostile commerce from the seas, and thereafter keeping the seas clear of hostile commerce, and at the same time capable of escaping from enemy vessels of superior fighting power. In this kind of naval strength, the United States is entirely deficient, whereas Great Britain is very strong. We could not possibly consider any arrangement which would prevent us from a development of full equality with Great Britain in facilities for carrying on cruiser warfare against commerce.

435.   *US Planning Section*

London,
early 1919

Building Program

General Situation

Admiral Benson has received the following despatch from the Navy Department:–

> 'The Department has asked Congress to authorise a second [three] year building program providing for ten additional dreadnoughts and six additional battle cruisers. ... Having studied the Admiralty's and any other plans and gotten the ideas of whatever officers you may deem advisable, please submit your views on the subject, upon your return. ...'

578   ANGLO-AMERICAN NAVAL RELATIONS 1917–1919

The Chief of Naval Operations would like the above quoted despatch taken as a subject for study and estimate of the questions involved. ...

In May 1918, at a time when the crushing defeat of Germany did not appear among the probabilities of the immediate future, the Planning Section prepared Memorandum No. 21 on the subject of the US Naval Building Policy.[1] At that time it was considered that ... the most likely combination of Powers against which the United States must be prepared to operate with its navy would be Germany, Austria and Japan.

****

We may assume that the Treaty of Peace with the Central Powers will
   (a) Dispose of the German naval menace to Great Britain.
   (b) Leave Germany much inferior in naval power to the United States.
   (c) Leave Austria with a negligible Navy.
   (d) Leave British Navy stronger relatively than it was before the war, and without any restraining influence of consequence in Europe.
   (e) Promote the US Navy to second place.

The events of the past few months will have indicated to Japan that American military and naval power is great enough, and the will to fight of the American people strong enough to render any warlike aggression against us by Japan highly unwise except Japan be in alliance with a strong European power.

We see that –
   (a) The world is to be left with one great Navy – *the British Navy*; and with one other navy that may possibly grow to be a rival of the British Navy – *the American Navy*.
   (b) No Navy or combination of Navies from which the American Navy is absent can greatly menace British supremacy on the sea.
   (c) No Navy or Combination of European Navies from which the British Navy is absent can greatly menace the American Navy.
   (d) No combination of any European Navy with the Japanese Navy in a war against the United States (except that Navy be British) is sufficiently probable to be a basis of plans for a building programme.

We may summarise the above deductions as follows:–

[1] See document no. 387.

Any additions to the British Fleet must be made with reference to the United States as a possible enemy.

Any additions to the United States Fleet must be made with reference to Great Britain as a possible enemy.

These are the facts of the case irrespective of the state of the Entente Cordiale existing between the two countries.

There are many factors which make war between the United States and Great Britain unlikely. Among these are

(a) Present sentiment.

(b) Economic dependence of Great Britain on the United States.

(c) Proximity of Canada to United States.

(d) Great amount of British wealth invested in the United States.

(e) Possible lack of Colonial support unless the war were considered highly just by the British Colonies.

(f) British labour situation.

(g) Sound business sense of the British government.

(h) Lack of aggression in American Aims.

But in spite of these happy obstacles to war, war may come; so we have to examine the possible causes of war, the missions imposed on naval forces by the war, and the resulting character of the possible campaigns.

Possible Causes of War

(a) *Trade Rivalry*

The war has caused a revival of the American Merchant Marine. The peaceful pressure it will exert towards getting its share of trade will arouse the anxiety of the British Government. Successful trade rivalry strikes at the very root of British interest and British prosperity, and may threaten even the existence of the British Empire. If British trade is seriously threatened, her people may feel that war is justified – as a measure of self-preservation.

(b) *Conflicting Views regarding Freedom of the Seas*

It is well known that British and American views regarding Freedom of the Seas are widely at variance so far as the actual application of belligerent rights is concerned. The freedom of action accorded by overwhelming superiority of naval power is not likely to lead to an interpretation of rules of warfare contrary to interest. One has but to scrutinise our diplomatic correspondence during the first years of this war when the United States was still neutral to see in the questions there discussed elements of danger.

(c) *Possible Repressive Measures on our Trade Expansion*
(d) *Considerations discussed in Planning Section Memorandum No.21*, and especially the instability of the present world organization.

Quite aside from the question of war with Great Britain there are reasons why the US Navy should be as powerful as any other Navy. We have taken the lead in certain world policies. We have been able to do this through the known unselfishness of our motives and chiefly through the sudden rise in importance of our naval and military power. We are interested in seeing the growth everywhere of American ideals of international justice and fair dealing. There is no surer way of furthering this growth than in providing diplomacy with the sanction of a naval power that by reason of its greatness shall be fearless.

In the unhappy event of a war between Great Britain and the United States it may be assumed that –

(1) No great oversea military campaign would be practicable for either country.

(2) That belligerent merchant vessels would be compelled to abandon trade between North America and Europe, unless they were in very heavily escorted convoys.

(3) Most other belligerent trade would be driven into convoys for protection against enemy cruisers.

(4) Both belligerents would use heavily armed merchant cruisers as commerce raiders.

(5) The missions of the fleets will be to destroy or sequestrate each other's merchant marine, endeavouring to get freedom to do so by decisive fleet or squadron engagements.

The flag of both countries will be flying throughout all the seas so that cruiser warfare will be worldwide. Such warfare will require secure fuelling and supply bases so distributed as best to support the world wide operations. Each country will be compelled to keep at home forces to meet local threats in the most vital areas.

Whichever country is the aggressor will seek to bring on a fleet engagement. Isolated bases are not secure – nor are post-war aims to be fully realized if the enemy is left with his naval strength unimpaired. We must therefore consider the outcome of a naval campaign to be dependent upon battles in which the fleets engage. Cruiser warfare will eventually break down if the bulwark on which it rests – the fleet – gives way. It may be to the interest of one country or the other to delay the final engagement.

During this time operations against bases, cruiser fights, prizes captured and recaptured in every part of the world, will bring the naval vessels of the two governments in contact. There is but one sound basis for designing vessels to participate in these contacts and that is superiority of type. There is but one certain way of ensuring equality of opportunity for them and that is by providing equality of strength supported by equal facilities.

American commercial routes all lie near British Naval Bases. The Canadian ports on the North, and the West Indian ports and Bermuda on the South, overlook all our great commercial routes in the Atlantic. The Canadian ports are of less importance than those farther south because such routes in the Atlantic as we may use in war will lie away from those ports and towards the West Indian ports. If we are to dominate the latter and guarantee security to the Canal, we must establish ourselves on the flank of their communications with a suitably equipped base on a well defended commodious harbor. Samana Bay is the sole position that is suitable and available to us. If we hold Samana Bay the only remaining harbors suitable for use of the British Fleet are the Gulf of Paria and the Gulf of Caricao. Eventually, if the British deemed it essential to continue to use their West Indian Bases they would have to bring their fleet to the support of those bases and doing so would expose themselves to all the dangers of a long line of communications, and of operations at a great distance from repair facilities. But if their fleet should come, we must be prepared to meet it capital ship for capital ship. It may be contended that a fleet so far from home cannot be as effective as one operating near its home base. This is true but even if the aggressor is compelled to withdraw, subsequent phases of the campaign may require equally distant operations on the part of the defending fleet.

From the foregoing considerations regarding the general strategy of a war with Great Britain, we conclude that the governing principles in naval preparations should be:–

(a) Superiority of type – ship for ship.
(b) Equality in strength in capital ships and cruisers.
(c) Equality of shore facilities in the essential operating areas.

****

From the above we see that the tendency of British naval opinion since Jutland is towards greater protection for battle cruisers and a retention of the 8-gun battery arrangement. It seems probable that no new programme of importance will be undertaken by the British until the execution of our programme is considerably more advanced than at present. We must therefore decide now from our own judgment of experience and tendencies what types of capital ships we should build.

****

Air Craft Carriers

The probability that heavier-than-air aircraft will become of increasing importance to fleet operations leads us to recommend at least two aircraft carriers for experimental and development work. The characteristics of these vessels cannot be laid down by non-technical officers except in the most general way. Data is now being collected on this subject and a special report will be made.

Conclusions

In view of the foregoing, and in view of the known present international conditions, we now modify the conclusions given in our Memorandum No. 21, to read as follows:–

1. *Basic Naval Policy of the United States*

The Navy of the United States shall be a self contained organization designed to exercise, in the Pacific, a commanding superiority of naval power, and, in the Atlantic, a defensive superiority of naval power, against all potential enemies who may seek to extend their sphere of influence over, or to impose their sovereignty on, any portion of the American continent or islands contiguous thereto, not now in their possession, or who may unjustly interfere with our international rights or our trade expansion.

2. In interpreting the basic naval policy we should consider for the present the British Navy as the maximum probable force which we must be prepared to meet. We should have always in mind the possibility of the co-operation of the British and Japanese Navies.

3. The present anti-submarine programme of construction, except destroyers, should be abandoned. No more anti-submarine vessels of any type should be laid down.

4. No anti-submarine submarines should be built.

5. The general Naval Programme should be –

Battleships   2
Note. These to have the characteristics of those
already appropriated for.
Battleships   4

****

Note. The above programme to be increased as necessary ship for ship to meet any new British building programme or any accessions to the British Fleet through the distribution of battleships of the German fleet to the Allies.

Battle Cruisers   6

Note. These are additional to those already provided for.

****

Fighting Scouts   48

****

Note. New British programme to be met vessel for vessel.

Super-Destroyers   36

Note. New British programme to be met vessel for vessel.

Scout Submarines   54

Aircraft Carriers   2

The Department's programme provides for 16 capital ships and 156 of undefined types.

The foregoing analysis leads to the conclusion that to balance the existing and projected British capital ships, but 12 are required.

Having in view a possible alliance between Great Britain and Japan, it is recommended that the four remaining capital ships be 25-knot battleships.[1]

****

436. *Press Statement by Daniels on US Postwar Building Programme*

c. 4 January 1919

Secretary of the Navy Daniels appeared before the House Naval Affairs Committee yesterday afternoon ... Secretary Daniels emphasized his earlier recommendation for the authorization of

---

[1] It is a little surprising, given the ready employment of US submarines on anti-submarine patrols off the eastern seaboard and from Berehaven and the Azores, and the recent British 'R' class (specially designed as 'hunter-killers'), that the US Navy's 'think tank' should dismiss this form of anti-submarine warfare out of hand. 'Fighting scouts' corresponds to the RN's 'light cruisers', though of 7–10000 tons rather than the 4–5000 tons of the British 'C' and 'D' classes. 'Super destroyers' may be rendered 'flotilla leaders' of which the US Navy had none. The Americans had been greatly impressed by the action of the two leaders *Swift* and *Broke* in April 1917

another three year building programme. In the course of his argument in behalf of his recommendation, Secretary Daniels said in part:

'No step backward, but a long step forward, should be taken by this Congress in strengthening the American Navy. The additional three-year programme recommended in my annual report is a conservative one intended to consolidate the policy of steady upbuilding of the Navy established in 1916. The General Board of the Navy, after extensive investigation and exhaustive consideration, has recommended a much larger programme extending to the year 1925. While their recommendations are entitled to, and have received, very careful consideration, the Department has not felt justified at this time in recommending such an extensive programme, or one extending over such a long period. At the same time, a year-by-year programme is not thought to be advisable; it is too much of the hand-to-mouth nature, and naval experts and thinking men interested in the Navy have seen its unwisdom and in 1916 succeeded in substituting a better plan. When the three year programme policy was adopted, it met with general approval throughout the country, and a reversion to hand-to-mouth methods now would be a retrograde step. The Department has felt that the least it could do at this time was to recommend a virtual duplication of this programme.

... I am asking that authorization be given for the construction of ten dreadnoughts, six battle cruisers, and ten scout cruisers to be laid down during the coming three years and one hundred and thirty other ships of such type and character as may give us a well-rounded Navy. The initial appropriation need not be large, for work on some of the big ships already authorized was necessarily deferred during the war in order that work might be concentrated upon destroyers and like small craft and merchant ships. Now the construction of the big ships will be pushed as rapidly as possible, the number of small craft being ample until more dreadnoughts and other big ships are added to the naval force. ... My thought is, and it finds expression in the estimates, that under present conditions we ought to make no change in the naval programme which the United States set for itself in 1916. We ought neither to commit ourselves to any gigantic expansion or to recede from the wise three year policy.

It is our duty to consider the obligations imposed upon America if the Peace Conference now occupied at Versailles ... completes its work satisfactorily as we all hope it will do. Let us assume that this Conference will give birth to some plan looking toward a concert of the nations for the maintenance of peace, whether it be a League of Nations ... or what not. ...

... power for the enforcement of judicial decisions sometimes needs to be considerable; and back of that must lie a tremendous police power of prevention ...

It seems self-evident that a world-police must be established to achieve this purpose, no matter what the constitution or plan of operation of the Peace League may be. That world-police will be very largely naval, for only a police equipped with and trained to ships could be world-mobile, ...

That being true it becomes obvious that if the United States is to participate in such a movement it must participate upon a scale commensurate with its wealth, intelligence, great population and scientific attainments. Any lesser participation would be a shirking of its duty. A contribution less in cost, strength or any detail of perfection, than that of any other member of the League, would be undignified and unworthy of a nation which by Providence has been so generously endowed as the United States.

I am quite certain that it would be improper for America even to consider the proposition of contributing to the world-police a number of units smaller than that contributed by the greatest other power. ... It would be contrary to all our traditions and all our ideals to assume that in the planning of a new and mighty Navy, America could be animated either by fear or by the intention of aggression.

What if, unhappily, the Peace Conference should fail to come to an agreement upon such a plan? Suppose the Powers do not now agree to curtail armament? Then it is entirely obvious to all that the United States, if she is to realise her destiny as a leader of the democratic impulse, if she is to play a proper part (as she, hand in hand with her incomparable Allies, has played it in this war) in the protection of small nations, the preservation of the freedom of the seas for them and for the world at large, must have a Navy that will be as powerful as that of any nation in the world.

It is my firm conviction that if the Conference at Versailles does not result in a general agreement to put an end to naval building on the part of all the nations, then the United States must bend her will and bend her energies, must give her men and her money to the task of the creation of incomparably the greatest Navy in the world. She has no designs upon the territory or the trade of any other nation or groups of nations. But she is pledged to the support of the Monroe Doctrine; she is pledged to the protection of the weak wherever they may suffer threats; she is incomparably strong in natural resources; if need be she must be incomparably strong in defense against aggressors and in offense against evil doers.

America is committed to the promise of entering into a general and genuine plan for the reduction of armaments. If the outcome of the Peace Conference shall be that all nations will concur in this idea then the United States will gladly join them in the worthy plan. For three years we have been committed to such a programme in such circumstances. But if such an agreement cannot be shortly arranged then we here in America must accept the burden which the failure automatically will thrust upon us and meet it by adding such units to our Navy as will secure our own safety and aid powerfully in protecting the peace of the world.

****

437. *Daniels to Wilson*

25 January 1919

… Unless conditions abroad dictate change my own view is that three year program should be adopted with proviso that if Peace Mission orders reduction of armament the President be authorized not to make contracts. Will you please cable your suggestion[?] If our friends in Congress are told that you feel this program will be helpful there is no doubt of success. If it is purely a domestic policy looking toward a bigger American Navy now there is strong sentiment to postpone authorization.[1]

438. *Wilson to Daniels*

Paris,
27 January 1919

I can say with very great conviction that it is necessary for the accomplishment of our objects here that the three-year building program should be adopted as recommended. I am willing that the

---

[1] This was probably an accurate divination of Congressional opinion, though as time went on, and especially after the 1920 elections which gave the Republicans solid majorities in both houses, it became certain that budget-cutting would be the order of the day. See Fry, pp. 39–46.

Proviso should be included that if by International agreement a reduction of armaments is arranged, I will be authorized to withhold further contracts until Congress is consulted but it would be fatal to go beyond that at this juncture.

439. *The Daily Mail*

London,
23 January 1919

United States Navy Strength: Views of Mr Franklin Roosevelt

****

... 'The United States has no intention of challenging anybody's supremacy', he said. 'Our building programme has nothing whatever in contemplation except the creation of a first-rate Fleet commensurate with the needs of a country that has 6,000 miles and more of coast-line on two seaboards which are linked by a strip of canal that one aeroplane could put out of action.

If Britain's security as an insular Power depends upon a powerful Navy, as it manifestly must, the defensive necessities of America, with her vast ocean front, are no less palpable. There is not a sane person in the United States who thinks of constructing a Fleet for the purpose of disputing Britain's position at sea. I have no hesitation whatsoever in describing such notions as utterly baseless.'[1]

****

440. *Sims to Daniels*

5 February 1919

Referring to your letter concerning alleged British criticisms of your recent statements regarding our building program, etc., I have had the matter looked up in the British press and I find that the impression created, first by the original announcement of our three year program, but, particularly, by the statements that you made before the House Naval Committee, is interpreted, practically universally, on this side as a threat, that is, a threat as to what America intends to do if the Peace Conference does not accomplish certain results.

[1] This is a characteristic Roosevelt statement, conceding nothing but disarming in its definiteness.

What confuses the issue is that there appears to be a doubt in all minds over here as to what exactly are the results which we insist upon. There is constant speculation in the press and in conversations upon this point.

Though there have been a number of comments in the British press concerning your statements, I cannot now find that in any case you have been incorrectly quoted. It is possible that the way you have been quoted has conveyed an impression which you did not intend. This is an evil which of course besets all men in public life. What I refer to is the way in which the headlines are sometimes cast, and also the fact that in all cases you were as usual, not fully quoted, but only certain isolated statements from your hearing or public addresses were selected.

I think I can best convey to you the interpretation placed upon your public statements by sending you the British *Fortnightly Review* for February, which contains an article by one of the leading British naval writers – Archibald Hurd. The title of the article, you will note, is 'The United States and Sea Power: A Challenge'.[1]

In view of the completeness of this review it will not be necessary to refer to the matter in detail, but I feel sure that, upon reading the article, you will recognise how difficult it would be to remove from the European mind the impression that the announcement of our building program is in the nature of a threat.

Of course it makes no difference at all as to what the intention was in originally announcing the program, or as to what your intention was in the statement before the House Committee. The only fact of importance in this connection is the practically universal impression that these announcements have made over here. As stated above, this impression is that of a threat or a challenge, and I do not see how any amount of explanation on this side can remove it.

Incidentally, I also find a more or less general impression that the so-called 'threat' discussed above is, as a matter of fact, more or less of a bluff – that we have little intention of actually converting our words into realities.

While I do not know enough about the Government's policies to express any opinion as to the advisability of making these announcements, or of carrying out the plan proposed, still I cannot help

---

[1] Archibald Hurd, 'The United States and Sea Power: A Challenge', *Fortnightly Review*, February 1919, pp. 175–89. Hurd (later knighted) was the premier British naval correspondent of the 1914–1945 era.

but feel that it is extremely regrettable that the nations on this side should have the distinct impression that they have been threatened.

Ever since we came into the war it has been one of the objects of the naval forces over here to try and bring about a better feeling between the Allies and the United States, particularly between Great Britain and the United States. The British have also been trying to do the same thing through their Ministry of Information, and our Government has done much in this line. Literally millions of dollars have been expended in this effort and most gratifying progress has been made. But, unfortunately, it is not too much to say that a great deal of the good accomplished by this effort has been neutralised by the feeling that has been created against us by the alleged challenge or threat of our recent announcements.

Of course, I assume there was no such intention on our part, but as showing how thoroughly established is this impression in European minds, Mr Hurd declares that your statement is in effect as follows:–

'Either join the Utopians, surrender the trident which you have, it is true, wielded for centuries with great advantage to humanity and ourselves in particular, or else we will take that trident from you.'

He justifies this interpretation by quoting the following from your statement:–

'If unhappily the Peace Conference shall fail to come to an agreement for a plan of disarmament ... then the United States must bend her will and her energies and must give her men and [her] money to the task of the creation of incomparably the greatest Navy in the world.'

There are also in this article statements to the same effect made by Admiral Badger, and there are now appearing in the European Press similar statements by Admiral Mayo, who characterises the Peace Conference as a 'Sewing Circle'.[1]

It is of course inevitable that these statements should be interpreted in connection with recent statements made by Mr Hurley, Mr Schwab and Mr Dollar,[2] advocating certain policies concerning the development of our merchant marine.

I think you will see from the above that, as I have said before, it

[1] Badger was still Senior Member, General Board, and Mayo CinC, Atlantic Fleet.
[2] Edward N. Hurley, Chairman, US Shipping Board and President, Emergency Fleet Corporation. Charles M. Schwab, Director-General, Emergency Fleet Corpor-

would appear impracticable to disabuse European minds of these impressions by anything that can be done on this side. It is possible that some announcement made from the other side might have the desired effect.

The statement that we should greatly increase our navy in order to do our share in policing the seas – keeping down piracy, etc. – appears not to be understood, as it is assumed that this service could be performed by a relatively small number of cruisers armed with 6-inch or 7-inch guns.

I need hardly say, I am sure, that in this letter I am simply reporting opinions or impressions regarding your statements that are current on this side, and that therefore in no case should they be assumed to be mine.

I have assumed that you would want me to be quite frank in explaining the impression in question – that otherwise the letter would be quite useless. This impression, being attributed largely to you, it of course follows as a natural consequence that it has rendered you to a certain extent unpopular on this side, especially in Governmental circles.[1]

441. *Memorandum for War Cabinet by Admiral Sir William Lowther Grant*

25 February 1919

[Note by Wemyss]

This paper was written by Admiral Sir W. Grant, at my request, on his return from America.[2]

[Note by Long]

A most interesting and informing paper. I agree with all the conclusions. I think I should circulate to Cabinet. ...[3]

British Policy as Regards the American Naval Programme

A considerable section of US educated or wealthy classes is actively pro-British and as such wholeheartedly endorse the British point of view as regards a predominant Navy. In fact, its advocacy

ation. Mr. Dollar has not been identified.
    [1] Sims, already determined to force a public debate on Daniels's stewardship, must have enjoyed writing this letter.
    [2] Grant had recently relinquished his command of the North America and West Indies Station.
    [3] Walter Hume Long (1st Viscount) (1854–1924): Conservative MP 1882–1921; President, Local Govt. Board, 1915–16; Colonial Secretary 1916–19; First Lord of Admiralty 16 January 1919–February 1921; Viscount 1921.

approaches the indiscreet and causes some irritation among those not holding the same strong opinions. This section has been largely reinforced during the past year or more owing to contact with and a better knowledge of British [people] of a representative type, who have been present in the country in considerable numbers. The value of this intimate association and mutual understanding can hardly be overstated. The majority of the remainder of the above classes, while not actively pro-British, recognises what Britain has done during the war and is prepared to take a sympathetic view of the British standpoint, provided that standpoint be placed squarely before it. It includes many Senators, Congressmen, Politicians and public men of the better and broader type. This class as a whole is disgusted by the manner in which the present demand for a big US Navy has been put forward, regarding it as logically rendering them open to the charge of insincerity when advanced simultaneously with advocacy for reduction of armaments and a League of Nations and as an undisguised attempt at bullying England when she is in a condition of exhaustion which the Americans themselves would similarly be in had they joined in the war earlier.

The bulk of the population are, in spite and because of their public and political education, not actively anti-British but blatantly pan-American. They can be swayed by careful leading along right lines and to counteract baneful influences, but any ill-judged action on our part might be fanned to produce among them such a wave of spread-eagleism as to force the Government to carry through the biggest Naval programme, even if the President does not really mean or wish to do so, and this in spite of the fact that the country at large is indifferent to a big Navy and will be strongly averse to the increased taxation involved and to the acceptance of any external responsibilities or liabilities beyond their cherished Monroe Doctrine. There are many Senators, Congressmen and Politicians who belong to this class, who, not moving in the same social circles, never hear the British point of view, and who, it is to be feared, are only too ready to listen to anything anti-British or to mistrust or distort anything said or done by the British.

It is a curious fact that, in spite of all argument and representation, the broader minded American without exception insists that the education and enlightenment of the American masses as to the honesty of British motives and as to the greatness of their achievements and self-sacrifice during the war must be undertaken by the British themselves and cannot and will not be done from within.

There is, of course, a large actively anti-British element in the US mainly Irish and German, but, unfortunately, persistently supported and encouraged by many politicians and others who have not the same excuse. These are wholly unscrupulous and will seize upon anything said or done, distort or even invent, in order to get what they regard as the best possible material to advance their own political ends or notoriety, and it is a sad sorry fact that such material will still always obtain a ready hearing in the US.

The large Navy idea is supported by the President and Secretary Daniels, the latter being probably the pawn of the former, and it has the support of all the thick and thin supporters of the President and of all the anti-British elements. It has the support of the Navy generally, who, apart from those who have served in Europe, are jealous of the British Navy, but would probably be satisfied with naval equality as between Britain and the US. The Navy, however, apart from the politicians, has little power or influence in the country.

The more enlightened elements, and especially those of the Republican party, will not willingly endorse it, especially to the point of creating ill-will between the two countries, and it will probably not be endorsed by the country at large unless we, by ill-advised action, render it possible for those who desire it to carry it through on a wave of popular spread-eagleism. Any action taken by us will require the greatest possible tact and discretion and should be such that it will be impossible for any word or action of ours to be used [for] publication by those who desire it for the formating of popular feeling.

The British case, so far as the Government is concerned, should, it is thought, be advanced so far as is possible in private and by argument. British and Imperial responsibilities and needs and their vital dependence on the protection of their communications and food supplies must be made clear, as also the impossibility of entrusting the safeguarding of these to others who, however loyally they might enter into partnership, could not be expected and undoubtedly would not under certain conditions, however admittedly justifiable, employ their forces in matters which their country would repudiate as outside their province or responsibility.

Sentiment carries weight in the US, and the feeling in Great Britain and throughout the Empire that their very existence depends upon a predominant Navy, that it has many times in the past been the only barrier between them and utter destruction, that it is believed by them to have preserved at the same time the freedom of the world at large, and that it is regarded by them as a birthright which no Government would dare to compromise, and that public sentiment would never allow such an abrogation, should be advanced, and then the unthinkable possibility that if the US persist the so-called League of Nations and reduction of armaments will resolve itself into competitive naval armaments between US and Great Britain, instead of between Great Britain and Germany, as it was before the war.

It must be made clear that under no circumstances whatever will Great Britain surrender her responsibility to her Empire or to the world at large, and that these responsibilities entail for her a predominant Navy, and this should be done in such a way that it is impossible for the President or his friends in his political campaign to quote from word or writing anything which could be distorted to carry US public opinion in the way he might conceivably desire.

The probable ultimate US desire will be to fix their Naval standard on what they call the 50–50 basis, i.e., an equality with this country (anything beyond this is almost certainly bluff) on the grounds that they cannot leave their interests to be protected by the British Fleet, especially while we are allied with the Japanese. They say we can fix our strength according to our responsibilities, which they recognise are great, requiring strength, and that they will then merely equal us. Any arguments based on strength proportional to interests and responsibilities and deprecating mistrust shown of us may be listened to but will very likely be met with the demand as to what agreement or guarantee can be given by us which can be convincing and can be used by those who have to assure the US public that a big Navy for them is unnecessary.

The fundamental idea now generally prevalent in US is that the future of the world is in the hands of the English speaking races, that these must be united in the closest union; and that the forces at their disposal will be used jointly for the sole purpose of preserving or enforcing peace. The extent to which the US should be the predominant partner in this union depends in the mind of the US citizen, upon his pan-American as opposed to his pro-British sympathies. Any idea of war between the two countries is regarded as unthinkable.

For these reasons any argument based upon possible conflict between the two countries must be eliminated. It would at once, if used, induce a competition in naval armaments between us. What we are asking US is to trust us and sink their national pride, which demands that the naval forces at disposal should be equally divided between us.

The argument that the respective naval armaments of the two countries must necessarily be apportioned to the share taken by each in the white man's burden might carry considerable weight.

At bottom their desire for equality can only be because they are not prepared to leave themselves, as they believe, at our mercy, and this argues mistrust of us. Such mistrust cuts to the root of their fundamental principle of complete union, at which they professedly aim, and appears to be really the only argument which can be used to induce them to accept our views as to the relative naval forces necessary to and to be maintained by the two countries respectively.

The time for us publicly to admit to creating a strength greater than we should otherwise desire will be when they actually commence their own increase, and not before. In the meantime, I would suggest we fix and publish the minimum strength we adopt as a policy and to which we intend to build up or gradually reduce, at the same time making it clear that this is done regardless of US, whose present programme is not taken seriously. Our standard will undoubtedly be adopted by US as their standard, to which they will relatively build. Then there will be great controversy in US, and on their Government will be pinned the odium of any increase in their relative power. When they have fixed their policy it will be quite time enough for us publicly to modify ours as may be necessary owing to their action.

442. *Benson to the American Commission to Negotiate Peace*

Hotel De Crillon,
Paris,
21 February 1919

I am so impressed with the principle involved that I strongly recommend sending the following cable to the President of the United States, as it is quite certain that our present Naval building program will be prominently brought before him immediately upon his arrival in Washington[1]:–

'In order to stabilize the League of Nations, it is vitally necessary that no one power included in it should dominate in military or naval strength. There should be at least two powers of equal Naval

---

[1] Wilson made a brief trip home, 14 February–13 March 1919.

strength. If this principle is accepted, it should be the deciding factor in our present Naval building program, as Great Britain and the United States are the only two great powers to be considered in this connection at the present time.'

443. *Daniels to Wilson*

Paris,
4 March 1919

... I feel with Admiral Benson, that no nation ought to have a force either on land or sea, to dominate, and in military and naval strength our country ought to be ready and willing to furnish, in proportion to its wealth and commercial importance, the necessary force to maintain the world's peace.

444. *Admiralty Memorandum for War Cabinet*

13 March 1919

Battle Cruiser Programme

The Board of Admiralty have again had under consideration the question of the completion or cancellation of *Howe, Rodney* and *Anson*, the three Battle Cruisers building in Private Yards, upon which work has been suspended since March 1917.

****

The Board of Admiralty have now decided that these three vessels should be removed from the slips and cancelled, the reasons which have led them to this decision being as follows:–

****

(7) It is understood that the War Cabinet take the view that the United States of America need not, for the present at any rate, be considered a potential enemy.

The Admiralty, however, feel bound to emphasise the facts stated in the Memorandum GT 6653 that the US Naval Programme provides for the building of six Battle Cruisers, and that if that Programme is proceeded with, our shortage in Battle Cruisers must be remedied, otherwise we shall before long, fall behind the

United States Navy in ships of that class.

It will be essential, therefore, that the question of our position as regards Battle Cruiser strength should be considered at the earliest moment possible after the Terms of Peace are finally settled, in the meantime the preparation of new designs for the Battle Cruiser type is being taken in hand.

445. *Daniels to Wilson*

Paris,
30 March 1919

Admiral Wemyss came over from London and Admiral Benson and I had a conference with him on Saturday,[1] and Mr Long, First Lord of the Admiralty, will be over tomorrow to have a conference at eleven o'clock in accordance with your suggestion. After we have talked the matter over, I would like to see you sometime Monday afternoon to give you the result of the interview and to get your point of view.[2]

****

I found Admiral Wemyss in hearty accord with Admiral Benson's feeling that the German Fleet should be sunk. ... If it is the best policy to sink any of them, it is best that all of them should be sunk by action of the Council[3] and not by the independent action of any nation.

I confess that at first the idea of sinking them did not appeal to me, but when I reflected that it is not sinking many millions of dollars that would be useful and they could not be used by any nation without a large investment of money to put in the munition works to supply the ammunition to fit the German ships, it would really constitute a liability rather than an asset. It is a great question – whether the Council ought to favour permitting this liability to rest upon the nations which are already greatly burdened with debt.

---

[1] The notorious 'Naval Battle of Paris'; see J. Daniels, *The Wilson Era*, vol. 2, pp. 367–88; Klachko, pp. 127–53; Tillman, *passim*.
[2] Wilson was now back in Paris.
[3] Presumably the Council of Four (Wilson, Lloyd George, Clemenceau and Orlando), from February 1919 the chief decision-making body at the Preliminary Peace Conference and the subsequent (May–June) Peace Congress.

446. *Memorandum by Benson on Anglo-American Talks on Naval Building at the Paris Peace Conference, March 1919*

Washington,
16 May 1921

****

... the Secretary of the Navy requested that I come over to his hotel immediately. I went over at once, and much to my surprise, upon entering the reception room found Admiral Sir [Rosslyn] Wemyss, First Sea Lord of the British Admiralty, in earnest conference with the Secretary of the Navy. I expressed considerable surprise, and after a few remarks between Admiral Wemyss and myself, the Admiral turned to the Secretary of the Navy, and with great earnestness asked him a question about as follows: 'Why are you so intent on increasing your Navy, and to what extent do you propose to carry it out?' ...

Of course, I was, naturally, very much irritated at the impertinence of such a question, and immediately broke in and said: 'Mr Secretary, please do not answer that question'. I then turned to Admiral Wemyss and with considerable warmth and shaking my finger at him, said: 'By what authority do you presume to come over here and ask such a question of our Secretary?' This of course, completely disconcerted Admiral Wemyss to such an extent that it practically ended the interview, and after agreeing to come to my quarters later on in the day, he withdrew.

****

Later in the day, Secretary Daniels, Admiral Wemyss and myself met in my quarters at the Crillon and agreed with Admiral Wemyss that we would meet Mr Walter Long, then First Lord of the British Admiralty in my quarters on the following morning.

At the time and date noted, the conference took place in my quarters at the Crillon, the only persons being present were the Secretary of the Navy, Walter Long, First Lord of the British Admiralty, and myself. The interview was opened by Mr Daniels making some casual remarks in regard to his visit, and Mr Walter Long replying and stating, as I recall it now, that he was acting in accordance with the directions of his Prime Minister. The conversation gradually settled down to the question of the building program, the reasons for our big naval program, and the great number of merchant ships that we were building.

Mr Long stated that they felt very apprehensive of the situation as it then appeared; that due to the fact that England was an island country and depended entirely on its commerce and merchant marine, that it could not look with equanimity upon the large merchant marine that was being built up by the United States, and the increased Naval program seemed to be intended as a means of controlling the sea from a naval viewpoint, and that Great Britain could not feel satisfied in coming out of the war with the tremendous losses she had sustained in men, money and ships, and in addition becoming a second-rate sea power commercially or otherwise. This is simply the general tenor of the conversation.

I stated very frankly to Mr Long that I had not only been a member of the General Board of the Navy for some time, but for several years its presiding officer; and that in all our naval studies we had never really contemplated the possibility of a war with Great Britain, and that I, for one, was quite frank in stating that thought had never occurred to me, that I felt that these two great English-speaking peoples would never be so inconsiderate of each other as to contemplate such action, and that I was quite sure that it was foreign to the views of naval officers generally. I stated we had frequently referred to the fact that we should have a navy equal to that of England, because, being in that position, we would be able to meet Germany possibly allied with Japan or some other nation, and that we felt strongly the danger to be apprehended from such a combination.

The conversation drifted along these lines, Mr Long making it quite evident that something must be done on our part to stop our building program. I finally said to Mr Long as follows: 'Mr Long, I gather from what you have said that what you mean in plain English is that Great Britain has always been supreme on the sea, both from a naval standpoint and commercially, and that she intends to continue so at all hazards'. After thinking for a while, he said: 'Well, Admiral, that is about the size of it'.

I then said to him: 'Well, Mr Long, if you and the other members of your Government continue to argue along the lines you are proceeding [upon] this morning, I can assure you that it will mean but one thing, and that is war between Great Britain and the United States'. His remark was: 'Admiral, that is a very strong statement'. I replied, 'Mr Long, we are discussing a very serious subject, and further, if the people of the United States only knew such a conference as this was going on in Paris, it would start a flame that nothing under Heaven could quench'.

Mr Long then turned to Mr Daniels and said: 'Mr Secretary, I am very much impressed with what the Admiral says, and the way in which he says it'. Mr Daniels replied: 'I do not think the Admiral has stated the case any too strongly'. Mr Long then said: 'In that case, you had better talk to your President, and I will talk to my Prime Minister'. That practically ended the interview.

****

What I want to emphasise is that this indicates a deliberate intention on the part of the representatives of the British Cabinet and the British Government to use every possible influence to block our naval building program, and also to put every possible obstacle in the way of the development of our merchant marine. I also wish to emphasise the fact that this all took place right in the midst of the Peace Conference, which clearly indicated the attitude of the British Government with regard to this development, and that same Government is still in power in Great Britain, and it only bears out the propaganda and other efforts that have been constantly made and are constantly being made to hamper, and, if possible, destroy our commercial development, and it is at the bottom of this propaganda for disarmament and other features tending to keep the United States in a position subordinate to the British Empire.

This action is paralleled by the action of the British de Bunson Commission that visited South American countries in 1918 with the object of building up commercial relations and negotiating secret treaties, which, if they had not been discovered and had been carried out, would have completely hampered any development of our trade in South and Central America.[1]

It is for reasons of this kind that I feel so strongly the necessity for every possible step being taken to meet and defeat the efforts of British propaganda.[2]

[1] The British mission to Latin America was led by Sir Maurice W. E. de Bunson (1852–1932): diplomat; former Ambassador to Portugal, Spain, Austria; served in war at FO; after war worked in City; mission said to have enjoyed 'remarkable success'.

[2] Benson drew up this statement to help friendly Congressmen exert pressure on the Harding administration as it moved to organise the Washington Conference on naval

447. *Daniels to Wilson*

Paris,
7 April 1919

Admiral Benson feels strongly that we should go on building until our Navy is as strong as Great Britain's, which of course would mean that we would have to ask for a big appropriation for new ships in the next Congress. Lloyd George is very earnest and very strong in saying that he would not give a snap of his finger for the League of Nations if we keep on building. I explained to him that the programme we were working on was enacted by Congress in 1916 and that much of the material was fabricated, the machinery under contract, and the armor ordered, and that Congressional direction to build these ships could not be changed except by Congressional action, and that even when they were built Great Britain would have 33 battleships to our 23; 13 battlecruisers to our 6; 79 light cruisers to our 10; 535 destroyers to our 370; and 219 submarines to our 98. He replied that that was true, but that he was concerned about nothing except capital ships, and that their 46 capital ships as compared with our 29 would look as if we had a large disparity in comparison with Great Britain, but in gun power and modern firing our later ships would be much superior and their older ships would be outclassed.[1]

Mr Long put it plainly afterwards that he wished us to agree to stop the 1916 programme, which we are now building and which was authorized by Congress, which would of course leave us much inferior to Great Britain. It is upon that line that he wishes to talk with me, and I have wished to have the President's views before having a further conference.

It is my judgement that if any agreement is to be made at all, it ought not to be between Great Britain and America, but ought to be between all the Allied nations, and that it is very questionable whether a conference between Mr Long and myself could reach any result that will be satisfactory to Mr Lloyd George. From his very strong expressions the other morning, there is no doubt that he feels that when Great Britain sinks the ships that she will get [from Germany] and quits building battlecruisers, we should stop the construction of capital ships. I do not think the American

limitation and Pacific problems, held in the winter of 1921–22.

[1] Lloyd George, no doubt reflecting an Admiralty briefing, was right. At least 9 British battleships and 4 battle cruisers were now obsolescent, compared with 2, possibly 4, American battleships.

people would stand for this or that Congress would authorize it. It would raise another argument against the League of Nations that in America would be so strong that we could not defend it successfully.

448. *Memorandum by US Naval Advisory Staff*

Paris,
7 April 1919

United States Naval Policy

There is no subject in connection with the League of Nations that has caused so much perplexity, both at home and abroad, as the apparent inconsistency of the United States in advocating a general reduction of armaments, while itself undertaking an intensified Naval Building programme.

It is natural that a hostile foreign press should seize upon this apparent inconsistency as an evidence of hypocrisy on the part of the American Government, which is accused of aiming to obtain an advantage over other Powers by inducing them to trust in the ideal strength of an unarmed League, while continuing itself to rely on the practical strength of an armed nation. We hope that the following examination of the subject will make clear to all that American aims are legitimate aims, and that the step America is taking is one demanded by world interest, and one that menaces the just aspirations of no Power whatever.

****

In the past our naval position has derived great strength from the potential hostility of the British and German fleets. Neither the German nor the British fleet could venture abroad without grave risk that the other would seize the opportunity thus presented to crush a rival. This condition gave to America a position of special strength both in council and in decision, because her navy was so strong that no other Navy could neglect its influence. All that is now changed. The German fleet has ceased to exist, with the result that we suddenly find the British Navy in a position of unparalleled strength. No navy is left in Europe capable of offering any real resistance to the British Navy.

Under present conditions the British Navy, with its world wide supporting organization, is strong enough to dominate the seas in whatever quarter of the globe that domination may be required

We do not consider this a condition calculated to advance either our own just interests or the welfare of the world. A Power so absolute that it may disregard other Powers with impunity is less apt to act with justice than if there be a balancing influence of force as well as of world opinion to oppose it. This is true within a League of Nations as well as without a League of Nations.

... Everyone, except ourselves, looks to British Naval Representatives for suggestions in naval matters, ... Since we are considering naval policy as affecting American interests, and since the British Navy is the only Navy in existence that can threaten the American Navy, British policies have a peculiar interest for us.

Every great commercial rival of the British Empire has eventually found itself at war with Great Britain and has been defeated. Every such defeat has strengthened the commercial position of Great Britain.

****

A present governing policy of Great Britain is the control and monopoly, so far as possible, of international communications. These include –

Submarine telegraph cables
Radio systems
Commercial Aircraft
Merchant Shipping
Fueling facilities
Fuel deposits.

The British negotiations at the Peace Conference are conducted with these objects frankly in view. Their attainment is possible largely through British strength at sea. No one can contend that such monopolies represent the promotion of interests that are just to all the world.

The possibility of future war is never absent from the minds of statesmen, so we see in the British negotiations a very careful attention to the preservation of their present military domination of the sea. Among the measures they contend for are:

1. *The distribution of the German and Austrian Fleets.*

Comment.   Great Britain now has more than half of all the dreadnoughts of the world; if the German and Austrian ships are distributed on the most probable basis of *losses during the present war*, the United States would have to add to its Navy double the number of dreadnoughts it already possesses, or else remain an inferior naval power. In any case this perfectly logical policy of Great Britain, if carried out, will place her in a position of supremacy for years to come.[1]

2. *The razing of fortifications commanding waterways that Great Britain does not control.*

Comment. This is a natural policy of a great sea power. Its object is to give, in time of war, the maximum possible freedom to that Power whose navy controls the sea. It is put forward as being a policy in the interest of freedom of the seas, but the true object is that given above.

3. *The most liberal possible interpretation of belligerent rights on the High Seas.*

Comment. Very few people realize how reluctant the British are to codify maritime international law. They naturally prefer the absence of law in order that during war their Navy may have complete freedom of action. The absence of Maritime Law during the present war has led to an expansion of so-called belligerent rights that certainly would never be accepted by an International Congress. As an example, if Canada should attempt to gain her independence from Great Britain by force, and if the United States remained neutral, it is the British contention that Great Britain could blockade every port of the United States and could so regulate our imports that we could spare none for exportation to Canada. This is not International law, but an application of the law of force to neutrals. The only reply is the presence of a potential force that will secure the abandonment of the contention.

These proposals take on a special significance because of a recent pronouncement. At a time when all the world is seeking to form a League of Nations that will secure justice to great and small nations alike, the British Prime Minister announces that the British alliance with France will continue for ever. In the Far East, Japan remains within the British alliance. We look in vain for any provision of the League Covenant that forbids such alliances. Such combinations seem to us to contain elements of grave danger and to demand of us extraordinary measures.

Our own present and prospective world position needs special consideration. We are setting out to be the greatest commercial rival of Great Britain on the seas. We know that increase of population, the development of our great national resources, and our lack of real dependence on the rest of the world, spread before

[1] As Wemyss's memorandum (see no. 433) and Daniels's report to Wilson (see no. 445) make clear, the British were opposed to the distribution of German ships.

us the promise of a greater future than any other Power may expect. The gradual realization of this promise is bound to excite enmity and to cause unjust opposition to our expanding world interests. Heretofore we have lived apart, but now we are to live in constant and intimate relations with the rest of the world. We must be able to enter every world conference with the confidence of equality. We can have this confidence in but one way and that is by actually being equal to the greatest. ...

****

... the soundness of the League as a practicable working scheme must stand the test of its ability to restrain, if necessary, its strongest member. This cannot be done by a heterogenous combination of naval craft assembled by the nations of the League, unless in that assemblage there is one group of a single nationality that is equal in strength to the strongest navy. ...

We want the world League to be secure, to endure, and to establish a new order – the reign of law among nations. This cannot be brought about if some one Power is to dominate the decisions of the League by a world wide predominance of naval strength. We do not need to argue that whoever dominates the sea exercises more control over world policies than any other Power may do. As the interdepedence of nations increases this dominance of sea power over world policies will become more and more complete. ...

As long as Great Britain insists on retaining her overwhelming naval force, the only answer for the purposes of the League is the building of an equal force by some nation capable of constructing and maintaining a fleet of equal strength and efficiency. The United States is the only Power that is today financially and physically capable of building such a fleet, or of undertaking a future building competition with Great Britain.

It is not believed, however, that any competition in armaments is necessary. Once the principle of two equal naval Powers within the League is made clear to our own people and to the British public, a means will be found to maintain a parity of the two fleets with the minimum of burden to the taxpayer. Equality of the two fleets can be brought about by the destruction of the German fleet, the bulk of which would go to Great Britain on any probable scheme of distribution, and by a further reduction of the British fleet that, while leaving Great Britain ample strength to protect her world commerce and colonies, would still make it possible for the United States with a reasonable increase of its fleet, to equal the size of the

British fleet.

****

With two navies of equal strength, the world would breathe free from the fear of a naval domination that has the power at any moment of threatening the economic life of any nation. The resulting mutual respect of Great Britain and the United States would go further than anything else toward the establishment of just maritime law upon the high seas both in peace and in war.

The success of the League of Nations will rest in large part on the honesty, integrity and strength of the United States. The political and economic weakness of Europe as a result of the world war have thrust upon us the burden of imparting vital force to a Covenant that attempts to reconcile the conflicting interests of the world.

Our ability to sustain the League in its formative period and establish it eventually on a secure foundation will depend chiefly on the strength we give it to *resist the domination of any single Power*. We ourselves have no desire to dominate the League, but we believe it to be our duty to the world to make our counsels heard as attentively as the counsels of any other Power.

****

We believe that a better way in which to obtain two equal navies in the world is for the British Navy to be reduced in strength, and for Great Britain and America to determine jointly from time to time what the strength of the two fleets shall be.

449.   *Admiralty Memorandum for the War Cabinet*

30 April 1919

League of Nations Covenant

The Board of Admiralty desire to call attention to the fact that, although the wording of Article VIII of the League of Nations Covenant has been revised to some extent since the Admiralty Memorandum of 3 March[1] was circulated to the War Cabinet, this Article still limits the freedom of this country to provide the means of defence thought necessary by its Naval and Military advisors, in a manner which the Admiralty consider to be dangerous.

The Admiralty Memorandum of 3 March suggested the omis-

---

[1] Not reproduced.

sion of the words in Article VIII which provide that the scale of the armaments of the various nations 'when adopted shall not be exceeded without the permission of the Executive Council'. Nevertheless, this provision, with a slight variation in the wording, still appears in the Covenant. The wording, as now published is:–

'After these plans shall have been adopted by the several Governments the limits of armaments therein fixed shall not be exceeded without the concurrence of the Council.'

The retention of this Clause is all the more objectionable because it has now been definitely laid down by Article V that, except where otherwise expressly provided, the decisions of the Council shall require the agreement of all the States represented.

The principle of unanimous decision, which in other parts of the Covenant safeguards the independent sovereignty of States, and has been included for that purpose, actually has the contrary effect in the case of the Clause referred to, since it follows from it that any one State represented in the council can prevent any other member of the League from making any increase in its armaments.

In the opinion of the Admiralty, the inclination of this provision is likely vitally to injure the success of the Covenant. Either the several States, knowing that they are giving away the power to make any subsequent changes in their armaments, will pitch their claims so high at the outset that the attempt to limit armaments will be entirely unfruitful, or the Covenant must be deliberately broken by a Nation when it feels that for some urgent reason or other an increase in its armaments is necessary to its safety.

450.   *Memorandum by Benson*

c. May 1919

****

It may be argued against the necessity for America's having a fleet equal to the British fleet, that there is nothing in the British fleet inimicable to the League of Nations or to the principles which should govern such a League; but we believe that this is not entirely true. The world will be left after this peace with but one power strong on the sea and everyone else weak. All actions of the League of Nations outside of Continental Europe will be actions depending in the first instance upon naval power, and consequently will be actions depending largely upon the will of those controlling the British Fleet. In addition to the power of the British fleet itself, there is the added tendency which is unavoidable, of the lesser Powers being swayed towards association with the stronger Power as a matter of pure interest. It is perfectly understandable that no weak Power will desire to associate itself with weakness rather than strength, even though right may be on the side of weakness. This tendency of Powers to group themselves about great strength has been observed right here in Paris wherever Naval Conferences have met. The discussion of measures and principles has hinged largely upon decisions previously arrived at by the British Naval Representatives. There has been an unmistakeable tendency of all Powers other than America to associate themselves with British decisions, although I personally know that in several instances the Naval Representatives of those Powers were not in accord with the decisions they approved in Conference. This tendency of yielding to British naval opinion has been so pronounced on occasions that the formula of asking the opinion of representatives of sometimes one and sometimes two of the Great Powers has been omitted – the inference being that the opinions of these Powers were British opinions. Manifestly this state of affairs, if continued into the future, is not one calculated to promote the survival of a League of Nations which has for its underlying principle equal opportunity for all the Powers of the world – both great and small. There must be some balancing force that will ensure a greater probability of just decisions.

I understand very well the predominant position in which the British Navy finds itself, not only through the strength of its ships, but through its world wide system of naval bases, fuelling facilities and communication facilities. It is true that the system of bases is essential to the maintenance of the British Empire as it exists today; but it is also true that the same system of bases would be most useful should at any time a Government arise in Great Britain that desired to use British naval power for unjust purposes. I feel that I do not have to assure anyone here present, that America has no ambitions that are hostile to any part of the British Empire or to British commerce; but America is concerned regarding the attitude of the British Empire towards the commerce of other nations. The

British doctrine of maritime rights is not in harmony with the American doctrine, and I realize that until America is in a position much stronger relatively than at present, it will be impossible to be certain that the British doctrine of maritime rights will agree more nearly with world interests, and more specifically with American interests. As an example it may be mentioned that, according to British doctrine of Freedom of the Seas, should Canada attempt to declare her independence, and should Great Britain attempt to prevent such separation, it would be within the power of the British Fleet, and within its right, to blockade every port on both the Atlantic and Pacific coasts of the United States. We, by joining in the present war, have appeared to give some support to this doctrine; but it is not our doctrine, and we do not believe in it, and we do not intend to remain in a naval position where we may be compelled to accept it.

451.   *John W. Davis[1] to Daniels*

American Embassy,
London,
30 April 1919

Answering your note of this morning I offer the following random suggestions for your House of Commons speech:–
1)   The customary tribute to Great Britain's part in the war with special stress, by reason of your official position, on the Navy. They never get too much of this and are inclined to notice its omission. They do not object to the suggestion that we also were in the war so long as we do not claim the credit for winning it.

****

Of course they would like to have you speak about the naval plans of the United States and would welcome any assurance they could draw from you that there was no thought of competitive armament. This is the sorest point in the British anatomy and could only be approached, if at all, *with the greatest delicacy*. I do not know how far you feel that you can or should enter on it. ...

---

[1] John W. Davis (1873–1955): Wall St attorney; Democrat; Representative from W. Virginia 1911–13; Solicitor-General in Wilson administration 1913–18; Ambassador to Britain September 1918–1921; President, American Bar Assn 1922; Democratic Presidential candidate 1924 (well beaten by Calvin Coolidge); later a fierce conservative critic of President F. D. Roosevelt.

452. *The Times*

London,
2 May 1919

Press Conference given by Secretary Daniels

It was pointed out to Mr Daniels that the British man in the street was asking why the United States Navy had an estimate of £600,000,000 for the Navy, which seemed rather a large sum for police work.

'Perhaps the man in the street has not read the Bill,' suggested Mr Daniels. 'The Naval Bill, with a £600,000,000 estimate for new construction, has a provision, which I helped to draw up, providing that if the League of Nations is established, it is in the discretion of the President to say that all the new ships may not be constructed. When the estimates were drawn up the Armistice had not been signed, and it was a question for each country to decide independently what it should do.

'I remember when Mr Winston Churchill[1] advocated a vacation in naval building in 1913. I approved of it in our country, and added, "Why a vacation? Why not an international agreement, which would be of permanent assistance, by agreements for such navies as would be sufficient to guarantee the world's peace".

'It is unthinkable that any nation in the League should undertake competitive naval building based on suspicion and distrust. I think that the day when the League of Nations was agreed to unanimously – which is the greatest event which any generation has witnessed for centuries – will make unnecessary the tremendous expenditure of money by each nation. Of course we must have in the League of Nations a mobile police force. The greatest pressure, of course, will be economic and social, but there must be behind that, certainly in the early days, a sufficient mobile navy of free nations to see that we are not going to have any more wars like the last.'

****

Referring to Britain's two-power standard, Mr Daniels said that Britain came to that decision before the war, when Germany was building against her. The decision was a wise one, but what Britain should do, now that there was no nation building against her, was a matter which this country must settle for herself. The League of

---

[1] Then First Lord of the Admiralty.

Nations was not a super-government, and did not undertake to decide for Britain, or the United States, or France, what their policy should be. The commitment to the theory of the League of Nations would no doubt cause reconsideration everywhere.

453. *The Daily Telegraph*

London,
2 May 1919

America's Navy

Mr Daniels's Speech

... Of one thing there must be no doubt; the end of competitive naval buildings has arrived. It would be a blunder, a calamity equal to a crime, if Great Britain and the United States should enter upon competitive naval buildings, either or both suspicious of the other. (Hear, hear).

****

The United States will, I am convinced, do nothing that international developments do not strictly require us to do, to add to the naval burdens of this or any other Power. As we recognise the political and geographical necessities which call for great British sea power, we are convinced that Britons, on their part, recognise that similar necessities exist in our case. We, too, have a prodigious coast-line. We have a great foreign trade, which is bound to grow, a carrying trade that will grow with it, and obligations growing out of our League of Nations covenant. The United States does not aspire, as we believe Great Britain does not aspire, to possess such strength at sea that we can impose our decrees arbitrarily on other free peoples. (Hear, hear). Such a tradition is wholly foreign to our political nature, and utterly out of tune with our traditions. But if the evolution of the League of Nations is not such as its friends and devotees in Europe and in America hope that it may be, if competition in armaments must continue, as in the past, unchecked by any other consideration than a nation's financial capacity – then, regrettable as the choice will be, repugnant as it will be to the American people, it will be essential, from the dictates of elementary national interest, that they shall build and maintain a fleet commensurate with the needs of national defence and with our international obligations.

Naval Co-operation

I believe I am the interpreter of American wisdom from one end of our country to the other when I say that the spirit of comradeship which Chichester and Dewey shared in Manila Bay[1] is the spirit which the American people devoutly trust may prevail between us to the end of time. Americans want naval co-operation, not naval competition, with Great Britain – co-operation in the maintenance of human liberties the world over, such co-operation as they carried out in European waters during the Great War, and such co-operation, under God's providence, as they will carry out again wherever and whenever freedom is assailed by the powers of evil and tyrannical aggression. ...

****

454. *The Pall Mall Gazette*

London,
2 May 1919

Mr Daniels's Visit

The Role of Great Britain and America

The visit of Mr Daniels, the Administrator of the American Navy, should clear up some of the confusion produced by his speeches upon 'the other side'. It was rather surprising for Englishmen to hear a few months ago from so high an authority that the United States proposed to outbuild us in naval construction, in case the question of armaments were not satisfactorily solved at Paris upon a League of Nations basis. Mr Daniels assured his audience yesterday that he looked on it as 'a calamity worse than a crime if the British people and the American people ever entered into a competition in Navy building'. That sentiment, we need not say, is shared to the fullest extent by every section of opinion in Great Britain. Obnoxious as the idea of hostility is in any direction, it would represent the most pessimistic of all outlooks for the world if this country and the United States should ever be found drifting into a position of jealous armed rivalry. Between them they ought to be able at this juncture to bring about a restraint of naval

---

[1] Captain Edward Chichester: Captain 1889; commanded *Immortalité*, cruiser, on China Station; later a baronet. Said to have facilitated Dewey's destruction of Spanish squadron in Manila Bay, 1 May 1898 and also reputed to have frustrated German SNO's wish to prevent Dewey from accomplishing his mission.

armament throughout the world, save only for the requirements of the common peace and the protection of each Power's imperative responsibilities. Those responsibilities will not be removed – although they may be lightened – by the institution of the League of Nations, and in our own case the safety of communications within an Empire extending to every part of the world creates liabilities to which there is no parallel. America might be self-supporting, and even prosperous, with scarcely a warship to her name. The British Empire could not exist and the United Kingdom would be confronted with starvation and bankruptcy if we were not ready at any moment to meet a challenge to the safety of the seas. These are considerations which British and American statesmen can discuss in all their hearings in the most friendly spirit, and we have little doubt of their being able to arrive at an understanding entirely consonant with the view of international policy to which both so firmly adhere.

455.   *Benson to President Wilson*

5 May 1919

****

... there will at all times be an European and an American interest which will always differ. It must be quite evident to you that in practically all questions that have come up Great Britain has been able to maintain her position and carry through her claims largely through the dominant influence exerted in consequence of her tremendous naval superiority. It is quite evident to my mind that if this condition of inequality of naval strength is to continue the League of Nations, instead of being what we are striving for and most earnestly hope for, will be a stronger British Empire.

For the six months that I have been constantly in conference with the representatives of the various powers I have tried in every possible way to interpret your views and to anticipate your ideals and objects of the League of Nations, and in these conferences have been prompted by these motives, and I have, from the very beginning, had forced upon me the fact above stated; that American interests, the American viewpoint, American aims and ideals were entirely foreign to those of the other powers and that in practically all important cases the representatives of the other powers have agreed with the representatives of Great Britain. The alliance between France and Japan and Great Britain, together with their interests, is so intimately connected that any addition to the naval strength of the former two powers will simply be so much more practically added to the strength of Great Britain. The conclusion therefore is most evident to my mind that everything should be done to decrease or at least to prevent an increase in the naval strength of Great Britain, France and Japan, as I am most thoroughly convinced that in order to stabilize the League of Nations and to have it develop into what we intended it to be the United States must increase her naval strength to such a force as will be able to prevent Great Britain at least from dominating and dictating to the other powers within the League.

It is with great hesitancy that I express myself as forcibly as I have in this letter, but I really feel that I would be neglecting my duty to you as well as to my country if I failed to do so.

****

456.   President Wilson to Benson

6 May 1919

... While it was impossible to get the words that you and I desired into the Treaty, I do not yet at all despair of bringing about the same result, chiefly because I do not believe that the taxpayers of these countries will consent to bear the burden of a larger naval establishment.

457.   Admiralty Memorandum for War Cabinet

7 May 1919

Relative Strength of Navies

It is desired that the War Cabinet should be aware of the relative strength of the Navies of the World at the present time and, so far as can be estimated, in 1923–4.

****

If vessels of the pre-*Orion* Classes and equivalent ships in other Navies[1] are omitted the relative estimated strength of the various Navies in Capital Ships in 1923–24 will be as follows:–

---

[1] The pre-*Orion* ships were: *Dreadnought* (1906), *Bellerophon, Téméraire, Superb*, (1909), *St Vincent, Collingwood* (1910), *Neptune, Colossus, Hercules* (1911), all now considered obsolete. The battle cruisers *Australia, New Zealand, Indomitable* and *Inflexible* could also be considered out of date.

Estimated Strength by 1923–24

	Dreadnought Battleships	Battle Cruisers	Total
Great Britain	24	6	30
United States	21	6	27
France	12	–	12
Italy 1921	4	–	4
Japan	8	6	14

This estimate includes the United States Programme which has actually been approved but not the further Programme now under consideration in America, which, if adopted, would render the position even more unsatisfactory.

458. *Daniels to Walter Long*

London,
8 May 1919

Upon our departure for home I am wiring to send to you and the British Admiralty our warm appreciation for two of the most delightful, informing and happiest weeks of our lives. The admirals and other officers accompanying me have had the most interesting conferences with officers of your service and our visit has not only been profitable but has strengthened the ties of friendship forged during the war between our two countries.

LIST OF DOCUMENTS AND SOURCES

1. *Public Record Office, Kew, London*
   Records of the Admiralty:
   (a) Papers of the First Lord of the Admiralty (ADM 116)
       (Sir Eric Geddes, Walter Long, 1917–21)
   (b) War Histories Collection, 1914–1918 (ADM 137).
2. *National Archives, Washington, DC*
   (a) Naval Records Collection, Office of Naval Records and
       Library, Subject File, 1911–1927, record group 45. (NSF/file,
       e.g., TP)
   (b) General Records of the Navy, Records of the General Board,
       record group 80. (GRN/ GB, file no., e.g., 425)
3. *Manuscript Division, Library of Congress, Washington, DC*
   (a) The Papers of Josephus Daniels (now microfilmed; check box
       numbers against those for reels). (Daniels, box no., e..g., 109)
   (b) The Papers of Admiral William Shepherd Benson, US Navy.
       (Benson, box no.)
   (c) The Papers of Admiral William Sowden Sims, US Navy.
       (Sims, box no.)
4. *Operational Archives Branch, US Naval Historical Center, Washington Navy Yard, Washington, DC*
   The Papers of Admiral William Veazie Pratt, US Navy (all
   from Series I, General Correspondence, 1898–1920).
5. *Franklin D. Roosevelt Library, Hyde Park, New York*
   (a) The Papers of Franklin D. Roosevelt, Assistant Secretary of
       the Navy File (FDR/ASN, box no., e.g., 15)
   (b) US Congress, Senate, *Naval Investigation: Hearings before
       the Sub-Committee of the Committee on Naval Affairs, US
       Senate*, 66th Congress, 2nd Session (1920), (typescript).
       (Senate, page no. of item)

PART I

1. Captain Guy Gaunt   3 February 1917   ADM 137/583
   to Captain W. R.
   Hall

2.	US Navy General Board to Secretary of the Navy Daniels	4 February 1917	GRN/GB 425
3.	Captain T. P. Magruder, US Navy, to F. D. Roosevelt	5 February 1917	FDR/ASN 15
4.	Admiralty to Gaunt	22 March 1917	ADM 137/654
5.	FO to Colville Barclay	22 March 1917	ADM 137/1436
6.	Ambassador Page to Secretary of State Lansing	23 March 1917	Sims 76
7.	President Wilson to Daniels	24 March 1917	Daniels 109
8.	Barclay to FO	25 March 1917	ADM 137/1436
9.	Admiralty to Vice-Admiral Sir M. Browning	29 March 1917	ADM 137/654
10.	Gaunt to Hall	19 March 1917	ADM 137/583
11.	General Board to Daniels	5 April 1917	GRN/GB 425

PART II

12.	Admiralty to Browning and Gaunt	2 April 1917	ADM 137/654
13.	Admiralty to Browning and Gaunt	3 April 1917	ADM 137/654
14.	Admiralty to Gaunt	7 April 1917	ADM 137/1436
15.	Admiral Sir John Jellicoe to Rear-Admiral Sims, US Navy	7 April 1917	Sims 68
16.	Memorandum by Jellicoe	9 April 1917	NSF/TP
17.	Browning to Admiralty	13 April 1917	ADM 137/1436

18.	Browning to Secretary of Admiralty (Graham Greene)	13 April 1917	ADM 137/1436
19.	Sims to Daniels	19 April 1917	Senate, 18
20.	Office Memo by Graham Greene	20 April 1917	ADM 137/1436
21.	Rear-Admiral Sir D. De Chair to Graham Greene	15 May 1917	ADM 137/1436
22.	De Chair to Admiralty	7 June 1917	ADM 137/1436

PART III

23.	Sims to Daniels	8 May 1917	Sims 54
24.	Admiralty to De Chair	25 May 1917	ADM 137/655
25.	Sims to Captain W. V. Pratt, US Navy	7 June 1917	Pratt
26.	Lieut R. Emmet, US Navy, to Sims	22 June 1917	Sims 55
27.	Page to Lansing	26 June 1917	NSF/TT
28.	Joseph Tumulty to President Wilson	29 June 1917	Daniels 109
29.	Sims to Daniels	29 June 1917	Senate 48
30.	W. Churchill (US) to President Wilson	July 1917	Sims 51
31.	Pratt to Sims	2 July 1917	Pratt
32.	Sims to Navy Dept	3 July 1917	Benson 8
33.	President Wilson to Daniels	2 July 1917	Daniels 110
34.	President Wilson to Sims	4 July 1917	NSF/TD
35.	Sims to President Wilson	after 4 July 1917	Sims 91
36.	Gaunt to Admiralty	5 July 1917	ADM 137/1437
37.	Lord Northcliffe to War Cabinet	5 July 1917	NSF/TT
38.	Jellicoe to Northcliffe	c. 10 July 1917	NSF/TT

39.	Daniels to Lansing	9 July 1917	Sims 54
40.	Sims to Daniels	16 July 1917	NSF/TP
41.	Browning to Jellicoe	20 July 1917	ADM 137/657
42.	Browning to Admiral W. S. Benson	26 July 1917	Daniels 66
43.	Sims to Daniels	31 July 1917	NSF/TT
44.	Browning to Jellicoe	10 August 1917	NSF/TT
45.	Sims to Pratt	18 August 1917	Pratt
46.	Sir Eric Geddes to Lloyd George	29 August 1917	ADM 116/1804
47.	Sims to Pratt	30 August 1917	Pratt
48.	Admiral H. T. Mayo, US Navy on the Admiralty	September 1917	NSF/TP
49.	Mayo to Benson	5 September 1917	NSF/TT
50.	Admiralty Operations Cttee	20 November 1917	ADM 137/1420
51.	Mayo to Daniels	8 September 1917	Benson 5
52.	Gaunt to Jellicoe	10 September 1917	ADM 137/1437
53.	Ambassador Spring-Rice to FO	12 September 1917	ADM 137/1437
54.	Jellicoe to Gaunt	14 September 1917	ADM 137/1437
55.	Gaunt to Hall	12 September 1917	ADM 137/658
56.	Deputy 1st Sea Lord to Gaunt	13 September 1917	ADM 137/658
57.	Gaunt to Benson	17 September 1917	NSF/TT
58.	Benson to Sims	24 September 1917	Benson 5
59.	Arthur Pollen to Roosevelt	26 September 1917	FDR/ASN 119
60.	Captain Dudley Pound to Vice-Admiral Sir R. Wemyss	c. 29 September 1917	ADM 137/1437
61.	Gaunt to Admiralty	6 October 1917	ADM 137/1437
62.	Navy Dept Memo for Benson	7 October 1917	Daniels 66

86.	Sims to Benson	14 January 1918	Benson 6
87.	Sims to Benson	15 January 1918	Pratt
88.	Admiral Sir L. Bayly to Sims	16 January 1918	Sims 47
89.	Daniels to Page	24 January 1918	Daniels 92
90.	Allied Naval Council: US Memo	12–14 March 1918	NSF/TX
91.	President Wilson to Daniels	31 January 1918	Daniels 66
92.	US Planning Section: Naval Air Effort	15 February 1918	ADM 137/2710
93.	Benson to Sims	4 March 1918	NSF/TT
94.	US Planning Section to Sims	7 March 1918	NSF/TX
95.	Memo by Admiralty Plans Division	15 March 1918	NSF/TX
96.	Sims to Benson	2 April 1918	Pratt
97.	Sims to Navy Dept	8 April 1918	NSF/OP
98.	Sims to G. A. Steel, Admiralty	11 May 1918	ADM116/1808
99.	Sims to Roosevelt	8 June 1918	Sims 82
100.	Sims to Captain H. I. Cone, US Navy	28 June 1918	NSF/TT
101.	Admiralty to Admiral Sir David Beatty	19 July 1918	ADM 137/1973
102.	Roosevelt to Daniels	27 July 1918	Daniels 94
103.	Sims to Benson	28 July 1918	Pratt
104.	Roosevelt to Family	30 July 1918	FDR/ASN 191
105.	US Intelligence Memo	3 August 1918	ADM 137/1964
106.	Sims to Navy Dept	4 August 1918	NSF/TD
107.	Sims to Bayly	8 August 1918	Sims 47
108.	Sims to Benson	10 August 1918	Pratt
109.	Roosevelt to Daniels	2 August 1918	Daniels 94
110.	Sims to Navy Dept	16 August 1918	NSF/TD
111.	Sims to Navy Dept	22 August 1918	NSF/TP
112.	Sims to Benson	2 October 1918	Benson 10
113.	Roosevelt to Daniels	16 October 1918	FDR/ASN 46
114.	Sims to Navy Dept	13 November 1918	NSF/WV
115.	Wemyss to Sims	16 November 1918	Sims 90

116.	Bayly to Sims	29 November 1918	Sims 47
117.	Admiral Lord Beresford to Sims	25 December 1918	Sims 50
118.	US Planning Section Memo	30 December 1918	NSF/TX
119.	Sims to Benson	24 January 1919	Benson 11
120.	Jellicoe to Sims	5 February 1919	Sims 68
121.	Sims to Bayly	6 March 1919	Sims 48
122.	Bayly to Sims	8 March 1919	Sims 48
123.	Geddes to Sims	24 March 1919	Sims 60
124.	Murray to Sims	26 March 1919	Sims 50
125.	W. S. Churchill to Sims	31 March 1919	Sims 50
126.	Rear-Admiral H. S. Knapp, US Navy to Murray	7 May 1919	Sims 50

PART IV

127.	Sims to Daniels	14 April 1917	Daniels 100
128.	Daniels to Cdr. J. K. Taussig, US Navy	14 April 1917	NSF/TD
129.	Sims to Daniels	18 April 1917	NSF/TD
130.	Jellicoe to De Chair	26 April 1917	ADM 137/655
131.	De Chair to Admiralty	27 April 1917	ADM 137/655
132.	Jellicoe to De Chair	27 April 1917	ADM 137/655
133.	De Chair to Jellicoe	28 April 1917	ADM 137/655
134.	Sims to Taussig	29 April 1917	NSF/TD
135.	Sims to Daniels	30 April 1917	NSF/TT
136.	Admiralty Memo on Convoys	1 May 1917	NSF/TT
137.	De Chair to Jellicoe	2 May 1917	ADM 137/655
138.	Admiralty to Gaunt	3 May 1917	ADM 137/655
139.	Gaunt to Admiralty	5 May 1917	ADM 137/655
140.	Sims to Bayly	8 May 1917	Sims 47
141.	Bayly to Sims	11 May 1917	Sims 47
142.	Sims to Daniels	8 May 1917	NSF/TD
143.	Sims to Navy Dept	11 May 1917	NSF/TD
144.	Lieut R. C. Grady, US Navy, to Sims	16 May 1917	NSF/TP
145.	Gaunt to Admiralty	23 May 1917	ADM 137/655
146.	Sims to Daniels	26 May 1917	Daniels 100

147.	Bayly to Sims	30 May 1917	Sims 47
148.	Sims to Bayly	1 June 1917	Sims 47
149.	Benson to Sims	June 1917	Benson 5
150.	Sims to Benson	13 June 1917	Senate 144
151.	Sims to Benson	14 June 1917	ADM 137/656
152.	Sims to Benson	14 June 1917	ADM 137/656
153.	Sims to Daniels	16 June 1917	Benson 5
154.	Daniels to Sims	20 June 1917	Senate 37
155.	Daniels to Sims	24 June 1917	NSF/OP
156.	Sims to Daniels	28 June 1917	Senate 86
157.	Jellicoe to Gaunt	30 June 1917	ADM 137/656
158.	Sims to Daniels	28 June 1917	Senate 70
159.	Jellicoe to Gaunt	29 June 1917	ADM 137/656
160.	Gaunt to Jellicoe	1 July 1917	ADM 137/656
161.	Gaunt to Jellicoe	3 July 1917	ADM 137/656
162.	Jellicoe to Gaunt	4 July 1917	ADM 137/656
163.	Sims to Daniels	c. 3 July 1917	Benson 5
164.	Sims to Pratt	3 July 1917	Pratt
165.	Gaunt to Jellicoe	5 July 1917	ADM 137/656
166.	Bayly to Sims	6 July 1917	Sims 47
167.	Daniels to Sims	7 July 1917	Senate 187
168.	Sims to Daniels	11 July 1917	Senate 187
169.	Sims to Daniels	8 July 1917	ADM 137/656
170.	Jellicoe to Sims	11 July 1917	Senate 92
171.	Sims to Lt-Cdr C. C. Belknap, US Navy	11 July 1917	Sims 48
172.	Bayly to Sims	16 July 1917	Sims 47
173.	Gaunt to Jellicoe	20 July 1917	ADM 137/657
174.	Jellicoe to Gaunt	22 July 1917	ADM 137/657
175.	Orders to a Convoy Escort Group	25 July 1917	NSF/IS-3
176.	Daniels to Sims	28 July 1917	Daniels 100
177.	Sims to Benson	30 July 1917	Senate 51
178.	Sims to Bayly	14 August 1917	Sims 47
179.	Sims to Pratt	30 August 1917	Pratt
180.	Gaunt to Admiralty	31 August 1917	ADM 137/1437
181.	Gaunt to Admiralty	2 September 1917	ADM 137/1437
182.	Page to Daniels	September 1917	Daniels 92
183.	Benson to Sims	5 September 1917	NSF/TT

184.	Sims to Navy Dept	11 September 1917	Senate 58
185.	Memo by Admiral Bayly	11 September 1917	Sims 47
186.	Sims to US Commander, Gibraltar	12 September 1917	NSF/OP
187.	Bayly to Admiralty	16 November 1917	ADM 137/1437
188.	Benson to Opnav	19 November 1917	Benson 9
189.	Asst Secretary of Admiralty to FO	3 December 1917	Sims 50
190.	Sims to Bayly	10 December 1917	Sims 47
191.	Jellicoe to Benson	17 December 1917	ADM 137/660
192.	Gaunt to Jellicoe	19 December 1917	ADM 137/660
193.	Sailing Orders to an Escort Group	2 January 1918	NSF/IS-2
194.	Sims to Opnav	9 January 1918	NSF/UP
195.	Minute by Captain W. W. Fisher	10 January 1918	ADM 137/1621
196.	Bayly to Sims	10 January 1918	Sims 47
197.	Admiralty Memo: US Air Operations	11 January 1918	ADM 137/2710
198.	Allied Naval Council: Convoys	22–23 January 1918	NSF/QC
199.	Bayly to Murray	26 January 1918	Sims 47
200.	Sims to Bayly	31 January 1918	Sims 47
201.	Memo by Director of Plans	11 February 1918	ADM 137/2707
202.	Memo by US Planning Section	19 February 1918	NSF/TX
203.	Benson to Sims	20 February 1918	NSF/TT
204.	Memo by US Planning Section	25 February 1918	ADM 137/2710
205.	Sims to Murray	23 February 1918	ADM 137/1621
206.	Sims to Benson	28 February 1918	Benson 6
207.	Minute by Director of Plans	1 March 1918	ADM 137/1621
208.	Murray to Sims	25 March 1918	ADM 137/1621
209.	Sims to Murray	28 March 1918	ADM 137/1621
210.	Sims to Benson	7 March 1918	Benson 6
211.	Bayly to Sims	10 March 1918	Sims 47

212.	Report by Director of Admiralty Intelligence	10 March 1918	NSF/OP
213.	Wemyss to Sims	26 March 1918	Sims 90
214.	Joint Appreciation by British and US Plans Divisions	28 March 1918	ADM 137/2708
215.	Joint Memo by British and US Plans Divisions	1 April 1918	NSF/TX
216.	Benson to Sims	5 April 1918	NSF/OP
217.	Sims to Opnav	7 April 1918	NSF/OP
218.	Joint Memo by British and US Plans Divisions	15 April 1918	ADM 137/2708
219.	Sims to Keyes	23 April 1918	Sims 68
220.	Captain Joel Pringle, US Navy, to Sims	24 April 1918	Sims 79
221.	Sims to Bayly	5 May 1918	Sims 47
222.	Sims to Murray	6 May 1918	ADM 137/1622
223.	Sims to Rear-Admiral H. O. Dunn, US Navy	7 May 1918	Sims 55
224.	Report of Admiralty Conference on Offensive Action	31 May 1918	ADM 137/2708
225.	Lieut W. A. Edwards, US Navy, to Murray	6 June 1918	ADM 137/1621
226.	Geddes to Sims	12 June 1918	ADM 116/1809
227.	Pringle to Sims	8 July 1918	NSF/OE
228.	Sims to President Wilson	13 July 1918	Benson 8
229.	Admiralty Memo: Sailings and Losses	17 July 1918	ADM 116/1810
230.	Sims to Captain N. A. McCully, US Navy	4 August 1918	NSF/OP
231.	Memo by Plans Division	28 August 1918	ADM 137/2709

232.	Memo by British and US Plans Divisions	30 August 1918	NSF/TX
233.	Notes by Plans Division	11 September 1918	NSF/TX
234.	Sims to Bayly	21 September 1918	Sims 47
235.	Sims to Bayly	24 September 1918	Sims 47
236.	Bayly to Sims	30 September 1918	Sims 47
237.	Sims to Bayly	2 October 1918	Sims 47
238.	US Office of Naval Intelligence Memo	17 October 1918	NSF/OE
239.	Bayly to Sims	20 October 1918	Sims 47
240.	Captain R. H. Leigh, US Navy, to Sims	30 November 1918	NSF/TT
241.	Murray to Sims	17 December 1918	NSF/TT
242.	Gunnery Dept, US Flotillas, Queenstown	24 December 1918	Sims 54
243.	Bayly to Admiralty	31 December 1918	Sims 47

PART V

244.	Sims to Opnav	21 July 1917	NSF/OP
245.	Sims to Pringle	31 July 1917	NSF/TT
246.	Benson to Sims	20 August 1917	Senate 67
247.	Sims to Benson	1 September 1917	Benson 5
248.	Sims to Beatty	30 October 1917	Sims 48
249.	Memorandum by Benson	November 1917	Benson 42
250.	Benson to Opnav	9 November 1917	Benson 5
251.	Daniels to Benson	13 November 1917	Senate 69
252.	Memo by Director of Plans	19 November 1917	ADM 137/2706
253.	Gaunt to Jellicoe	15 November 1917	ADM137/659
254.	Beatty to Sims	5 December 1917	Sims 48
255.	Sims to Benson	20 December 1917	Benson 5
256.	Memo by Director of Plans	13 January 1918	ADM 137/2707

280.	De Chair to Roosevelt	12 July 1917	FDR/ASN 14
281.	Benson to Sims	18 August 1917	Senate 198
282.	Sims to Rear-Admiral R. Earle, US Navy	25 September 1917	Sims 55
283.	Jellicoe to Benson	17 October 1917	ADM 137/659
284.	Benson to Sims	21 October 1917	NSF/TT
285.	Navy Dept to Sims	21 October 1917	Senate 201
286.	Jellicoe to Benson	22 October 1917	ADM 137/659
287.	Senior Member, General Board, to Daniels	24 October 1917	GRN/GB425–5
288.	Roosevelt to Daniels	29 October 1917	FDR/ASN 15
289.	Navy Dept to Sims	2 November 1917	Senate 202
290.	Benson to Daniels	9 November 1917	NSF/TT
291.	Memo by Rear-Admiral (Mining)	10 December 1917	ADM 137/2706
292.	Memo by US Planning Section	31 December 1917	NSF/TX
293.	Joint Memo by British and US Planning Staffs	12 January 1918	NSF/TT
294.	Memo by US Planning Section	12 March 1918	NSF/TX
295.	Memorandum by Beatty	5 June 1918	ADM 137/1963
296.	Memo by Plans Division	24 July 1918	ADM 137/2711
297.	Sims to Captain R. R. Belknap, US Navy	25 July 1918	Sims 48
298.	Memo by Wemyss for War Cabinet	31 July 1918	ADM 116/1771
299.	Sims to Benson	30 August 1918	Pratt
300.	R. R. Belknap to Sims	22 September 1918	Sims 48
301.	R. R. Belknap: Mines in War	undated	NSF/ZAN

323.	Memo by Geddes for War Cabinet	13 June 1918	ADM 116/1810
324.	Sims to Rear-Admiral J. Strauss, US Navy	July 1918	NSF/TT
325.	Sims to Opnav	26 July 1918	NSF/TT
326.	Niblack to Sims	29 July 1918	NSF/OP
327.	Benson to Sims	7 August 1918	NSF/TT
328.	Roosevelt to Daniels	2 August 1918	FDR/ASN 93
329.	Roosevelt to Family	2–11 August 1918	FDR/ASN 191
330.	Roosevelt to Daniels	13 August 1918	Daniels 94
331.	US Command, Gibraltar: American Effort in Mediterranean	c. November 1918	NSF/ZOR
332.	Grant to Murray	4 February 1919	ADM 137/1574
333.	Grant to Murray	4 February 1919	ADM 137/1574

PART VIII

334.	Gaunt to Admiralty	8 May 1917	ADM 137/1436
335.	Graham Greene to Gaunt	18 May 1917	ADM 137/1436
336.	CO, USS *Chattanooga*, to Commander, 3rd Sqdn, Patrol Force, US Atlantic Fleet	28 May 1917	NSF/TT
337.	Agreement between CinC, US Pacific Fleet, and Commodore commanding British Forces	29 June 1917	NSF/TT
338.	Admiralty to Captain K. Wade	5 July 1917	ADM 137/656
339.	Jellicoe to Browning	3 August 1917	ADM 137/657
340.	Browning to Jellicoe	3 August 1917	ADM 137/657
341.	Gaunt to Hall	7 August 1917	ADM 137/657

342.	Memo by Geddes for War Cabinet	4 September 1917	ADM 116/1768
343.	Sims to Navy Dept	9 October 1917	Senate 102
344.	Commander, American Patrol Detachment to CinC	10 November 1917	NSF/TT
345.	Commander, American Patrol Detachment, to Commander, 7th Naval District	30 November 1917	NSF/OP
346.	Benson to Sims	28 November 1917	NSF/TT
347.	Admiralty to Gaunt	20 December 1917	ADM 137/660
348.	Admiral W. B. Caperton, US Navy, to Daniels	14 January 1918	NSF/TT
349.	Benson to Sims	20 February 1918	NSF/TT
350.	Sims to Benson	25 February 1918	NSF/TT
351.	Sims to Benson	1 March 1918	NSF/TT
352.	Benson to Sims	3 March 1918	NSF/TT
353.	Sims to Murray	16 March 1918	ADM 137/1621
354.	Murray to Sims	3 April 1918	ADM 137/1621
355.	Vice-Admiral Sir W. L. Grant to Admiralty	18 March 1918	ADM 137/767
356.	Gaunt to Wemyss	23 March 1918	ADM 137/767
357.	Deputy First Sea Lord to Gaunt	26 March 1918	ADM 137/767
358.	Grant to Murray	1 April 1918	ADM 137/504
359.	Benson to Sims	7 April 1918	NSF/KD
360.	Sims to Benson	11 April 1918	NSF/KD
361.	Commandant, 1st Naval District, to Opnav	25 April 1918	NSF/TT
362.	Hall to Grant	15 May 1918	ADM 137/768
363.	Benson to Sims	5 June 1918	ADM 137/768
364.	Grant to Admiralty	6 June 1918	ADM 137/768
365.	Grant to Admiralty	15 June 1918	ADM 137/768
366.	Grant to British SNO, New York	14 June 1918	ADM 137/1619
367.	Grant to Admiralty	21 July 1918	ADM 137/903
368.	Admiralty to Grant	22 July 1918	ADM 137/903

397.	Memo by Director of Plans	September 1918	ADM 137/2710
398.	Conference between First Lord and Naval Members of Board	5 September 1918	ADM 116/1809
399.	Memo by Director of Statistics	22 September 1918	ADM 137/2710
400.	Wemyss to Geddes	3 October 1918	ADM 116/1809
401.	Notes for Conference with Navy Dept	October 1918	ADM 116/1809
402.	Memo of Conference at Navy Dept	8 October 1918	ADM 116/1809
403.	Memo of Meeting between US and British Officers	8 October 1918	NSF/TT
404.	Geddes to Daniels	10 October 1918	ADM 116/1809
405.	House to Balfour	13 October 1918	ADM 116/1809
406.	Geddes to Lloyd George	13 October 1918	ADM 116/1809
407.	Pratt to Sims	15 October 1918	Sims 78
408.	Admiralty Memo for War Cabinet	October 1918	ADM 137/2710
409.	Planning Cttee Opnav to Benson	7 October 1918	Benson 42
410.	Memo by US Planning Section	October 1918	NSF/TX
411.	Memo by Rear-Admiral Sir S. Fremantle and Comments by US Planning Section	October 1918	NSF/TX
412.	Sims to Bayly	15 October 1918	Sims 47
413.	Memorandum by Geddes	16 October 1918	ADM 116/1809
414.	Memorandum by Wemyss	17 October 1918	ADM 116/1810
415.	Benson to Daniels	3 November 1918	Pratt
416.	Memo by US Planning Section	7 November 1918	NSF/TX

INDEX

[Ranks are those then held; career details are in the footnotes]

ADAMS, Lieut E. G., USN, 472
Admiralty, anti-submarine warfare, 6,
23, 40–1, 43, 75, 76, 241, 285–6,
296–7, 300, 302–5, 311, 312, 317,
318; battle cruiser raid, 348, 352–4,
356–8; Convoy, 72, 103–4, 235,
236, 249, 446; League of Nations,
574, 605–6; Mediterranean, 403–4,
412; North Sea Barrage, 180, 368,
370, 371, 374–5, 378, 379–81, 382,
383–4, 392; organisation, 59–60,
67, 75, 117–18, 123, 147–8, 149,
165, 383; peace terms, 543–4, 547–
51, 554–60, 575–6, 595–6; Plans
Division, 60, 134, 141, 157–9, 177,
183–5, 203, 276, 277–8, 280, 287–
91, 292–3, 301–8, 328, 335–8, 342,
385, 387, 389–91, 393–4, 407–9,
410–11, 516, 563; War policy, 8,
71, 75, 76–7, 78–9, 83, 98–104,
120–23, 125, 135–41, 241, 284;
post-war policy 483–94, 595; and
Sims, 25, 38–41, 43, 60–6, 70, 82,
119–20, 133, 141–2, 143–4, 145–7,
161–2, 169–70, 185, 187–8, 247–9,
275–6, 315–16; USN, assistance
required, 14, 15, 18, 28–9, 49–51,
67–8, 77–8, 110–11, 134–5, 325–6,
328, 330, 332, 334, 335–8, 480,
482–3, 496–501, 504–39; USN;
building programme, 561–6, 573–4,
590–4, 596–9, 613–14; US Navy
Dept, 10, 15, 17, 33, 34, 47–9, 60–
4, 68, 76–7, 84–5, 91–2, 93, 94–8,
104–17, 126–8, 143, 149, 160, 182,
243–4, 291, 439–41, 443, 446–7,
454–5, 456–8, 460–3, 465, 467–71.
Adriatic: 48, 136, 137, 138–9, 150, 156,
176, 179, 180, 282, 305, 308, 375,
397, 398, 399, 400, 406–12, 414–15,
416, 417, 418, 419, 420, 425, 426,
427, 428, 432, 433
Aegean: 150, 179, 308, 416, 418, 419,
422, 427, 428

Allied Naval Council: 60, 64, 95, 98,
99–104, 126, 142–3, 150–5, 158,
179, 266–71, 278–9, 282, 283–4,
399, 406–7, 411, 412, 416, 426, 485,
527, 544, 551, 553–4, 559–61, 596
American Expeditionary Forces,
transportation of: 20, 57, 84, 129,
134, 173, 181, 194, 200, 225–6, 230,
243, 245, 247, 310, 350, 352, 357,
409, 412, 413, 441, 467–8, 517, 525,
531, 538
Anderson, Capt E.A., USN, 451
Anti-submarine warfare: 6, 13, 14, 15,
19–20, 23, 25, 28, 29, 30, 31, 38–
43, 44, 49, 67, 69, 71–6, 77–8, 79,
81–2, 84–5, 86–7, 88, 92, 97–8, 101,
109, 122–3, 124–5, 129, 134, 137,
147, 150, 154, 176, 185, 193, 194,
196, 201, 202–3, 207, 209–10, 193–
321, 367–94, 464–71, 515–16, 522,
525, 530–1, 538–9; hunting, 151,
155, 203–5, 267, 272, 274, 275, 282,
285–6, 290–1, 304, 306, 432–3, 517,
525, 529, 531–2
Argentina: 90
Armistice: 55, 64, 65, 200, 471, 484,
541–7, 553–61, 571–2, 573, 575–6
Asquith, H.H: 255
Australia: 269
Austria-Hungary: 20, 48, 176, 308, 398–
9, 400, 412, 419, 425, 427, 428, 482,
487, 502–3, 539–41, 575, 578, 602
Azores Islands: 102, 103, 105, 115, 128,
131, 171, 202, 203, 242, 244, 248–9,
255–6, 266, 291, 348, 350, 351, 557

BABCOCK, Lt-Cdr J.V., USN, 218,
371, 456
Badger, R-Adm C.J., USN, 10, 35, 46,
589
Baker, Newton D.: 485
Balfour, A.J: 15, 16, 26, 27, 45, 48, 57,
67, 68, 113, 114, 176, 180, 238, 368,
382, 417, 425, 441, 480–1, 497–8,

Navy Records Society
(Founded 1893)

The Navy Records Society was established for the purpose of printing unpublished manuscripts and rare works of naval interest. The Society is open to all who are interested in naval history, and any person wishing to become a member should apply to the Hon. Secretary, c/o Barclays Bank PLC, Murray House, 1, Royal Mint Court, London EC3N 4HH. The annual subscription is £15, which entitles the member to receive one free copy of each work issued by the Society in that year, and to buy earlier issues at much reduced prices.

A list of works in print is shown below; very few copies are left of those marked with an asterisk. The prices to members and non-members respectively are given after each volume, and orders from members should be sent, enclosing no money, to Mrs. Annette Gould, 5, Goodwood Close, Midhurst, West Sussex GU29 9JG. Those marked 'TS' and 'SP' are published for the Society by Temple Smith and Scolar Press, and are available to non-members only from the Gower Publishing Group, Gower House, Croft Road, Aldershot, Hampshire GU11 3HR. Those marked 'A & U' are published by George Allen & Unwin, and are available to non-members only through bookshops.

The Society has already published:

Vols. 1 and 2. *State Papers relating to the Defeat of the Spanish Armada, Anno 1588* Vols I & II, ed, Professor J. K. Laughton. (£12.00 ea./£45.00 set TS)

Vol. 11. *Papers relating to the Spanish War, 1585–87*, ed. Julian S. Corbett. (£15.00/£35.00 TS)

Vol. 16. *Logs of the Great Sea Fights, 1794–1805*, Vol. I, ed. Vice-Admiral Sir T. Sturges Jackson. (£12.00/£20.00)

Vol. 18. *Logs of the Great Sea Fights, 1794–1805*, Vol. II, ed. Vice-Admiral Sir T. Sturges Jackson. (£12.00/£20.00)

Vol. 20. *The Naval Miscellany*, Vol. I, ed. Professor J. K. Laughton. (£15.00/£20.00)

646   ANGLO-AMERICAN NAVAL RELATIONS 1917–1919

Vol. 31. *The Recollections of Commander James Anthony Gardner,*
1775–1814, ed. Admiral Sir R. Vesey Hamilton and Professor J. K.
Laughton. (*£15.00/£20.00*)

Vol. 32. *Letters and Papers of Charles, Lord Barham, 1758–1813,*
Vol. I, ed. Sir J. K. Laughton. (*£15.00/£20.00*)

Vol. 38. *Letters and Papers of Charles, Lord Barham, 1758–1813,*
Vol. II, ed. Sir J. K. Laughton. (*£15.00/£20.00*)

Vol. 39. *Letters and Papers of Charles, Lord Barham, 1758–1813,*
Vol. III, ed. Sir J. K. Laughton. (*£15.00/£20.00*)

Vol. 40. *The Naval Miscellany,* Vol. II, ed. Sir J. K. Laughton.
(*£15.00/£20.00*)

Vol. 41. *Papers relating to the First Dutch War, 1652–54,* Vol. V,
ed. C. T. Atkinson. (*£10.00/£20.00*)

Vol. 42. *Papers relating to the Loss of Minorca in 1756,* ed.
Captain H. W. Richmond. (*£15.00/£20.00*)

Vol. 43. *The Naval Tracts of Sir William Monson,* Vol. III, ed. M.
Oppenheim. (*£10.00/£20.00*)

Vol. 45. *The Naval Tracts of Sir William Monson,* Vol. IV, ed. M.
Oppenheim. (*£10.00/£20.00*)

*Vol. 46. *The Private Papers of George, Second Earl Spencer,* Vol.
I, ed. Julian S. Corbett (*£15.00/£20.00*)

Vol. 47. *The Naval Tracts of Sir William Monson,* Vol. V. ed. M.
Oppenheim. (*£10.00/£20.00*)

Vol. 49. *Documents relating to Law and Custom of the Sea,* Vol. I,
ed. R. G. Marsden. (*£15.00/£20.00*)

Vol. 50. *Documents relating to Law and Custom of the Sea,* Vol. II,
ed. R. G. Marsden. (*£10.00/£20.00*)

Vol. 52. *The Life of Admiral Sir John Leake,* Vol. I, ed. G. A. R.
Callender. (*£10.00/£20.00*)

Vol. 53. *The Life of Admiral Sir John Leake,* Vol. II, ed. G. A. R.
Callender. (*£10.00/£20.00*)

Vol. 54. *The Life and Works of Sir Henry Mainwaring,* Vol. I, ed.
G. E. Manwaring. (*£10.00/£20.00*)

Vol. 60. *Samuel Pepys's Naval Minutes,* ed. Dr. J. R. Tanner.
(*£15.00/£20.00*)

Vol. 65. *Boteler's Dialogues,* ed. W. G. Perrin. (*£10.00/£20.00*)

Vol. 66. *Papers relating to the First Dutch War, 1652–54,* Vol. VI,
ed. C. T. Atkinson. (*£10.00/£20.00*)

Vol. 67. *The Byng Papers,* Vol. I, ed. W. C. B. Tunstall (*£15.00/*
£20.00)

Vol. 68. *The Byng Papers,* Vol. II, ed. W. C. B. Tunstall. (*£15.00/*
£20.00)

Corrigenda to *Papers relating to the First Dutch War, 1652–54*, ed. Captain A. C. Dewar. (*Free*)

Vol. 70. *The Byng Papers,* Vol. III, ed. W. C. B. Tunstall. (*£10.00/ £20.00*)

*Vol. 71. *The Private Papers of John, Earl of Sandwich*, Vol. II, ed. G. R. Barnes and Lt Cdr J. H. Owen. (*£15.00/£20.00*)

Vol. 73. *The Tangier Papers of Samuel Pepys*, ed. Edwin Chappell. (*£15.00/£20.00*)

Vol. 74. *The Tomlinson Papers*, ed. J. G. Bullocke. (*£10.00/£20.00*)

Vol. 77. *Letters and Papers of Admiral the Hon. Samuel Barrington*, Vol. I, ed. D. Bonner-Smith (*£10.00/£20.00*)

Vol. 79. *The Journals of Sir Thomas Allin, 1660–1678*, Vol. I, ed. R. C. Anderson. (*£10.00/£20.00*)

Vol. 80. *The Journals of Sir Thomas Allin, 1660–1678*, Vol. II, ed. R. C. Anderson. (*£10.00/£20.00*)

Vol. 89. *The Sergison Papers, 1688–1702*, ed. Cdr R. D. Merriman, (*£10.00/£20.00*)

Vol. 104. *The Navy and South America, 1807–1823*, ed. Professor G. S. Graham and Professor R. A. Humphreys. (*£10.00/£20.00*)

Vol. 107. *The Health of Seamen*, ed. Professor C. C. Lloyd. (*£10.00/£20.00*)

Vol. 108. *The Jellicoe Papers*, Vol. I, ed. A. Temple Patterson. (*£8.00/£20.00*)

Vol. 109. *Documents relating to Anson's Voyage round the World, 1740–1744*, ed. Dr Glyndwr Williams. (*£10.00/£20.00*)

Vol. 111. *The Jellicoe Papers*, Vol. II, ed. A. Temple Patterson. (*£10.00/£20.00*)

Vol. 112. *The Rupert and Monck Letterbook, 1666*, ed. Rev. J. R. Powell and E. K. Timings. (*£10.00/£20.00*)

Vol. 113. *Documents relating to the Royal Naval Air Service*, Vol. I., ed. Captain S. W. Roskill. (*£10.00/£20.00*)

Vol. 114. *The Siege and Capture of Havana, 1762*, ed. Professor David Syrett. (*£10.00/£20.00*)

*Vol. 115. *Policy and Operations in the Mediterranean, 1912–14*, ed. E. W. R. Lumby. (*£15.00/£20.00*)

Vol. 116. *The Jacobean Commissions of Enquiry, 1608 & 1618*, ed. Dr. A. P. McGowan. (*£10.00/£20.00*)

Vol. 117. *The Keyes Papers*, Vol. I, ed. Dr Paul G. Halpern. (*£10.00/£20.00*)

Vol. 119. *The Manning of the Royal Navy: Selected Public Pamphlets 1693–1873*, ed. Professor J. S. Bromley. (*£8.00/£20.00*)

Vol. 120. *Naval Administration, 1715–1750*, ed. Professor D. A.

Baugh. (*£8.00/£20.00*)

Vol. 121. *The Keyes Papers*, Vol. II, ed. Dr Paul G. Halpern. (*£8.00/£20.00*)

Vol. 122. *The Keyes Papers*, Vol. III, ed. Dr Paul G. Halpern. (*£8.00/£20.00*)

Vol. 123. *The Navy of the Lancastrian Kings: Accounts and Inventories of William Soper, Keeper of the King's Ships 1422–1427*, ed. Dr Susan Rose. (*£10.00/£20.00*)

Vol. 124. *The Pollen Papers: The Privately Circulated Printed Works of Arthur Hungerford Pollen, 1901–1916*, ed. Dr Jon T. Sumida (*£10.00/£20.00 A & U*)

Vol. 125. *The Naval Miscellany*, Vol. V, ed. N. A. M. Rodger. (*£8.00/£30.00 A & U*)

Vol. 126. *The Royal Navy in the Mediterranean, 1915–1918*, ed. Professor Paul G. Halpern (*£10.00/£38.50 TS*)

Vol. 127. *The Expedition of Sir John Norris and Sir Francis Drake to Spain and Portugal, 1589*, ed. Professor R. B. Wernham. (*£10.00/£32.50 TS*)

Vol. 128. *The Beatty Papers*, Vol. I, 1902–1918, ed. B. McL. Ranft (*£10.00/£38.50 SP*)

Vol. 129. *The Hawke Papers: A Selection: 1743–1771*, ed. Ruddock F. Mackay (*£8.00/£37.50 SP*)